THE PERSONALITY CULT OF
STALIN
IN SOVIET POSTERS, 1929-1953
ARCHETYPES, INVENTIONS & FABRICATIONS

THE PERSONALITY CULT OF
STALIN
IN SOVIET POSTERS, 1929-1953
ARCHETYPES, INVENTIONS & FABRICATIONS

ANITA PISCH

PRESS

Published by ANU Press
The Australian National University
Acton ACT 2601, Australia
Email: anupress@anu.edu.au
This title is also available online at press.anu.edu.au

National Library of Australia Cataloguing-in-Publication entry

Creator: Pisch, Anita, author.

Title: The personality cult of Stalin in Soviet posters, 1929 - 1953 : archetypes, inventions and fabrications / Anita Pisch.

ISBN: 9781760460624 (paperback) 9781760460631 (ebook)

Subjects: Stalin, Joseph, 1879-1953--Symbolism.
                Political posters, Russian.
                Symbolism in politics--Soviet Union.
                Symbolism in mass media.
                Symbolism in art.

Dewey Number: 741.670947

All rights reserved. No part of this publication may be reproduced, stored in a retrieval system or transmitted in any form or by any means, electronic, mechanical, photocopying or otherwise, without the prior permission of the publisher.

Cover design and layout by ANU Press. Cover image adapted from: '26 years without Lenin, but still on Lenin's path', Mytnikov, 1950, Izdanie Rostizo (Rostov-Don), edn 15,000.

This edition © 2016 ANU Press

CES Prize
This publication was awarded a Centre for European Studies Publication Prize in 2015. The prize covers the cost of professional copyediting.

Contents

Acknowledgements vii

List of illustrations ix

Abbreviations xxi

Introduction 1

1. The phenomenon of the personality cult —
   a historical perspective 49
2. The rise of the Stalin personality cult 87
3. Stalin is like a fairytale sycamore tree — Stalin as a symbol . . . 191
4. Stalin saves the world — Stalin and the evolution
   of the Warrior and Saviour archetypes 291

Conclusion 441

Appendix 1: Breakdown of posters in the research
sample by year 447

Appendix 2: Frequency trends in posters with images of Stalin
in the research sample, and Stalin's appearances in *Pravda* 449

Appendix 3: Posters of Stalin and Lenin by year 451

Bibliography 453

Index 499

Acknowledgements

This research began as PhD research in the School of Art History and Curatorship at The Australian National University (ANU). I would like to gratefully acknowledge the expert guidance and support of my thesis supervisor, Professor Sasha Grishin, throughout the three years of my research, as well as from the other members of my supervisory panel, Dr Andrew Montana and Dr Kevin Windle. Professor Grishin has been generous with his time and knowledge, and managed to make me laugh at times when I thought I had forgotten how. Dr Windle assisted with some of the translations of the 'curlier' Russian captions and Dr Kirill Nourzhanov assisted with the translation of the Uzbek poster captions. Thanks are also due to Dr Zoja Bojic and to Margaret Travers.

The staff of the graphics department at the Russian State Library in Moscow were very helpful and hospitable during my two periods of fieldwork, and I would particularly like to thank Dr Liubov Rodionova for facilitating my research at the library, the legendary Nina Baburina for her assistance in targeting folders containing Stalin posters, and Dr Svetlana Artamonova for her assistance in gaining access to other relevant library holdings and her willingness to answer my queries and discuss various aspects of my research. Dr Olga Litvinova was extremely helpful at the Museum of Contemporary History in Moscow, granting me access to all posters in the collection that contain an image of Stalin. Svetlana Khrodakovskaia was happy to discuss with me the poster collection at the Museum of Political History in St Petersburg.

Dr Liudmila Riabova of the History Department at the St Petersburg State University provided assistance by facilitating my participation in the 'Russia's statehood: The authorities and society across the twentieth century' conference at which I was able to present some of my research findings and discuss them with scholars from a number of academic disciplines. I am particularly indebted to Svetlana Petrova for her assistance in the presentation of my conference paper. I am also grateful to Dr Tatiana Tabolina of the Russian Academy of Sciences for her interest in, and encouragement of, my research and for her feedback.

I thank the dedicated librarians at the National Gallery of Australia Research Library, ANU libraries, the National Library of Australia and the Baillieu Library at the University of Melbourne. I would like to particularly thank staff at the Chifley Library at ANU for answering my queries concerning interlibrary loans and for assisting me to access a variety of materials that have proved invaluable to my research.

I am grateful to my colleagues in Art History at ANU for their helpful comments and critiques of oral presentations of my research at our regular gatherings and for providing a wonderful milieu in which to work.

This research and my fieldwork and conference attendance in Russia were made possible through the financial support provided by the Australian National University Postgraduate Award and ANU College of Arts and Social Sciences research support fund. The publication of this book has been supported by the generous financial and professional assistance provided by ANU Centre for European Studies Publishing Prize – I am particularly grateful to Christine Huber of the Humanities and Creative Arts Editorial Board for guiding me through this process. Special thanks also go to my eagle-eyed editor, Justine Molony, for her excellent and professional work in editing the manuscript. I would like to acknowledge the assistance and professionalism of the team at ANU Press — especially Emily Tinker, Publications Coordinator, for her expertise in the publication process; and Teresa Prowse, Digital Design/Publishing Officer, for her excellent design of the cover and layout.

No prolonged project is possible without the support of family and friends. Sputi Piosik has been unwavering in his friendship and merry spirit. My long-suffering family have put up with my bouts of irritability and anxiety and offered constant support and love. My mother is, as always, my rock and, along with David, Theresa and Alana, have never faltered in their belief in me. My father, the first in our family to receive a PhD, was always a role model of scholarly courage and sadly passed away before I completed my research. I know he was delighted I was following my dream.

List of illustrations

Fig. 2.1 'Komsomol political education system mid-Volga organisation V.L.K.S.M for 1930–31', unidentified artist, 1930, (Samara), 28 x 75 cm, edn 5,000 165

Fig. 2.2 'Under the Lenin banner for socialist construction', Gustav Klutsis, 1930. 166

Fig. 2.3 'With the banner of Lenin we were victorious in the battle for the October revolution ...', Viktor Deni, 1931, Izogiz (Moscow, Leningrad), 52 x 72 cm, edn 20,000 167

Fig. 2.4 'Shock work at the machine is combined with the study of Marxist–Leninist theory', A.M. Rumiantsev, 1931, Izogiz (Moscow), 85 x 58 cm, edn 40,000 168

Fig. 2.5 'With the banner of Lenin ...', Viktor Deni, 1933, Izogiz (Moscow), 77 x 109 cm, edn 60,000 169

Fig. 2.6 'With the banner of Lenin ...', Gustav Klutsis, 1933, Izogiz, 62 x 88 cm, 300,000 170

Fig. 2.7 'With the banner of Lenin ...', Iraklii Toidze, 1933, Izogiz (Moscow, Leningrad), 62 x 94 cm (edn of 300); 82 x 110 cm, edn 1,000. 171

Fig. 2.8 'Long live the great party of Lenin–Stalin — leader and organiser of the victorious building of socialism!', L. Stenberg, 1937 171

Fig. 2.9 'Chronicle of the arrests, exiles and escapes of Comrade Stalin', unidentified artist, 1938 172

Fig. 2.10 'Be as the great Lenin was', Vasilii Elkin, 1938, Izogiz (Moscow, Leningrad), 60 x 94 cm, edn 100,000 173

Fig. 2.11 'Be as the great Lenin was', A.I. Madorskii, 1938, edn 15,000 174

Fig. 2.12 'Be as the great Lenin was', A.I. Madorskii, 1939,
60 x 90 cm, edn 20,000. 175

Fig. 2.13 'Departing from us ...', Vladimir Kaidalov, 1940,
UzFimgiz (Tashkent), 60 x 92 cm, edn 7,000. 176

Fig. 2.14 'Under the banner of Lenin, under the leadership
of Stalin — forward to new victories!', Petr Golub, 1945,
Iskusstvo, 85.5 x 61 cm, edn 200,000 177

Fig. 2.15 '1918–1943 Long live the XXV anniversary of the
Leninist–Stalinist Komsomol', Vladimir Serov, 1943,
Iskusstvo (Leningrad), 70 x 52 cm, edn 5,000. 178

Fig. 2.16 'The banner of Lenin ...', L. Stenberg, 1949, Iskusstvo
(Moscow, Leningrad), 85 x 56.5 cm, edn 100,000. Another
edition of 100,000 was issued in 1951. 179

Fig. 2.17 '26 years without Lenin, but still on Lenin's path',
Mytnikov, 1950, Izdanie Rostizo (Rostov-Don), edn 15,000 . 180

Fig. 2.18 'In the name of communism', Viktor Govorkov, 1951,
Iskusstvo (Moscow), 86 x 97 cm, edn 600,000 181

Fig. 2.19 'Glory to the great leaders of October',
Naum Karpovskii, 1951, Iskusstvo (Moscow),
64.5 x 87.5 cm, edn 100,000. 181

Fig. 2.20 'Glory to Lenin, glory to Stalin, glory to great October',
V. Reshetnikov, 1952, Latgosizdat, edn 3,000 182

Fig. 2.21 'Long live the great, united party of Lenin–Stalin ...',
unidentified artist, 1952 182

Fig. 2.22 'Long live the Bolshevik Party, the Lenin–Stalin Party,
the vanguard of the Soviet people forged in battle, the
inspiration and organiser of our victories!', Vladislav Pravdin,
1950, Iskusstvo (Moscow, Leningrad), 64.5 x 87.5 cm,
edn 1,000,000. 183

Fig. 2.23 'Raise higher the banner of Marx, Engels, Lenin, and
Stalin!', Gustav Klutsis, 1933, edn 50,000 and then an edition
of 30,000. In 1936 an edition of 250,000 was released. 183

Fig. 2.24 'Long live the great, invincible banner of Marx–Engels–
Lenin', Nikolai Dolgorukov, 1934, 163.5 x 56 cm 184

LIST OF ILLUSTRATIONS

Fig. 2.25 'Long live the great invincible banner of Marx–Engels–Lenin–Stalin!', Vladislav Pravdin & Zoia Pravdina, 1938, Iskusstvo (Moscow, Leningrad), 62 x 94 cm, edn 100,000... 185

Fig. 2.26 'Long live the great invincible banner of Marx–Engels–Lenin–Stalin! Long live Leninism!', unidentified artist, 1940, edn 6,000 185

Fig. 2.27 'Long live the great invincible banner of Marx–Engels–Lenin–Stalin!', Nikolai Denisov & Nina Vatolina, 1941, Iskusstvo (Moscow, Leningrad), edn 100,000 186

Fig. 2.28 'Glory to great Stalin!', Vladimir Kaidalov, 1949, Gosizdat (Tashkent), edn 5,000....................... 187

Fig. 2.29 'But there is one branch of science ...', Bainazar Al'menov, 1951, Tatgosizdat (Kazan), edn 13,000 188

Fig. 2.30 'Long live the great invincible banner of Marx, Engels, Lenin, Stalin', A. Kossov, 1953, Iskusstvo (Moscow), 66 x 92 cm, edn 500,000............................ 189

Fig. 2.31 'Under the banner of Marx–Engels–Lenin–Stalin, under the guidance of the Communist party — forward, to the victory of communism!', Boris Belopol'skii, 1955, 54.5 x 87 cm..................................... 189

Fig. 3.1 'Thank you Comrade Stalin for our happy life!', Nikolai Zhukov, 1940, Iskusstvo (Moscow, Leningrad), 62 x 92 cm, edn 100,000............................ 261

Fig. 3.2 'Stalin's kindness illuminates the future of our children!', Iraklii Toidze, 1947, Iskusstvo (Moscow, Leningrad), 61 x 43 cm 262

Fig. 3.3 'Stalin is the wisest of all people ...', Vartan Arakelov, 1939, Iskusstvo (Moscow, Leningrad), edn 75,000 263

Fig. 3.4 'So — greetings, Stalin, and live for a hundred years ...', Konstantin Cheprakov, 1939, UzFimGiz (Tashkent), 62 x 94 cm 264

Fig. 3.5 'For communism! ...', Mikhail Reikh, 1948, Uzdarnashr (Tashkent), edn 10,000 265

Fig. 3.6 'We are warmed by Stalin's affection ...', unidentified artist, 1949, 47 x 61 cm 266

Fig. 3.7 'Great Stalin is the beacon of communism!',
Viktor Ivanov, 1949, Iskusstvo (Moscow, Leningrad),
74 x 52.5 cm, edn 300,000 267

Fig. 3.8 'Stalin takes care of each of us from the Kremlin',
Viktor Govorkov, 1940, Iskusstvo (Moscow, Leningrad),
62 x 92 cm, edn 100,000............................ 268

Fig. 3.9 'The captain of the Soviet Union leads us from victory
to victory!', Boris Efimov, 1933, Izogiz (Moscow, Leningrad),
62 x 94 cm, edn 200,000............................ 269

Fig. 3.10 'Glory to Stalin, the great architect of communism!',
Boris Belopol'skii, 1951, Iskusstvo (Moscow), edn 500,000 . . 269

Fig. 3.11 'Glory to great Stalin, the architect of communism!',
N. Petrov & Konstantin Ivanov, 1952, Iskusstvo (Moscow),
edn 200,000 270

Fig. 3.12 'Thank you beloved Stalin for our happy childhood',
Viktor Govorkov, 1936, Izogiz, 71 x 103.2 cm............ 270

Fig. 3.13 'On the joyous day of liberation ...', Viktor Koretskii,
1943, Iskusstvo (Moscow, Leningrad), edn 50,000 271

Fig. 3.14 'XXV years of the Komsomol', Vladimir Fedotov, 1943 . . 272

Fig. 3.15 'We'll surround orphans with maternal kindness
and love', Nikolai Zhukov, 1947, 79 x 57 cm............. 273

Fig. 3.16 'Best friend of children. Glory to great Stalin!',
Elena Mel'nikova, 1951, Iskusstvo (Moscow), edn 50,000. . . 273

Fig. 3.17 'Glory to Stalin's falcons — the conquerors of aerial
elements!', Viktor Deni & Nikolai Dolgorukov, 1937........ 274

Fig. 3.18 'Long live the Soviet pilots — the proud falcons of
our motherland!', Nina Vatolina & Nikolai Denisov, 1938. . . 275

Fig. 3.19 'To the new achievements of Soviet aviation!',
Vladislav Pravdin, 1950 275

Fig. 3.20 'Stalin raised us to be loyal to the people!', Petr Golub,
1948, Iskusstvo (Moscow, Leningrad), 86 x 61 cm 276

Fig. 3.21 'And Stalin raised us to be loyal to the people,
inspired us to work and to deeds!', Leonid Golovanov,
1949, Iskusstvo (Moscow, Leningrad), 76.5 x 56 cm,
edn 300,000 277

LIST OF ILLUSTRATIONS

Fig. 3.22 '"Long life and prosperity to our motherland!" I. Stalin', F. Litvinov, 1949, Krymizdat, edn 10,000 278

Fig. 3.23 'We have overthrown capitalism ...', Mikhail Kuprianov, 1933, (Moscow), edn 4,000 279

Fig. 3.24 'Without a revolutionary theory there can be no revolutionary movement ...', Pikalov, 1933, Izogiz (Leningrad), 77 x 109 cm, edn 30,000. 280

Fig. 3.25 'Shock workers of the fields engage in fighting for the socialist reconstruction of agriculture ...', Gustav Klutsis, 1932. 281

Fig. 3.26 'Our noble people', Konev, 1935, Obshchestvo sodeistviia oborone i aviatsionno-khimicheskomu stroitel'stvu SSSR (Kharkov), 85 x 60 cm, edn 20,000 282

Fig. 3.27 'Stalinists! Extend the front of the Stakhanovite movement!', Genrikh Futerfas, 1936. 283

Fig. 3.28 'Long live our teacher, our father, our leader, Comrade Stalin!', Nikolai Avvakumov, 1946, Iskusstvo (Moscow, Leningrad), edn 200,000. 284

Fig. 3.29 'Long live our leader and teacher the great Stalin!', Vladislav Pravdin & Nikolai Denisov, 1948, Iskusstvo (Moscow, Leningrad) 285

Fig. 3.30 'Reach for prosperity!', Viktor Ivanov, 1949. 286

Fig. 3.31 'Under the banner of Lenin, under the leadership of Stalin, forward to the victory of communism!', Iraklii Toidze, 1949, Iskusstvo (Moscow, Leningrad), 85 x 61 cm 287

Fig. 3.32 'Long live the equal-rights woman in the USSR, an active participant in the administration of the nation's state, economic, and cultural affairs!', Marina Volkova & Natalia Pinus, 1938. 288

Fig. 3.33 '"Such women didn't and couldn't exist in the old days" I.V. Stalin', Mikhail Solov'ev, 1950, Iskusstvo (Moscow), 101 x 68 cm, edn 200,000. 289

Fig. 4.1 'I.V. Stalin', unidentified artist, 1930, Litografia CKKPO (Krasnodar), edn 25,000 375

Fig. 4.2 'The Civil War 1918–1920', unidentified artist,
1938, 92 x 62.5 cm 376

Fig. 4.3 'Defence of the USSR', unidentified artist, 1938,
92 x 62.5 cm. 377

Fig. 4.4 'Comrade I.V. Stalin at the Front of the Civil War',
S. Podobedov, 1939, RKKA 378

Fig. 4.5 'Military Oath', S. Podobedov, 1939. 379

Fig. 4.6 'Long live our leader and teacher, best friend
of the Red Army, our dear and beloved Stalin!',
S. Podobedov, 1940, RKKA 379

Fig. 4.7 'Long live our dear invincible Red Army!',
Dmitrii Moor & Sergei Sen'kin, 1938 380

Fig. 4.8 'To continue the policy of peace and of strengthening
business relations with all countries …', M. Kaminskii,
1939, Mistetstvo (Kiev), 60 x 92 cm, edn 20,000. 381

Fig. 4.9 'Long live the organiser and leader of the victorious
Red Army great Stalin!', S. Podobedov, 1938, RKKA. 382

Fig. 4.10 'Long live the creator of the first cavalry, best friend
of the Red Cavalry — Comrade Stalin!', unidentified artist,
1939, RKKA 383

Fig. 4.11 'Stalin's spirit makes our army and country strong
and solid', Viktor Deni & Nikolai Dolgorukov, 1939 384

Fig. 4.12 'The foreign policy of the Soviet Union is clear
and explicit', unidentified artist, 1940, Izostat 385

Fig. 4.13 'If the leader calls …', Viktor Koretskii, 1941,
Izvestiia, 35 x 25 cm. 386

Fig. 4.14 '"The spirit of the great Lenin and his victorious
banner inspires us now in the Patriotic War as it did
23 years ago." Stalin', unidentified artist, 1941, Iskusstvo
(Moscow, Leningrad), 82.5 x 59.5 cm, edn 10,000 387

Fig. 4.15 'Under the banner of Lenin–Stalin we were victorious
in the great October Socialist Revolution …', A.V. Vasil'ev
and S.F. Yanevich, 1941, Izdanie (Leningrad), edn 20,000. . . 388

LIST OF ILLUSTRATIONS

Fig. 4.16 '"All our forces — to support our heroic Red Army and our glorious Red Navy! All the power of the people — to defeat the enemy!" Stalin', Iraklii Toidze, 1941, edn 6,000 389

Fig. 4.17 'We swore an oath to our leader to fight the enemy …', Konstantin Cheprakov, 1941, Gosizdat (Tashkent), 60 x 94 cm, edn 10,000 390

Fig. 4.18 'Under the name of Stalin we won. Under the name of Stalin we will win!', unidentified artist, 1941, Iskusstvo (Leningrad), edn 25,000 391

Fig. 4.19 'The spirit of the great Lenin and his victorious banner inspires us now in the Patriotic War as it did 23 years ago', Boris Mukhin, 1942, Iskusstvo (Moscow, Leningrad), 90 x 60 cm, edn 20,000 392

Fig. 4.20 'We can and must clear our Soviet soil of the Hitlerite filth!', V. Mirzoe, c. 1942, Sakhelgami, edn 1,500 393

Fig. 4.21 'Under the invincible banner of the great Lenin — forward to victory!', Nikolai Kogout, 1942, Gosizdat, edn 15,000 394

Fig. 4.22 'The path to our glory is immutable — Fascism will die! …', Pen Varlen, 1942, Gosizdat (Tashkent), edn 10,000 394

Fig. 4.23 'Under the banner of Lenin, forward, to victory!', Vladimir Serov, 1942, Iskusstvo (Leningrad), 89 x 63 cm, edn 10,000 395

Fig. 4.24 'Comrades of the Red Army …', Viktor Ivanov & Ol'ga Burova, 1942, Iskusstvo (Moscow, Leningrad), 88 x 59 cm, edn 30,000 396

Fig. 4.25 'Okno UzTAG No. 123', Nadezhda Kashina, 1942, Okno UzTAG (Uzbekistan), 84 x 183 cm 397

Fig. 4.26 'Okno TASS No. 590', Pavel Sokolov-Skalia, 1942, TASS (Moscow), 218 x 102 cm, edn 400 398

Fig. 4.27 'During the war …', Vlasob', 1943, (Baku), edn 5,000 . . 399

Fig. 4.28 'For the Soviet fatherland ...', Nikolai Zhukov
& Viktor Klimashin, 1943, Iskusstvo (Moscow, Leningrad),
edn 25,000 400

Fig. 4.29 '"The spirit of the great Lenin and his invincible banner
inspire us now in the patriotic war" (I. Stalin)', Veniamin
Pinchuk, 1943, Iskusstvo (Leningrad), edn 4,000 401

Fig. 4.30 'For our great motherland!', Nina Vatolina, 1944,
Iskusstvo (Moscow, Leningrad), edn 50,000 401

Fig. 4.31 'Under the leadership of Comrade Stalin, forward to
complete victory over our enemy!', A.A. Babitskii, 1944,
Iskusstvo (Moscow, Leningrad), 90 x 59 cm, edn 5,000 402

Fig. 4.32 '"Glory to the great heroic Red Army, defending the
independence of our country and winning victory over
the enemy!" I. Stalin', Vladimir Kaidalov, 1945, Dal'giz,
edn 5,000 403

Fig. 4.33 'Great Stalin — first deputy of the Supreme Soviet
of the USSR', Stepan Razvozzhaev, 1945, Izdanie (Irkutsk),
edn 25,000 404

Fig. 4.34 'Long live the creator of the constitution of socialist
society, the leader of the Soviet people, great Stalin!',
unidentified artist, portrait by Karpov, Undated, c. 1945,
Izdatelstvo Krasnyi Krym, edn 10,000 405

Fig. 4.35 'The Soviet people are full of gratitude and love
for dear STALIN — the great organiser of our victory',
Viktor Koretskii, 1945, Iskusstvo (Moscow, Leningrad),
edn 75,000 406

Fig. 4.36 'Long live generalissimus STALIN — great leader and
general of the Soviet people!', Viktor Deni, 1945, Iskusstvo
(Moscow, Leningrad), edn 50,000 407

Fig. 4.37 'Forward, to new victories of socialist construction!',
Iraklii Toidze, 1946, Iskusstvo (Moscow, Leningrad),
103 x 68 cm, edn 50,000 408

Fig. 4.38 '1917–1946 Glory to the Red Army, defending the gains
of the great October socialist revolution!', Viktor Koretskii,
1946, Iskusstvo (Moscow, Leningrad), 96 x 63 cm,
edn 70,000 409

Fig. 4.39 'Long live the V.K.P.(b) — the party of Lenin–Stalin, inspirer and organiser of our great victories!', Iraklii Toidze, 1946, Iskusstvo (Moscow, Leningrad), edn 250,000 410

Fig. 4.40 'Long live the leader of the Soviet people — great Stalin', Onufriichuk, 1946, Mistetstvo, edn 50,000. 411

Fig. 4.41 'Long live the leader of the Soviet people — great Stalin!', Boris Mukhin, 1947, Iskusstvo (Moscow, Leningrad), edn 300,000. 412

Fig. 4.42 'Long live the leader of the Soviet people, great Stalin!', Boris Mukhin, 1947, Iskusstvo (Moscow, Leningrad) 413

Fig. 4.43 'Long live the leader of the Soviet people — great Stalin', Vladislav Pravdin & Nikolai Denisov, 1947, Iskusstvo (Moscow, Leningrad), edn 200,000 414

Fig. 4.44 'Glory to the leader of the Soviet people — great Stalin!', Georgii Bakhmutov, 1947, Mistetstvo, edn 70,000 415

Fig. 4.45 'Stalin is our fighting banner', Aleksandr Druzhkov & I. Shagin, 1948, Iskusstvo (Moscow, Leningrad) 416

Fig. 4.46 'Glory to great Stalin!', Boris Mukhin, 1948, Iskusstvo (Moscow, Leningrad) 417

Fig. 4.47 'It is our good fortune ...', N. Petrov, 1948, Iskusstvo (Moscow, Leningrad) 418

Fig. 4.48 'Long live the V.K.P.(b) inspirer and organiser of the victory of the Soviet people!', B.I. Lebedev, 1948, Izdatelstvo (Moldavia), edn 5,000. 419

Fig. 4.49 'Long live the party of Lenin–Stalin, inspirer and organiser of our victories!', F. Litvinov, 1948, Krymizdat 420

Fig. 4.50 'Long live the VKP(b) ...', Aleksandr Druzhkov, 1948, Iskusstvo (Moscow, Leningrad). 421

Fig. 4.51 'We will struggle to reap a big cotton harvest!', Vladimir Kaidalov, 1950, 86 x 58.5 cm 422

Fig. 4.52 '"We stand for peace and we defend the cause of peace." I. Stalin', Boris Berezovskii, 1947, Iskusstvo (Moscow, Leningrad), 118 x 68 cm 423

Fig. 4.53 '"Long life and prosperity to our motherland!" I. Stalin', Iraklii Toidze, 1947, Iskusstvo (Moscow, Leningrad) 424

Fig. 4.54 'Stalin is our great standard-bearer of peace!', Viktor Ivanov, 1950, Iskusstvo (Moscow, Leningrad), 83.4 x 56.4, edn 100,000. 425

Fig. 4.55 'Great Stalin is the banner of friendship of the peoples of the USSR!', Viktor Koretskii, 1950, Iskusstvo (Moscow, Leningrad), edn 200,000 426

Fig. 4.56 'Great Stalin is the best friend of the Latvian people!', Petr Golub, 1950, Iskusstvo (Moscow, Leningrad), edn 20,000 427

Fig. 4.57 '"We stand for peace and we defend the cause of peace." I. Stalin', Boris Belopol'skii, 1952, Iskusstvo (Moscow), 82 x 64 cm, edn 300,000 428

Fig. 4.58 '"The world will be saved and enhanced if people take responsibility for maintaining peace into their own hands and defend it to the end." I. Stalin', Boris Belopol'skii, 1952, Iskusstvo (Moscow), 69 x 56 cm, edn 100,000 429

Fig. 4.59 'Happy New Year, beloved Stalin!', Konstantin Ivanov, 1952, Iskusstvo (Moscow), 55.5 x 37 cm, edn 50,000 430

Fig. 4.60 'Long live the Leninist VKP(b), organiser of victorious socialist construction', Viktor Deni & Nikolai Dolgorukov, 1934, Izogiz (Moscow, Leningrad), 62 x 94 cm, edn 6,500 .. 431

Fig. 4.61 'Glory to great Stalin!', V. Paradovskii, 1947, Kirgosizdat, edn 2,190 432

Fig. 4.62 'Cadres decide everything', Gustav Klutsis, 1935, Izogiz (Moscow, Leningrad), 77 x 109 cm, edn 20,000 433

Fig. 4.63 'Long live the Stalinist Order of Heroes and Stakhanovites!', Gustav Klutsis, 1936, 71.3 x 101.2 cm. 434

LIST OF ILLUSTRATIONS

Fig. 4.64 'Our government and the Party does not have other interests …', Viktor Koretskii, 1938, Izogiz (Moscow, Leningrad), 86 x 61.3 cm, edn 300,000 435

Fig. 4.65 'The reality of our program …', I. Shagin, 1947, Iskusstvo (Moscow, Leningrad), edn 300,000 436

Fig. 4.66 'Under the leadership of the great Stalin — forward to communism!', Boris Berezovskii, Mikhail Solov'ev & I. Shagin, 1951, Iskusstvo (Moscow), edn 500,000 437

Fig. 4.67 'Glory to the first candidate for deputy of the Supreme Soviet of the USSR, great Stalin!', Viktor Govorov, 1946, Ogiz 438

Fig. 4.68 'We gathered under the red banner of Lenin …', Nikolai Denisov, 1949, Iskusstvo (Moscow, Leningrad), 89 x 60 cm, edn 100,000. 439

Fig. 4.69 'I would like comrades to systematically influence their deputies …', Be-Sha (Boris Shapoval) & Rozenberg, 1940, Mistetstvo (Kiev), edn 40,000 440

The following repositories hold copies of the posters included in this volume:

- The Museum of Contemporary History, Moscow
- The Russian State Library, Moscow
- The State Historical Museum, Moscow
- The State Museum of the History of the Blockade of Leningrad, St Petersburg, Russia
- Hoover Institution Archives, Stanford, California, United States
- The Jane Voorhees Zimmerli Museum, New Brunswick, New Jersey, United States
- Tom and Jeri Ferris Collection of Russian and Soviet Culture, University of Southern California, United States
- The David King Collection, London.

See the image sources for location details relating to each image.

Abbreviations

AKhR	Assotsiatsia Khudozhnikov Revolutsii / Association of Artists of the Revolution
AKhR/R	Assotsiatsia Khudozhnikov Revolyutsionnoi Rossii / Association of Artists of Revolutionary Russia
ASSR	Autonomous Soviet Socialist Republic
MOSSKh	Moskovskaia organizatsiia Soiuza sovetskikh khudozhnikov / Moscow Section of the Union of Soviet Artists
NEP	New Economic Policy
NKVD	Narodnyi Komissariat Vnutrennikh Del / The People's Commissariat for Internal Affairs
Okna TASS	Okna telegrafnoie agentstvo Sovetskogo Soiuza / Telegraph Agency of the Soviet Union windows
ORPP	Obshchestvo Revolyutsionnikh Rabotnikov Plakata / Union of Russian Revolutionary Poster Artists
RABIS	Rabouchee iskusstvo / Worker's Art, an organ of the Central Committee of the Communist Party.
RGALI	Rossiiskii Gosudarstvennyy Arkhiv Literatury i Iskusstva / Russian State Archive of Literature and Art
RGASPI	Rossiiskii Gosudarstvennyi Arkhiv Sotsial'no-politicheskoi Istorii / Russian State Archive of Socio-Political History
ROSTA	Rossiiskoie telegrafnoie agentstvo / Russian Telegraph Agency

RSFSR	Russian Soviet Federative Socialist Republic
TsDAHOU	Tsentral'nyi Derzhavnyi Arkhiv Hromads'kykh Ob'iednan' Ukrainy / The Central State Archive of Public Organisations of Ukraine
USSR	Union of Soviet Socialist Republics
UzTAG	Uzbekskoe Telegrafnoe Agentstvo / Uzbek Telegraph Agency
VKhUTEMAS	Vysshiye Khudozhestvenno-tekhnicheskie Masterskie / Higher Art and Technical Studios
VKP(b)	Vsesoiuznaia Kommunisticheskaia Partiia (bol'shevikov) / All-Union Communist Party (Bolshevik)
VLKSM	Vsesoyuznyy Leninskiy Kommunistícheskiy soyúz molodozhi / The All-Union Leninist Young Communist League (Komsomol)

Introduction

In the arts of representation are found the real origins and organs of social control ... What then is a king? He is a king's portrait, and that alone makes him king ...
Louis Marin[1]

[N]ow the image of the leader is unthinkable outside of his portrait
Bill Keller[2]

Politics will eventually be replaced by imagery. The politician will be only too happy to abdicate in favor of his image, because the image will be much more powerful than he could ever be.
Marshall McLuhan[3]

Some people may say that Lenin is recommending moral persuasion instead of violence! But it is foolish to imagine we can solve the problem of organising a new science and technology for the development of communist society by violence alone.
Vladimir Il'ich Lenin[4]

---

1   Louis Marin, *Portrait of the king*, Minneapolis, University of Minnesota Press, 1988, p. 218.
2   Bill Keller, 'Skul'ptura na vystavke', *Iskusstvo*, 2, 1941, pp. 45–47, quoted in Jan Plamper, *The Stalin cult: a study in the alchemy of power*, New Haven, Yale University Press, 2012, p. 197.
3   Marshall McLuhan, remark at the American Booksellers Association luncheon, Washington DC, June 1969, quoted in the *Vancouver Sun*, 7 Jun. 1969, cited in Robert Andrews, *The new Penguin dictionary of modern quotations*, London, Penguin, 2003, books.google.com.au/books?id=VK0vR4fsaigC&pg=PT1111&lpg=PT1111&dq=marshall+mcluhan+The+new+penguin+dictionary+of+modern+quotations&source=bl&ots=F-iC0c8wiM&sig=BAMUDrIXRMbypg0Znsg_NMOkFgE&hl=en&sa=X&ved=0ahUKEwiR2qiQ3IbQAhXFtpQKHa81AvoQ6AEIGzAA#v=onepage&q=marshall%20mcluhan%20The%20new%20penguin%20dictionary%20of%20modern%20quotations&f=false (accessed 1 Nov 2016).
4   V.I. Lenin, *Collected works*, vol. 29, George Hanna (trans.), Moscow, Progress Publications, 1965, p. 72.

THE PERSONALITY CULT OF STALIN IN SOVIET POSTERS, 1929–1953

Although the literature on Stalinist propaganda is enormous, there has been no dedicated study on the marketing of Stalin's personality cult in posters during the Stalinist period. This book is an attempt to fill this lacuna. Research on Iosif Stalin and the Soviet Union under his leadership is extensive and encompasses a wide number of academic disciplines, including history, political science, psychology, sociology, film, music, literature and the visual arts. In recent years, as material in the Soviet archives has become available to researchers since the collapse of communism in 1989, many scholars have used the archives to access material to confirm hypotheses that were earlier little more than informed conjecture. With so much material about Stalin already published, it is increasingly difficult to be familiar with all aspects of the Stalinist literature, and researchers in the field must exercise caution not to merely reiterate material that already exists elsewhere.

While it is true that almost every facet of Stalinist history, politics and biography has been examined by specialists in these fields, there has been limited research conducted on art under Stalin, and a comparatively small amount of research devoted to the posters of the Stalin era, especially examined from the iconographic perspective of the art historian. Historian Jan Plamper suggests that one reason for this derives from the very nature of Stalinist art. He argues that socialist realism had totalising ambitions that not only sought to fill all available space, but also to deny the existence of art criticism and art history as discrete disciplines by making them indistinguishable from the material found in visitor's comment books at exhibitions. Thus, according to Plamper, the absence of conventional art historical exegeses of socialist realism paintings today seems to testify to the success of 'socialist realist empire-building ambitions'.[5]

From the beginning of the Soviet regime, posters were seen as a vitally important medium for communicating with and educating the vast population of the territories of the USSR. While the medium of film came to rival the poster in importance in the late 1930s, the poster remained, throughout the years of Stalin's leadership, a primary form of propaganda produced under strict centralised control that closely reflected the regime's evolving priorities. Posters containing an image of Stalin provide evidence for analysis of the way in which the

---

5   Plamper, *The Stalin cult*, p. 115.

leadership wished to present itself and the regime, and indicate those values that were considered most important to the creation of the new man and the new civilisation. Stalin came increasingly to symbolise the Party and the state, and the persona generated for him in propaganda reflects how the state saw itself or, at the very least, wished to appear in the eyes of the people. Although scholars including Victoria Bonnell,[6] Graeme Gill,[7] and Jeffrey Brooks[8] have all made extensive reference to the propaganda poster in their historical and sociological research, all but Bonnell (see below) have done so within a broader context of the history of the Stalinist years. The posters are employed for illustrative purposes, as examples of a particular theme or trend under discussion.

In this book, the Stalin propaganda posters are examined from an art historical iconographic and iconologic perspective, employing methodology that was first developed by Erwin Panofsky,[9] and Fritz Saxl.[10] This methodology focuses on imagery and the meaning of works of art, rather than on form. The iconographic analysis commences with a detailed and intensive study of the imagery employed in a large number of posters of Stalin, and the iconologic analysis explores the meaning inferred from this imagery, examined within the historic context in which the posters were produced. It is argued that the portrayal of Stalin in posters was not intended to reflect his personal qualities as a man, or even as a leader, but that his persona was constructed along archetypal and mythic lines in order to symbolise the essential qualities of Bolshevism as an ideology, and more concrete but impersonal entities, such as the Party and the state. The intention behind the use of Stalin as a symbol was primarily didactic. While Marxist ideology was a central concern for Stalin and

---

6   Victoria E. Bonnell, *Iconography of power: Soviet political posters under Lenin and Stalin*, Berkeley, University of California Press, 1998.
7   Graeme J. Gill, *Symbols and legitimacy in Soviet politics*, New York, Cambridge University Press, 2011.
8   Jeffrey Brooks, *Thank you, Comrade Stalin! Soviet public culture from revolution to Cold War*, Princeton University Press, 2000.
9   Erwin Panofsky, *Meaning in the visual arts: papers in and on art history*, New York, Doubleday, 1955.
10 Fritz Saxl, *Lectures*, vols 1 & 2, London, Warburg Institute, 1957; and, Fritz Saxl, *A heritage of images: A selection of lectures by Fritz Saxl*, Harmondsworth, Penguin, 1970. Also see Mark Cheetham et al., *The subjects of art history*, Cambridge University Press, 1998; Brendan Cassidy (ed.), *Iconography at the crossroads*, Princeton University Press, 1993; Mieke Bal & Norman Bryson, 'Semiotics and art history', *Art Bulletin*, June 1991, pp. 174–298; M.A. Holly, *Panofsky and the foundations of art history*, Ithaca, New York, Cornell University Press, 1984.

the top Party elite, it usually assumed a lower priority among the general population in their everyday struggle to survive in conditions of varying privation. In order to transform man and society, and to create a new civilisation, which was the ultimate goal of Marxist–Leninist ideology, the population had not only to be made aware of socialist tenets and principles, but to wholeheartedly adopt them as their own and work harmoniously towards the achievement of a real transformation in their physical environment. Due to the largely agrarian nature of Soviet society and low levels of literacy in the population, propaganda that focused on complex ideological notions, or that assumed considerable prior knowledge, was found to be unsuccessful in educating the population as a whole. Ideology had to be simplified, goals had to be made clear, and impersonal entities were given a face that was both representative and instantly recognisable. As this process evolved, the image of the leader came to increasing prominence. Unlike painted portraits of Stalin,[11] posters usually left less room for ambiguity by virtue of greater freedom to montage objects in the one image. They also had the capacity for distortions of scale and perspective and the accompanying caption could direct the viewer to the intended meaning.

The approach adopted in this research is primarily an art historical one, however the art history discipline itself has become, to some extent, multidisciplinary. Primary emphasis is placed on an iconographic, iconological and semiotic study where the Stalinist imagery is placed within an iconographic tradition. Simultaneously, this tradition is interrogated in a broader sociological context, taking into account a multitude of approaches that are adopted by political scientists, historians, psychologists, psychoanalysts and other researchers. The author's own background in art history, psychology, philology, political science and modern history is, to some extent, reflected in the approaches adopted. It is hoped that the material uncovered in this study may in turn inform the current discourse in Stalinist studies across a number of other disciplines.

In order to obtain a thorough understanding of the purpose and meaning of Stalin posters, research for this book draws on several fields of enquiry. One of the primary areas of research focuses on the

---

11 Plamper focuses on the image of Stalin in Soviet oil painting in *The Stalin cult* (2012).

INTRODUCTION

development and uses of political posters, both in Stalin's Soviet Union and outside. A good general history of the graphic arts for political purposes can be found in Robert Philippe's *Political graphics*,[12] and Jeffrey T. Schnapp's *Revolutionary tides*.[13] An excellent overview of the history of the political poster in Eastern Europe is *Political posters in Central and Eastern Europe, 1945–95*, by James Aulich and Marta Sylvestrová.[14] For a comprehensive examination of the Russian Civil War poster, see Vyacheslav Polonskii's *Russkii revolyutsionnyi plakat*,[15] and B.S. Butnik-Siverskii's *Sovetskii plakat epokhi grazhdanskoi voiny, 1918–1921*.[16] For an examination of posters in the context of art in the early years of Stalinism in the USSR see C.G. Holme's *Art in the USSR*, published in 1935.[17] Peter Kenez also examines pre-Stalinist posters in the context of Soviet propaganda on the whole in *The birth of the propaganda state*, published in 1985.[18] Writing more recently, since the opening of the archives, Graeme Gill[19] and Malte Rolf[20] both examine the poster in the wider propaganda context.

Stephen White's *The Bolshevik poster*[21] of 1998 examines the pre-revolutionary influences on the Soviet political poster and provides an excellent history of the development of the poster under Lenin's and Stalin's leadership. White's study includes biographies of leading poster artists and outlines the formal structures in place for the production of posters, their dissemination, and ongoing feedback to poster artists. White's primary focus is on the posters of the Civil War period, which he sees as the peak of Bolshevik poster production,

---

12 Robert Philippe, *Political graphics: art as a weapon*, New York, Abbeville Press, 1982.
13 Jeffrey T. Schnapp, *Revolutionary tides: the art of the political poster 1914–1989*, Geneva, Skira, 2005.
14 James Aulich & Marta Sylvestrová, *Political posters in Central and Eastern Europe, 1945–95: signs of the times*, Manchester University Press, 1999.
15 Vyacheslav Polonskii, *Russkii revolyutsionnyi plakat*, Moscow, Gosizdat, 1925.
16 B.S. Butnik-Siverskii, *Sovetskii plakat epokhi grazhdanskoi voiny, 1918–1921*, Moscow, Izd. Vses. Knizhnoi palaty, 1960.
17 C.G. Holme, *Art in the USSR: architecture, sculpture, painting, graphic arts, theatre, film, crafts*, London, The Studio, 1935.
18 Peter Kenez, *The birth of the propaganda state: Soviet methods of mass mobilization, 1917–1929*, Cambridge University Press, 1985.
19 Gill, *Symbols and legitimacy in Soviet politics*.
20 Malte Rolf, 'A hall of mirrors: Sovietizing culture under Stalinism', *Slavic Review*, 68:3, 2009, pp. 601–30.
21 Stephen White, *The Bolshevik poster*, New Haven, Yale University Press, 1998.

with perhaps a further peak in the years of the Great Patriotic War.²² He devotes only one chapter out of six to posters produced after the Civil War.

An extensive source of information on Soviet posters is Bonnell's *Iconography of power*.²³ Bonnell's research, conducted with primary sources from the Russian State Library's poster collection, examines the historical antecedents of the Soviet political poster and the circumstances under which political posters were created. She approaches the topic thematically, dealing with the iconography of the worker, the representation of women and Bolshevik demonology across the Lenin and Stalin years. Bonnell touches on material of particular relevance to the current research in chapters on the iconography of the *vozhd'* (leader)²⁴ and the apotheosis of Stalinist political art.

Three recent monographs have also provided useful information for this research. Margarita Tupitsyn focuses on the work of Gustav Klutsis and Valentina Kulagina,²⁵ while Erika Wolf²⁶ and Robert Bird et al.²⁷ have examined the career of Viktor Koretskii in publications in 2012 and 2011 respectively. Two sources were consulted for biographical information on Soviet poster artists. The incomplete multi-volume *Khudozhnikii Narodov SSSR*²⁸ contains brief biographies of many poster artists, and Matthew Cullerne Bown's *A dictionary of 20th century Russian and Soviet painters, 1900s–1980s*²⁹ provides brief biographical sketches of some graphic artists who were also

---

22 White, *The Bolshevik poster*, p. 130.
23 Bonnell, *Iconography of power*.
24 The term *vozhd'* derives from the Church Slavonic for leader. At the time of the Russian Revolution, it was primarily used to denote a military leader, and was first applied to Lenin in around 1918 (see Bonnell, *Iconography of power*, p. 140).
25 Margarita Tupitsyn, *Gustav Klutsis and Valentina Kulagina: photography and montage after constructivism*, New York, International Center of Photography, 2004.
26 Erika Wolf, *Koretsky: the Soviet photo poster: 1930–1984*, New York, The New Press, 2012.
27 Robert Bird, Christopher P. Heuer, Matthew Jesse Jackson, Tumelo Mosaka & Stephanie Smith (eds), *Vision and communism: Viktor Koretsky and dissident public visual culture*, New York, New Press, 2011.
28 V.V. Andreyanova, *Khudozhnikii Narodov SSSR: Biobibliograficheskii Slovar'*, 1, Moscow, Izdatel'stvo 'Iskusstvo', 1970; V.V. Andreyanova, *Khudozhnikii Narodov SSSR: Biobibliograficheskii Slovar'*, 2, Moscow, Izdatel'stvo 'Iskusstvo', 1972; V.V. Andreyanova & I.I. Nikonova, *Khudozhnikii Narodov SSSR: Biobibliograficheskii Slovar'*, 3, Moscow, Izdatel'stvo 'Iskusstvo', 1976; I.I. Nikonova, *Khudozhnikii Narodov SSSR: Biobibliograficheskii Slovar'*, 4:1, Moscow, Izdatel'stvo 'Iskusstvo', 1983.
29 Matthew Cullerne Bown, *A dictionary of 20th century Russian and Soviet painters, 1900s–1980s*, London, Izomar, 1998.

INTRODUCTION

known as painters. A 2009 journal article by Maria Gough examines the emergence of photomontage in the work of John Heartfield and Gustav Klutsis.[30] An invaluable comprehensive catalogue of Okna TASS (windows of the Telegraph Agency of the Soviet Union) posters was compiled by Aleksei Morozov in 2013.[31] Many other sources were consulted for general research or comparative purposes in order to situate the Soviet political poster in the context of other propaganda posters.[32]

During Stalin's leadership, all production of propaganda materials was centralised under government control, which lead to homogeneity of themes, and often of methods, across artistic fields. It is thus necessary to view the political poster in the context of the whole of Soviet artistic production. Key texts dealing with art and literature under

---

30   Maria Gough, 'Back in the USSR: John Heartfield, Gustav Klucis, and the medium of Soviet propaganda', *New German Critique*, 36:2, 2009, pp. 133–84.
31   Aleksei Morozov, *Agit-Okna, Okna TASS, 1941–1945*, Moscow, Kontakt-Kultura, 2013.
32   Dawn Ades & Alison McClean, *Revolution on paper: Mexican prints 1910–1960*, Austin, University of Texas Press, 2009; James Aulich, *War posters: weapons of mass communication*, New York, Thames & Hudson, 2011; David Craven, *Art and revolution in Latin America, 1910–1990*, 2nd edn, New Haven, Yale University Press, 2006; David Craven, Teresa Eckmann, Tere Romo & Ilan Stavans, *Latin American posters: public aesthetics and mass politics*, Sante Fe, Museum Of New Mexico Press, 2006; David Crowley, *Posters of the Cold War*, London, Victoria & Albert Museum, 2008; Milton Glaser & Mirko Ilic, *The design of dissent: socially and politically driven graphics*, Gloucester, Rockport Publishers, 2006; Robert Hariman & John Louis Lucaites, *No caption needed: iconic photographs, public culture, and liberal democracy*, University Of Chicago Press, 2007; David Kunzle, *Che Guevara: icon, myth, and message*, Washington, D.C., Study of Political Graphics, 1997; Peter Paret, Beth Irwin Lewis & Paul Paret, *Persuasive images: posters of war and revolution from the Hoover Institution archives*, Princeton University Press, 1992; Collection, The USSR Lenin Library, *Soviet political posters: 1917/1980*, Boston, Penguin, 1986; Maria Lafont, *Soviet posters: the Sergo Grigorian Collection*, Fort Worth, Prestel Publishing, 2007; *Building the collective: Soviet graphic design 1917–1937*, 2nd edn, New York, Princeton Architectural Press, 1996; N.I. Baburina, *The Soviet political poster 1917–1980: from the USSR Lenin Library Collection*, Harmondsworth, Penguin Books, 1985; Alla Rosenfeld (ed.), *Defining Russian graphic arts: from Diaghilev to Stalin, 1898–1934*, New Jersey, Rutgers University Press, 1999; Margarita Tupitsyn, *Glaube, Hoffnung — Anpassung, Sowietische Bilder 1928–1845*, Oberhausen, Plitt Verlag, 1996; Richard Hollis & Elena Barkhatova, *Russian constructivist posters*, France, Pyramyd, 2010; John Milner, *El Lissitzky: design*, Easthampton, Antique Collectors' Club, Ltd, 2010; Boris Mukhametshin, *Anti-posters: Soviet icons in reverse*, Riverside, Xenos Books, 1987; Stephen M. Norris, *A war of images: Russian popular prints, wartime culture, and national identity, 1812–1945*, DeKalb, Northern Illinois University Press, 2006; *Chinese propaganda posters*, Köln, Taschen, 2011; Melissa Chiu, *Art and China's revolution*, New Haven, Yale University Press, 2008; Ekaterina V. Haskins & James P. Zappen, 'Totalitarian visual "monologue": reading Soviet posters with Bakhtin', *Rhetoric Society Quarterly*, 2010, 40:4, pp. 326–59.

Stalin include those by Matthew Cullerne Bown,[33] Jan Plamper,[34] Jeffrey Brooks,[35] David Elliott,[36] Sheila Fitzpatrick,[37] Katerina Clark,[38] Graeme Gill,[39] Evgeny Dobrenko,[40] Rosa Ferré,[41] Peter Kenez,[42] James von Geldern,[43] Irina Gutkin,[44] Dawn Ades,[45] Thomas Lahusen,[46] Régine

---

33 Matthew Cullerne Bown, *Art under Stalin*, New York, Holmes and Meier Pub., 1991; Bown, *A dictionary of 20th century Russian and Soviet painters*; Matthew Cullerne Bown, *Socialist realist painting*, New Haven, Yale University Press, 1998; Matthew Cullerne Bown & Brandon Taylor (eds), *Art of the Soviets: painting, sculpture, and architecture in a one-party state, 1917–1992*, Manchester University Press, 1993.

34 Plamper, *The Stalin cult*; Jan Plamper, 'Abolishing ambiguity: Soviet censorship practices in the 1930s', *Russian Review*, 60:4, 2001, pp. 526–44; Jan Plamper, 'The Stalin cult in the visual arts, 1929–1953', PhD dissertation, University of California, Berkeley, 2001.

35 Jeffrey Brooks, 'Socialist realism in *Pravda*: read all about it!', *Slavic Review*, 53:4, 1994, pp. 973–91; Jeffrey Brooks, 'Stalin's politics of obligation', *Totalitarian Movements and Political Religions*, 4:1, 2003, pp. 47–67; Jeffrey Brooks, 'The Russian nation imagined: the peoples of Russia as seen in popular imagery, 1860s–1890s', *Journal of Social History*, 43:3, 2010, pp. 535–57; Brooks, *Thank you, Comrade Stalin!*

36 David Elliott, *New worlds: Russian art and society, 1900–1937*, New York, Rizzoli, 1986; David Elliott, 'Guerillas and partisans: Art, power and freedom in Europe and beyond, 1940–2012', *Framework*, Helsinki, 10, Supp., 2009, pp. 22–25.

37 Sheila Fitzpatrick, *The Commissariat of Enlightenment: Soviet organization of education and the arts under Lunacharsky October 1917–1921*, Cambridge, The University Press, 1970; Sheila Fitzpatrick, *The cultural front: power and culture in revolutionary Russia*, Ithaca, New York, Cornell University Press, 1992.

38 Katerina Clark, 'Eisenstein's two projects for a film about Moscow', *The Modern Language Review*, 101:1, 2006, pp. 184–200; Katerina Clark, *The Soviet novel: history as ritual*, University of Chicago Press, 1981; Katerina Clark & Evgeny Dobrenko, *Soviet culture and power. A history in documents, 1917–1953*, New Haven, Yale University Press, 2007.

39 Gill, *Symbols and legitimacy in Soviet politics*.

40 E.A. Dobrenko & Eric Naiman, *The landscape of Stalinism: The art and ideology of Soviet space*, Seattle, University of Washington Press, 2003; Clark & Dobrenko, *Soviet culture and power*; Evgeny Dobrenko, 'Creation myth and myth creation in Stalinist cinema', *Studies in Russian and Soviet Cinema*, 1:3, 2007, pp. 239–64; Evgeny Dobrenko, 'Pushkin in Soviet and Post-Soviet culture', in Andrew Kahn (ed.), *The Cambridge companion to Pushkin*, Cambridge, Cambridge University Press, 2006.

41 Rosa Ferré, *Red cavalry: creation and power in Soviet Russia from 1917 to 1945: 07.10.2011 – 15.01.2012*, Madrid, La Casa Encendida, 2011.

42 Kenez, *The birth of the propaganda state*; Abbott Gleason, Peter Kenez & Richard Stites, *Bolshevik culture: experiment and order in the Russian Revolution*, Bloomington, Indiana University Press, 1985.

43 James von Geldern, *Bolshevik festivals, 1917–1920*, Berkeley, California, 1993; James von Geldern & Richard Stites (eds), *Mass culture in Soviet Russia: tales, songs, poems, movies, plays and folklore, 1917–1953*, Bloomington, Indiana University Press, 1995.

44 Irina Gutkin, *The cultural origins of the Socialist realist aesthetic: 1890–1934*, Evanston, Northwestern University Press, 1999.

45 Dawn Ades, *Art and power: Europe under the dictators 1930–45*, London, Thames and Hudson in association with Hayward Gallery, 1995.

46 Thomas Lahusen, *How life writes the book: real socialism and socialist realism in Stalin's Russia*, Ithaca, New York, Cornell University Press, 1997; Thomas Lahusen & E.A. Dobrenko, *Socialist realism without shores*, Durham, Duke University Press, 1997.

Robin,[47] Gleb Prokhorov,[48] Marek Bartelik,[49] Victoria Bonnell,[50] David Brandenberger,[51] Igor Golomshtok,[52] Boris Groys,[53] Hans Gunther,[54] Oliver Johnson,[55] David King,[56] Maureen Perrie,[57] Karen Petrone,[58] Susan E. Reid,[59] and Richard Stites.[60] Further research in this area is detailed in the bibliography.

A central argument of this book is that the Russian tradition of icon painting associated with the Orthodox Church has been a strong influence on the form and content of the political poster. In *The avant-garde icon*,[61] Andrew Spira argues that Russian art of the 19th and 20th centuries is underpinned by the artforms associated with traditional Russian icon painting. *The meaning of icons*[62] by Léonide Ouspensky

---

47 Régine Robin, *Socialist realism: an impossible aesthetic*, Stanford University Press, 1992.
48 Gleb Prokhorov, *Art under socialist realism: Soviet painting, 1930–1950*, East Roseville, Craftsman House, 1995.
49 Marek Bartelik, 'Concerning socialist realism: recent publications on Russian art', *Art Journal*, 58:4, 1999, pp. 90–95.
50 Victoria E. Bonnell, 'The peasant woman in Stalinist political art of the 1930s', *The American Historical Review*, 98:1, 1993, pp. 55–82.
51 David Brandenberger, *National Bolshevism: Stalinist mass culture and the formation of modern Russian national identity, 1931–1956*, Cambridge, Harvard University Press, 2002; Kevin M.F. Platt & David Brandenberger, *Epic revisionism: Russian history and literature as Stalinist propaganda*, Madison, University of Wisconsin Press, 2006.
52 Igor Golomshtok, *Totalitarian art in the Soviet Union, the Third Reich, Fascist Italy and the People's Republic of China*, New York, Icon Editions, 1990.
53 Boris Groys, *The total art of Stalinism: avant-garde, aesthetic dictatorship, and beyond*, Princeton University Press, 1992; Boris Groys & Max Hollein (eds), *Dream factory communism. The visual culture of the Stalin era*, Ostfildern-Ruit, Hatje Cantz Verlag, 2003.
54 Hans Gunther (ed.), *The culture of the Stalin period*, London, Macmillan, 1990.
55 Oliver Johnson, 'The Stalin Prize and the Soviet artist: status symbol or stigma?', *Slavic Review*, 70:4, 2011, pp. 819–43.
56 David King, *Red star over Russia: a visual history of the Soviet Union from 1917 to the death of Stalin: posters, photographs and graphics from the David King collection*, London, Tate, 2009; David King, *The commissar vanishes: the falsification of photographs and art in Stalin's Russia*, New York, Metropolitan Books, 1997.
57 Maureen Perrie, 'Folklore as evidence of peasant mentalite: social attitudes and values in Russian popular culture', *Russian Review*, 48:2, 1989, pp. 119–43.
58 Karen Petrone, *Life has become more joyous, Comrades. Celebrations in the time of Stalin*, Bloomington, Indiana University Press, 2000; Karen Petrone, 'Iconography of power', *The Russian Review*, 58:2, 1999, p. 333.
59 Susan E. Reid, 'All Stalin's women: gender and power in Soviet art of the 1930s', *Slavic Review*, 57:1, 1998, pp. 133–73; Susan E. Reid, 'Socialist realism in the Stalinist terror: the *Industry of Socialism* art exhibition, 1935–41', *The Russian Review*, 60:2, 2001, pp. 153–84.
60 Richard Stites, *Soviet popular culture: entertainment and society since 1900*, Cambridge University Press, 1992.
61 Andrew Spira, *The avant-garde icon: Russian avant-garde art and the icon painting tradition*, Aldershot, Lund Humphries/Ashgate, 2008.
62 Léonide Ouspensky & Vladimir Lossky, *The meaning of icons*, 2nd edn, Crestwood, St Vladimir's Seminary Press, 1982.

and Vladimir Lossky is one penetrating and insightful resource on the meaning of icons, their history, and the way in which they are used for the purposes of didactic instruction in the Russian Orthodox Church.

It is not sufficient to merely consider Stalinist art in isolation. In any society, but most particularly in the centralised and controlled socialist systems of the 20th century, art both reflects and creates the cultural milieu in which it operates. It is crucial to understand this wider social, economic and political context if one is to understand the meanings and functions of propaganda in the Soviet system. A vast array of material has been published on the historical, political and social conditions in the USSR under Stalin. For a full listing of materials consulted see the bibliography. Key texts include those by Stalinist scholars Balázs Apor, Jan Behrends, Polly Jones and E.A. Rees;[63] Claes Arvidsson and Lars Erik Blomquist;[64] Marina Balina and E.A. Dobrenko;[65] David Brandenberger;[66] Jeffrey Brooks;[67] Katerina Clark and Evgeny Dobrenko;[68] Sarah Davies;[69] Orlando Figes;[70]

---

63   Balázs Apor, Jan C. Behrends, Polly Jones & E.A. Rees, *The leader cult in communist dictatorships: Stalin and the Eastern Bloc*, Hampshire, Palgrave, 2004.
64   Claes Arvidsson & Lars Erik Blomquist, *Symbols of power: The esthetics of political legitimation in the Soviet Union and Eastern Europe*, Stockholm, Almqvist och Wiksell, 1987.
65   Marina Balina & E.A. Dobrenko, *Petrified Utopia: happiness Soviet style*, London, Anthem Press, 2009.
66   Brandenberger, *National Bolshevism*; D.L. Brandenberger & A.M. Dubrovsky. '"The people need a tsar": the emergence of National Bolshevism as Stalinist ideology, 1931–1941', *Europe–Asia Studies*, 50:5, 1998, pp. 873–92; David Brandenberger, 'The cult of Ivan the Terrible in Stalinist Russia', *The Russian Review*, 62:1, 2003, pp. 172–73; David Brandenberger, *Propaganda state in crisis: Soviet ideology, indoctrination, and terror under Stalin, 1927–1941*, New Haven, Yale University Press, 2011.
67   Brooks, 'Stalin's politics of obligation'; Brooks, 'The Russian nation imagined'; Brooks, *Thank You, Comrade Stalin!*.
68   Clark & Dobrenko, *Soviet culture and power*.
69   Sarah Davies, 'The "Cult" of the Vozhd': representations in letters from 1934–41', *Russian History*, 24:1–2, 1997, pp. 131–47; Sarah Davies, *Popular opinion in Stalin's Russia: terror, propaganda and dissent, 1934–1941*, Cambridge University Press, 1997; Sarah Davies & James Harris (eds), *Stalin: a new history*, Cambridge University Press, 2005.
70   Orlando Figes, *The whisperers: private life in Stalin's Russia*, New York, Metropolitan Books, 2007; Orlando Figes & Boris Kolonitskii, *Interpreting the Russian Revolution: the language and symbols of 1917*, New Haven, Yale University Press, 1999.

INTRODUCTION

Sheila Fitzpatrick;[71] J. Arch Getty;[72] Graeme Gill;[73] Jochen Hellbeck;[74] Klaus Heller and Jan Plamper;[75] David L. Hoffman;[76] Catriona Kelly;[77] Peter Kenez;[78] Christina Kiaer and Eric Naiman;[79] Stephen Kotkin;[80] Eric Naiman;[81] Jan Plamper;[82] Kevin Platt and David Brandenberger;[83]

71   Sheila Fitzpatrick, 'Cultural revolution revisited', *Russian Review*, 58:2, 1999, pp. 202–09; Fitzpatrick, *The cultural front*; Sheila Fitzpatrick, *Everyday Stalinism: ordinary life in extraordinary times — Soviet Russia in the 1930s*, New York, Oxford University Press, 1999; Sheila Fitzpatrick, *Stalinism: new directions*, London, Routledge, 1999.
72   J. Arch Getty, 'Samokritika rituals in the Stalinist Central Committee, 1933–1938', *Russian Review*, 58:1, 1999, pp. 49–70; J. Arch Getty, 'State and society under Stalin: constitutions and elections in the 1930s', *Slavic Review*, 50:1, 1991, pp. 18–35; J. Arch Getty & Oleg V. Naumov, *The road to terror: Stalin and the self-destruction of the Bolsheviks, 1932–1939*, New Haven, Yale University Press, 1999.
73   Graeme Gill, *The origins of the Stalinist political system*, Cambridge University Press, 1990; Graeme J. Gill, *Stalinism*, 2nd edn, London, Macmillan Press, 1998; Gill, *Symbols and legitimacy in Soviet politics*; Graeme Gill, 'Personality cult, political culture and party structure', *Studies in Comparative Communism*, 17:2, 1984, pp. 111–21; Graeme Gill, 'Political myth and Stalin's quest for authority in the party', in T.H. Rigby, Archie Brown & Peter Reddaway (eds), *Authority, power and policy in the USSR: essays dedicated to Leonard Schapiro*, London, Macmillan, 1980, pp. 98–117; Graeme Gill, 'The Soviet leader cult: reflections on the structure of leadership in the Soviet Union', *British Journal of Political Science*, 10:2, 1980, pp. 167–86.
74   Jochen Hellbeck, 'Fashioning the Stalinist soul: the diary of Stepan Podlubnyi (1931–1939)', *Jahrbücher für Geschichte Osteuropas*, Neue Folge, 44:3, 1996, pp. 344–73.
75   Klaus Heller & Jan Plamper (eds), *Personality cults in Stalinism*, Goïttingen, V&R Unipress, 2004.
76   David L. Hoffmann (ed.), *Stalinism: The essential readings*, Malden, Blackwell Publishing, 2003; David L. Hoffmann, *Stalinist values: the cultural norms of Soviet modernity, 1917–1941*, Ithaca, New York, Cornell University Press, 2003.
77   Catriona Kelly, *Children's world: growing up in Russia, 1890–1991*, New Haven, Yale University Press, 2007; Catriona Kelly, *Comrade Pavlik: the rise and fall of a Soviet boy hero*, London, Granta, 2005; Catriona Kelly, 'Riding the magic carpet: children and leader cult in the Stalin era', *The Slavic and East European Journal*, 49:2, 2005, pp. 199–24.
78   Kenez, *The birth of the propaganda state*.
79   Christina Kiaer & Eric Naiman, *Everyday life in early Soviet Russia: taking the Revolution inside*, Bloomington, Indiana University Press, 2006.
80   Stephen Kotkin, *Magnetic Mountain: Stalinism as a civilization*, Berkeley, University of California Press, 1995.
81   Eric Naiman, *Sex in public: the incarnation of early Soviet ideology*, Princeton University Press, 1997.
82   Plamper, *The Stalin cult*.
83   Platt & Brandenberger, *Epic revisionism*.

Bernice Glatzer Rosenthal;[84] Robert Service;[85] Harold Shukman;[86] Lewis Siegelbaum, A.K. Sokolov, L. Kosheleva and S.V. Zhuravlev;[87] Richard Stites;[88] Ronald Suny;[89] and Robert Tucker.[90]

A substantial field of research over several decades has detailed the biography of Stalin. An early contribution to the field that is of particular interest is the biography written by Alexandrov et al.[91] under Stalin's supervision in 1947, which was published with specific didactic and propagandistic intent. This text provides one of the best available indicators of how Stalin and his cohort intended his persona to be presented to the people. Other Stalinist 'insider' accounts include those by Stalin's daughter Svetlana Alliluyeva,[92] Vyacheslav Molotov,[93] Viktor Serge,[94] Ilia Ehrenburg,[95] Aleksandra Kollontai,[96]

---

84   Bernice Glatzer Rosenthal, *New myth, new world: from Nietzsche to Stalinism*, Pennsylvania State University Press, 2002.
85   Robert Service, *A history of 20th century Russia*, Cambridge, Harvard University Press, 1999.
86   Harold Shukman, *Redefining Stalinism*, London, Frank Cass, 2003.
87   Lewis H. Siegelbaum, A.K. Sokolov, L. Kosheleva & S.V. Zhuravlev, *Stalinism as a way of life: a narrative in documents*, New Haven, Yale University Press, 2000.
88   Stites, *Soviet popular culture*.
89   Ronald Grigor Suny, *The Soviet experiment: Russia, the USSR and the successor states*, 2nd edn, New York, Oxford University Press, 2011.
90   Robert C. Tucker, *Stalinism: essays in historical interpretation*, New York, W.W. Norton and Company, 1977; Robert C. Tucker, 'The rise of Stalin's personality cult', *American Historical Review*, 84, 1979, pp. 347–66; Robert C. Tucker, 'The theory of charismatic leadership', *Dædalus*, 97:3, 1968, pp. 731–56.
91   G.F. Alexandrov, M.R. Galaktionov, V.S. Kruzhkov, M.B. Mitin, V.D. Mochalov & P.N. Pospelov, *Joseph Stalin: a short biography*, Moscow, Foreign Languages Publishing House, 1947.
92   Svetlana Alliluyeva, *Only one year*, Paul Chavchavadze (trans.), New York, Harper and Row, 1969; Svetlana Alliluyeva, *Twenty letters to a friend*, Priscilla Johnson McMillan (trans.), New York, Harper & Row, 1967.
93   F. Chuev, *Molotov remembers: inside Kremlin politics — conversations with Felix Chuev*, Albert Resis (ed.), Chicago, Terra Publishing Center as Sto sorok besed s Molotovym, Ivan R. Dee, Inc., 1993.
94   Victor Serge, *Memoirs of a revolutionary 1901–1941*, Peter Sedgwick (trans.), London, Oxford University Press, 1963.
95   Ilya Ehrenburg, *Men, years — life*, vol. 5, *The war: 1941–45*, Tatiana Shebunina & Yvonne Kapp (trans.), London, MacGibbon and Kee, 1964; Ilya Ehrenburg, *Men, years — life*, vol. 6, *Post-war years: 1945–1954*, Tatiana Shebunina & Yvonne Kapp (trans.), London, MacGibbon and Kee, 1966.
96   Beatrice Farnsworth, 'Conversing with Stalin, surviving the terror: the diaries of Aleksandra Kollontai and the internal life of politics', *Slavic Review*, 69:4, 2010, pp. 944–70.

INTRODUCTION

and Milovan Djilas.[97] A contemporary hostile view of Stalin can be found in the writings of Lev Trotskii.[98] Notable Stalin biographies from the period before 1990 include Isaac Deutscher's *Stalin*;[99] Robert McNeal's *Stalin*;[100] and Robert Tucker's *Stalin as revolutionary, 1879–1929*.[101] More recent biographies, which adopt a new perspective on Stalin that is informed by material in the archives, include Robert Service's *Stalin*;[102] and the two recent books by Simon Sebag Montefiore, *Young Stalin* and *Stalin: the court of the Red Tsar*.[103]

Although a broad examination of many aspects of society under Stalin provides a crucial context for understanding the Stalin political poster, it is necessary to also look further afield to provide a more complete context for this material. Throughout recorded history there have been a number of personality cults around prominent historic figures, going back to classical antiquity with Alexander the Great, Julius Caesar, and Caesar Augustus; and later the Holy Roman Emperor Maximilian I, and Napoleon Bonaparte. Research in this area has sought to understand the phenomenon of the personality cult throughout history, and the ways in which the cults have manifested through time. Surviving art objects and contemporary accounts of artistic production from each period provide a rich record of how such cults were expressed in each era.[104]

---

97 Milovan Djilas, *Conversations with Stalin*, London, Rupert Hart-Davis, 1962.
98 Leon Trotskii, *My life*, www.marxists.org/archive/trotsky/1930/mylife/ch41.htm (accessed 25 May 2012); Leon Trotsky, *The history of the Russian Revolution*, Ann Arbor, University of Michigan Press, 1957.
99 Isaac Deutscher, *Stalin; a political biography*, 2nd edn, New York, Oxford University Press, 1966.
100 Robert McNeal, *Stalin: man and ruler*, New York University Press, 1988.
101 Robert C. Tucker, *Stalin as revolutionary, 1879–1929*, New York, W.W. Norton and Company, 1973.
102 Robert Service, *Stalin: a biography*, Cambridge, Bellknap Press, 2006.
103 Simon Sebag Montefiore, *Young Stalin*, New York, Alfred A. Knopf, 2007; S. Sebag Montefiore, *Stalin: the court of the Red Tsar*, London, Weidenfeld and Nicolson, 2003.
104 In *Rituals and power*, S.R.F. Price examines the personality cults of antiquity, from Alexander the Great to the Caesars (*Rituals and power: the Roman imperial cult in Asia Minor*, Cambridge University Press, 1984). Eric Badian's *Alexander the Great* provides a comprehensive foundational study of the cult of Alexander the Great and how it came into existence ('Alexander the Great between two thrones and Heaven', *Journal of Roman Archaeology*, supp. ss 17, 1996, pp. 11–26). In *The divinity of the Roman emperor*, Lily Ross Taylor explores the processes by which Julius Caesar came to be deified, and how his successor, Caesar Augustus, was able to consolidate his divinity through reference to his lineage from Julius Caesar (*The divinity of the Roman emperor*, Middletown, American Philological Association, 1931). Larry Silver's book *Marketing Maximilian* is a primary source of information on the cult of Holy Roman Emperor Maximilian I, who ultilised the newly invented printing press and artists including Albrecht

There also exists a specifically Russian context for the cult of personality and Stalin must be considered in the context of the tsars who led Russia before him. The available literature on Russian history is vast and cannot be covered adequately within the scope of this book. A selection of sources that provide a background to the history of Russian leadership include Abbott Gleason's *A companion to Russian history*;[105] Geoffrey Hosking's *Russia and the Russians*;[106] Michael Cherniavsky's *Tsar and people*;[107] Richard Hellie's 'The structure of Russian imperial history';[108] Richard Wortman's *Scenarios of power*;[109] and Edward L. Keenan's 'Muscovite political folkways'.[110] As the Second World War loomed in Europe, Stalin and the Soviet leadership appealed to this great Russian past to gain legitimacy and to mobilise the people for the sacrifices necessary to the war effort. There is extensive literature available on Stalin's 'rehabilitation' of Aleksandr Nevskii, Ivan IV and Peter the Great, which takes advantage of the recent availability of material in the Soviet archives. *Epic revisionism*,[111] edited by Kevin M.F. Platt and David Brandenberger, is a collection of essays in which notable scholars from several disciplines explore the return to canonical status of a number of historic and literary personalities who had been disregarded after

---

Dürer and Hans Burgkmair to spread the symbols of his authority with an unprecedented access to his target audience (*Marketing Maximilian: the visual ideology of a Holy Roman Emperor*, Princeton University Press, 2008). The scholarly literature on the cult of Napoleon also proves valuable to an investigation of the major premises of this book. Examination of the art produced in France in support of Napoleon's reign shows a continuation and elaboration on the themes that emerged in earlier personality cults. In *Napoleon and history painting*, Christopher Prendergast conducts a detailed study of some of the most well-known paintings of Napoleon that were executed in his own time by artists such as Antoine-Jean Gros, Jacques-Louis David, and Jean-Auguste-Dominique Ingres, with an eye to the symbolism employed, ambiguity (both intentional and unintentional), satire and the establishment of lineage and legitimacy for the emperor (*Napoleon and history painting: Antoine-Jean Gros's La Bataille d'Eylau*, Oxford, Clarendon Press, 1997). David Welch and Simon Lee both examine art as propaganda in the personality cult of Napoleon (David Welch, 'Painting, propaganda and patriotism', *History Today*, 55:7, 2005, pp. 42–50; Simon Lee, *Art and ideas: David*, London, Phaidon Press, 1998).
105 Abbott Gleason, *A companion to Russian history*, Chichester, Wiley-Blackwell, 2009.
106 Geoffrey A. Hosking, *Russia and the Russians: a history*, Cambridge, M.A., Belknap Press of Harvard University Press, 2001.
107 Michael Cherniavsky, *Tsar and people: studies in Russian myths*, New Haven, Yale University Press, 1961.
108 Richard Hellie, 'The structure of Russian imperial history', *History and Theory*, 44, Dec. 2005, pp. 88–112.
109 Richard Wortman, *Scenarios of power: myth and ceremony in Russian monarchy*, vol. 1, Princeton University Press, 1995.
110 Edward L. Keenan, 'Muscovite political folkways', *Russian Review*, 45:2, 1986, pp. 115–81.
111 Platt & Brandenberger, *Epic revisionism*.

the 1917 Revolution. In addition to this anthology, there is a wide selection of journal articles discussing 'socialism in one country', the rehabilitation of the tsars, and Russian art during the Second World War by scholars including David Brandenberger,[112] Maureen Perrie,[113] Katerina Clark,[114] Sheila Fitzpatrick,[115] Thomas Lahusen,[116] E.A. Dobrenko and Eric Naiman,[117] and Lars T. Lih.[118]

Other personality cults of the 20th century provide a further historic context for examination of the Stalin cult. While the abovementioned readings provide a 'vertical' perspective from which to view Stalin, a horizontal perspective also contributes to a greater understanding of the phenomenon of his personality cult. Adolf Hitler, Benito Mussolini and Mao Zedong chronologically overlapped with Stalin, and each used the arts to generate and maintain personality cults, making use of the technologies that became available in the 20th century. A number of sources compare Stalin and Hitler, such as *Hitler and Stalin* by Alan Bullock,[119] *Lenin, Stalin and Hitler* by Robert Gellately,[120] Åke Sandler's *Stalin and Hitler*,[121] and *June 1941* by John Lukacs.[122] Igor Golomshtok undertakes a comparative view of art under the 'totalitarian' regimes of Stalin, Hitler, Mussolini and Mao, and argues that art functions in a totalitarian system to transform dry ideology into images and myths for consumption by the general

---

112 Brandenberger & Dubrovsky, "The people need a tsar"; David Brandenberger & Kevin F.M. Platt, 'Terribly romantic, terribly progressive, or terribly tragic: rehabilitating Ivan IV under I.V. Stalin', *The Russian Review*, 58:4, 1999, pp. 635–54; Brandenberger, *National Bolshevism*; Brandenberger, 'The cult of Ivan the Terrible in Stalinist Russia'.
113 Maureen Perrie, *The image of Ivan the Terrible in Russian folklore*, Cambridge University Press, 1987; Maureen Perrie, *The cult of Ivan the Terrible in Stalin's Russia*, Houndmills, Palgrave, 2001.
114 Clark, *The Soviet novel*; Clark, 'Eisenstein's two projects for a film about Moscow'.
115 Fitzpatrick, *The cultural front*; Fitzpatrick, *Stalinism*.
116 Thomas Lahusen & Gene Kuperman, *Late Soviet culture: from perestroika to novostroika*, Durham, Duke University Press, 1993; Lahusen & Dobrenko, *Socialist realism without shores*.
117 Dobrenko & Naiman, *The landscape of Stalinism*.
118 Lars T. Lih, 'The cult of Ivan the Terrible in Stalin's Russia', *The Journal of Modern History*, 75:4, 2003, pp. 1004–05.
119 Alan Bullock, *Hitler and Stalin: parallel lives*, New York, Knopf, 1992.
120 Robert Gellately, *Lenin, Stalin, and Hitler: the age of social catastrophe*, New York, Alfred A. Knopf, 2007.
121 Åke Sandler, *Stalin and Hitler: a lesson in comparison*, Stanford, 1953.
122 John Lukacs, *June 1941: Hitler and Stalin*, New Haven, Yale University Press, 2006.

public.¹²³ In his article 'Stalinism vs Hitlerism ...'¹²⁴ Ernest Raiklin, however, argues for the existence of substantial differences between the societies of the Soviet Union and Nazi Germany.

In addition to viewing Stalin posters in a historical context, it is also useful to examine the psychological phenomena associated with the personality cult and their relevance to the forms and content of propaganda. Research of this nature provides insights into how personality cults arise, and the many factors that maintain them. As there is a strong and consistent use of visual topoi throughout the history of the personality cult, and as the topoi themselves appear to be archetypal in their symbolism, and are the defining feature of much of the art generated in the service of personality cults, some understanding of the psychological mechanisms at work is helpful. Research has been undertaken in the field of leadership studies, with particular reference to charismatic and ideological leaders.¹²⁵

---

123 Golomshtok, *Totalitarian art*.
124 Ernest Raiklin, 'Stalinism vs Hitlerism: the basic intentions and results', *International Journal of Social Economics*, 38:4, 2011, pp. 358–81.
125 Tucker, 'The theory of charismatic leadership'; Antonio Costa Pinto & Stein Ugelvik Larsen, 'Conclusion: fascism, dictators and charisma', *Politics, Religion & Ideology*, 7:2, 2006, p. 255; J.O. Hertzler, 'Crises and dictatorships', *American Sociological Review*, 5:2, 1940, pp. 157–69; Michelle C. Bligh & Jill L. Robinson, 'Was Gandhi "charismatic"? Exploring the rhetorical leadership of Mahatma Gandhi', *The Leadership Quarterly*, 21, 2010, pp. 844–55; Helen Constas, 'The U.S.S.R. — from charismatic sect to bureaucratic society', *Administrative Science Quarterly*, 6:3, 1961, pp. 282–98; Deanne N. Den Hartog, Robert J. House, Paul J. Hanges & S. Antonio Ruiz-Quintanilla, 'Culture specific and cross-culturally generalizable implicit leadership theories: are attributes of charismatic / transformational leadership universally endorsed?', *Leadership Quarterly*, 10:2, 1999, pp. 219–56; Roger Eatwell, 'Introduction: new styles of dictatorship and leadership in interwar Europe', *Totalitarian Movements and Political Religions*, 7:2, 2006, pp. 127–37; Roger Eatwell, 'The concept and theory of charismatic leadership', *Totalitarian Movements and Political Religions*, 7:2, 2006, pp. 141–56; Richard R. Fagen, 'Charismatic authority and the leadership of Fidel Castro', *The Western Political Quarterly*, 18:2, 1, 1965, pp. 275–84; Ronald Glassman, 'Legitimacy and manufactured charisma', *Social Research*, 42:4, 1975, pp. 615–37; Bert Hoffman, 'Charismatic authority and leadership change: lessons from Cuba's post-Fidel succession', *International Political Science Review*, 30, 2009, pp. 229–48; Robert J. House & Jane M. Howell, 'Personality and charismatic leadership', *Leadership Quarterly*, 3:2, 1992, pp. 81–108; Ralph P. Hummel, 'Charisma in politics. Psychosocial causes of revolution as pre-conditions of charismatic outbreaks within the framework of Weber's epistemology', PhD dissertation, New York University, 1972; Aristotle A. Kallis, 'Fascism, "charisma" and "charismatisation": Weber's model of "charismatic domination" and interwar European fascism', *Politics, Religion and Ideology*, 7:1, 2006, pp. 25–43; Donald McIntosh, 'Weber and Freud: on the nature and sources of authority', *American Sociological Review*, 35:5, 1970, pp. 901–11; Michael D. Mumford, Jazmine Espejo, Samuel T. Hunter, Katrina E. Bedell-Avers, Dawn L. Eubanks & Shane Connelly, 'The sources of leader violence: a comparison of ideological and non-ideological leaders', *The Leadership Quarterly*, 18, 2007, pp. 217–35; Jan Pakulski, 'Legitimacy and mass compliance: reflections on Max Weber and Soviet-type societies', *British Journal of Political Science*, 16:1, 1986, pp. 35–56; Jeremy T. Paltiel, 'The cult of personality:

Psychoanalytic approaches to the Stalin cult have been considered[126] and, for the first time to this author's knowledge, the concept of mortality salience has been applied to the personality cult of Stalin.[127]

One notable feature of the personality cult that manifests strongly in Stalin posters is the way in which the forms and symbols of religion are employed in the service of a regime professing an atheist philosophy. A number of concepts and fields of research assist in understanding the way in which religious imagery came to be associated with Bolshevism, and Stalin came to be portrayed in a manner that suggested a dual, Christ-like nature, or deity. Central to this argument is the concept of political faith as religion in the Soviet Union and other 'totalitarian states'. There exists a huge academic discourse in this area, including a journal, *Totalitarian Movements and Political Religions*, that is devoted exclusively to the field.[128]

---

some comparative reflections on political culture in Leninist regimes', *Studies in Comparative Communism*, 16:1–2, 1983, pp. 49–64; Philip Pomper, 'Nečaev, Lenin, and Stalin: the psychology of leadership', *Jahrbücher für Geschichte Osteuropas, Neue Folge*, 26:1, 1978, pp. 11–30; Guenther Roth & Claus Wittich (eds), *Max Weber: economy and society: an outline of interpretive sociology*, vol. 2, Berkeley, University of California Press, 1978; Dankart A. Rustow, 'Atatürk as founder of a state', *Daedalus*, 97:3, Philosophers and Kings: Studies in Leadership, 1968, pp. 793–828; Philip Smith, 'Culture and charisma: outline of a theory', *Acta Sociologica*, 43, 2000, pp. 101–10; Jill M. Strange & Michael D. Mumford, 'The origins of vision: charismatic versus ideological leadership', *The Leadership Quarterly*, 13, 2002, pp. 343–77; Carol Strong & Matt Killingsworth, 'Stalin the charismatic leader? Explaining the "cult of personality" as a legitimation technique', *Politics, Religion and Ideology*, 12:4, 2011, pp. 391–411; Stephen Turner (ed.), *The Cambridge companion to Weber*, Cambridge University Press, 2000; Max Weber, Hans Heinrich Gerth & Charles Wright Mills, *Max Weber: essays in sociology*, Oxford University Press, 1946; Max Weber, *On charisma and institution building*, The University of Chicago Press, 1968; Max Weber, *The Russian Revolution*, Gordon C. Wells & Peter Baehr (trans., eds), Cambridge, Polity Press, 1995.
126 David Luck, 'Psycholinguistic approach to leader personality: Hitler, Stalin, Mao and Liu Shao Ch'i', *Soviet Studies*, 30:4, 1978, pp. 491–515; Betty Glad, 'Why tyrants go too far: malignant narcissism and absolute power', *Political Psychology*, 23:1, 2002, pp. 1–37; Jerrold M. Post, 'Narcissism and the charismatic leader–follower relationship', *Political Psychology*, 7:4, 1986, pp. 675–88; Jerrold M. Post, 'Current concepts of the narcissistic personality: implications for political psychology', *Political Psychology*, 14:1, 1993, pp. 99–121.
127 Florette Cohen & Sheldon Solomon, 'The politics of mortal terror', *Current Directions in Psychological Science*, 2011, 20:316, pp. 316–20.
128 Peter Lambert & Robert Mallett, 'Introduction: the heroisation–demonisation phenomenon in mass dictatorships', *Totalitarian movements and political religions*, 8:3–4, 2007, pp. 453–63; Nicholas Berdyaev, *The Russian Revolution: two essays on its implications in religion and psychology*, London, Sheed and Ward, 1931; Jay Bergman, 'The image of Jesus in the Russian revolutionary movement', *International Review of Social History*, 35, 1990, pp. 220–48; Marina Cattaruzza, 'Introduction to the special issue of *Totalitarian Movements and Political Religions*: political religions as a characteristic of the 20th century', *Totalitarian Movements and Political Religions*, 6:1, 2005, pp. 1–18; William C. Fletcher, 'Soviet sociology of religion: an appraisal', *Russian Review*, 35:2, 1976, pp. 173–91; Emilio Gentile & Robert Mallett, 'The sacralisation of politics: definitions, interpretations and reflections on the question of secular religion and totalitarianism', *Totalitarian

THE PERSONALITY CULT OF STALIN IN SOVIET POSTERS, 1929–1953

The study of the Soviet poster is hampered by the fact that there is no comprehensive collection or catalogue of these posters. The Russian State Library in Moscow, known as the V.I. Lenin Library between 1925 and 1992, is the official copyright library of Russia (and the USSR between 1922 and 1991). In theory, one copy of every publication had to be lodged at this library, including all published posters. In practice, this has not always been the case and there are many lacunae, especially in the poster collection. The collection, which reputedly numbers about 400,000 posters and includes pre-revolutionary and post-Soviet posters, is catalogued in a card index divided thematically and chronologically. The posters themselves are stored in huge folios and are clustered in chronological bundles and then sorted thematically. This means that it is possible to directly access virtually all of the posters held at the library that deal with Stalin. There is also an incomplete subsidiary card index dealing with authors/artists of the posters. For this research I accessed all folders holding images of Stalin, as far as possible. Some of the posters listed in the index cards are no longer extant or could not be located. In many instances, neither the index cards nor the posters themselves contained all of the relevant publication information, including details of the artist, the size of the print run and the exact place of publication. There is

---

Movements and Political Religions, 1:1, 2000, pp. 18–55; Robin Edward Hutt, 'Symbolism in religion, with special reference to Orthodox worship and its relevance for the free church tradition', Masters thesis, Durham University, 1985, etheses.dur.ac.uk/7637/ (accessed 10 Nov. 2013); Adolf Keller, *Church and state on the European continent*, London, The Epworth Press, 1936; Christel Lane, 'Legitimacy and power in the Soviet Union through socialist ritual', *British Journal of Political Science*, 14:2, 1984, pp. 207–17; Christel Lane, *The rites of rulers: ritual in industrial society: the Soviet case*, Cambridge University Press, 1981; Timothy W. Luke, 'Civil religion and secularization: ideological revitalization in post-revolutionary communist systems', *Sociological Forum*, 2:1, 1987, pp. 108–34; Hans Maier, 'Political religions and their images: Soviet communism, Italian fascism and German national socialism', *Politics, Religion and Ideology*, 7:3, 2006, pp. 267–81; Marin, *Portrait of the king*; Klaus Georg Riegel, 'Marxism & Leninism as a political religion', *Totalitarian Movements and Political Religions*, 2005, 6:1, pp. 97–126; Natalia Skradol, 'Remembering Stalin: mythopoetic elements in memories of the Soviet dictator', *Totalitarian Movements and Political Religions*, 2009, 10:1, pp. 19–41; Michael Smith, 'Stalin's martyrs: the tragic romance of the Russian Revolution', *Totalitarian Movements and Political Religions*, 2003, 4:1, pp. 95–126; Mark D. Steinberg, 'Workers on the cross: religious imagination in the writings of Russian workers, 1910–1924', *Russian Review*, 53:2, 1994, pp. 213–39; Nina Tumarkin, 'Religion, Bolshevism and the origins of the Lenin cult', *Russian Review*, 40:1, 1981, pp. 35–46; Olga Velikanova, *Making of an idol: on uses of Lenin*, Göttingen, Muster-Schmidt-Verlag, 1996; Fenggang Yang, 'Religion in China under communism: a shortage economy explanation', *Journal of Church and State*, 52:1, 2010, pp. 3–33; David B. Zilberman, 'Orthodox ethics and the matter of communism', *Studies in Soviet Thought*, 17:4, 1977, pp. 341–419.

also room for inherent confusion as some of the posters, especially offset lithographs, were produced in different sizes and editions, and reproduced in subsequent years.

Commencing in 1934, *Letopis' izobrazitel'nogo iskusstva*[129] published four annual issues, continuing through to the present. All of the art volumes list the photographic reproductions of paintings, 'posters', 'photographic newspapers', postcards, handbills and any other publications with graphic content. A study of these between 1934 and 1953 reveals some of the lacunae in the Russian State Library holdings. For the purposes of this iconographic study it is difficult to determine whether the listed posters do or do not contain an image of Stalin. Although clearly the posters isolated in this study may not represent a comprehensive collection of posters with an image of Stalin, they do represent a substantial proportion of such posters and are a sufficient representation through which to draw substantiated conclusions.

In addition to the poster collection at the Russian State Library, the poster collection at the Museum of Contemporary History in Moscow was also accessed, yielding 43 posters that include an image of Stalin, although these overlapped with those contained in the State Library collection. The poster collections of the State Historical Museum in Moscow and the Museum of the Great Patriotic War were also accessed. Additional posters meeting the criteria for this research were found in a number of books that either contained Soviet poster collections, made reference to posters, or were monographs devoted to the most well-known Soviet poster artists, and in online collections.

These search methods yielded a total of 389 posters that contained an image of Stalin.[130] In determining what constituted 'an image of Stalin', it was decided that all types of visual representation of the face or body of Stalin were eligible for inclusion, encompassing photographs, sketches and line drawings, paintings, silhouettes, representations of Stalin as a statue or a frieze, Stalin's image on a banner, and images of Stalin in newspapers and books as they are represented in the posters. No images fitting the research criteria were discarded. This broad interpretation of the 'image of Stalin' was adopted because the way in

---

129 *Annals of the Fine Arts.*
130 See Appendix 1 for a chart breaking down by year the number of posters illustrated with an image of Stalin.

which his image appeared on posters was fluid and dynamic over time, and changes in depiction coincided with external events or crises, the demands of internal policy, and trends in the development of the personality cult around Stalin.

The posters of this sample are analysed as art objects that were produced for the broad purpose of propaganda for the Soviet regime, under which a number of more defined purposes can be outlined, as discussed below. Although produced as a form of state art aimed at the masses, the posters as objects carry heavy political, ideological and sociological baggage and can only be understood within these contexts. This iconographic approach to the posters, coupled with a cross-disciplinary approach to the contexts in which they were produced, has both benefits and limitations. The focus on primary materials — the posters themselves — within the narrow confines of this topic, has brought to light many previously unpublished posters and has added substantially to the material available for scholarly analysis. This study's concentration on the image of Stalin in the posters, and close examination of a such a large number of posters, limits its application to making broader generalisations about Soviet propaganda posters on the whole. This study does not undertake a comprehensive comparative analysis of Stalin's image across all propaganda media, nor does it compare the image and persona of Stalin with those of other socialist/communist leaders or with his contemporaries in other countries. While these are potentially fruitful areas of study, they are beyond the scope of this investigation. This study does not focus on the material conditions and contractual arrangements under which poster artists and other artists worked in the USSR, although where these can be shown to have a bearing on the types of posters produced, they are discussed.[131]

---

131 There are several excellent studies that use archival resources to document these conditions, including Plamper's *The Stalin cult* (2012). Plamper's book also documents in considerable detail who was responsible for producing and censoring cult products, and how much control Stalin exerted over the dissemination and use of his image. The detail of Plamper's argument is not reproduced in this study, although Plamper's findings will inform this writer's argument. See also Plamper, 'Abolishing ambiguity'; Bown, *Art under Stalin*; Bown & Taylor, *Art of the Soviets*; Bown, *Socialist realist painting*; Rosa Ferré, *Red cavalry*; Groys, *The total art of Stalinism*; Oliver Johnson, 'The Stalin Prize and the Soviet artist'; Reid, 'All Stalin's women'; Reid, 'Socialist realism in the Stalinist terror'.

In Chapter One the key concepts informing the research will be explored and a brief historical overview of the use of art as propaganda in leader cults from the ancient world to Stalinist times will be undertaken. It will be demonstrated that the cult of Stalin was not a unique phenomenon but drew heavily from its historical precedents. The political science concept of the 'political religion' will be investigated and it will be argued that Bolshevism fits all the criteria for inclusion in this category. This concept is crucial to a proper understanding of the Stalin personality cult not only because it provides a rationale for features of the cult that may seem surprising in a secular, anti-religious context, but also because the traditions, images and rituals of the Russian Orthodox Church continued to be strongly expressed, albeit often in mildly disguised form, in Soviet propaganda, despite its avowedly atheist stance.

Myth and ritual are crucial components of any society, and when the Bolsheviks seized power they attempted to break with the past and to invent a new tradition. As myths develop from the collective unconscious and grow out of a shared cultural experience, as well as demonstrating many commonalities across all human traditions, Soviet myths inevitably drew on universal archetypes and had much in common with their Russian predecessors and with other myths from other societies. The propaganda used to disperse these myths drew on ancient forms, whilst also incorporating new technologies. One point of divergence between the newly forged Soviet myths and rituals and those of some other societies is that the Soviets sought consciously to instil a collective culture that emphasised the values of collective welfare and happiness rather than focusing on individual fulfilment.

The model of leadership engaged in by the Bolshevik Party will also be examined as an example of charismatic leadership, with reference to the concepts of legitimacy outlined by the sociologist Max Weber. Brief reference will be made to some of the salient features and special challenges that accompany the charismatic situation. The concept of charismatic leadership is important to an understanding of the perceived need to build a cult of personality around a leader in order to bestow legitimacy upon the regime. While there is a common perception that the Russians prefer strong autocratic leadership to more democratic forms of government, this has not always historically been the case, and the creation of a strong leader persona at the helm of the nation had more to do with the lack of any traditional or legal legitimacy for the government, and to the presence of forces hostile to the regime, than to any alleged national predisposition.

Chapter Two will explore how Stalin's charismatic leader persona was created. Despite appearing an unlikely candidate for charismatic leadership, Stalin was perceived as approachable and accessible in his early years, as personally charming by people who met him and by close comrades, and also as highly intelligent by those who knew him well. Beset by internal strife and external pressures, the Bolshevik regime required a rallying symbol at its head, a figure who could appeal to and mobilise people of all nationalities from all walks of life. Those who would not be mobilised were deemed 'enemies of the people' and exiled, imprisoned or executed. It will be argued that a number of devices were employed to construct a symbolic persona embodied by the name 'Stalin', including binary coding to contrast the leader with the demonic enemy; the creation of a hagiography that functioned in the same manner as the lives of the saints to create an instructional myth for the education of believers; and the veneration of an apotheosised Lenin symbol to legitimate Stalin as leader and, by extension, the Party and its ideological vision for government. There will also be a brief examination of the ways in which artistic production was co-opted and regulated by the state in order that all art served the function of propaganda and education of the masses. Finally, there will be an examination of the role of the Soviet propaganda poster in maintaining the leader cult in Soviet society.

Chapters Three and Four will be devoted to a detailed examination of the plurality of meanings embodied by the symbolic persona of Stalin as depicted in propaganda posters. Many of the metaphors associated with Stalin will be examined, including his association with steel and with the sun, which emerge from pre-Soviet traditions of leadership emblems. The association of Stalin with the archetypes of the Architect, the Helmsman, the Magician, the Teacher and, most notably, the pervasive archetype of the Father will be explored in considerable detail. Analysis of these archetypes will be informed by what Jeffrey Brooks calls the 'politics of obligation', and the way in which notions of obligation and reciprocity pervaded Soviet society and contributed to the utility of these archetypes will be examined.

In Chapter Four the exploration of the archetypes associated with the Stalin persona in posters will continue, focusing on the Warrior and Saviour archetypes. It will be argued that although a warrior identity for Stalin was emphasised in posters from the early years of his leadership and was indeed a natural extension of the self-image of most of the Old Bolsheviks, the Warrior archetype as identified with the top leadership was primarily resident in the person of Kliment Voroshilov, marshal of the Soviet Union until 1941, when the Soviet Union became embroiled in the Great Patriotic War. After victory in the war, the Warrior archetype came to be merged with that of the Saviour, as Stalin was credited with leading the nation to victory. As the Cold War deepened and the Soviet Union became the major sponsor of the international peace movement, the Saviour archetype came to dominate in portrayals of Stalin in propaganda posters.

Although the notion of Stalin as Saviour only gained momentum after the Great Patriotic War, Stalin was depicted in posters as a sacred personage from the mid-1930s, when he was frequently portrayed in a similar or identical manner to the apotheosised Lenin and given superhuman attributes. There is considerable evidence that some people treated portraits and posters of Stalin and Lenin as icons, hanging them in the 'icon corner' in their homes and praying to them and that, despite official censure for such behaviour, some propaganda was created to intentionally evoke the Orthodox icon. It will be argued that, despite religion being anathema to Lenin, propaganda posters consciously paralleled and invoked religious experience in order to arouse enthusiasm and zeal in the population for the immense tasks of industrialisation, collectivisation, winning the war and creating a new type of civilisation. The image of Stalin in propaganda posters across the decades of his leadership, when examined in broad perspective, reveals that not only was that image ubiquitous by its omnipresence, but that it was all-encompassing, holding a multitude of semantic meanings, encapsulating a number of archetypes and also, somewhat surprisingly, encompassing traits of both male and female genders.

From 1929 until 1953, the retouched image of Stalin became a central symbol in Soviet propaganda across all artistic and cultural genres. Images of an omniscient Stalin appeared in the media of socialist realist painting, statuary, monumental architecture, friezes, banners and posters. Stalin was lauded in poetry, theatre, film and song; oaths were sworn to him; thanksgiving ceremonies were held to honour him; and millions of Soviet soldiers in the Great Patriotic War ran into battle with his name on their lips.[132] The 'Stalin' who was celebrated in propaganda bore but scant resemblance to the man Iosif Vissarionovich Dzhugashvili whose humble origins, criminal past, penchant for violent solutions and unprepossessing appearance[133] made him an unlikely recipient of uncritical charismatic adulation. The Bolsheviks needed a wise, nurturing and authoritative figure to embody their revolutionary vision and to legitimate their hold on power. The persona of 'Stalin' arose through a process that involved both the deliberate manufacture of a charismatic leader through propaganda, and the wish-fulfilling projections of an unnerved, destabilised and largely uneducated, illiterate and superstitious population of a sage guide through troubled times. This leader would come to embody the sacred and archetypal qualities of the Father of the nation, the great Warrior and military strategist, the wise Teacher and the Saviour of the land. Stalin's image in propaganda posters became a symbol of Bolshevik values and the personification of a revolutionary new type of society. Transforming a leader into a symbol that embodies an ideological vision is a key tactic in mobilising a population to identify as a cohesive whole, to strive for common goals and to behave in prescribed ways.

When the Bolsheviks seized power in the October Revolution of 1917, they were not secure in their rule. Lenin hoped that the Russian Revolution would be a spark for a broader rebellion — Europe, including Russia, was still in the grip of the First World War, and it was hoped that this instability would see communist parties across Europe brought to power, which would then support the revolution in Russia. This expected domino effect did not occur and the Bolsheviks in Russia found themselves isolated in power in a country with a largely feudal economy that was still suffering from the ravages and deprivations of war. As early as 1881, the revolutionary leader Vera Zasulic wrote to Karl Marx on behalf of the revolutionary socialists to ask whether he thought all countries of the world had to pass

---

132 Ehrenburg, *Men, years — life*, vol. 6, p. 304. Literary historian Lazar Lazarev claims, however, that in his experience of the war, soldiers did not run into battle shouting 'For Stalin!': '... in fact we never mentioned Stalin, and when we went into battle it was "For the Motherland!" that we shouted. The rest of our war cries were obscenities' (quoted in Figes, *The whisperers*, p. 434).

133 Ilia Ehrenburg recalled: 'On one occasion I found myself standing close to him ... He was not like his portraits. An old man, short of stature, with a face that looked pitted by the years, a low forehead, a pair of sharp, lively eyes ...' (Ehrenburg, *Men, years — life*, vol. 6, p. 302).

INTRODUCTION

through all phases of capitalist production on their way to socialism. Zasulic implored Marx to answer as soon as possible because, for the Russian socialists, this was a matter of 'life and death'. Marx replied in a brief and guarded missive from London on 8 March 1881 that the Russian socialists *could* jump directly to the communist phase, but would only achieve success by starting with the land held in common by the peasants, eliminating all other harmful influences, and with subsequent revolutions in Western Europe. Marx noted that his theories, as outlined in *Das Kapital*, applied only to the highly industrialised and modernised Western democracies, where all property was privately owned.[134]

After 1917, the Bolsheviks found themselves waging war on two fronts — the military and the ideological. Russia was torn apart by a civil war that lasted approximately four years. The situation was complex and variable across the vast empire and conflict did not occur merely along class lines, but was complicated by nationalist concerns in some ethnic territories. In an informative study of nationality and class in the 1917 revolutions, Ronald Suny points out that, while most of the non-Russian peoples of the tsarist empire were peasant, they differed radically from one another in their internal class differentiation and their degree of national consciousness. Thus, while in some areas, such as the Ukraine, national and economic class divisions coincided almost exactly — the Ukrainians were almost entirely peasants, the landowners and officials were Poles and Russians, the commercial bourgeoisie was largely Jewish — in other parts of the empire the population was almost entirely peasant with low levels of national consciousness. Often concepts of identity were tied to the village or region, rather than to nation, race or class. Across the empire the Civil War, which was triggered by the disintegration of the unifying imperial authority and which was characterised by economic disintegration and the upheaval of the old social order, was fought on a variety of grievances and issues by combatants with varying agendas.[135]

---

134 See Richard Sakwa, *The rise and fall of the Soviet Union, 1917–1991*, London, Routledge, 1999, pp. 2–3.
135 Ronald Grigor Suny, 'Nationality and class in the revolutions of 1917: a re-examination of social categories', in Nick Lampert & Gábor T. Rittersporn (eds), *Stalinism: its nature and aftermath*, Hampshire, Macmillan, 1992, p. 226.

Despite the fact that the Bolshevik elite shared some grievances with the peasantry, there was not much common ground from which to mobilise the peasants against the monarchic regime. Serfdom was abolished in Russia in 1861 as part of a large-scale agrarian reform under Tsar Aleksandr II, yet the material situation of many peasants did not improve. The revolution of 1905 in which Tsar Nicholas II's troops fired on petitioners was seen by many as an indication that the tsar was no longer the protector of the people.[136] Ideological arguments assumed little importance for the peasants when compared with greater concerns such as how to feed the family. The Bolsheviks sought to win over the peasantry with the promise of a better life under a socialist system and freedom from oppression, and appealed to the peasants with tangible promises including the seizure of land from rich landowners, and the redistribution of this land on an equitable basis. Much of the peasantry turned against the Bolsheviks as the Civil War became increasingly protracted.

The situation in the urban centres, although better for the Bolsheviks, was still far from certain. Unemployment and inflation were high — the ruble was worthless and workers were paid in kind and then had to barter for food. Industrial output had dropped to one-fifth of that before the war, with the steel works producing only 5 per cent of prewar output.[137] Marxism promised the elimination of class, and state ownership of the means of production. Ideologically, it promised power and dignity to the worker, as the proletariat took over the reins of government. To make matters worse for the Bolsheviks, they could not even count on unequivocal support from the intelligentsia. For example, writer Maksim Gor'kii expressed his concerns in *Novaya Zhizn*[138] as early as January 1918:

> The 'Government of Soviets' is putting into the heads of the workers the notion that the establishment of a socialist system is possible in Russia.

---

136 In her examination of folklore themes as a means to shed light on peasant attitudes to government and authority, Maureen Perrie finds the picture that emerges is not straightforward. While sometimes appearing as a negative or foolish figure in folklore, the tsar is more often portrayed as the benevolent protector of the poor, with boyars, landowners and the clergy as the perpetrators of evil and injustice. The 'good tsar' was a stereotypical figure, not necessarily embodied by the current monarch, but referencing backward to the historic past ('Folklore as evidence of peasant mentalite').
137 Deutscher, *Stalin*, p. 223.
138 *New Life*.

Novaya Zhizn, in a number of articles which met no objections as to their substance from the government organs, asserted — and will assert in the future — that the necessary conditions for the introduction of socialism are nonexistent in our country and that the Smolny government treats the Russian worker like brushwood: it kindles the brushwood in order to see — will a European revolution be ignited by the Russian bonfire?[139]

By 1921 about 800,000 soldiers had lost their lives fighting in the Civil War and as many as 8 million civilians died as a result of war, starvation and disease.[140]

In addition to winning military battles, Lenin and the Bolshevik Party were faced with the tasks of gaining and consolidating power in a large and ethnically diverse empire; establishing legitimacy for a government that had no traditional or legal right to rule; and also with beginning to institute the tasks of the socialist revolution — to not only change the behaviour of the people it governed, but to transform their thoughts and consciousness as well. With their history as underground revolutionaries and a tradition of using journalism, pamphleteering and essay writing to attract and organise followers, it was natural for the Bolsheviks to turn to methods of propaganda to support their aims.

Upon seizing power, the Bolsheviks' first act was to nationalise the publishing industry. On 9 November 1917, Lenin issued the 'Decree on the Press', which closed down all newspapers that preached 'open opposition or insubordination to the worker–peasant government'.[141] The control of information, and the production and dissemination of propaganda became chief tasks of the new regime. The term propaganda is a slippery one, and definitions of the term say as much about the people defining it, their era, and their political viewpoint, as they do about the term itself.[142] To employ the term at its most

---

139 Maxim Gorky, 'The fruits of demagogy', *Novaya Zhizn*, 3:217, 1918, in Maxim Gorky, *Untimely thoughts: essays on revolution, culture and the Bolsheviks, 1917–18*, Herman Ermolaev (trans.), New York, Paul S. Eriksson, Inc., 1968, p. 122.
140 John Simkin, Spartacus Educational, spartacus-educational.com/RUScivilwar.htm (accessed 2 Nov. 2016).
141 Brooks, *Thank you, Comrade Stalin!*, p. 3.
142 As communications scholar Nicholas J. O'Shaughnessy observes: 'To attempt to define propaganda is to tread lightly on a conceptual minefield. How we define propaganda is in fact the expression of the theories we hold about propaganda' (*Politics and propaganda*, Manchester, Manchester University Press, 2004, p. 14).

basic level of meaning, 'propaganda' refers to the manipulation and employment of language and symbols in the service of an ideological or social purpose.[143] The term is used colloquially in a somewhat pejorative manner today, but should not automatically carry negative connotations.[144] As Nicholas O'Shaughnessy notes, 'The word propaganda is a description of style, function and political content, but it is not in itself a final judgment, however it might be used in popular discourse'. Propaganda was to serve several purposes under the socialist regime: to legitimate the Party and its leadership, to express the Bolshevik 'vision' of a new society, to publicise government policy, to mobilise the population to participate in campaigns related to industrialisation and collectivisation, to clearly and publicly identify enemies of the regime and to enlist popular support in eliminating these enemies. The Bolshevik vision included such massive tasks as educating the population according to Marxist–Leninist principles and engineering a new type of person in a new type of society, and was often phrased in terms that were not only utopian, but that borrowed from the language and symbols of religion.

This sacralisation of politics did not happen subconsciously or unintentionally. Within the revolutionary movement, there was a strand of socialist thought to which Lenin was vehemently opposed, the idea of *bogostroitel'stvo* ('god-building'), which claimed such notable adherents as Gor'kii, Anatolii Lunacharskii, Vladimir Bonch-Bruevich and Aleksandr Bogdanov. The god-builders accepted the basic human need for religion, but sought to replace supernatural beliefs with a belief in science, and belief in god with belief in humanity (as a collective, rather than the worship of any one individual). Science and the belief in humanity would ultimately liberate the whole world, and the science of Marxism–Leninism would abolish all barriers of class, race and nation.

---

143 I am not distinguishing at this point between the term 'propaganda' that, after Plekhanov, was the attempt to get many ideas across to a small group of Party members and the intelligentsia, and the term 'agitation', which consisted of a small number of simplified messages aimed at the masses, and am subsuming both terms under the general term 'propaganda' according to its current use in academic discourse.
144 Nicholas J. O'Shaughnessy, 'The death and life of propaganda', *Journal of Public Affairs*, 12:1, 2012, p. 34.

INTRODUCTION

With such lofty aims as creating a 'heaven on earth', and 'engineering' a new type of Soviet person, it is hardly surprising that the creation and dissemination of propaganda held crucial importance for the Bolsheviks, both when establishing the new regime and later, under Stalin, in maintaining power in the face of exceptionally challenging circumstances. It was a central tenet of Bolshevik ideology that art and culture would belong to 'the masses' and, more specifically, reflect the tastes and preferences of the 'proletariat' or working class. As Lenin famously said, under a socialist government, art would no longer serve the elite of society, the 'upper ten thousand suffering from boredom and obesity; it will rather serve the millions and tens of millions of labouring people, the flower of the country, its strength and its future'.[145] Whether or not the small proletariat in existence in the 1920s was to be allowed to express its own preferences, or whether these needed to be guided and shaped from above, was a matter of contention in the early Bolshevik regime. Under Lenin's leadership, this debate was resolved in favour of the latter proposition.

After the October Revolution, Lenin, the Bolshevik leadership and members of the intelligentsia, including Vladimir Maiakovskii, Vladimir Tatlin and Aleksandr Rodchenko, called for artists to take to the streets and use their creative talents in the service of the Revolution. Large numbers of artists and designers supported the Revolution by contributing their talent to the propaganda machine. According to Pavel Tretiakov, businessman and patron of the arts, 'The "art-worker" must stand beside the man of science as a psycho-engineer, a psycho-constructor ... Propaganda towards the forging of the new man is in essence the only content of the works of the Futurists'.[146]

In making art and culture available for mass consumption, all fields of artistic endeavour and communications were potential vehicles for the dissemination of propaganda and the inculcation of the core values of Bolshevism. This preoccupation with art and culture was to continue into the Stalinist era, with Stalin becoming minutely involved in many areas of cultural production. Stalin watched every film before its release,

---

145 V.I. Lenin, *Polnoe sobranie sochinenii*, vol. 12, p. 104, quoted in Vladimir Pavlovich Tolstoi, I.M. Bibikova, & Catherine Cooke, *Street art of the Revolution: festivals and celebrations in Russia, 1918–33*, New York, Vendome Press, 1990, p. 11.
146 Pavel Tretiakov quoted in Golomshtok, *Totalitarian art*, p. 26.

giving his approval or veto,[147] and sometimes suggesting changes that had to be implemented before the film could be released.[148] Stalin was involved in editing slogans for press publications.[149] He was also involved in scientific and scholarly debates, making major corrections to works of non-fiction and, ultimately, in 1950, contributing his own dissertation on linguistics to the academic arena,[150] followed in 1952 by a long pamphlet on political economy.[151]

The 1919 program of the Petrograd Collective of Communist–Futurists declared:

> A Communist structure demands a Communist consciousness. All forms of everyday life, morality, philosophy and art must be restructured according to Communist principles. Without this, any future development of the Communist revolution is impossible.[152]

Most of the existing artistic genres — painting, sculpture, architecture, literature, theatre, music, porcelain and, indeed, some new ones (for example, film, agit-trains[153] and agit-ships, festivals and parades) — were pressed into the service of these aims. This massive undertaking saturated Soviet society with the values, symbols and imagery of the Bolshevik cause. Symbols create a lens through which people perceive and shape their present reality, remember and interpret the past, and make predictions about the future. In order to initiate the necessary dramatic transformation in people and society, the Bolshevik leadership had to not only seize power, but to capture and redefine the discourse.

---

147 Sarah Davies, 'Stalin as patron of cinema: creating Soviet mass culture, 1932–1936', in Davies & Harris, *Stalin*, pp. 202–25; Djilas, *Conversations with Stalin*, p. 95.

148 Plamper provides evidence that Stalin corrected the wording of his own quotes and, for films, suggested that scenes be reshot, changed endings, and suggested that musical scores be rewritten (*The Stalin cult*, pp. 133–34). Maria Belodubrovskaya argues that, at least in relation to the dominant biopic genre, Stalin's interventions were less direct than is usually claimed ('The jockey and the horse: Joseph Stalin and the biopic genre in Soviet cinema', *Studies in Russian and Soviet Cinema*, 5:1, pp. 29–53).

149 Brandenberger, *Propaganda state in crisis*, p. 101; Plamper, *The Stalin cult*, p. 133.

150 Stalin's *Marxism and problems of linguistics* was published in the 20 June, 4 July, and 2 August, 1950 issues of *Pravda*.

151 I.V. Stalin, *Economic problems of socialism in the USSR*, published in the USSR by Gospolitizdat, 1952, and by Foreign Languages Press, Peking in 1972.

152 Quoted in Golomshtok, *Totalitarian art*, p. 22.

153 Agitation trains — trains that travelled the country delivering propaganda messages. Andrew Spira contends that the idea for the agit-trains may derive from a mobile church in a train that was despatched under Tsar Nicholas II in 1896 (*The avant-garde icon*, p. 186).

INTRODUCTION

While Marxist ideas may have been accessible to the intelligentsia and, indeed, debated in endless meetings, the Bolshevik leadership realised the need to translate the basic concepts of Marxism–Leninism into a format that could be understood and adopted by the proletariat and the peasantry. In general, the peasantry did not have a grasp of ideological concepts and were unfamiliar with the words used by the Bolsheviks and other participants in the political arena.[154] In the early days of Bolshevik rule, Party members were sent out amongst the people to attempt to ascertain the effectiveness of propaganda campaigns. The information brought back to the centre revealed that both urban and rural workers had little understanding of the language used in propaganda and media such as the newspapers.[155] In order to dominate meaning, shape society and change thought, the new language of Marxism–Leninism had to infiltrate society and obliterate the old systems of meaning and interaction, and to do so in a manner accessible to a population that, in 1917, was largely functionally illiterate.[156] The poster was a comparatively cheap and accessible medium that was particularly suited to this time and to the purposes of mass propaganda. The visual impact of messages conveyed through the use of simple and bold colour schemes and eye-catching design in posters transcends language barriers, although a shared visual literacy

---

154 Many of the words appearing in the press were new and imported from other languages, or were abbreviations of the names of the new committees and administrative bodies set up by the Bolsheviks. Peter Kenez observes that, in 1923, peasants were unfamiliar with even the most commonly used acronyms such as those for the USSR and Sovnarkom (*The birth of the propaganda state*, p. 256). Orlando Figes and Boris Kolinitskii observe that imported words were both misunderstood and mispronounced by bewildered peasants: 'Thus the word "republic" (*respublica*) appeared as *rezh'publiku* ("cut the public"), *despublika* and *razbublika* in various peasant letters; "regime" (*rezhim*) became *prizhim* ("suppress"); "constituent" (*uchreditel'noe*) was transformed into *chereditelnoe* (on the basis that the Constituent Assembly would decide everything "in its turn" or *cheredom*); "revolution" (*revoliutsiia*) was pronounced and written as *revutsia, levoliutsiia* and *levorutsia*; the "Bolsheviks" (*bol'sheviki*) were confused with a party of *bol'shaki* (peasant elders) and of *bol'shie* (big people); while "annexation" (*anneksiia*) was thought by many peasant soldiers to be a small Balkan kingdom neighbouring *kontributsiia* (the word used at this time for indemnity) and at least on one occasion was confused with a woman called Aksinia' (*Interpreting the Russian Revolution*, p. 129).
155 Readers of *The Workers' Newspaper*, a newspaper specifically aimed at the masses and written at a lower level of sophistication and complexity than *Pravda* and *Izvestiia*, complained that they needed 'ten dictionaries' to read the paper (Brooks, *Thank you, Comrade Stalin*, p. 12).
156 According to Stephen White, the 1897 census of the Russian Empire found that only 28.4 per cent of the total population aged between nine and 49 was literate, with considerable regional variation (e.g. Estonia, 96.2 per cent: Russia, 29.6 per cent: Uzbekistan, 3.6 per cent); whereas, by 1920, the overall level of literacy within the territory under Soviet rule had increased to 44.1 per cent, with national variations and significant variations between urban (73.5 per cent) and rural (23.8 per cent) dwellers (*The Bolshevik poster*, pp. 18–19).

and culture is necessary for the intended audience. Exposure to the *lubok* (an illustrated broadsheet) and the iconography of the Russian Orthodox Church meant that most of the population shared a visual literacy that included stylisation, symbolism, exaggeration, caricature, inverse perspective, distortions of scale and the use of multiple scenes to tell a story.

The poster was not a new phenomenon in Russian life. St Petersburg had hosted an important international exhibition of artistic posters in 1897 and, at the beginning of the 20th century, there was a small commercial industry primarily producing movie and advertising posters. Under the Bolsheviks, the use of the poster was greatly expanded and modified in design and purpose. Poster campaigns were central to propaganda efforts throughout the Soviet era and were well suited to deal with the government's need to publicise widely and quickly a large number of policies and initiatives, to identify enemies of the people, and to promote united goals and visions. Director of the editorial and publishing wing of the Red Army during the Civil War, Vyacheslav Polonskii, enthusiastically proclaimed the value of poster art:

> With the help of this handiwork of the streets and squares, that rapprochement between art and the people that other dreamers have been awaiting will come about ... It is not pictures hanging in museums, or book illustrations passed from hand to hand among book lovers, or frescoes, which are accessible to only the few, but the poster and *lubok*, which are produced in the millions for the masses and the streets, that will bring art to the people, show them what can be done and how with brush and paint, intrigue them by their artistry, and unleash the pent-up reserves of artistic possibilities.[157]

In the early years of the new regime, the issue of each new poster was announced in *Pravda* and posters were also reviewed there. The magazine *Bednota*[158] reproduced posters on its pages, ensuring that their message reached even remote villages.[159] In the 1930s, there were two journals devoted to the reproduction, review and analysis of posters — *Produktsiia izobrazitel'nykh iskusstv*,[160] begun in 1932,

---

157 Polonskii, *Russkii revolyutsionnyi plakat*, p. 3.
158 *The Poor*.
159 Alla Rosenfeld, 'The world turned upside down: Russian posters of the First World War, the Bolshevik revolution, and the Civil War', in Rosenfeld, *Defining Russian graphic arts*, p. 147.
160 *Art Production*.

INTRODUCTION

and *Plakat i khudozhestvennaia reproduktsiia*,[161] from 1934 to 1935.[162] Indeed, posters were deemed so important to the propaganda effort that many of the propaganda posters of the early years had the words 'Anyone who takes down this poster commits counterrevolution' printed across the base.[163]

Stalin's image became a prominent feature of propaganda posters in the early 1930s and remained so, with some fluctuations, until his death in 1953. Stalin was portrayed through propaganda as a charismatic leader and his image was idealised, emphasising the charismatic relationship between Stalin and the citizenry. The notion of charismatic leadership derives from the work of Weber.[164] According to Weber's theory of political legitimation, there are three pure types of legitimate domination: traditional, charismatic, and rational.[165] 'Charismatic' legitimation rests 'on devotion to the exceptional sanctity, heroism or exemplary character of an individual person, and of the normative patterns or order revealed or ordained by him'.[166] By its very nature, revolution creates charismatic leadership that relies on the motivating persona of the leader for popular support. Legitimacy, as conceived by Weber is a socio-political relationship, not a psychological state or ideological claim. Charismatic domination is not defined purely by the personal qualities of the leader, but by the existence of a following

---

161 *Poster and Artistic Reproduction*.
162 Bird et al., *Vision and communism*, p. 21.
163 White, *The Bolshevik Poster*, p. 112; Baburina, *The Soviet political poster 1917–1980*, p. 3.
164 There is a vast literature discussing the virtues and limitations of Weber's notions of legitimacy and charismatic legitimation and it is beyond the scope of this study to enter into this sociological debate. Plamper makes a good case for the application of Edward Shils' notion of 'sacrality' to the Stalin cult, as being more flexible and having stronger religious connotations than Weber's 'charisma' (*The Stalin cult*, p. xvi). Graeme Gill outlines seven means of legitimacy that were sought by the Soviet leadership during the Stalinist years (*Symbols and legitimacy in Soviet politics*, p. 24). The broad notion of charismatic legitimation, as outlined by Weber, can be meaningfully applied to the Stalin cult and illuminates some of the basic premises underlying the argument in this book.
165 'Traditional' grounds rest 'on an established belief in the sanctity of immemorial traditions and the legitimacy of those exercising authority under them'. The tsar and his successors were deposed in the revolution of February 1917 (and later assassinated with his extended family, the doctor, the nurse and the dog), thus traditional authority in Russia was swept away. 'Rational' grounds rest 'on a belief in the sanctity of enacted rules and the right of those elevated to authority under such rules to issue commands'. The provisional government under Aleksandr Kerenskii, which replaced the tsar, was overthrown by force and, with only 24 per cent of the vote in the Constituent Assembly elections in November 1917, the Bolsheviks could not make a strong claim to legal–rational legitimacy.
166 Weber in Roth & Wittich, *Max Weber*, p. 215.

that is oriented to the leader.[167] To some extent, an infantilising bond is created between the charismatic leader and his followers[168] and such conditions may have facilitated the development of a personality cult around an authoritative, charismatic leader like Stalin, and certainly contributed to the success of the Father, Saviour and Teacher archetypes in Stalinist symbolism. [169]

The phenomenon of the personality cult goes hand-in-hand with Weber's notion of charismatic leadership. The two concepts are often used interchangeably, with the same criteria applied to both terms. As it may be argued that not every charismatic leader develops a manifest personality cult, some clarification is necessary. As has already been noted, the charismatic leader is the recipient of devotion and loyalty from followers due to perceived qualities and abilities. Adulation is thus directed to the leader as an individual, not as the holder of a particular office. Charismatic leaders tend to come to the fore during crises and, if they are successful, manage to bring some order to the chaos, and deliver their followers from imminent danger.

The charismatic leader created by the October Revolution was Lenin. With the need to institute law and order after the Revolution and Civil War, a 'routinisation of charisma' began to occur. After the struggle of the Revolution with its promise of utopia, and the desperate struggles of the Civil War, came the routine business of governing, with all its political rhetoric, bureaucratic bulkiness, taxation and

---

167 'Psychologically this recognition is a matter of complete personal devotion to the possessor of the quality, arising out of enthusiasm, or of despair and hope'. Weber in Roth & Wittich, *Max Weber*, p. 242.
168 Sociologist Ronald Glassman adopts a Freudian perspective on the followers of a charismatic leader: 'humans allow themselves to fall into this altered state of perception and interaction because (1) they tend to fall into states of existential despair, (2) they become anxious about actually upcoming dangerous situations, and (3) under such circumstances, because of the long dependency-and-love period of human childhood, humans may turn toward a parental figure and assume a childlike dependency and subordinate attitude of behavior' ('Legitimacy and manufactured charisma', p. 617).
169 In fact, in an article on the psychology of Soviet corruption, Jeffry Klugman argues that passivity and obedience are a part of Soviet culture inculcated through cultural norms in Soviet parenting: 'Perhaps for lack of space, perhaps to maintain supervision, children are included in adult gatherings, becoming passive spectators. Teenagers are discouraged from having chores or earning money. Childhood thus becomes a training ground for both passive dependency and compliance with an intrusive authority', and 'Via the indulgent privileges accorded to members, the need for support from above for both membership and advancement, and the required submission to Party discipline, Party membership expresses the passive dependent side of the original parenting relationship' ('The psychology of Soviet corruption, indiscipline, and resistance to reform', *Political Psychology*, 7:1, 1986, pp. 67–82, pp. 68, 70).

INTRODUCTION

mundanity. The extraordinary became submerged in the routine of the ordinary. Weber employs a dramatic metaphor: 'every charisma is on the road from a turbulently emotional life that knows no economic rationality to a slow death by suffocation under the weight of material interests'.[170] This routinisation of charisma began to set in while Lenin was still alive[171] and, as Lenin's physical presence as Bolshevik leader diminished due to the severity of his illness, the first inklings of a personality cult were being constructed around him.

When Lenin died in January 1924, the fledgling Bolshevik regime was faced with a crisis of succession. This was particularly risky for a regime that was born under charismatic legitimation, because there were no traditional or legal traditions in place for the transfer of power to a successor. The regime was particularly vulnerable at this time and one way of dealing with this situation was to attempt to transfer the charisma of the first leader to a successor, who then also partakes of charismatic legitimation.[172] A potential new leader strives to demonstrate his close links to the first charismatic leader and employs propaganda that highlights a 'lineage' or seemingly natural succession.

One of the options that may be open to the charismatic leader who faces routinisation or a succession crisis, is to formally enter the structures of power by accepting or seizing political office. The term 'personality cult' may be said to refer to the circumstance in which a charismatic leader accepts political office or formal political leadership of some sort, and sets about generating, maintaining and controlling his public image or persona. Alternately, one could say that the term refers to the specific charismatic situation in which charisma is generated 'from above' (from the leadership) rather than rising 'from

---

170 Roth & Wittich, *Max Weber*, p. 1120.
171 In Weber's words: 'Emotional revolutionism is followed by the traditionalist routine of everyday life; the crusading leader and the faith itself fade away, or, what is even more effective, the faith becomes part of the conventional phraseology of political philistines and banausic technicians' (Weber, Gerth, Mills, *Max Weber*, p. 125).
172 Weber discusses the routinisation of charisma and the crisis of succession at length. It is beyond the scope of this book to examine these concepts in detail, or to look at the means by which the charisma attached to Lenin came eventually to be grafted onto Stalin. The personality cults of both Lenin and Stalin were created largely with the purpose of serving as vehicles for this transfer.

below' (from the masses).[173] Generation of charisma from above usually involves the use of mass media and propaganda tools to construct a carefully tailored persona for the leader.

With Lenin's death, construction of the personality cult became centralised in the Commission for the Immortalisation of Lenin's Memory, and his personality cult expanded rapidly, assisted by the genuine grief felt by followers at his early demise. Stalin came to power among the Bolsheviks at least in part because he was the most successful in establishing an identity as Lenin's disciple, student and mentee, and in demonstrating the extent to which he had become indispensable to Lenin. While this was critical in the early years of his leadership, over time Stalin gained increasing charismatic legitimacy in his own right.

The marketing of Stalin's constructed image in the media and propaganda served to legitimise his increasingly despotic rule and the rule of the Bolshevik Party through the generation and maintenance of a personality cult built around his persona, and also functioned as a mechanism for communicating the Party's vision. Stalin not only articulated the Bolshevik vision of society but, through the use of his image in propaganda, came to embody it. Jill Strange and Michael Mumford outline five mechanisms through which a leader's articulation of a vision appears to influence followers' actions.[174] First, the vision specifies the direction, purpose and uniqueness of the future goal; second, vision motivates followers into action towards these future goals; third, vision provides a sense of meaning and identity; fourth, vision provides the common framework around which people coordinate activities; and fifth, vision institutionalises prescriptive beliefs that may serve as a basis for development of organisational norms and structures.

If the tasks of the new revolutionary society in the USSR were to be achieved, it was essential that the leader articulate the Bolshevik vision in a clear and inclusive manner. By applying Strange and Mumford's mechanisms to the situation in the USSR we can see that first, Bolshevik propaganda stressed the historic significance of the advent

---

173 For a more comprehensive discussion of this issue see Vinay Kumar Srivastava, 'Mao cult, charisma and social science', *China Report*, 21, 1985, pp. 359–70, pp. 363–64.
174 Strange & Mumford, 'The origins of vision', p. 344.

of socialism and the Soviet people's unique place in world history as the vanguard of a higher phase in world economic and political evolution. Socialism was the preparatory stage of communism[175] and, when the transition to communism was complete, time and history would cease, as the peoples of the world would live in a classless, harmonious, unchanging utopia of material plenitude and spiritual maturity — a real 'heaven on earth'.

Second, though this future was some way off, it was attainable, and propaganda provided evidence that progress was being made and the appropriate milestones reached, and motivated the population to continue to work towards future goals. The Stakhanovite movement became a national phenomenon due to newspaper publicity of the 1935 Stakhanovite conference, and a concerted poster campaign that promoted the concept of socialist competition and exceptional achievement, and made national heroes of the Stakhanovite workers. Collective group achievements such as the Metro, the Dnieper Dam, Magnitogorsk,[176] and the Moscow–Volga Canal, became widely celebrated phenomena thanks to posters that, while ultimately attributing all credit for their success to Stalin, encouraged an attitude of collective ownership of the finished product. The propagandising of spectacular socialist successes had the dual function of reassuring the population that they were on the way to achieving their collective goals (and their sacrifices were worthwhile), whilst also reflecting well on the leader and shoring up legitimacy for the Party. As Weber pointed out, charismatic authority is inherently unstable, and:

> The charismatic leader gains and maintains his authority solely by proving his strength in life. If he wants to be a prophet, he must perform miracles; if he wants to be a warlord, he must perform heroic deeds. Above all, however, his divine mission must 'prove' itself in that those who faithfully surrender to him must fare well. If they do not fare well, he is obviously not the master sent by the gods.[177]

---

175 The Stalin Constitution of 1936 instituted in law the fact that socialism had now been achieved.
176 An industrial city in Chelyabinsk Oblast that, under Stalin's Five Year Plans, was to be developed into a city of the future, built around a huge iron and steel plant. For a fascinating account of this process and its challenges, see Stephen Kotkin, *Magnetic Mountain: Stalinism as a civilization*, Berkeley, University of California Press, 1995.
177 Max Weber, *On charisma and institution building*, pp. 22–23.

Third, Stalinist propaganda posters provided the population with a strong sense of identity for inclusion in the new socialist utopia — the people pictured in the posters were usually either proletarians or peasants and were portrayed in typical garb, sometimes carrying identifying tools of trade, or undertaking typical worker or peasant tasks.[178] In early posters, Stalin could be seen walking beside the workers in his workman's boots — the first among equals.[179] Children were also often featured in posters, reinforcing the notion of Stalin as the father–protector and emphasising the infantilised bond between Stalin and the people.[180]

Fourth, policy directions and visions of their implementation were brought to life in the drawings and photomontages depicted on the posters. The goals and projections of the five-year plans, and successes in aviation, electrification and construction were indicated with charts and graphs in the posters of the late 1920s and early 1930s and publicised with catchy slogans such as 'Five into four', which encouraged the population to achieve the targets of the five-year plan in only four years.[181] Finally, the message contained in well-publicised slogans such as 'Cadres decide everything', gained dogmatic authority through association with Stalin's name and image, and became institutionalised in practice through their ubiquitous presence in posters.[182]

As the person who articulated society's vision, Stalin became both an inspiration to the populace and a symbol of strong, wise authority requiring implicit obedience and spiritual faith, and leaving little room for individual thought and interpretation. Even someone as widely travelled and experienced as Ilia Ehrenburg could only look back on the Stalinist years and reflect: 'The cult of personality had not

---

178 For example, Viktor Nikolaevich Deni & Nikolai Andreevich Dolgorukov, 'We've got a Metro!', 1935; P. Yastrzhembsky, 'Glory to the creator of USSR constitution, the great Stalin!', 1937; Konstantin Pavlovich Cheprakov, 'So — greetings, Stalin, and live for a hundred years, shine like the sun, live for victory! And lead us on the way to victory! Accept the country's joyous greetings!' 1939; A.M. Venediktov, 'You cleared the way for our freedom, Soviet rule gave glory to our country', 1949; and, Naum Pavlovich Karpovskii, 'Long live the Komsomol generation!', 1948.
179 For example, Gustav Klutsis, 'The reality of our program — it's real people ...', 1931.
180 See Chapter Three.
181 For example, Gustav Klutsis, 'Five into four', 1930; and, Viktor Deni, 'The five-year plan in four years', 1930.
182 For example, Gustav Klutsis, 'Cadres decide everything', 1935 (Fig. 4.62).

INTRODUCTION

converted me to unthinking faith but it had swayed my judgments: I could not see the future of the country as other than bound up with what was daily called "the wisdom of our leader of genius".'[183] It is a challenging prospect to attempt to determine whether Stalin's charismatic persona was created as a vehicle for transmitting the socialist propaganda message, or whether, as much recent research in the field of leadership studies suggests, the nature of the visionary and transformational message in a society that has in the recent past been characterised by exploitation and corruption (under the tsars) almost inevitably leads to the endowment of the bearer of that message with charismatic properties.[184] One reason for broaching this question in relation to Stalin is that, as evidenced by eyewitness accounts, Stalin did not appear to have many of the traits that one traditionally associates with a charismatic presence. He was not possessed of great oratorical skill, spoke Russian with a strong Georgian accent,[185] and appeared to be self-effacing. Stalin is known to have tried to curb some of the excesses of his cult of personality. He rejected the idea of a personal biography for many years and, when one was produced, he edited the text of his biography and removed some of the more extreme adulatory passages. In July 1933, he opposed a proposed exhibition on his life that was organised by the Society of Old Bolsheviks and, in February 1938, he rejected the publication of Vera Smirnova's *Tales of Stalin's childhood* by Detizdat, the Komsomol publishing house.[186] Several other Party members, particularly Trotskii, were renowned for their brilliant and fiery oratory. Stalin, like Mahatma Gandhi in India,[187] spoke simply, directly, somewhat monotonously, and without

---

183 Ehrenburg, *Men, years — life*, vol. 6, p. 302.
184 'vision may be conceived of a set of beliefs about how people should act, and interact, to attain some idealized future state' (Strange & Mumford, 'The origins of vision', p. 344).
185 Molotov recalls that, when Stalin mispronounced a word on the podium, all subsequent speakers felt obliged to repeat the mistake: 'If I'd said it right', Molotov reminisced, 'Stalin would have felt I was correcting him.' He was very 'touchy and proud' (quoted in Montefiore, *Stalin*, p. 304).
186 See Sarah Davies, 'Stalin and the making of the leader cult in the 1930s', in Apor et al., *The leader cult in communist dictatorships*, pp. 33–34. Stalin also rejected Nikolai Ezhov's suggestion in 1937 that Moscow be renamed Stalinodar, and attempted to quash Ivan Koniev's suggestion after the Great Patriotic War that he be given the rank of Generalissimus. Simon Sebag Montefiore recounts the occasion on which Lazar Kaganovich coined the term 'Stalinism' during a dinner at Zubalova (Stalin's dacha): "'Everyone keeps talking about Lenin and Leninism but Lenin's been gone a long time ... Long live Stalinism!' 'How dare you say that?' retorted Stalin modestly. "Lenin was a tall tower and Stalin a little finger"' (*Stalin*, p. 66).
187 Bligh and Robinson use the case study of Mahatma Gandhi to argue that charismatic leadership owes more to the nature of the 'vision' or message, than to the personal characteristics

rhetorical device.[188] E.A. Rees contrasts Stalin's style of public speech with that of his contemporary, Adolf Hitler: 'Compared to Hitler's mesmeric, demonic oratory, Stalin's speeches were slowly delivered, based on the relentless presentation of figures and argument to make his case. Stalin's appeal was primarily to the intellect'.[189] Despite his lack of theatrical flair, some eyewitnesses expressed a preference for Stalin's style of speech over that of more accomplished orators.[190] In filmed recordings of Stalin's speeches, he seems uncomfortable in the spotlight, however, he was also a keen strategist and, from the earliest days of his public speaking, was aware of the effectiveness of his low-key, anti-oratorical approach: 'your big cannon is no use here when you need to shoot short distances'.[191]

The question of whether the leader's charisma is seen as the vehicle by which the message is delivered, and is therefore of central importance, or the message itself is primary, with the leader becoming charismatic in the eyes of followers through his ability to articulate that vision, appears to be one of the 'chicken-and-egg' variety and, as such, may not have a definitive answer. Exploration of this topic has implications for an understanding of the role of propaganda in society and, in particular, for an examination of the role of the image of Stalin in Bolshevik propaganda. Does the most effective propaganda focus on the visionary message or on the visionary leader? If propaganda begins with a focus on the visionary and transformational message, is there a degree of inevitability that it will end with a focus on the leader as the embodiment of that message? To approach the question from another angle: do propagandists set out with the deliberate purpose of creating a mortal deity? Or, in broadcasting the visionary

---

and oratory skills of the leader ('Was Gandhi "charismatic"?', p. 845).
188 According to Strange and Mumford, one of the 29 characteristics that identifies the ideological subtype of the charismatic type of leader is: 'The leader will communicate in such a way that the attention is not placed on himself, but on his ideas' ('The origins of vision', p. 351).
189 E.A. Rees, 'Introduction: leader cults: varieties, preconditions and functions', in Apor et al., *The leader cult in communist dictatorships*, p. 17.
190 For example, in her personal diary of 1936, Galina Vladimirovna Shtange (wife of a professor at the Moscow Electromechanical Institute of Railroad Engineers (MEMIIT)) noted: 'Stalin speaks very slowly and distinctly — extremely simply, so simply that each word penetrates into your consciousness and I think the man cannot be found who would not be able to understand what he says. I really love that, I don't like highfaluting, bombastic speeches that are aimed at creating an acoustic effect' ('Diary of Galina Vladimirovna Shtange' (1936), in Veronique Garros et al. (eds), *Intimacy and terror: Soviet diaries of the 1930s*, New York, New Press, 1995, p. 205).
191 Stalin quoted in Montefiore, *Young Stalin*, p. 135.

message, does the necessity for easily apprehended symbols mean that propagandists follow a path that inevitably leads to the deification of the leader?

The situation becomes even more complex when we delve further into psychological studies of charismatic leadership. The nature of the pre-existing society (the one that is being rejected and replaced) and the nature of the transformational/revolutionary message appear to prescribe the type of leader that will emerge.[192] It appears that social and environmental factors play a large role in determining the type of leader who will emerge, the type of message that will be received by the revolutionary masses, the characteristics the leader must embody, and the charismatic relationship the leader will have with his followers. These environmental factors interact in a complex and cyclical manner

---

192   In a 2007 study on leader violence, Mumford et al. found that group, organisational and environmental conditions may play a greater role in predicting leader violence than the personal characteristics of the leader ('The sources of leader violence', pp. 217–35). Mumford and Strange propose that 'ideological leadership' is a subgenre of charismatic leadership with some distinguishing features, and argue that Stalin's style of leadership fits the ideological subgenre: 'ideological leadership may be viewed as a form of charismatic leadership where greater emphasis is placed on values and standards in vision formation than is typically the case for charismatic leaders' ('The origins of vision', p. 373). While speculative at this point, if one extrapolates from these findings to suggest that, in many respects, the charismatic leader is a product of the prevailing social conditions (as the Marxists claim and Stalin himself insisted), we once again arrive at the prospect that his image in propaganda reflects the qualities expected of and perceived in the leader by society, rather than qualities intrinsic in the leader himself. See Stalin's 1931 interview with Emil Ludwig (R. MacNeal (ed.), I.V. Stalin, *Sochineniya*, 13, Stanford, Hoover Institute of War, Revolution and Peace, 1967, p. 255). The idealised elevation of the charismatic leader appears to become more inevitable still when we factor in leadership research suggesting that the type of person who is likely to become a charismatic leader of the personalised ideological type is commonly narcissistic, selective in interpretation of information, projects negative intentions on others, and engages in biased self-serving appraisals of others. House and Howell follow McClelland in defining:
> socialized charismatic leadership as leadership which (a) is based on egalitarian behavior, (b) serves collective interests and is not driven by the self-interest of the leader and (c) develops and empowers others ... socialized leaders tend to be altruistic, to work through legitimate established channels and systems of authority when such systems exist, and to be self-controlled and follower-oriented rather than narcissistic. Theoretically personalized leaders rely on personal approval or rejection of followers to induce others to comply with their wishes. They show disregard for the rights and feelings of others and they tend to be narcissistic, impetuous, and impulsively aggressive. ('Personality and charismatic leadership', p. 84)

This personality type may be more inclined than most other people to insist on the correctness of his own values and beliefs over others, and to accept laudatory praise as his due. See Mumford et al., 'The sources of leader violence', p. 233.

with certain personal qualities of the charismatic leader. It is difficult to establish to what extent propaganda drives this process or merely reflects the prevailing situation.

The above questions aside, it will be argued that the Stalin who appeared in propaganda posters was not a 'real person', but an idealised image that was either manufactured in a manner not dissimilar to branding in modern marketing, or that served as a sort of projected wish-fulfilment on the part of the population. In several private statements to his intimates, Stalin appears to have had no illusions about the separation between the man, Iosif Dzhugashvili, and his persona.[193] Stalin's Politburo colleagues often had the sense that he was acting:[194] 'Krushchev called him a "man of faces"; Lazar Kaganovich remarked that there were four or five different versions of Stalin; and Molotov and Anastas Mikoian both sensed at various times that Stalin was just playacting.'[195] Yuri Zhdanov is quoted as reporting a family argument in which Vasilii, Stalin's younger son, stated that he is a Stalin too! According to Zhdanov, Stalin replied: 'No you're not ... you're not Stalin and I'm not Stalin. Stalin is Soviet power. Stalin is what he is in the newspapers and portraits, not you, no not even me.'[196] Stalin proclaimed a Marxist perspective on the role of the leader in society, asserting that leaders should not be glorified as individuals, but could be promoted as the embodiment of the cause. Great men arise from the circumstances of the times.[197] Molotov recalls that at first 'Stalin struggled with his cult and then came to rather like it'.[198] When the writer Mikhail Sholokhov criticised the adulation directed at Stalin, Stalin replied smiling, 'What can I do? The people need a god.'[199]

---

193 During the Great Patriotic War, Stalin declined the opportunity to swap his captured son, Yakov, for the German General von Paulus on the grounds that his son was not the equivalent of the General and that such a swap would be insensitive to all the other citizens whose sons had been taken prisoner-of-war. Yakov eventually perished in the POW camp. Stalin was questioned about this by a Georgian compatriot after the war and replied, 'What would they have said of me, our millions of Party fathers, if having forgotten about them, I had agreed to swapping Yakov? No, I had no right ... Otherwise, I'd no longer be "Stalin"' (Chuev, *Molotov remembers*, p. 209).
194 By way of contrast, Pavel Sudoplatov, a Chekist, thought 'it was hard to imagine such a man could deceive you, his reactions were so natural, without the slightest sense of him posing' (Montefiore, *Stalin*, p. 55).
195 Montefiore, *Young Stalin*, p. 42.
196 Quoted in Montefiore, *Stalin*, p. 4.
197 Stalin famously expressed this conviction in his 1931 conversation with Ludwig (*Sochineniya*, vol. 13, p. 255).
198 F. Chuev, *Sto sorok besed s Molotovym*, Moscow, 1991, p. 261.
199 Quoted in Montefiore, *Stalin*, p. 143.

INTRODUCTION

In order to create the persona of the great and bountiful leader, much obfuscation of Stalin's true history and character had to occur. There is an extensive literature on the falsification of history under Stalin and, in particular, the inaccuracy of Stalin's official biography.[200] While providing many valuable insights, to focus on this aspect of Stalin's leadership is to somewhat miss the point. The Soviet leadership, many of whom carried their revolutionary pseudonyms or 'cadre names' throughout their political careers, never intended biography to be a genre that revealed the literal truth regarding the minutiae of personal character, history and upbringing. 'You speak about history,' Stalin told his Politburo colleagues, 'but one must sometimes correct history.'[201] Personal lives and individual character were irrelevant to the cause and, in fact, even in the earliest days of the regime, under Lenin's leadership, the highest praise a Bolshevik could bestow on a comrade was that (s)he had no personal life.[202] Biography was constructed as a genre of literature with a purely didactic purpose, which was aimed at mobilising a poorly educated and only newly literate population.[203] Its aim was to show the path to be taken to communist enlightenment, and it operated as a guide to the individual's path and struggle, and also as a parable for the larger struggle of the Bolshevik Party at a macroscopic level.

Under Stalin, the falsification and rewriting of history eventually extended to all areas of public discourse and even into the private sphere. Paintings on popular revolutionary subjects, such as the salvo from the Aurora and the storming of the Winter Palace, were published in history textbooks and took on the status of documentary images.[204] Not only was history rewritten or created afresh, thereby eliminating everything that did not fit with the official Party line, but evidence was altered — in particular, photographs. The leadership ensured that people who had fallen from favour were painted/inked out of photographs or, sometimes, when shoring up a historical claim,

---

200 For example, after 1929 Stalin used a false date of birth. Stalin was born on 6 December 1878 (old style calendar) but, during his leadership, began to officially list his birthday as 21 December 1879.
201 Stalin, quoted in Montefiore, *Stalin*, p. 142.
202 For example, in 1925 a Bolshevik was praised in a *Pravda* newspaper obituary for his asceticism: 'Comrade Nesterenko had no personal biography and no personal needs' (cited in Brooks, *Thank you, Comrade Stalin!*, p. 24).
203 For an interesting and in-depth argument of this case, see D. Brandenberger, 'Constructing the cult: a case study of Stalin's official biography', in Davies & Harris, *Stalin*.
204 Golomshtok, *Totalitarian art*, Introduction.

removed seamlessly, so that it appeared that they had never been there in the first place.[205] Terrified of being found in possession of compromising material after a family member was arrested, people took to their family photo albums with scissors or ink. It was not enough, though, for enemies of the people to disappear from historic occasions. Stalin had also to be seen to be present at the most decisive moments in revolutionary history, whether or not he had actually been there. David King sees Stalin's need to control his image and the context in which it appeared in the public arena as one of the principle motivating factors in adopting socialist realism as the official artistic form for the socialist state:

> from the time of [Stalin's] birth in 1879 [sic] until he was appointed General Secretary in 1922, there probably exist fewer than a dozen photographs of him. For a man who claimed to be the standard-bearer of the Communist movement, this caused grave embarrassment, which could only be overcome by painting and sculpture. Impressionism, expressionism, abstraction — for Stalin none of these artistic movements were capable of showing his image properly. So he made realism — socialist realism — the central foundation of the Stalin cult. A whole art industry painted Stalin into places and events where he had never been, glorifying him, mythologising him.[206]

Works of art, such as a painting depicting the young Stalin helping a wounded comrade who had been shot during a demonstration, were commissioned in the service of the creation of a mythic biography befitting a Bolshevik leader.[207]

So, too, in propaganda posters, Stalin did not exist as a man, but operated in a symbolic and allegorical realm that gradually saw him increasingly removed from the everyday and mundane, and moved

---

205 In later versions of a famous photograph of Lenin speaking in Red Square, Trotskii has disappeared. Teachers instructed their pupils to rip pages containing images of denounced people out of their school textbooks (King, *The commissar vanishes*, p. 10). In 1934, constructivist Aleksandr Rodchenko published his book *Ten years of Uzbekistan*, which celebrated the first 10 years of Soviet rule in the area and featured a number of official portraits of the Uzbek leadership. Three years later, as this leadership was purged on Stalin's orders, these images had to disappear. David King was able to examine Rodchenko's own copy of the book: 'Rodchenko's response in brush and ink came close to creating a new art form, a graphic reflection of the real fate of the victims. For example, the notorious secret-police torturer Yakov Peters had suffered an ethereal, Rothko-like extinction. The face of party functionary Akmal Ikramov, veiled in ink, had become a terrifying apparition' (*The commissar vanishes*, p. 10).
206 King, *The commissar vanishes*, p. 13.
207 Golomshtok, *Totalitarian art*, p. 187.

towards a form of deity. The Stalin symbol was complex and many-faceted and, like all symbols, exhibited shifts in meaning and emphasis over time. At the most basic level, as Stalin explained to his son Vasilii, 'Stalin' symbolised Soviet power and the socialist state. He was seen as the source of all bounty, the dispenser of all goods and services, the inspiration for, and strategist behind, all victories, and the supreme mentor and patriarch to the people[208] — first to the people of the Soviet Union and, after the Great Patriotic War, to the people of the world. Stalin's image was represented to the populace through the archetypes of the Father, the Warrior, the Teacher and the Saviour.

The Father archetype was one of the strongest and most prevalent images associated with Stalin's persona. Despite the Bolshevik regime's break with the autocratic past, many of the symbols and traditions associated with tsarist authority were co-opted by the new regime in the quest for legitimacy. Stalin was frequently referred to in the press by 'father' epithets and was often portrayed in posters in a paternal or patriarchal role. Stalin was also referred to in posters and other propaganda by the term *rodnoi*, which implied a familial relationship or kinship, as that of a father to children, between him and the Soviet populace. This patriarchal relationship was to extend throughout Soviet society, which consisted of vast networks of patronage that ran both vertically and horizontally. Thus the notions of gift-giving, obligation, bounty, reciprocity, and even mentorship, were integral to Soviet life, and Stalin merely sat at the top of the pyramid, as the ultimate dispenser of goods and benefits to a network below.[209] As such, Stalin was the patriarch of all the Soviet peoples, all nationalities and all ethnicities. After the Great Patriotic War, with the 'liberation' of the peoples of Eastern Europe and the Soviets' active involvement in the world peace movement, Stalin was portrayed in posters as the patriarch and protector of all of the peoples of the world.

Like so many of the 'great men' of history, Stalin's public image drew on the Warrior archetype, with Stalin represented in postwar propaganda as a successful military leader and strategist. Victory in

---

208 For a detailed examination of Stalin and the 'politics of obligation' see Brooks, 'Stalin's politics of obligation', and Brooks, *Thank you, Comrade Stalin!*
209 These networks of patronage were reinforced by the strong familial connections that existed among the top Bolsheviks. Entire family clans held leadership positions, and intermarried with each other in tight-knit circles.

the war was sometimes even attributed directly to Stalin.[210] After the war, Stalin rarely appeared in public and delegated many public functions to his close deputies. Stalin's disappearance from public life meant that his only presence for the people was through the image projected in propaganda, with its mythic, allegoric, archetypal and spiritual dimensions. Thus Stalin became less like a man, and more like a god.

A third major archetype contributing to the Stalin persona was that of the Teacher, with Soviet propaganda frequently referring to Stalin as 'teacher', 'great teacher' or 'dear teacher'. Of course, Stalin took great pains to point out that he was only a humble student/disciple/mentee of the great Lenin. The archetype, however, had a strong tradition in Russian society, originating with the intelligentsia in the mid-19th century when higher education became accessible to individuals from the non-gentry classes.[211] Teachers facilitated the education, spiritual development, and social advancement of their mentees through widespread systems of patronage. Under the Soviet system, as all resources became concentrated in the hands of the state, systems of mentorship came increasingly under the control of the state, with Stalin at its head as the ultimate mentor and teacher.

There are countless portrayals of Stalin and Lenin together in a variety of propaganda media. In propaganda posters, Stalin's image was frequently linked with that of Lenin in order to show that Stalin was Lenin's truest disciple, the continuer of the faith, and Lenin's legitimate successor to the Soviet leadership. In the early years of his leadership, Stalin was depicted as taking a subordinate role, listening to Lenin's guidance or reading Lenin's works. From the mid-1930s, however, Stalin was usually portrayed as Lenin's equal and, at times, even appeared to be giving advice to Lenin. Eventually, in the late 1940s and the 1950s, with victory in the war to recommend him, Stalin no

---

210 As Isaac Deutscher points out, Marshal Zhukov gained enormous popularity for his role in the war victory and, on the first Victory Day, he stood side by side with Stalin on the Lenin mausoleum to receive the gratitude and adulation of the pressing crowds. The situation had already changed by the second Victory Day: 'in 1946 Marshal Zhukov completely disappeared from the public eye. From then on his role in the defence of Stalingrad and even Moscow was gradually blurred in the official accounts of the war, until, on the third anniversary of the battle of Berlin, *Pravda* managed to commemorate the event without mentioning Zhukov even once' (*Stalin*, p. 547).
211 Barbara Walker, 'Iosef Stalin: "Our teacher, dear"', in Heller & Plamper, *Personality cults in Stalinism*, p. 47.

longer needed always to appeal to Lenin's legitimating influence and was able to claim the title of 'Teacher' in his own right. He even began to publish authoritative texts, which appeared on bookshelves next to those of Lenin and Marx.[212]

One of the most interesting archetypes used to portray Stalin in the avowedly atheist Soviet society was the archetype of the Saviour. Lenin, whose abhorrence of the personality cult was legendary, was frequently associated with Christ and this archetype was easily transferred, along with most other manifestations of the Lenin cult, onto the figure of his successor. The incorporation of the visual language of the icon of the Russian Orthodox Church into the Soviet propaganda poster drew visual analogies between Stalin and the sacred and divine figures with whom the Russian population was familiar.[213] Stalin was not only associated with the figure of Christ but, somewhat surprisingly, was endowed with many of the qualities of the Mother of God. That the use of a number of archetypes to portray Stalin was a deliberate propaganda strategy is evidenced by the fact that, in the 1930s, exhibitions of Stalin portraits were held and structured around themed rooms carrying titles such as 'Stalin as military commander' and 'Stalin as Marxist theoretician'.[214]

The Soviet propaganda poster provides, among other things, a striking case study of the centrality of art to human society and of the power of art to shape society at all levels — physically, emotionally and spiritually. The Soviet poster encouraged the Soviet people to make physical changes in their environment, such as performing superhuman feats in the workplace, and to build new cities and railways. It encouraged diverse peoples with often conflicting interests and values to identify as a nation, to pursue common goals, to rally behind a supreme leader and to survive indescribable hardship to win the Great Patriotic War. The Soviet poster also promoted a new type of atheistic, egalitarian society with core values that were markedly different from the preceding society and those in the capitalist countries surrounding the Soviet Union.

---

212 Ethan Pollock's 'Stalin as the coryphaeus of science: ideology and knowledge in the post-war years' (Davies & Harris, *Stalin*), outlines the process by which Stalin was called in by scholars to arbitrate the scholarly debates in Soviet linguistics.
213 From around the 1880s, new technology in Russia allowed the accumulated layers of varnish, repainting and soot on icons to be stripped back to reveal their original detail and vivid colour.
214 Plamper, *The Stalin cult*, p. 181.

While it would be disingenuous to claim that the entire Soviet population embraced the Stalin persona uncritically, there is ample evidence to indicate that the majority of people did embrace and support the goals of the regime, and were deeply invested in the creation of a new and better society.[215] Support came not only from Old Bolsheviks, dedicated Party members and cynical careerists, but also from workers, peasants (although this group proved to be particularly intransigent), writers and artists, and members of the intelligentsia both inside and outside the Soviet regime. The image of Stalin embodied the vision of an unprecedented new type of society in which opportunities were open to all who chose to follow the Bolshevik line and re-create themselves in the image of the Party.

---

215 Stephen Kotkin discusses the difficulty in gauging the sincerity of belief of participants in the 'Bolshevik crusade' in his study of Magnitogorsk. He notes that the high value placed on public displays of allegiance and the lack of source materials make it difficult to assess the level of support for the regime amongst citizens. Kotkin approaches the task, instead, by examining radical 'unbelief' and concluding that 'there seems to have been little support or grounds for radical unbelief in the Communist cause for those living inside the USSR under Stalin, however, this does not mean that universal, uncritical acceptance was the result ... Elements of "belief" and "disbelief" appear to have coexisted within everyone, along with a certain residual resentment'. Kotkin states further that 'When a compelling revolutionary vision resembling the "higher truth" of a revealed religion is refracted through patriotic concerns and a real rise in international stature, we should not underestimate the popular will to believe or, more accurately, the willing suspension of disbelief'. He notes that revolutionary truth was maintained by the collective power of millions of people participating in the system for a variety of reasons, which include belief in the cause (*Magnetic Mountain*, pp. 225–30).

The phenomenon of the personality cult — a historical perspective

Men make their own history, but they do not make it as they please; they do not make it under self-selected circumstances, but under circumstances existing already, given and transmitted from the past. The tradition of all dead generations weighs like a nightmare on the brains of the living. And just as they seem to be occupied with revolutionizing themselves and things, creating something that did not exist before, precisely in such epochs of revolutionary crisis they anxiously conjure up the spirits of the past to their service, borrowing from them names, battle slogans, and costumes in order to present this new scene in world history in time-honored disguise and borrowed language. Thus Luther put on the mask of the Apostle Paul, the Revolution of 1789–1814 draped itself alternately in the guise of the Roman Republic and the Roman Empire, and the Revolution of 1848 knew nothing better to do than to parody, now 1789, now the revolutionary tradition of 1793–95.

Karl Marx[1]

Every period has its great men, and if these are lacking, it invents them.

Claude Adrien Helvétius[2]

---

1 Karl Marx, '18th Brumaire of Louis Bonaparte. Karl Marx 1852,' *Marxists Internet Archive*, www.marxists.org/archive/marx/works/1852/18th-brumaire/ch01.htm (accessed 4 Jul. 2011).
2 Helvétius, quoted in Leon Trotskii, *My life*, www.marxists.org/archive/trotsky/1930/mylife/ch41.htm (accessed 2 Nov. 2016).

Before turning to an examination of the way in which the image of Stalin was marketed in propaganda posters during his leadership, it is necessary to define some key terms and to explore some of the central concepts that enhance understanding of the intent and context for Soviet propaganda. In establishing what is meant by the term 'personality cult', it becomes evident that the production of propaganda for the masses is a defining component of this phenomenon. Modern personality cults are possible due to the capability to disseminate images of the leader and his[3] achievements over wide distances and to saturate public space with cult products. Further exploration of the features of personality cults will lead to the concept of political religion in which secular ideology becomes a matter of faith and the citizenry a community of believers. An understanding of political religions helps to explain the persistence of so many religious forms and rituals in a society committed to atheism.

It is important to note that the cult of Stalin did not exist in isolation and was, in fact, part of a broader network of cults that both preceded Stalin's and coexisted with it, and which also had historical precedents dating back to ancient times. By examining the cult of Stalin in the context of other leader and personality cults, it becomes evident that the cult of Stalin was not an extraordinary phenomenon that arose under a particular political system at a particular time in history, but part of a long tradition. There was a degree of inevitability about the rise of a charismatic leader cult in an uprooted society that needed to industrialise rapidly whilst surrounded by largely hostile forces.

Definition of the term 'personality cult'

The phenomenon of the personality cult has been studied across a variety of disciplines and from numerous hypothetical and research perspectives. It has been explored as a historical phenomenon,[4]

---

3   Since most leaders with personality cults are male, I will use the masculine pronoun. Jan Plamper argues that a defining feature of the modern personality cult is that the cult leader is male (*The Stalin cult: a study in the alchemy of power*, New Haven, Yale University Press, 2012, p. 25).
4   For example, Jost Dulffer, 'Bonapartism, fascism and National Socialism', *Journal of Contemporary History*, 11:4, 1976, pp. 1109–28; Maria Chamberlin, 'Charismatic leaders: Napoleon, Stalin, Mao Zedong and Kim Il Sung', Masters thesis, California State University, 2010, gradworks.umi.com/14/87/1487113.html (accessed 2 Nov. 2016); J.O. Hertzler, 'Crises and dictatorships', *American Sociological Review*, 5:2, 1940, pp. 157–69; Mattei Dogan, 'Comparing

1. THE PHENOMENON OF THE PERSONALITY CULT

as a manifestation of politics as religious faith,[5] from a psychological perspective,[6] through the lens of leadership studies,[7] and as a mass media phenomenon.[8] Studies have focused on the personality of the leader; the characteristics of the followers; the nature of the relationship between the leader and followers; the mechanisms that generate and maintain the personality cult; the causes of the cult; the effects of the cult; and the art, literature, architecture and science generated by societies of which a personality cult is a feature.

---

two charismatic leaders: Ataturk and de Gaulle', *Comparative Sociology*, 6, 2007, pp. 75–84; Wale Adebanwi, 'The cult of Awo: the political life of a dead leader', *Journal of Modern African Studies*, 46:3, 2008, pp. 335–60; Karl Marx, '18th Brumaire of Louis Bonaparte'; Dragoş C. Mateescu, 'Kemalism in the era of totalitarianism: a conceptual analysis,' *Turkish Studies*, 7:2, 2006, pp. 225–41; Hans Kohn, 'Napoleon and the age of nationalism', *Journal of Modern History*, 22:1, 1950, pp. 21–37; Dankart A. Rustow, 'Atatürk as founder of a state', *Daedalus*, 97:3, *Philosophers and kings: studies in leadership*, 1968, pp. 793–828; Balázs Apor, Jan C. Behrends, Polly Jones & E.A. Rees, *The leader cult in communist dictatorships: Stalin and the Eastern Bloc*, Hampshire, Palgrave, 2004; Robert C. Tucker, *Stalinism: essays in historical interpretation*, New York, W.W. Norton and Company, 1977.

5 For example, Peter Lambert & Robert Mallett, 'Introduction: the heroisation–demonisation phenomenon in mass dictatorships', *Totalitarian Movements and Political Religions*, 8:3–4, 2007, pp. 453–63; Roger Eatwell, 'Introduction: new styles of dictatorship and leadership in interwar Europe', *Totalitarian Movements and Political Religions*, 7:2, 2006, pp. 127–37; Antonio Costa Pinto & Stein Ugelvik Larsen, 'Conclusion: fascism, dictators and charisma', *Politics, Religion & Ideology*, 7:2, 2006, pp. 251–57; Emilio Gentile & Robert Mallett, 'The sacralisation of politics: definitions, interpretations and reflections on the question of secular religion and totalitarianism', *Totalitarian Movements and Political Religions*, 1:1, 2000, pp. 18–55.

6 For example, Josep R. Llobera, *The making of totalitarian thought*, Oxford, Berg, 2003; Bruce Mazlish, 'Group psychology and problems of contemporary history', *Journal of Contemporary History*, 3:2, 1968, pp. 163–77; Michael D. Mumford, Jazmine Espejo, Samuel T. Hunter, Katrina E. Bedell-Avers, Dawn L. Eubanks & Shane Connelly, 'The sources of leader violence: a comparison of ideological and non-ideological leaders', *The Leadership Quarterly*, 18, 2007, pp. 217–35; David Luck, 'Psycholinguistic approach to leader personality: Hitler, Stalin, Mao and Liu Shao Ch'i', *Soviet Studies*, 30:4, 1978, pp. 491–515; Robert C. Tucker, 'The rise of Stalin's personality cult', *American Historical Review*, 84, 1979, pp. 347–66.

7 For example, Deanne N. Den Hartog, Robert J. House, Paul J. Hanges, S. Antonio Ruiz-Quintanilla, 'Culture specific and cross-culturally generalizable implicit leadership theories: are attributes of charismatic / transformational leadership universally endorsed?', *Leadership Quarterly*, 10:2, 1999, pp. 219–56; Robert J. House & Jane M. Howell, 'Personality and charismatic leadership', *Leadership Quarterly*, 3:2, 1992, pp. 81–108; Jill M. Strange & Michael D. Mumford, 'The origins of vision: charismatic versus ideological leadership', *The Leadership Quarterly*, 13, 2002, pp. 343–77; Robert C. Tucker, 'The theory of charismatic leadership', *Daedalus*, 97:3, 1968, pp. 731–56.

8 Hans Speier, 'The truth in hell: Maurice Joly on modern despotism', *Polity*, 10:1, 1977, pp. 18–32; Plamper, *The Stalin cult*; Robert C. Tucker, *Stalin in power: the revolution from above, 1928–1941*, New York, W.W. Norton and Company, 1990.

THE PERSONALITY CULT OF STALIN IN SOVIET POSTERS, 1929–1953

The term 'cult' came to be coupled with the term 'personality' in modern European languages in the first half of the 19th century,[9] although it does not seem to have appeared in the Russian language until much later. It is frequently claimed that the term '*Kul't lichnosti*'[10] was first used in Russia in Nikita Krushchev's 1956 Secret Speech to the Twentieth Party Congress of the VKP(b), in which he denounced the 'cult of the individual' surrounding the then-deceased Stalin;[11] although Georgi Malenkov, who very briefly succeeded Stalin as premier and first secretary of the Communist Party, used the term in relation to Stalin shortly after Stalin's death in April 1953, in a speech to the Central Committee.[12] Personality cults were seen as inherently anti-Marxist, with Marx and Friedrich Engels speaking out in 1877 against the aggrandisement that was occurring around them as their fame grew.[13]

The precise definition given to the term personality cult varies slightly according to historical era, and also to the discipline and orientation of the writer, although the differences in usage across academic fields are subtle. In general, the most well-known examples of leaders with personality cults — for example, Stalin, Mao Zedong, Adolf Hitler, Napoleon Bonaparte, Maximilian I, Caesar Augustus and Alexander

---

9   Jan Plamper, 'Introduction', in Klaus Heller & Jan Plamper, *Personality cults in Stalinism* (eds), Goittingen, V&R Unipress, 2004, p. 22.
10 Meaning cult of personality / cult of the individual.
11 Nikita Krushchev, 'Speech to 20th Congress of the C.P.S.U.', 24–25 Feb. 1956, www.marxists.org/archive/khrushchev/1956/02/24.htm (accessed 2 Nov. 2016).
12 'By order of the Praesidium, I find it necessary to put in front of you one basic question, having great meaning for the future strengthening and cohesion of the leadership of our Party and the Soviet government. I am speaking about the question of the incorrect, un-Marxist understanding of the role of personality in history, which, I must clearly say, has received widespread distribution among us, and as a result has turned into the harmful propaganda of the cult of personality. It is unnecessary to prove that such a cult has nothing in common with Marxism and seems to have come from something else' (Georgi Malenkov, cited in Karl E. Loewenstein (trans.), 'Ideology and ritual: how Stalinist rituals shaped the thaw in the USSR, 1953–4', *Totalitarian Movements and Political Religions*, 8:1, 2007, pp. 93–114, p. 99). See also Mark Kramer, 'Political violence in the USSR', in Robert Conquest & Paul Hollander (eds), *Political violence: belief, behaviour and legitimation*, Palgrave Macmillan, New York, 2008, p. 73.
13 'Neither of us [here Marx refers to Engels as well as himself] cares a straw for popularity. Let me cite one proof of this: such was my aversion to the personality cult that at the time of the International, when plagued by numerous moves — originating from various countries — to accord me public honour, I never allowed one of these to enter the domain of publicity, nor did I ever reply to them, save with an occasional snub. When Engels and I first joined the secret communist society, we did so only on condition that anything conducive to a superstitious belief in authority be eliminated from the Rules' (Karl Marx, 'Letter to Wilhelm Blos in Hamburg, London, 10 November 1877', in 'Letters: Marx – Engels correspondence 1877', marxists.anu.edu.au/archive/marx/works/1877/letters/77_11_10.htm (accessed 2 Nov. 2016)).

the Great — are equally identifiable as such by 'the man in the street', as by specialists across a number of disciplines. An examination of some of the definitions of the term informs what is encompassed by this concept. Historian Jan Plamper begins by outlining the history of the word 'cult', from its origins with religious and ritualistic usage in Ancient Roman times, to the semantic shift in meaning when coupled with secular referents during the Enlightenment and the French Revolution. He sees the Romantic era's 'cult of genius' as being the closest predecessor to the 'cult of personality', manifesting in acts of appreciation, such as the erection of public statues of Johann von Goethe and the holding of a Friedrich Schiller festival in 1839.[14]

According to historian E.A. Rees, who here uses the term 'leader cult', but is essentially talking about the same phenomenon:

> A leader cult is an established system of veneration of a political leader, to which all members of society are expected to subscribe, a system that is omnipresent and ubiquitous and one that is expected to persist indefinitely. It is thus a deliberately constructed and managed mechanism, which aims at the integration of the political system around the leader's persona.[15]

Political scientist Pao-min Chang has described the personality cult as 'the artificial elevation of the status and authority of one man ... through the deliberate creation, projection and propagation of a godlike image'.[16] Historian Árpad von Klimó believes that personality cults should be viewed as secularised forms of religious rituals and adds: 'Here we define "cult of personality" as a sum of symbolic actions and texts which express and ritualise the particular meanings ascribed to a particular person in order to incorporate an imagined community.'[17] In a similar vein, Plamper defines the generally accepted usage of personality cult as 'god-like glorification of a modern political leader with mass media techniques, and excessive glorification of this leader'.[18] Key features of each of these definitions are the elevation

---

14   Plamper, in Heller & Plamper, *Personality cults in Stalinism*, pp. 22–23.
15   E.A. Rees, 'Introduction: leader cults: varieties, preconditions and functions', in Apor et al., *The leader cult in communist dictatorships*, p. 4.
16   Pao-min Chang, quoted in Jeremy Taylor, 'The production of the Chiang Kai-shek personality cult, 1929–1975', *The China Quarterly*, 185, 2006, pp. 96–110 (no page no.).
17   Árpad von Klimó, '"A very modest man": Béla Illés, or how to make a career through the leader cult', in Apor et al., *The leader cult in communist dictatorships*, p. 47.
18   Plamper, in Heller & Plamper, *Personality cults in Stalinism*, p. 33.

and glorification of an individual, the use of symbolism and ritual,[19] the fact that the image or persona of the leader is manufactured and heavily managed, the use of mass media for the dissemination of the cult,[20] and parallels to religious phenomena.

Political religions

The concept of 'political religion' is central to any analysis of charismatic leadership, and to an understanding of personality cults in particular. As previously noted, the term 'cult' derives from a specifically religious connotation, and personality cults surrounding political leaders share much common ground with religious worship.[21] As historian Marina Cattaruzza explains, the term 'political religion' is today almost always associated with the authoritarian regimes of the 1930s — Stalin's Russia, Hitler's Germany and Mussolini's Italy.[22] Political religions are phenomena of the modern era, 'developing only after the construction of a political sphere independent from religion and after religion had been turned into a private matter, relegated

---

19   As Christel Lane indicates, there is wide disagreement across a number of disciplines as to how the word 'ritual' is defined. Lane's definition of the term serves adequately the purposes of this book: 'Ritual ... is a stylized, repetitive, social activity which, through the use of symbolism, expresses and defines social relations. Ritual activity occurs in a social context where there is ambiguity or conflict about social relations, and it is performed to resolve or disguise them. Ritual can be religious or secular' (*The rites of rulers: ritual in industrial society: the Soviet case*, Cambridge University Press, 1981, p. 11).
20   Plamper distinguishes between modern personality cults and their premodern predecessors on the basis of five characteristics: modern personality cults derive their legitimacy from 'the masses' while monarchical cults were aimed at an elite, the use of mass media by modern cults allows a far wider dissemination of cult products than in the premodern era, modern personality cults emerged only in closed societies, modern personality cults were born of a secular age from which God had been expelled, and the modern personality cult was exclusively patricentric in contrast to premodern cults in which females were elevated (*The Stalin cult*, p. xvii).
21   As J. Maritain has observed: 'Communism is so profoundly, so substantially a religion — an earthly religion— that it ignores the fact that it is one' (*Umanesimo integrale* (Rome, 1946) cited in Gentile & Mallett, 'The sacralisation of politics', p. 49). Statements like that by Lev Trotskii, in which he anticipated the future that mass belief in Bolshevism would create as 'a real paradise on this earth for the human race', which would unite and embody 'all that is most beautiful and noble in the old faiths', borrow from the language and imagery of religion (cited in Timothy W. Luke, 'Civil religion and secularization: ideological revitalization in post-revolutionary communist systems', *Sociological Forum*, 2:1, 1987, pp. 108–34, p. 114).
22   This observation in relation to political religions parallels Plamper's defining characteristics of the modern personality cult as occurring in closed societies from which God has been expelled (*The Stalin cult*, p. xvii).

to a private dimension'.²³ Italian philosopher Benedetto Croce sees religious belief as fundamental to human existence and argues that, when formal religion is suppressed, people will try to form a religion of their own.²⁴

The first elaboration of the sacralisation of politics at a theoretical level began in 1762 with Jean-Jacques Rousseau's concept of 'civil religion',²⁵ which was to be founded on principles of popular sovereignty, would replace Christianity, and unite political and religious power into a political unity.²⁶ The concept of political religion derives from that of civil religion, but diverges from it in some key areas: it is intolerant of and openly hostile to other religions and ideologies, or seeks to subordinate and submerge them; it places the interests of the community above those of the individual; it seeks to manage and control all areas of human existence; and it sanctifies the use of violence against its enemies. Gentile and Mallett state that political religions occur when politics takes on the characteristics of religion by 'confer[ring] a sacred status on an earthly entity (the nation, the country, the state, humanity, society, race, proletariat, history, liberty, or revolution) and render[ing] it an absolute principle of collective existence'.²⁷ This sacralised secular entity becomes the main source of values for individual and mass behaviour, and an object of veneration through myth and ritual. Political religion is characterised by the existence of an 'elect community', a 'messianic

---

23   Marina Cattaruzza, 'Introduction', *Totalitarian Movements and Political Religions*, spec. iss., *Political religions as a characteristic of the 20th century*, 6:1, pp. 1–18, p. 2.
24   'The entire contemporary world is again in search of a religion … Religion is born of the need for orientation as regards life and reality, of the need for a concept that defines life and reality. Without religion, or rather without this orientation, either one cannot live, or one lives unhappily with a divided and troubled soul. Certainly, it is better to have a religion that coincides with philosophical truth, than a mythological religion; but it is better to have a mythological religion than none at all. And, since no one wishes to live unhappily, everyone in their own way tries to form a religion of their own, whether knowingly or unknowingly' (Benedetto Croce, 'Per la rinascita dell'idealismo', cited in Gentile & Mallett, 'The sacralisation of politics', p. 31).
25   According to Rousseau, the dogmas of civil religion 'ought to be few, simple, and exactly worded, without explanation or commentary. The existence of a mighty, intelligent and beneficent Divinity, possessed of foresight and providence, the life to come, the happiness of the just, the punishment of the wicked, the sanctity of the social contract and the laws: these are its positive dogmas. Its negative dogmas I confine to one, intolerance, which is a part of the cults we have rejected' (*The social contract: or principles of political right*, G.D.H. Cole (trans.), vol. 4, chpt. 8, 1762, www.constitution.org/jjr/socon_04.htm#008 (accessed 24 May 2012).
26   Gentile & Mallett, 'The sacralisation of politics', p. 35.
27   Gentile & Mallett, 'The sacralisation of politics', pp. 18–19.

function', 'political liturgy', and a 'sacred history'.[28] In 1916, amidst the mass death and destruction of the First World War, Antonio Gramsci proposed that socialism:

> is precisely that religion that must destroy Christianity. Religion in the sense that it too is a faith, that has its mystics and practitioners; and religion because it has substituted the idea of the transcendental God of the Catholics with faith in man and in his superior power as a single spiritual reality.[29]

As early as 1920, before the death of Lenin and before the era of the great totalitarian regimes of the 20th century, British Communist Bertrand Russell claimed, after visiting the Soviet Union, that Bolshevism was a religion much like Islam.[30] In 1925 British economist John Maynard Keynes identified Leninism as a new religion[31] and, in 1931, exiled Russian religious and political philosopher Nikolai Berdyaev observed:

> Like every religion, [Bolshevism] carries with it an all-embracing relation to life, decides all its fundamental questions, and claims to give meaning to everything ... it takes possession of the whole soul and calls forth enthusiasm and self-sacrifice.[32]

---

28 Gentile & Mallett, 'The sacralisation of politics', p. 23.
29 Antonio Gramsci, *Cronache torinesi 1913–1917*, cited in Gentile & Mallett, 'The sacralisation of politics', p. 37.
30 Bertrand Russell, *The practice and theory of Bolshevism*, London, George Allen and Unwin, 1920.
31 Keynes' observations are insightful, if somewhat disparaging and idiosyncratic: 'Like other new religions, Leninism derives its power not from the multitudes but from a small number of enthusiastic converts whose zeal and intolerance make each one the equal in strength of a hundred indifferentists. Like other new religions, it is led by those who can combine the new spirit, perhaps sincerely, with seeing a good deal more than their followers, politicians with at least an average dose of political cynicism, who can smile as well as frown, volatile experimentalists, released by religion from truth and mercy, but not blind to facts and experience, and open therefore to the charge (superficial and useless though it is where politicians, lay or ecclesiastical, are concerned) of hypocrisy. Like other new religions, it seems to take the color and gaiety and freedom out of everyday life and offer a drab substitute in the square wooden faces of its devotees. Like other new religions, it persecutes without justice or pity those who actively resist it. Like other new religions, it is unscrupulous. Like other new religions, it is filled with missionary ardor and ecumenical ambitions. But to say that Leninism is the faith of a persecuting and propagating minority of fanatics led by hypocrites is, after all, to say no more or less than that it *is* a religion, and not merely a party, and Lenin a Mahomet, and not a Bismarck' (*Essays in persuasion*, New York, Rupert Hart-Davis, 1965, p. 4).
32 Nicholas Berdyaev, *The Russian Revolution: two essays on its implications in religion and psychology*, D.B. (trans.), London, Sheed and Ward, 1931, p. 60.

1. THE PHENOMENON OF THE PERSONALITY CULT

One of the ways in which the veneration of man became manifest in the Soviet Union was in the cults of heroes and martyrs. Celebrated figures included Bolsheviks killed in the October Revolution and the Civil War; socialists killed in strikes, revolutions and skirmishes prior to the 1917 Revolution; great revolutionary figures of the past; and some of the towering humanist figures of Russian literature. Statuary, festivals and parades celebrated these famous people in a manner that is reminiscent of the veneration previously accorded to religious martyrs and heroes. As Lambert and Mallett point out: 'At its root, after all, the word "hero" conveys an interweaving of man with god. From classical antiquity onward, the hero was invested with powers that were expressly *super*human.'[33] Lenin was a prime mover in the creation of the celebrations and rituals to honour heroes and martyrs, but he viewed these figures as educational and exemplary, rather than as sacred. In a famous tract from 1905, in which Lenin referred to religion as the 'opium of the people', he rejected outright any form of religious sentiment as damaging and exploitative:

> Religion is one of the forms of spiritual oppression which everywhere weighs down heavily upon the masses of the people, over burdened by their perpetual work for others, by want and isolation ... Those who toil and live in want all their lives are taught by religion to be submissive and patient while here on earth, and to take comfort in the hope of a heavenly reward. But those who live by the labour of others are taught by religion to practise charity while on earth, thus offering them a very cheap way of justifying their entire existence as exploiters and selling them at a moderate price tickets to well-being in heaven. Religion is opium for the people. Religion is a sort of spiritual booze, in which the slaves of capital drown their human image, their demand for a life more or less worthy of man.[34]

Despite Marxism's atheistic stance, there are inherent in Marxism (and indeed Marxism–Leninism) many tenets that are wholly compatible with a religious and/or spiritual outlook. Marxism promises adherents a utopian future at the conclusion of linear time, in which equality, harmony and an end to suffering await humankind. It also values asceticism, places emphasis on the inner transformation of the individual, and calls for absolute faith and self-sacrifice in

---
33 Lambert & Mallett, ' Introduction', p. 454.
34 V.I. Lenin, 'Socialism and religion', *Novaya Zhizn*, 28, 3 Dec. 1905, www.marxists.org/archive/lenin/works/1905/dec/03.htm (accessed 2 Nov. 2016).

order to achieve this end. The Bolshevik Party was portrayed as a sacred entity crusading on a worldwide mission of Leninism.[35] Feliks Dzerzhinskii justified the violent actions of the Cheka, the infamous Bolshevik secret police, in terms of 'requiring sacrifices in order to shorten up the road to salvation for others'.[36] In later years, under Stalin, a 'lack of faith', which could consist of the mere suspicion of inappropriate thoughts, rather than actual subversive action, became sufficient grounds for the application of the death penalty. Indeed, it was always anticipated that Marxism–Leninism would embark on a crusade that would ultimately engulf the whole world. It aimed to unite and liberate the entire population of the globe, ultimately abolishing barriers of class, race and nation.

Anatolii Lunacharskii, who was one of the primary young theorists of the god-building movement, saw a humanist religion as providing the emotional bond that would link human beings together.[37] Such a religion was key to involving the masses in the building of a socialist society. In 1907 Lunacharskii wrote from exile, 'Scientific socialism is the most religious of all religions, and the true Social Democrat is the most deeply religious of all human beings'.[38] The term 'god-building' referred to the 'development of the human spirit into an "All-Spirit" (*Vsedusha*)',[39] and this process was to begin with the socialist revolution. The god-builders believed in spiritual immortality, as this generation would be linked to all future generations by the same

---

[35] 'The charismatic glorification of the party as a saviour, messiah, a salvation army for a backward society in overwhelming social and cultural misery, gives the *intelligentsia* a mission to fulfil for their "inner needs", a firm conviction to march on the progressive sides of historical development, and an undivided commitment to the holy cause of the party. The fusion of the conflicting demands of "individual heroism and organizational impersonalism" found expression "in the form of an organizational hero — the Bolshevik Party". Leninism became a world mission' (Klaus-Georg Riegel, 'Marxism–Leninism as a political religion', *Totalitarian Movements and Political Religions*, 2005, 6:1, pp. 97–126, p. 104).
[36] Feliks Dzerzhinskii cited in Riegel, 'Marxism–Leninism as a political religion', p. 103.
[37] 'The faith of an active human being is a faith in mankind of the future; his religion is a combination of the feelings and thoughts which make him a participant in the life of mankind and a link in that chain which extends up to the superman ... to a perfected organism ... If the essence of any life is self-preservation, then a life of beauty, goodness, and truth is self-realization' (A.V. Lunacharskii, 'Osnovyp ozitivnoie stetiki', in S. Doratovskii & A. Charushnikov (eds), *Ocherki realisticheskogo mirovozzreniia*, St Petersburg, 1904, pp. 181–82, cited in Nina Tumarkin, 'Religion, Bolshevism and the origins of the Lenin cult', *Russian Review*, 40:1, 1981, pp. 35–46, p. 42).
[38] A.V. Lunacharskii, 'Budushchee religii', p. 23, cited in Tumarkin, 'Religion, Bolshevism and the origins of the Lenin cult', pp. 42–43.
[39] Tumarkin, 'Religion, Bolshevism and the origins of the Lenin cult', p. 43.

bonds that linked all of humankind in the present, but also, for some, there was a belief in the possibility of physical immortality through advances in science. Leonid Krasin, like Aleksandr Bogdanov, believed that science would one day make resurrection possible,[40] and it was the god-builder Krasin who took charge of the preservation of Lenin's body after his death in 1924.[41] From a purely pragmatic viewpoint, if one is to be resurrected in the future, the physical body must be preserved.

It is interesting to note how well this dovetails with Russian Orthodox faith. In the Christian tradition, the embalmed corpse symbolises the non-putrefaction of the body, a sign of holiness and saintliness, which is a widespread and longstanding belief amongst the Soviet public, although the incorruptibility of remains is not in fact a requirement for canonisation in the Russian Orthodox Church.[42] The tale of *Khitryi Lenin*[43] illustrates Lenin's entry into folklore and myth as an immortal who still walks the earth in his embalmed body. The idea that a revered and heroic leader could sleep after death, to be awakened in the future when his country needed him, was a myth found not only throughout Russian folklore, but in the mythology of many nations.[44]

Lenin's domination of the Party line, his railings against any vestige of religious thought or sentiment, and his disavowal of the methodology of the god-builders, were ultimately unable to prevent spiritual and mystical attitudes from infecting Bolshevik thoughts and practices. In 1920, a poster containing the 'Ten commandments of the proletarian' was published by the Central Committee. Perhaps, as Lunacharskii (and indeed Croce and Rousseau) postulated, people need a set of spiritual beliefs if they are to maintain enthusiasm for the tasks of bettering themselves and creating a new kind of society.[45]

---

40   The Biocosmist-Immortalist group's manifesto of 1922 reads: 'For us, essential and real human rights are the right of being (immortality, resurrection, rejuvenation) and the right of mobility in the cosmic space (and not the alleged rights proclaimed in the declaration of the bourgeois revolution of 1789)' (cited in Boris Groys, 'The immortal bodies', *Res: Anthropology and Aesthetics*, 53/54, 2008, pp. 345–49, p. 348).
41   Tumarkin, 'Religion, Bolshevism and the origins of the Lenin cult', p. 44.
42   Nina Tumarkin, *Lenin lives! The Lenin cult in Soviet Russia*, Cambridge, Harvard University Press, 1997, p. 5.
43   *Clever Lenin*. See Tumarkin, *Lenin lives!*, pp. 198–99.
44   The legend of King Arthur immediately springs to mind for those in the English-speaking world.
45   In his 1968 Nobel Prize-winning novel *The first circle*, Aleksandr Solzhenitsyn allowed the character of the true believer socialist prisoner, Rubin, to be a mouthpiece for this viewpoint:

In fact it was the cult of personality, which was (ironically) built on the foundation stones of Lenin's demise and deification, that was to provide the ideological and spiritual focus for the Soviet regime for the next seven decades.[46] The cult of Lenin and its importance to the cult of Stalin will be discussed in Chapter Two. Chapter Four examines in detail the way in which the traditions and rituals of the Russian Orthodox Church pervaded Soviet propaganda in mildly disguised form, and explores the propaganda value of the image of Stalin as an icon.

Ritual and the supremacy of the collective over the individual

As already discussed, the term 'cult' derives from the religious sphere, but it is important to note that in the ancient world, the sharp differentiation between religious and secular spheres that characterises many Western democracies today did not exist. Classics scholar Ittai Gradel cautions against interpreting imperial personality cults from a modern, often Christian, perspective, noting that the term 'religio' meant 'reverence, conscientiousness and diligence towards superiors, commonly, but not exclusively, the gods'.[47] With the advent of political religions in the autocratic regimes of the 20th century, there was once again a blurring of the barriers between the secular and religious realms, with a corresponding 'reverence, conscientiousness and diligence towards superiors' manifested through ritual and the 'politics of obligation'.[48]

'In the old days people had leaned on the Church and the priests for moral guidance. And even nowadays, what Polish peasant woman would take any serious step in life without consulting her priest?
It could be that the country now needed firm moral foundations, even more urgently than the Volga – Don Canal or the great new dam on the Angara River.
The question was: how to set about creating them?
This was the whole point of the "Proposal for the Establishment of Civic Temples", of which Rubin had already made a rough draft' (Aleksandr Solzhenitsyn. *The first circle*. Michael Guybon (trans.). New York, Harper and Row, 1968).
46   As Tumarkin wryly observes: 'It is an irony of history that the god-builders acted to deify human genius in the person of Lenin, for whom all religion was anathema and god-building was particularly repugnant, and that Lenin should have become, by the efforts of some of his oldest friends, the Man–God of Communism' ('Religion, Bolshevism and the origins of the Lenin cult', p. 46).
47   Ittai Gradel, *Emperor worship and Roman religion*, Oxford, Clarendon Press, 2002, p. 6.
48   The 'politics of obligation' will be discussed in greater detail in Chapter Three.

The leader cult and its manifestation through ritual can have a unifying effect on a society, stressing social, political and moral cohesion. Many of the concepts that Simon Price discussed in relation to the Roman imperial cults can be applied, with some modifications in terminology, to the leader cults of the 20th century:

> The imperial cult stabilised the religious order of the world. The system of ritual was carefully structured; the symbolism evoked a picture of the relationship between the emperor and the gods. The ritual was also structuring; it imposed a definition of the world. The imperial cult, along with politics and diplomacy, constructed the reality of the Roman empire.[49]

In a similar manner in the Soviet Union of the 20th century, the personality cult of the leader stabilised the political order and, through carefully structured ritual, provided a definition of the relationship between the leader and the people, and a definition of the world — at least the world as it should be in the imminent socialist utopian future. Jeffrey Brooks sees the 'politics of obligation' as legitimating Stalin's leadership and the Bolshevik regime at a time when 'the officially sanctioned image of the world diverged sharply from the actualities of daily life',[50] and the nature of these reciprocal relationships was often defined and elaborated through ritual, including both semi-private personal rituals to replace the sacraments of the church and massive public street parades and re-enactments of historic events. A number of new Soviet rituals and festivals were introduced.[51] For example, in 1920, the Orthodox ritual of baptism was replaced by the Soviet

---

49 S.R.F. Price, *Rituals and power: the Roman imperial cult in Asia Minor*, Cambridge University Press, 1984, p. 247.
50 Jeffrey Brooks, 'Stalin's politics of obligation', *Totalitarian Movements and Political Religions*, 4:1, 2003, pp. 47–48, p. 50.
51 Lenin's death commemoration (on 21 January till 1929, thereafter on 22 January, merged with Bloody Sunday commemoration); Bloody Sunday commemoration (22 January); Red Army Day (23 February); Women's Day (originally last Saturday in February by the old calendar, then 8 March); Overthrow of the Autocracy (12 March); Day of the Paris Commune (18 March); Lena Massacre commemoration (17 April); May Day (1 May); Day of the USSR (6 July); Anniversary of October Revolution (7 November); Anniversary of 1905 Revolution (19 December).

ritual of '*Oktiabrina*'.⁵² Christel Lane sees the mass rituals of Stalinism as instruments of cultural management that facilitated acceptance of a general system of Marxist–Leninist norms and values.⁵³

Soviet propaganda did indeed frequently depict a calm and joyous world, which was observably at odds with lived reality. At the Seventeenth Party Congress, writer F.I. Panferov⁵⁴ urged his fellow writers and artists to use their creative talent to portray the peasants' joy at collectivisation.⁵⁵ Collectivisation had been strongly opposed by the majority of peasants, who frequently decided to slaughter their animals and burn their crops rather than surrender them to the *kolkhoz* (collective farm). Party officials went out into the countryside and physically forced the process, using terror and inducing famine to ensure that quotas were met. In the posters, paintings and literature of the day, the peasants beam and rejoice in gratitude at the gift that the state has given them. Many writers and artists were aware of the truth, having seen the starving peasants at the railway stations as they travelled the countryside documenting socialism's marvels. Nevertheless, they cooperated with the Party in portraying reality as it should be, arguably working in service of a higher truth.

Because the world celebrated in Soviet literature, film and music appears somewhat at odds with the reality of Soviet life, there is a frequent tendency to speculate as to whether or not participants in celebrations and rituals in the Stalinist era were 'sincere' in their practice — that is, whether there was genuine emotion attached to the words and actions of public obeisance — with the implication that participants took part in such rituals purely out of hope for advancement, or for fear of the consequences of not doing so (or a mixture of both). Price's comments in relation to attempts to understand the imperial personality cult

---

52   'Octobering'. See David King, *Red star over Russia: a visual history of the Soviet Union from 1917 to the death of Stalin: posters, photographs and graphics from the David King collection*, London, Tate, 2009, p. 168; Graeme J. Gill, *Symbols and legitimacy in Soviet politics*, New York, Cambridge University Press, 2011, p. 74.
53   Lane, *The rites of rulers*, p. 25.
54   Fedor Ivanovich Panferov was the author of the trilogy of novels *Mother Volga (The blow*, 1953; *Meditation*, 1958; and, *In the name of the young*, 1960); State Prize winners *The struggle for peace* (books 1–2) 1945–47 and, *In the land of the vanquished*, 1948; and also held political office in the Supreme Soviet of the USSR. For further details see hrono.ru/biograf/bio_p/panferov_fi.php (accessed 3 Jan. 2014).
55   F.I. Panferov, 'XVII s'yezd VKP(b) Rech' tovarishcha Panferova, Zasedaniye 8 fevralya 1934 g., utrenneye', hrono.ru/vkpb_17/25_3.html (accessed 3 Jan. 2014).

of Ancient Rome from a contemporary standpoint, may apply equally well to our own attempts to pass judgment on the participants in Soviet rituals, coming, as we do, from a different era, and a different political and spiritual milieu:

> The problem with emotion as the criterion of significance of rituals is not just that in practice we do not have the relevant evidence, but that it is covertly Christianizing. The criterion of feelings and emotions as the test of authenticity in ritual and religion is in fact an appeal to the Christian value of *religio animi*, religion of the soul, that is, the interior beliefs and feelings of individuals.[56]

For the Bolshevik Party, touting a Marxist view of history and, indeed, influenced by thinkers like Friedrich Nietzsche,[57] the collective took precedence over the individual. Article 27 of the Rules of the Communist Party states: 'The highest principle of party leadership is collectivism …' and articles 30, 34 and 38 vest supreme authority in the Party Congress, in the Central Committee between congresses, and in the Politburo and the Secretariat between plenums of the Central Committee.[58] In his examination of the imagery used in political religions, Hans Maier describes the transformation in society after the Russian Revolution:

> The people who marched here were not individuals, but a collective. The new human being had left behind his 'little ego, twitching with fear and rickets'; he had surrendered the 'farce of individuality' in favour of a mass existence. His salvation no longer lay with his interior life, his psychic development, and his personal culture. Instead, it lay with the duplication of his external functions, the melding of individuals into a unity. United marching, united action, united struggle, street and field as mass media — revolutionary artists and poets characterised the 'new human being' using such images.[59]

---

56 Price, *Rituals and power*, p. 10.
57 For an excellent analysis of the numerous ways in which Nietzschian philosophy pervaded Bolshevism, see Bernice Glatzer Rosenthal, *New myth, new world: from Nietzsche to Stalinism*, Pennsylvania State University Press, 2002.
58 Cited in Graeme Gill, 'The Soviet leader cult: reflections on the structure of leadership in the Soviet Union', *British Journal of Political Science*, 10:2, 1980, pp. 167–86, p. 176.
59 Hans Maier, 'Political religions and their images: Soviet communism, Italian fascism and German National Socialism', *Politics, Religion and Ideology*, 7:3, 2006, pp. 267–81, p. 274.

In societies founded on principles of 'the collective' and 'the overall good', the 'interior beliefs and feelings of individuals' may be considered to be of lesser importance and validity than societal goals and the outward behaviour of the people as a whole. Participation in rituals, and the generation and acceptance of propaganda, expresses faith in the goals of the regime, and loyalty to the Party and to Marxist–Leninist ideology and vision. It demonstrates a willingness to bring about change at both the level of the individual and as a collective. Further, as Brooks notes, in societies built around collective principles, the outward manifestation of faith may be more important than the individual's inner convictions, with 'correct performance, rather than belief ... most important to Soviet authorities. The significance of correct performance may explain why people were punished for small mistakes, such as printers' errors'.[60] The rites, symbols and language of Bolshevism were so pervasive as to be virtually inescapable, with Stalinism presented as a new form of civilisation.[61]

Implicit in the collectivist worldview is a tendency to categorise people and, as in the Soviet case, to view them through a Marxist lens as members of particular classes, rather than as unique individuals with their own peculiar sets of circumstances. It is almost a truism that the ability to name things and people, and thus to put people into categories, is a fundamental form of political power. Categorisation of people defines their relation to the community, and will even shape people's understanding of themselves. It is thus that, in November 1918, Martin Latsis, Chairman of the Eastern Front Cheka, could state:

> We are not waging war against individual persons. We are exterminating the bourgeoisie as a class. During the investigation, do not look for evidence that the accused acted in deed or word against Soviet power. The first questions that you ought to put are: To what class does he belong? What is his origin? What is his education or profession? And it is these questions that ought to determine the fate of the accused. In this lies the significance and essence of the Red Terror.[62]

---

60 Jeffrey Brooks, *Thank you, Comrade Stalin! Soviet public culture from revolution to Cold War*, Princeton University Press, 2000, p. 68.
61 See Gill, *Symbols and legitimacy in Soviet politics*, p. 2.
62 Latsis quoted in Riegel, 'Marxism–Leninism as a political religion', p. 106.

1. THE PHENOMENON OF THE PERSONALITY CULT

Categorisation is good for thinking about human beings, but also good for manipulating, dominating and exploiting them. Many of the propaganda posters of the Civil War period and into the early 1930s were designed specifically to help identify classes of enemies, such as priests and kulaks (peasants), and to conflate members of these classes with monsters, fiends, vampires, or portray them as subhuman. The emphasis on the supremacy of the collective over the individual was also clearly demonstrated in the ritual aspects of the show trials of the 1930s, and in the Soviet ritual known as '*samokritika*' or 'self-criticism'.[63]

This emphasis on the collective and on ritualised behaviour and interactions has several implications for the study of Soviet propaganda posters. First, people, including the leader, are often represented as types, rather than as carefully delineated individuals. A crowd may consist of representatives of a number of typical professions, or a smattering of Soviet national groups identifiable by distinct national costume. These types may change and evolve according to the needs of propaganda and sometimes also to reflect a changing reality or, more often, to reflect the anticipated end result of a process of change that is just beginning. Second, the posters model ideal relationships between the leader and subjects, and institutionalise hierarchy and patterns of obligation.[64] Third, the emphasis on the collective and the depiction of crowds in propaganda posters reinforces the notion of a unified society working together towards mutually desired goals. And fourth, ritualistic depictions employ visual symbolism that is laden with semantic value and which evokes, sometimes at the semiconscious or subconscious level, the rich historical background from which it arises. Traditions in which art is used as propaganda to promote or maintain support for a political leader date back more than 2,000 years.

---

63   *Samokritika* was an apology ritual wherein an official was publicly accused of some Party infraction and expected to admit his mistake in accordance with mutually understood rules and formulae. Typically, a senior official from outside an organisation presided over a meeting which encouraged criticism of the organisation's leadership from below and empowered those present to criticise or denounce their leaders. For a detailed examination of the ritualistic nature of *samokritika* see J. Arch Getty, 'Samokritika rituals in the Stalinist Central Committee, 1933–1938', *Russian Review*, 58:1, 1999, pp. 49–70.
64   Chapter Four discusses how the visual language of the Russian Orthodox Church is reinterpreted in a Soviet setting in order to facilitate ideal relationships.

THE PERSONALITY CULT OF STALIN IN SOVIET POSTERS, 1929–1953

Personality cults in art — a brief historical survey

Personality cults surrounding political leaders did not begin with the totalitarian regimes of the last century, nor are they confined to a particular ideology or specific political systems. They can be found in a variety of places and times throughout human history. There are valuable insights to be gained by conducting a quick survey of some of the salient features of personality cults from antiquity right up to the time immediately preceding Stalin's rule. It will be demonstrated that, although many of the features of the cult of Stalin and the accolades and exceptional attributes heaped on him may at first seem to be unique and tailored specifically to the expression of Stalin's outstanding leadership, they are in fact generic and formulaic when viewed in the context of the personality cults that preceded him.

The first known case of a divine cult of a living human is usually dated as occurring at the end of the 5th century BC with the Spartan general Lysander, who was venerated on Samos.[65] Personality cults occurred in the Egypt of the Pharaohs, around Alexander the Great, the Roman emperors, the Japanese emperors, Napoleon, Napoleon III and the Russian tsars, as well as in a number of other imperial systems, fascist governments, and socialist regimes. The use of art to publicise and promote the persona of the leader has a similarly long history. For example, the Ancient Romans excelled in sculpture and, in particular, the portrait bust, the use of which was restricted to patricians. Large numbers of busts of the emperor were created and distributed throughout the empire to be set up in public places and in private homes. Every Roman citizen was required to burn incense in front of the emperor's bust to demonstrate loyalty and allegiance.[66] Caesar Augustus was portrayed in various roles: military commander (*imperator*); first citizen of Rome (*princeps*); and chief

---

65 See Price, *Rituals and power*, p. 26; and, Frank William Walbank, *The Hellenistic world*, London, Fontana, 1981, pp. 212–13.
66 The persecution of early Christians began partly because of their refusal to perform this ritual of civic duty.

priest (*pontifex maximus*).[67] These roles related to his official titles and duties and expressed the persona of the ruler in his various formalised relationships to his subjects, but were also archetypal.

Similarly, throughout the Soviet Union, every public room or office usually contained several busts of Lenin and Stalin, and they took their place in Lenin corners and Stalin rooms alongside icons. When busts and portraits of the leader appeared in official buildings, they legitimated proceedings and assumed a proxy role for the leader. As David King points out, in the final decade of Stalin's life, and as he retreated from public view, portraits and busts came increasingly to 'stand in' for Stalin in all public arenas: 'The bronze Stalin, the marble Stalin, were invulnerable to the bullets of the "Zinovievite bandits". The flesh and blood Stalin could safely stay out of the public gaze. Sculpture became the real Stalin — heavy, ponderous, immortal.'[68] In his seminal work *Portrait of the King*, French philosopher and historian Louis Marin elaborates the concept of simultaneous presence and absence which occurs with 're-presentations' of the king via portraiture. The portrait of the king invokes presence and the force of legitimation, authorisation, and the power of institution, thereby creating subjects.[69] The power of the king's portrait derives in part from the fact that it simultaneously represents three bodies of the king: 'as sacramental body it is visibly *really present* in the visual and written currencies; as historical body it is visible as *represented*, absence becomes presence again in "image"; as political body it is visible as *symbolic fiction signified* in its name, right, and law.'[70] As Marin argues, the king is only really king in images, and for his power to have substance, a belief in the iconic emblems of his leadership, as re-presented in the portrait, is necessary.[71]

---

67 Hugh Honour & John Fleming, *A world history of art*, London, Macmillan Reference Books, 1982, p. 210.
68 David King, *The commissar vanishes: the falsification of photographs and art in Stalin's Russia*, New York, Metropolitan Books, 1997, p. 13.
69 'What is re-presenting, if not presenting anew (in the modality of time) or in the place of (in the modality of space)? The prefix *re-* introduces into the term the value of substitution ... At the place of representation then, there is a thing or person absent in time or space, or rather an other, and a substitution operates with a double of this other in its place ... Such would be the first effect of representation in general: to do as if the other, the absent one, were here and the same; not presence but effect of presence. It is surely not the same, but it is as if it were, and often better than, the same' (Louis Marin, *Portrait of the king*, Minneapolis, University of Minnesota Press, 1988, p. 5).
70 Marin, *Portrait of the king*, p. 13.
71 Marin, *Portrait of the king*, p. 8.

THE PERSONALITY CULT OF STALIN IN SOVIET POSTERS, 1929–1953

Propaganda imagery in Ancient Rome was not confined to portrait busts. Monumental architecture assumed increasing importance, as it would 2,000 years later in the Soviet Union. Triumphal arches were created as a fusion of architecture and sculpture and, although they could be used as literal gateways in triumphal processions, they didn't necessarily provide entry to anything in particular — their purpose was ornamental, rather than functional. Colossal cult statues of the Roman emperors, some seven to eight metres tall, were also erected across the Roman Empire, on the same scale as cult statues of the gods. Images of the emperor were carried in processions at imperial festivals and on other occasions. All of these practices were to be revived and used extensively for propaganda purposes in the Soviet Union, with statuary reaching heights of up to 40 metres. In fact, a 100-metre-high statue of Lenin was intended to top the Palace of Soviets, which was planned for the site of the Cathedral of Christ the Saviour in Moscow, although this overambitious plan never came to fruition. Portraits of Stalin and Lenin (and other Soviet leaders) were carried on poles in processions, and are depicted in this manner in propaganda posters.

The area of most particular interest to this study, the political poster, is perhaps most closely paralleled in numismatics. Darius the Great of Persepolis distributed his image to the populace across a wide empire by placing it on coins. As part of the propaganda involved in their struggle to succeed Julius Caesar in Ancient Rome, Antony and Octavian both issued coins with their portraits situated in the position which had previously been reserved for the gods. Brutus, too, issued coins with emblems of his ancestors inhabiting the place reserved for the gods. Coins struck in Asia feature emblems of Dionysus and portraits of Antony with an ivy crown on his head. Antony identified himself closely and publicly with Dionysus and, like Octavian, made attempts to establish a divine lineage for himself.

Coins were an excellent means of propaganda as, apart from their purely pragmatic use as currency within the economic system, they were small, portable, widely distributed, and often in public view. At times they may also have taken on apotropǽic qualities.[72] In *Portrait*

---

[72] See Stefan Skowronek, *On the problems of the Alexandrian mint: allusion to the divinity of the sovereign appearing on the coins of Egyptian Alexandria in the period of the early Roman Empire: 1st and 2nd centuries A.D.*, Varsovie, Ed. scientifiques de Pologne, 1967, p. 74.

1. THE PHENOMENON OF THE PERSONALITY CULT

of the king, Louis Marin references a 1602 text by Rascas de Bagarris[73] in which state counsel advises the king to mint commemorative coins with his own image in order to miraculously transform discourse into history.[74] The aim of propaganda is to convert discourse to history and Soviet propaganda, in particular, sought to embed the world it represented in the viewer's mind as an already accomplished fact. As with the portrait of the king on a coin, the audience for the propaganda poster is required to simultaneously look and read.

Many of the coins minted with a portrait of the ruler alluded to the divinity of emperors, both deceased and living, using familiar and widely understood symbols to illustrate these connections. Many of the symbols used on Roman coins (and indeed in other forms of propaganda) were those associated with apotheosis, and made explicit visual reference to the divinity of the emperor. For example, laurel wreaths, crowns, ears of corn and globes symbolised divine attributes, and the emperor depicted with his right hand uplifted signified salvation, magic force and apotropæic greeting.[75] Stalin's image in propaganda posters is frequently surrounded by laurel or oak leaves and alongside ears of corn and images of the globe. Stalin is also depicted in oratorical poses with his right hand raised.[76] Stefan Skowronek observes that, for the Roman emperors, divine honours were often only a political tool and, in many cases, were not taken seriously by the emperors themselves.[77] He postulates that the Roman emperors were deeply invested in their political programs, but not in their own personality cults; that is, 'the Imperial cult was not the result of religious impulses, but led to the manifestation of feelings of loyalty towards the Emperor'.[78] I will argue that Stalin, too, viewed his personality cult as a political tool to model ideal relations between the leader and the masses in order to mobilise the citizenry to pursue the goals of the regime as laid down by the Bolshevik vanguard.

---

73 *Discours qui montre la nécessité de rétablir le très ancient et auguste usage public des vrayes et parfaits médailles.*
74 Tom Conley, 'Foreword: The king's effects,' in Marin, *Portrait of the king*, p. xi.
75 Skowronek, *On the problems of the Alexandrian mint*, p. 79.
76 See Chapter Four.
77 Skowronek, *On the problems of the Alexandrian mint*, p. 72.
78 Skowronek, *On the problems of the Alexandrian mint*, p. 80.

Historic parallels to, and precedents for, the cult of Stalin are not confined to the Classical world. Holy Roman Emperor Maximilian I of Habsburg faced many of the same leadership challenges as the emperors of Ancient Rome, and as the Bolsheviks when they seized power in 1917. Like Stalin, Maximilian headed a large empire with disputed borders, diverse populations and widely varied traditions of local government. A brief examination of some aspects of the personality cult of Maximilian I brings us a step closer to the modern world, as Maximilian was the first major leader to utilise the printing press in the service of his propaganda. The printing press enabled the comparatively inexpensive production of a large number of visual images and text, which were portable and thus easily distributed to a mass audience. By commissioning skilled artists (most notably Albrecht Dürer and Hans Burgkmair) to create, for example, an original woodblock featuring his stylised image, which would then be reproduced in bulk, the emperor was able to influence and control the persona that would be viewed by the public in all corners of the empire.

Images of Maximilian were laden with symbolism, forming a rich visual language that testified to his personal qualities, his archetypal qualities as a leader, his lineage, and the legitimacy of his office. Maximilian did not abandon other forms of art and propaganda for which there was such rich and extensive precedent. Taking his cue from the Roman emperors before him, he appeared in statuary and his deeds were proclaimed on triumphal arches and through the issue of coins. Like the emperors striving for divinity before him, Maximilian planned a large number of public works to demonstrate not only his historical links to the Roman Empire, but also his spiritual and ideological links to the Emperor Constantine, displaying his Christian piety and faith, his leadership qualities and his warrior identity. As Maximilian worried that his claims to traditional legitimacy were not sufficient to ensure a stable and peaceful rule, he both 'beefed up' these claims with some creative genealogy,[79] and also used his manufactured image to appeal to his subjects on charismatic grounds.

---

79 Maximilian took great pains to establish his claims of traditional legitimacy, investing large amounts of money in 'scholarly' investigations of his genealogy. He asked Stabius to draw up a family tree headed by Noah that included Osiris and Hercules Libycus; and had this genealogy submitted to the faculty of Vienna University where it was found to be consonant with Old Testament scriptures. Depending on political necessity, Maximilian would shift emphasis between claims to be descended from the Trojans and from the Ancient Romans. By grafting his

1. THE PHENOMENON OF THE PERSONALITY CULT

In another parallel to Stalin's leadership, many of Maximilian's planned elaborate projects did not come to fruition, and records of his intentions survive only in the form of preliminary drawings and woodcuts showing plans for statues and monuments.[80] The surviving drawings and prints for Maximilian's planned great monuments show an extraordinarily rich visual language of symbols and archetypes associated with leadership and divinity, and demonstrate remarkable continuity with those used to indicate the divinity of figures like Alexander the Great, Julius Caesar and Caesar Augustus. It is hardly surprising, then, that we find much of the same symbolism cropping up in the art and propaganda associated with the leader cults that followed Maximilian and, later, in posters of Stalin.

The French Revolution saw the emergence of a number of cults centred around revolutionary leaders, most notably Maximilien de Robespierre and Jean-Paul Marat, who made appearances in propagandistic paintings and a proliferation of portrait busts. These figures were pushed into the background when Napoleon came onto the scene. A brief glance at the cult of Napoleon illuminates the major premises of this book in three ways. First, the art produced in France in support of Napoleon's leadership shows a continuation and elaboration on the themes that emerged in earlier personality cults. Under Napoleon's director of artistic patronage, Vivant Denon, a group of official artists was assembled to produce works that celebrated Napoleon's triumphs.[81] Artists such as Jacques-Louis David, Antoine-Jean Gros and Jean-Auguste-Dominique Ingres painted portraits of the emperor that emphasised his military prowess, his links to the Roman emperors, and took particular pains to establish an ideological but *non*-genealogical lineage by showing Napoleon walking firmly in the footsteps of other great men of the past. It is at this point in European history, where no claim to traditional legitimacy exists, that propaganda promoting the charisma and ideology of the leader comes to the fore. In his detailed analysis of Napoleon and history

---

family tree onto that of the French royal houses, he could claim Merovingian ancestry as well (Larry Silver, *Marketing Maximilian: the visual ideology of a Holy Roman Emperor*, Princeton University Press, 2008, p. 55).
80 One such project was to be his grand tomb monument, which was only finally completed by his grandson Ferdinand, some 80 years after it was first begun in 1502 (Silver, *Marketing Maximilian*, p. 63).
81 See David Welch, 'Painting, propaganda and patriotism,' *History Today*, 55:7, 2005, pp. 42–50, p. 45.

painting, Christopher Prendergast examines the symbolism of the trimmings of Napoleon's coronation as a quest to confer legitimacy on his usurpation of the monarchy, without making reference to the Bourbons, by suggesting a lineage that drew on a more distant past.[82] Napoleon reached back to Ancient Rome and also to the more local association with Charlemagne by paying homage to him at Aix-la-Chapelle; by wearing Carolingian paraphernalia at his coronation;[83] by being crowned dressed in a Roman tunic; and, by adopting bees, which were associated with the Merovingian kings, as his personal symbol.[84] Stalin's appeal to a pantheon of Russian heroes of the past, including two tsars (Ivan Grozny and Peter the Great), as imminent war threatened the Soviet Union, and the visual representations of his ideological lineage[85] were major tactics in shoring up legitimacy for his leadership.

Second, Stalin's propagandists employed the same archetypes in their depictions of Stalin as the French artists employed in their portraits of Napoleon. Understandably for someone with Napoleon's military background, the primary topos was that of the Warrior and, like Stalin after him, there was a later shift from the topos of the Warrior to that of the Saviour, employing quasi-sacral images of forgiving, blessing and healing.[86] Napoleon was also portrayed as a 'fatherly' figure, the other major archetype employed in the Stalin cult.[87]

Third, the posthumous cult of Napoleon, which spread across Europe after his death, at times approached the sort of adulation encountered in 21st-century celebrity-obsessed popular culture. In his article on 'Lisztomania', the cult of Ferencz 'Franz' Liszt, Dana Gooley describes 19th-century European society as not only obsessed with Liszt, but also with the persona of Napoleon, with students at the Ecole polythechnique walking and dressing like Napoleon.[88] The cult had

---

82   Christopher Prendergast, *Napoleon and history painting: Antoine-Jean Gros's La Bataille d'Eylau*, Oxford, Clarendon Press, 1997, p. 35.
83   Some of this paraphernalia was not authentic and was created especially for the coronation.
84   Prendergast, *Napoleon and history painting*, pp. 35–36.
85   Chapter Two details Stalin's appeal to a lineage from Lenin, and also from Marx and Engels.
86   For a more detailed discussion of this transition, see Prendergast, *Napoleon and history painting*, p. 84.
87   See Prendergast, *Napoleon and history painting*, p. 164.
88   'In Paris the cult of Napoleon sank in so deeply that it affected people's everyday behavior. Frances Trollope commented in 1835 that all of the students at the Ecole polythechnique were walking and dressing like Napoleon, and a frontpage article in the Gazette Musicale identified

its origins amongst the Romantic literati in England, then bloomed in France when Napoleon died in 1821, and gained renewed impetus after the Paris Revolution of 1830. The cult of Napoleon became popular in Russia, England, France and Germany in the 19th century and, to a lesser extent, across the rest of Europe. In Germany and France portraits of Napoleon could be found in almost every house.[89] It is particularly interesting to note that Russia experienced a cult of Napoleon, despite its success in forcing Napoleon to retreat from Russian soil in the Patriotic War of 1812. Napoleon's identity as a conquering enemy and his subsequent ignominious flight and abandonment of his remaining men, seems to have done little to sully his reputation as a great general and a great emperor.[90] The cult of Napoleon Bonaparte was later used as a vehicle to power by his nephew Louis Napoleon (Napoleon III).

One of the most elaborate cults of a revolutionary leader prior to Lenin, and perhaps one of the most similar,[91] was that of George Washington, which served in part to legitimate the American Revolution. Washington's cult featured an exemplary (and somewhat fabricated) biography, a plethora of historical paintings, monumental statuary and the appearance of portraits in virtually every family home.[92]

"The Napoleon" as a ubiquitous social type: [Napoleons are] that class, made up of many people in the civil sphere, whom we see overcome with the silly pretention of imitating, copying, and aping the great man ... Today the common ambition is turned toward Napoleon; it is he who serves as the standard measure, him who is chosen as the model and type ... [There is now] an innumerable, infinite, immense race of Napoleons in all political, literary, musical and industrial categories. Everywhere you go you bump into a Napoleon; the Napoleons travel the streets, in carriage, on foot or by horse, and most often by foot'; Dana Gooley, 'Warhorses: Liszt, Weber's "Konzertstück", and the cult of Napoléon', *19th-century Music*, 24:1, 2000, pp. 62–88, p. 67.

89   Gooley, 'Warhorses', p. 68.

90   In *War and Peace*, Leo Tolstoi laments the veneration of Napoleon at the expense of the conquering but self-effacing Field Marshal Kutuzov: 'For Russian historians (strange and terrible to say!) Napoleon, that most insignificant tool of history who never anywhere, even in exile, showed human dignity — Napoleon is the object of adulation and enthusiasm: he is grand. But Kutuzov, the man who from first to last in the year 1812, from Borodino to Vilna, was never once, by word or deed, false to himself, who presents an example, exceptional in history, of self-denial and present insight into the future significance of what was happening — Kutuzov appears to them as some colourless, pitiable being, and whenever they speak of him in connection with the year 1812 they always seem a little ashamed of the whole episode' (*War and Peace*, vol. 2, Rosemary Edmonds (trans.), London Folio Society, 1971, p. 576).

91   Soviet historian I.I. Shitts cites the cult of Kemal Attaturk in Turkey as being the inspiration for the Soviet leader cults (*Dnevnik 'Velikogo Pereloma'* (mart 1928 – avgust 1931)), Paris, YMCA Press, 1991.

92   See Tumarkin, *Lenin Lives!*, p. 2.

Soviet personality cults

There were a number of personality cults in existence in close proximity to Lenin's era. Trotskii disparagingly characterised the immediate post-revolutionary period as being full of likely candidates for Bonaparte-style cults, just waiting for propitious, post-revolutionary circumstances.[93] In the period before the seizure of power by the Bolsheviks in October 1917, there were cults around several leaders or potential leaders such as General Lavr Kornilov, an intelligence officer and Imperial Army general during the First World War, Prime Minister Aleksandr Kerenskii, and even Trotskii himself.[94] Cultic practice in the Soviet Union extended beyond the Party leaders and their potential successors in leadership circles. In the years of Stalin's rule, there was a hierarchy of cults, with the minor cults of other leadership figures, regional figures and, after the war, Eastern European leader cults, orbiting like satellites around the central and predominant cult of the Supreme Leader, Stalin. Other Politburo members, Party bosses in major cities and regional centres, and even the directors of large-scale enterprises, all had their own minor cults and towns, streets, factories and schools were named after them, their portraits were often carried through the streets in celebratory parades, biographies written and distributed, birthdays celebrated publicly and, sometimes after their deaths, their apartments were turned into museums.[95]

The nominal head of the Soviet State,[96] Mikhail Kalinin, was one member of the Politburo who had his own thriving mini-cult. Kalinin was of genuine peasant origin and, prior to the Revolution, had worked on a farm, as a butler and on the railroads. While most of the Party leadership could be regarded as members of the intelligentsia (and were seen to have a vanguard role on the way to the Communist

---

93 'The misfortune of the Russian candidates for Bonaparte lay not at all in their dissimilarity to the first Napoleon, or even to Bismarck. History knows how to make use of substitutes. But they were confronted by a great revolution which had not yet solved its problems or exhausted its force' (Leon Trotsky, 'Kerensky and Kornilov, (elements of Bonapartism in the Russian Revolution)', *The history of the Russian Revolution*, vol. 2, *The attempted counter-revolution*, www.marxists.org/archive/trotsky/1930/hrr/ch29.htm (accessed 14 Jul. 2012).
94 See Chapter Four for further details.
95 See Apor et al., *The leader cult in communist dictatorships*, p. 10.
96 Chairman of the Presidium of the Supreme Soviet of the USSR from 1922 to 1946 and chairman of the Central Executive Committee of the Congress of Soviets of the Russian SFSR from 1919 to 1938.

1. THE PHENOMENON OF THE PERSONALITY CULT

utopia), much was made of the fact that Kalinin emerged from one of the classes in whose name the Bolsheviks governed and he was often photographed in full peasant dress at his village, or at the House of Peasants in Moscow.

Several other high-profile Politburo members had cults as well, including Grigorii Zinoviev[97] and marshal of the Soviet Union, Kliment Voroshilov, whose cult was built around the military archetype until that role became part of Stalin's persona during the Great Patriotic War. Stalin may have been the 'man of steel', but Lazar Kaganovich, who was people's commissar for transport and was responsible for building the Moscow Metro, also had a cult following and was known as 'Iron Lazar' and the 'Iron Commissar'.[98] Nikita Krushchev, Lavrenti Beria and Andrei Zhdanov all had regional cults and were paid tribute in songs such as 'Song of Krushchev' and 'Song for Beria'. Indeed there was even an 'Ode to Ezhov', the dreaded people's commissar for state security who was executed under Stalin in 1940.[99] Vyacheslav Molotov and Voroshilov featured in propaganda posters in their own right, with Molotov taking centre stage from Stalin in one Uzbek poster by Cheprakov of 1939 (Fig. 3.4).

After 1948, the People's Democracies of Eastern Europe, which had fallen under Soviet influence after the Great Patriotic War, adopted socialist systems of government and became increasingly 'Sovietised'. The Party leaders were supported by and answerable to Moscow, and were obliged to adopt the Soviet model of government, regardless of national cultural idiosyncrasies. In each of these countries, personality cults were manufactured around the persona of the leader, making use of many — 'teacher', 'friend', 'caretaker', 'father of the nation'

---

[97] In his memoirs Viktor Serge describes the cultish obsequiousness shown to Grigorii Zinoviev by some members of the public, and Zinoviev's palpable embarrassment: 'A comrade who was a former convict had a sumptuously coloured cover designed by one of the greatest Russian artists, which was intended to adorn one of Zinoviev's pamphlets. The artist and the ex-convict had combined to produce a masterpiece of obsequiousness, in which Zinoviev's Roman profile stood out like a proconsul in a cameo bordered by emblems. They brought it to the President of the International, who thanked them cordially and, as soon as they were gone, called me to his side. "It is the height of bad taste", Zinoviev told me in embarrassment, "but I didn't want to hurt their feelings. Have a very small number printed, and get a very simple cover designed instead"' (*Memoirs of a revolutionary 1901–1941*, Peter Sedgwick (trans.), London, Oxford University Press, 1963, p. 113).
[98] S. Sebag Montefiore, *Stalin: the court of the Red Tsar*, London, Weidenfeld and Nicolson, 2003, p. 170.
[99] Montefiore, *Stalin*, p. 277.

— but not all, of the epithets used to glorify Stalin. In Yugoslavia, Josip Broz took on the partisan name of 'Tito'[100] and was characterised by such epithets as 'the best son of our people', 'the creator of the war victory', and 'organiser of the people's army'.[101] Some accolades were reserved only for Stalin himself, as cultural anthropologist Izabella Main points out, 'only the Soviet leader could be described as "the engineer of history", "the genius architect of communism" or "the great genius of mankind"'.[102]

Writers and artists also sometimes gained cult-like followings. For example, Nadezhda Mandelshtam[103] recalls in her memoirs the 'cult-like devotion' around Andrei Belii, author of the seminal text *Symbolism*.[104] Aleksandr Pushkin and Nikolai Chernishevskii[105] were cult figures during Soviet times,[106] with huge celebrations taking place on the 100th anniversary of Pushkin's birth in 1937. Maksim Gor'kii was a contemporary Soviet writer who also had a cult. Bernice Rosenthal notes that there was a cult for almost every field of endeavour: Anton Makarenko in education, Nikolai Marr in linguistics, Ivan Pavlov in psychology, Trofim Lysenko in biology, Konstantin Stanislavskii in theatre, with films made about Gor'kii, Makarenko, and Pavlov.[107] Lysenko's portrait was hung in all scientific institutions, busts of him were widely available for purchase, monuments were erected in his honour, and a hymn to Lysenko was included in the repertoire of the State Chorus.[108]

---

100 From the Serbo-Croat words '*ti to*', which means 'You do this', often used by Josip Broz in issuing orders during the war (Stanislav Sretenovic & Artan Puto, 'Leader cults in the Western Balkans (1945–90): Josip Broz Tito and Enver Hoxha', in Apor et al., *The leader cult in communist dictatorships*, p. 210).
101 Sretenovic & Puto, 'Leader cults in the Western Balkans (1945–90)', p. 209.
102 Izabella Main, 'President of Poland or "Stalin's most faithful pupil"? The cult of Boleslaw Bierut in Stalinist Poland', in Apor et al., *The leader cult in communist dictatorships*, p. 184.
103 Widow of the poet Osip Mandelshtam who wrote a scathing poetic portrait of Stalin in 1933 and was later to die in a prison camp.
104 Nadezhda Mandelstam, *Hope against hope: a memoir*, Max Hayward (trans.), New York, Atheneum Publishers, 1970, p. 186.
105 Author of the novel *What is to be done?*
106 For an interesting discussion of this phenomenon, see Evgeny Dobrenko, 'Pushkin in Soviet and post-Soviet culture', in Andrew Kahn (ed.), *The Cambridge companion to Pushkin*, Cambridge, Cambridge University Press, 2006, pp. 202–20.
107 Rosenthal, *New myth, new world*, p. 387.
108 Rosenthal, *New myth, new world*, p. 419.

1. THE PHENOMENON OF THE PERSONALITY CULT

The cultic phenomenon was not only confined to powerful or influential individuals. One of the legendary figures of the Great Patriotic War, Zoia Kosmodemianskaia, became the subject of several novels, essays, films and artworks. At the age of 18, at great personal risk, she acted under Stalin's orders to sabotage buildings as the Germans advanced on local villages. She was captured, brutalised, humiliated and interrogated but refused to disclose any information to the Germans, other than giving the false name of 'Tania'. She was hanged by the Germans on 29 November 1941, with her story becoming widely known after the publication of an article by Petr Lidov in *Pravda* in October 1942.[109] Kosmodemianskaia was the first woman to be awarded (posthumously) the title Hero of the Soviet Union in the Great Patriotic War. Many girls have since been named in her honour.

During the Stalinist era, there was even a cult around a 13-year-old boy, Pavlik Morozov, who was allegedly martyred through being murdered by his family after informing on his father for selling false identity papers. *Pravda* published a long series of articles on this story, continually shaping the myth until it became a 'conversion narrative' in which a young village boy tried to lead his peasant community from their backward ways into the light of socialist utopia. Morozov was even featured in propaganda posters, such as the 1952 poster by O. Korovin titled 'Pavlik Morozov'. Recent investigations in the archives by scholars such as Catriona Kelly[110] have suggested that, while Morozov did exist and was murdered, the published story surrounding his death was largely fabricated.

Whether or not cults such as those of Morozov and Kosmodemianskaia were accurate in their details, or partially fabricated, it is clear that their founding narratives were honed and polished to serve an

---

109 Petr Lidov, 'Five German photographs', *Pravda*, 24 Oct. 1942. The article finished with the words: 'When they halt for shelter, fighting men will come bow to the earth before her ashes and to say a heartfelt Russian thank-you. To the father and mother who bore her into the world and raised her a heroine; to the teachers who educated her; to the comrades who forged her spirit. Her undying glory will reach all corners of the Soviet land, millions of people will think about a distant snowy grave with love, and Stalin's thoughts will go to the graveside of his faithful daughter' (cited in Petr Lidov, 'Tanya', in James von Geldern & Richard Stites (eds), *Mass culture in Soviet Russia: tales, songs, poems, movies, plays and folklore, 1917–1953*, Bloomington, Indiana University Press, 1995, p. 344).
110 Catriona Kelly, *Comrade Pavlik: the rise and fall of a Soviet boy hero*, London, Granta, 2005; Catriona Kelly, *Children's world: growing up in Russia, 1890–1991*, New Haven, Yale University Press, 2007, pp. 79–80.

exemplary and instructional role for the population — particularly Soviet youth in these two cases. In her memoirs, Nadezhda Mandelshtam provides a striking example of the efficacy of this sort of propaganda. During her exile in Kalinin she met a 14-year-old boy who was also in exile with his family, and was said to be distantly related to Stalin. The boy spent days denouncing his parents as traitors and lamenting the fact that, unlike Pavlik, he had not denounced his parents in time: 'He used a formula which had been instilled in him during his very careful upbringing: "Stalin is my father and I do not need another one" ...'[111]

Cults also grew up around groups and organisations. There was the cult of the Revolution, the cult of the proletariat, the cult of the Party, the cult of the freedom fighter and the cult of the hero. In the immediate aftermath of the Revolution, fallen freedom fighters were venerated as martyrs and revolutionary saints. They were celebrated in song, poetry, biography and statuary. Their images were carried in street parades or displayed in iconic fashion. The cult of the hero dates to the decree on heroes published in *Izvestiia*[112] on 18 April 1934, which identified the Soviet hero as the 'the best of the Soviet people', those who had accomplished inspiring deeds which in turn were inspired by Stalin.[113]

The people need a tsar

It is often claimed that the deposition of the tsar did not displace the need in the Russian population for a strong, autocratic ruler.[114] Research conducted by Orlando Figes and Boris Kolonitskii indicates that many of the older peasants were distraught at the overthrow of the tsar,[115] who was seen as the embodiment of the life and soul of the nation. His portrait was often hung as an icon and some peasants

---

111 Mandelstam, *Hope against hope*, pp. 254–55.
112 News.
113 Rosenthal, *New myth, new world*, p. 388.
114 For example, Rees, in Apor et al., *The leader cult in communist dictatorships*, p. 9; and, Orlando Figes & Boris Kolonitskii, *Interpreting the Russian Revolution: the language and symbols of 1917*, New Haven, Yale University Press, 1999, p. 103.
115 '"The Church was full of crying peasants" one witness recalled. "What will become of us?" they constantly repeated — "They have taken the Tsar away from us?"' F. Isupov, *Pered izgnaniem, 1887–1919*, Moscow, 1993, p. 187 quoted in Figes & Kolonitskii, *Interpreting the Russian Revolution*, p. 138.

crossed themselves when his name was mentioned. From the time of Ivan the Terrible, tsars and princes were often depicted in official portraiture as having haloes as they went into battle (both spiritual and physical) on behalf of their subjects.[116] Aside from its sacred connotations, the halo was a symbol of kingship. Klaus-Georg Riegel sees strong similarities between the blend of the sacred and secular found in the person of the tsar, and that to be found in modern political religions: 'The Tsarist hierocracy — a close affiliation of autocratic monarchy and Orthodox Christianity — represented a fusion of secular and sacral power typical of the modern political religions to come.'[117]

Faith in the tsar as the protector of the people was severely shaken by the events of *Krovavoie Voskresen'ie* (Bloody Sunday)[118] in 1905. Unarmed and peaceful workers, led by Orthodox priest Georgii Gapon, had come to the Winter Palace to present a petition to the tsar, singing 'God save the tsar' and carrying icons and portraits of the tsar, in the belief that he would be prepared to listen to their grievances.[119] Although Nicholas II had left the Winter Palace, the petitioners were gunned down by Nicholas' Imperial Guard, belying the notion that this tsar was the ordained protector of the people. As in the past, the myth of the benevolent tsar or 'tsar-deliverer' was easily transferable to the next strong leader who promised to save the country and its people. In 1923, British Ambassador George Buchanan recounted a conversation he had with a Russian soldier, in which the soldier said: 'Yes, we need a republic, but at its head there should be a good Tsar.'[120]

Stalin is famously quoted as having said: 'Don't forget that we are living in Russia, the land of the tsars ... the Russian people like it when one person stands at the head of the state', and 'The people need a tsar, i.e. someone to revere and in whose name to live and labour.'[121]

---

116 Sergei Bogatyrev, 'Bronze tsars: Ivan the Terrible and Fedor Ivanovich in the décor of early modern guns', *SEER*, 88:1/2, 2010, pp. 48–72, p. 69.
117 Riegel, 'Marxism–Leninism as a political religion', p. 100.
118 22 January/9 January old calendar, 1905.
119 The petitioners were attempting to draw the tsar's attention to poor and unsafe work conditions, low wages, long working days, and the introduction of conscription, in the hope that the tsar would intervene on their behalf.
120 George Buchanan, *My mission to Russia and other diplomatic memoirs*, vol. 2, London, Cassell and Company Ltd, 1923, p. 86.
121 D.L. Brandenberger & A.M. Dubrovsky source these statements as follows: R.A. Medvedev, *K sudu istorii: genezis i posledstviya stalinizma*, New York, 1974, p. 628; 'Dnevnik Marili Anisimovny Svanidze', in 'Iosif Stalin v ob"yatyiakh sem'i: iz lichnogo arkhiva, Sbornik dokumentov', Yu. G. Murin & V.N. Denisov (eds), Moscow, 1993, p. 176. Similar statements are

Evidently Stalin believed that Russia could only be governed by the firm hand of a vanguard leadership, but also that this was the wish of the people as well. In fact, in the years immediately following the October Revolution, Lenin and most of the other Bolshevik leaders frequently reiterated their belief that the country was not ready to be ruled directly by the proletariat, and that power had to be concentrated in the hands of a small, centralised Bolshevik minority if Russia was to survive and overcome the many obstacles it faced — and if indeed the Bolsheviks were to maintain power. According to Lenin, such strong, centralised leadership was legitimated by revolutionary circumstance which arose from class struggle.[122]

It is beyond the scope of this study to debate whether or not, and under what circumstances, Russia may need a 'tsar' at the helm of government. Psychologist Bruce Mazlish, in his exploration of group psychology and the study of history, argues against the notion of a 'national character' that predisposes the inhabitants of a particular country to adopt certain unitary character traits or codes of psychological need, and states that 'national character' is a 'non-existent analytical tool'.[123] In fact, as historian Edward L. Keenan argues, Russia is not historically predisposed to autocratic rule and has demonstrated a preference for oligarchic or collegiate rule with a politically weak nominal autocrat, except in times of rapid socio-economic change and political turbulence.[124] What is significant, though, is that this perception exists, it is often reiterated, and that those in leadership roles during the Soviet era appear to have accepted and promoted the necessity for a strong, authoritarian figure to lead

---

reported in A. Antonov-Ovseyenko, *The time of Stalin: portrait of a tyranny*, New York, 1981, p. 223; A. Antonov-Ovseenko, *Portret Tirana*, Moscow, 1995, p. 344; and, Edvard Radzinsky, *Stalin*, Moscow, 1997, p. 356 (although the latter may have lifted his quotation, attributed to Petr Chagin, from an English-language edition of Medvedev's book; e.g. Roy Medvedev, *Let history judge: the origins and consequences of Stalinism*, George Shriver (ed. & trans.), New York, 1989, p. 586 and n. 98 ('"The people need a tsar": the emergence of national Bolshevism as Stalinist ideology, 1931–1941', *Europe-Asia Studies*, 50:5, 1998, pp. 873–92, p. 873).

122 'a revolution differs from a "normal" situation in the state precisely because controversial issues of state life are decided by the direct class and popular struggle ... This fundamental fact implies that in time of revolution it is not enough to ascertain "the will of the majority" — you must *prove to be the stronger* at the decisive moment and in the decisive place; you must *win*' (V.I. Lenin, 'Constitutional illusions', *Rabochy i soldat*, 4 & 5 (22 & 23) Aug. 1917, *Collected works*, vol. 25, Stepan Apresyan & Jim Riordan (trans.), Moscow, Progress Publishers, 1964, pp. 197, 201, 203–04.

123 Mazlish, 'Group psychology', p. 168.

124 Edward L. Keenan, 'Muscovite political folkways', *Russian Review*, 45:2, 1986, pp. 115–81, p. 118.

the country, even to the extent that many endorsed the use of terror against their own people. Propaganda that aimed to elevate and glorify this strong figure found an audience in the Party, in the bureaucracy, and also in the general population. The severity of the measures taken to repress dissent is an indication of how threatening it was perceived to be. Merely eliminating dissenters, however, was not enough to harness the population for the task of building a new state. For this colossal effort, the population had to be actively engaged to participate in the process, and to commit wholeheartedly to the Party's goals.

Succession dilemmas and the manufacture of charisma

As already noted, one of the major reasons that propaganda was needed to create the image of a powerful, infallible leader who could work miracles, was because neither Lenin nor Stalin (nor, in fact, the Bolshevik Party itself) could lay claim to power based on either traditional (i.e. monarchic succession) or rational–legal grounds. Lenin was in power, although without holding an official title as head of state, for only seven years before his death, four of which saw the nation embroiled in civil war. He carried authority due to his intense charismatic relationship with his Party, in the initial phases, and after with the nation as a whole. It could be argued that the manufacture of the full-blown cult of Lenin served the function of legitimating the Bolshevik regime after the death of its charismatic leader, and then of legitimating Stalin as leader. Or, to put it in Weberian terms, in the 1920s the Bolshevik Party was faced with the challenges of a routinisation of charisma and, then, with the problem of succession when Lenin died. This challenge was met initially by transferring the personal charisma of the leader to the impersonal mechanism of the Party through the cult of Lenin, and by focusing on appeals to ideological legitimation. Once Stalin consolidated his personal power, the propaganda mechanism of the Party set about manufacturing a charismatic personality for Stalin that, over the three decades of his rule, gradually saw the transfer of all legitimacy to reside only in his persona. When Stalin died in 1953, the Weberian dilemma of succession once more raised its head, charisma was again transferred to the Party, and Stalin's cult of personality was denounced.

The origins of charismatic legitimation can probably be traced as far back as late tribal societies and the succession battles that occurred in the increasingly complex early agricultural societies. When challenges occurred to hereditary/traditional leadership, legitimacy claims were enhanced by artificial attempts to stage-manage the charismatic process and create what Ronald Glassman calls 'psychic grandeur', using padding, stilts, magic symbols and myths and legends.[125] While the concept of 'manufactured charisma' may initially appear to be both cynical and exploitative on the part of the leadership, the deliberateness and calculation involved in setting up the personality cult does not necessarily belie a sincerity of belief in the ultimate goals of the regime, or in the leader's mission. Graeme Gill suggests that the manufacture of a personality cult around the figure of the leader was not only for the benefit of the general public. In fact, he sees the cult as being a unifying and rallying force for the inner circle and true believers, glorifying their past and promising a bright future in the face of the struggles of the present.[126] In 1930 Voroshilov wrote to Stalin: 'Dear Koba ... Mikoyan, Kaganovich, Kuibyshev and I think the best result would be the unification of the leadership of the Sovnarkom and to appoint you to it as you want to take the leadership with all strength.'[127] Anastas Mikoian also wrote: 'Nowadays we need strong leadership from a single leader as it was in Illich [Lenin's] time and the best decision is you to be the candidate for the Chairmanship ... Doesn't all of mankind know who's the ruler of our country?'[128]

The personality cult can be viewed primarily as a political tool with a lengthy and well-documented record of success in conferring legitimacy on a leader who lacks traditional or legal–rational authority, or for whom these grounds of legitimation are under challenge. In such circumstances, charismatic legitimation can serve to bolster authority for as long as the charismatic leader is able to deliver on the promises made to his supporters. Charismatic leaders emerge from revolutionary situations by articulating and embodying the revolutionary vision and the ideals of the new society. The charismatic relationship tends to be relatively shortlived because, in the face of obstacles and opposition,

---

125 See Ronald Glassman, 'Legitimacy and manufactured charisma', *Social Research*, 42:4, 1975, pp. 615–37, pp. 618–19.
126 Graeme Gill, 'Personality cult, political culture and party structure', *Studies in Comparative Communism*, 17:2, 1984, pp. 111–21, p. 119.
127 Voroshilov quoted in Montefiore, *Stalin*, p. 62.
128 Mikoian quoted in Montefiore, *Stalin*, p. 62.

the leader is unable to deliver on the revolutionary promises in the long term, the routine and mundane tasks of government overwhelm the revolutionary spirit,[129] and the charismatic leader dies and has no traditional or established means of transferring his charisma to a successor. The manufacture of charisma through the creation of a personality cult that is initially attached to the dead (or dying) leader, but comes to include the successor, provides a means of transferring charisma to either an impersonal party or to a designated successor. If the new leader is to maintain power in the long term, charisma must come to reside in his person and he must be demonstrated to embody the party's vision and ideology and to symbolise collective values. A symbolic identity is created around the new leader, drawing on ritual, myth and ancient archetypes to endow him with a charismatic persona.

Myth

Myth is an essential component of all societies. It explains where a society has come from, provides a notion of collective identity and indicates a collective destination. When a revolution occurs and the old order is overthrown, a radical break with the past is required, and much of the symbolism, ritual and myth associated with the old order is discarded and replaced with new myths that support the values of the new society. This was the essential reasoning behind Lenin's decree 'on the dismantling of monuments erected in honour of the tsars and their servants and on the formulation of projects for monuments of the Russian socialist revolution', of August 1918. Lenin had an understanding of the role of myth in society, and was influenced by his reading of Georges Sorel, for whom myths were mobilising ideas that could spur the workers into action. Mythology did not have to be objectively true, but it did have to be embodied in powerful symbols. Myths were to carry an emotional charge that reached people at an unconscious level and could be grasped only by intuition alone.

---

129 In his article on Max Weber and Sigmund Freud, Donald McIntosh notes that the transition from rebellious band to responsible administrators and organisers is psychologically very difficult for the revolutionary leadership, and that it is striking how often the task of building the new society is left to the successor. McIntosh cites as examples Jesus and the Apostles Peter and Paul, Caesar and Augustus, Robespierre and Napoleon, Gandhi and Nehru, and Lenin and Stalin ('Weber and Freud: on the nature and sources of authority', *American Sociological Review*, 35:5, 1970, pp. 901–11, p. 906).

For Sorel, myths are not lies, propaganda or ideology in the modern sense of these words; they are not cynically manufactured either. Myths are already present, in a latent form, within the mass itself. They are already anchored in the collective unconscious, and should simplify the world and identify enemies.[130] Although the Bolsheviks may have originally cast new characters in the major roles, and branded their rituals and celebrations with their own symbols and colours, the basic form and narrative content of their myths, and their use of archetypal characters, drew from the universal collective unconscious and thus demonstrated remarkable consistencies with the myths of past societies. By the late 1930s, Stalinist propaganda was even reaching back to the great Russian mythological past to demonstrate a continuity of values and principles. There is a degree of inevitability in this, as it is almost impossible to produce an image without context and which is devoid of any cultural baggage: to do so would make it virtually incomprehensible.

The Bolshevik quest for the new man, the new society, and the new morality are all facets of the yearning for a new myth. Bernice Rosenthal argues that the Bolshevik drive to create a new culture does not in fact derive from their reading of Marx and Engels, who never developed a detailed theory of culture, believing that it would change following changes in the economic base of the superstructure. The quest for the new man had preoccupied Russian radicals since the 1860s[131] and gained impetus for the Bolsheviks from their reading of Nietzsche,[132] Richard Wagner, and their Russian popularisers.

While ideology underpins the dominant conceptions of social reality in a society, it is inherently unsuited to the everyday tasks of communication between leaders and citizens.[133] What was needed by the Bolshevik Party leadership in order to conduct this dialogue and create a new man, a new society and, indeed, a new civilisation, was a metanarrative that incorporated a Soviet mythology to motivate the masses to act in accordance with the ideological tenets of Marxism.

---

130 See David Gross, 'Myth and symbol in Georges Sorel', in S. Drescher, D. Sabean & A. Sharlin (eds), *Political symbolism in modern Europe: essays in honour of George L. Mosse*, New York, Transaction, 1982, pp. 104–57, pp. 104–05.
131 Rosenthal, *New myth, new world*, p. 9.
132 Nietzsche could still be openly discussed in Russia until 1917. See Rosenthal, *New myth, new world*, p. 3.
133 Gill, *Symbols and legitimacy in Soviet politics*, p. 3.

1. THE PHENOMENON OF THE PERSONALITY CULT

As Gill points out, all myths throughout the world have three themes in common: 'the existence of an evil conspiracy against the community, the presence of a saviour who can release the community from this threat, and the coming of a golden age.'[134] As will be seen in Chapters Three and Four, Soviet propaganda was dominated by these themes. A large genre of posters, although very few that actually contain an image of Stalin, was devoted to identifying and ridiculing the enemy — first, class enemies, then enemies of the people and the fascist German enemy. Stalin was depicted in propaganda as the only person who could reliably identify these enemies, and as the saviour who delivered victory over fascism to the Soviet people and was to bring peace to the whole world. Much of Soviet propaganda depicted a calm and joyous communist utopia just around the corner.

One of the dominant myths in Soviet society was built around the life of Stalin. The biography of Stalin documented how a cobbler's son from a poor and humble family used the strength of his will, courage and Bolshevik values to rise to leadership of the nation. Although the bones of this story are true, the incidents related in the biography are mythical and formulaic. James von Geldern and Richard Stites see this mythology of opportunity as having a strong base in the working class (upward social mobility for the working class was state policy) and as being widely accepted by the Soviet citizenry: 'The popular audience did not reject the cult of Stalin as something directed against its interests, but accepted it as a myth of success available to anyone. National heroes were symbols of common endeavor, and their successes were shared by all.'[135]

In her study of the cult of Stalin for children, Catriona Kelly examines the representation of Stalin as a hero for children in Soviet fairytales (*skazka*)[136] where his 'magical' qualities consisted not only in his power of self-transformation, but also in his ability to watch over and protect everyone.[137] As will be seen in Chapter Three, Stalin was often depicted in posters as watching over the nation, children

---

134 Gill, *Symbols and legitimacy in Soviet politics*, p. 4.
135 von Geldern & Stites, *Mass culture in Soviet Russia*, p. xix.
136 In an interesting parallel, 2004 saw the publication in the Soviet Union of a book of *Fairytales about our president*, which uses a series of *lubki* to illustrate the exploits of President Vladimir Putin.
137 Catriona Kelly, 'Riding the magic carpet: children and leader cult in the Stalin era', *The Slavic and East European Journal*, 49:2, 2005, pp. 199–224.

in particular, and the Spassky tower of the Moscow Kremlin often appeared almost as a fairytale castle. Stalin became the subject of odes, eulogies and pseudo-folktales and folk songs, using native traditions to create stories around the Stalin persona. Despite the fact that some of them were illiterate, several folksingers and narrators were elected full members of the Union of Soviet writers, were elected to positions in government and were given awards.[138]

Conclusion

When examining the cult of personality from a historical perspective, beginning with the ancient world and exploring historical developments in Europe up to modern times, it is apparent that the basic features of charismatic leadership, and the cults of personality manufactured around charismatic leaders, show more similarities with each other than differences, regardless of geography or epoch. This is hardly surprising, because charismatic leaders and the conditions that create them have existed across societies through time, and the problems faced by these leaders and their states are remarkably consistent. Despite the fact that the very nature of political propaganda is such that it promotes each of these leaders as uniquely talented and blessed, or at the very least as one of a rare breed, in many respects their public personas are almost interchangeable, with their personality cults sharing several key genres, symbols and literary characteristics.

---

138 Felix J. Oinas, 'The political uses and themes of folklore in the Soviet Union', *Journal of the Folklore Institute*, 12:2/3, 1975, pp. 157–75, p. 163.

2
The rise of the Stalin personality cult

> The task of the construction of images of Lenin and Stalin, the geniuses who created Socialism, and their closest comrades, is one of the most responsible creative and ideological tasks that art has ever faced.
>
> Aleksandr Gerasimov[1]

> 'Tell me,' Sklyansky asked, 'what is Stalin?'
> 'Stalin,' I said, 'is the outstanding mediocrity in the party.'
>
> Lev Davidovich Trotskii[2]

The personality cult of Stalin draws from a long tradition in which leaders in precarious positions of power sought to strengthen legitimacy and unite their citizens into an entity that identified as a collective whole. This chapter is devoted to examining how a persona was created for Stalin via the mechanism of the cult. The question will be approached from two angles: first, by an overview of artistic production under Stalin; and, second, by outlining some of the devices that were used to construct the symbolic persona encompassed by the name 'Stalin'. The cult of Stalin was built on the foundations of the Lenin cult, allowing Stalin to gain legitimacy as Lenin's most appropriate successor, and Stalin was subsequently positioned as

---

[1] Quoted in Igor Golomshtok, *Totalitarian art in the Soviet Union, the Third Reich, fascist Italy and the People's Republic of China*, New York, Icon Editions, 1990, p. 226.
[2] Leon Trotskii, 'Lenin's death and the shift of power', *My life*, www.marxists.org/archive/trotsky/1930/mylife/ch41.htm (accessed 25 May 2012).

a great Marxist theoretician and revolutionary thinker, alongside Marx, Engels and Lenin. The propaganda apparatus created a formulaic Stalin biography that was to be used to educate the 'simple people', and demonised 'the enemy' as a backdrop against which Stalin could appear as a wise man and saviour. In order to generate effective and consistent propaganda for the purpose of educating the masses, all artistic and cultural production was brought under state control with all artists employed by the state to create products that elucidated the Bolshevik vision and promoted socialist and communist goals.

Art under Stalin

In order to most effectively market the Stalin image to the Soviet public, a line of consistent praise of Stalin had to be established and all competing points of view to be eliminated. It is self-evident that the only certain way in which this could be achieved was if all cultural production was centralised under the control of the state. While the first years of the Bolshevik regime had seen the flourishing of a plethora of artistic styles and forms of expression, with artists and writers embracing novel and revolutionary forms to express the reality of a new and revolutionary society, as the 1920s drew to a close the state began to exercise ever-increasing control over the production of propaganda materials, and to reject avant-garde and formalist approaches as being incomprehensible and meaningless to the masses. This was a somewhat peculiar assertion because the Soviet public had longstanding traditions with regard to visual and sacred art and were, in fact, visually literate, accustomed to abstraction, stylisation, caricature and the grotesque. In addition, as the years under Soviet rule passed, the population was becoming increasingly educated, particularly with regard to science and culture, and thus comprised an increasingly sophisticated audience. The tendency to move away from avant-gardism and towards realism under Stalin had, like most other aspects of Stalinist society, its roots in Lenin's period of leadership. Lenin is known to have had conventional artistic tastes and to have disliked avant-garde art, particularly futurism.[3] Within Lenin's lifetime, the leader portrait and the propaganda poster had already emerged as significant genres in cultural production. For example,

---

3   See Matthew Cullerne Bown, *Art under Stalin*, New York, Holmes and Meier Pub., 1991, p. 23.

the *All-Union agricultural and domestic–industrial exhibition* in Moscow in August 1923 featured a giant portrait of Lenin assembled out of thousands of living plants and a Lenin corner, a derivative of the Red corner in which icons were traditionally hung in Russian homes. Matthew Cullerne Bown suggests that Lenin may have been fundamentally opposed to these displays but unable to prevent them due to his advancing illness.[4]

After Lenin's death in 1924, state control of art began gradually to tighten. Communist professors were appointed to art schools as a matter of policy, and the commissioning of works of art became more widespread.[5] From 1926 to 1929, several decrees were passed by the government to inhibit contact with foreigners, travel abroad, the admission of foreign artists to the Soviet Union, and which required that Soviet citizens who wished to return home after studying abroad pass exams on Soviet society. A decree issued in December 1928 stated that the sole function of literature was now to be communist education. Graeme Gill notes, however, that right up until the early 1930s, an artistic world that was only loosely connected to the regime persisted such that there continued to be significant variation in the projection of symbols and meaning in art and considerable freedom of expression.[6]

After 1929, most Stalin portraits, including copies, were commissioned under *kontraktatsiia*.[7] Artists were contracted by branches of the central state commissioning agency, VseKoKhudozhnik,[8] to produce a given number of works in a particular timeframe. These could be works on a given theme, or based on a field trip to construction projects[9] or collectivised farms although, by the late 1930s,[10] artists would usually be given a specific title to illustrate.[11] VseKoKhudozhnik

---

4   Bown, *Art under Stalin*, p. 30.
5   Bown, *Art under Stalin*, p. 40.
6   Graeme J. Gill, *Symbols and legitimacy in Soviet politics*, New York, Cambridge University Press, 2011, p. 11.
7   Contract system.
8   The All-Russian Cooperative Union of Fine Arts.
9   One of the most notorious of these was the book edited by Maksim Gor'kii on prison labourers' work on the Belomor Canal. An edition called *The White Sea Canal* was published by Bodley Head in London in 1935 and a US edition, *Belomor*, was published in New York by H. Smith and R. Haas in the same year.
10   Khudfond (Khudozhestvennyi Fond, Art Fund) took over *kontraktatsiia* in the late 1930s.
11   For further detail see Christina Kiaer, 'Was socialist realism forced labour? The case of Aleksandr Deineka in the 1930s', *Oxford Art Journal*, 28 Mar. 2005, pp. 321–45, p. 334.

would then sell the works to other institutions with artists guaranteed a buyer and payment for their work. In March 1930 a resolution was issued 'On measures for creating favourable working conditions for artists', which set down minimum budgets for acquiring works by Soviet artists for the union republics, regional departments of education, social insurance funds, and trade unions, with allocated funding increasing over time.[12] Finally, in April 1932, all artists' organisations were abolished and all artists had to work under the aegis of a single union in their town or region. As members of the artists' union, most artists received salaries comparable to an engineer with average qualifications, which they attempted to supplement through *kontraktatsiia*.[13] In his August 1934 speech on Soviet literature to the First All-Union Congress of Soviet Writers, Maksim Gor'kii justified the centralisation of cultural production as enabling creative professionals to comprehend their corporate strength and as harmoniously merging all aims towards a unity to guide all the creative work in the country.[14]

Centralisation under VseKoKhudozhnik saw an increase in collective and brigade work, particularly in media, such as public sculpture, the design of public spaces and major events like the *All-Union agricultural exhibition*. Artist contracts were not easy to come by and Galina Yankovskaya and Rebecca Mitchell have documented that: 'From 1931 to 1935, only 397 people received contracts, which is incommensurate with the number of cooperative artists. Eight out of ten painters in Moscow and twenty-four out of fifty in the provinces did not participate in this system.'[15] Despite centralisation of control of artistic production there was a dizzying array of organisations, institutions and bureaucratic agencies to be negotiated in order to gain access to commissions. Knowledge of how to navigate this bureaucracy was highly prized and heavily guarded.[16]

---

12   Galina Yankovskaya & Rebecca Mitchell, 'The economic dimensions of art in the Stalinist era: artists' cooperatives in the grip of ideology and the plan', *Slavic Review*, 65:4, 2006, pp. 769–91, p. 774.
13   Jan Plamper, *The Stalin cult: a study in the alchemy of power*, New Haven, Yale University Press, 2012, p. 181.
14   Maxim Gorky, 'Soviet literature', speech delivered to the Soviet Writers Congress, 1934, www.marxists.org/archive/gorky-maxim/1934/soviet-literature.htm (accessed 23 Jul. 2013).
15   Yankovskaya & Mitchell, 'The economic dimensions of art in the Stalinist era', p. 777.
16   See Plamper, *The Stalin cult*, p. 172.

State control of art increased throughout the 1930s. On accessing material only recently made available in the Soviet archives, Katerina Clark remarked on the extent to which, during the 1930s, members of the Politburo were engaged in legislating cultural matters:

> What is truly extraordinary is that the heads of state of a country that boasted being the largest in area ('one sixth of the world') and was for much of this period undergoing draconian modernization and the build-up of its military, coupled with a protracted socio-political–economic revolution, spent so much of their time on cultural matters, even in the most critical moments of inner-party struggle, the terror, or of war. Among the members of the Politburo, Stalin was the most actively involved.[17]

Stalin took for himself the portfolio of commissar of cultural enlightenment from 4 June 1934 till 27 November 1938 when it was passed to the notorious Andrei Zhdanov. The timing of Stalin's assumption of this portfolio is interesting. It came just four months after the Seventeenth Party Congress in January 1934, at which opposition to Stalin had surfaced, and when the possibility of a challenge to his leadership was in the air — 300 votes were cast against Stalin.[18] It also occurred just before the First All-Union Congress of Soviet Writers, at which the future direction of Soviet art was formalised and institutionalised. By picking up the culture portfolio at this time, Stalin was ensuring that he would have a controlling influence over cultural production in the regime, demonstrating yet again how pivotal mass culture was to the Soviet leadership.

Significantly, it was in 1934 that the image of Stalin became ubiquitous in the media and propaganda. Soviet cultural production from this point on became increasingly self-referential or, what Malte Rolf has referred to as a 'hall of mirrors' in which '[c]ultural items constantly reflected other bits of the rhetoric, symbols, or ritual of the Soviet cultural canon' and there was little reference to anything outside the officially endorsed canon.[19] The repetition of canonic themes and

---

17 Katerina Clark, 'The cult of literature and Nikolai Ostrovskii's "How the steel was tempered"', in Klaus Heller & Jan Plamper (eds), *Personality cults in Stalinism*, Göttingen, V&R Unipress, 2004, p. 415.
18 Sara Fenander, 'Author and autocrat: Tertz's Stalin and the ruse of charisma', *Russian Review*, 58:2, 1999, pp. 286–97, p. 289, p. 292.
19 Malte Rolf, 'A hall of mirrors: Sovietizing culture under Stalinism', *Slavic Review*, 68:3, 2009, pp. 601–30, p. 601.

images also manifested in the peculiarly socialist practice of copying artworks. As there was no 'art for art's sake' and no marketplace geared around the procurement of 'unique' pieces, works were produced for didactic and propagandistic purposes. Paintings, sculptures and posters were copied, chopped up and reassembled and translated into other media with the aim of filling public space with approved images. Sculptures were based on standardised models and institutions and organisations could only buy pictures that were stamped with the seal of the representative of the Main Repertory Committee.[20] Stalin was much more than the sole authoritative voice on all art-related matters in the Soviet Union, he became art's principle subject matter and, by the mid-1930s, Soviet public space was saturated with all manner of images of the leader.

Despite the centralised governmental control of artistic production, it would be incorrect to assume that it was only the government that gave such a pre-eminent place to art and literature in society. Cultural matters were important to the public as well. Alongside the professional art organisations, a myriad of amateur and workers' artist societies flourished. Factories and workplaces set up artists' clubs for their workers. The Union of Soviet Artists set up Commissions for the Creativity of the People, which visited workplaces and organised evening schools and artists' circles for amateur artists and craftspeople. Instruction was given on how to paint and sculpt portraits of the leader, and in the techniques of socialist realism.

In 1931–32, German photomonteur John Heartfield visited the USSR to experience first-hand the developments in poster and propaganda art. Archival photographs show Heartfield surrounded by Red Army soldiers gathered at worktables, all cutting and assembling photographs and text into photomontage posters. In his lecture to the Moscow Polygraphics Institute on 24 July 1931, Heartfield expressed his conviction that photomontage was not only a medium for dissemination to the masses through mechanical reproduction, but also a participatory medium, to be practised by the masses themselves.[21] The public was not only interested in participation in the creation of art, but in viewing it as well. At the height of the siege of Leningrad,

---

20 Yankovskaya & Mitchell, 'The economic dimensions of art in the Stalinist era', p. 787.
21 Maria Gough, 'Back in the USSR: John Heartfield, Gustav Klucis, and the medium of Soviet Propaganda', *New German Critique*, 36:2, 2009, pp. 155–56.

in the terrible winter of 1941–42, a major exhibition, *Leningrad in the days of the Patriotic War*, was opened in the Leningrad Union of Artists. In January 1942 this exhibition was airlifted over the blockade and shown in Moscow.

Socialist realism

Socialist realism was announced as the officially endorsed method[22] for works of art and literature at the first Soviet Writers' Congress in 1934. The term seems to have first appeared in print in May 1932,[23] and was attributed to Stalin, who told writers and leaders at a meeting at Gor'kii's house: 'The artist ought to show life truthfully. And if he shows our life truthfully, he cannot fail to show it moving to socialism. This is and will be socialist realism.'[24] The enthusiasm for a return to Russian realism was not merely a top-down initiative. The majority of the members of the painting section of MOSSKh[25] were former members of AKhR/R[26] and thus stylistically conservative. The Party line was in sympathy with the preferences of the majority of artists,[27] and was perceived by many politically engaged artists as a means of establishing a more equitable access to commissions.[28] Socialist realism was regarded by the Party as the most progressive form of art that had ever existed, as was still being claimed in the *Encyclopædic dictionary of literature*, published in the USSR in 1987, which proclaimed it 'the leading artistic method of the modern era'.[29]

In her article on Aleksandr Deineka, Christina Kiaer examines the question of whether socialist realism was forced labour, and argues that, in Deineka's case, the turn to greater realism was the result of

---

22 Although socialist realism is often discussed as if it were a 'style' of art, it was in fact declared to be a 'method' in 1934, defining itself in opposition to formalism as 'freedom from the dogma of style'. See Ekaterina Degot, 'Socialist realism from the viewpoint of critical art', in Rosa Ferré, *Red cavalry: creation and power in Soviet Russia from 1917 to 1945: 07.10.2011 – 15.01.2012*, Madrid, La Casa Encendida, 2011, p. 489.
23 Bown, *Art under Stalin*, p. 89.
24 Jeffrey Brooks, *Thank you, Comrade Stalin! Soviet public culture from revolution to Cold War*, Princeton University Press, 2000, p. 108.
25 Moscow Section of the Union of Soviet Artists.
26 AKhR/R is Association of Artists of Revolutionary Russia, 1922–28; AKhR is Association of Artists of the Revolution, 1928–32.
27 Bown, *Art under Stalin*, p. 94.
28 Kiaer, 'Was socialist realism forced labour?', p. 322.
29 Bown, *Art under Stalin*, p. 13.

an evolution in the artist's vision of what constituted appropriate revolutionary art, a process that was responsive to changing historical circumstances.[30] Susan Reid makes the case that Soviet artists were 'far from either the unified body wishfully imagined by Soviet mythology or the browbeaten bunch implied by received Western narratives of the "imposition" of Socialist Realism'.[31] Artists like Deineka were allowed some latitude in the work they produced and Deineka at least seems to have felt that he was able to speak his mind openly.[32] Indeed, at least in these early days before the purges of 1937–38, intense discussion about art occurred and dissenting views were put forward, as is evidenced in a diary entry by Valentina Kulagina, graphic artist and wife of artist Gustav Klutsis, dated 6 April 1936:

> Yesterday attended a discussion on socialist realism. The formalists spoke — Denisovsky, Shterenberg, Tyshler — and all unanimously refused to apologize for their form[alist] 'mistakes', attacking the talentless 'mediocrities' who have 'neither formalism nor naturalism', who never rock the boat and therefore feel like 'real' artists.[33]

Socialist realism is neither conventional realism, nor is it 'naturalism'. The 6 May 1934 edition of *Pravda* carried a definition of socialist realism that was taken from the statutes of the new union:

> Socialist realism, the basic method of Soviet artistic literature and literary criticism, demands truthfulness from the artist and a historically concrete portrayal of reality in its revolutionary development. Under these conditions, truthfulness and historical concreteness of artistic portrayal ought to be combined with the task of the ideological remaking and education of working people in the spirit of socialism.[34]

The qualifying phrase 'in its revolutionary development' hints at the real kernel of socialist realism. Reality was to be reflected through the prism of the Bolshevik Revolution and to be shaped to the aim of educating the workers. Put another way, socialist realism takes for its subject, not life as it is, but life as it ought to (or will) be, the end

---

30   Kiaer, 'Was socialist realism forced labour?', p. 321.
31   Susan E. Reid, 'Socialist realism in the Stalinist terror: the *Industry of Socialism* art exhibition, 1935–41', *The Russian Review*, 60:2, 2001, pp. 153–84, p. 161.
32   See Kiaer, 'Was socialist realism forced labour?', pp. 321–45.
33   In Margarita Tupitsyn, *Gustav Klutsis and Valentina Kulagina: photography and montage after constructivism*, New York, International Center of Photography, 2004, p. 221.
34   Brooks, *Thank you, Comrade Stalin!*, p. 108.

result and satisfaction of processes already underway. Socialist realism extracts a basic human truth from myth and folklore, marrying it with socialist ideals, to create a reality for consumption by the viewer/reader. For the god-builder Gor'kii, socialist realism is only possible within the socialist society. Its aims are transcendent and spiritual, and stop at nothing short of the transformation of the earth and the birth of the new man.[35]

In his insightful analysis of socialist realism and the nature of Soviet truth, Petre Petrov argues against interpreting socialist realism as merely a tissue of lies and deception. Beginning with the proposition that the general consensus on socialist realism is that it represents a 'bogus reality' and 'rape of the real' deliberately designed to hide the truth, he approaches Soviet society through the lens of historical dialectics, 'the mode of inquiry that sees reality, not as an immediate *datum*, but as the concrete process of defining and redefining what is real'.[36] Petrov argues that these deceptions pervaded the fabric of Soviet life so thoroughly that there was hardly anything left over and thus were also part of objective experience and empirical reality: 'If people thought of themselves as builders of a brighter future, as many did, there is much argumentative work to be done before one could conclude that such people inhabited a pseudoreality, while cynics and dissidents had their feet firmly planted in life-as-it-is.'[37] Petrov proposes that a more appropriate line of enquiry is to examine how Stalinist ideology itself refashioned the notion of truth and the real.

---

35 'Life, as asserted by socialist realism, is deeds, creativeness, the aim of which is the uninterrupted development of the priceless individual faculties of man, with a view to his victory over the forces of nature, for the sake of his health and longevity, for the supreme joy of living on an earth which, in conformity with the steady growth of his requirements, he wishes to mould throughout into a beautiful dwelling place for mankind, united into a single family' (Gorky, 'Soviet literature').
36 Petre Petrov, 'The industry of truing: socialist realism, reality, realization', *Slavic Review*, 70:4, 2011, pp. 873–92, p. 867.
37 Petrov, 'The industry of truing', p. 878.

The Soviet propaganda poster

The Soviet propaganda poster is but one facet of the 'hall of mirrors' that constituted Soviet cultural production. It was one of the several comparatively new art forms that came to prominence after the October Revolution. Over the decades of the Soviet regime, extensive poster campaigns were launched in support of a vast array of initiatives: to educate the people about the drive for collectivisation, to promote the five-year plans, to rally people for the war effort, to convey the utopian society at the end of the socialist rainbow, and to promote the personality cults of Lenin and Stalin. Their purpose was not only to educate and inform, but also to enlist the population to transform the world through the use of a new language, the formulation of new goals, and the creation of a new form of civilisation. In the service of these aims, a large number of posters featured the images and words of the leader as guidance, exhortation, encouragement and inspiration to create the new society. While this process was begun in Lenin's time, it was during the decades of Stalin's rule that the image of the leader in posters became omnipresent.

Robert Bird et al. date the earliest predecessors of the wall poster to Ancient Roman times and note that wall paintings advertising everything from circuses, elections and goods for sale were present in Pompeii in the 1st century BC. Similar sorts of advertisements printed on broadsheets by woodcut appeared in Muscovy in the Middle Ages.[38] The rise of the poster in its current form occurred in part due to material circumstances. Lithography was invented in 1796 and chromolithography in 1837, with paper-making machines arriving in 1825 and faster drying inks in the 1870s. The modern-day poster was born around the 1870s with the addition of text to lithographic images and there were poster exhibitions in Europe as early as the mid-1880s.[39] These technical innovations meant that, suddenly, huge runs of printed colour works on paper could be made available for distribution. Improvements in transport networks over large distances meant that this printed material could be distributed over wide territories and reach audiences that were formerly too

---

38   Robert Bird, Christopher P. Heuer, Matthew Jesse Jackson, Tumelo Mosaka & Stephanie Smith (eds), *Vision and communism: Viktor Koretsky and dissident public visual culture*, New York, New Press, 2011, p. 10.
39   Joseph Ansell & James Thorpe, 'The poster', *Art Journal*, 44:1, 1984, pp. 7–8.

remote to exchange communications with the large centres. In the words of El Lissitskii: 'the poster is the traditional book ... flung in all directions'.[40]

These technical innovations do not wholly account for the emergence of the political poster. As Jeffrey Schnapp argues, perhaps the primary reason for the sudden prominence of the political poster in Europe is the expansion of suffrage to increasing numbers of people, and the socio-political need to influence the new voters: 'The state, political movements, labor unions, not to mention sellers of goods and providers of services, all required a fast and efficient conduit to the multitudes, multitudes that could not always be counted on to read newspapers.'[41] Because public opinion now counted, there was a need to find techniques of mass persuasion with the aim of providing information, but also 'in the sense of being provided with rituals, symbols, and narratives, with mobilizing signs, slogans, beliefs, and myths that insure social cohesion and promote participation in the life of the nation'.[42] Posters were an ideal medium to meet these goals, largely because they occupied public space and were potentially visible to large numbers of people as they went about their daily business. Indeed, Engels argued in 1894 that posters were the 'main means of influencing the proletariat' making every street a 'large newspaper'.[43]

Posters had to be simple, bold, eye-catching and legible at a distance. They competed for space and attention in the public arena and were often encountered only briefly, so had to communicate their message quickly, unambiguously and with impact. This was particularly true of posters designed for the urban environment. It is interesting to note that, in 1931, as the Central Committee called for scientific analysis of how posters were received by the viewer, they began with the hypothesis that peasants could be engaged with more complex designs than city dwellers. The theory went that peasants had more time than workers to stop and contemplate the design 'devotionally'.[44] The

---

40   El Lissitskii, quoted in Bird et al., *Vision and communism*, p. 13.
41   Jeffrey T. Schnapp, *Revolutionary tides: the art of the political poster 1914–1989*, Geneva, Skira, 2005, p. 21.
42   Schnapp, *Revolutionary tides*, p. 20.
43   Karl Marx & Friedrich Engels, *Sochineniya*, vol. 6, 2nd edn, Moscow, Gospolitizdat, 1957, p. 478, cited in Stephen White, *The Bolshevik poster*, New Haven, Yale University Press, 1998, p. 111.
44   Bird et al., *Vision and communism*, p. 15.

truth of this may be in part attested to by the fact that poster reviews often highlighted the lack of authenticity in the depiction of rural scenes, including gross inaccuracies in regard to 'machinery, terrain, people, clothing, labor activities, and animals'.[45] Several absurdities committed by apparently urban-based artists resulted in laughter and dismissal of the poster by a peasant audience. The poster was also a suitable medium for populations in which literacy was low but that had a tradition of visual imagery. Russian peasant language was full of symbolism, deriving not only from religion, but also from the supernatural and an elaborate demonology of spirits and devils which could influence all aspects of human life. As Nina Tumarkin observes: 'in the Russian popular mentality, the vocabulary of real power drew upon images of the supernatural. In traditional peasant culture the miraculous and phantasmagorical were a regular part of daily life.'[46]

There was a brief but significant historical precedent in pre-revolutionary Russia for the use of posters and poster-like materials. In 1897, St Petersburg hosted the *First International Poster Exhibition*, despite the fact that the Russian industry was not yet highly developed — of the 727 posters displayed from 13 countries, including France, Germany, the United States and Great Britain, only 28 were from Russia.[47] This exhibition signalled the end of the small industry of poster production as a purely commercial affair in Russia, and the beginning of the poster as an artform and, from 1897 onward, a large number of artists and designers from outside the commercial sphere became involved in poster production. Artists like Mikhail Vrubel, Leon Bakst, Evgenii Lansere, and Viktor and Apollinari Vasnetsov were all involved in pre-revolutionary poster production in Russia.[48]

Russian posters of the early 20th century existed mainly to advertise consumer goods and movies, and featured beautiful women, sometimes dressed in folk costume; strong men at work; and Russian architecture. From the earliest days of the Bolshevik regime, however, it was the political poster that quickly assumed a central place in the graphic

---

45   Victoria E. Bonnell, 'The peasant woman in Stalinist political art of the 1930s', *The American Historical Review*, 98:1, 1993, pp. 55–82, p. 70.
46   Nina Tumarkin, *Lenin lives! The Lenin cult in Soviet Russia*, Cambridge University Press, 1997, p. 70.
47   Alla Rosenfeld, *Defining Russian graphic arts: from Diaghilev to Stalin, 1898–1934*, New Jersey, Rutgers University Press, 1999, pp. 18–19.
48   White, *The Bolshevik poster*, p. 12.

arts. The graphic arts were experiencing rough times during the Civil War, as journals closed down, putting illustrators out of work; and businesses were unable to function, cutting down on advertising work, thus closing off the traditional avenues of employment for graphic artists. From August 1918, political posters suddenly flourished and what Vyacheslav Polonskii refers to as 'poster mania' occurred.[49]

Beginning with the publishing section of the Central Executive Committee of the Soviets, each Soviet agency responsible for some sort of propaganda began to commission posters, with the Red Army becoming a major patron of graphic artists.[50] Poster artists could work for either side in the Civil War and Peter Kenez notes that most of the well-known artists worked for the Whites, leaving the way open for emerging artists to work for the Revolutionary Army.[51] Dmitrii Moor was one of the few graphic artists working for the Red Army at this time who signed his work, the eventual outcome of the Civil War still being too uncertain to confidently predict. Polonskii observed that if the Whites had won Moscow, Moor would likely have been hanged.[52] Poster art was seen as a major contributor to the success of the Red Army in the Civil War, as a means of bringing art to the masses, and as a medium for the transformation of society. In the propagandistic publication of 1935, *Art in the USSR*, C.G. Holme claims 'The poster artists of the U.S.S.R. may justly be called the historic vanguard of our pictorial art. For this group of artists was really the first to take up militant front positions, in the true sense of these words, during the civil war period of 1918–20'.[53] Trotskii wanted posters to be put up 'in every workshop, every department, every office',[54] and lauded Moor in a special decree in 1922 as a 'hero of the pencil and the paintbrush'.[55]

---

49 Quoted in Peter Kenez, *The birth of the propaganda state: Soviet methods of mass mobilization, 1917–1929*, Cambridge University Press, 1985, p. 112.
50 Kenez, *The birth of the propaganda state*, p. 112.
51 Kenez, *The birth of the propaganda state*, p. 113.
52 Vyacheslav Polonskii, 'Russkii revolyutsionnyi plakat', Moscow, Gospolizdat, 1925, p. 66.
53 C.G. Holme, *Art in the USSR: architecture, sculpture, painting, graphic arts, theatre, film, crafts*, London, The Studio, 1935, p. 68.
54 Bird et al., *Vision and communism*, p. 21.
55 L.D. Trotsky, *Sochenineniya*, seriya 6, 21, Moscow, Giz, 1927, p. 242, cited in White, *The Bolshevik poster*, p. 112.

By the end of 1920, 3,100 posters had hit the streets[56] and there were 453 agencies producing posters, the largest of these being Litizdat,[57] which was established in October 1919 with Polonskii at its head.[58] Litizdat was given the task of producing propaganda and educational materials in a wide variety of formats including posters, periodicals, pictures, drawings, proclamations, brochures and books. White notes that:

> almost 70 per cent of the 29.8 million copies of publications in all categories between June 1919 and January 1921, for instance, were proclamations, appeals, posters or open letters to the troops, and posters and *lubok* [illustrated broadside] pictures alone accounted for some 20 per cent of total production over the same period.[59]

Both Moor and Viktor Deni[60] designed posters for Litizdat. Posters had reached such prominence as a means of cultural expression that, in February 1924 in Moscow, a poster exhibition, *The poster in the last six years*, became the first retrospective to be held in Soviet Russia.[61]

The political poster of the early Soviet period was influenced to some extent by the *lubok*[62] and the icon. The *lubok*, which had wide circulation among the peasantry, typically combined illustrations with text, and its subject matter included religion and folklore as well as political developments and social issues of the day. Several of the Russian avant-garde artists became interested in the *lubki* as part of a wider exploration of folk art in the 1910s. Kazimir Malevich and Vladimir Maiakovskii became the designer and caption writers

---

56 Gill, *Symbols and legitimacy in Soviet politics*, p. 11.
57 The Literature and Publishing Department of the Political Administration of the Revolutionary Military Council of the Republic.
58 See Victoria E. Bonnell, *Iconography of power: Soviet political posters under Lenin and Stalin*, Berkeley, University of California Press, 1998, p. 25; B.S. Butnik-Siverskii, *Sovetskii plakat epokhi grazhdanskoi voiny, 1918–1921*, Moscow, Izd. Vses. Knizhnoi palaty, 1960; and, White, *The Bolshevik poster*, pp. 39–40.
59 White, *The Bolshevik poster*, p. 39.
60 Stephen White provides evidence that Lenin appreciated Deni's work (*The Bolshevik poster*, p. 60).
61 Elena Barkhatova, '"Modern icon", or "tool for mass propaganda"? Russian debate on the poster', in Rosenfeld, *Defining Russian graphic arts*, p. 133.
62 White provides an excellent history of the *lubok* and its influence on the Soviet poster in *The Bolshevik poster* (1998).

respectively for a new First World War publication, *Today's Lubok*, which produced a series of more than 50 patriotic posters. Moor was also involved in the production of *Today's Lubok*.⁶³

After the Revolution, the satirical *lubok* form was used as a news bulletin by the Bolsheviks, and also to lampoon and ridicule the enemy — the White generals, capitalists, *oblomovs*,⁶⁴ and priests, among others. In 1918 *Pravda* proclaimed the poster a 'powerful weapon of socialist propaganda, influencing the broadest possible public. Attracting to itself the attention of the masses, it makes the first impression on their consciousness, which lectures and books can subsequently deepen'⁶⁵ and, in 1925, theoretician N. Tarabukin proclaimed the poster a 'weapon of mass influence'.⁶⁶ In 1918 ROSTA (Russian Telegraph Agency) was established with three main areas of responsibility — collecting and disseminating information, agitation, and supervision of the Soviet press. With chronic paper and ink shortages making publication of books and newspapers difficult, the first ROSTA Window posters appeared in Moscow in 1919 with the object of combining 'the functions of poster, newspaper, magazine and information bulletin'.⁶⁷ In the tradition of the *lubok*, they featured colourful graphics and often satirical text, but were also enhanced by the experimentation in style, form and colour that was brought to the artform by the artists of the avant-garde. Maiakovskii, who worked on the ROSTA windows, enthused: 'ROSTA Windows are something fantastic. It is a handful of artists serving, by hand, a huge nation of a hundred and fifty million. It's instantaneous news wires remade into a poster; it's decrees instantly published as ditties. It is a new form introduced directly by life.'⁶⁸ Holme enthused retrospectively in 1935:

---

63 White, *The Bolshevik poster*, p. 3.
64 The terms 'oblomov' and 'oblomovism' derive from Ivan Goncharov's popular novel, *Oblomov* (1859). The central character, Oblomov, is indecisive and apathetic, and takes the first 50 pages of the novel to get from his bed to his chair. 'Oblomovshchina' (oblomovism) refers to a condition of fatalistic apathy and sloth. Chonghoon Lee notes that the condition was a central concern of Soviet psychiatric and neurological research and was viewed as a 'national disease' which was denounced in the drive for industrialisation and the search for heroes of labour ('Visual Stalinism from the perspective of heroisation: posters, paintings and illustrations in the 1930s', *Totalitarian Movements and Political Religions*, 8:3–4, 2007, pp. 503–21, p. 503).
65 *Pravda*, 6 Oct. 1918, quoted in White, *The Bolshevik poster*, p. 112.
66 N. Tarabukin quoted in Barkhatova in Rosenfeld, *Defining Russian graphic arts*, p. 147.
67 Viktor Duvakin, 'Introduction to V.V. Mayakovsky', *Groznyi smekh. Okna satiry ROSTA*, Moscow–Leningrad, Iskusstvo, 1938, p. v, cited in White, *The Bolshevik poster*, p. 67.
68 Vladimir Maiakovskii, 'Terrifying laughter,' quoted in Barkhatova in Rosenfeld, *Defining Russian graphic arts*, pp. 134–35.

It is difficult to imagine the Moscow or Petrograd of 1919–20 without those 'satire [Rosta] windows', brightly illuminated till the early hours of the morning and attracting large throngs of spectators. The 'Rosta Windows' constituted a remarkable supplement to the exhortations of the leaders, which were, posted on the walls near-by, to the appeals of the Party, and to the telegraphic news bulletins from the battle-fronts of the civil war.[69]

Russian Orthodox icons were also a significant influence on the development of Soviet poster art, a fact that was (somewhat surprisingly) noted in a Soviet publication in 1922 in which Aleksei Sidorov described the poster as a 'contemporary icon'.[70] James Aulich and Marta Sylvestrová see in both the Soviet political poster and the orthodox icon 'a lack of distinction between the represented and that which is represented, a blurring between what is pictured and what is real which occurs through a process of magical identification'.[71] Both icons and political posters are neither decorative nor pictorial, but instructive and symbolic. A wealth of visual information is encoded in the images for the initiated believer, for whom the image functions at a pre-rational level to facilitate the link between man and god in the case of the icon, and citizen and the regime (often as embodied through the Stalin leader symbol) in the case of the poster.

One of the most famous early Bolshevik poster artists, Aleksandr Apsit, trained as an icon painter,[72] while the atheist Moor spent his early years studying icons, concentrating on composition, form, colour, and the use of narrative and illustrative techniques.[73] Moor later put his knowledge of icons to use in satirical drawings for anti-religious publications. The engraver Ivan Pavlov stated that Moor's renditions of the saints were so successful that peasants often hung them in their icon corners, unaware of the satirical intent.[74] In an unpublished essay, Moor acknowledged that the poster form derived from both peasant woodcuts and 'the religious paintings of the vestibules of churches

---

69   Holme, *Art in the USSR*, pp. 68–69.
70   A.A. Sidorov, 'Iskusstvo plakata', *Gorn*, 1922, no. 2, pp. 122–27, p. 125, cited in White, *The Bolshevik poster*, p. 5.
71   James Aulich & Marta Sylvestrová, *Political posters in Central and Eastern Europe, 1945–95: signs of the times*, Manchester University Press, 1999, p. 7.
72   Bonnell, *Iconography of Power*, p. 32.
73   D.S. Moor, 'Avtobiografiya', 1934, TsGALI f 1988, op. 2 ed. Khr 13, cited in White, *The Bolshevik poster*, p. 6.
74   I.N. Pavlov, *Moya zhizn i vstrechi*, Moscow, Iskusstvo, 1949, p. 260, cited in White, *The Bolshevik poster*, p. 43.

2. THE RISE OF THE STALIN PERSONALITY CULT

[and] in a certain number of icons, particularly of the 15th century'.[75] Deni also directly borrowed religious motifs in early satirical work for the Bolshevik regime. As Robert Philippe has observed in a more general sense in his study on art as a weapon, political prints depicting the personalities and events of political, social, military and religious life have always served to decorate the walls of people's houses: 'In this sense they are the heirs of the sacred picture. They testify to convictions, and provide reassurance of ways of being.'[76] While the appropriation of the icon tradition gave many political posters a sacred and devotional aura, the satirical and parodic traditions that grew out of the *lubok* and satirical magazines undercut this to some extent by priming the possibility of subversive interpretations.

In the early 1930s, control of poster design became centralised, with all commissions proceeding from state departments, and the materials needed to engage in art practice only available through the state. On 11 March 1931 the Central Committee issued a 'Resolution on poster agitation and propaganda' that centralised control over allocating and ratifying Soviet poster commissions into the exclusive hands of Izogiz,[77] which came under the direct oversight of the Central Committee.[78] The resolution named visual art as a 'powerful tool in the reconstruction of the individual, his ideology, his way of life, his economic activity' and as a means of 'entering the consciousness and hearts of millions of people',[79] and also called for specific measures to gather more accurate information on viewer reception and response to posters. At the same time, the Union of Russian Revolutionary Poster Artists (ORPP) was established, headed by Moor.

The centralisation of poster production was not unwelcome to some artists and critics, who had expressed concerns in the press that the standard of poster design was in decline and that valuable and scarce materials were being wasted on hack work. Centralisation was a means of ensuring that commissions and materials were directed to the best artists.[80] Gill points out that, while some degree of diversity and artistic

---

75   Lektsii D. S. Moora o plakatnom iskusstve I ego istroii' (n.d.) TsGALI f. 1988, op 1 ed. Khr. 68, cited in White, *The Bolshevik poster*, p. 6.
76   Robert Philippe, *Political graphics: art as a weapon*, New York, Abbeville Press, 1982, p. 172.
77   Art Department of the State Publishing House.
78   Gough, 'Back in the USSR', pp. 142–43.
79   *Brigada khudozhnikov* 1–3, 1931, 1–3, cited in Bonnell, *Iconography of Power*, p. 37.
80   For an elaboration of this viewpoint see White, *The Bolshevik poster*, p. 120.

freedom remained in the other visual arts, posters were always more carefully regulated and thus a more rigid expression of the regime's priorities due to the fact that the regime generated commissions and monopolised the means of printing and reproduction.[81] By the beginning of the 1930s, posters made by enthusiastic amateur demonstrators to carry in parades were quickly confiscated and destroyed.[82] Themes, texts and images for official posters were dictated to commissioned artists,[83] who then had to submit their work to the censors for approval. The rigour and uncertainty of censorship is attested to in a 1935 diary entry by Kulagina:

> Yesterday, Gustav handed in his poster Stalin and Voroshilov[84] … to the Glavlit for the 3rd time — and Irinova (now it's Irinova!) didn't want to sign off on it and he had to take it to central Glavlit … and then this morning he went to the central Glavlit — Gurinov signed it and then immediately after that Irinova signed it too. I find such things outrageous — one moment it's this and that is bad, and Stalin doesn't look like himself — and then all of a sudden all is well.[85]

Despite the fact that all posters were commissioned under strict guidelines, many posters submitted were either rejected, or sent back for major revision.[86] In July 1930 a decree of the Council of People's Commissars resulted in 200 artists being sent to construction sites and collective farms for two months each to create propaganda about the first Five-Year Plan and the progress of the collectivisation drive. Thirty per cent of the work they produced was rejected by the purchasing committees of VseKoKhudozhnik and Izogiz.[87] In April 1931 a meeting of the review board under Izogiz occurred in which 22 posters that Izogiz intended to publish were to be discussed. Most of them were

---

81 Gill, *Symbols and legitimacy in Soviet politics*, p. 11.
82 Ekaterina V. Haskins & James P. Zappen, 'Totalitarian visual "monologue": reading Soviet posters with Bakhtin', *Rhetoric Society Quarterly*, 2010, 40:4, pp. 326–59, p. 335.
83 A diary entry by Kulagina dated 11 January 1933 provides a good example of how this process worked: 'Was at Izogiz today, got an assignment for a poster on the theme of Stalin's report [In January 1933, Stalin announced the completion of the first Five-Year Plan ahead of schedule, in four years]. It has to be ready in three days' (Tupitsyn, *Gustav Klutsis and Valentina Kulagina*, p. 206).
84 Gustav Klutsis, 'Long live the workers and peasants Red Army — loyal guard of the Soviet borders', 1935.
85 Diary entry dated 11 March 1935 in Tupitsyn, *Gustav Klutsis and Valentina Kulagina*, p. 216.
86 For an interesting insight into how this occurred from the artists' point of view, see Tupitsyn, *Gustav Klutsis and Valentina Kulagina*.
87 Bown, *Art under Stalin*, p. 41.

2. THE RISE OF THE STALIN PERSONALITY CULT

severely criticised, with half of them rejected outright.[88] A 1933 entry in Kulagina's diary reads: 'Yakovlev made a report on the state of the poster sector. He didn't have anything good to say. Criticized all the May Day posters. Gustav was praised, Elkin was harshly criticized; of Pinus's poster he said that it was published by mistake (too sugary and philistine).'[89]

By 1933 propaganda posters had become such an established artform that a large retrospective exhibition celebrating 15 years of the creative work of poster artists and cartoonists opened in Moscow, including albums of work by Deni, Moor, the Kukryniksy,[90] and Boris Efimov. Holme wrote of the exhibition: 'We saw before us a gallery of works testifying to the creation of an entirely new art in posters and cartoons. This new art could also be seen in numerous art editions and albums containing the best posters and cartoons of the Soviet masters.'[91] It may have been this exhibition to which Kulagina referred when she wrote in her diary on 16 December 1933: 'But there is no inventiveness, no creativity. Or formalism is what destroys someone like me? But it seems to me that one always has to look for something pointed — and at Izogiz, they like posters that are barely distinguishable from one another.'[92]

In the mid-1930s the range of expression in political posters declined still further, with an increased focus on a narrower pool of symbols and motifs. While in 1934 more than 240 posters were produced in print runs averaging about 30,000, by 1937 the total number of posters produced was only 70, but the print runs increased for some posters to the hundreds of thousands.[93] Public space was frequently saturated with posters and visual repetition occurred not only because the pool of images from which poster artists drew was confined, but also because posters could be displayed in multiples of the same image. There is evidence that Klutsis designed some of his posters with the intention that they be displayed in serial repetition.[94] By 1935, the emphasis

---

88   Bonnell, 'The peasant woman in Stalinist political art of the 1930s', p. 68.
89   Tupitsyn, *Gustav Klutsis and Valentina Kulagina*, p. 206.
90   Artists collective of Mikhail Kuprianov, Porfiri Krylov and Nikolai Sokolov.
91   Holme, *Art in the USSR*, p. 70.
92   Tupitsyn, *Gustav Klutsis and Valentina Kulagina*, p. 210.
93   See Rolf, 'A hall of mirrors', p. 610; Bonnell, *Iconography of power*, p. 43; Klaus Waschik & Nina Baburina, *Werben fur die Utopie: Russische Plakatkunst des 20. Jahrhunderts*, Bietigheim-Bissingen, Edition Tertium, 2003, p. 254.
94   See Tupitsyn, *Gustav Klutsis and Valentina Kulagina*, p. 54.

in posters was moving away from a focus on the everyman hero of labour and towards a focus on Stalin as a leader–hero. Stalin's image took central place in a number of posters, and artists like Klutsis, who had worked predominantly in photomontage to create cut-and-paste images combining his own staged worker–hero photos with large crowd scenes, now turned their attention to retouching images of Stalin to remove facial scars and creases in clothing.[95] Ekaterina Haskins and James Zappen argue that the Stalin posters are the most blatantly monologic of all of the propaganda posters:

> In contrast to the industrialization and collectivization posters, which exhibit some tension between the authoritative and the internally persuasive word and even, in the case of the collectivization posters, explicitly invite a response, the Stalin posters seek to neutralize any possible internal ideological struggle and to silence any possible dissent by representing the authoritative word of the beloved leader as the only word.[96]

The poster text, which always directs the reader to the correct interpretation of the image by narrowing down the choice of possible meanings, now consisted almost exclusively of the pronouncements of Stalin, with an occasional word of praise about Stalin by Molotov or Voroshilov. Even posters that appear to be about Lenin's legacy now present Lenin as interpreted by Stalin — the pronouncement of Stalin lends legitimacy to the doctrine of Lenin. Other people in the posters exist only in relation to Stalin — they gaze up at him with awe, carry his portrait in parades, study his texts, salute him, sing songs about him and follow him into the utopian future. In the words of Haskins and Zappen, 'The visual composition thus certifies Stalin's symbolic role in the Soviet pantheon and casts the Soviet people as an approving chorus'.[97]

In the late 1930s, formalism and any kind of experimental work were increasingly decried and socialist realism became the predominant artistic method. A number of even the most celebrated poster artists were publicly criticised in the 1930s and 1940s, including Klutsis,[98]

---

95 Tupitsyn, *Gustav Klutsis and Valentina Kulagina*, p. 34.
96 Haskins & Zappen, 'Totalitarian visual "monologue"', p. 348.
97 Haskins & Zappen, 'Totalitarian visual "monologue"', p. 348.
98 See Bonnell, *Iconography of power*, p. 40.

Moor,[99] Deni,[100] Viktor Koretskii,[101] Deineka,[102] Vasilii Elkin,[103] Natalia Pinus[104] and Vladimir Lebedev.[105] The Congress of Victors of 1934 declared that socialism had been achieved, with this formalised by the Soviet Constitution of 1936, and poster images increasingly depicted the fulfilment of socialism, and the happiness of the Soviet citizen. Stalin was depicted not only as the father of all Soviet children, but as the father of the nation and its heroes, including the Stakhanovites, polar explorers and record-breaking aviators.[106] By 1939 a rigid canon of Stalin images was fixed: '[Stalin's] appearances in *Pravda* adhered to a certain rhythm, which more or less followed the calendar of Soviet holidays. Year after year Stalin appeared on the same occasions and the same holidays — often with the same pictures.'[107]

The Great Patriotic War saw a marked revival in the production of war posters, with many of the surviving Civil War artists returning to serve their country. With the fortunes of war so dismal in 1941 and 1942, there was an initial decrease in posters of Stalin, however, once fortunes turned and as victory seemed assured, Stalin's image again resumed its place as a central rallying symbol for the regime. After the resurgence of the poster during the war, with its dramatic scope for heroic warriors and loyal, hardworking citizens contrasting with a satirised or demonised enemy, poster artists faced the challenge of finding images to depict peace. The family took centre stage amid scenes coloured in subtle, pastel hues and images of the imminent utopia as the nation moved from socialism to communism. Images of victory celebrations moved on to a renewed call for reconstruction and hence, further sacrifice, sometimes using the slogans of prewar construction, but with new images that suggested springtime and white collar workers replacing the miners and builders of earlier times. Stalin was depicted again as a father of the people, but this time his brood had expanded to include the conquered nationalities and,

---

99 See White, *The Bolshevik poster*, p. 138.
100 See White, *The Bolshevik poster*, p. 138.
101 See Erika Wolf, *Koretsky: the Soviet photo poster: 1930–1984*, New York, The New Press, 2012, pp. xi, 7, 9–11.
102 See White, *The Bolshevik poster*, p. 138.
103 See Tupitsyn, *Gustav Klutsis and Valentina Kulagina*, p. 206.
104 See Tupitsyn, *Gustav Klutsis and Valentina Kulagina*, p. 206.
105 See White, *The Bolshevik poster*, p. 138.
106 To be examined in greater detail in Chapter Three.
107 Plamper, *The Stalin cult*, p. 63.

ultimately, the people of the whole world, to whom Stalin was portrayed as a saviour and bringer of peace. Stalin was also sometimes depicted in a manner that was strongly suggestive of the Orthodox icon.

In 1948 the campaign against cosmopolitanism was launched, with renewed attacks on formalism and an anti-Semitic bias.[108] In the same year the Central Committee issued a decree 'On shortcomings and Measures for Improvement of the Publication of Political Posters', calling for improvements in poster production on all levels — artistic method, ideological content, and printing process. This culminated in a meeting in 1951 to assess the progress made with regard to the Central Committee's resolution of 1948. Formalism was attacked and Koretskii, despite having been celebrated as a Stalin Prize[109] winner, came under particular attack, with specific reference made to the extensive use of photography in his graphic art practice. From 1952 Koretskii virtually discontinued his use of photographs and employed a more painterly technique. Koretskii survived these attacks and continued as a leading poster artist until *perestroika* in the late 1980s, at which time he devoted himself to painting.[110]

A point that is often ignored or underestimated in studies of Stalinist propaganda posters is the extent of the impact of purely practical factors on poster design. While it is often difficult to piece together today all of the situational factors that existed at any given time during poster production, a careful reading of a variety of sources provides clues. Wherever possible, these factors must be taken into account in an iconographical reading as they impact on the numbers of posters produced, printing methods, and elements of design and colour. Until well into the 1930s the Soviet regime experienced continual paper shortages. In fact, paper shortages at the time of the October Revolution were a contributing factor to the rise of the poster at this time. The Revolution and Civil War had substantially disrupted the printing industry. The loss of the Baltic regions, which supplied about half of the nation's paper needs, was one factor,[111] as was the loss of qualified printers, lack of spare parts and fuel, and the pro-Menshevik

---

108 For an insight into how this affected Jewish artists like Koretskii see Wolf, *Koretsky*, pp. 8–9.
109 The Stalin Prize was a state prize awarded across a number of cultural and scientific fields between 1941 and 1954 — thereafter, the USSR State Prize.
110 See Wolf, *Koretsky*, pp. 10–11.
111 A.I. Nazarov, *Oktyabr I kniga*, Moscow, Nauka, 1968, p. 167 cited in White, *The Bolshevik poster*, p. 19.

sympathies of the printers' union.[112] The Bolshevik regime needed to reach mass audiences with its propaganda material and displaying large posters in public venues proved to be a more efficient use of paper than printing millions of copies of smaller bulletins, newspapers and books for individual consumption.[113] Paper shortages continued to plague the new regime into the next decade, with Kulagina recording in her diary on 31 July 1932 that paper shortages in that year had resulted in a cutback on poster commissions to artists.[114]

Poster design was influenced by factors such as the availability of ink, the timeframe in which the poster was to be produced, the printing method used, and the availability of portraits of the leader. Polonskii pointed out in relation to Civil War posters that not only was the paper of very poor quality, but inks were in limited supply and a further limitation on the use of inks was due to the quick turnaround time required. Posters had to be current, sometimes being released within hours or days of new events, and each additional colour added to the production time.[115] Stephen White observes: 'As a result, only one or two colours were used in most cases; only in exceptional circumstance, when a week or two was in hand, could three or four colours be employed. Posters produced in this more leisurely manner tended to be on fairly general themes ... .'[116]

Sometimes a number of factors conspired to make poster production difficult. White notes that, by the late 1920s, the political poster could not react 'promptly and with adequate resources' to current events due to 'a combination of centralization and financial stringency, together with some insensitive personnel appointments'.[117] The New Economic Policy (NEP) also meant that shop windows were once again

---

112 White, *The Bolshevik poster*, p. 19.
113 This chronic paper shortage in the early days of Bolshevik power contributed to the rise of another revolutionary medium for propaganda — propagandistic porcelain. The state Porcelain Factory, maker of official porcelain for the tsar, was full of undecorated porcelain blanks at the biscuit stage. These were decorated with the symbols, slogans and images of Red propaganda, then fired and put into circulation (Nina Lobanov-Rostovsky, 'Soviet propaganda porcelain', *The Journal of Decorative and Propaganda Arts*, 11:2, 1989, pp. 126–41, pp. 128–29).
114 Kulagina cited in Tupitsyn, *Gustav Klutsis and Valentina Kulagina*, p. 203.
115 Polonskii cited in White, *The Bolshevik poster*, p. 64.
116 White, *The Bolshevik poster*, p. 64.
117 White, *The Bolshevik poster*, p. 126.

in use to display consumer goods and that organisations had to show both financial accountability and to pay for posters that had hitherto been provided by the State for free.

The inability to get access to the leadership is a further factor that influenced the content of posters and provides one reason for poster images being so highly repetitive. In a 1935 letter to Kulagina, Klutsis complains of not being allowed close enough to the leadership in Red Square to get good close-up photos without a telephoto lens. Jan Plamper notes that while Stalin may have posed for portraits on rare occasions in the 1920s, it is unclear whether he ever posed for portraits thereafter.[118] What remained as source material for artists was only the official photos published in the media, and these were all vetted, as had been the case with images of Lenin.[119] Artists had access to a comparatively small pool of images of the leaders, and these images were cut and pasted into a variety of situations and backgrounds. The Russian State Library in Moscow still holds folios which contain copies of the officially sanctioned portrait images of Stalin, separated into two categories marked 'Fond' and 'Rekomend'.[120] Many of the portrait images in these folders form the basis of Stalin portraits on posters.

Commercial concerns affecting the artist are yet another factor that influenced the form and content of Stalinist posters. Many artists who normally worked in other media undertook graphic propaganda work in order to make a living and commissions were competitive. From 1931, Izogiz assigned particular slogans to artists who then submitted a draft to their editor for approval.[121] From this time, posters were usually printed with detailed publishing information in small typescript at the bottom of the page. This detail included not only the name of the artist, but also the name of the editor responsible for approving the poster.[122] Practical considerations relating to the rates

---

118 Plamper, *The Stalin cult*, p. 141.
119 Plamper describes the process by which photographs of Stalin were submitted to Comrade Poskryobyshev of Stalin's secretariat for approval, and discusses evidence that Stalin looked at photos himself and participated in the decision-making on whether or not to publish them (*The Stalin cult*, p. 34).
120 No one at the library is able to explain precisely how these categories were used.
121 Erika Wolf discusses this process in relation to the career of Viktor Koretskii (*Koretsky*, pp. 3–4).
122 The degree of detail is inconsistent and many posters do not contain complete information, with some even lacking the name of the artist or the year of publication.

of pay of the artist could also come into consideration. In his 1932 essay 'A worldwide achievement', Klutsis noted that RABIS[123] 'directed a 25 per cent reduction in pay to artists and poster makers using the method of photomontage'.[124] Yankovskaya and Mitchell observe that, after the Great Patriotic War, standard norms for pricing works of art were introduced. According to these rules, the larger an artistic canvas was in square metres, the higher the fee earned by the artist; topical compositions were paid higher than landscapes and still lifes; works with crowds of people paid higher than those with a single figure; a full-length portrait paid higher than smaller upper torsos; and a portrait of someone in uniform paid higher than the same person in civilian clothing.[125] These incentives may understandably have led to a tendency towards gigantism. There was also considerable incentive to create works that would win prizes. The Stalin Prize First Class carried with it a bonus of 100,000 rubles and impacted on salaries and pensions,[126] while exemplary work for the regime was acknowledged with access to improved non-communal living quarters.[127]

Stalin's charisma

With the entire apparatus of cultural and artistic practice under centralised control, and production across all media generated by one officially endorsed methodology, the Soviet leadership was in an ideal position to saturate the marketplace with their product. The nature of this product was complex and all-encompassing, and was marketed as a new form of civilisation. In order for fundamental changes in behaviour and massive transformation of the landscape to occur, the population had to be engaged and mobilised to adopt the ideology (and goals and vision) of the leadership as their own. One of the primary strategies adopted by the Bolsheviks in order to achieve this was to endow the leader with a persona that symbolised abstracts,

---

123 *Rabouchee iskusstvo*, or Worker's Art, an organ of the Central Committee of the Communist Party.
124 Gustav Klutsis, 'A worldwide achievement', Cynthia Martin (trans.), originally published as 'Mirovoe dostizhenie', *Proletarskoe Foto*, no 6, 1932, pp. 14–15 in Tupitsyn, *Gustav Klutsis and Valentina Kulagina*, p. 238.
125 Yankovskaya & Mitchell, 'The economic dimensions of art in the Stalinist era', p. 789.
126 Oliver Johnson, 'The Stalin Prize and the Soviet artist: status symbol or stigma?', *Slavic Review*, 70:4, 2011, pp. 819–43, p. 822.
127 Tupitsyn, *Gustav Klutsis and Valentina Kulagina*, p. 201.

such as Bolshevik values and ideology, as well as concrete entities such as the Party and the state. The leader had to appear charismatic, and this charisma had to endure in the long term, overcoming the perils inherent in the inevitable routinisation of charisma.

Despite Trotskii's (not entirely disinterested) description of Stalin as a provincial 'mediocrity', and socialist revolutionary Nikolai Sukhanov's[128] description of him as a 'grey blur',[129] in the early years of the Bolshevik regime, there is ample evidence that many people found Stalin personally charming. Simon Sebag Montefiore has conducted extensive research in the newly opened archives and concludes that the foundation of Stalin's power in the Party was not fear but charm, with his close associates addressing him affectionately and informally, and able to disagree with him.[130] Marshal Georgii Zhukov saw Stalin as thoughtful and attentive,[131] Lavrenti Beria commented that 'he dominated his entourage with his intelligence',[132] and Voroshilov wrote to Avel Enukidze in June 1933, describing Stalin as 'remarkable' and as possessing a 'great mind'.[133] The painter Evgeni Katsman was delighted by Stalin's hospitality,[134] and Stalin's adopted son Artiom said he made 'we children feel like adults and feel important'.[135] In his memoirs written in 1964, Ilia Ehrenburg recounts how Stalin

---

128 Sukhanov was shot on Stalin's orders on 27 August 1939.
129 N.N. Sukhanov, *The Russian Revolution, 1917: a personal record*, London, Oxford University Press, 1955, pp. vii, xii, 230.
130 'Stalin possessed the dominant will among his magnates, but they also found his policies generally congenial. He was older than them all except President Kalinin, but the magnates used the informal "you" with him. Voroshilov, Molotov and Sergo [Ordzhonikidze] called him "Koba" … Mikoyan … called him Soso … in 1930, all these magnates, especially the charismatic and fiery Sergo Orzhonikidze, were allies, not protégés, all capable of independent action' (S. Sebag Montefiore, *Stalin: the court of the Red Tsar*, London, Weidenfeld and Nicolson, 2003, p. 49).
131 'The appearance of JV Stalin, his quiet voice, the concreteness and depth of his judgments, the attention with which he heard the report, made a great impression on me' (Zhukov, quoted in Montefiore, *Stalin*, p. 42).
132 Beria, quoted in Montefiore, *Stalin*, p. 42.
133 'A remarkable man, our Koba. It is simply incomprehensible how he can combine the great mind of the proletarian strategist, the will of a statesman and revolutionary activist, and the soul of a completely ordinary kind comrade … It is good that we have Koba' (RGASPI, f.667, op.1, d.17, ll.5–6, quoted in Kevin McDermott, 'Archives, power and the 'cultural turn': reflections on Stalin and Stalinism', *Totalitarian Movements and Political Religions*, 2004, 5:1, pp. 5–24, p. 10). McDermott notes the possibility that Voroshilov may have been 'subconsciously' writing for a wider audience.
134 'Joseph Vissarionovich immediately made everything simple and clear. His calmness and cheerful hospitality delighted us' (RGALI, f. 2368, op. 2, d.36, ll. 20–21, cited in Plamper, *The Stalin cult*, p. 138).
135 S Montefiore, *Stalin*, p. 42.

had a way of charming those to whom he talked, including influential writers Henri Barbusse, Rolland Romain and Lion Feuchtwanger.[136] Writing in 1966, without the benefit of the archival material available today, Isaac Deutscher, a subscriber to Trotskii's view of Stalin as a mediocrity, begrudgingly acknowledged some of the foundations of Stalin's personal appeal as laying in his self-effacing modesty, his approachability and his ability to listen.[137] Stalin's personal charm, his apparent modesty, his high intelligence, and an ability to appear as an 'everyman', approachable and chameleon-like, provided a foundation upon which his charismatic persona could be built. However, these qualities alone are not enough to mobilise a population to undergo great sacrifices in the service of a grand vision. The charismatic leader must ultimately appear to have 'superhuman' qualities and none of the foibles and weaknesses that are the mark of the ordinary man.

From the days of Lenin and Trotskii, the Party leadership upheld the firm conviction that the ultimate goal of the communist utopia was worth any sacrifice. The Party had to be kept in power to guide this process at any cost. It was with this intent that Stalin and his intimates set about the deliberate task of manufacturing charisma around the person of the leader[138] — a charismatic persona encompassed by

---

136 'Barbusse wrote: "It can be said that in no one have Lenin's thoughts and words been embodied better than Stalin." After meeting him Romain Rolland said: "He is amazingly human." Feuchtwanger thought himself a sceptic, an old stager. Stalin must have been laughing up his sleeve when he told Feuchtwanger how much he disliked having his portrait everywhere, but the old stager believed him' (Ilya Ehrenburg, *Men, years — life*, vol. 5, *The war, 1941–45*, Tatiana Shebunina & Yvonne Kapp (trans.), London, MacGibbon and Kee, 1964, p. 305).
137 'What was striking in the General Secretary was that there was nothing striking about him. His almost impersonal personality seemed to be the ideal vehicle for the anonymous forces of class and party. His bearing seemed of the utmost modesty. He was more accessible to the average official or party man than the other leaders. He studiously cultivated his contacts with the people who in one way or another made and unmade reputations, provincial secretaries, popular satirical writers, and foreign visitors. Himself taciturn, he was unsurpassed at the art of patiently listening to others … His private life, too, was beyond reproach or suspicion' (Isaac Deutscher, *Stalin; a political biography*, 2nd edn, New York, Oxford University Press, 1966, pp. 275–76). In a similar vein, and with the benefit of archival material, J. Arch Getty observes that, from the earliest days of Party life, one of Stalin's greatest strengths was his ability to work in a committee: 'to listen, to moderate, to referee, to steer the discussion toward a consensus. This had earned him the respect, co-operation, and loyalty of senior Bolsheviks' ('Stalin as prime minister: power and the Politburo', in Sarah Davies & James Harris (eds), *Stalin: a new history*, Cambridge University Press, 2004, p. 100).
138 That the manufacture of charisma for the Stalin persona was deliberate is beyond question. For a discussion of the evidence supporting this assertion see Plamper, *The Stalin cult*, p. 29; Benno Ennker, '"Struggling for Stalin's soul": the leader cult and the balance of power in Stalin's inner circle', in Heller & Plamper (eds), *Personality cults in Stalinism*, pp. 163–65; James L. Heizer, 'The cult of Stalin, 1929–1939', PhD thesis, University of Kentucky, 1977, p. 62.

the pseudonym 'Stalin'. Stalin explicitly spoke out against the cult developing around himself[139] and, as Sarah Davies documents, significantly edited the *Kratkii Kurs*[140] so that it was less focused on Stalin and the other *vozhdi*.[141] In a 1930 letter to an Old Bolshevik, Ia. M. Shatunovskii, Stalin stated:

> You speak of your 'devotion' to me. Perhaps that phrase slipped out accidentally. Perhaps. But if it isn't an accidental phrase, I'd advise you to thrust aside the 'principle' of devotion to persons. It isn't the Bolshevik way. Have devotion to the working class, its party, its state. That's needed and good. But don't mix it with devotion to persons, that empty and needless bauble of intellectuals.[142]

On the basis of the archival information available, Davies concludes that, while Stalin was generally critical of his cult,[143] he was not against the promotion of the leader as an embodiment of the cause and could see the advantages of the cult for the mobilisation of the 'backward masses'.[144] Davies summarises Stalin's attitude to his cult as follows: 'To close relatives he maintained that it was a necessary, if temporary, evil, to be tolerated for the sake of the "masses" who were accustomed to worshipping the tsar.'[145]

Paradoxically, a major component of the cultic persona of Stalin was his personal modesty. Plamper observes that, unlike the contemporaneous cults of Hitler in Germany and Mussolini in Italy, which did not fabricate images of modesty, the Stalin cult was presented as 'an oxymoron, a cult *malgré soi*'.[146] Modesty was the primary personality trait listed in a 1939 publication for Pioneers, *Vozhatyi*,[147] which described Stalin in the following manner:

---

139 Sarah Davies, 'Stalin and the making of the leader cult in the 1930s', in Balázs Apor, Jan C. Behrends, Polly Jones & E.A. Rees, *The leader cult in communist dictatorships: Stalin and the Eastern Bloc*, Hampshire, Palgrave, 2004, p. 33.
140 *Istoriia Vsesoiuznoi Kommunisticheskoi partii (bolshevikov) Kratkii kurs*, Moscow, Gospolitizdat, 1938. [History of the All-Union Communist Party (Bolshevik). Short Course.]
141 Davies, in Apor et al., *The leader cult in communist dictatorships*, p. 36.
142 I.V. Stalin, *Sochineniia*, 13, 1946–52, Moscow, Gospolitizdat, p. 19.
143 Davies cites numerous examples of Stalin's detachment from his own cult, and of his apparent modesty (in Apor et al., *The leader cult in communist dictatorships*, pp. 29–30).
144 Davies, in Apor et al., *The leader cult in communist dictatorships*, p. 30.
145 Davies, in Apor et al., *The leader cult in communist dictatorships*, p. 38.
146 Plamper, *The Stalin cult*, p. 19.
147 Pioneer Leader, organ of the Komsomol Central Committee and the Central Council of the Pioneer Organisation.

> Modesty and simplicity. Crystalline honesty and principled behavior in everything and always. Clarity of goals and toughness of character, overcoming all and every obstacle. Persistence and personal courage. These are the traits of character of great Stalin. These are the Bolshevik traits with which we should inoculate the Pioneers.[148]

Largely due to the Marxist distaste for glorification of the individual, Lenin's abhorrence of any kind of cultish behaviour, and to general Bolshevik asceticism, Stalin had to appear as if he was actively discouraging the excesses of the adulation directed at him, which was always to seem as if coming from below.[149] One useful mechanism for producing just such an effect was the Stalin Prize. The Stalin Prize was conceived in 1939 to coincide with Stalin's 60th birthday celebrations and was first presented in 1941. The prizes were conceived as a Soviet equivalent to the Nobel Prize and, in addition to substantial financial and material rewards, also carried some (although ambivalent) symbolic capital. Artistic works that contributed to the genre of the leader cult enjoyed a 'privileged' status in the competition, with roughly half of the prizes in the field of painting awarded to works on the leader cult over the 13-year history of the prize.[150] Oliver Johnson argues that the Stalin Prizes were part of the modesty formula 'whereby the vainglorious mechanisms of cult management were attributed to an independent panel of specialists, casting the leader himself as a passive or even reluctant beneficiary of spontaneous artistic celebration'.[151]

Although Stalin's modesty was best conveyed through the medium of words, his visual image was also contrived to depict traits of humility that may appear at odds with the effusive aggrandisement occurring in posters. Until 1943, when he accepted military rank, Stalin appeared in posters and in public in a plain military-style tunic or unadorned greatcoat, usually wearing workman's boots. This contrasted with portrayals of Lenin, who always appeared in suit and tie, and clearly as a member of the intelligentsia. Stalin was also frequently depicted with his hand in his jacket, in what the English-speaking world refers

---

148 *Vozhatyi* 14, 1939, p. 5, cited in Catriona Kelly, 'Riding the magic carpet: children and leader cult in the Stalin era', *The Slavic and East European Journal*, 49:2, 2005, pp. 199–224, p. 201.
149 Plamper contends that Stalin placed documents that demonstrated his personal modesty at the 'easy-to-reach upper levels' of the archives and that, on digging deeper into the archives, documents can be found suggesting Stalin's 'jealous control and expansion' of his cult (Plamper, *The Stalin cult*, p. 124).
150 Johnson, 'The Stalin Prize and the Soviet artist', p. 833.
151 Johnson, 'The Stalin Prize and the Soviet artist', p. 834.

to as the 'Napoleonic pose'. Stalin sometimes adopted this pose in media photographs, which suggests that perhaps this was habitual or comfortable for him. While portrait painters and poster artists may have been copying nature when presenting Stalin in this manner, the prevalence and deliberateness of this gesture in media in which the original image is easily altered and manipulated, suggest that it conveyed a specific meaning. Of the 389 posters in the research sample, 21 depict Stalin with the hand-in pose, spanning the years of his leadership from 1931 to 1951. Unlike in the English-speaking world, the gesture is not interpreted as 'Napoleonic' in Russia,[152] and it makes little intuitive sense for Stalin to copy a gesture associated with Napoleon. In fact, as Arline Meyer notes, the 'hand-in-waistcoat' pose is encountered with relentless frequency in 18th-century English portraiture, possibly both because it was a habitual stance of men of breeding and because of the influence of classical statuary. Meyer traces classical references to the 'hand withdrawn' back to the actor, orator, and founder of a school of rhetoric, Aeschines of Macedon (390–331 BC), who claimed that speaking with the arm outside the cloak was considered ill-mannered.[153] The gesture is discussed as a classical rhetorical gesture by John Bulwer in 1644[154] and by François Nivelon in 1737.[155] Nivelon states that the 'hand-in-waistcoat' pose signifies 'boldness tempered with modesty', and Bulwer notes that 'the hand restrained and kept in is an argument of modesty, and frugal pronunciation, a still and quiet action suitable to a mild and remiss declamation'.[156] Five of Stalin's appearances in posters in this pose involve Stalin depicted as a statue, and Stalin took pride in his mild, anti-oratorical mode of speech. A reading of this gesture that suggests 'boldness tempered with modesty' is in keeping with the persona created for Stalin in Soviet propaganda.

---

152 Several conversations that I had with Russians in 2013 revealed that none of them associated this pose with Napoleon. No one was able to assign it any clear meaning other than to suggest that it may be associated with military leadership. As Stalin was depicted in this pose long before he accepted military rank, and while the Warrior archetype was primarily associated with Kliment Voroshilov, it is unlikely that the gesture was meant to be interpreted in this way.
153 Arline Meyer, 'Re-dressing classical statuary: the eighteenth-century "hand-in-waistcoat" portrait', *The Art Bulletin*, 77, 1995, pp. 45–64.
154 See John Bulwer's double essay 'Chirologia, the natural language of the hand', and 'Chironomia, the art of manual rhetoric', in *Chirologia: or the naturall language of the hand. Composed of the speaking motions, and discoursing gestures thereof. Whereunto is added Chironomia: or, the art of manuall rhetoricke. Consisting of the naturall expressions, digested by art in the hand, as the chiefest instrument of eloquence*, London, Thomas Harper, 1644.
155 François Nivelon, *The rudiments of genteel behaviour*, 1737.
156 Meyer, 'Re-dressing classical statuary'.

Stalin's biography

The personality cult of Stalin is often seen as beginning in earnest with Stalin's 50th birthday celebrations on 21 December 1929.[157] This date is interesting because neither the date nor the year correspond with Stalin's real birthdate, which was 18 December 1878.[158] Thus, Stalin, for reasons of his own, chose to falsify his birthday, although all of his early records, such as those from the seminary, clearly show the 1878 date. By 1929 Stalin had a much firmer grip on the reins of power than he did in 1928. Perhaps 50th birthday celebrations and the cultic phenomena surrounding them were simply more politically expedient in 1929 than the previous year.[159] Such creative and expedient use of biographical data came to be a prominent feature of the Stalin era, although it should also be noted that many monarchs today have their birthdays publicly celebrated on a different date to their actual date of birth.

During Stalin's rule, universal education programs initiated by the Bolsheviks paid off with major improvements in literacy and cultural exposure of the general population. In literature, the genres of the novel and biography became immensely popular, with biography (or the biopic) forming a major genre of film. Novels showed an everyman following the path of enlightenment.[160] Biographies presented in microcosm through the titular figure the life and history of the Party. The popular 1934 film *Chapaev* was made about a real man, Vasilii Chapaev, and lay claim to historical truth. When Chapaev's family saw the film they protested that it bore little resemblance to actuality. Stalin was aware of this when he saw the film and made a

---

157 See Bonnell, *Iconography of power*, p. 156; Catriona Kelly, 'Riding the magic carpet: children and leader cult in the Stalin era', *The Slavic and East European Journal*, 49:2, 2005, pp. 199–224, p. 200; and Robert C. Tucker, 'The rise of Stalin's personality cult', *American Historical Review*, 84, 1979, pp. 347–66. Davies argues, however, that the praise heaped on Stalin at this time was an exception to the rule, with the focus typically being on anonymous collective leadership. She dates the emergence of the full-blown cult to 1933 (*Popular opinion in Stalin's Russia: terror, propaganda and dissent, 1934–1941*, Cambridge University Press, 1997, pp. 147–48).
158 6 December, old calendar. S. Sebag Montefiore, *Stalin*, p. 21; Brooks, *Thank you, Comrade Stalin!*, p. 60.
159 Jeffrey Brooks speculates that Stalin may have wanted to match the age of his 'arch-rival' Trotskii, or may have wished to 'elevate[d] himself in a way that would have been difficult a year earlier' (*Thank you, Comrade Stalin!*, p. 60).
160 For an extensive exploration of the socialist realist novel, see Katerina Clark, *The Soviet novel: history as ritual*, University of Chicago Press, 1981.

now famous comment afterwards: 'They're lying like eyewitnesses'. The directors of the film explained the higher notion of truth that was being served in their portrayal of Chapaev: 'having rejected narrow biography [*biografichnost'*], we were brought to a more complete realization of the true features of Chapaev through an entire artistic process. His son and daughter, having watched the film, recognized their father in it — only after several viewings!'[161]

A major motivating force for the creation of biographies of the leaders, especially Stalin, was the lack of knowledge of Party members about the identities and roles of their own leadership. This was regarded as a failing in propaganda work and even in the mid-1930s members were expelled from the Party on these grounds.[162] In 1939 a 16-page publication titled *In commemorating the sixtieth anniversary of J.V. Stalin: what to write about the life and activities of Comrade Stalin* was published to assist writers of birthday greetings to Stalin. The chapter headings provide an outline of the events considered important in the life of the *vozhd'*: 'The revolutionary decades of Comrade Stalin in the Caucasus', 'Comrade Stalin in the period of preparation and construction of the October Revolution', 'The heroic struggle of Comrade Stalin on the front of the Civil War', 'Stalin — the great organizer of the victory of socialism in our country', and 'Stalin — the great continuer of the teachings of Marx, Engels and Lenin'.[163] A similar guide for the writers of children's letters was published in a pedagogical journal.[164] These publications highlight the focus on a standardised and formulaic biography for didactic purposes.

Soviet writers attempted to produce a satisfactory biography of Stalin for several years. In the 1940s, Stalin believed that biography had a defined role to play in the education of the Soviet public. While cadres should now be educated in the scientific laws of Marxism–Leninism through a study of theory and ideology in the collected works of Lenin and Stalin, these were still too sophisticated for 'the masses', who were best served through the exemplary lives outlined

---

161 Evgeny Dobrenko, 'Creation myth and myth creation in Stalinist cinema', *Studies in Russian and Soviet Cinema*, 1:3, 2007, pp. 239–64, p. 248.
162 Davies, *Popular opinion in Stalin's Russia*, p. 168.
163 Bernice Glatzer Rosenthal, *New myth, new world: from Nietzsche to Stalinism*, Pennsylvania State University Press, 2002, p. 386.
164 Rosenthal, *New myth, new world*, p. 386.

in biography.¹⁶⁵ In 1946 Stalin asked that a new biography of Lenin be prepared: 'this is a proven way of helping the simple people begin their study of Marxism.'¹⁶⁶

The official version of Stalin's biography was published in 1947. It was largely myth. Once again, this approach to biography has historical precedents, most notably in the hagiographies of medieval saints in the Russian Orthodox Church. As Clark points out: 'The 1917 Revolution, the Civil War, and certain crucial moments in Stalin's life became a kind of canonized Great Time that conferred an exalted status on all who played a major part in them (World War II has since been added to the list).'¹⁶⁷ Indeed, as early as 1926, in a speech delivered at a welcoming committee in Tbilisi, Stalin described his life thus far as structured around *skitanii* (wandering)¹⁶⁸ and a series of three baptisms: the first was amongst the Tbilisi workers where he learned about practical work; the second was as a fighter amongst the workers of Baku between 1905 and 1907; and the third was in Leningrad amongst the Russian revolutionaries and involved the guidance of Lenin.¹⁶⁹ Catriona Kelly's research into the Stalin cult for children shows that the version of the cult aimed at children was not quintessentially different to that for adults and functioned through a 'trickle-down effect' through the Komsomol¹⁷⁰ and Pioneers.¹⁷¹ Children were encouraged to treat Stalin as a role model and his biography was essentially a condensed form of the hagiography for adults. Key points included Stalin's exemplary childhood, his study at the seminary, his work in the underground, his arrests and exiles, the first meeting with Lenin, his role in the Revolution and the Civil War, and his achievements as *vozhd'* — the

---

165 RGASPI, 558/11/1122/3-4, cited in Davies, in Apor et al., *The leader cult in communist dictatorships*, p. 36; RGASPI, 629/1/54/23-26, cited in Davies, in Apor et al., *The leader cult in communist dictatorships*, p. 37.
166 RGASPI, 629/1/54/23-26, cited in Davies, in Apor et al., *The leader cult in communist dictatorships,*, p. 37.
167 Clark, *The Soviet novel*, p. 40.
168 Stalin's use of the word *skitanii* (wandering) in talking of his period of prison and exile evokes, as Alfred Rieber points out, 'the secret underground and illegal monasteries of the Old Believers that sheltered religious wanderers' ('Stalin, man of the borderlands', *The American Historical Review*, 106:5, 2001, pp. 1651–91, p. 1673).
169 See Rieber, 'Stalin, man of the borderlands', p. 1673.
170 The All-Union Leninist Young Communist League (or VLKSM) for youth aged 14 to 28 years. It was originally formed in 1918 as the Russian Young Communist League, or RKSM.
171 The Vladimir Lenin All-Union Pioneer Organisation for children aged 10 to 14, founded in 1922 and dissolved in 1991. Pioneers wore red scarves and undertook activities similar to the scouts. Children under nine years old could join the Little Octobrists.

victory of socialism, the achievements of the Red Army and Soviet aviation, the 1936 constitution and the Stakhanovite movement.[172] In the *Short biography*, Stalin is even credited with saving Lenin's life, making him a true hero:

> It was Stalin who saved the precious life of Lenin for the Party, for the Soviet people and for humanity at large, by vigorously resisting the proposal of the traitors Kamenev, Rykov and Trotsky that Lenin should appear for trial before the courts of the counter-revolutionary Provisional Government.[173]

The biography crafted for Stalin in propaganda posters (and indeed in all other artforms) relates to Stalin's Bolshevik leader persona.[174] The man Dzhugashvili disappeared from view many years prior to Stalin's assumption of the leadership. As a member of the Bolshevik underground he adopted, among others, the pseudonym 'Koba', from a heroic and avenging character in the 1883 novel *The patricide* by Alexander Kazbegi. Some time later, possibly around 1910, he adopted the pseudonym 'Stalin', which derives from the Russian word *stal'* — steel. This latter persona was preserved throughout his leadership until his death in 1953.

In *Young Stalin*, Montefiore suggests that Stalin needed to create a falsified public persona because of his early involvement in 'the dirty business' of politics, including criminal activity in his underground work for the Bolshevik Party.[175] The often clumsy transparency of the fabrication of an alternate past has led to a common reactive tendency to dismiss as falsehood all claims that Stalin had achieved anything in his early Party days, which is as erroneous in one direction as the cultic claims are in the other. While the desire to muddy the waters of his Georgian past may have been one motivating factor behind the creation of Stalin's mythic biography, it can be argued that the formulaic structure of the created biography and the tenets of the

---

172 See Kelly, 'Riding the magic carpet', p. 201.
173 G.F. Alexandrov, M.R. Galaktionov, V.S. Kruzhkov, M.B. Mitin, V.D. Mochalov & P.N. Pospelov, *Joseph Stalin: a short biography*, Moscow, Foreign Languages Publishing House, 1947, p. 53.
174 A 2003 exhibition curated by Tatiana Kurmanovkaya at the Museum of Russian Contemporary History in Moscow bore the title *Stalin: man and symbol*.
175 Montefiore argues that Stalin's personal history had to remain hidden 'either because it was too gangsterish for a great, paternalistic statesman or because it was too Georgian for a Russian leader' (*Young Stalin*, New York, Alfred A. Knopf, 2007, p. xxvii).

socialist–realist method suggest that its primary purpose was didactic. It mattered little whether or not Stalin's image in propaganda had any but the scantest basis in reality. What did matter was that the persona of the leader could inspire, exhort, and provide security for the populace and, perhaps most important of all, that the huge unwieldy masses from a variety of ethnicities, classes, backgrounds, and levels of education, all harnessed their energies in the direction of unanimous, uniform goals.

Stalin and the enemy

The *raison d'être* of the vanguard socialist government is to fight and win class war, prior to the eventual withering away of the state apparatus.[176] By its very nature the legitimacy of the socialist government is predicated on the existence of an enemy. If the enemy disappears and one wishes to maintain power, an enemy must be invented. The Soviet Union was indeed born out of real conflict and struggle; was surrounded by hostile forces before, during and after the Great Patriotic War; and was under varying degrees of threat from the enemy within, the demonisation of which served its own propaganda purposes.[177] As anthropologist Philip Smith has observed, the symbolic coding of charismatic leadership hinges on binary codings and salvation narratives:

> images of 'evil' must be present in the forest of symbols surrounding each charismatic leader. There must be something for them to fight against, something from which their followers can be saved … . As a general rule of thumb, charismatic authority will attain its greatest force when images of evil are at their most threatening.[178]

---

176 Peter Lambert & Robert Mallett, 'Introduction: the heroisation–demonisation phenomenon in mass dictatorships', *Totalitarian Movements and Political Religions*, 8:3–4, 2007, pp. 453–63, p. 459.
177 Gill lists the following enemies of the people at the end of the 1920s: the Industrial Party, Right Opportunists, Trotskyists, skeptics about the first Five-Year Plan, spies, kulaks, priests, drunkards, bureaucrats, shirkers, wreckers, capitalists, former White Guardists and international capital (Gill, *Symbols and legitimacy in Soviet politics*, p. 96).
178 Philip Smith, 'Culture and charisma: outline of a theory', *Acta Sociologica*, 2000, 43, pp. 101–10, pp. 103–05.

THE PERSONALITY CULT OF STALIN IN SOVIET POSTERS, 1929–1953

The demonisation of opposition into the hated enemy — 'saboteurs, Swastika-bearing Russian Orthodox priests and even Leon Trotsky himself became the vilified demons of the Soviet cosmology, to be cast out and destroyed mercilessly'[179] — works on several levels. As historian David Hoffmann has noted, it may have arisen from the intrinsic mentality of Stalin and the other Party leaders, which had been shaped by the Revolution and Civil War and in which vanquishing opponents was literally a matter of life and death.[180] Stalin once said to Lev Kamenev: 'The greatest delight is to mark one's enemy, prepare everything, avenge oneself thoroughly and then go to sleep.'[181] Stalin was also quite pragmatic about the killing of large numbers of innocent people in order to make sure that the enemy was destroyed.[182] In a propaganda sense, at the most basic level, demonisation served to divide the population into 'us' and 'them', encouraging citizens to identify with people and values that belong to 'us', and reject alien values as belonging to 'them'. Abbott Gleason,[183] Victoria Bonnell,[184] and Iurii Lotman and Boris Uspenskii[185] all observe that polarisation is a particular and longstanding feature of Russian culture, both in the upper classes, and among the peasantry. In Soviet

---

179 Lambert & Mallett, 'Introduction', p. 460.
180 David L. Hoffmann, *Stalinist values: the cultural norms of Soviet modernity, 1917–1941*, New York, Ithaca, Cornell University Press, 2003, p. 182.
181 Quoted in Montefiore, *Stalin*, p. 235.
182 'If our cadres are weakly trained, this means that the state is at risk. Take the case of the followers of Bukharin. Their leaders, losing their roots among the people, began to cooperate with foreign intelligence. But besides their leaders, there was a mass following, and they were not all spies and intelligence agents. We could assume that ten–fifteen–twenty thousand and maybe more were Bukharin's people. We could consider that the same number or more were Trotsky's people. But were all these spies? Of course not. But what happened to them? They were people who could not accept the sharp turn to the collective farm; they could not fathom this change, because they were not politically trained, they did not know the laws of socialist and economic development ... For that reason we lost a part of our cadres, but we gained a huge cadre of workers, and we received new cadres and we won over the people to the collective farms and we won over the peasantry' (Stalin, quoted in Oleg Khlevniuk, Alexander Vatlin & Paul Gregory (eds), *Stenogrammy zasedanii Politburo TsKRKP(b) 1923–1938*, vol. 3, Moscow, Rosspen, 2007, p. 686).
183 Abbott (Tom) Gleason, 'Views and re-views: Soviet political posters then and now: essay', library.brown.edu/cds/Views_and_Reviews/essay.html (accessed 2 Nov. 2016).
184 Victoria Bonnell has an excellent chapter on Soviet demonology in propaganda under Lenin and Stalin in *Iconography of Power*, p. 187.
185 Iurii M. Lotman & Boris A. Uspenskii, 'Binary models in the dynamic of Russian culture (to the end of the 18th century)', in Iu. M. Lotman, Lidiia Ginzburg, Boris Andreevich Uspenskii, Alexander D. Nakhimovsky & Alice S. Nakhimovsky, *The semiotics of Russian cultural history: essays*, Ithaca, New York, Cornell University Press, 1985.

times, argues Gleason, under a dialectical Marxist ideology, binary oppositions between what was deemed 'ours' and 'not ours' were only intensified.[186]

Silke Satjukov and Rainer Gries note that a clear conception of both the hero and the demon is necessary to assist the individual in adopting the correct ideological stance under the various forms of class struggle.[187] From the beginning of the battle for succession after Lenin's death, Stalin presented his policies as being those of the Party, and those of his rivals as belonging to the 'factional opposition'.[188] First Trotskii was demonised. Even whilst under attack at the Thirteenth Party Congress in May 1924, Trotskii upheld the notion of Party unity, identifying himself as one of 'us'.[189] Later, Kamenev and Grigorii Zinoviev were portrayed as belonging to the Left opposition and, after this, Nikolai Bukharin and his followers were vilified as the Right opposition. Erik van Ree argues that Stalin saw the Party as an organic entity and had a 'mystical' view of Party unity that aimed at: 'the complete, psychological submersion of the individual party member in the larger collective.'[190] In 1928 Iurii Piatikov stated: 'We are a party of people who make the impossible possible ... and if the party demands it ... we will be able by an act of will to expel from our brains in twenty-four hours ideas that we have held for years. Yes, I will see black where I thought I saw white, because for me there is no life outside the party.'[191] Stalin shared with other Old Bolsheviks a view of the Party as being the central guiding ideological force in the journey towards communism, making factionalism, by definition,

---

186 Gleason, 'Views and re-views'.
187 S. Satjukov & R. Gries, 'Feindbilder des Sozializmus. Eine theoretische einführung', in S. Satjukov & R. Gries, *Unsere Feinde. Konstruktionen des Anderem im Sozialismus*, Leipzig, Leiziper Universitätsverlag, 2004.
188 Richard Lowenthal, 'The post-revolutionary phase in China and Russia', *Studies in Comparative Communism*, 16:3, 1983, pp. 191–201, p. 197.
189 'Comrades, none of us wants to be or can be right against the party. In the last analysis, the party is always right, because the party is the sole historical instrument that the working class possesses for the solution of its fundamental tasks ... . It is only possible to be right with the party and through it since history has not created any other way to determine the correct position' (L.D. Trotskii, *Thirteenth Congress of the All-Union Communist Party (Bolsheviks): stenographic report*, Moscow, State Press for Political Literature, 1936, pp. 158–59).
190 Erik van Ree, 'Stalin's organic theory of the party', *Russian Review*, 52:1, 1993, pp. 43–57, p. 43.
191 Quoted in Mikhail Heller & Aleksandr M. Nekrich, *Utopia in power, the history of the Soviet Union from 1917 to the present*, New York, Summit Books, 1986, p. 289. Piatikov, a former secretary of the Central Committee, was expelled by the Party for Trotskyist–Zinovievite leanings, but was reinstated in 1928 after renouncing Trotskyism. He was executed in 1937.

intolerable. Once discussion was over and a decision had been taken, all Party members must fall into line behind that decision and present a unified front to the world. Any dissent was seen as treacherous and the dissenter publicly labelled an 'enemy of the people'. In 1937, 200,000 people braved temperatures of −27°C in Red Square to hear the court's verdict in the show trials denouncing the opposition as followers of 'Judas–Trotskii'.[192]

Stalin was able to go further than merely situating himself on the side of morality and the correct path. Stalin's propaganda set him up as indispensable, because only he could identify the numerous enemies of the regime. Political scientist Jeremy Paltiel argues that this apparent ability became the mechanism by which all power came to reside in the person of Stalin. Where, prior to the purges, the Stalin image had symbolised the Party and the state, the destruction of the Party apparatus during the purges left only one authoritative certainty — Stalin himself.[193] One of the primary effects of the purges of the late 1930s was to strengthen the identification of citizens with the leader, and to increase hostility towards enemies. This occurred most overtly through publicity and propaganda that identified 'enemies of the people', put them on trial, found them guilty, and then punished or executed them. Not everyone, however, believed in the guilt of all of those put on trial, particularly as more and more of the population were devoured by the machinery of the purge, and people were asked to accept that a high proportion of the upper echelons of the Soviet hierarchy, including most of the Old Bolsheviks who had been responsible for the success of the Revolution, were traitors who had been actively working against the regime all along.[194] Kulagina rejected outright the notion that her husband and her father could possibly be guilty:

---

192 Montefiore, *Stalin*, p. 214.
193 Jeremy T. Paltiel, 'The cult of personality: some comparative reflections on political culture in Leninist regimes', *Studies in Comparative Communism*, 16:1–2, 1983, pp. 49–64, p. 63.
194 The memoirs of an Old Bolshevik, 'V.K.', are quoted by Roy Medvedev to illustrate the point that, although many did not believe in the guilt of all those accused during the show trials, some still supported the Terror on principle: 'Of course I never imagined that Bukharin and Trotsky were Gestapo agents or that they wanted to kill Lenin; moreover, it was clear to me Stalin never believed it either. But I considered the trials of 1937–38 to be a far-sighted political tactic, and thought that Stalin had done the right thing in resolving to discredit all forms of opposition once and for all in such grim fashion. After all, we were a besieged fortress; we had to close ranks; there was no room for doubts or uncertainty. Did all those theoretical controversies have any meaning for the "broad masses"? Most "ordinary people" could not even

the more time goes on, the stronger I believe that he [Klutsis] got caught up in an absurd moment when multitudes of other innocent people got caught up as well, if you think about it logically — surely it can't be that every third person in the Soviet Union is guilty — I know my father, I know my husband — I know them to be men of great honor, I know that Gustav would not stand even the least critical talk about our country, always tried to argue the opposite, I know how he worked, how he labored, how proud he was of all our achievements, I know how self-sacrificing he is, how truly honest — not just in word like many people who are now thriving.[195]

Recent work in the field of terror management theory[196] in psychology offers a potential explanation for the strengthening of support for the leadership despite the evident absurdity of many of the charges laid against purge victims. The extensive reach of the purges, like other acts of terror, is likely to have induced mortality salience in the Soviet population. That is, seeing so many people arrested, fearing footsteps in the night and the knock on the door, knowing that the penalty for being found guilty of treason was often execution, is likely to have reminded people of their own mortality. Experimental research by Florette Cohen and Sheldon Solomon, published in 2011, examines how political preferences are altered when existential concerns are aroused.[197] By priming subjects to become aware of their own mortality, sometimes subliminally, Cohen and Solomon established that mortality salience promotes support for charismatic leaders who are seen to share the subject's cultural world views and increases aggression against those who hold rival beliefs.[198]

---

see the difference between Left and Right ... Therefore all deviationists, all types of sceptics had to be portrayed as scoundrels so repulsive that others would recoil in horror; they would become total outcasts, hated and cursed by the people ... In prison I became an even more obstinate Stalinist than before ...' (*On Stalin and Stalinism*, Ellen de Kadt (trans.), Oxford University Press, 1979, pp. 107–08).
195 Kulagina's diary entry, cited in Tupitsyn, *Gustav Klutsis and Valentina Kulagina*, pp. 233–34.
196 A field of research in psychology, founded by Tom Pyszczynski, Jeff Greenberg and Sheldon Solomon in 1991, based on the writings of Ernest Becker in the 1970s, which suggests that 'existential concerns have a unique and potent effect on support for political candidates, voting intentions, and attitudes about domestic and foreign policy' (Florette Cohen & Sheldon Solomon, 'The politics of mortal terror', *Current Directions in Psychological Science*, 2011, 20:316, pp. 316–20, p. 316).
197 Cohen & Solomon, 'The politics of mortal terror', pp. 316–20.
198 Cohen & Solomon, 'The politics of mortal terror', p. 316.

An important component of the formula outlined by Cohen and Sheldon is that the charismatic leader shares the cultural world views of the citizens. Cultural world views are unlikely to be literally true, but are 'shared fictions' sustained by social consensus which 'minimize death anxiety by imbuing the world with order, meaning, and permanence and by providing a set of standards of behavior that, if satisfied, confer self-esteem and the promise of symbolic and/or literal immortality'.[199] The generation of shared cultural world views is very much the work of propaganda, which, as Nicholas O'Shaughnessy points out, 'does not necessarily ask for belief. It is an invitation to share a fantasy'.[200] The method of socialist realism was particularly conducive to creating a fantasised reality, while the saturation of Soviet public space with propaganda images illustrating the new communist reality provided an all-encompassing world view that was intricately entwined with the persona of Stalin. Alex Inkeles and Raymond Bauer provide evidence that the general mores and values of the Soviet leadership were shared by the general populace, with opposition arising only when these were not implemented in practice.[201] The simultaneous juxtaposition through news media and propaganda of Stalin's role in delivering all the benefits of outstanding Soviet achievements and a newly joyous life with the presence of pervasive threatening hostile forces all around, played on both overt and subconscious mechanisms to cement the identification of the people with their leader.

There is another way in which mortality salience was constantly invoked in Stalinist propaganda — the almost constant presence of Lenin. Throughout the years of his leadership, Stalin was consistently depicted alongside Lenin. Lenin's image held the potential for bolstering support for Stalin's leadership at the level of the unconscious mind because Lenin was dead, and was frequently depicted as 'dead'; that is, in apotheosised form. Posters such as those that urged 'Be as

---

199 Cohen & Solomon, 'The politics of mortal terror', pp. 316–17.
200 Nicholas J. O'Shaughnessy, 'The death and life of propaganda', *Journal of Public Affairs*, 12:1, 2012, pp. 29–38, p. 38.
201 'popular values do not clash with most of the values *implied* in the Soviet system itself. On the contrary, there is a general marked congruence between popular values and the goals the system purports to pursue' (Alex Inkeles & Raymond Augustine Bauer, *The Soviet citizen: daily life in a totalitarian regime*, Harvard University Press, 1959, cited in Davies, *Popular opinion in Stalin's Russia*, p. 185).

the great Lenin was'[202] or depicted Stalin delivering his elegiac oath[203] made it impossible to ignore human mortality, while at the same time promising salvation and redemption through following Lenin's teachings (as interpreted by Stalin), a powerful pairing of emotions with a long tradition in the church.

After the murder of Sergei Kirov in 1934, Stalin's image also served as a reminder of human mortality. Michael Smith argues that one of the many 'mantles' worn by Stalin, one which is often overlooked, is the mantle of 'martyr survivor' — 'the one who mourned, who suffered with the sadness of loss ... he was the one who literally carried the remains of his fallen comrades to their premature graves'.[204] Stalin was not only depicted in propaganda posters alongside the spirit of Lenin, but was also pictured in the press standing guard over Lenin's body and carrying Lenin's coffin to the crypt. Stalin as a mourner was to become a frequent theme in the newspapers. He appeared in *Pravda* as a pallbearer 14 times,[205] helping to bury Mikhail Frunze, Feliks Dzerzhinskii, Kirov, Gor'kii, Zhdanov[206] and, indeed, his own wife, Nadia. Kirov's murder led to the unravelling of a vast conspiracy that was to dominate the media for the next four years. The narrative to emerge from this act was that a wave of assassinations had been planned, with Kirov, Gor'kii and Valerian Kuibyshev successfully executed, while Stalin, Voroshilov, Molotov and Kaganovich were all assassins' targets. This imminent threat of death, which gave impetus to the purges, meant that Stalin's image continually invoked mortality salience, while his propaganda presented him as the means to salvation that would literally manifest in the deliverance of the communist utopia. Even without the overt use of Christian symbolism, Stalin's persona became increasingly Christlike, encapsulating in the one person both the potential for martyrdom and the promise of salvation.

---

202 Vasilii Elkin, 'Be as the great Lenin was', 1938 (Fig. 2.10); A.I. Madorskii, 'Be as the great Lenin was', 1938 (Fig. 2.11); A.I. Madorskii, 'Be as the great Lenin was', 1939 (Fig. 2.12). Discussed in greater detail below.
203 Vladimir Kaidalov, 'Departing from us, comrade. Lenin urged us to strengthen and extend the union republics. We swear to you, comrade. Lenin, that we will fulfil with honour your behest', 1940; Vladimir Kaidalov, 'Departing from us, comrade. Lenin urged us to strengthen and extend the union republics. We swear to you, comrade. Lenin, that we will fulfil with honour your behest', 1951.
204 Michael Smith, 'Stalin's martyrs: the tragic romance of the Russian Revolution', *Totalitarian Movements and Political Religions*, 4:1, 2003, pp. 95–126, p. 108.
205 Plamper, *The Stalin cult*, p. 42.
206 Smith, 'Stalin's martyrs', pp. 107–08.

Plamper conducted extensive research into the portrayal of Stalin in *Pravda* during his leadership and has noted that, in 1936, in preparation for the show trial of Kamenev and Zinoviev, a number of articles appeared on the theme of 'Stalin in danger', with titles like 'Take care of and guard Comrade Stalin', and 'Take care of your leaders like a military banner'.[207] In 1937 and 1938 there was a 'precipitous drop' in Stalin pictures and Plamper posits that this was most likely to avoid linking him with the purges although, whenever violence in politics increased, there was an increase in 'love and tenderness' towards Stalin. Stalin was also kept out of pictorial representations of the Molotov–Ribbentrop pact.[208] In fact, even in *samokritika* rituals, Stalin was never the focus of attention. He sat off to one side, rather than in the centre, and there were no portraits of him on display.[209]

Stalin was only occasionally depicted in posters alongside images of 'the enemy',[210] with most of these occurring during the Great Patriotic War. He was frequently depicted with heroes in the form of other celebrated leaders, Stakhanovites, Arctic explorers and record-breaking pilots, and workers and peasants leading everyday heroic lives. By separating Stalin's image from pictures of violence or the enemy, and reinforcing Stalin's heroic status through news articles and the attribution of great Soviet feats in aviation,[211] exploration and construction to Stalin's inspiration and intervention, the propaganda mechanism was able to clearly delineate 'us' from 'them', to outline the correct ideological stance for the citizen, to boost approval ratings of the leader through the subconscious mechanism of mortality salience, and to depict Stalin as indispensable to the nation as the only person capable of identifying the numerous enemies trying to destroy the socialist experiment.

---

207 Plamper, *The Stalin cult*, pp. 47–48.
208 Plamper, *The Stalin cult*, p. 48.
209 J. Arch. Getty, 'Samokritika rituals in the Stalinist Central Committee, 1933–1938', *Russian Review*, 58:1, 1999, pp. 49–70, p. 56.
210 See Chapter Four for a further exploration of this subject.
211 Jay Bergman argues that Stalin ensured that the timing of the first Moscow show trial was fixed to coincide with Valerii Pavlovich Chkalov's record-breaking flight in order that the two events could be juxtaposed in the media ('Valerii Chkalov: Soviet pilot as new Soviet man', *Journal of Contemporary History*, 33:1, 1998, pp. 135–52, p. 138).

The cult of Lenin

The cult of Lenin, which flourished after his death in 1924, served as a model for that of Stalin, while also coexisting with it.[212] By linking himself to Lenin, Stalin promoted his candidacy for leadership, and provided legitimacy for his leadership after he consolidated power in his own hands. The development of the Lenin cult was supremely important to Stalin, because the cult of Lenin could be used as a means by which what Andrew Spira calls the 'religious energy of the people' could be directed at the Party 'without appearing to direct it towards himself'.[213] Indeed, the primary initial *raison d'être* for the creation of the Lenin cult, as Lenin was increasingly forced out of political life due to his illness, was the transfer of charisma to the Party. When a few years later Stalin consolidated his leadership, the focus of the cult remained on the Party, however the Party itself came to be increasingly symbolised by the persona of Stalin. In many ways too, as Alice Mocanescu points out in her article on the cult of Nicolae Ceauşescu, Lenin's cult, attached as it was to someone who was already dead, provided an opportunity to test out the response of the population and their level of acceptance of certain solutions.[214] Eventually the propaganda saw Lenin and Stalin become merged into one hyphenated identity of Lenin–Stalin (somewhat reminiscent of the entity Marx–Engels), although Stalin also came to be celebrated as an extraordinary individual in his own right.

The process of deification of Lenin was a result of motivating factors from both 'above' and 'below' — that is, the adulation of Lenin derived from both the genuine feelings of grief experienced by the public at the loss of their charismatic leader, and the overt actions of the leadership to portray Lenin as immortal, and to place his persona outside the confines of time and space. The cult of Lenin had quasi-religious overtones. A personality cult began to grow around Lenin after he survived an assassination attempt by Fania Kaplan on 30 August 1918. Zinoviev used religious concepts in a speech he made about Lenin to the Petrograd Soviet on 6 September 1918, which was

---

212 Indeed, Lenin's cult persisted long after Stalin's cult was denounced and suppressed.
213 Andrew Spira, *The avant-garde icon: Russian avant-garde art and the icon painting tradition*, Aldershot, Lund Humphries/Ashgate, 2008, p. 200.
214 Alice Mocanescu, 'Practising immortality: schemes for conquering "time" during the Ceauşescu era', *Studies in Ethnicity and Nationalism*, 10:3, 2010, pp. 413–34, p. 414.

then published in an edition of 200,000: 'He is really the chosen one of millions. He is leader by the grace of God. He is the authentic figure of a leader such as is born once in 500 years ...'.[215] Editor of *Bednota* and director of Agitprop, Lev Sosnovskii, described Lenin as 'Christlike' in *Petrogradskaia Pravda* on 1 September 1918 and endowed Lenin with a Christlike dual nature, both man and god: 'Ilich is the mortal man and Lenin is the immortal leader and universal symbol,' whilst suggesting that the wounding of Lenin was akin to the voluntary sacrifice of a man who consciously made himself vulnerable.[216] The Central Committee issued a written statement on Lenin's death that was distributed in millions of copies:

> Lenin lives in the soul of every member of our party. Every member of our party is a particle of Lenin. Our entire communist family is a collective embodiment of Lenin. Lenin lives in the heart of every honest worker. Lenin lives in the heart of every poor peasant.[217]

Writing in 1926, Malevich anticipated the full potential of the cult of Lenin:

> The artists created a reality of Christ which did not exist ... They will also create a portrait of Lenin in the future ... In the image he has been transposed from material existence into sanctity, he has emerged from materialistic communism into spiritual religious communism, he rises above the materialistic plan of the action; like God he orders matter to take on a new order of relationships in his name.
>
> ... All production must serve the new church, for everything that is born now is born in Leninism, every step is born on the path of Leninism, Lenin is in everything, no step can be taken without Lenin, just as no goal can be reached without God.[218]

---

215 Zinoviev quoted in Bown, *Art under Stalin*, p. 29.
216 Lev Sosnovskii, cited in Bonnell, *Iconography of power*, p. 141; and Tumarkin, *Lenin lives!*, p. 84. On 27 January 1924, Sosnovskii wrote in tribute to Lenin in *Pravda* of 'two Lenins', one human, the other divine. It was the human Lenin who had died while the divine one would have eternal life ('Il'ich-Lenin', *Pravda*, 27 January 1924, p. 2, cited in Jay Bergman, 'The image of Jesus in the Russian revolutionary movement', *International Review of Social History*, 35, 1990, pp. 220–48, p. 244).
217 Quoted in Tumarkin, *Lenin lives!*, p. 148.
218 T. Andersen (ed.), *Malevich: the world as non-objectivity — unpublished writings, 1922–5*, vol. 3, Copenhagen, Borgens Forlag, 1976, pp. 320–21, p. 331.

Prior to Lenin's incapacitation and death, it was the writings of Marx and Engels that held the status of dogma for the Bolsheviks, while Lenin the revolutionary was seen primarily as a man of deed and action.[219] Lenin's teachings and writings became collectively known as 'Leninism', a term that appears to have been first used in January 1923,[220] when Lenin was already politically sidelined due to ill health. While effusive praise of Lenin had always occurred in the public arena, both Tumarkin and Robert Tucker mark the shift in emphasis in which Lenin's words were elevated to the status of dogma as beginning at the Twelfth Party Congress in April 1923 as part of the power struggles already occurring within the Politburo and Central Committee in Lenin's absence.[221] In Kamenev's opening speech at the congress he stated: 'We know only one antidote against any crisis, against any wrong decision: the teaching of Vladimir Ilyich.'[222]

In 1923 the Lenin Institute was established (opening formally in 1924) to collect and protect Lenin's writings. In his tribute to Lenin dated 22 January 1924, Trotskii articulated the question: 'How shall we continue?' and answered on behalf of the mourning nation, 'With the lamp of Leninism in our hands'.[223] Adherence, devotion and demonstrable loyalty to Leninism became the sole criterion for legitimacy as each of the key players in the power struggle sought to prove that he was the truest pupil and disciple of Lenin. In a 1931 interview with German biographer Emil Ludwig, Stalin described Lenin as a brave 'mountain eagle' who stood 'head and shoulders' above other socialist leaders.[224] In similar fashion to the stories of

---

219 For example, In March/April 1924, revolutionary writer Viktor Serge was still attempting to argue that Lenin was not primarily a writer: 'Lenin is no writer: he only writes out of necessity, exactly what is needed for daily activity, with no more regard for form or style than is absolutely necessary to attain his aim: to convince, to clarify, to refute, to dissuade, or to discredit, as the case may be. His style, bereft of any literary pretensions, has the simple straightforwardness of the spoken word ... Lenin, so intransigent a Marxist, is no dogmatist. For is not dogma always the resort of cowardly or weak spirits, incapable of adapting themselves to reality?' ('Lenin in 1917' (March/April 1924), originally published in French in *Faits et Documents*, no. 2, 1925, Al Richardson (trans.), www.marxists.org/archive/serge/1924/xx/lenin.html#f22 (accessed 16 Jul. 2012)).
220 Tumarkin, *Lenin lives!*, p. 120.
221 Tumarkin, *Lenin lives!*, p. 122; Robert C. Tucker. *Stalin as revolutionary, 1879–1929*, New York, W.W. Norton and Company, 1973.
222 Tucker, *Stalin as revolutionary*, p. 279.
223 Leon Trotskii, 'Lenin dead, Tiflis Station, January 22, 1924', John G. Wright (trans.), www.marxists.org/archive/trotsky/1924/01/lenin.htm (accessed 25 May 2012).
224 'When I've compared him with the other leaders of our party, it's always seemed to me that Lenin stood head and shoulders above his comrades-in-arms — Plekhanov, Martov, Aksel'rod

other child heroes, stories of Grandpa Lenin's exemplary youth were manufactured and packaged into an instructional narrative aimed at young children, encouraging them to study diligently and act with integrity. The image of a curly-headed young Lenin became the badge and banner of the Oktiabriata[225] and children pledged their loyalty under this banner.[226]

Not everyone fell under Lenin's spell. Writing in *Novaya Zhizn'*,[227] just weeks after the October Revolution, Gor'kii was scathing about Lenin's character and attitude to the masses, whilst also acknowledging some of his outstanding personal qualities.[228] Though supremely confident in the righteousness and necessity of the Bolshevik line, Lenin was always publicly and vehemently opposed to manifestations of hero-worship around his person. Old Bolshevik and contemporary of Lenin, Vladimir Bonch-Bruevich claimed that Lenin was appalled by what he read about himself in the newspapers after the 1918 assassination attempt.[229] Despite Lenin's objections to his cult, Tumarkin sees the Lenin persona created by the cult as being wholly in line with Lenin's

---

and others — and that in comparison with them, Lenin was not simply one of the leaders, but a leader of the highest sort, a mountain eagle who did not know fear in battle and who bravely led the party ahead along the unknown paths of the Russian revolutionary movement' (J.V. Stalin, 'Talk with the German author Emil Ludwig', 13 December 1931, Hari Kumar (trans.), in J.V. Stalin, *Works*, Moscow, Foreign Languages Publishing House, 1955, vol. 13, pp. 106–25, www.marxists.org/reference/archive/stalin/works/1931/dec/13.htm (accessed 12 Jul. 2012)).

225 The Oktiabriata was formed in 1923–24 for children born in 1917, and was a precursor to the Pioneers (the V.I. Lenin All-Union Pioneer Organisation). Dutiful and successful children were expected to progress through the Oktiabriata to the Pioneers and then onto the Komsomol, before becoming adult Party members.

226 'I, a young pioneer of the Soviet Union, in the presence of my comrades solemnly promise to love my Soviet Motherland passionately, and to live, learn and struggle as the great Lenin bade us and as the Communist Party teaches us' (Pioneers' Promise quoted at www.pwhce.org/doc1rus.html (accessed 18 Jul. 2012)).

227 *New Life*.

228 'Lenin himself, of course, is a man of exceptional strength. For twenty-five years he stood in the front rank of those who fought for the triumph of socialism. He is one of the most prominent and striking figures of international social democracy; a man of talent, he possesses all the qualities of a "leader" and also the lack of morality necessary for this role, as well as an utterly pitiless attitude, worthy of a nobleman, toward the lives of the popular masses ... he considers himself justified in performing with the Russian people a cruel experiment which is doomed to failure beforehand' (Maxim Gorky, '"Untimely thoughts"', *Novaya Zhizn*, 177, November 10, 1917', *Untimely thoughts: essays on revolution, culture and the Bolsheviks, 1917–18*, Herman Ermolaev (trans.), New York, Paul S. Eriksson, Inc, 1968, p. 88).

229 Bonch-Bruevich quoted Lenin: 'It is shameful to read ... they exaggerate everything, call me a genius, some kind of special person ... All our lives we have waged an ideological struggle against the glorification of the personality, of the individual; long ago we settled the problem of heroes. And suddenly here again is a glorification of the individual!' (quoted in Tumarkin, *Lenin lives!*, p. 90).

view of himself: 'The object of his cult — an immortal Lenin who personifies the Communist Party and is the author of the guiding line to socialism — is the reflection of Lenin's conception of himself evident in his writings, in the organization of the party he founded and led, and in his style of leadership.'[230] Lenin's stance of public modesty and asceticism, and disavowals of the excesses of his cult, were later adopted by Stalin in relation to his own cult, and may form part of the perceived correct persona for an eminent Bolshevik leader.

Establishing lineage

The actions that were taken to immortalise Lenin after his death can be seen as a key part of the strategy employed by the leadership to legitimate the Bolshevik Party by demonstrating continuity with Lenin's leadership. After Lenin's death, there was no clear charismatic candidate to take his place. Trotskii appeared to many to be the most likely candidate to seize Lenin's mantle, but he was ill and far away from Moscow when Lenin died, and was evidently tricked by Stalin's faction into missing Lenin's funeral.[231]

Within the context of the struggle for succession that occurred after Lenin's death, the personality cult of Lenin became a vehicle to power and legitimacy for any candidate who could successfully prove his indisputable lineage to the man-god. Tucker makes the purpose of this strategy clear: 'Stalin followed the strategy of cult building via the assertion of Lenin's infallibility. By making the party's previous *vozhd'* an iconographic figure beyond criticism, Stalin ... implicitly nominated the successor-*vozhd'* for similar treatment.'[232]

Although Stalin certainly made use of the Lenin cult, both as a model for his own cultic rituals and as a means to promote his leadership, research in the Soviet archives by Benno Ennker[233] has established that, contrary to claims by historians like Pomper, Tumarkin and

---

230 Tumarkin, *Lenin lives!*, p. 25.
231 Leon Trotsky, 'Chapter xlv: Lenin's death and the shift of power', *My life*, www.marxists.org/archive/trotsky/1930/mylife/ch41.htm (accessed 25 May 2012).
232 R.C. Tucker, *Stalin in power: the Revolution from above, 1928–1941*, New York, W.W. Norton & Company, 1992, p. 154.
233 Benno Ennker, *Die Anfänge des Leninkults in der Sowjetunion*, Cologne, Böhlau, 1997, pp. 315–19.

Tucker, Stalin was not directly involved in the creation of the cult of Lenin. The Commission for the Immortalisation of the Memory of V.I. Lenin was headed by Molotov and had Voroshilov as a member. Both were close comrades of Stalin, and Voroshilov was head of the Red Army, a patron of painting in general and of the artists Isaak Brodskii and Evgeni Katsman in particular, and was thus centrally involved in the generation of first the Lenin cult and then the cult of Stalin.[234] Once Stalin had consolidated his leadership after the battle for succession, his propaganda built on the cult of Lenin and it was certainly in Stalin's best interests to allow the cult of Lenin to flourish.

The appeal to an established lineage is a phenomenon that occurs throughout the history of charismatic leadership, and is often perpetrated through the use of a variety of artistic media. The 'logo' of Darius the Great, king of the Persian Achaemenid Empire, in which he was depicted as an archer, was used by his successors for generations after his death, as was Alexander the Great's portrait on coinage. Caesar Augustus linked himself firmly to the deified Julius Caesar by fostering the cult and promoting the apotheosis of Julius Caesar. Maximilian I asserted a visual and genealogical lineage from the Caesars, as well as Constantine, the Trojans, the Merovingians, and Noah, as can be seen in the monumental woodcut, *The triumphal arch* by Albrecht Dürer;[235] and Napoleon I robed himself in the regalia of a Roman emperor in Jean-Auguste-Dominique Ingres' painting *Napoleon on his imperial throne*.[236] Napoleon, like Stalin and the other Kremlin contenders, could not claim direct or blood lineage to great figures from the past. Instead, Napoleon had to establish an ideological lineage. One of the ways in which Napoleon achieved this was by using a high profile venue, the Denon wing of the Louvre Museum, and the power of art to visually link his own image to St Louis, Francois I, and Louis XIV, in the museum that was renamed at this time the Musée Napoleon.[237]

---

234 Plamper, *The Stalin cult*, p. 24.
235 1517, woodblock print, 295 cm x 357 cm.
236 1806, Musée du Louvre, Paris.
237 See Christopher Prendergast, *Napoleon and history painting: Antoine-Jean Gros's La Bataille d'Eylau*, Oxford, Clarendon Press, 1997, p. 2.

Stalin, who had originally been a favourite of Lenin's, had somewhat fallen out of favour shortly before Lenin's death,[238] and Lenin had expressed concerns regarding the suitability of Stalin's personal qualities for the role of leader in what has come to be known as 'Lenin's testament', but was really just one of several letters to the Central Committee by which Lenin attempted to continue to participate in political life from his sickbed.[239] Lenin's judgments about Stalin and, indeed, some damning testimony about Trotskii, were held back from the Party for four months after his death. Once they were disclosed at a plenary session of the Central Committee in May 1924, it was decided to suppress the documents and not disclose them publicly. Zinoviev proposed that Stalin remain in the leadership position and was quickly supported by Kamenev, while Trotskii remained silent.[240] It was thus known amongst the inner circle of the Party that Stalin had not been endorsed for succession by Lenin, although nor had any other candidate received full positive support.[241] After Lenin's death, it was to take several years of political manoeuvring before Stalin was to emerge as his successor.

---

238 Stalin spoke rudely to Lenin's wife Nadezhda Krupskaia and, also, along with Sergo Ordzhonikidze, alienated some of the Caucasian Bolsheviks through his ill-mannered and rough treatment of them.
239 'Comrade Stalin, having become Secretary-General, has unlimited authority concentrated in his hands, and I am not sure whether he will always be capable of using that authority with sufficient caution ... Stalin is too rude and this defect, although quite tolerable in our midst and in dealing among us Communists, becomes intolerable in a Secretary-General. That is why I suggest that the comrades think about a way of removing Stalin from that post and appointing another man in his stead' (Vladimir Ili'ich Lenin, 'Letter to the Congress', 1922, www.marxists.org/archive/lenin/works/1922/dec/testamnt/congress.htm (accessed 1 Sep. 2011)).
240 'Comrades, the last wish of Ilyich, every word of Ilyich, is without doubt law in our eyes. More than once we have vowed to fulfil everything which the dying Ilyich recommended us to do. You know well that we shall keep that promise ... But we are happy to say that on one point Lenin's fears have not proved well founded. I mean the point about our general secretary. You have all been witnesses of our work together in the last few months; and, like myself, you have been happy to confirm that Ilyich's fears have not been realised' (Zinoviev, quoted in Tony Cliff, 'The campaign against Trotsky', *Trotsky: fighting the rising Stalinist bureaucracy 1923–1927*, www.marxists.org/archive/cliff/works/1991/trotsky3/02-campaign.html (accessed 13 Nov. 2013)).
241 Tumarkin sees Lenin's 'testament' as an indication of the extent to which Lenin identified himself with the Party and the regime, so that 'in fact the new institutions were fitted so completely to Lenin's leadership that they seemed a direct extension of his person'. She believes that Lenin wished, whether consciously or not, to sabotage the possibility of his replacement: 'He simply could not conceive of his regime functioning without him and was unable to envision himself incapable of continuing concentrated work' (*Lenin lives!*, p. 59).

Stalin gained control of the Politburo at the Fifteenth Party Congress on 18 December 1927. Stalin, like leaders stretching back for more than 2000 years before him, demonstrated that not only had he been a close companion and confidant of Lenin, but also that he had always supported his political positions and was a devoted adherent to his dogma: 'As for myself, I am just a pupil of Lenin's, and the aim of my life is to be a worthy pupil of his.'[242]

One of the ways in which Stalin sought to promote his candidacy as a successor to Lenin was to establish himself as one of the interpreters of Leninism. It was not enough merely to accumulate power through strategic associations, convenient staff appointments and Machiavellian manoeuvrings. Stalin needed to make a significant contribution to Marxist ideology and to gain credentials as a Party theoretician. In 1924 Stalin gave a series of lectures at the Sverdlov University, which were then published as the book *The foundations of Leninism*. In this ambitious book Stalin attempted to comprehensively systematise Lenin's teachings across a broad spectrum of subject areas, supporting his assertions with large numbers of illustrative quotes from Lenin. While other members of the Party leadership delivered talks and papers on aspects of Leninism, none had attempted such comprehensive coverage, and Stalin's book became the most influential writing on Leninism at the time.[243]

One of the primary ways in which Stalin publicly illustrated his closeness to Lenin, was by ensuring that his image was visually linked with that of Lenin.[244] A large number of political posters that feature the image of Stalin, juxtapose this image with the image of Lenin. This

---

242 Stalin, 'Talk with the German author Emil Ludwig'.
243 Trotskii took exception to this approach, claiming that dogmatism was contrary to Lenin's style, which was flexible and responsive to circumstances: 'Lenin cannot be chopped up into quotations suited for every possible case, because for Lenin the formula never stands higher than the reality; it is always the tool that makes it possible to grasp the reality and to dominate it. It would not be hard to find in Lenin dozens and hundreds of passages which, formally speaking, seem to be contradictory. But what must be seen is not the formal relationship of one passage to another, but the real relationship of each of them to the concrete reality in which the formula was introduced as a lever. The Leninist truth is always concrete!' (Leon Trotsky, 'Tradition and revolutionary policy', *The new course*, December 1923, www.marxists.org/archive/trotsky/1923/newcourse/ch05.htm (accessed 26 Sep. 2012)).
244 Stalin's propaganda apparatus went as far as cutting and pasting photographs and commissioning paintings showing Stalin and Lenin together on occasions where they had not been together in order to promote this idea of Stalin's lineage. Stalin was also depicted in fake historical scenes as standing, speaking and pointing while Lenin listens. See Brooks, *Thank you, Comrade Stalin!*, p. 61.

2. THE RISE OF THE STALIN PERSONALITY CULT

occurs in a number of ways throughout the years of Stalin's leadership and subtle variations in the way in which this was done reflect the evolution of the Stalin cult over time. Of the 389 posters comprising my sample of posters with images of Stalin, he appears with an image of Lenin in 138 posters — a little over one-third of them. The first posters I have located in which Stalin appears with Lenin are both from 1930. One is a poster promoting the value of political education with the title 'Komsomol political education system mid-Volga organisation V.L.K.S.M for 1930–31' (Fig. 2.1). Lenin and Stalin appear as equals on either side of the poster, outlined in a sacral red Bolshevik aura although, as a full-length figure, Lenin is larger and therefore more prominent than the smaller bust of Stalin. Both men are quoted, along with Engels, and their authoritative texts are depicted around the page. A number of textboxes of various shapes and sizes outline available circles and schools for the self-education of youth.

The other poster of 1930 is a well-known poster by Klutsis in which Stalin's head is only half visible and literally in Lenin's shadow. The heads of the two leaders dwarf the diagonally arranged scenes of construction. The strong diagonals and vivid reds against black-and-white suggest movement and determination. 'Under the Lenin banner for socialist construction' (Fig. 2.2) is the first of Klutsis's posters to include Stalin, but it is Lenin, already dead for six years, who is seen to be at the forefront of the movement towards construction and industrial expansion. Stalin appears behind, but literally merged, with Lenin and the overt message is that Stalin, the disciple of the great master, is emerging as the new 'Lenin of today'. In her examination of mythopoetic elements in memories of Stalin, Natalia Skradol posits that the transfer of special characteristics from one great man to his successor can only be accomplished when there is a moment of physical contact between the two:

> allegorised either as an act of midwifery on the part of Stalin, or as a smooth continuation of a most intimate co-existence with each man being an extension of the other, punctuated by death. Physical contact is indispensable for the sacred royal unction ritual, as a figure endowed with divine authority performs the marking of the new ruler.[245]

---

[245] Natalia Skradol, 'Remembering Stalin: mythopoetic elements in memories of the Soviet dictator', *Totalitarian Movements and Political Religions*, 2009, 10:1, pp. 19–41, p. 34.

By merging Lenin and Stalin into one conjoined face, Klutsis employs mythic symbolism to denote the transfer of power and conferring of legitimacy from Lenin to Stalin.[246]

Klutsis had been a member of the Latvian rifle guard, which formed Lenin's personal bodyguard during the days of the October Revolution, and thus witnessed Lenin's leadership at close range. He had a strong personal allegiance to Lenin[247] and was fully committed to employing his artistic talent in service of the goals of the regime,[248] securing many commissions for posters during the early to mid-1930s. One is tempted to speculate that, by placing Stalin so deeply in Lenin's shadow, Klutsis was asserting the unique qualities of Lenin as Bolshevik leader. Weight is given to this interpretation by Margarita Tupitsyn's assertions that the exaggerated claims made in propaganda for Stalin's 50th birthday celebrations[249] would have 'infringed on Klutsis's consciousness' due to his personal experiences with Lenin.[250] It is interesting to note that, at some time between 21 September 1930 and 31 August 1931, Klutsis was expelled from the Party, accused of not paying member's dues for five months, of distancing himself from the Party's work, and of exhibiting 'political illiteracy'. After repenting his mistakes, Klutsis was immediately reinstated.[251]

---

246 In Chiaureli's 1946 movie *Klyatva* (*The oath*), Lenin's spirit is transferred to Stalin while he sits on a park bench in Gor'kii. The movie can be viewed at www.youtube.com/watch?v=-dlP5g_UTrY.
247 In her monogram on Klutsis and Kulagina, Margarita Tupitsyn notes that Klutsis's experiments in applying formalist methodology to socio-political iconography always included an image of Lenin, as he was the figure that Klutsis most admired (*Gustav Klutsis and Valentina Kulagina*, p. 19).
248 In his autobiography, Klutsis summed up his role as an artist of the revolution: 'My task was to make the revolutionary struggle of the working class and Soviet reality the contents of my creative output, converting it into artistic images comprehensible to the masses [...] Before me was the challenge to transform the poster, the book, the illustration, the postcard into mass conductors of Party slogans' (quoted in Christina Lodder, 'The experiments at the Vkhutemas School', in Ferré, *Red cavalry*, p. 168).
249 These included claims that Stalin was 'the Great Leader — the organizer of the October Revolution, the creator of the Red Army, and distinguished military commander ... leader of the world proletariat, and the great strategist of the Five-Year Plan' (Mikhail Geller & Aleksandr M. Nekrich, *Utopiia u vlasti: Istoriia Sovetskogo Soiuza s 1917 goda do nashikh dnei*, London, Overseas Publication Interchange, 1982, p. 246).
250 See Tupitsyn, *Gustav Klutsis and Valentina Kulagina*, p. 61.
251 Tupitsyn, *Gustav Klutsis and Valentina Kulagina*, p. 188. Klutsis was arrested and executed in 1938 due to his 'alleged participation, beginning in 1936, in the Latvian fascist-nationalist organization, operating at the time in Moscow'. Prometheus, a Latvian organisation, was established in Moscow in 1923 and shut down by government decree in 1937 (Tupitsyn, *Gustav Klutsis and Valentina Kulagina*, p. 15). It is worth noting, however, that around the time of

2. THE RISE OF THE STALIN PERSONALITY CULT

Despite fully consolidating his leadership in 1929, Stalin did not yet have a high public profile. Forced collectivisation was unpopular and had disastrous consequences. Food was rationed, millions of peasants died in the famine of 1930–33 and, as Jeffrey Brooks points out, 1933 was the decade's worst year for 'excess deaths' (the euphemism for murder and famine),[252] and a year in which Moscow experienced a water shortage.[253] Stalin's low public profile may have been due to the lack of good news to spread to the population and an attempt to dissociate him from negative news.[254] Until 1934, Stalin appeared with Lenin in between a quarter and a third of Stalin posters. Lenin was usually depicted in an apotheosised form, by providing inspiration on a banner, as in Deni's 1931 'With the banner of Lenin we were victorious in the battle for the October revolution …' (Fig. 2.3), or as an outlined head, this time alongside that of Marx, in A.M. Rumiantsev's 1931 'Shock work at the machine is combined with the study of Marxist-Leninist theory' (Fig. 2.4). Lenin was also sometimes shown as 'solid' and substantial, sometimes accompanied by his texts and, in a 1932 poster by Klutsis, 'October to the world',[255] as the great teacher of Stalin, showing him the way forward.

In 1933 there was a sudden leap in the number of images of Stalin in posters, coinciding with an increase in his appearances in *Pravda*. On 7 November 1933, foreign correspondent Eugene Lyons walked down Gork'ii Street in Moscow, counting the portrait posters of Lenin and Stalin as he went. Images of Stalin outnumbered images of Lenin 103 to 58.[256] The posters of this year presented Stalin as a leader in his own right although, in most cases, his image was still differentiated

---

Klutsis's arrest, *Pravda* attacked photomontage as one of Izogiz's 'serious defects', and other photomontage practitioners were being arrested, including the director of Izogiz, Boris Malkin (Wolf, *Koretsky*, p. 5).
252 Jeffrey Brooks, 'Socialist realism in *Pravda*: read all about it!', *Slavic Review*, 53:4, 1994, pp. 973–91, p. 977.
253 John E. Bowlt, 'Stalin as Isis and Ra: socialist realism and the art of design', *The Journal of Decorative and Propaganda Arts*, no. 24, *Design, culture, identity: the Wolfsonian Collection*, 2002, pp. 34–63, p. 54.
254 Plamper argues that, as Stalin had controlled the media since at least 1927, the choice to keep a low profile and minimise his cult was his own (*The Stalin cult*, p. 29).
255 For an image, see www.artpoisk.info/artist/klucis_gustav_gustavovich_1895/k_mirovomu_oktyabryu.
256 Eugene Lyons, *Moscow carousel*, New York, Alfred A. Knopf, 1935, pp. 140–41. It must be borne in mind that this figure relates to the display of images, not the production of posters, and evidence from the current sample suggests that Stalin's appearances with Lenin in posters maintained the same proportion of the total as in previous years.

from that of Lenin by grounding him in the reality of the current time, or sketching him tonally or in flesh tones. Lenin was apotheosised by being sketched in faint outline, by appearing as a statue, or by being shown in silhouette.

The idea of the banner of Lenin[257] came to prominence, with Stalin invoking the victorious and inspirational banner of Lenin in three posters of 1933, all of which featured the concluding quotation from Stalin's lengthy and detailed political report to the Sixteenth Congress of the VKP(b) on 27 June 1930.[258] Two of the best known names in Soviet graphic art, Klutsis and Deni, were contracted to produce posters on this theme, while the third, Iraklii Toidze, was in the early years of a highly successful career in political poster art. Deni's poster (Fig. 2.5) features sketches of the head of Lenin, and head and neck of Stalin, almost equal in size, on either side of a radio transmitter that broadcasts the words 'Long live the proletariat revolution of the whole world', set against a plain backdrop. Lenin's head, sketched in faint tones, seems to float in the picture plane, while Stalin, anchored by his neck and collar and sketched in darker tones, casts a shadow and appears more solid. Although it is Lenin's inspiration that is invoked in the text, Stalin invokes it through his quotation, as the truest disciple and interpreter of Leninism.

Klutsis' poster on the same theme (Fig. 2.6) is dominated by the large curve of a red banner that hovers over the Soviet leaders.[259] Lenin looms large and monolithic, cast in stone in front of the banner and behind Stalin, who is larger than the other figures. While Stalin is singled out as worthy of extra attention, the poster makes clear that his firm foundation is Leninism. Toidze's[260] poster (Fig. 2.7) juxtaposes the present and the past with Stalin adopting a static hand-in pose behind a red podium that forms a wedge in the bottom right corner of the poster. Arrayed behind him are the Soviet people, male and

---

257 To be discussed in greater detail later in this chapter.
258 'With the banner of Lenin we were victorious in the battle for the October Revolution./ With the banner of Lenin we were victorious in attaining decisive achievements in the struggle to build socialism. / With the same banner we will be victorious in our proletarian revolution throughout the world. / Long live Leninism!' This text appears on propaganda posters from as early as 1931.
259 Stalin, Molotov, Kaganovich, Voroshilov, Ordzhonikidze, Mikhail Kalinin, Kirov, Kuibyshev, Stanislav Kossior and Mikoian.
260 The publishing details on the poster give Toidze's family name as 'Taidze', however, Toidze's signature is printed on the bottom right of the poster and it can thus be safely attributed to him.

female, of various nationalities and in the garb of various occupations, looking up and ahead and smiling. Behind them are three banners and behind these are two historical scenes — the storming of the Winter Palace with Lenin atop the turret of a tank in iconic pose, urging the revolutionaries forward; and a smaller scene with a younger Stalin, mimicking Lenin's pose, speaking at the Sixth Party Congress of August 1917 in Petrograd.[261] Stalin and Lenin are portrayed by Toidze as joint leaders of the Revolution, with Lenin taking precedence, while Stalin stands alone and dominates the poster as the leader of today.

Between 1934 and 1936, the general tendency to treat the images of Stalin and Lenin differently continued, using techniques such as placing Lenin on a banner,[262] on a poster on the wall,[263] or as a statue,[264] while Stalin is situated on the ground, sometimes amongst people, and more corporeal in appearance.[265] Interestingly, while in 1934 more than half of the few posters produced containing an image of Stalin also contained an image of Lenin, in 1935 there were no posters that I have located where Stalin and Lenin appear together. In this year Stalin appeared with Kaganovich in celebration of the opening of the Metro;[266] with Voroshilov in celebration of the Red Army,[267] aviation

---

261 This significant congress was held semi-legally between the February and October revolutions. Lenin was in exile and unable to attend, and Stalin delivered the Political Report on behalf of the Bolshevik Party.
262 See Viktor Deni & Nikolai Dolgorukov, uncaptioned poster, 1934 and Mizin 'The Leninist Komsomol was and still is the young reserve of our revolution', 1934.
263 See Iraklii Toidze, 'Under the banner of Lenin, under the leadership of Stalin — forward to the victory of communism!', 1936.
264 See I.V. Stebaev & G. Logvin, 'XV years of the LKSMU: The Leninskii Komsomol was and remains a young reserve for our revolution', (Ukrainian) 1934 and K.V. Zotov, 'We're growing up under Lenin and Stalin's banner!', 1934.
265 The sole exception to this is a poster by Deni, who often employed sketched portraits rather than photographs in his work. Both Stalin and Lenin are sketched in similar style, however Lenin, on the left of the poster, is clearly associated with 1917 and an image of the past. Lenin points to the progress made under Stalin on the right of the poster, who is associated with socialist construction taking place in 1934. Viktor Deni, '1917–1934 raise higher the banner of Lenin — it carries us to victory!', 1934.
266 See Viktor Deni & Nikolai Dologorukov, 'We've got a Metro!', 1935.
267 See Gustav Klutsis, 'Long live the Workers' and Peasants' Red Army, the loyal guards of the Soviet borders!', 1935.

and the Motherland;[268] with Aleksei Stakhanov;[269] and with the Politburo Central Committee.[270] In 1936 Stalin was also often featured with other members of the Politburo.[271]

Bernice Rosenthal divides the Stalin cult into three distinct periods. In the first period, until 1933, Stalin used the Lenin cult to position himself as Lenin's heir; in the second period, between 1933 and 1936, Stalin elevated himself above the Party; and, it is only in the final stage, from 1936 to 1953, that Stalin was spoken of in superhuman terms.[272] Close examination of the propaganda posters of the time lends support to much of this theory. It is argued here, however, that Stalin took pains throughout the entire period of his leadership to emphasise his role as Lenin's heir. Before 1933, he was not consistently distinguished from his Politburo colleagues, except on the occasion of his 50th birthday. From 1933 onward, Stalin was increasingly singled out for special accolades, although he still often appeared alongside Politburo colleagues. During these years, when Stalin appeared with Lenin, they usually inhabited different realms, Stalin being earthbound, while Lenin was presented in apotheosised form. It was only in 1936 that Stalin was referred to in superhuman terms and, from 1937, posters evidence a change in the earlier tendency to treat the images of Stalin and Lenin differently. From this time, Stalin frequently appeared without Lenin, but when they did appear together, they were often (although not always) treated similarly — for example, Efim Pernikov's 'The Soviet Constitution is the only truly democratic constitution in the world' in which both men's images are carried as processional banners, although Stalin's banner is much larger with a laudatory

---

268 See Gustav Klutsis, 'Long live our happy socialist motherland. Long live our beloved great Stalin!', 1935.
269 See A. Reznichenko, 'The Stakhanovite movement ...', 1935.
270 See Gustav Klutsis, 'Politburo CC VKP(b),' 1935.
271 See Nikolai Dolgorukov, 'Swell the ranks of the Stakhanovites', 1936; G. Klutsis, 'Long live the Stalinist Order of Heroes and Stakhanovites!', 1936 (Fig. 4.63); and, Genrikh Futerfas, 'Stalinists! Extend the front of the Stakhanovite movement!', 1936 (Fig. 3.27).
272 Rosenthal, *New myth, new world*, p. 374.

2. THE RISE OF THE STALIN PERSONALITY CULT

caption. In their 1937 posters both Stenberg (Fig. 2.8)[273] and Galina Shubina[274] place Lenin and Stalin on a large red banner and treat the images of each in identical fashion.[275]

One of the most interesting pairings of Lenin and Stalin of 1937, and one which provides a partial exception to the above proposition, occurs in Toidze's '"I am pleased and happy to know how our people fought and how they have achieved a world-historic victory. I am pleased and happy to know that the blood freely shed by our people, was not in vain, that it has produced results!" I. Stalin'.[276] The top half of the poster deals with the present. Stalin stands at a raised podium in front of a banner with a bas-relief of Lenin's head enclosed in a medallion. Below Stalin is a crowd of citizens, all paying tribute, including a young child — symbol of the new nation; an old man holding a bound copy of the 1936 Stalin constitution; an aviator; and, in the centre, elevated above the others but below Stalin, is the Rodina, symbol of the motherland, bearing aloft a cornucopia of harvest. Stalin reciprocates the tribute paid to him by applauding the crowd.[277] 1937 is depicted as a year of success and abundance, and Lenin appears as a kind of Soviet saint or deity whose presence confers approval upon the scene below.

The middle of the poster consists of a broad red text box containing the poster caption, which is a quotation from Stalin from the 'Report on the draft constitution of the U.S.S.R.'[278] The bottom of the poster depicts a scene from the Bolsheviks' mythic past. Lenin and a younger Stalin stand side by side, towering over, but separated from, the troops rushing into action during the Civil War. While the scene at the top is static and the red banner does not move, all but Lenin and Stalin are in motion in the scene below, cavalry surging forward and the

---

273 No initial or first name recorded on the poster. Stenberg, 'Long live the great party of Lenin-Stalin — leader and organiser of the victorious building of socialism!', 1937.
274 Galina Shubina, 'Long live the first of May!', 1937.
275 Coinciding with this change in the way in which Lenin and Stalin were depicted together was the release of the film *Lenin in October*, which depicts Stalin by Lenin's side, providing counsel on his every move. See Dawn Ades, *Art and power: Europe under the dictators 1930–45*, London, Thames and Hudson in association with Hayward Gallery, 1995, p. 251.
276 See redavantgarde.com/en/collection/show-collection/1431--i-am-pleased-and-happy-to-know-what-our-people-fought-for-and-how-they-achieved-world-historic-victory-pleasant-and-happy-to-know-that-the-blood-profusely-shed-by-our-people-was-not-in-vain-that-it-had-produced-results-stalin.html?authorId=197.
277 See Chapter Three for a discussion of gratitude, obligation and reciprocity.
278 Delivered at the Extraordinary Eighth Congress of Soviets of the U.S.S.R., 25 Nov. 1936.

banner billowing in the wind. Muscles ripple and strain, sabres are raised and pistols cocked, clouds swirl in the sky and a beam of light falls upon the head of the lead horse, making it resemble a unicorn, and endowing the scene with a sense of the mythic or supernatural. Stalin and Lenin are shown here as equals, although Lenin points the way forward to victory. Stalin and Lenin are treated differently in the part of the poster that deals with 1937, but are treated similarly as co-leaders of the Party during the Revolution and Civil War in the part dealing with the past.

In 1938 and 1939 Stalin's appearances with Lenin remained at around 34 per cent and 24 per cent respectively of total Stalin posters. In 1938 Stalin often appears alone in the form of a photographic bust portrait, particularly in posters that promote the regional elections of the Soviet Union of that year[279] but, also, in a curious poster documenting in detail Stalin's arrests, exiles and escapes from exile between 1902 and 1917 (Fig. 2.9).[280] Stalin appears with Molotov under a banner with Lenin's head,[281] and with Voroshilov to promote Soviet aviation[282] and to make a show of Soviet military strength.[283] Stalin appears on equal footing at the top of the page with a photographic portrait of Lenin in a poster that reproduces his speech to the electoral meeting on 11 December 1937 at the Bolshoi Theatre,[284] and in posters by Moor and Sergei Sen'kin which publicise the Agricultural Act[285] and celebrate the might of the Red Army.[286] In her discussion of the giant photographic portraits of Lenin and Stalin hung in Red Square on Soviet holidays, Dawn Ades discusses a phenomenon that is equally applicable to the

---

[279] For example, I. Yang, 'Voters of Stalin's constituency vote in Moscow June 26, 1938 in the elections to the Supreme Soviet of the RSFSR for the great leader of the people, dear and beloved Iosif Vissarionovich Stalin', 1938; Unknown artist, 'June 26, 1938 — the day of the elections to the Supreme Soviet of the RSFSR to the Supreme Council of the Autonomous Chuvash Republic', 1938; and, Marenkov, 'Iosif Vissarionovich Stalin …', 1938.
[280] See unknown artist, 'Chronicle of the arrests, exiles and escapes of Comrade Stalin', 1938 (Fig. 2.9).
[281] See Viktor Koretskii, '"Our government and the party does not have other interests and other concerns, other than those which the people have", Stalin', 1938 (Fig. 4.64).
[282] See Nina Vatolina & Nikolai Denisov, 'Long live Soviet pilots — proud falcons of Motherland!', 1938.
[283] See Viktor Deni & Nikolai Dolgorukov, 'The enemy's fate is predetermined: we have crushed them before and we will keep on crushing', 1938.
[284] Unidentified artist, 'Speech of Comrade Stalin at the election meeting for voters … Moscow, 11 December 1937', 1938.
[285] Dmitrii Moor & Sergei Sen'kin, 'The USSR is the country of the largest socialist agriculture in the world', 1938.
[286] Dmitrii Moor & Sergei Sen'kin, 'Long live our dear invincible Red Army!', 1938 (Fig. 4.7).

smaller posters by Moor and Sen'kin of 1938. The arrangement of Lenin and Stalin on either side of a block of text is directly reminiscent of the Russian Orthodox icon, and invites comparison with Sts Peter and Paul and, particularly, Sts John Chrysostom and Basil, who are:

> normally depicted facing inward towards each other and with the holy texts unfolding between them, as in a sixteenth-century Novgorod icon in the Russian Museum. The modern variant shows the two Soviet leader-saints, now both figuratively and literally in command of the Word.[287]

Lenin is always situated on the viewer's left. This not only associates him with 'the past', but also signifies sacrality. Plamper points out in his discussion of imagery in *Pravda* that the upper left quarter of the front page was always especially sacred.[288] When Stalin is pictured with Voroshilov or Molotov, it is his image that occupies the upper left corner.

The years 1938 to 1939 were also notable for the appearance of three posters with identical captions and similar visual elements in which Stalin and Lenin are visually differentiated, with Lenin appearing in apotheosised form in the sky, on a banner and as a statue. The captions are taken from Stalin's electoral speech of 11 December 1937,[289] part of which is reproduced on each of the posters,[290] in which Stalin advises elected deputies to 'Be as the great Lenin was'. Each of the posters depicts Stalin delivering a speech. The 1938 poster by Elkin

---

287 Ades, *Art and power*, p. 251.
288 Plamper, *The Stalin cult*, p. 40.
289 See J.V. Stalin, 'Speech delivered by Comrade J. Stalin at a meeting of voters of the Stalin Electoral Area, Moscow', 11 December 1937, www.marxists.org/reference/archive/stalin/works/1937/12/11.htm and www.youtube.com/watch?v=iaU_ak19YwY (accessed 30 Oct. 2013). In the speech Stalin discusses the progressive law, enshrined in the constitution, which enables voters to call deputies to account for their actions during their term of office. Stalin advises voters to hold underperforming or misbehaving deputies accountable for their actions and to expect their deputies to behave in the way that Lenin did.
290 'The electors, the people, must demand that their deputies should remain equal to their tasks, that in their work they should not sink to the level of political philistines, that in their posts they should remain political figures of the Lenin type, that as public figures they should be as clear and definite as Lenin was, that they should be as fearless in battle and as merciless towards the enemies of the people as Lenin was, that they should be free from all panic, from any semblance of panic, when things begin to get complicated and some danger or other looms on the horizon, that they should be as free from all semblance of panic as Lenin was, that they should be as wise and deliberate in deciding complex problems requiring a comprehensive orientation and a comprehensive weighing of all pros and cons as Lenin was, that they should be as upright and honest as Lenin was, that they should love their people as Lenin did.'

(Fig. 2.10), one of the artists who documented the construction of the Moscow–Volga Canal,[291] shows Stalin behind a podium with right palm outstretched in a traditional oratorical gesture and left hand clutching a sheaf of papers. A crowd of workers stretching back to the horizon look and listen attentively. The top half of the poster is dominated by a large, pale image of Lenin's head gazing out to the left, traditionally associated with the past. The 1938 poster by A.I. Madorskii (Fig. 2.11) shows Stalin behind a podium,[292] while Lenin is emblazoned upon a banner. Madorskii's 1939 poster (Fig. 2.12) depicts an indoor scene with Stalin in front of a huge stone bust of Lenin that is draped in the flag of the USSR.[293] In each of these posters Lenin is invoked as an inspiration from the past, whose steady example is to be practised in the present and future. Despite Lenin's visual dominance of the images, it is Stalin's words that feature, and Stalin appears as the sole authoritative interpreter of Lenin's legacy for the future. The importance given to this speech of Stalin's is evidenced by the fact that two more posters of 1939 also took it as their subject.[294] In the majority of posters from 1939, the year of Stalin's 60th birthday celebrations, Stalin is pictured alone, sometimes assuming a position originally taken by Lenin, such as an outline silhouette on a banner[295] or in the sky,[296] a sole figure on a large banner,[297] or as a statue.[298]

---

[291] I.I. Nikonova, *Khudozhnikii Narodov SSSR: Biobibliograficheskii Slovar'*, 4:1, Moscow, Izdatel'stvo 'Iskusstvo', 1983, p. 19.
[292] This portrait of Stalin is taken from a photograph from his speech at the Stakhanovite conference of 1935.
[293] The Stalin portrait here appears to be drawn from the actual photographs of the 11 December speech.
[294] Both posters are by unidentified artists and were published by Izdaniye Obkoma VKP(b), the Regional Committee of the VKP(b) in 1939.
[295] See Aleksandr Druzhkov, 'Long live the organiser of our invincible aviation, best friend of Soviet pilots, great Stalin!', 1939.
[296] See Aleksandr Druzhkov & I. Shagin, 'Long live the Soviet physical culture athletes!', 1939.
[297] See M. Lebedev & S. Podobedov, 'Stalin is our battle banner', 1939; Vasilii Elkin, 'Long live Comrade Stalin — banner of invincible Soviet aviation!', 1939; Unidentified artist, 'Long live the leader and teacher of workers of all the world, best friend of the Red Army, dear and beloved Stalin', 1939; P. Yastrzhembskii, 'The All-Union Agricultural Exhibition. Opening August 1 (1939)', 1939; and, Marina Volkova, 'To our glorious physical culture men and women athletes of the Soviet country — an impassioned greeting!', 1939.
[298] See S. Podobedov, 'Long live the organiser and leader of the victorious Red Army great Stalin!', 1939 (Fig. 4.9); Vartan Arakelov, 'Stalin is the wisest of all people ...', 1939 (Fig. 3.3); Viktor Koretskii, 'Workers of collective and Soviet cooperative farms and machine and tractor stations' operators ...', 1939; and, K. Ryvkin, 'The Soviets of Worker Deputies of the Capital are leading the fight to fulfil the Stalinist Plan for the Reconstruction of Moscow', 1939.

2. THE RISE OF THE STALIN PERSONALITY CULT

In 1940, posters in which Stalin appears with Lenin make up only 25 per cent of total posters. In one of these posters, Lenin is only visible as a face on a tiny processional barrier in an indistinct crowd, while the profile of Stalin dominates the poster[299] and, in another, he appears in the form of the Order of Lenin, which sits like a stamp of approval over a schematic map of the planned reconstruction for the transformation of Tashkent, Uzbekistan, into a cultured city.[300] A 1940 poster from Tashkent by Vladimir Kaidalov quotes from Stalin's funerary oath to Lenin on 26 January 1924: 'Departing from us, Comrade Lenin urged us to strengthen and extend the union republics. We swear to you, Comrade Lenin, that we will fulfil with honour your behest' (Fig. 2.13). A giant head of Lenin sits above the Kremlin in a crimson sky. Beneath it, a crowd of people in Uzbek dress carry large red banners and look up at Stalin, who stands at the podium, arm raised to swear his oath. The portion of Stalin's oath that is quoted on the poster refers to socialist work to be undertaken in the union republics. In 1940 Tashkent was in the early stages of a total reconstruction that would see a 'cultured city' rise out of the demolition of a city of single-storey mudbrick houses, the opening of the Tashkent canal, and the opening of the children's railway. Plans to refashion the city's inhabitants into high-rise dwellers were meeting with resistance, and this poster calls upon the apotheosised Lenin to legitimate Stalin's plan, whilst also showing Stalin to be a man of his word.

With the outbreak of the Great Patriotic War in 1941, there was a sharp decline in the number of posters produced that contained an image of Stalin, however, appearances with Lenin jumped to 50 per cent of the total in this sample, and stayed roughly at this level until 1946, the year in which Stalin was glorified as responsible for victory in the war. It is not unexpected that, in the disastrous early years of the war, with Stalin's decision-making ability called into question, he may have elected to keep a low public profile, both in terms of public appearances and in terms of propaganda images, and also that the figure of Lenin may have been more frequently paired with Stalin to

---

299 See Nikolai Zhukov, 'Thank you Comrade Stalin for our happy life', 1940 (Fig. 3.1).
300 See B. Zhukov, 'We are the birthplace of the most happy, daring, all-powerful people, where grey-haired old men are cheerful, where there is the carefree laughter of children (From the welcome to the builders of BFK by Comrade Stalin)', 1940.

shore up Stalin's legitimacy. What is surprising is that, in 1946, when Stalin's legitimacy as leader in his own right was highest, he appeared with Lenin in 55 per cent of posters.

The posters of the war years express mixed trends, with the images of Stalin and Lenin differentiated in terms of treatment in 14 posters between 1941 and 1945 (inclusive); and Stalin and Lenin treated in similar or identical fashion in 13 posters during the same period. Lenin continued to be invoked as a protective banner, while Stalin's leadership at the time was stressed.[301] Typical of this treatment is future Hero of Socialist Labour Petr Golub's poster of 1945, 'Under the banner of Lenin, under the leadership of Stalin — forward to new victories!' (Fig. 2.14). Lenin appears as a bas-relief enclosed in a medallion on a gold-fringed red banner, while Stalin stands to attention in his marshal's uniform in the foreground, before a pink-tinged Kremlin that appears to rise out of the mist in the manner of an enchanted castle. Victory in the war has recently been attained and it is Stalin's leadership that will continue the momentum to new victories of socialism.

In other instances Lenin and Stalin appear on the banner together and the banner is invoked in both their names as the banner of 'Lenin–Stalin', almost as if they form one entity, an entity representing the Party, the state and Soviet power.[302] Vladimir Serov's 1943 poster '1918–1943 Long live the XXV anniversary of the Leninist–Stalinist Komsomol' (Fig. 2.15) shows determined young male and female Komsomol members, some in military uniform, others dressed as partisans, rushing forward to defend the motherland.[303] The All-Union Leninist Young Communist League (Komsomol)[304] was the

---

301 See A.A. Babitskii, 'Under the leadership of Comrade Stalin, forward to complete victory over our enemy!', 1944 (Fig. 4.31); and, M. Karpenko, 'Under the banner of Lenin, under the leadership of Stalin — forward the complete defeat of the German invaders!', 1944.
302 See A.V. Vasil'ev & S.F. Yanevich, 'Under the banner of Lenin-Stalin we were victorious in the great October Socialist Revolution. Under the banner of Lenin-Stalin we will be victorious in the Great Patriotic War. Raise the banner of Lenin-Stalin. It carries us to victory', 1941 (Fig. 4.15); Vladimir Serov, 'Long live the 25th anniversary of the Leninist–Stalinist Komsomol', 1943; and, Nikolai Zhukov & Viktor Klimashin, 'For the Soviet fatherland the sons of all the peoples of the Soviet Union go into battle. Long live the Red Army — the army of brotherhood and friendship of the peoples of the USSR! Under the banner of Lenin-Stalin forward to the west!', 1943 (Fig. 4.28).
303 As discussed in Chapter Four, it is unusual to associate females with combat in Soviet propaganda, and the women here are not overtly carrying weapons. As Komsomol members they are, however, depicted as prepared to defend the nation.
304 Vsesoyuznyy Leninskiy Kommunistícheskiy soyúz molodozhi (VLKSM).

youth division of the Communist Party and, as the name suggests, was primarily associated with Lenin. It was unusual to append Stalin's name to the Komsomol moniker, although his name did come to be strongly associated with the war effort.

Between 1947 and 1950, Stalin's appearances with Lenin range from about 30 to 50 per cent in posters. In a strikingly simple poster of 1949 by L. Stenberg (Fig. 2.16) Stalin's discipleship to Lenin is emphasised in the poster caption, while his equality of status with Lenin is reinforced visually. The image is dominated by an undulating banner in rich red tones. At the top of the banner, Stalin and Lenin appear in golden bas-relief profile. At the bottom of the banner, also in gold, are a sprig of oak leaves, and one of laurel leaves, both symbols of heroism, strength and victory. The caption in large gold letters fills most of the poster: 'The banner of Lenin, the party's banner is raised high and carried on by Stalin — the disciple of Lenin, the best son of the Bolshevik Party, and a worthy successor and the great continuer of the work of Lenin.'

A 1950 poster by painter and graphic artist Boris Belopol'skii depicts Lenin on a banner hovering over Stalin's right shoulder, almost in the manner of a protective spirit. Stalin's figure dominates the poster, his white marshal's jacket luminous against the rich red of the banner. Stalin is depicted behind a podium in oratorical pose, and the text of the poster is taken from his report to the Eighteenth Party Congress on 10 March 1939 on the work of the Central Committee; that is, before the war interrupted the progression of socialism towards communism: '"We move further, forward towards Communism." I. V. Stalin'. Stalin stands in this poster as the figure who is continuing and expanding upon Lenin's work, and as the man who will ultimately bring the dream of communism to fruition.

An intriguing poster by Mytnikov, published at Rostov-on-Don in 1950, employs the generic slogan 'Under the banner of Lenin, under the leadership of Stalin — forward to the victory of communism!' at its base, but has an unusual caption at the top of the poster — '26 years without Lenin, but still on Lenin's path' (Fig. 2.17). An almost white-haired Stalin stands with his face in semi-shadow, his brows pinched as if in grief. According to Clark, in socialist realist literature the furrowed brow or pinched face are signs of the revolutionary's dedication and sacrifice.[305] Although his skin is generally smooth and unblemished, Stalin appears tired and aged. Behind him, a massive red banner billows in a yellow sky, resembling a wall of fire. The tiny Spassky tower is in shadow, with the sky behind it glowing yellow and the golden fringe of the banner resembling flames. The words on the banner read 'Long live the Party of Lenin–Stalin!'

Dominating the banner, on a scale similar to Stalin's head, is that of Lenin in grayscale. Lenin also looks out of the poster, but far further to the left (the past) than Stalin. Lenin's hair, normally portrayed as flat and sparse, curls forward around his forehead above his ears, and his usually trim goatee is thick and lush and appears to circle his chin. This is an unusual depiction of Lenin, but bears some resemblance to depictions of St Nicholas the Wonderworker in Russian Orthodox icons. St Nicholas, whose feast day is 6 December (19 December, Old Calendar) is the 'miracle-working' saint and one of the most beloved figures in the iconography of the church, known for his gentleness, humility, love of all people and purity of heart. Tales of his life highlight a reputation for giving anonymous and secret gifts to aid people in need and he is reported to have divided his substantial inheritance among the poor. He is known to intercede for petitioners in response to heartfelt prayer through his icon in practical and tangible ways, particularly in matters of healing and rescue, and is also the patron saint of travellers, particularly seafarers. Nicholas is usually depicted with a high, bald forehead, his hair curling in on either side, and with a trim circular beard and moustache. By placing Lenin on the red banner over Stalin's right shoulder, visually referencing St Nicholas, and making textual reference to his exemplary role, Mytnikov is perhaps drawing a parallel between Lenin and Nicholas's gentle nature, humility, and fame for redistributing the wealth of the rich among the poor, whilst also suggesting that the apotheosised Lenin can intercede on behalf of both Stalin and the Soviet citizen. While Lenin is a saint in the Soviet pantheon, Stalin is the dedicated and self-sacrificial revolutionary who bears aloft the Lenin banner.

After 1950 the overall number of posters of Stalin declined, with posters with Lenin making up 57 per cent of 1951 posters. Stalin and Lenin are juxtaposed as equals in Viktor Govorkov's 'In the name of

---

305 Clark, *The Soviet novel*, p. 57.

2. THE RISE OF THE STALIN PERSONALITY CULT

communism' (Fig. 2.18) in which the past and the present are depicted with realistic parallel scenes involving Lenin and Stalin. Both men are planning the electrification of the nation on a map of the USSR. Lenin holds a book titled *Plan for the electrification of the RSFSR, 1920*, while Stalin is associated with a book titled *Electrification of the USSR*. As he marks out the Main Turkmen Canal, he is seen to be expanding on the work begun by Lenin — Lenin's plan extends across the Russian republic, while Stalin's encompasses the whole of the Soviet Union.

Stalin and Lenin are depicted as having been joint leaders during the October Revolution in a 1951 poster by Ukrainian-born Naum Karpovskii with the caption 'Glory to the great leaders of October!' (Fig. 2.19). A black-haired and dashing young Stalin stands beside Lenin in front of scenes of battle during the Civil War. Lenin's right arm is extended as if showing the way, and both Stalin and Lenin gaze into the distance towards the future. Thus, while Lenin's role as teacher is featured, the young Stalin is nevertheless depicted as an equal leader of the October Revolution. In 1952 Stalin was depicted with Lenin in posters published by Latgosizdat[306] in Riga, and by Azernesr[307] in Baku. The Latvian poster by V. Reshetnikov (Fig. 2.20) carries the slogan 'Glory to Lenin, glory to Stalin, glory to great October', while the lock over the canal has the inscription 'Stalin is the world/Stalin is peace'.[308] The distinguished and greying head of Stalin dominates the poster, while Lenin's head forms part of the fabric of the banner billowing behind him. A 1952 poster by an unidentified artist shows Lenin and Stalin as equals with the caption 'Long live the great, united party of Lenin–Stalin, intelligence, honour and conscience of our communist era!' (Fig. 2.21) and both portraits are treated in similar fashion.[309]

---

306 Latvian publishing house.
307 Publishing house in Azerbaijan.
308 Stalin eto mir! The word 'mir' in Russian means both 'world' and 'peace'.
309 Stalin appears more 'Asiatic' in this poster than he does in those published in Moscow and Leningrad.

The significance of the banner

The red banner is the most frequently employed motif in the Soviet propaganda poster. Of the 389 posters in the research sample, the banner appears in 275,[310] and several more utilise a plain red backdrop that evokes both the banner and also the red background sometimes found in Russian Orthodox icons. Scenes that do not feature banners are frequently indoor settings, or close-cropped photographic portraits, particularly black-and-white photographs of Stalin's head.

The colour red had several connotations in the Soviet Union. The Russian word for 'red', *krasnyi*, shares a common etymology with the word for 'beautiful', *krasivyi*, and red is associated with beauty. Red is a sacred colour in the Russian Orthodox Church, and symbolises life, love, warmth and the victory of life over death as made manifest in the Resurrection. It is also the colour of blood and, as such, can signify martyrdom in general, and Christ's sacrifice of his life for humankind in particular, with a red background on an icon symbolising eternal life or martyrdom. Orthodox priests traditionally wear cassocks of dark red or purple on feast days associated with Christ and the elevation of the cross and those associated with martyrs. Bright red cassocks are worn on the feast days of Sts Peter and Paul, and can be worn on Pascha (Easter) and at Christmas.

The association of the red flag with communism dates to the Paris Commune of 1871, where it was raised at the seized Hotel de Ville by proletarian revolutionaries. Marx wrote extensively on the Paris Commune in his book about the civil war in France, mentioning specifically the symbolic power of the red flag:

> When the Paris Commune took the management of the revolution in its own hands; when plain working men for the first time dared to infringe upon the governmental privilege of their 'natural superiors' … the old world writhed in convulsions of rage at the sight of the Red Flag, the symbol of the Republic of Labor, floating over the Hôtel de Ville.[311]

---

310 Just over 70 per cent.
311 Karl Marx, 'The third address May 1871 [The Paris Commune], *The Civil War in France*, 1871', www.marxists.org/archive/marx/works/1871/civil-war-france/ch05.htm (accessed 7 Nov. 2013).

2. THE RISE OF THE STALIN PERSONALITY CULT

The Russian communists adopted the red flag as the symbol of their movement and, when the Bolsheviks seized power, they made the red flag, with yellow hammer and sickle insignia, the flag of the nation. The political antecedents of the red flag/banner include willingness to defend oneself and engage in battle,[312] an attitude of defiance,[313] the revolutionary spirit,[314] willingness to sacrifice, the blood of martyrs and, more specifically, the communist cause.

Battle banners held a particular significance during war. To capture an enemy's banner was to take a great prize, and to lose one's banner meant court martial and disbandment of the unit.[315] During the victory parade after the Great Patriotic War, soldiers hurled captured German banners at Stalin's feet and Stalin can be seen in propaganda standing atop these banners in an unmistakable sign of victory and symbol of humiliation for the defeated Germans.[316] This gesture was a repetition of the incident after the Patriotic War of 1812 in which the Russian generals threw the captured banners of Napoleon's troops at the feet of Emperor Aleksandr II.

The red banner is also often used protectively in a manner reminiscent of the veil of the Virgin in Russian Orthodox icons. According to Russian Orthodox belief, Mary Theotokos appeared before St Andrew in Blachernae Church in Constantinople in the 10th century, moving through the air and then praying for Christ's intercession and protection for mankind. After praying, the Virgin spread her veil over the congregation in a gesture of protection. Icons of the Feast of Intercession show the Virgin in an aureole in the upper part of the

---

312 From the 13th century, a 'baucans', a plain red streamer flown from the masthead of a ship, signified the intention to give battle and to fight to the death ('Dictionary of vexillology: Baucans', *Flags of the world*, www.crwflags.com/fotw/flags/vxt-dvb3.html#baucens (accessed 7 Nov. 2013)).
313 Dating from the 17th century, a red flag symbolised defiance and the intention to resist ('Dictionary of vexillology: flag of defiance', *Flags of the world*, www.crwflags.com/fotw/flags/vxt-dvf3.html#flagofdefiance (accessed 7 Nov. 2013)).
314 During the French Revolution it was associated with the revolutionary spirit of the common people and the Marquis de Lafayette raised a red flag over the Champs-de-Mars on 17th July 1791. Red was also the colour associated with the Phrygian cap that became a symbol of the revolution. The Jacobins flew a red flag as a symbol of the blood sacrifice made by martyrs to the cause.
315 Karel C. Berkhoff, *Motherland in danger: Soviet propaganda during World War II*, Cambridge, Harvard University Press, 2012, p. 55.
316 For example, Stefan Gints, 'The triumph of victory …', 1945.

icon holding the veil in her outstretched arms. Below, and on either side of her, are a host of saints and angels with whom most Orthodox churchgoers would be familiar.

Marxism–Leninism had all the characteristics of a political religion and the Soviet population, particularly the older generation that grew up in pre-Soviet times, was visually literate with regard to iconography and Christian symbolism. When Christian baptisms were replaced by the Soviet *Oktiabrina* ritual in 1920, the red banner took the place traditionally reserved for the icon.[317] During the 1940s, after the outbreak of the Great Patriotic War, Stalin reversed the earlier Soviet policy of persecution of the Church, releasing surviving priests from the prison camps, and allowing some churches to open and minister to the public. In December 1941, as the Germans approached Moscow, Stalin ordered that the sacred Theotokos of Vladimir be taken up in an aeroplane and flown around Moscow, invoking the Virgin's intercession and protection from the invading Germans.

Many Stalinist propaganda posters depict huge red banners that fill the sky and hover protectively over the crowds below them. These banners often carry images of the great communist revolutionary thinkers Marx, Engels, Lenin and Stalin — alone or together in combination. The text on the posters specifically invokes the banner as a protective and inspirational object, whether protecting the troops going into battle, as will be seen in Chapter Four, inspiring citizens to further sacrifice in the name of the victory of communism, or even protecting and legitimating the leadership. A 1950 poster by Pravdin serves as an illustration of this point. 'Long live the Bolshevik Party, the Lenin–Stalin Party, the vanguard of the Soviet people forged in battle, the inspiration and organiser of our victories!' (Fig. 2.22) features two red banners that dominate the sky. The largest of the two, which occupies almost all of the top half of the landscape-format poster, is intensely red and decorated with gold braid — it ripples as if in a gentle breeze. It is emblazoned with the head and shoulders of Lenin in fleshy tones, associating Lenin with eternal life, as in the icon, and also acknowledging his sacrifice for the sake of the people.[318]

---

317 David King, *Red star over Russia: a visual history of the Soviet Union from 1917 to the death of Stalin: posters, photographs and graphics from the David King collection*, London, Tate, 2009, p. 168.
318 Despite surviving an assassination attempt by Dora Kaplan in 1918, Lenin was frequently viewed as a martyr to the cause and began to be associated with Christ. Lenin died in 1924 of natural causes but was still celebrated as a martyr. See Bergman, 'The image of Jesus in the

Lenin looks out to his right, his eyes focused on a distant vision. Beneath him, the figure of Stalin dominates the centre foreground, his head jutting up into the red field created by the banner, with Lenin hovering over his right shoulder like a protective 'good angel'. Stalin's gaze mimics that of Lenin and he partakes of the implication of eternal life already bestowed upon Lenin. Behind Stalin, and also underneath Lenin's banner, are the figures of the leadership. They are differentiated from Stalin by appearing smaller and their gazes turn in a number of directions, with Andrei Andreev and Mikoian looking directly at the viewer.

Behind the first banner and in the background is a second large banner that hovers over the anonymous faces of 'the masses', carrying text which reads: 'Under the banner of Lenin, under the leadership of Stalin — forward to the victory of communism!', making literal the well-worn slogan. If we read Pravdin's poster as an icon replacing Orthodox iconography with Soviet iconography, it is the apotheosised Lenin who floats in the upper part of the poster, contained within an implicit aureole. His red banner spreads over the Party leaders, guiding and protecting them as they lead the people forward to victory. Stalin, the largest figure in the poster and, therefore, the most important, is the chief saint, while the other leaders flanking him fill the ranks of the minor saints. The common people follow behind Stalin and are also guided and protected by a Lenin banner. Like the icon, the poster is a primarily visual medium which relies on the impact of the image to deliver its message. Text is simple and serves to reinforce the visual message and also to provide additional clues as to how the image should be read, but it is the image that embeds in the viewer's mind. By visually referencing the characteristics of the Russian Orthodox icon, the posters encouraged the viewer to respond in a spiritual manner to the form and content of the poster, and to draw parallels, both conscious and unconscious, between the central figure in the posters and the key spiritual figures of the Orthodox faith. This was facilitated by Russian traditions of leadership in which the tsar held both secular and spiritual powers and was viewed as the sacred protector of the people.

Russian revolutionary movement', pp. 220–48.

THE PERSONALITY CULT OF STALIN IN SOVIET POSTERS, 1929–1953

Stalin and the legacy of Marx–Engels–Lenin

Aside from Stalin's frequent appearances with Lenin, he also appeared in posters with the pantheon of great communist thinkers, tracing his ideological lineage further back in history than his immediate predecessor Lenin, to Marx and Engels. *Pravda* marked the 50th anniversary of Marx's death on 14 March 1933 by lauding Stalin's contributions to Marxist ideology: 'Stalin's name ranks with the great names of the theoreticians and leaders of the world proletariat — Marx, Engels, and Lenin.'[319] Stalin's place in the canon is demonstrated unambiguously in a well-known poster by Klutsis as early as 1933 — 'Raise higher the banners of Marx, Engels, Lenin, and Stalin!' (Fig. 2.23). The image is dominated by the heads of Marx, Engels, Lenin and Stalin, each on their own red banner. Victoria Bonnell makes the following observation in reference to Klutsis's poster:

> The photographs of Marx, Engels and Lenin show them looking off to one side; Stalin, by contrast, is the only one of the four who makes direct eye contact with the viewer. The artist's choice was deliberate, since there existed at the time well-known portraits of both Marx and Lenin gazing directly at the viewer. The direct gaze sets Stalin apart from the others and gives his image a particular magnetism.[320]

One can expand somewhat on Bonnell's reading of the poster. It is Marx and Engels whose heads are turned to the viewer's right side. They do not engage the viewer, looking perhaps to the future and their own visionary predictions, but most definitely in the direction of the heads of Lenin and Stalin — the heroes of the past looking to the future, which is occurring in the present. Lenin and Stalin are both almost full-face to the viewer, however, as Bonnell points out, Lenin's eyes are swivelled to the viewer's right. Lenin, too, looks to Stalin for the leadership of the present day. The baton has been passed from Marx and Engels, to Lenin, who now passes it on to Stalin. Stalin is neither focused on a mythical past, nor on a visionary future, but gazes out at the viewer from a firmly entrenched position in the present. The crowd scenes surrounding each of the giant banners further illustrate this point. Marx and Engels are surrounded by fighters from the French and German revolutions of 1789 and 1848 respectively, wielding

---

319 Tucker, 'The rise of Stalin's personality cult', p. 366.
320 Bonnell, *Iconography of power*, p. 158.

swords and muskets, fighting on foot and horseback. The numbers of soldiers engaged in the battle are relatively few. Under Lenin's banner the October revolutionaries storm the Winter Palace in October 1917, while above, the crowds rush in to join the fight.[321] Stalin's banner reveals something new in that he is flanked by dense crowds of workers — some, like the woman in the foreground, beaming happily; others looking determined, steadfast and attentive; all carrying tools rather than weapons. Gone is the classical architecture that surrounds Marx and Engels, replaced around the figure of Stalin by scenes of Soviet construction, which include the wall of the Dnieper Dam — Soviet construction constituting the new 'battlefront'. Stalin's 'revolution'[322] began around 1928 with forced collectivisation, the revocation of the NEP, the Shakhty Trial,[323] and the introduction of the five-year plans.[324] Despite the fact that Stalin's revolution did not result from the violent overthrow of the existing order, the nature of his reforms was such that they provided a revolutionary break with the past and, from this perspective, Stalin can be viewed as the fourth great revolutionary thinker in the process of evolution that was leading to the communist utopia. Klutsis's poster unequivocally sets Stalin alongside the other great revolutionaries and pillars of socialist thought while, at the same time, emphasising his relevance to the current time. Variations on this formula would recur often throughout the years of Stalin's rule, with several posters visually referencing this one. Indeed, this poster was

---

321 The storming of the Winter Palace was a small affair involving relatively few people but became, in the mythic propaganda about the Revolution, a key event with a cast of thousands. Re-enactments of the event in the first years after the Revolution involved thousands of military personnel and civilians.

322 Sheila Fitzpatrick and Richard Lowenthal are two of many scholars who examine the concept of the 'Stalin revolution'. See Sheila Fitzpatrick, *Everyday Stalinism: ordinary life in extraordinary times — Soviet Russia in the 1930s*, New York, Oxford University Press, 1999, p. 4; and, Lowenthal, 'The post-revolutionary phase in China and Russia', p. 198.

323 Trial conducted in 1928 in which a group of engineers from the Donbass was accused of sabotaging the Soviet economy. Stalin used this case as evidence of his assertion that class struggle was intensifying.

324 Sheila Fitzpatrick summarises the nature of Stalin's revolution in the following way: 'The term "Stalin's revolution" has been used for this transition, and that conveys well its violent, destructive, and utopian character. But this revolution was largely the result of state initiative, not popular movements, and it did not result in a change of political leadership. The point of the revolution, in Stalin's eyes, was to lay the economic foundations for socialism by rooting out private enterprise and using state planning to promote rapid economic development' (*Everyday Stalinism*, p. 4).

so successful that it was released in a first edition of 50,000, a second edition of 30,000, a 1936 edition of 250,000 and, in 1937, it was produced in more than 20 languages of the Soviet republics.[325]

In her examination of Stalin's attitude to his cult of personality, Davies indicates the numerous ways in which Stalin tried to curb and moderate the excesses of the cult. She points out that in 1934, for example, Stalin crossed out his name in the phrase 'banner of Marx–Engels–Lenin–Stalin', although, she says, by 1939 he allowed it to remain.[326] In fact, a poster from 1938 employs the 'Marx–Engels–Lenin–Stalin' formula in the caption,[327] indicating that Stalin was already comfortable with this formulation by 1938. In this light, Klutsis's poster of 1933 appears at first to be something of an anomaly. The differences between this and later posters are subtle, but important. Klutsis's caption refers to the 'banners of Marx, Engels, Lenin and Stalin' and the visual imagery places each of the great thinkers on his own banner. In later posters, where Stalin's name is appended to those of the other three, it is in hyphenated form, and the visual image shows all four heads emblazoned on a single banner. In these latter cases it is one protective banner which is invoked, and the four merge into a unifying force that symbolises the Party, the state and communism.

Prior to 1938, the merged hyphenated identity was reserved solely for the apotheosised thinkers. A 1934 poster by graphic artist and journalist Nikolai Dolgorukov carries the slogan 'Long live the great, invincible banner of Marx–Engels–Lenin' (Fig. 2.24) on a long triangulated banner that falls like a shaft of light from the heavens over Stalin's right shoulder, although the poster does not carry an image of Marx, Engels or Lenin. Instead, the upper torso of Stalin is depicted in giant scale jutting into the sky, as if forming part of fortifications of the Kremlin wall. Stalin looks down and out of the poster, his right hand raised as if waving to the crowd or perhaps conferring a blessing. The sky is full of aircraft while, below, a huge military parade stretches across Red Square with the mounted figure of Voroshilov montaged

---

325 Bonnell, *Iconography of Power*, p. 158.
326 See Davies, in Apor et al., *The leader cult in communist dictatorships*, p. 39.
327 See Vladislav Pravdin & Zoia Pravdina, 'Long live the great invincible banner of Marx–Engels–Lenin–Stalin!' (Fig. 2.25), discussed below.

into the scene. Although Stalin assumes gigantic proportions and projects into the sky, he is still firmly tied to the corporeal world of military parades and developing the might of the Red Army.

A 1937 poster by G. Mirzoev carries the same slogan as Dolgorukov's poster, but this time attributes it as a quotation from Stalin: '"Long live the great and invincible banner of Marx–Engels–Lenin!" (I. Stalin)'.[328] Stalin dominates the foreground, his features lit from above in golden tones. He is separated from Marx, Engels and Lenin, who are featured on a small banner that protrudes from the globe and billows over it in a premonition of world revolution. Once again, Stalin inhabits the world of the living, in contrast to the three communist gods.

Changes in the relationship between Stalin and Marx, Engels and Lenin began to appear in 1938. Stalin appears alongside the three in a poster by husband and wife team Vladislav Pravdin and Zoia Pravdina, with the new caption of 'Long live the great invincible banner of Marx–Engels–Lenin–Stalin!' (Fig. 2.25). In front of a rich red banner the heads of Marx, Engels, Lenin and Stalin, all in three-quarter view, are lined up. Not only has Stalin's name been added to the banner as part of the hyphenated identity but, in contrast to earlier posters on this theme, Stalin is now treated in exactly the same manner as the other communist luminaries — his portrait is identical in size and manner of execution, and his gaze is in the same direction. No longer to be viewed as a mere 'pupil', 'disciple' or mouthpiece for Lenin, he takes his place as an equal alongside the other great theoreticians.

Stalin makes an interesting appearance with Marx, Engels and Lenin in a notable 1939 poster by Pavel Sokolov-Skalia, who was a well-known painter as well as graphic artist, head of Okna TASS, theatre artist and cinema artist for *Mosfilm*.[329] In 'The train is going from the station of socialism to the station of communism',[330] Stalin appears with the pillars of communism on a banner that decorates the side of a train pushing up a slope, and he is also portrayed in the window of the engine room as the train driver. The poster is sub-captioned 'Tried and tested locomotive engineer of the Revolution, Comrade Stalin'.

---

328 See www.eremeevs.com/index.php?lotid=277316.
329 At the time of this poster, Sokolov-Skalia was teaching at the Grekov Studio of War Artists (Matthew Cullerne Bown, *A dictionary of 20th century Russian and Soviet painters, 1900s–1980s*, London, Izomar, 1998).
330 See sovietart.me/posters/year/1939/6.

The four heads appear so that it is Marx who is at the head of the train, and Stalin bringing up the rear. Beneath the picture of the train is a graph with the title 'implementation schedule of the movement of the Bolshevik train' which shows the various stops on the journey to socialism, beginning with the foundation of the newspaper *Iskra* in 1900, progressing through the armed uprising of December 1905, the founding of the newspaper *Pravda* in 1912, and the October Revolution of 1917. Another graph titled 'current schedule' shows the one-stop journey from socialism to communism. This playful graphic depicts Stalin as both the last in the line of great communist thinkers, and as the man currently responsible for steering the nation's journey to the final destination envisaged by Marx and Engels.

A 1940 poster by an unidentified artist begins with the formulaic caption, then adds a little more: 'Long live the great invincible banner of Marx–Engels–Lenin–Stalin! Long live Leninism!' (Fig. 2.26). The text dominates the panoramic format of the poster, with a smaller section on the left of the poster occupied by a banner containing the four heads of Stalin, Lenin, Engels and Marx, each depicted as if cast in stone in identical manner. Beneath the heads, the first part of the large caption is repeated: 'Long live the great invincible banner of Marx–Engels–Lenin–Stalin!' Stalin's image has unambiguously found its place amid the communist gods.

The Great Patriotic War saw the revolutionary thinkers theme disappear for a period of time with only one 1941 poster by Nikolai Denisov and Nina Vatolina carrying the slogan 'Long live the great invincible banner of Marx–Engels–Lenin–Stalin!' (Fig. 2.27). Perhaps ideology took a back seat to more critical matters at this time. The poster is dominated by the busts of the four theorists, all gazing to the viewer's left at the same distant point. Stalin is not differentiated from the other three in pose or manner of treatment, although his head is the closest and largest, ostensibly due to perspective. While the portraits are realistic, they have a chiselled, immovable quality about them, and appear as remote and incorporeal, as belonging to the realm of heroes and gods, rather than the everyday mundane.

In 1946, the first volume of Stalin's *Collected works* appeared and, in 1947, *Stalin: a short biography* was finally published. The biography outlines at great length Stalin's contribution to Marxist thought and makes explicit the claim that Stalin has developed communist ideology to a *further* stage than Lenin.³³¹ In 1949 there was a return to the theme of the four great communist figures, although Kaidalov's poster (Fig. 2.28) is all about Stalin, whose lavish 70th birthday celebrations occurred in this year. The poster makes visual reference to Marx, Engels and Lenin, but names only Stalin in the text. Kaidalov differentiates Stalin stylistically from the other great thinkers. Marx, Engels and Lenin appear to be part of the fabric of the gold-fringed banner and are incorporeal, while Stalin, in full colour and resplendent in his marshal's uniform, takes up a position in the foreground in three-quarter view, bathed in an intense white light. Although the caption is in the Russian language, the poster was published in Tashkent by Gosizdat³³² and the tiny people beneath the huge banner hold aloft bouquets of the cotton crop. In gold and white tones, the people themselves resemble a crop, part of the bounty of the Soviet republics whose energies are being harvested to build communism. In the background the holy Kremlin in red merges with Soviet banners and birthday fireworks light up the sky. The simple caption is also a departure from the visually similar posters up to this date. 'Glory to great Stalin!' is cut into grey stone and surrounded by a wreath of cotton leaves, giving it a feel of monolithic importance, permanence, and an association with victory. Although Stalin is removed from the banner and brought back into the real world, his treatment in this poster, and its unambiguous caption, serve to mark him out as worthy of particular adulation in the present.

The next poster to deal with the Marx–Engels–Lenin-Stalin theme was again published outside of the major centres, by Tatgosizdat³³³ in Kazan, Tatarstan (Fig. 2.29), and quotes Stalin on the necessity to train all cadres, regardless of specialty, in the laws of Marxism–

---

331 'The chapter on "Dialectical and Historical Materialism" is a masterly statement of the principles of dialectical and historical materialism, expounded with the utmost conciseness and lucidity. Here Stalin gives a general account of all that has been contributed to the dialectical method and materialistic theory by Marx, Engels and Lenin, and further develops the doctrine of dialectical and historical materialism in conformity with the latest facts of science and revolutionary practice ... .
Stalin's "Dialectical and Historical Materialism," written by an incomparable master of the Marxist dialectical method, and generalizing the vast practical and theoretical experience of Bolshevism, *raises dialectical materialism to a new and higher level, and is the pinnacle of Marxist-Leninist philosophical thought* ... .
That which Lenin had not lived to do in development of the theory of the state, was done by Stalin' (Alexandrov et al., *Joseph Stalin*, pp. 140–41, p. 145).
332 State Publishing House of the Russian republic.
333 Publishing house of Tatarstan.

Leninism.[334] The 1951 poster by illustrator of folktales and fairytales Bainazar Al'menov shows the four pillars of communism as part of a billowing banner that fills the top half of the picture plane.[335] The banner is rich red in colour and adorned with gold tassels. Beneath it, also in rich red with gold trim, are four slender books, one by each of the men pictured above, which outline the immutable laws of Marxism–Leninism. Stalin's work resides unambiguously beside those of the three great thinkers.

In 1953, the year in which Stalin died, there was yet another return to the banner of Marx–Engels–Lenin–Stalin with a poster released in Moscow by A. Kossov (Fig. 2.30), bearing the caption 'Long live the great invincible banner of Marx, Engels, Lenin, Stalin'. The four profiles of equal size, treated in identical fashion, adorn a huge red banner that takes up almost the entire visual field of the poster. Beneath the banner is a scene of celebration and jubilation in which a crowd of tiny figures dressed in colourful national costumes carry banners with the slogans 'Forward to Communism!', 'Glory to the Party of Lenin and Stalin!', 'For peaceful work!', and 'For the happiness of the people!'. Stalin continued to be portrayed as part of the banner of Marx–Engels–Lenin–Stalin until at least 1955, when he appeared with Marx, Engels and Lenin in a poster by Belopol'skii (Fig. 2.31). By this time Stalin had been dead for two years, and the poster shows the four profiles as if they are all hewn from the one stone. The caption of the poster makes clear that the Marx–Engels–Lenin–Stalin banner was still viewed as a legitimating tool for the Party, with the four communist leaders being invoked to inspire the people and confer legitimacy on the Party's continued efforts toward the achievement of full communism: 'Under the banner of Marx–Engels–Lenin–Stalin, under the guidance of the Communist party — forward, to the victory of communism!'

---

334 'But there is one branch of science which Bolsheviks in all branches of science are in duty bound to know, and that is the Marxist–Leninist science of society, of the laws of social development, of the laws of development of the proletarian revolution, of the laws of development of socialist construction, and of the victory of communism.' I. Stalin.

335 Stalin and Lenin both appear particularly 'Asiatic' in their banner profiles. Stalin was often given facial features reminiscent of the general racial characteristics of the place in which the poster was published. In the Asian parts of the Soviet Union he tended to have Asiatic features, while in the European parts he looked more European. Stalin described himself to Georgi Dimitrov as a 'Russified Georgian–Asian' (*obrusevshii gruzin-aziat*) — see Plamper, *The Stalin cult*, p. 46. Lenin was part Kalmyk on his father's side.

The claim that Stalin belonged with the other great communist writers was not merely empty rhetoric. Stalin's works had outsold those of the other great thinkers since the early 1930s.[336] By 1949, almost 17 million copies of *Problems of Leninism* were in print in 52 languages.[337] Stalin certainly wished to be taken seriously as a communist ideologue, as is evidenced by his interventions in the discourses on linguistics, science and economics. Tucker sees Stalin's 1924 *Foundations of Leninism* as an effective way for Stalin to 'prove himself a Bolshevik leader of large theoretical horizons'.[338] In an informative article on Stalin as the 'coryphaeus of science', Ethan Pollock analyses Stalin's interventions in the field of science and argues that Stalin's interest should not be viewed as deriving from excessive vanity or even political expediency. Instead, he sees the time Stalin devoted to these matters as being indicative of their significance in Soviet society.[339]

Stalin did not claim to have particular expertise in a variety of specialist fields. When he publicly intervened in the debate on Marrist linguistics by writing an article for *Pravda*, he began by pointing out that he had been approached by a group of young comrades to contribute to the discussion, and that he did so on the basis of his knowledge of the laws of Marxism.[340] Stalin was well and widely read in a number of areas, and had spent a lifetime studying and developing further the ideology of Marxism–Leninism. He spent 16 years trying to get Soviet political economists to produce an appropriate textbook on Marxist–Leninist economics.[341] Stalin was intimately involved in the discussions about the book, editing the manuscript and producing copious notes that were then distributed to the authors. He evidently felt he was

---

336 Tucker cites overall figures for the release of the classic Marxist texts in the years 1932–33: 'seven million copies of the works of Marx and Engels, fourteen million of those of Lenin, and sixteen and a half million of those of Stalin, including two million copies of Stalin's *Problems of Leninism*' ('The rise of Stalin's personality cult', p. 366).
337 Tucker, 'The rise of Stalin's personality cult', p. 366.
338 Tucker, *Stalin as Revolutionary*, p. 319.
339 Pollock points out that Marxism–Leninism was viewed as an ideology based in science and that, accordingly, science should flourish and lead to the discovery of absolute truths if practised in accordance with Marxist principles ('Stalin as the coryphaeus of science: ideology and knowledge in the post-war years', pp. 271–88, in Davies & Harris, *Stalin*, p. 273).
340 'I am not a linguist … but as to Marxism in linguistics, as well as in other social sciences, this is a subject with which I have a direct connection' (I.V. Stalin, quoted in Pollock, 'Stalin as the coryphaeus of science', in Davies & Harris, *Stalin*, pp. 277–78. The original of Stalin's article can be found at RGASPI f. 558, op. 1, d.5301).
341 'Soviet power has been around for 33 years and we don't have a book on political economy. Everyone is waiting' (I.V. Stalin, RGASPI f.17, op. 133, d.41, ll.8-25, cited in Pollock, 'Stalin as the coryphaeus of science', in Davies & Harris, *Stalin*, p. 284). Pollock observes: 'Stalin hoped the

qualified to make a valuable contribution to the science of Marxism–Leninism, a contribution born from the cauldron of actual experience in endeavouring to work in a socialist system. His predecessors did not have such experience, Lenin having died within seven years of the Revolution, many years short of the achievement of socialism in the USSR.

Conclusion

The personality cult of Stalin was a complex phenomenon that defies facile or superficial explanation. It was certainly generated as a 'top-down' phenomenon by the Soviet leadership with the purpose of rallying the citizenry around the central symbolic figure of Stalin. The state's centralised control of artistic production facilitated the generation, maintenance and widespread dissemination of Stalin's symbolic persona, although this centralised system of contractual work was often supported by the artists themselves, some of whom were able to gain access to stable and relatively secure incomes. The political poster industry was particularly tightly regulated, in part by virtue of the fact that the state controlled not only the distribution of contracts, but also the availability of materials and the printing presses. Artists created a charismatic persona around Stalin as leader, with a mythic and exemplary hagiography, increasingly superhuman abilities, and the blessing of the state's founder. Stalin came to function as a symbol for the Party, the state and the nation, as well as for more abstract concepts, such as the new man, the new society and the Bolshevik vision. Chapter Three will explore the symbolism associated with the Stalin persona and his identification with the Father and Teacher archetypes.

---

book would provide a stunning critique of capitalism and a powerful description of communism as Marx's kingdom of freedom. In short, the book would be a 'New Testament' of Marxism–Leninism' (Pollock, 'Stalin as the coryphaeus of science', in Davies & Harris, *Stalin*, p. 282).

2. THE RISE OF THE STALIN PERSONALITY CULT

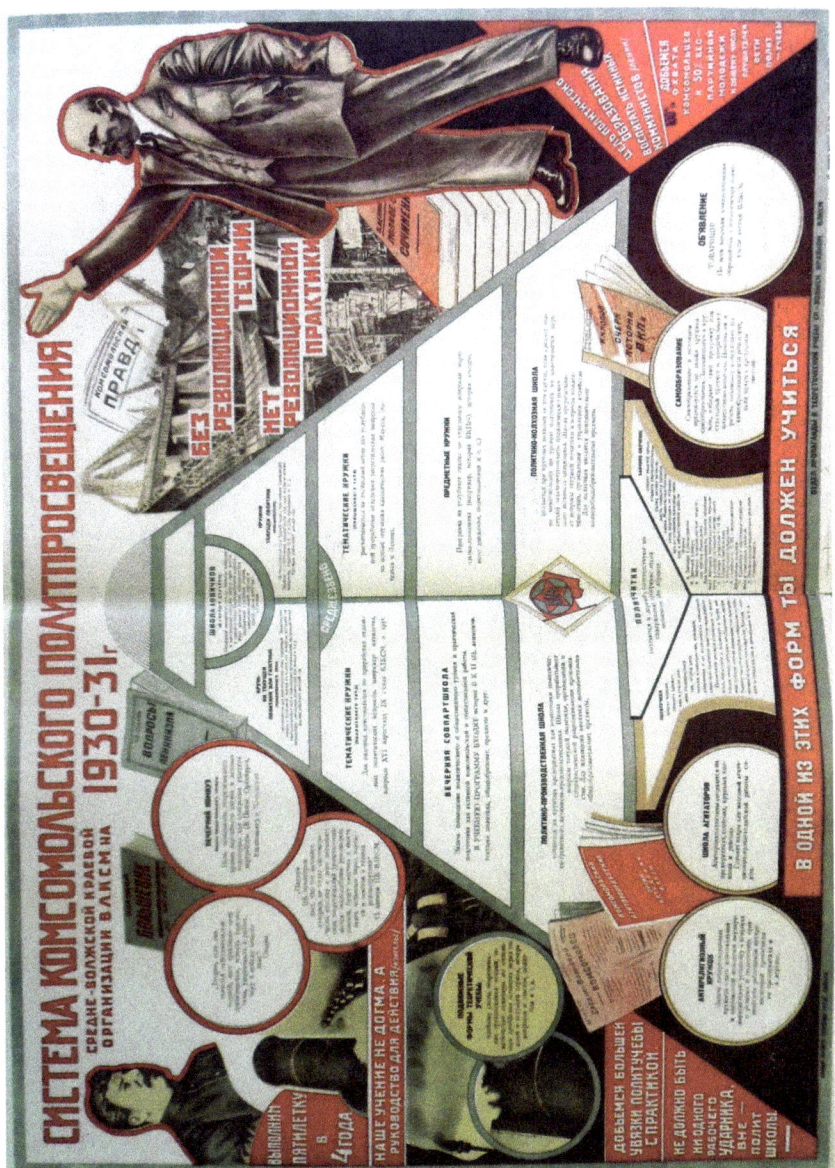

Fig. 2.1 'Komsomol political education system mid-Volga organisation V.L.K.S.M for 1930–31', unidentified artist, 1930, (Samara), 28 x 75 cm, edn 5,000

Source: Russian State Library

Fig. 2.2 'Under the Lenin banner for socialist construction', Gustav Klutsis, 1930

Source: Russian State Library

Fig. 2.3 'With the banner of Lenin we were victorious in the battle for the October revolution …', Viktor Deni, 1931, Izogiz (Moscow, Leningrad), 52 x 72 cm, edn 20,000

Source: redavantgarde.com/en/collection/show-collection/737--with-lenin-s-banner-we-have-won-fights-for-october-revolution-.html?authorId=8

Fig. 2.4 'Shock work at the machine is combined with the study of Marxist–Leninist theory', A.M. Rumiantsev, 1931, Izogiz (Moscow), 85 x 58 cm, edn 40,000

Source: Hoover Institution Archives

2. THE RISE OF THE STALIN PERSONALITY CULT

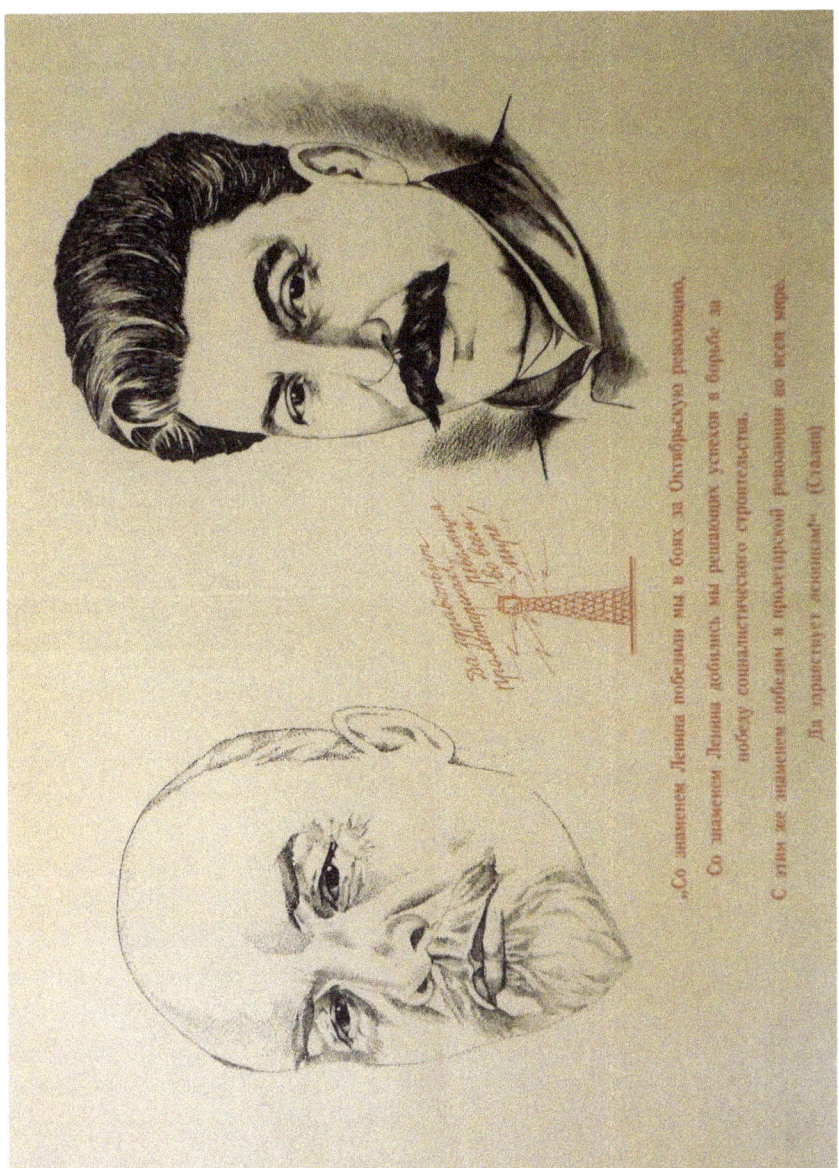

Fig. 2.5 'With the banner of Lenin …', Viktor Deni, 1933, Izogiz (Moscow), 77 x 109 cm, edn 60,000

Source: Russian State Library

Fig. 2.6 'With the banner of Lenin ...', Gustav Klutsis, 1933, Izogiz, 62 x 88 cm, 300,000

Source: Russian State Library

2. THE RISE OF THE STALIN PERSONALITY CULT

Fig. 2.7 'With the banner of Lenin …', Iraklii Toidze, 1933, Izogiz (Moscow, Leningrad), 62 x 94 cm (edn of 300); 82 x 110 cm, edn 1,000

Source: Russian State Library

Fig. 2.8 'Long live the great party of Lenin–Stalin — leader and organiser of the victorious building of socialism!', L. Stenberg, 1937

Source: Russian State Library

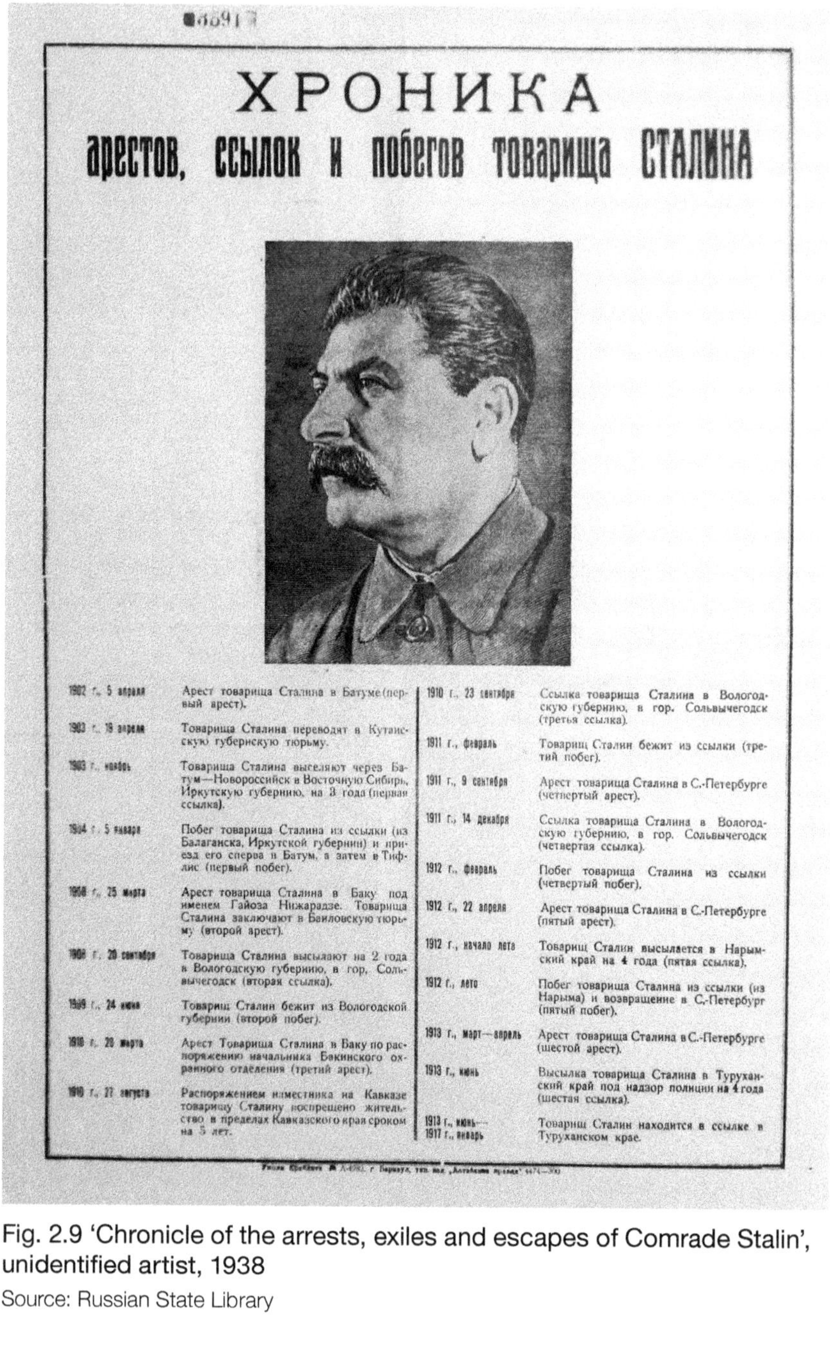

Fig. 2.9 'Chronicle of the arrests, exiles and escapes of Comrade Stalin', unidentified artist, 1938

Source: Russian State Library

Fig. 2.10 'Be as the great Lenin was', Vasilii Elkin, 1938, Izogiz (Moscow, Leningrad), 60 x 94 cm, edn 100,000
Source: Russian State Library

Fig. 2.11 'Be as the great Lenin was', A.I. Madorskii, 1938, edn 15,000
Source: Russian State Library

2. THE RISE OF THE STALIN PERSONALITY CULT

Fig. 2.12 'Be as the great Lenin was', A.I. Madorskii, 1939, 60 x 90 cm, edn 20,000

Source: Russian State Library

THE PERSONALITY CULT OF STALIN IN SOVIET POSTERS, 1929–1953

Fig. 2.13 'Departing from us …', Vladimir Kaidalov, 1940, UzFimgiz (Tashkent), 60 x 92 cm, edn 7,000
Source: Russian State Library

2. THE RISE OF THE STALIN PERSONALITY CULT

Fig. 2.14 'Under the banner of Lenin, under the leadership of Stalin — forward to new victories!', Petr Golub, 1945, Iskusstvo, 85.5 x 61 cm, edn 200,000

Source: Russian State Library

Fig. 2.15 '1918–1943 Long live the XXV anniversary of the Leninist–Stalinist Komsomol', Vladimir Serov, 1943, Iskusstvo (Leningrad), 70 x 52 cm, edn 5,000

Source: redavantgarde.com/en/collection/show-collection/676-long-live-the-hhvth-anniversary-of-lenin-and-stalin-s-komsomol-.html?authorId=15

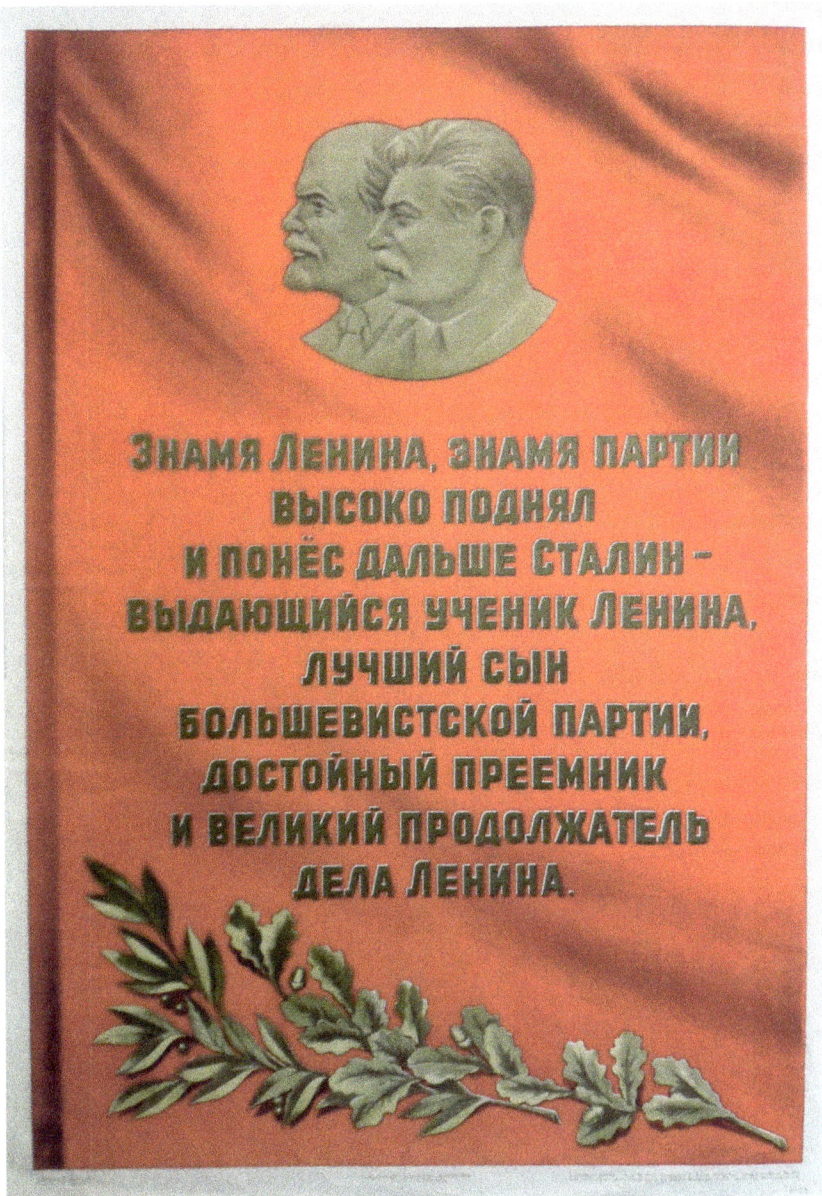

Fig. 2.16 'The banner of Lenin …', L. Stenberg, 1949, Iskusstvo (Moscow, Leningrad), 85 x 56.5 cm, edn 100,000. Another edition of 100,000 was issued in 1951

Source: Russian State Library

THE PERSONALITY CULT OF STALIN IN SOVIET POSTERS, 1929–1953

Fig. 2.17 '26 years without Lenin, but still on Lenin's path', Mytnikov, 1950, Izdanie Rostizo (Rostov-Don), edn 15,000
Source: Russian State Library

2. THE RISE OF THE STALIN PERSONALITY CULT

Fig. 2.18 'In the name of communism', Viktor Govorkov, 1951, Iskusstvo (Moscow), 86 x 97 cm, edn 600,000

Source: Russian State Library

Fig. 2.19 'Glory to the great leaders of October', Naum Karpovskii, 1951, Iskusstvo (Moscow), 64.5 x 87.5 cm, edn 100,000

Source: Russian State Library

Fig. 2.20 'Glory to Lenin, glory to Stalin, glory to great October', V. Reshetnikov, 1952, Latgosizdat, edn 3,000

Source: Russian State Library

Fig. 2.21 'Long live the great, united party of Lenin–Stalin …', unidentified artist, 1952

Source: ostaline.su/staliniana/posters/view.html?node=42411&letter=867&sort=names&card=37974

2. THE RISE OF THE STALIN PERSONALITY CULT

Fig. 2.22 'Long live the Bolshevik Party, the Lenin–Stalin Party, the vanguard of the Soviet people forged in battle, the inspiration and organiser of our victories!', Vladislav Pravdin, 1950, Iskusstvo (Moscow, Leningrad), 64.5 x 87.5 cm, edn 1,000,000

Source: Russian State Library

Fig. 2.23 'Raise higher the banner of Marx, Engels, Lenin, and Stalin!', Gustav Klutsis, 1933, edn 50,000 and then an edition of 30,000. In 1936 an edition of 250,000 was released

Source: Russian State Library

Fig. 2.24 'Long live the great, invincible banner of Marx–Engels–Lenin', Nikolai Dolgorukov, 1934, 163.5 x 56 cm

Source: The Jane Voorhees Zimmerli Art Museum

Fig. 2.25 'Long live the great invincible banner of Marx–Engels–Lenin–Stalin!', Vladislav Pravdin & Zoia Pravdina, 1938, Iskusstvo (Moscow, Leningrad), 62 × 94 cm, edn 100,000
Source: Russian State Library

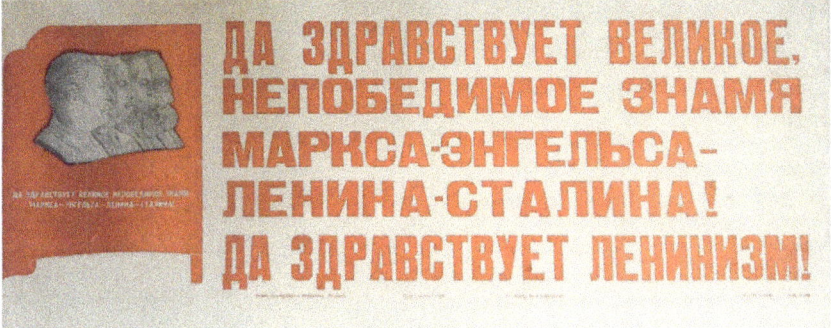

Fig. 2.26 'Long live the great invincible banner of Marx–Engels–Lenin–Stalin! Long live Leninism!', unidentified artist, 1940, edn 6,000
Source: Russian State Library

Fig. 2.27 'Long live the great invincible banner of Marx–Engels–Lenin–Stalin!', Nikolai Denisov & Nina Vatolina, 1941, Iskusstvo (Moscow, Leningrad), edn 100,000

Source: Russian State Library

2. THE RISE OF THE STALIN PERSONALITY CULT

Fig. 2.28 'Glory to great Stalin!', Vladimir Kaidalov, 1949, Gosizdat (Tashkent), edn 5,000
Source: Russian State Library

Fig. 2.29 'But there is one branch of science …', Bainazar Al'menov, 1951, Tatgosizdat (Kazan), edn 13,000

Source: Russian State Library

2. THE RISE OF THE STALIN PERSONALITY CULT

Fig. 2.30 'Long live the great invincible banner of Marx, Engels, Lenin, Stalin', A. Kossov, 1953, Iskusstvo (Moscow), 66 x 92 cm, edn 500,000

Source: redavantgarde.com/en/collection/show-collection/1051-long-live-the-great-and-invincible-banner-of-marx-engels-lenin-stalin-.html?authorId=386

Fig. 2.31 'Under the banner of Marx–Engels–Lenin–Stalin, under the guidance of the Communist party — forward, to the victory of communism!', Boris Belopol'skii, 1955, 54.5 x 87 cm

Source: Russian State Library

3
Stalin is like a fairytale sycamore tree — Stalin as a symbol

Gratitude's a dog's disease.
Iosif Stalin[1]

There was a fight in a line at the factory; people were hurt and a couple of policemen showed up. People just can't seem to appreciate how happy their lives are.
Andrei Stepanovich Arzhilovsky (ex-prisoner, executed by firing squad, 5 September 1937)[2]

Depending on your point of view, Stalin may or not be like a fairytale sycamore tree, but this metaphor, from a panegyric by Kazakh poet Dzhambul, serves to illuminate a central tenet of this book: that 'Stalin', as he appeared in Soviet posters, was a construct. Indeed, we are all 'constructs' in terms of our perceived and performed identities in society. Stalin, however, is a construct produced by a large group of people for mass consumption with specific goals in mind. Stalin existed as a symbol for such concrete entities as the Bolshevik Party and the state, but also for more abstract concepts like communist progress, Bolshevik values and vision, and peace. The Party's propaganda apparatus tightly controlled the use of his image and

---

[1] Quoted in Simon Sebag Montefiore, *Stalin: the court of the Red Tsar*, London, Weidenfeld and Nicolson, 2003, p. 43.
[2] 'Diary of Andrei Stepanovich Arzhilovsky', in Véronique Garros, Natalia Korenevskaya & Thomas Lahusen (eds), *Intimacy and terror: Soviet diaries of the 1930s*, New York, New Press, 1995, p. 150.

his persona drew on emblems of leadership and sacred imagery from both the Russian and the European past, from newly forged Bolshevik symbols, and on universal archetypes. In this chapter some of the symbols and archetypes associated with Stalin in propaganda posters will be explored.

Stalin as symbol

Writing in 1936, Swiss theologian Adolf Keller observed that, in contemporary authoritarian societies, the state itself had become a myth, and was increasingly depicted as possessing personal, and often divine, characteristics that came to be embodied in the symbolic persona of the leader:

> The State is a mythical divinity which, like God, has the right and might to lay a totalitarian claim on its subjects; to impose upon them a new philosophy, a new faith; to organise the thinking and conscience of its children ... It is not anonymous, not abstract, but gifted with personal qualities, with a mass-consciousness, a mass-will and a personal mass-responsibility for the whole world ... This personifying tendency of the myth finds its strongest expression in the mysterious personal relationship of millions with a leader ... The leader ... is the personified nation, a superman, a messiah, a saviour.[3]

States that are beset by turmoil, economic failure, social conflict or war invariably respond to these threats by seeking to strengthen the symbolic legitimation of the leadership. The leader cult attempts to create a point of reference for an entire belief system, centred on one man who embodies the doctrine. The cult is ubiquitous and aspires to universality of belief with the aim of integrating the masses into a 'community of believers'. As E.A. Rees states:

> Leader cults are part of the general process whereby the new power is symbolised and celebrated — in flags, hymns and anthems, medals, awards, prizes, stamps and coins, in the renaming of towns, streets and institutions. Leader cults are closely tied to the founding myths of new states.[4]

---

3   Adolf Keller, *Church and state on the European continent*, London, Epworth Press, 1936, pp. 56–59.
4   E.A. Rees, 'Introduction: leader cults: varieties, preconditions and functions', in Balázs Apor, Jan C. Behrends, Polly Jones & E.A. Rees, *The leader cult in communist dictatorships: Stalin and the Eastern Bloc*, Hampshire, Palgrave, 2004, pp. 7–8.

In a state that is in the process of reinventing itself, the leader cult becomes the means by which new rituals and traditions are instituted, employing symbols to bring consensus and a sense of shared identity in societies beset by latent conflict or indifference to the dominant ideology.[5]

The tendency of the Party to view their leader in mythic, symbolic and representational terms was already in evidence with regard to Lenin as early as 1923. For example, on 7 November 1923, *Pravda* declared: 'Lenin is not only the name of a beloved leader; it is a program and a tactic ... and a philosophical world view ... Lenin is the suffering for an idea ...'.[6] After Lenin's death, charisma came briefly to reside in the Party, however a charismatic leader's persona could provide a more concrete and personalised symbol for Bolshevik values and vision. Rees sees Stalin's cult in pragmatic terms, as an entity that 'reflected the reality that Stalin could command more public support than either the state or the party, and certainly more support than the regime's representatives and agents in the localities'.[7] In fact, Nina Tumarkin argues that, by 1934, Lenin and his cult had been relegated to a supporting role as a sort of 'sacred ancestor' of Stalin.[8]

As noted in the Introduction, Stalin regarded the Stalin name as symbolic of a created persona rather than as relating to his personal qualities as an individual.[9] This view of Stalin as a 'symbol of the Party' was shared by other members and was made explicit in propaganda posters. Nikolai Bukharin was asked in 1933 why he and the other Party members had entrusted the leadership to such a 'devil' as Stalin. Bukharin replied:

> You do not understand, it was quite different; he was not trusted, but he was the man whom the party trusted; this is how it happened: he is like the symbol of the party, the lower strata, the workers, the people trust him; perhaps it is our fault, but that's the way it happened, that is why we all walked into his jaws ... knowing probably that he would devour us.[10]

---

5   An excellent in-depth study of Soviet ritual can be found in Christel Lane, *The rites of rulers: ritual in industrial society: the Soviet case*, Cambridge University Press, 1981.
6   Nina Tumarkin, *Lenin lives! The Lenin cult in Soviet Russia*, Cambridge University Press, 1997, p. 132.
7   Rees, 'Introduction', in Apor et al., *The leader cult in communist dictatorships*, p. 11.
8   Tumarkin, *Lenin lives!*, p. 252.
9   Montefiore, *Stalin*, p. 4.
10 Quoted in Lydia Dan, 'Bukharin o Staline', *Novyi Zhurnal* 75, 1964, p. 182 (ellipsis in original).

A 1940 poster by Nikolai Zhukov (Fig. 3.1) features a quotation from Vyacheslav Molotov on the Stalin symbol: 'We have a name that has become the symbol of the victory of socialism. It is the name of the symbol of the moral and political unity of the Soviet people! You know what that name is — STALIN!' In the *Short biography* released in 1947, Stalin's value as the symbol of a plethora of Bolshevik values is made explicit in the text: 'In the eyes of the peoples of the U.S.S.R., Stalin is the incarnation of their heroism, their love of their country, their patriotism,'[11] 'Stalin's name is a symbol of the courage and the renown of the Soviet people, and a call to heroic deeds for the welfare of their great country,'[12] and 'The name of Stalin is a symbol of the moral and political unity of Soviet society.'[13] Writing in 1971, with the benefit of historical perspective, Roy Medvedev also regarded Stalin as a rallying symbol to unify and give hope to a suffering population during the Great Patriotic War: 'Stalin's image became a sort of symbol existing in the popular mentality independently from its actual bearer. During the war years, as the Soviet people were battered by unbelievable miseries, the name of Stalin, and the faith in him, to some degree, pulled the Soviet people together, giving them hope of victory.'[14] Evidence exists that this was true for at least some soldiers. The writer Konstantin Simonov quoted an officer on the Stalingrad front who said he 'gained all his strength from the idea that our great leader directs everything in our enormous cause from his office in Moscow and thus invests in him, an ordinary colonel, part of his genius and spirit'.[15]

The importance of maintaining central control over the image of Stalin was in evidence as early as December 1929 when, in preparation for celebration of Stalin's 50th birthday, Glavlit[16] published exact

---

11   G.F. Alexandrov, M.R. Galaktionov, V.S. Kruzhkov, M.B. Mitin, V.D. Mochalov & P.N. Pospelov, *Joseph Stalin: a short biography*, Moscow, Foreign Languages Publishing House, 1947, p. 201.
12   Alexandrov et al., *Joseph Stalin*, p. 202.
13   Alexandrov et al., *Joseph Stalin*, p. 203.
14   Roy Aleksandrovich Medvedev, *Let history judge: the origins and consequences of Stalinism*, New York, Knopf, 1971, p. 749.
15   Quoted in Orlando Figes, *The whisperers: private life in Stalin's Russia*, New York, Metropolitan Books, 2007, p. 410.
16   Jan Plamper notes that study of Glavlit censorship processes is substantially hindered by the fact that Glavlit archives from 1922 to 1937 are missing. Archival scholars are able to redress this situation to some extent by consulting the archives of regional Glavlit organisations. See Jan Plamper, 'Abolishing ambiguity: Soviet censorship practices in the 1930s', *Russian Review*, 60:4, 2001, pp. 526–44, p. 527. A. Fursenko and V. Afiani note the incompleteness of the Stalin archives, particularly from the 1940s, and advise using them cautiously: 'The integrity of Stalin's

regulations with regard to the use of Stalin's image in the press, prohibiting the use of printer's blocks bearing Stalin's image other than those issued by the Press-klishe[17] section of the ROSTA press agency.[18] From the mid-1930s the journal *Iskusstvo*[19] ran several articles guiding artists on how to portray the leader. The first edition of *Iskusstvo* in 1935 featured full-page portraits of Lenin and Stalin, with Stalin depicted adopting the 'hand-in' pose. The sixth edition in 1937 included illustrated articles titled 'Lenin in portraits, 1933–37', 'New portraits of Comrade Stalin', and 'Characteristics of the art of the epoch of Stalin', each running for several pages.[20] From around 1934 Stalin was visually distinguished from other leaders in propaganda, suggesting that he was the 'first among equals' and had exceptional, although human, qualities. Plamper observes that Stalin was distinguished from others by his size, his position in the picture plane, the colour of his clothing (which was often retouched), by the fact that his arm was often raised higher than those of others, by the fact that his hands never touched his face, by the direction of his gaze outside the picture plane,[21] by props such as his pipe, and by special mention in the poster caption.[22]

---

archives and historical links between documents was disrupted long ago' ('The death of Iosif Stalin', *International Affairs*, 49:3, 2003, pp. 188–99, p. 191). Kevin McDermott also advises using circumspection with the Soviet archives due to the lack of 'smoking guns', such as a personal diary by Stalin or stenographic records from the Politburo; the informal nature of much of the interaction between Politburo members; and the fact that a policy of misinformation was often actively employed by the Secret Police and others in the regime ('Archives, power and the "cultural turn": reflections on Stalin and Stalinism', *Totalitarian Movements and Political Religions*, 2004, 5:1, pp. 5–24, p. 8).

17 Type Supply.
18 Catriona Kelly, 'Riding the magic carpet: children and leader cult in the Stalin era', *The Slavic and East European Journal*, 49:2, 2005, pp. 199–224, p. 200.
19 Art.
20 Bernice Glatzer Rosenthal, *New myth, new world: from Nietzsche to Stalinism*, Pennsylvania State University Press, 2002, p. 380.
21 There are some interesting statements about the direction of Stalin's gaze in the Stalinist literature. Rosenthal states: 'Stalin's status as the new god was indicated by his position vis-à-vis other people. Stalin looks down, but they look up' (*New myth, new world*). James Aulich and Marta Sylvestrová state: 'Instead, the hero Stalin looks down on the world from his pedestal and, as the mediator between the profane and the divine, he has magical and superhuman powers' (*Political posters in Central and Eastern Europe, 1945–95: signs of the times*, Manchester University Press, 1999, p. 88). Plamper states: 'Knowledge of icons will not explain the direction of Stalin's gaze, which was invariably directed at a focal point outside the picture …' (*The Stalin cult: a study in the alchemy of power*, New Haven, Yale University Press, 2012, pp. xv, 11). In fact, in political posters, Stalin does three things with his eyes — he looks at the viewer, he looks down on the people, or he looks out of the picture plane into what one presumes is a vision of the future.
22 Plamper, *The Stalin cult*, p. 38.

The need to closely control Stalin's image is also evident in the type of censorship and 'retouching' performed on photographs of Stalin. In his books *The commissar vanishes* and *Red star over Russia*, David King documents the thorough censorship of photographic images, which included not only the deletion of newly undesirable figures from group scenes, but also the insertion of people into scenes at which they were not present, the merging of photographic images, and the insertion of extra objects into a scene.[23] In her study of photographs of Stalin, Leah Dickerman notes the use of specific devices: 'smoothing Stalin's pockmarked face and removing litter from his path; inserting text on banners so that the idea becomes legible; enlarging an adulatory crowd through montage …'.[24] Such censorship was often heavy-handed and obvious and there was no attempt to keep the role of censors beneath the public radar. Dickerman argues that the public and visible nature of censorship was itself an attempt by the state to demonstrate its dominance over the medium of photography, especially as the source images were often well known.[25] Such censorship, Plamper notes, also had as a primary goal the removal of ambiguity.[26] The number of possible meanings that could be ascribed to images was narrowed and contained, a process that was aided further in the case of propaganda posters by the caption text.

Such thorough state control of representations of the leader did not originate with the Stalinist regime. In fact, the photographic depiction of Bolshevik Party leaders was centralised and placed under the control of the secret police as early as 1924.[27] Nor was this phenomenon peculiar to the Soviet Union. As noted in the Introduction, leaders throughout history have sought to control the production and dissemination of their images amongst the citizenry using court-commissioned artists to create their portraiture, and officially sanctioned methods of reproduction. Elizabeth I of England issued edicts to regulate the way

---

23 David King, *Red star over Russia: a visual history of the Soviet Union from 1917 to the death of Stalin: posters, photographs and graphics from the David King collection*, London, Tate, 2009; and, David King, *The commissar vanishes: the falsification of photographs and art in Stalin's Russia*, New York, Metropolitan Books, 1997.
24 Leah Dickerman, 'Camera obscura: socialist realism in the shadow of photography', *October*, 93, 2000, pp. 138–53, p. 141.
25 Dickerman, 'Camera obscura', p. 143, 148.
26 Plamper, 'Abolishing Ambiguity', pp. 526–44.
27 Plamper, *The Stalin cult*, p. 24.

in which her image could be depicted on canvas.[28] In Taiwan during the 1930s, contemporaneous with the cult of Stalin, the Officers' Moral Endeavour Association (OMEA, *lizhishe*) fostered painters such as Liang Zhongming and Xu Jiuling who then drilled other artists in the correct portrayal of Chiang Kai-Shek and actively sought to learn from Soviet and American propaganda techniques.[29] In 1955, a team of Soviet artists arrived in China to teach Chinese artists to paint in a socialist realist style.[30] The Chinese propaganda apparatus soon set up its own guidelines for painting portraits of Mao Zedong, which took into account some purely Chinese cultural predispositions.[31] Regulation of Mao's image went a step further, with the government decreeing how the portraits were to be handled and hung.[32]

The Stalin persona, like most symbols, was multifaceted, malleable, and subject to change over time. In the early days of Stalin's rule, the Party leadership was presented as a somewhat anonymous collective with few pictures of leaders appearing in the press and Stalin often appearing alongside other leaders[33] or generic workers[34] in posters. Sarah Davies and James Heizer both note that in 1929, when Stalin did appear, he was generally depicted as 'iron-willed, cold, distant, and ruthless',[35] however, in some poster images between 1927 and 1932,

---

28 Nicholas J. O'Shaughnessy, 'The death and life of propaganda', *Journal of Public Affairs*, 12:1, 2012, pp. 29–38, p. 31.
29 See Jeremy E. Taylor, 'The production of the Chiang Kai-shek personality cult, 1929–1975', *The China Quarterly*, 185, 2006, pp. 96–110.
30 See David Elliott, 'Guerillas and partisans: art, power and freedom in Europe and Beyond, 1940–2012', *Framework, Helsinki*, 10, Supp, 2009, pp. 22–25, p. 24.
31 Mao's portrait was to be painted in a style reminiscent of Soviet socialist realism, however, this became 'further developed' in China: 'Cool colours were to be avoided; Mao's flesh should be modelled in red and other warm tones. Conspicuous displays of brushwork should not be seen; Mao's face should be smooth in appearance. The entire composition should be bright, and should be illuminated in such a way as to imply that Mao himself was the primary source of [the sun] light. If Mao were in the centre of a group of people, all surfaces that faced him should appear to be illuminated. In this way, slogans such as "Mao is the sun in our hearts" could be made tangible' (Julia F. Andrews, *Painters and politics in the People's Republic of China: 1949–1979*, London, University of California Press, 1994, p. 360).
32 Mao portraits had to be handled with special care, nothing could be hung above them, and the frame was not to have any spots or blemishes. See *Chinese propaganda posters*, Köln, Taschen, 2011, p. 20.
33 For example, Gustav Klutsis, 'The USSR is the leader of the world proletariat', 1931.
34 For example, Gustav Klutsis, 'These are real people, this is you and me', 1931.
35 Sarah Davies, *Popular opinion in Stalin's Russia: terror, propaganda and dissent, 1934–1941*. Cambridge University Press, 1997, p. 147; and, James L. Heizer, 'The cult of Stalin, 1929–1939', PhD thesis, University of Kentucky, 1977, p. 55.

Stalin can be seen with a faint Giacondian smile.[36] Otherwise, posters tend to focus on workers and the progress of industrialisation — Stalin is not the central image and depictions of him consist largely of head shots in which his expression is neutral and few clues are given as to his personal qualities.

Davies sees 1933 as the year in which the full-blown cult of Stalin began to emerge, and 1934 as the year in which it 'exploded'.[37] By 1933 Stalin was sometimes referred to with the epithet *liubimyi* (beloved)[38] and, by 1935, his portrait image was softening somewhat as he smiled or waved at crowds.[39] Despite the increasing tendency to eulogise Stalin, beginning in 1934, he was still only the *man* who leads the Party, first and foremost of the leaders of the people. Stalin was frequently shown in the media meeting and mixing with the people. This new emphasis on the relationship between the leader and the people can be demonstrated by the remarks of Aleksandr Ugarov, second secretary of the Leningrad *obkom*,[40] in connection with the preparation for the Day of the Constitution on 6 July 1935: 'This affair has to be organised in an essentially different way from in previous years. The political explanations should be organised so that people feel that Soviet leaders are coming to them and telling them about the achievements of Soviet democracy.'[41] By 1936, the cult progressed still further, with the emphasis on developing a fanatical cult following for the Party leadership and in particular, Stalin, as in this local Party report:

> During agitation and propaganda in the press there must be more popularisation of the *vozhdi*, and love for them must be fostered and inculcated in the masses, and unlimited loyalty, especially by

---

36 As in the 'Young Communist League of Political Education, Middle Volga', organisation poster of 1930 (artist unidentified), Viktor Deni's 'With the banner of Lenin …', 1930; Klutsis's 'These are real people, this is you and me', 1931.
37 Sarah Davies, *Popular opinion in Stalin's Russia: terror, propaganda and dissent, 1934–1941*, Cambridge University Press, 1997, p. 148.
38 Davies points out that Kirov was also referred to by the epithet *liubimyi* at the same time and that Kirov was perceived as more humane and caring than Stalin ('The "cult" of the vozhd': representations in letters from 1934–41', *Russian History*, 24:1–2, 1997, pp. 131–47, p. 133; and, Davies, *Popular opinion in Stalin's Russia*, p. 178).
39 Gustav Klutsis, 'Long live the USSR — a forerunner of unity for the workers of every nationality in the world', 1935; Gustav Klutsis, 'Long live our happy socialist motherland, long live our beloved great Stalin!', 1935; and, Gustav Klutsis, 'Cadres decide everything', 1935 (Fig. 4.62).
40 Provincial Committee.
41 Davies, *Popular opinion in Stalin's Russia*, pp. 148–50.

cultivating the utmost love for comrade Stalin and the other leaders amongst children and young people, inculcating Soviet patriotism, bringing them to fanaticism in love and defence of comrade Stalin and our socialist motherland.[42]

By the late 1930s, adulation for Stalin in propaganda was increasing. Stalin became the leader responsible for all of the new socialist construction taking place, the inspiration for record-breaking flights and new feats of exploration, the creator of the glorious new constitution and the only person capable of identifying and purging the regime's enemies. The German invasion of the Soviet Union in 1941 appears to have genuinely taken Stalin by surprise and undermined his confidence, especially as he had publicly maintained that Germany would not invade.[43] The façade of rampaging success became impossible to maintain. Stalin's appearances in the press decreased, although he was still quoted, and his image in propaganda posters also diminished. After victory Stalin reappeared as more triumphant than before the war and with a mandate for leadership in his own right, somewhat independent of his need to appeal to Lenin's legacy. Victory was celebrated, with Stalin as its author, and his image was often treated like an icon. By 1949 Stalin was also portrayed as a saviour and bringer of peace.[44]

The persona of Stalin not only evolved and adapted to circumstances over a long period of time, but also exhibited considerable breadth, holding the widest possible appeal to diverse audiences. There was a tension between the need to control Stalin's image through centralisation and censorship, which restricted meaning to within narrowly defined constructs, and the need to offer a plurality of meanings to reach the widest possible audience. This latter led to 'overcoding' of the image and a situation where symbols associated with the image contained a multitude of meanings that, if not wholly contradictory, sometimes sat together uneasily or appeared to be mutually exclusive. In other words, Stalinist symbolism can appear confusing if examined broadly and objectively and with a view to finding coherent and consistent meaning. In his study of Napoleon and history painting, Christopher Prendergast notes the same tendency

---

42 Cited in Davies, *Popular opinion in Stalin's Russia*, p. 150.
43 To be discussed in Chapter Four.
44 See Chapter Four.

with propagandistic portrayals of Napoleon, arising largely from the fact that there was an attempt to show Napoleon simultaneously as a victorious general and a benevolent leader.[45] The Stalin cult also had to reconcile within the one persona both his image as an iron-willed military victor (both in the Civil War and later in the Great Patriotic War) and the appearance of being a humane and caring leader providing for Soviet citizens. These two elements were expressed by the Warrior and the Father archetypes, and were somewhat reconciled (if not entirely convincingly) in the adoption of the Saviour archetype. Thomas Mathews' observations with regard to portraits of Christ apply equally well here. Mathews notes that the images correspond to what people needed from Christ, rather than to any intrinsic qualities and this has resulted in a plethora of representations of Christ that, as a whole, have little consistency and sometimes demonstrate bewildering contradictions.[46]

Stalin's relationship with Lenin, as depicted in propaganda, was another area of ambiguity, and highlights the androgyny of the symbolism associated with some charismatic leaders.[47] In her study of mythopoetic elements in memories of Stalin, Natalia Skradol explores how Stalin's mythology places him both as Lenin's son and as a sort of symbolic husband to Lenin. In this latter schema, Lenin is the mother figure who gives birth to the regime, and dies doing so, while Stalin receives the newborn into his hands and raises it. This notion is made explicit in a striking poster of 1947 by Iraklii Toidze (Fig. 3.2) which is discussed in detail in Chapter Four.

---

[45] The resultant 'overcoding', arising from the tension between the nature of the event depicted and the propaganda requirements of the depiction, lead to a confusing plurality of messages: 'Napoleon can only with difficulty be authoritative ruler, tragic victim, redemptive saviour and humanitarian benefactor in a scene of war, for which in any case he was primarily responsible in the first place ...', Prendergast argues that Napoleon is the first case in which propaganda consistently tried to reconcile these two images (*Napoleon and history painting: Antoine-Jean Gros's La Bataille d'Eylau*, Oxford, Clarendon Press, 1997, p. 168).

[46] Mathews goes on to note the power of images to encourage adulation and worship, even when objective analysis of the image finds it lacking in any real substance: 'often images overwhelm the ideas they are supposed to be carrying, or dress up with respectability ideas that in themselves are too shoddy to carry intellectual weight. Images not only express convictions, they alter feelings and end up justifying convictions. Eventually, of course, they invite worship' (*The clash of gods: a reinterpretation of early Christian art*, Princeton University Press, 1999, p. 11).

[47] To be discussed in greater detail in relation to religious symbolism and the icon in Chapter Four.

Igor Golomshtok observes in relation to Soviet genre painting under Stalin that the fundamental task of Soviet art was to interpret the Stalin symbol through a multitude of prisms: 'Stalin — let alone Lenin — was more a symbol than a man, and the role of Soviet art was to decipher this symbol, to reveal different aspects of the existence of this superman in thousands upon thousands of genre paintings.'[48] The French biographer of Stalin, Henri Barbusse, got to the crux of the matter when he observed that Stalin had 'the face of a worker, the head of a scholar, and in the clothing of a simple soldier'.[49] This 'triple nature' immediately invites a comparison with the 'Holy Trinity' and highlights the ability of the Stalin persona to both combine several natures in one being, and to appear as different things to different people, a sort of magical shape-shifting ability that befits a magician or a deity.[50] Alfred J. Rieber sees the roots of Stalin's multiple and sometimes contradictory identities as deriving from deeper, sometimes unconscious sources from within Stalin himself as he struggled to reconcile his Georgian beginnings with his proletarian values and political life in Russia.[51]

Stalin: 'Man of Steel'

It is well known that the alias adopted by Stalin, inconsistently at first from around 1910, and which later came to substitute for his own surname and to symbolise his persona, translates as 'Man of Steel'. Stalin, like Lenin and the other Bolshevik revolutionaries, had used

---

48   Igor Golomshtok, *Totalitarian art in the Soviet Union, the Third Reich, fascist Italy and the People's Republic of China*, New York, Icon Editions, 1990, p. 300.
49   Cited in Maya Turovskaya, 'Easy on the heart; or, "Strength through joy"', in Marina Balina & E.A. Dobrenko, *Petrified utopia: happiness Soviet style*, London, Anthem Press, 2009, p. 247.
50   This manner of presenting the leader does not merely belong to a 'naïve' Soviet past. In their article on Vladimir Putin and Putiniana, Julie A. Cassiday and Emily D. Johnson note that the cult around Putin is 'inherently polysemantic, highly mobile and easily individualized', with Putin's image nebulous and all-embracing, a reflection in which everyone can see what he wishes to see. They argue that the nostalgic cult that has developed around Putin serves the same purpose as the cult of Stalin ('Putin, Putiniana and the question of a post-Soviet cult of personality', *SEER*, 88:4, 2010, pp. 685–86).
51   For the purposes of analysis he uses the constructs of three analytical frames — 'the cultural (traditional Georgian), the social (proletarian), and the political (hegemonic Russian)' — each of which contained its own kernel of truth, 'layering of fabrications' and set of ambiguities, to explore the ambiguities and tensions in the public image of Stalin and posits that, once in power, Stalin deliberately maintained a multiplicity of meanings in order to destabilise others and to confirm his role as the 'master interpreter' and supreme authority (Alfred J. Rieber, 'Stalin, man of the borderlands', *The American Historical Review*, 106:5, 2001, pp. 1651–91, pp. 1656–57).

many cadre names during his underground career. The two others to endure throughout his lifetime, especially amongst close comrades from the early days, were 'Soso' and 'Koba'. There are, perhaps, a confluence of reasons for Dzhugashvili choosing the moniker 'Stalin' and also for why it stuck.[52] Montefiore suggests that the appellation 'Man of Steel' suited Stalin's character[53] and, undoubtedly, his conception of himself. Montefiore also draws a parallel with the case of Lenin, who had 160 aliases, but kept Lenin because it was the byline he used on his *What is to be done?* pamphlet, the article with which he made his reputation. Stalin used the Stalin byline on his article on nationalities, which made his reputation.[54] The name Stalin sounded Russian and was similar to 'Lenin'. In addition, Stalin's Bolshevik comrades were doing much the same thing: Scriabin became Molotov (Hammer Man) and Rosenfeld became Kamenev (Man of Stone).[55]

The use of 'steel' as a metaphor in portrayals of Stalin implied personal qualities of courage, determination, ruthlessness, toughness, and unbreakability. These qualities were compatible with those required in an underground revolutionary, and translated well into the leadership role, especially under the dire circumstances that existed in the fledgling Soviet regime, but also in view of the continued threats posed by internal and external enemies throughout Stalin's rule. Stalin may also have had earlier metaphoric associations with the tough metals from his Georgian childhood. Rieber posits that the cult of iron and steel was a widespread and possibly unique phenomenon in the Caucasus, especially in the oral tradition of epic Ossetian tales. One of the most popular heroes is Soslan Stal'noi[56] who was a defender (and sometimes vengeful destroyer) of his kinfolk.[57]

---

52 Montefiore suggests that it is possible, although he doubts that Stalin would have admitted it, that a girlfriend by the name of Ludmilla Stal was the original inspiration behind the pseudonym, as Stalin frequently fashioned aliases out of the names of his women (*Young Stalin*, New York, Alfred A. Knopf, 2007, p. 278).
53 Montefiore, *Young Stalin*, p. 279.
54 Montefiore, *Young Stalin*, p. 278.
55 Lev Davidovich Bronshtein had also used numerous aliases in his underground period, 'Trotskii' being the name he took from one of his jailers in Odessa when travelling on a forged passport.
56 Soslan the Iron Man.
57 Rieber, 'Stalin, Man of the Borderlands', p. 1681.

Iron and steel also had important metaphoric associations for Soviet society. During the 1930s Lazar Kaganovich earned the nickname 'Iron Lazar', possibly for both his iron will in executing the orders of Stalin, and because of his position as people's commissar for the railways, in charge of building the Moscow Metro. Iron and steel were crucial to Soviet efforts to industrialise rapidly, and construct impressive new Soviet cities, including the planned reconstruction of Moscow. During the 1930s Stalin was frequently depicted amid scenes of mammoth socialist construction, surrounded by vast structures of concrete and steel, and also as showing the way forward with steady outstretched arm and steely gaze. This display of 'iron will' continued in the posters of the war years, with Stalin becoming the rallying symbol of the determination of the nation to hold out against the fascist threat and to force victory. Stalin was closely associated with achievements in Soviet aviation and the aircraft of the Soviet Airforce were referred to as *staln'ye ptitsy* (birds of steel),[58] while flyers became known as *Stalinskim sokolam* (Stalin's falcons). The steely determination of Stalin's gaze and posture added force to the words of poster captions, usually Stalin's own words from speeches in which he exhorted and cajoled the citizenry to join their will for victory to his own. When Stalin refused to evacuate Moscow and the Kremlin with the rest of the government, he was seen to be living up to his appellation of 'Man of Steel'.

Stalin and the sun

One of the key symbols associated with Stalin in propaganda is the sun, with its related qualities of light and warmth. The sun is a recurrent motif throughout propaganda associated with leaders since pre-Christian times, when leaders appealed to their sun gods to look favourably upon their leadership, their battles and their harvests. Plamper traces the association of this trope with the leader in Russia back to the 17th-century court poet Simeon Polotskii.[59] Associating a leader with the sun suggests that he is the bringer of life and of bounty to the people. That Stalin approved of the use of this symbol for his leadership seems apparent because research into his personal

---

58 For example, *Pravda*, 19 Aug. 1933, cited in Plamper, *The Stalin cult*, p. 37.
59 Plamper, *The Stalin cult*, p. 93.

library has shown that, in a book about Napoleon, Stalin annotated the passage 'Had Napoleon been forced to choose a religion, he would have chosen to worship the sun, which fertilizes everything and is the true god of the earth', with the word 'Good', and circled the word 'sun' in red.[60]

The sun became a central image in Stalinist propaganda, with Stalin unambiguously equated with the sun in poetry and song, while propaganda posters frequently associated Stalin with light in general. At a meeting of shock workers in February 1936, the Dagestani folk poet Suleiman Stalskii referred to Stalin as the sun who 'illuminates the world'.[61] Hymns and songs dedicated to Stalin celebrate him with the words 'Like the sun, you have illumined the expanse',[62] or 'Glory to the golden sun, glory to the stars on the Kremlin, Glory to our native Stalin',[63] or 'Glory to our mother earth! Glory to the red sun in the Kremlin!'[64] In a 1937 editorial in *Literaturnaia Gazeta*[65] it was suggested that Stalin's warmth was so powerful that it could even protect his falcons against the freezing Arctic temperatures.[66] Perhaps one of the most laboured metaphorical associations of Stalin with the light of the sun occurs in a poem by Kazakh poet Dzhambul. This panegyric forms the text of a poster by Vartan Arakelov which was released in 1939, the year of Stalin's 60th birthday celebrations (Fig. 3.3).[67] Stalin is celebrated as the father of children of all nations

---

60 Evgenii Gromov, *Stalin: Vlast' I iskusstvo*, Moscow, Respublika, 1998, pp. 44–45.
61 Jeffrey Brooks, *Thank you, Comrade Stalin! Soviet public culture from revolution to Cold War*, Princeton University Press, 2000, p. 94.
62 Aram Khachaturian, 'Pesnia o Staline' [A song about Stalin], Moscow, Muzgiz, 1945, vol. 2, cited in John E. Bowlt, 'Stalin as Isis and Ra: socialist realism and the art of design', *The Journal of Decorative and Propaganda Arts*, 24, *design, culture, identity: The Wolfsonian Collection*, 2002, pp. 34–63, p. 54.
63 Aleksandr Prokof'ev, 'Slava Stalinu' [Glory to Stalin], in *Pesni o Staline* (Songs about Stalin), L.O. Belov et al., (eds), *Moscow: Gosudarstvennoeiz datel'stvok hudozhestvennoil iteratury*, 1950, p. 197, cited in Bowlt, 'Stalin as Isis and Ra', p. 54.
64 Anatoly Sofronov, 'Pesnia slavy' [A song of glory], cited in Bowlt, 'Stalin as Isis and Ra', p. 54.
65 *Literary Gazette*.
66 Editorial, *Literary Gazette*, 1937, no. 28, 26 May, p. 1, cited in Katerina Clark, *The Soviet novel: history as ritual*, University of Chicago Press, 1981, p. 126. A similar assertion with regard to the polar explorers appears in *Pravda*, 25 May 1937, p. 1, cited in Plamper, *The Stalin cult*, p. 40.
67 Stalin is the wisest of all people
You couldn't get a more beloved father.
Radiating light beams onto
Children of all nations, of all tribes.
Stalin is like a fairytale sycamore tree.
His power is visible from everywhere.
Every leaf is an expensive diamond

3. STALIN IS LIKE A FAIRYTALE SYCAMORE TREE

and tribes, and the source of a radiating and shimmering light, which reflects onto everyone. Despite the fatherly connotations of the text, this poster image of Stalin emphasises his remoteness from the realm of man and endows him with the qualities of a deity. Stalin is made of stone, an honour reserved for founding fathers and those who have accomplished exceptional feats. The statue is immutable and immortal. It stands amid lush blossoms, above children, looking protectively out over the scene and beyond, a god that guarantees abundance and safety, and invites veneration and worship. The children, from various nationalities, cannot hope to access Stalin personally and instead do so through his representative in the earthly realm, the poet Dzhambul, who sings words of praise of Stalin to the children, accompanying himself on the dombra.

The 1939 Uzbek poster, 'So — greetings, Stalin, and live for a hundred years …' (Fig. 3.4) by Konstantin Cheprakov, dates from the immediate prewar era in which Stalin's munificence extended beyond the borders of Russia and out to all the nationalities and states of the Soviet Union. Uzbekistan is one of the many countries that at that time made up the Union of Soviet Socialist Republics. This poster illustrates the gratitude to Stalin of the Uzbek people for the building of the 270-kilometre-long Great Fergana Canal to irrigate the cotton fields, and thus create cotton independence for the Soviet Union. Stalin is surrounded by a flowing multitude of Uzbek peasants bearing flowers and displaying the fruits of their irrigated fields. Stalin gives and receives congratulations to Molotov who, due to his position in the composition and the distinctive colour of his clothing, occupies centre stage. Interestingly, Molotov is also the centre of light in the poster, with a subdued Stalin in muted tones placed off in the shadows to the right.

Despite Stalin's reluctance to assume the limelight in the visual component of the poster, the text of the poster — 'So — greetings, Stalin, and live for a hundred years, shine like the sun, live for victory! And lead us on the way to victory! Accept the country's joyous

---

Shining soft light on you.
Remember forever, pioneer:
Stalin is your best role model.
Like a father, his smile shines on
Children of all nations, of all tribes.
Dzhambul

greetings!' — makes it clear to whom the Uzbek people owe their gratitude for the canal which is to be their lifeblood. In fact, Stalin is responsible for more than just water for the crops, he also provides the sunshine. Molotov takes centre stage because Stalin allows him to do so, a manifestation of Stalin's modesty and humility. The text makes clear that all of the illustrated bounty is due to the blessing bestowed by Stalin. By appearing to be a spontaneous outpouring of gratitude from the hearts of the people, both the image and the text illustrate the correct relationship between the leaders and the people.

A 1948 Uzbek poster by Mikhail Reikh (Fig. 3.5) also celebrates abundance and Stalin as the sun. The poster is dominated by a bust of Stalin emblazoned across a red sky. Stalin appears like the rising sun, illuminating the Uzbek people below who look to the sky, arms outstretched to offer thanks to the source of fertility and abundance. In their arms they hold offerings of bouquets of cotton and ears of wheat, and blossoming roses surround the poster caption. The caption, in both Uzbek and Russian, names Stalin as the sun and is taken from a letter signed by 26,474,646 Komsomol and youth on 3 November 1947: 'For communism! So youth exclaims, and this cry is heard in the distance. Youth swears allegiance, Comrade Stalin is the Sun of all the earth!'

Stalin's association with warmth and the sun is also the subject of a 1949 poster by an unidentified artist, 'We are warmed by Stalin's affection' (Fig. 3.6). The poster features a smiling bust of Stalin, with military collar but without cap, surrounded by the smaller heads of 15 children. Beneath Stalin is a laurel wreath that, with his military uniform and the fireworks and searchlights below, visually references victory in the Great Patriotic War. The children, who look ethnically Georgian, are encased in flowers, many of their heads appearing to grow out of the petals. The five children at the base of the poster appear to rise up from a bowl of fruit. Fruit, flowers and children all testify to the fecundity and abundance of the socialist utopia. Behind the youngest child, in the centre at the base, the spire of the Spassky tower rises, leading straight to the portrait of Stalin and thus linking the two symbols. Stalin is located at the position of deity, but also appears as the father of the children, a point that has particular resonance because of Stalin's Georgian roots. Above their heads, but beneath Stalin, fireworks and searchlights illuminate the violet sky. Stalin glows with a white light and, in the heavenly realm that he inhabits,

3. STALIN IS LIKE A FAIRYTALE SYCAMORE TREE

the entire background consists of the white light that emanates from him. The text of the poster is in Russian and Georgian and celebrates the joys of childhood, sunny Georgia and Stalin: 'We are warmed by Stalin's affection, We carry joy and happiness, / We are sunny Georgian children, / Singing a song to Stalin!' It is flanked by scenes of Georgian life — traditional architecture juxtaposed with new construction, and a train rushing through lush fields of crops.

Numerous posters depict Stalin as the source of light[68] or as illuminated by a light from above,[69] and Stalin was associated with both natural and artificial light. A notable example of this variant of the metaphor

---

68 Marina Volkova & Natalia Pinus, 'Long live the equal rights woman in the USSR', 1938; Viktor Koretskii, 'Workers of collective and Soviet cooperative farms and machine tractor station operators …', 1939; Iraklii Toidze, 'All our forces to support our Red Army …', 1941 (Fig. 4.16); Vasilii Bayuskin & A. Shpier, 'The Great Patriotic War', 1942; A.A. Kazantsev, 'Forward to the definitive defeat of the enemy', 1944; Stefan Gints, 'The triumph of victory …', 1945; V. Selivanov, 'Glory to our great people', 1945 (in which rays of sunshine emanate from the Stalin victory medal); Petr Shukhmin, 'Long live the great organiser and inspirer of historic victory …', 1945; I. Achundov, [text in Azerbaijani], 1946; Nikolai Avvakumov, 'Long live our teacher, our father, our leader, Comrade Stalin!', 1946 (Fig. 3.28); Ruben Shkhiyan, 'In order to build, we need to know …', 1947; Naum Karpovskii, 'Labour with martial persistence so your kolkhoz becomes part of the vanguard …',1948; Naum Karpovskii, 'Long live the Komsomol generation', 1948; Vladislav Pravdin & Nikolai Denisov, 'Glory to great Stalin!', 1948; Vladislav Pravdin & Nikolai Denisov, 'Long live our leader and teacher, the great Stalin!', 1948; Leonid Golovanov, 'And Stalin raised us to be loyal to the people, inspired us to work and to deeds', 1949 (Fig. 3.21); Iraklii Toidze, 'Long live the best friend of miners, great Stalin!', 1949; Viktor Koretskii, 'Great Stalin is the banner of friendship of peoples of the USSR!', 1950 (Fig. 4.55); N. Talipov, 'Long live Comrade Stalin …', 1950; Nina Vatolina, 'Thank you comrade Stalin for our happy childhood!', 1950; Boris Berezovskii, Mikhail Solov'ev & I. Shagin, 'Under the leadership of great Stalin — forward to communism!', 1951 (Fig. 4.66); Mikhail Gordon, 'Under the banner of Lenin, under the leadership of Stalin — forward to the victory of communism!', 1951; Elena Mel'nikova, 'Best friend of children, glory to great Stalin!', 1951; B.V. Vorontsov, 'Iosif Vissarionovich Stalin', 1951.
69 M. Zhukov, 'The leader of the people of the USSR and workers of the whole world', 1938 (in which the sun forms part of the emblem of the Turkmen Soviet Socialist Republic); Viktor Deni & Nikolai Dolgorukov, 'Stalin's spirit makes our army and country strong and solid', 1939 (Fig. 4.11); Vladimir Kaidalov, 'Departing from us …', 1940 (Fig. 2.13); Naum Karpovskii, 'People praise life in song …', 1940; Viktor Klimashin, 'The All-Union Agricultural Exhibition', 1940; Iraklii Toidze, 'The party is unbeatable …', 1940; U. Zubov, 'Under the guidance of great Stalin, forward to new victories', 1941; Vladimir Serov, 'Under the banner of Lenin, forward to victory', 1942 (Fig. 4.23); Pavel Sokolov-Skalia, 'Long live the VKP(b) — leaders and organisers of the Komsomol', 1943; M. Karpenko, 'Under the banner of Lenin, under the leadership of Stalin — forward to the complete defeat of the German invaders', 1944; Viktor Govorov, 'Glory to the first candidate for deputy of the Supreme Soviet of the USSR, great Stalin!', 1946 (Fig. 4.67); Boris Berezovskii, '"We stand for peace and we defend the cause of peace." I. Stalin', 1947 (Fig. 4.52); Petr Grechkin, 'Under the banner of Lenin, under the leadership of Stalin …', 1947; Naum Karpovskii, 'Long live the invincible banner of Lenin–Stalin', 1947; Iraklii Toidze, 'Stalin's kindness illuminates the future of our children', 1947 (Fig. 3.2); Nikolai Denisov & Vladislav Pravdin, 'Under the banner of Lenin, under the leadership of Stalin — forward to the victory of communism!', 1948; Vasilii Suryaninov, 'Stalin is our banner!', 1948; Vladimir Kaidalov, 'Glory to great Stalin!', 1949; F. Litvinov, 'Long life and prosperity to our motherland!', 1949 (Fig. 3.22);

is Stalin Prize winner Viktor Ivanov's 'Great Stalin is the beacon of communism!' of 1949 (Fig. 3.7). Stalin stands alone in his study, in front of a bookshelf containing the collected works of Marx and Engels, Lenin, and his own writings. Although he is lit from above, the text makes it clear that it is Stalin who is the guiding light of communism. Several posters celebrating Stalin's role in guiding the nation to victory in the Great Patriotic War show the sky lit up with fireworks and searchlights.[70] During holiday celebrations Stalin's image was sometimes projected onto clouds in the night sky, so that he appeared to be hovering over the crowds on a beam of light like a protective deity.[71]

Stalin was also associated with electric light. Lenin had been strongly associated with electricity as a result of concerted propaganda campaigns to electrify the nation using the slogan: 'Communism is Soviet power plus the electrification of the whole country.'[72] Lightbulbs were commonly referred to as 'Ilich's little lamps' and Lenin was thanked for delivering electricity to new communes. Tumarkin parallels this situation with the Orthodox tradition of linking the saints with water sources they miraculously found.[73] During Stalin's leadership, electrification remained strongly tied to Lenin, although Stalin was also associated with bringing power to the nation through massive industrial projects like the Dnieper Dam. Some posters

---

F. Litvinov, 'Raise higher the banner of Lenin–Stalin — banner of our great victory!', 1949; Viktor Ivanov, 'For national happiness!', 1950; Vladimir Kaidalov, 'We will struggle to reap a big cotton harvest!', 1950; B. Lebedev, 'Under the banner of Lenin, under the leadership of Stalin ...', 1950; Mikhail Solov'ev, 'Such women didn't and couldn't exist in the old days', 1950 (Fig. 3.33); V. Musinov, 'Great Stalin is the hope of the world', 1951; Boris Belopol'skii, '"The world will be saved and enhanced if people take responsibility for maintaining peace into their own hands and defend it to the end." I. Stalin', 1952 (Fig. 4.58).

70 A.A. Babitskii, 'Under the leadership of Comrade Stalin, forward to complete victory over our enemy!', 1944 (Fig. 4.31); Stefan Gints, 'The triumph of victory', 1945; Vladimir Kaidalov, 'Glory to the great heroic Red Army ...', 1945; Boris Mukhin, 'Glory to the great heroic Red Army ...', 1945; V. Selivanov, 'Glory to our great people ...', 1945; Petr Shukhmin, 'Long live the great organiser and inspirer of historic victory against German imperialism ...', 1945; V. Medvedev, 'Long live the 30th anniversary of the great October Socialist Revolution', 1947; F. Litvinov, 'Long live the party of Lenin–Stalin, inspirer and organiser of our victories!', 1948 (Fig. 4.49); Petr Golub', 'Long life and prosperity to our motherland!', 1949; Vladimir Kaidalov, 'Glory to great Stalin!', 1949; Naum Karpovskii, 'Glory to the great leaders of October!', 1951 (Fig. 2.19).

71 This eyecatching event is captured on the cover of *Ogonyok*, December 1949.

72 This is a quotation from a speech by Lenin in 1930 that subsequently became a propaganda slogan. V.I. Lenin, 'Our foreign and domestic position and party tasks', speech delivered to the Moscow Gubernia Conference Of The R.C.P.(b.), 21 Nov. 1920, in V.I. Lenin, *Collected Works*, vol. 31, 4th edn (Julius Katzer, trans.) Moscow, Progress Publishers, 1965, pp. 408–26.

73 Tumarkin, *Lenin lives!*, p. 131.

visually juxtapose images of Stalin and Lenin, suggesting that Stalin was carrying on Lenin's pioneering work in electrification in the present day.[74]

This focus on light in the Stalin era also extended to an obsession with light fittings and lamps, which occupied a special place in the interior design of railway stations, theatres, and public buildings. The lights in the Metro stations were so resplendent they were described as an 'artificial underground sun'.[75] A famous poster of 1940 by honoured graphic artist Viktor Govorkov,[76] 'Stalin takes care of each of us from the Kremlin' (Fig. 3.8), shows Stalin seated at his desk in the Kremlin, working through the night, softly illuminated by his desk lamp. This lamp was to become part of the mythology of Stalin and an emblem of his care for the Soviet people. Each night, whether or not he was actually at the Kremlin, a lamp was lit in the window as a symbol of Stalin's constant vigilance and diligence.

Stalin as the helmsman and engine driver

Although the epithet 'The Great Helmsman' is usually associated in current terminology with Mao Zedong, Stalin was also known by this epithet and appeared in political posters as the captain of a ship, or as the driver of a train. The helmsman image has a long history of association with skilled leadership and was a common motif in Byzantine court literature,[77] and Ancient Greek and Ancient Roman literature and philosophy. Maurizio Vito also notes a usage of the helmsman metaphor by St John Chrysostom in which the helmsman is endowed with gifts that belong to divine providence.[78] When a helmsman appears as a character in literature, he is often the mouthpiece for the author's political views and, by nature of his role, demonstrates strong leadership qualities. The helmsman symbol is part of a larger field of metaphors in which the ship represents the

---

74 For example, Viktor Govorkov, 'In the name of communism', 1951 (Fig. 2.18).
75 Bowlt, 'Stalin as Isis and Ra', pp. 49–50.
76 Govorkov studied under Dmitrii Moor and Sergei Gerasimov and was awarded the title of Honoured Artist of the RFSFR in 1971. V.V. Andreyanova & I.I. Nikonova, *Khudozhnikii Narodov SSSR: Biobibliograficheskii Slovar'*, vol. 3, Moscow, Izdatel'stvo 'Iskusstvo', 1976, p. 64.
77 Alice Mocanescu, 'Practising immortality: schemes for conquering "time" during the Ceaușescu era', *Studies in Ethnicity and Nationalism*, 10:3, 2010, pp. 413–34, p. 418.
78 Maurizio Vito, *Terra e Mare: Metafore e Politica in Conflitto*, Rome, Aracne Editrice, 2012.

state, navigation represents knowledge, skill and care, and the journey becomes an odyssey. Michel Foucault notes the use of this group of metaphors in classical poetry and philosophy and observes that the navigation metaphor implies three types of knowledge possessed by the skilled helmsman associated with medicine, political government and self-government.[79] The helmsman image carries within it multiple implications. The helmsman is able to care for himself and for others, exerts both self-control and political leadership, and has the wisdom to take account of the many aspects necessary to navigate a skilled course through often tempestuous waters (navigating by the stars, understanding the weather and wind, knowledge of the currents, knowledge of how the ship operates). Finally, there is the understanding that he holds his position with divine consent.

A 1933 poster by highly decorated satirist, caricaturist, ROSTA and TASS artist Boris Efimov[80] depicts Stalin as the helmsman steering the ship of the USSR (Fig. 3.9). In his greatcoat and plain workman's cap, a hearty and broad-shouldered Stalin grasps the helm with two large firm hands, his vigilant gaze out over his left shoulder keeping watch against enemies and potential threats. Next to him, the Soviet flag flaps in the breeze and behind him, in the top left of the poster, is the midsection of a huge ship with its red star emblem. The bottom right of the poster contains the text in small red letters, 'The captain of the Soviet Union leads us from victory to victory!' The text advises the viewer that not only is Stalin keeping the Soviet Union safe from harm, but he is also steering a journey of multiple victories — in fact the entire journey consists of a journey from one port of victory to another (from socialism to communism). It is implicit that without him the ship would sink. The poster is somewhat unusual in that is does not refer to Stalin by name in the text but uses the 'captain' metaphor instead.

---

79 'The path towards the self will always be something of an Odyssey ... This dangerous journey to the port, the port of safety, implies a knowledge, a technique, an art ... Three types of technique are usually associated with this model of piloting: first, medicine; second, political government, third, the direction and the government of oneself' (Michel Foucault, Frédéric Gros, François Ewald & Alessandro Fontana, *The hermeneutics of the subject: lectures at the Collège de France, 1981–1982*, New York, Palgrave-Macmillan, 2005, pp. 248–49).

80 Efimov was a highly decorated Soviet artist who was awarded the titles of People's Artist of the RSFSR in 1959; People's Artist of the USSR in 1967; Corresponding Member of the Academy of Arts in 1954; USSR State Prize Winner in 1950, 1951 and 1972; and the Order of Lenin in 1980 (I.I. Nikonova, *Khudozhnikii Narodov SSSR: Biobibliograficheskii Slovar'*, 4:1, Moscow, Izdatel'stvo 'Iskusstvo', 1983, pp. 66–68).

This poster must have been considered an important propaganda tool because it was issued in an edition of 200,000 in 1933, before such big editions became commonplace.

Another trope related to the helmsman is that of the locomotive driver. Due to the far more recent emergence of the train and the railroad, this metaphor cannot boast the same long history of use as the helmsman metaphor, although, for obvious reasons, it is related to (perhaps even an updated extension of) the helmsman metaphor, in keeping with the Soviet emphasis on modernity and progress. There is one significant difference between the ship and the train: a helmsman must use all his knowledge and skill to navigate a safe route among many possible other routes, while the train driver has no choice of alternate routes and must follow the tracks. The train driver's role involves keeping the engine running, avoiding pitfalls, and managing speed and braking. The locomotive is often used as a metaphor for history, and there is inevitability about the destination along a route that was already laid out before the engine driver sat at the controls. This makes the train a particularly apt metaphor for the communist journey. According to Marxist theory, scientific laws govern history, and the final destination of communism is inevitable. The leader is a caretaker of the state until it is no longer needed and withers away. Once the destination is reached, neither the train nor the train driver will be needed.

The metaphor of the train is employed in a 1939 political poster by Pavel Sokolov-Skalia discussed in Chapter Two. This poster shares with the 1933 Efimov poster the notion of a strong, wise leader who has firm control, as well as that of the journey from success to success. In both posters Stalin is shown as in firm control of a huge and powerful machine. In the 1939 poster, the text makes explicit that Stalin is 'tried and tested', a man of knowledge and experience. He is the only one of the four Marxist theorists depicted on the banner decorating the side of the train to have real and enduring experience in making a socialist society work. This is why he drives.

Implicitly related to the symbolic identities of helmsman and train driver are the 'path'[81] metaphors that frequently appear in the text of posters, and which are visually represented by the outstretched arm and pointed hand, and the direction of the leader's gaze. The 'line' or 'path' is the correct way in which to achieve socialism and communism, and implies that there is only one correct direction, ideology or strategy. In Soviet propaganda, this direction is indicated by the leader (who may be driving a train down the railroad tracks, pointing or gazing) and the citizenry are duty-bound to follow him because no other way is correct or acceptable. Jeffrey Brooks points out that, although this metaphor was frequently used by Lenin, it is not borrowed from Marx and Engels, who employed vaguer metaphors for development and growth.[82] This metaphor is also implied in the 'Forward to the victory of communism' posters that are discussed in Chapter Four.

Stalin the architect

The notion of Stalin as the architect of Soviet communism dates to the time of the burgeoning of the Stalin cult in 1934. On 1 January 1934, in *Pravda*, Karl Radek published a laudatory article on Stalin titled 'The architect of socialist society', which was then reissued as a pamphlet[83] in an edition of 225,000.[84] Written after his expulsion from the Party for 'oppositionist activities' in 1927, and readmission to Party ranks after capitulating to Stalin in 1930, the booklet has the intriguing subtitle: 'the ninth in a course of lectures on "The history of the victory of socialism", delivered in 1967 at the School of Inter-Planetary Communications on the fiftieth anniversary of the October Revolution', and its content is so excessively eulogistic that it is difficult to determine just how one should read it. After signing

---

81 M. Karpenko, 'On the path of Lenin to joy and glory, with Stalin in our hearts we are going to victory!', undated; Unknown artist, 'The path to victory — implementation of the six conditions of Comrade Stalin', 1932; Pen Varlen, 'The path to victory — implementation of the six conditions of Comrade Stalin', 1942; Aleksandr Venediktov, 'You cleared the path for our freedom, Soviet rule gave glory to our country', 1949; A. Mytnikov, '26 years without Lenin, but still on Lenin's path', 1950 (Fig. 2.17).
82 Brooks, *Thank you, Comrade Stalin!*, p. 48.
83 Karl Radek, *The architect of socialist society*, Moscow, Co-operative Publishing Society of Foreign Workers in the USSR, 1934.
84 Rosenthal, *New myth, new world*, p. 375.

3. STALIN IS LIKE A FAIRYTALE SYCAMORE TREE

a document capitulating to Stalin in 1929,[85] Radek was readmitted to the Party in 1930 and went on to lead Cominform and deliver a keynote address at the Writers Conference of 1934. He was arrested in the purges of 1937 and subsequently died in the gulag during a sentence of 10 years hard labour. Radek argues that Stalin, rather than Lenin, was the architect of socialism. He acknowledges that Stalin stood on the shoulders of Lenin, but claims that in executing Lenin's will, Stalin had to take many daring independent decisions and to develop Lenin's teachings in the same manner that Lenin had further developed those of Marx.[86] Interestingly, Radek employs the helmsman metaphor with Stalin called upon by history 'to take the helm and steer the proud ship of Lenin through storm and stress',[87] describes Stalin as 'a pillar of fire' who 'marched in front of mankind and led the way',[88] and speaks of Stalin as being 'steeled in the tireless struggle against the scores of shades of the petty bourgeois movement'.[89] These and related metaphors recur with monotonous regularity throughout the pamphlet, constituting a listing of the canon of tropes associated with Stalin.

When Radek wrote in 1934, the Congress of Victors had just declared the full achievement of socialism and the new task of progressing to the higher stage, communism, had commenced. By the time the two posters celebrating Stalin as the architect of communism appeared, Stalin was an old man, already over 70, and the quest to introduce a communist society had been taking place for 17 years, complicated by the need for defence in the Great Patriotic War. A 1951 poster by Boris Belopol'skii carries the caption 'Glory to Stalin, the great architect of communism!' (Fig. 3.10) and was issued in a massive edition of half a million copies, which suggests that it was viewed as an important piece of propaganda. The poster, in pale blues and muted browns typical of the pastel shades of the 'era of abundance', is dominated by Stalin, depicted with attributes of leadership (his marshal's uniform) and standard props (unlit pipe in the right hand and scroll in the left). At the literal level, the scroll is suggestive of an architect's blueprints, but at a symbolic level it also references the scroll or logos held by

---

85 See L. Trotsky, *The challenge of the left opposition (1928–29)*, New York, Pathfinder, 1981, p. 157.
86 Radek, *The architect of socialist society*, p. 10.
87 Radek, *The architect of socialist society*, p. 23.
88 Radek, *The architect of socialist society*, p. 23.
89 Radek, *The architect of socialist society*, p. 25.

Christ. Behind Stalin, bathed in a white glow that appears to emanate from him, is the new hydroelectric work being undertaken across the Soviet territories. The inscription on the dam wall is carved in stone and reads '"Communism is Soviet power plus the electrification of the whole country." Lenin', an iconic Lenin slogan, to which Radek also draws attention in his pamphlet.[90] In the far distance is a small statue of Lenin, the man upon whose foundation Stalin was building. There are two groups of figures in the poster, both existing only in order to react (and illustrate for the viewer the correct attitude to take) to Stalin. The group of men on the left, who appear to be professional workers associated with bringing the communist dream to fruition, stare up at Stalin with awe and respect. In the bottom-right corner, passers-by on a barge hail Stalin with visible enthusiasm. Stalin pays no attention to them and gazes out to the viewer's right at a future that only he can see. By focusing on Stalin, the other figures demonstrate that it is Stalin who embodies the communist future. Like a priest or shaman, Stalin acts as a sort of intermediary between the vision and the people.

The second poster, by N. Petrov and Konstantin Ivanov (Fig. 3.11), was published in 1952 and carries the same slogan as the Belopol'skii poster. This poster uses black-and-white photography as a means of documentary evidence of the progress of Soviet society. Stalin is superimposed in front of a view of Moscow and is looking up the Volga River. The city appears to be bustling with pedestrians, cars and river traffic, and is bathed in a white light which also shines on Stalin from above. Stalin again looks out of the picture, this time to the viewer's left, which is usually associated with the past, and suggests that Stalin is surveying what has already been achieved. The poster plays on the two levels of meaning of the architect symbol. Stalin is literally shown as responsible for the planning and rebuilding of Moscow, which commenced in 1935, but also responsible for planning and building the new communist society. Moscow was seen as a symbol for the whole federation, her transformation a metaphor for the moral and political transformation of the whole of Soviet society. Katerina Clark points out that, although only parts of Moscow were rebuilt, it was usually represented as being totally rebuilt, and photographs of models were often presented (as in the case of the Palace of Soviets) as if the new

---

90 Radek, *The architect of socialist society*, pp. 40–41.

buildings already existed.[91] Moscow was also represented — in Stalin's 'Greetings on her 800th anniversary' in 1947, for example — as a sort of symbolic saviour of the West, having liberated the West from the Tartar yoke, repulsed the Polish–Lithuanian invasion in the Time of Troubles, repelled Napoleon in 1812, and won the Great Patriotic War against the fascists.[92]

Archetypes of reciprocity

The Stalin cult made use of a number of symbols and archetypes to demonstrate the many facets of the leader and his relationship to the people, which in turn served as a model for both the new Soviet person and the new society. Two of the most pervasive and fundamental archetypes associated with Stalin are those of the Father and the Teacher. These archetypes are distinct, but closely related, as both involve notions of responsibility, care and mentoring relationships, but only the Father archetype implies kinship between participants. It is here that the relationship between the leader and his people enters the realm of myth and also, it may be argued, that the deepest realms of the unconscious are tapped by cult propaganda. Before investigating how the Father and Teacher archetypes manifested in the cult of Stalin, it is necessary to briefly examine the nature of Soviet society and how these archetypes tapped into systems of reciprocal obligation already in existence.

The constructs of the 'economy of the gift' and the 'politics of obligation,' as explored by Brooks,[93] are important concepts in understanding the way in which Soviet society functioned under Stalin, and also in making sense of propaganda which fostered a sense of obligation to the leader. These terms refer to an economic system whereby the citizenry receives ordinary goods and services as gifts from the leadership.[94] In *What was socialism, and what comes next?*,

---

91   Katerina Clark, 'Eisenstein's two projects for a film about Moscow', *The Modern Language Review*, 101:1, 2006, pp. 184–200, p. 186.
92   See Clark, 'Eisenstein's two projects for a film about Moscow', p. 192.
93   Brooks, *Thank you, Comrade Stalin!*
94   Brooks, *Thank you, Comrade Stalin!*, p. xv.

anthropologist Katherine Verdery uses the simple analogy of the all-American lemonade stand to emphasise one of the pertinent points of divergence between capitalist and socialist systems:

> In capitalism, those who run lemonade stands endeavour to serve thirsty customers in ways that make a profit and outcompete other lemonade stand owners. In socialism, the point was not profit, but the relationship between thirsty persons and the one with the lemonade — the Party center, which appropriated from producers the various ingredients (lemons, sugar, water) and then mixed the lemonade to reward them with, as it saw fit. Whether someone made a profit was irrelevant: the transaction underscored the center's paternalistic superiority over its citizens — that is, its capacity to decide who got more lemonade and who got less.[95]

Verdery goes on to point out that goods produced in the socialist countries were either gathered and held centrally, or almost given away to sections of the population at low prices. The socialist contract guaranteed food and clothing, but not quality, availability or choice, and the goods produced often could not compete on world markets with goods produced in capitalist countries. The point was not to sell the goods, but to control redistribution, because that was how the leadership confirmed its legitimacy with the public.[96]

In song, film, theatre and posters, Stalin was promoted as the benefactor of all society. All bounty came from Stalin in his role as head of state. While in numerous ways the cult of Lenin formed a prototype for the cult of Stalin, the two cults differed in one important respect. As Brooks points out, nobody had to thank Lenin for their 'happy childhood', nor were they indebted to him personally. Lenin was not the wellspring of all accomplishments and, although he received gifts, he wasn't deluged with them in the way that Stalin was as his cult grew.[97] The celebration of Stalin's 70th birthday on 21 December 1949, was overseen by a specially assembled 'Committee for Preparations of Comrade Stalin's Birthday', with the festivities costing 5.6 million rubles and attracting thousands of pilgrims.[98] Trainloads of gifts

---

95 Katherine Verdery, *What was socialism, and what comes next?*, Princeton University Press, 1996, p. 25.
96 Verdery, *What was socialism, and what comes next?*, p. 26.
97 Jeffrey Brooks, 'Stalin's politics of obligation', *Totalitarian Movements and Political Religions*, 4:1, 2003, pp. 46–67, p. 49.
98 Montefiore, *Stalin*, p. 537.

arrived from around the world,[99] and from nationalities within the territories of the USSR.[100] Accompanying the gifts, were display cases full of letters of love and gratitude to Stalin, some hand-embroidered on linen or silk, or contained in elaborately carved caskets, others simple and seemingly heartfelt.[101] In Lenin's time, citizens were made aware that they were obligated, but they owed their gratitude to the Revolution, the Party and the state, rather than to the leader. By the mid-1930s, Stalin had become a symbol for the Party, with the two entities synonymous, so that expressing gratitude to Stalin (which was easier than directing gratitude to a faceless entity) was equivalent to giving thanks to the Party and the state. Nikolai Ssorin-Chaikov and Olga Sosnina point out: 'Within this idiom of gratitude, the gifts to Stalin are counter-gifts for socialism; a gift from the socialist state as a beautiful artifact given to its citizens and embodied in the care and the "love of the leader".'[102] Viewing Stalin as the source of all benefits

---

99 For example, East Germany sent 70 freight car loads, and a select group of 8,000 of the gifts from both abroad and from artisans, housewives and children throughout the Soviet Union, formed a massive exhibition at the Pushkin Museum. As social anthropologists Nikolai Ssorin-Chaikov and Olga Sosnina have documented: 'These gifts ranged from models of military hardware ... to exemplars of industrial and petty-commodity production ... to samples of natural resources and applied art objects such as a pipe "from the US to the Soviet people" with the carved figurines of Stalin and Truman playing chess' ('The faculty of useless things: gifts to Soviet leaders', in Klaus Heller & Jan Plamper, *Personality cults in Stalinism*, Goïttingen, V&R Unipress, 2004, p. 277). Stalin apparently never visited the exhibition, appeared unimpressed with his celebrations and 'sat like a statue, not looking at anyone ... as if not listening to the speeches in his tribute' (Nikolai Ssorin-Chaikov, 'On heterochrony: birthday gifts to Stalin, 1949', *Journal of the Royal Anthropological Institute*, 12, 2006, pp. 355–75, p. 364).
100 For example, the massive rug woven by the workers of Azerbaijan, covering an area of 70 m² and weighing 167 kilograms, which featured a gigantic portrait of Stalin and about 70 pictorial narratives surrounding him.
101 For example, Guards Sergeant-Major Igor Nikolskii carved a tobacco box made from plexiglass for Stalin, accompanied by the following missive: 'A participant of the war, who has traveled its hard road from beginning to end, I wish to send you my thanks for our victory. The tobacco box is made out of a piece of a downed German plane. I am not a jeweler. My tools were an awl, a penknife, a drill, and a brush; my workshop was the open air. I made it as best I could. The box holds neither gold nor jewels, but only the boundless love of a Russian soldier for his leader, Generalissimo Stalin. Please accept this gift from a soldier of the Great Patriotic War. I have written my thoughts and given of my best' (Igor Nikolski, quoted in Boris Polevoi, 'To Stalin from the peoples of the world', 1950, in James von Geldern & Richard Stites (eds), *Mass culture in Soviet Russia: tales, songs, poems, movies, plays and folklore, 1917–1953*, Bloomington, Indiana University Press, 1995, pp. 457–58).
102 Ssorin-Chaikov & Sosnina, 'The faculty of useless things', in Heller & Plamper, *Personality cults in Stalinism*, p. 284.

had the additional effect of removing agency from all other actors in society, and thus reinforced Stalin's totalitarian control and undercut the moral standing of his opponents.[103]

The gift of care, guidance and leadership from a benevolent Stalin to a grateful populace formed a central theme of Stalinist propaganda. By definition, gifts come without strings attached although, in practice, as Marcel Mauss points out, there is almost always[104] a reciprocal obligation, and what separates the gift from economic transactions is the unspecified time delay between the two events.[105] This time delay allows a mutual pretence that the two events are not causally related and reciprocity remains hidden by mutual consent. The reciprocal obligation owed to Stalin for his bountiful gifts took the form of spontaneous and extravagant displays of gratitude.

Staged 'thanking ceremonies' became a part of the ritual of Soviet public life. They were held in schools, and also as part of other important occasions, such as the opening of Party congresses and the celebrations for the anniversary of the October Revolution. A woman brought up in the late 1930s recalled that the ritual of thanking Stalin was 'akin to thanking God for one's daily bread'.[106] The pervasive public secular ritualistic offering of thanks and praise may be somewhat unfamiliar phenomena to those raised in a Western democratic society in the 21st century, however, the ritual of thanking Stalin was not without precedent in Russian society. Traditionally, the tsar had been seen as the father figure and benefactor of the nation, as expressed in the proverb: 'Without the Tsar, the land is a widow; without the Tsar, the people is an orphan.'[107] Many of the characteristics of the people's relationship to the tsar, including the tradition of diplomatic

---

103 Brooks, 'Stalin's politics of obligation', p. 47.
104 Mauss argues that there is always a reciprocal obligation of some sort. However, Hélène Cixous, in her discussion of the 'feminine economy', argues that the gifts given by a mother to a child, for example, expect no reciprocation, and it is only the predominating 'masculine economy' that is characterised by reciprocal obligation ('Sorties: out and out: attacks/ways out/ forays', in Alan D. Schrift, *The logic of the gift: toward an ethic of generosity*, New York, Routledge, 1997).
105 Marcel Mauss, *The gift: forms and functions of exchange in archaic societies*, Ian Gunnison (trans.), New York, W.W. Norton and Company, 1967 (1923).
106 Larisa Vasil'eva, *Deti Kremlya*, Moscow, 1997, p. 85, cited in Catriona Kelly, 'Grandpa Lenin and Uncle Stalin: Soviet leader cult for little children', in Apor et al., *The leader cult in communist dictatorships*, p. 108.
107 Brooks, 'Stalin's politics of obligation', p. 51.

gift giving to the tsars,[108] were carried over to their relationship with the next strong leader–saviour who took the helm of government. Russian traditions of bribery, official favours and even the Orthodox gift of the sacraments, through which the believer can attain eternal life, all contributed to a culture of obligation.[109]

In addition to the official state-controlled economy, a second economy coexisted during Soviet times, which grew directly from the culture of gift giving. The term *blat* has an interesting and revealing etymology,[110] but was not generally used in 'polite society' (being considered 'un-Soviet'), and was usually alluded to with euphemisms.[111] It refers to the widespread practice of obtaining life's essentials, which were often unavailable through official channels, using a system of 'connections' and 'acquaintances'. Three points are crucial in understanding *blat* — the first is that, as there was no private ownership of anything, everything must be accessed through the state and state officials. The second point is that, although the transactions involved the misappropriation and misdirection of collectively owned property, *blat* did not tend to refer to incidents of outright bribery, which were seen as separate and usually criminal acts. *Blat* involved social networks and relationships, and the extending of favours, often separated in time, so that they took on the quality of reciprocal gift giving. The third point is that this second economy of *blat* was dependent on the official economy, which controlled the means of production, and was the source of all goods and services. If one had eliminated the state-controlled economy, rather than flourishing with opportunities for capitalist entrepreneurship, the second economy would have died.

---

108 In fact, the Imperial Porcelain factory, which was renamed the Lomonosov Porcelain factory in Soviet times, was able to maintain a continuous business manufacturing gifts for Russia's leaders, from the 18th century right through Soviet times.
109 See Brooks, 'Stalin's politics of obligation', p. 51.
110 According to Alena E. Ledeneva, '*blat*' was an old word that acquired new meaning in the Soviet era, despite being banned from official discourse. It was originally used to refer to less serious types of criminal activity, and when used, as most often, in the phrase *po blatu*, referred to obtaining something illicitly, by protection or patronage. In its current usage it seems to refer simply to obtaining something through connections (*Russia's economy of favours: blat, networking and informal exchange*, Cambridge University Press, 1998, p. 12).
111 Ledeneva, *Russia's economy of favours*, p. 13.

Blat was all pervasive because it was necessary for survival, and Soviet society consisted of vast networks of patronage that ran both vertically and horizontally. Notions of gift giving, obligation, bounty, reciprocity, and even mentorship, were integral to Soviet life, and Stalin merely sat at the top of the pyramid, as the ultimate dispenser of goods and benefits to a network below. These networks of patronage were reinforced by the strong familial connections among the top Bolsheviks. Entire family clans held leadership positions, and intermarried with each other in tight-knit circles. During the latter part of Stalin's leadership, dutiful and obedient subordinates were given packets of cash, cars, apartments,[112] dachas, holidays and other benefits directly as rewards for service and loyalty, and stores came into existence that sold only to a restricted clientele, regardless of how much money someone outside the circle may manage to accumulate. None of these goods was ever 'owned' by the recipients, everything belonged to the state, and could be removed at the whim of Stalin. Montefiore observes: 'It used to be regarded as ironic to call the Soviet élite an "aristocracy" but they were much more like a feudal service nobility whose privileges were totally dependent on their loyalty.'[113]

Notions of obligation and reciprocal duty saturated Soviet society at all levels and took a central position in the regime's rituals, including such rituals as *samokritika* in which misguided subjects were required to apologise publicly to society for failing in their duty. These notions arose not only out of Bolshevik ideology and *partiinost'*,[114] but also from long Russian cultural and religious traditions that predated the Revolution. The use of archetypes to formalise and give expression to these concepts not only served to create the appearance of the existence of a long tradition in the fledgling regime, but enabled the populace to embrace their leader in a manner to which they were already accustomed, at both the conscious and subconscious level.

---

112 When Anastas Mikoian first moved to Moscow, Stalin allowed him to stay in his own apartment. When Mikoian declared how much he loved the apartment, Stalin gave it to him (Montefiore, *Stalin*, p. 44).

113 Montefiore, *Stalin*, p. 45.

114 *Partiinost'* can generally be defined as 'partymindedness' or 'partisanship'. The *Great Soviet encyclopædia* entry for the term is as follows: 'The Communist Party consistently upholds the principle of *partiinost'*. Defending and substantiating the goals and tasks of the working class and the policies of the Communist Party, Marxist–Leninist theory mercilessly criticises the exploiters' system, its politics, and its ideology …' (G.L. Smirnov, 'Partiinost', in A.M. Prokhorov & M. Waxman (eds), *Great Soviet encyclopædia*, 3rd edn, New York, Macmillan, 1973).

This served to enhance the legitimacy of the leadership so that, as *Pravda* stated in 1941, the leaders were seen as 'the lawful heirs to the Russian people's great and honourable past'.[115]

Stalin was not only the source of all bounty, but also the source of all accomplishments. Great care was taken to ensure that Stalin was strongly associated with all the regime's achievements, while dissociated from catastrophes and failures, such as forced collectivisation, famine and the German invasion. Failures were blamed on sabotage, 'meddling', and the overzealous pursuit of targets by local officials.[116] Despite the many difficulties faced by the Soviet Union in dragging its economy into the 20th century,[117] the achievements touted in propaganda were not always empty rhetoric. There were significant accomplishments during Stalin's reign, even though some of these were achieved at the expense of 'slave labour' from the gulags and cost many human lives.

One of the ways in which the sense of obligation was reinforced in Soviet society was through the use of propaganda centred specifically around the theme of thanking and benefaction. I have divided posters on this theme into seven categories, according to the aspect of obligation and gratitude that they best reflect: posters that highlight the debt owed to Stalin for a happy childhood;[118] posters that highlight

---

115 Cited in Kevin M.F. Platt, 'Rehabilitation and afterimage: Aleksei Tolstoi's many returns to Peter the Great', in Kevin M.F. Platt & David Brandenberger, *Epic revisionism: Russian history and literature as Stalinist propaganda*, Madison, University of Wisconsin Press, 2006, p. 53.
116 Stalin's article 'Dizzy with success' illustrates the way in which he neatly dodged his accountability for the excesses of collectivisation. His motives were always pure and unimpeachable: 'How could there have arisen in our midst such blockheaded exercises in "socialization", such ludicrous attempts to over-leap oneself, attempts which aim at by-passing classes and the class struggle, and which in fact bring grist to the mill of our class enemies? They could have arisen only in the atmosphere of our "easy" and "unexpected" successes on the front of collective-farm development. They could have arisen only as a result of the blockheaded belief of a section of our Party: "We can achieve anything!", "There's nothing we can't do!" They could have arisen only because some of our comrades have become dizzy with success and for the moment have lost clearness of mind and sobriety of vision. To correct the line of our work in the sphere of collective-farm development, *we must put an end to these sentiments*' ('Dizzy with success', *Pravda*, 60, 02 Mar. 1930, from J. V. Stalin, *Problems of Leninism*, Peking, Foreign Languages Press, 1976, pp. 483–91, p. 490).
117 A revealing example of just how difficult this rapid industrialisation could be can be found in Stephen Kotkin's study of Magnitogorsk (*Magnetic Mountain: Stalinism as a civilization*, Berkeley, University of California Press, 1995).
118 For example, Viktor Govorkov, 'Thank you beloved Stalin for our happy childhood', 1936 (Fig. 3.12); Dmitrii Grinets, 'Thanks to the Party, thanks to dear Stalin for a happy, joyful childhood', 1937; Nina Vatolina, Viktor Deni & Vladislav Pravdin, 'Thank you Comrade Stalin for our happy childhood!', 1938; Nina Vatolina, 'Thank you dear Stalin for our happy childhood!',

the debt owed by women for their new equality in society to Stalin and the Party;[119] posters that thank Stalin, the Party and/or the Red Army for winning the war;[120] posters that acknowledge Stalin as the benefactor of all humankind;[121] posters that associate Stalin and the Party with great Soviet achievements;[122] posters that acknowledge

---

1939; Nikolai Zhukov, 'Thank you Comrade Stalin for our happy life!' (Fig. 3.1), 1940; Iraklii Toidze, 'Stalin's kindness illuminates the future of our children!', 1947 (Fig. 3.2); Nina Vatolina, 'Thanks to dear Stalin for our happy childhood!', 1950.
119 For example, Nikolai Mikhailov, 'Stalin among delegates', 1937; Marina Volkova & Natalia Pinus, 'Long live the equal-rights woman in the USSR ...', 1938 (Fig. 3.32); Mikhail Solov'ev, 'Such women didn't and couldn't exist in the old days', 1950 (Fig. 3.33).
120 For example N. Bondar, 'Long live our dear Stalin! Long live the liberated workers of Bessarabia!', undated; Semen Gel'berg, 'Long live the All-Union Communist Party of Bolsehviks, the party of Lenin–Stalin — the inspirer and organiser of our victory', c. 1945; Vladimir Kochegura, 'Long live the party of Lenin–Stalin. Inspirer and organiser of our victory!', c. 1945; Aleksandr Zhitomirskii, 'Stalin is the greatness of our era, Stalin is the banner of our victory!', 1942 (although victory was yet a long way off); Viktor Koretskii, 'On the joyous day of liberation ...', 1943 (Fig. 3.13); Viktor Deni, 'Long live generalissimus STALIN — great leader and general of the Soviet people!', 1945 (Fig. 4.36); Vladimir Kaidalov, '"Glory to the great heroic Red Army, defending the independence of our country and winning victory over the enemy!" I. Stalin', 1945 (Fig. 4.32); Viktor Koretskii, 'The Soviet people are full of gratitude and love for dear STALIN — the great organiser of our victory', 1945 (Fig. 4.35); Boris Mukhin, 'Glory to the great heroic Red Army ...', 1945; V. Selivanov, 'Glory to our great people, to the victorious people!', 1945; Petr Shukhmin, 'Long live the great organiser and inspirer of historic victory', 1945; Viktor Ivanov, 'Long live the party of Lenin–Stalin!', 1946; Viktor Koretskii, '1917–1946. Glory to the Red Army. Defending the gains of the great October socialist revolution!', 1946; Iraklii Toidze, 'Long live the V.K.P.(b) — the party of Lenin–Stalin, inspirer and organiser of our great victories!', 1946 (Fig. 4.39); Mikhail Solov'ev, 'Glory to the armed forces of the USSR and their victory over Japan!', 1947; V. Ivanov, '1918–1948. Glory to the party of Lenin and Stalin — the organiser of victorious armed forces of the USSR!', 1948; B.I. Lebedev, 'Long live the V.K.P(b) inspirer and organiser of the victory of the Soviet people!', 1948 (Fig. 4.48); F. Litvinov, 'Long live the party of Lenin–Stalin, inspirer and organiser of our victories!', 1948 (Fig. 4.49); Boris Mukhin, 'Glory to great Stalin!', 1948 (Fig. 4.46); N. Petrov, '... it is our good fortune that in the difficult years of the war ...', 1948 (Fig. 4.47); F. Litvinov, 'Raise the banner of Lenin–Stalin — the banner of our great victory!', 1949; Vladislav Pravdin, 'It is our blessing that during the difficult years of war ...', 1949.
121 For example Boris Berezovskii, '"We stand for peace and we defend the cause of peace." I. Stalin', 1947 (Fig. 4.52); Petr Golub, 'Great Stalin is the best friend of the Latvian people!', 1950 (Fig. 4.56); Viktor Ivanov, 'Stalin is our great standard-bearer of peace!', 1950 (Fig. 4.54); Viktor Koretskii, 'Great Stalin is the banner of friendship of the peoples of the USSR!', 1950 (Fig. 4.55); V. Musinov, 'Great Stalin is the hope of the world!', 1951; Boris Belopol'skii, '"We stand for peace and we defend the cause of peace." I. Stalin', 1952 (Fig. 4.57); Boris Belopol'skii, '"The world will be saved and enhanced if people take responsibility for maintaining peace into their own hands and defend it to the end." I. Stalin', 1952 (Fig. 4.58).
122 For example, B. Lebedev, 'Long live the party of Lenin–Stalin. Leader and organiser of the strong Soviet people!', undated; B. Lebedev, '"Socialism for the USSR is what has been achieved and won." I. Stalin', undated; V. Deni, 'With the banner of Lenin we won in the battles for the October Revolution ...', 1930; Viktor Deni, 'With the banner of Lenin we won in the battles for the October Revolution ...', 1931; Unidentified artist, 'Under the banner of the VKP(b), and its Leninist Central Committee ...', 1933; Unidentified artist, 'The current workers, our Soviet workers want to live with all of their material and cultural needs covered ...', 1933; Viktor Deni,

3. STALIN IS LIKE A FAIRYTALE SYCAMORE TREE

and encourage those who strive to do their duty;[123] and, posters that appear to acknowledge that obligation is a two-way street.[124] Of these

---

'With the banner of Lenin we won in the battles for the October Revolution ...', 1933; Gustav Klutsis, With the banner of Lenin we won in the battles for the October Revolution'...', 1933; Iraklii Taidze (sic – Toidze), 'With the banner of Lenin we won in the battles for the October Revolution ...', 1933; Konstantin Vialov, 'The party has ensured that the USSR has transformed ...', 1933; Viktor Deni & Nikolai Dolgorukov, 'Long live the Leninist VKP(b), organiser of victorious socialist construction', 1934 (Fig. 4.60); Viktor Deni & Nikolai Dolgorukov, 'We've got a metro!', 1935; Nikolai Denisov & Nina Vatolina, 'Long live the great creator of the Soviet constitution', 1936; Gleb Kun, Vasilii Elkin & Konstantin Sobolevskii, 'Greetings to great Stalin. The Moscow–Volga Canal is open!', 1937; Stenberg, 'Long live the great party of Lenin–Stalin — leader and organiser of the victorious building of socialism', 1937; P. Yastrzhembskii, 'Glory to the creator of USSR constitution, the great Stalin!', 1937; Nikolai Denisov & Nina Vatolina, 'Long live the great creator of the Soviet constitution, beloved leader of the peoples, Comrade Stalin!', 1937; Unidentified artist, 'Comrade Stalin Iosif Vissarionovich ...', 1938; Unidentified artist, 'Long live the great Stalin, creator of the constitution and victorious socialism', 1938; Unidentified artist (Armenian language), '12 June. With enormous gratitude and best regards, we send greetings to great Stalin!', 1938; Vasilii Elkin, 'Long live great Stalin, leader of the people, the creator of the constitution of victorious socialism and true democracy!', 1938; Unidentified artist, 'Long live the creator of the first cavalry (horse army), best friend of the Red Cavalry — Comrade Stalin!', 1939 (Fig. 4.10); Unidentified artist, 'Long live the creator of the constitution of socialist society, the leader of the Soviet people, great Stalin!', 1945(?) (Fig. 4.34); M.L. Ioffe, 'Glory to great Stalin, creator of the constitution of the USSR', 1946; Iraklii Toidze, 'Long live the V.K.P.(b) — the party of Lenin–Stalin, inspirer and organiser of our great victories!', 1946 (Fig. 4.39); Aleksandr Druzhkov, 'Long live the VKP(b)', 1948 (Fig. 4.50); Unidentified artist, 'We are warmed by Stalin's affection ...', 1949 (Fig. 3.6); Leonid Golovanov, 'And Stalin raised us to be loyal to the people ...', 1949 (Fig. 3.21); Iraklii Toidze, 'Long live the best friend of miners, great Stalin!', 1949; Aleksandr Venediktov, 'You cleared the path for our freedom, Soviet rule gave glory to our country', 1949; Nikolai Denisov, 'Long live great Stalin, creator of the constitution of the victorious socialism!', 1950; A.A. Mytnikov, 'Long live the creator of the most democratic constitution in the world great Stalin!', 1950; Vladislav Pravdin, 'Long live the Bolshevik Party, the Lenin–Stalin Party', 1950; Vladislav Pravdin, 'To the new achievements of soviet aviation!', 1950; N. Talipov, 'Long live Comrade Stalin — creator of the most democratic constitution in the world!', 1950; B.V. Vorontsov, 'Iosif Vissarionovich Stalin', 1951.

123 For example, Konev, 'Our nobles. Greetings to the best shock workers — heroes of socialist labour', 1935 (Fig. 3.26); Polyakov, 'Worthy sons and daughters of the great party of Lenin–Stalin', 1935; Reznichenko, 'The Stakhanovite movement', 1935; Iu. Tsishevskii, 'Expand the ranks of the Stakhanovites of the socialist fields', 1935; Nikolai Dolgorukov, 'Swell the ranks of the Stakhanovites', 1936; Genrikh Futerfas, 'Stalinists! Extend the front of the Stakhanovite movement!', 1936 (Fig. 3.27); Gustav Klutsis, 'Long live the Stalinist Order of Heroes and Stakhanovites!', 1936 (Fig. 4.63); Viktor Deni & Nikolai Dolgorukov, 'Glory to Stalin's falcons – the conquerors of aerial elements!', 1937 (Fig. 3.17); Viktor Deni, 'Long live our dear Stalinist falcons ...', 1938; Nina Vatolina & Nikolai Denisov, 'Long live Soviet pilots — proud falcons of Motherland!', 1938; Aleksandr Druzhkov, 'Long live the organiser of our invincible aviation, best friend of Soviet pilots, great Stalin!', 1939; Vasilii Elkin, 'Long live Comrade Stalin — banner of invincible Soviet aviation!', 1939.

124 For example, unidentified artist, '"The current workers, our Soviet workers want to live with all of their material and cultural needs covered ... he's entitled to it, and we are obliged to provide him with these conditions." Stalin', 1933; Iraklii Toidze, 'I am pleased and happy to know how our people fought ...', 1937; Vladimir Kaidalov, 'Departing from us, Comrade Lenin urged us to strengthen and extend the union republics ...', 1940 (Fig. 2.13); E. Fedotov, 'XXV years of the Komsomol', 1943; Naum Karpovskii, 'Labour with martial persistence so your

subgenres of the gratitude theme, posters that associate Stalin and the Party with great Soviet achievements and posters that thank Stalin/the Party/the Red Army for winning the war are by far the most numerous and could be considered together to make up a general theme of gratitude for 'Soviet victories'.[125] Indeed, after the Great Patriotic War, propaganda posters often referred to Soviet 'victories' in a manner that encompassed winning the war, the attainment of socialism, the imminent attainment of communism, and record-breaking feats in workplaces, aviation and polar exploration all at once. Posters that highlight the debt owed to Stalin for a happy childhood, and posters that highlight the debt owed by women for their new equality in society to Stalin and the Party usually engage the Father archetype in relation to Stalin, as discussed below.

When examining the archetypes associated with Stalin, it is important to remember that it is only rarely that Stalin is seen to embody only one archetype in any given poster. He is often representing at least two, and sometimes more. Sometimes he makes symbolic gestures that can be read on a number of levels, at other times his visual image may suggest one archetype while the text specifies others, often several in the one caption — Stalin can be, all at once, 'father, teacher, leader, friend, and inspirer and organiser of victories'. As noted earlier, this can lead to a somewhat confusing blend of images and symbols which occasionally attempt clumsy reconciliations of traits that are essentially irreconcilable. It also means that attempts to separate out posters as representing particular archetypes are somewhat problematic. While the key archetypes will be addressed separately in this study for ease of interpretation, it must always be borne in mind that there is often considerable overlap between archetypal identities, and also some fairly transparent contradictions.

---

kolkhoz becomes part of the vanguard. The reward for honest work is wealth, fame and honor!', 1948; Viktor Koretskii, 'Beloved Stalin is the people's happiness!', 1949; Vladislav Pravdin, 'Work well so that Comrade Stalin thanks you', 1949; Aleksei Kokorekin, 'Be prepared to struggle for the cause of Lenin–Stalin!', 1951; M. Solomyanii, (in Ukrainian) 'Excellent study will please the leader!', 1952.

125 Many of these posters will be discussed in Chapter Four.

Stalin as the father of the nation

The major archetype associated with Stalin was that of *Otets Narodov*, the father of the people. In many ways, Stalin inherited the mantle of father from Lenin who, in turn, inherited it from the tsars,[126] although the scope of Lenin's 'family' was initially somewhat confined when compared to that of Stalin after him and the tsars before him. Under Stalin, Lenin was frequently depicted in propaganda for children as 'Grandpa Lenin'[127] — in this schema Stalin is Lenin's son who must step up and take responsibility for the family when Lenin, the father, dies. Statements by leading members of the Party after Lenin's death indicate profound despair at the prospect of continuing without him, just as there had been deep distress among some of the peasants on hearing of the deposition of the tsar.[128] Trotskii's words of 22 January 1924, echoing the well-known proverb about the tsar, highlight Lenin's paternal role in the eyes of the Party: 'And now Vladimir Ilyich is no more. The party is orphaned. The workmen's class is orphaned.'[129] Indeed, Lenin may have somewhat subscribed to this view himself. As Tumarkin observes, Lenin repeatedly spoke of Soviet Russia in terms which suggested it was a child in need of care and nurturing.[130] It is interesting to note that, in these early years after the Revolution, with Civil War only a couple of years behind the fledgling nation, and class struggle still at the forefront of propaganda, Trotskii does not refer to Lenin as the father of the whole nation. This is a time of the dictatorship of the proletariat as led by the vanguard party, where not everyone is equal, nor entitled to the benefits of socialist citizenship.

---

126 Michael Cherniavsky notes that Peter the Great was known popularly as *'Batiushka Tsar'* (Father Tsar), a term which was also widely used throughout the 17th century, and also that the Senate granted Peter the title of *'Otets Otechvesta'* (Father of the Fatherland). Until 1917, *'Batiushka Tsar'* was paralleled by the commonest epithet for Russia, *'Matushka Rus'* (Mother Russia) (*Tsar and people: studies in Russian myths*, New Haven, Yale University Press, 1961, pp. 83–84). The traditional term *batiushka* had been primarily used in relation to priests, tsars and fathers, but was used to refer to Stalin in 1938 in publicity about the Papinin-led polar expedition (Jan Plamper, 'Georgian Koba or Soviet "father of peoples"? The Stalin cult and ethnicity', in Apor et al., *The leader cult in communist dictatorships*, p. 134).
127 See Tumarkin, *Lenin lives!*, p. 62.
128 It is often claimed that the deposition of the tsar did not displace the need in the Russian population for a strong, autocratic ruler. See, Rees, 'Introduction', in Apor et al., *The leader cult in communist dictatorships*, p. 9, and Orlando Figes & Boris Kolonitskii, *Interpreting the Russian Revolution: the language and symbols of 1917*, New Haven, Conn. and London, 1999, p. 103.
129 Leon Trotskii, 'Lenin dead, Tiflis Station, January 22, 1924', John G. Wright (trans.), www.marxists.org/archive/trotsky/1924/01/lenin.htm (accessed 25 May 2012).
130 Tumarkin, *Lenin lives!*, p. 59.

Trotskii names Lenin as the father of the Party and the working class. In contrast, Stalinist propaganda from the mid-1930s took pains to portray Stalin as a father of all people of all the Soviet nations, with this extending to the 'liberated' nations after the Great Patriotic War, and the entire world during the peace movement of the years of the Cold War. By extension, once class conflict had been eliminated and socialism achieved, Lenin too could be seen as a founding father of the whole nation.

The notion of the powerful male leader as a father to his people is widespread and, as David Hoffmann points out, even in Britain in the 20th century, the king was depicted as the father of the people with the nation taking on a female persona as a motherland, and compatriots seen as brothers and sisters.[131] The relationship of father to son encompasses several notions: the father raises the son to be a successful and dutiful citizen, the father nurtures and protects the son, the father teaches and guides the son, and the son reciprocates by being successful, showing gratitude and respect, and by making the father proud. In Stalinist society, particular emphasis was laid on the civic duty of parents to correctly educate their children in the spirit of communism, even instilling in them a willingness to lay down their lives for their country.[132] In order to carry authority and enhance legitimacy, it is important that the leader be seen as a father to the citizenry, rather than as a sibling or peer. This is particularly important in a regime like that of Soviet Russia, where the traditional father, the tsar, had been overthrown, and a power vacuum existed. The father figure must be rapidly replaced and re-established to prevent chaos. The Soviet population were so accustomed to thinking of Stalin as a father figure that many people were stunned when Stalin addressed them as 'brothers and sisters' in a speech in November 1941.[133]

---

131 David L. Hoffmann, *Stalinist values: the cultural norms of Soviet modernity, 1917–1941*, Ithaca, New York, Cornell University Press, 2003, p. 158.
132 See Hoffmann, *Stalinist values*, p. 107.
133 Speech delivered at the Red Army parade in Red Square on the anniversary of the October Revolution, 1941. In this famous speech Stalin begins by directly appealing to Soviet citizens from all walks of life in all circumstances, and uncharacteristically refers to the people as 'brothers and sisters': 'Comrades, men of the Red Army and Red Navy, commanders and political instructors, working men and working women, collective farmers — men and women, workers in the intellectual professions, brothers and sisters in the rear of our enemy who have temporarily fallen under the yoke of the German brigands, and our valiant men and women guerillas who are destroying the rear of the German invaders!' (*Tovarishchi krasnoarmeytsy i krasnoflottsy, komandiry i politrabotniki, rabochiye i rabotnitsy, kolkhozniki i kolkhoznitsy,*

3. STALIN IS LIKE A FAIRYTALE SYCAMORE TREE

Viewing Lenin and Stalin as fathers of the people had a further dimension. For a child, a parent has always existed and atemporality is a feature of both the cult of Lenin and the cult of Stalin. For Lenin it is embodied in the famous words of poet Vladimir Maiakovskii: 'Lenin lived! Lenin lives! Lenin will live!'[134] and in the tale of *Khitryi Lenin*.[135] For Stalin this timelessness was a prominent feature of many 'reminiscences' of ordinary people's encounters with him, bearing in mind that the authenticity of these accounts cannot be verified (i.e. they may have been written by propagandists rather than genuine 'simple folk'): 'He was talking so persuasively, clearly and simply, that many of us at that moment felt as if comrade Stalin had been with us not for one month, but for many years, that we had already heard those words a long time ago and that they had taken deep roots in our consciousness.'[136] This phenomenon is also particularly apparent in the reactions of citizens to Stalin's death.

A happy childhood

The use of the Father archetype in depictions of the leader enables the symbolic persona to convey both authority and benevolence simultaneously, as well as inherently encapsulating the notion of a reciprocal relationship of rights and obligations. One of the most interesting ways in which this is manifested is in the propaganda posters on the theme of the happy childhood. These posters show happy, well-fed children in joyous mood, expressing their gratitude to the man responsible, the fatherly figure of Stalin. As Catriona Kelly observes:

---

rabotniki intelligentskogo truda, brat'ya i sestry v tylu nashego vraga, vremenno popavshiye pod igo nemetskikh razboynikov, nashi slavnyye partizany i partizanki, razrushayushchiye tyly nemetskikh zakhvatchikov!) (I.V. Stalin, 'Rech' na Krasnoy ploshchadi 7 noyabrya 1941 goda', www.marxists.org/russkij/stalin/t15/t15_14.htm (accessed 19 Aug. 2013)).

134 V.V. Maiakovskii, 'Komsomolskaia', quoted in Trevor J. Smith, 'The collapse of the Lenin personality cult in Soviet Russia, 1985–1995', *The Historian*, 60, 1998, p. 325.

135 Tumarkin, *Lenin lives!*, pp. 198–99.

136 'In the night to 1 January 1902: Old Batumi workers yell about their meeting with Comrade Stalin' ('V noch' na 1-e ianvaria 1902 goda: Rasskaz starykh batumskih rabochikh o vstreche s tovarishchem Stalinym') (*Pravda*, 01 Jan. 1937, p. 2, cited in Natalia Skradol, 'Remembering Stalin: mythopoetic elements in memories of the Soviet dictator', *Totalitarian Movements and Political Religions*, 2009, 10:1, pp. 19–41, p. 22).

'Happiness', traditionally understood as a state of fortuitous delight descending on a person unexpectedly, by act of God as it were, now became the just desert of all Soviet citizens, but above all children. But 'happiness' still had to be earned; pleasure was the reward for subordination of the self.[137]

Happiness in Soviet terms did not refer to the emotional state of the individual or to the pursuit of individual fulfilment. Happiness, like everything else, was conceived of as a collective principle.[138] Universal happiness was a duty, and to be happy was an act of loyalty to the state and to the leader. Nadezhda Mandelstam recounts:

> Everybody seemed intent on his daily round and went smilingly about the business of carrying out his instructions. It was essential to smile — if you didn't, it meant you were afraid or discontented. This nobody could afford to admit — if you were afraid, then you must have a bad conscience.[139]

The theme of 'A happy childhood'[140] was adopted for the 1936 May Day celebrations in Moscow.[141] One of the more interesting manifestations of this propaganda theme was announced in an *Izvestiia* article of 1937: 'The Moscow Bolshevik Factory is preparing special varieties of high-quality cookies to be called "Happy Childhood" and "Union". The cookies will be packaged in beautifully designed boxes.'[142] The first propaganda poster on this theme appeared in 1936. Viktor Govorkov's 'Thank you beloved Stalin for our happy childhood' (Fig. 3.12) carries one variant of the iconic slogan, 'Thank you dear

---

137 Catriona Kelly, *Children's world: growing up in Russia, 1890–1991*, New Haven, Yale University Press, 2007, p. 94.
138 As Albert Baiburin and Alexandra Piir note: 'Whether private individuals actually were happy was a matter of indifference, so far as the Soviet government was concerned; no interest was taken in this question. Happiness acquired an absolute significance: "universal happiness"; the happiness of all working people, of the world proletariat, of the Soviet population generally … . Thus, it was enough for someone to be a Soviet citizen and to live in the Soviet Union to experience universal happiness … Those who enjoyed this privileged access to happiness in an overall sense were in turn able to enjoy happiness at various subsidiary levels: dying for the Motherland, or (a less elevated, but still worthy and useful version of the same fate) labouring tirelessly for the benefit of the nation' (Baiburin & Piir, 'When we were happy: remembering Soviet holidays', in Balina & Dobrenko, *Petrified utopia*, p. 166).
139 Nadezhda Mandelstam, *Hope against hope: a memoir*, Max Hayward (trans.), New York, Atheneum Publishers, 1970, p. 365.
140 The trope of the happy childhood pre-dates the Stalin era and can be seen in classic Russian literature, such as Leo Tolstoi's *Detstvo* (see 'A joyful Soviet childhood: licensed happiness for little ones', in Balina & Dobrenko, *Petrified utopia*, p. 5).
141 'Diary of Galina Vladimirovna Shtange', in Garros et al., *Intimacy and Terror*, p. 169.
142 *Izvestiia*, 15 Oct. 1937, quoted in Garros et al., *Intimacy and Terror*, p. 46.

3. STALIN IS LIKE A FAIRYTALE SYCAMORE TREE

Comrade Stalin for our happy childhood!' This slogan appeared everywhere in the world of the Soviet child — over nursery doorways, on walls in schools, on magazine and book covers — and was chanted by children at celebrations. Govorkov's poster shows Stalin dressed in white (suggesting purity, simplicity, and also making him appear full of light), surrounded by children with toys, flowers and artworks. In the background, children play in miniature cars and on scooters, watched by their mother, who is of secondary importance after Stalin.[143] Stalin's figure dominates the poster, his gaze is focused on a young boy who shows him a drawing of the Kremlin. Other boys hold model ships and aeroplanes, while the girls are passive and express gratitude by gesture, and by the gift of flowers. The colour palette is mostly muted and pastel red, green and white — the colours of festivity, which emphasises the relaxed and idyllic nature of the scene. Though happy and relaxed, the children are also orderly. From the mid-1930s onwards, the ideal Soviet child was consistently depicted as obedient and grateful.[144]

In the 1937 poster 'Thanks to the Party, thanks to dear Stalin for our happy, joyful childhood' by Dmitrii Grinets,[145] Stalin adopts a fatherly pose with three children. The portrait format of the poster emphasises the intimacy and physical closeness of the scene, which is reminiscent of a family home. By depicting such a scene, with Stalin standing in as the father for non-related children, the suggestion is made that he is the father of all children of all nationalities of the USSR, intimately concerned with the prospects and fate of each child in his care. Stalin holds the smallest child against his chest, while his focus is keenly on the elder boy who plays the violin for him. The youngest boy shows ambition to join the armed forces, wearing military garb and clutching a toy aeroplane in his right arm. The older boy wears a Pioneer scarf and will be a successful musician. It is only the young girl, wearing traditional headdress, who is given no costume or prop

---

143 In her memoirs, Nadezhda Mandelshtam recalled Boris Pasternak's wife, Zinaida Nikolayevna, saying: 'My children love Stalin most of all, and me only second' (*Hope against hope*, p. 51).
144 For example, as Catriona Kelly notes, the 1937 film *Cradle song*, showed Stalin surrounded by children and included footage of the Eighteenth Party Congress where Young Pioneers sang songs of praise to Stalin. In the film, children were portrayed as one of two stable points, along with Stalin, in a nation characterised by the 'frenetic motion of trains and planes criss-crossing the country' (see Kelly, *Children's world*, p. 93).
145 For an image, see Dawn Ades, *Art and power: Europe under the dictators 1930–45*, London, Thames and Hudson in association with Hayward Gallery, 1995, p. 243.

to indicate her future vocation. Perhaps her gratitude and devotion are a sufficient contribution. The caption of the poster, which is in Ukrainian and occupies the bottom third of the poster, reinforces this notion of gratitude, and is uncommon for its time in that it emphasises the thanks owed to the Party, as well as to Stalin. The word *ridnomu* (and its Russian equivalent *rodnomu*) does not translate precisely in English. Used as a term of endearment, the word also connotes a kin or familial relationship with the person to whom it is applied.

The 1938 poster 'Thank you Comrade Stalin for our happy childhood!', by Nina Vatolina, Nikolai Denisov, Vladislav Pravdin and Zoia Rykhlova-Pravdina, features a similar colour scheme and several of the same objects as the Govorkov poster of 1936. Significantly in this poster, the action takes place in front of a New Year tree, which had been banned since 1916, but was reinstated in 1935.[146] The tree in the 1938 poster is decorated with traditional candles and garlands, but also with small aircraft, parachutes and red stars. The model aeroplane and ship are typical Soviet toys, inspiring boys to emulate Soviet heroes in aviation and exploration.[147] By including these toys in the poster, oblique reference is also made to the great Soviet achievements in these fields. Stalin is not only providing a happy childhood, but also offers the children the potential for happy and fulfilling futures. In the 1938 poster, Stalin is surrounded by fair-haired Russian children who are situated on the same level in the picture plane as he although, by virtue of his status as adult male, he looks down on the children protectively. The scene is relaxed and informal, with four of the children gazing up at Stalin with affection while a fifth child has his back turned to Stalin and gazes directly at the viewer. The implication is that a Soviet childhood is a time of sacred innocence, unbounded joy, and material plenitude (the flowers in the bottom right-hand

---

146 Pavel Postyshev, second secretary of the Central Committee of the Communist Party of Ukraine, wrote a letter to *Pravda* in 1935 calling for the installation of the New Year tree in schools, homes, children's clubs and at Pioneers' meetings. Much was made of the reinstitution of the New Year tree by *Izvestiia*. On 1 January 1937, *Izvestiia* reported: 'On New Year's Eve nearly A QUARTER OF A MILLION HOLIDAY TREES were lit up in the capital alone. The spruce tree has come to symbolise our country's happy youth, sparkling with joy on the holiday ... The clinking of glasses filled with champagne. At the stroke of midnight, hundreds of thousands of hands raised them in a toast to the health of their happy motherland, giving tribute in the first toast of the year to the man whose name will go down through the ages as the creator of the great charter of socialism' (quoted in Garros et al., *Intimacy and terror*, p. 12).

147 Catriona Kelly notes that official New Year tree ceremonies, which in practice were open to a fairly limited elite group, 'were in part a way of tutoring the offspring of the Soviet elite in new roles (hence the giving of telephones as gifts ...)' (*Children's world*, p. 112).

corner are a further indication of material wealth). As the slogan suggests, all of these things are provided by the dominating paternal presence of Stalin, who is, by association, a kind of secular Father Christmas. This association is not spurious, as on 30 December 1936 Stalin appeared on the cover of the newspaper *Trud*[148] as Grandfather Frost, usurping the traditional role of the secularised version of Saint Nicholas, and making literal his role as mythical children's benefactor.

In 1935–36, Stalin began to appear with children more frequently in newspaper photographs. Plamper dates the launch of the image of Stalin as father to a newspaper article in 1935 in which he appeared with 11-year-old Pioneer Nina Zdrogova on the tribune of the Lenin Mausoleum, saluting a physical–cultural parade.[149] The image of the ruler with devoted child was to become one of the most significant genres across the various media in the cult of personality. One of these newspaper photographs, V. Matvievskii's 'Young girl and the Leader', 1936,[150] became particularly iconic, with copies posted in schools, children's clubs and institutions. It even appeared in a later propaganda poster as an icon.[151] The photograph was taken at a meeting between Party leaders and a delegation from the Buriat–Mongolian ASSR.[152] Gelia Markizova, aged seven, the daughter of one of the delegates, presented Stalin with a large bouquet of flowers, and he reciprocated with a kiss.[153] In this, and other newspaper reports of children meeting Stalin, such precise details of the ritual exchange were always noted.

As well as surrounding himself with children, Stalin also surrounded himself with flowers, both in photographs and posters. Flowers had formed a part of the personality cults of Aleksandr Kerenskii and General Lavr Kornilov in 1917,[154] however, after the October Revolution flowers disappeared from political life, as they were not consistent with the severe and sparse style of early Bolshevism and its ascetic idealism. Flowers re-emerged onto the public arena in

---

148 *Labour*.
149 Plamper, 'Georgian Koba or Soviet "father of peoples"?', in Apor et al., *The leader cult in communist dictatorships*, p. 130.
150 See history1900s.about.com/od/people/ss/Stalin.htm#step7, image number 7. About education: Joseph Stalin (accessed 2 Nov. 2016).
151 Nikolai Zhukov, 'We'll surround orphans with maternal kindness and love', 1947 (Fig. 3.15).
152 Autonomous Soviet Socialist Republic.
153 In December 1937, Gelia's father was arrested and later shot, and her mother, Dominika Fedorovna Markizova, was arrested and later sent to Southern Kazakhstan, where she died under mysterious circumstances in November 1940.
154 See Chapter Four.

the mid-1930s, even showing up in military parades, and became a constant presence in propaganda posters until the Great Patriotic War. Flowers symbolise celebration, festivity, fertility and abundance. The exchange of flowers for a 'gift' from Stalin became part of the ritual of ceremonial occasions. The use of flowers as symbols in Stalinist political posters embraced many of these traditional associations, as well as reinforcing the ritual that was becoming canonical. Flowers enhance the atmosphere of celebration and signify a rite of passage — a meeting with Stalin was a special milestone in the life of these select, fortunate children. The giving of flowers is a gesture of tribute and thanks to someone who has served or protected you. Flowers highlight the lush abundance of the imminent socialist utopia, which is already manifesting in the joyous lives led by these children. If Stalin took on the role of the great Father, wedded to the Soviet motherland, flowers and children symbolised the fertility of this union. While Russia had largely been regarded as a 'fatherland' in tsarist times, under Stalin it came increasingly to be called the 'motherland'. David Brandenberger notes that, before 1934 in Soviet Russia, the word *rodina* had been used only to refer to ethnically homogenous home territories. As of 1934, Stalin began to continually insert the word *rodina* into slogans for press publications when referring to the Soviet Union as a whole.[155] This became increasingly poignant during the years of the Great Patriotic War with several dramatic propaganda posters inciting men to protect the vulnerable motherland, often as embodied in a cowering woman, from Nazi atrocities.

Just one year after the 1938 'happy childhood' poster, as war erupted in Europe and threatened the Soviet Union, key changes were already beginning to surface in propaganda posters. In Vatolina's 1939 version of 'Thank you dear Stalin for our happy childhood' the children are from various nationalities within the Soviet Union, although Russian children still predominate. In earlier posters the children occupied the same space in the picture plane as Stalin, but now he is geographically isolated from them — nominally, away at the Kremlin, but in fact floating above them in the sky, looking down on them like an omnipotent god. This god-like quality is reinforced by the difference in scale in the two halves of the poster — Stalin's head is that of a titan and it dominates the heavens. There is no sky, only light

---

[155] David Brandenberger, *Propaganda state in crisis: Soviet ideology, indoctrination, and terror under Stalin, 1927–1941*, New Haven, Yale University Press, 2011, p. 101.

3. STALIN IS LIKE A FAIRYTALE SYCAMORE TREE

(as in an icon) and the sacred spire of the Spassky tower, topped by its red star, stands like the steeple of a church bathed in fairytale light. The Kremlin is the earthly home of the benign deity and in the poster forms a link between the realms of the heavens (inhabited by Stalin) and earth (inhabited by the children). The children bring lush bunches of flowers but these remain symbolic offerings which will not actually reach Stalin. While the children salute and gaze with reverential awe, Stalin looks down on them as a symbolic father, offering protection and benefaction and radiating white light across the various lands and territories of the union. Here Stalin's transformation from man to myth commences.

During the Great Patriotic War, Stalin's image appeared in posters less frequently than in the years immediately before the war, and when it did appear, it was primarily to rally the population for the war effort. Visually, he was portrayed in posters as leading the people into battle, and I have located only one poster of the early war years in which he is referred to as father.[156] During the war, the family, extended to include the larger 'family' of workmates and fellow soldiers, continued to be a focal point for propaganda, while there was also an increased focus on the biological family as being under threat from the Nazi invasion. By 1943, with the tide of the war turning in the Soviet Union's favour, Stalin began to appear in propaganda more frequently and was even sometimes depicted as 'standing in' for absent fathers. In Viktor Koretskii's 1943 'On the joyous day of liberation …' (Fig. 3.13) a portrait of Stalin is hung on the wall like an icon and has talismanic properties; however, the child is also treating the portrait as if it were a portrait of his own father. The peasant man in the poster appears too old to be the husband of the young woman, or father of the child, and it can be safely assumed that, with the war still raging outside the window, the child's father is away defending the nation. The family gather instead around a portrait of Stalin who, in this early version of the poster, is not wearing insignia of rank and looks humble and approachable. This reading of the poster is supported by the lengthy poster caption in which Stalin is referred to as 'our friend and father'.

---

156 Konstantin Cheprakov, 'We swore an oath to our leader to fight the enemy. We will keep the covenant of our fathers. Lead us into battle victory, wise Stalin — Clear the enemy, father of fighters!', 1941 (Fig. 4.17). This poster, with text in both Uzbek and Russian, was published in a small edition of 10,000 in Tashkent.

Stalin is also referred to as a father and apparent husband of Lenin in a 1943 poster by Vladimir Fedotov (Fig. 3.14). This curious poster, produced on cheap paper without details of place of publication or size of edition, celebrates 25 years of the Komsomol, although the poster image itself is about the war effort. In the poster caption, a verse by Kazimir Lisovskii,[157] Lenin takes on the maternal qualities of love and nurturing, while Stalin adopts the role of the father and raises the Komsomol generation — these are not children, but young people of fighting age. Lenin's banner is draped protectively over the young fighters, like the veil of the Virgin, and it is his spirit that is invoked to intercede on their behalf, while Stalin leads the troops on the battlefield in the earthly realm.

In influential graphic artist Nikolai Zhukov's[158] 'We'll surround orphans with maternal kindness and love' (Fig. 3.15) of 1947, a young orphan, born during the war years, lies in a clean bed, warm and protected under a red quilt. The young woman who cares for the child comforts it with her right hand while the left hand is raised in a gesture which suggests both protection and blessing. She is wholly absorbed in the child's care, her gaze intently on the child's face. She represents the motherland, the manifestation of the caring Soviet state. As we only see the back of the child's head, and even gender is indeterminate, the child figure has a universality that encompasses not only all orphans, but all of the children of the USSR. Stalin's portrait with Gelia Markizova is on the wall and it stands in for the father the child has lost in the war.

---

157 In labour and battle we are stronger
We gave the Motherland our youthful enthusiasm.
Great Lenin lovingly nurtured us,
Stalin reared us with a father's care.
Military winds are raging over us,
With enemies not yet decisively finished.
In the battle the banner of Lenin covers us
And beloved Stalin is conducting us to victory!
158 Zhukov, a highly decorated People's Artist of the USSR (1963) with an Order of Lenin (1967), Order of the Red Banner of Labour (1962) and Order of the Red Star, was also a Soviet pilot and was the artistic director of the Studio of Military Artists from 1943. Жуков, Николай Николаевич — Википедия, ru.wikipedia.org/wiki/%D0%96%D1%83%D0%BA%D0%BE%D0%B2,_%D0%9D%D0%B8%D0%BA%D0%BE%D0%BB%D0%B0%D0%B9_%D0%9D%D0%B8%D0%BA%D0%BE%D0%BB%D0%B0%D0%B5%D0%B2%D0%B8%D1%87 (accessed 2 Nov. 2016).

3. STALIN IS LIKE A FAIRYTALE SYCAMORE TREE

In Konstantin Ivanov's 'Happy New Year, beloved Stalin!', of 1952, Stalin's portrait is hung like an icon by a young boy at New Year. It is interesting to compare the 1952 Ivanov poster with the 1938 poster by Vatolina, Denisov, Pravdin and Pravdina. Both are set amid New Year celebrations and feature a New Year tree. In the earlier poster, Stalin is physically present in the scene, a benefactor and bestower of gifts. His interactions with the children are familiar and paternal. The New Year tree is hung with baubles that predict the fulfilling futures offered to the children. In the later poster Stalin is present only as a portrait on which the child gazes in rapture. The small portion of the tree that is visible carries red stars as decorations, but none of the other earlier portents of the happy future, and is adorned with tinsel, traditional baubles, a candy cane, a fish and a rabbit, suggesting abundance. The child is alone in this poster, without siblings, peers or parents. Perhaps the child is an orphan. Stalin stands in for the absent father, but here, as in the Zhukov poster, he is a remote presence and his relationship with the child is anything but familiar.

With the war years behind the Soviet Union, there was a rapid return to the notion of thanking Stalin for a happy childhood. In June 1946 a children's festival was held that began with the reading of a letter of gratitude to Stalin by a Pioneer, and was followed by a parade of Pioneers with balloons and flowers released from aircraft flying overhead.[159] In his final years, Stalin almost never appeared in public, and worked locked away in his dacha, just outside Moscow, or at one of his several holiday dachas located around the empire. This increasing remoteness was paralleled in journalistic and literary texts which featured less frequent opportunities for children to have direct contact with Stalin, and emphasised more contacts in remote or mediated forms, such as receiving a letter or telegram from Stalin.[160]

In 1950 another 'Thanks to dear Stalin for our happy childhood!' poster by Vatolina was released. A grey-haired Stalin appears in military uniform, standing on a podium. Although he touches the arm of the young Pioneer boy, he is separated in the picture plane from the two children and elevated above them. The girl carries a bunch of flowers to give to Stalin, but holds it off to the side, reaching up

---
159 Kelly, *Children's world*, p. 124.
160 Kelly, 'Grandpa Lenin and Uncle Stalin', in Apor et al., *The leader cult in communist dictatorships*, p. 109.

to touch Stalin with her right hand, as one might touch a holy icon. A huge bunch of red roses forms a barrier between them and the girl cannot reach him. The colour palette in Vatolina's 1950 poster is more vivid than in the earlier posters; the flowers are depicted in a more realistic style and occupy a large space in the image. The figure of Stalin floats in an undifferentiated background of pure light, which illuminates the face of the boy. In the 1936 and 1938 posters, children are relaxed and celebrating, not all of them look at Stalin and where they do look at him, it is with friendship and affection, from within the same space. Frequently, one of the children engages the viewer by looking directly out from the image. In the later posters, the children have diminished in number and importance and are restrained and respectful. It is clear that merely to be admitted to Stalin's presence is an honour and reward. The boy appears in profile and the girl is viewed from the rear; no child engages the viewer or embodies the 'happy childhood' of the poster's text. In 1950 a happy childhood consists entirely in being loyal and dutybound to Stalin. As Stalin is portrayed wearing military uniform, the formality of the occasion is reinforced, and the viewer is also reminded that all citizens owe Stalin a debt of gratitude for victory in the war.

After 1950, the 'happy childhood' theme slipped into the background and poster artists focused on depicting obedient children performing their duty to Stalin, who is now almost always represented in one of three ways: as a visionary on a mission to save the world, as a portrait/icon, or as a frieze. Stalin's special relationship with the Pioneers is illustrated in the 1951 poster, 'Best friend of children. Glory to great Stalin!' by well-known artist Elena Mel'nikova (Fig. 3.16). Stalin appears as a giant portrait hanging behind rows of unified, obedient children, who salute, wave flags and appear to be engaged in an oath-taking ceremony. The Soviet regime bound children to Stalin by the taking of oaths of allegiance and duty at initiation ceremonies into the Pioneers and Komsomol, and posters such as this reinforced the sense of obligation the children owed their leader. It is interesting to note that this is one of the relatively few posters of this era in which Stalin does not appear in military uniform. The text emphasises the friendly nature of the relationship between Stalin and the young Pioneers, and makes no reference to Stalin as a 'father'. There is no interaction as

Stalin looks out into the distance and the children have their backs turned to him. Neither the Warrior nor the Father archetype is being emphasised here.

Propaganda posters that overtly thanked Stalin for a happy childhood operated on several levels in Stalin's cult of personality. On one level, they appealed to children and instructed them in appropriate behaviour and attitude towards the *vozhd'*. By depicting Stalin increasingly as a mythical and iconic figure, children were further encouraged to an attitude of unquestioning obedience and spiritual faith that filled the vacuum left by the suppression of the Orthodox religion in Soviet society. With increasing emphasis on family values in Soviet society from the mid-1930s, even the lessons to be drawn from the cult of Pavlik Morozov were subtly repackaged, with the emphasis shifting away from the denunciation of his parents, and moving to his obedience and hard work as a school pupil.[161] *Komsomolskaia Pravda* declared in 1935: 'Young people should respect their elders, especially their parents.'[162] The 'happy childhood' posters, like most Soviet propaganda posters, were not primarily directed at children. The real targets were adults, many of whom faced a real spiritual crisis with the outlawing of religion, who were invited to embrace the blissful utopia manufactured by the state's artists. Obedient and faithful children not only served as models for appropriate adult behaviour, but were expected to re-educate their parents according to the new ways.

Fathers and sons

This ongoing re-education campaign to model new relationships in a new society employed the methodology of socialist realism across all genres of artistic production. In her examination of the Soviet novel, Clark discusses the two 'types' of biographies written in the 1930s — biographies of 'fathers' and biographies of 'sons'.[163] Fathers were usually represented by Party leaders like Stalin, Sergei Kirov, Kliment Voroshilov and Sergo Ordzhonikidze, or leaders in their fields like Anton Makarenko, Maksim Gor'kii and Nikolai Marr, while sons were

---

161 Figes, *The whisperers*, p. 162.
162 Figes, *The whisperers*, p. 162.
163 Clark, *The Soviet novel*, pp. 123–26.

Soviet heroes, like aviators and explorers.[164] While both fathers and sons served as examples to be emulated, the sons differed from the fathers in that they exhibited a childish and 'irresponsible' side and required guidance from the more stable and responsible father figure. Additionally, sons had not undergone the sorts of trials and suffering experienced by the fathers. As Clark points out, the sons did not move up to the status of fathers, remaining permanently indebted to and under the authoritative guidance of the father figures.

The relationship between Stalin and a number of these 'sons' of the nation was another prominent theme in propaganda posters during the mid-1930s. As already noted, in Soviet propaganda Stalin was not only the provider of all bounty to citizens of the Soviet Union, nor simply the benefactor of humankind. He was also the central facilitator of all motion, and the source of all achievement. Every accomplishment by any Soviet citizen reflected back on Stalin, who was an inspiration and muse to all. The notion of individual accomplishment due to exceptional personal abilities did not fit with a Marxist–Leninist view of history, which stressed that individuals were only able to accomplish great feats because they recognised the nature and significance of revolutionary times and were able to act in accordance with circumstances.[165] A significant genre of Soviet propaganda emerged to document and publicise great Soviet achievements, to credit them all to the Revolution, the Party, and ultimately the brilliance of the great enabler whom history had placed in the role of the leader. Stalin was effusively credited with not only facilitating all of the successes of the Soviet Union, but with such apparently miraculous abilities as keeping his aviators and polar explorers warm against the Arctic cold. Stalin was able to do this by virtue of the breadth and depth of his paternal care.

---

164 Clark, *The Soviet novel*, pp. 124–28.
165 This indeed is how Stalin saw himself, as revealed in an interview he gave to Emil Ludwig in 1931: 'Marxism does not deny that prominent personalities play an important role, nor the fact that history is made by people. In *The poverty of philosophy* and in other works of Marx you will find it stated that it is people who make history. But of course, people do not make history according to their own fancy or the promptings of their imagination. Every new generation encounters definite conditions already existing, ready-made, when that generation was born. And if great people are worth anything at all, it is only to the extent that they correctly understand these conditions and know how to alter them' (J.V. Stalin, 'Talk with the German author Emil Ludwig', 13 December 1931', Hari Kumar (trans.). In J.V. Stalin, *Works*, vol. 13. Moscow, Foreign Languages Publishing House, 1955, pp. 106–25, www.marxists.org/reference/archive/stalin/works/1931/dec/13.htm (accessed 12 Sep. 2012)).

3. STALIN IS LIKE A FAIRYTALE SYCAMORE TREE

One area of particular success and Soviet pride was aviation. Beginning in 1933, Aviation Day was celebrated by the Soviets every year, on 18 August, in much the same spirit as May Day and Revolution Day. The 1953 *Great Soviet encyclopedia* entry on aviation runs to several pages and credits Russia and the Soviet Union with being at the forefront of almost every aviation-related advance since 1731. The entry documents in great detail each theoretical and scientific contribution to the field of aviation, and downplays or discredits developments from other nations.[166] The year 1936 saw the beginning of a flourishing subgenre of posters that celebrated Soviet achievements in aviation. According to Kaganovich, aviation was 'the best expression of our accomplishments',[167] and at one time or other the Soviets held 62 aviation-related world records.[168] The propaganda promoting Soviet aviation served several related purposes. The industry showed genuine technological proficiency, and advances made in the field were a source of national pride for Soviet citizens, and thus served to legitimate the leadership in goal-rational terms. The charismatic leader only maintains leadership for as long as he is seen to be delivering on promises and the fact that these achievements reached beyond Soviet borders, and indicated Soviet superiority in this field to the rest of the world, not only provided a wider stage on which to demonstrate Soviet achievement, but also served as excellent propaganda to promote the success of the socialist system to the rest of the world. In addition, with the possibility of war in Europe on the horizon, demonstrations of Soviet aerial superiority served as a deterrent to the Germans and any others who might wish to challenge the USSR on the field of battle.

Soviet aviators, and their analogous colleagues, the polar explorers, performed daring feats and achieved world firsts, providing the Soviet people with a pantheon of new cultic heroes outside the traditional military and political spheres (and, hence, they were no threat to Stalin's own cult). Indeed, the first female heroes of the Soviet Union were pilots. An important component of the hero status that was accorded aviators was their 'victory over nature', a key concept in

---

166 See 'Aviation' from *The Great Soviet encyclopædia*, 1953, in von Geldern & Stites, *Mass culture in Soviet Russia*, p. 486.
167 Quoted in Jay Bergman, 'Valerii Chkalov: Soviet pilot as new Soviet man', *Journal of Contemporary History*, 33:1, 1998, pp. 135–52, p. 137.
168 Bergman, 'Valerii Chkalov', p. 137.

the Soviet agenda to industrialise rapidly and to bring a comfortable standard of living to the populace. As Bergman notes, the phraseology 'Stalin's falcons' and 'birds of steel' linked the new heroes to the folkloric heroes of the past — 'Kievan and Muscovite princes were often described in Russian folklore as falcons, and some of the heroes in these tales miraculously transformed themselves into birds'[169] — while at the same time still allowing the regime to separate itself from its tsarist predecessors (and Lenin), who did not have an aviation industry. The final paragraph of the aviation entry in the 1953 *Great Soviet encyclopædia* makes this point explicit:

> Thus, Russian scientists, engineers and inventors, working on the creation of flying machines, pioneered solutions to the basic problems of aviation. However, the decrepitude of Russia's bourgeois-landowner system, the incompetence of its tsarist rulers, and the country's technico-economical backwardness did not allow the initiatives of Russian innovators in aeronautics and aviation opportunities broad practical development. Innovators were given no support. Tsarist functionaries fawning before fancy foreigners ignored the discoveries and inventions of the Russian compatriots. Many valuable works by Russian scientists and inventors were credited to foreigners. Only the Great October Socialist Revolution gave designers, scientists, engineers, inventors and rationalizers limitless opportunities for creative work and the realization of their projects.[170]

The promotion of aviators as 'new Soviet men' partially addressed the awkwardness around the concept of the heroic individual, as the element of teamwork could always be reinforced — it took a pilot, a copilot and navigator (and Stalin) to make these heroic flights. This tension was never totally resolved and, in the late 1930s, in aviation as elsewhere, individual heroic cultic figures emerged and were promoted by the Soviet leadership. One of the most notable of these was Valerii Pavlovich Chkalov, the son of a boilermaker, who in 1937 was the first person to fly (with his copilot and navigator) from Moscow to the United States via the North Pole. Chkalov became the subject of posters, postage stamps and press articles, and appeared in photographs and paintings alongside Stalin. While Chkalov gained considerable cultic and heroic status in his own right, his achievements were always linked

---

169 Bergman, 'Valerii Chkalov', p. 139.
170 'Aviation', from *The Great Soviet encyclopedia*, in von Geldern & Stites, *Mass culture in Soviet Russia*, p. 486.

to Stalin's patronage, most notably through portraying the relationship between Stalin and Chkalov as that of father and son. A *Pravda* article of 1936 described the meeting between Stalin and Chkalov after the successful mission to the Kamchatka Peninsula as one in which they embraced like father and son, and Georgii Baidukov, Chkalov's copilot, recorded in his memoirs that, at Chkalov's funeral, Stalin 'sorrowfully bade farewell to his own most beloved son'.[171] In an article titled 'Our father' in *Izvestiia* in August 1938, just months before his death, Chkalov made this relationship explicit: 'In laudatory speeches, songs, and verses the Soviet people call Stalin a lodestar and a sun. But most of all, he is the embodiment of one word, the most tender and human word of all — father.'[172] There was perhaps some basis, no matter how small, for Stalin sharing the credit for these heroic flights. As with many other aspects of Stalin's leadership, Stalin was minutely involved in the planning of historic flights, discussing routes taken and other involved details of the flights. Sometimes this level of planning served his specific needs. The proposed August 1936 flight route was altered by Stalin to decrease its chances of failure, as Stalin was counting on the propaganda value of the successful flight during the upcoming show trials and purges.[173]

The 1937 poster 'Glory to Stalin's falcons — the conquerors of aerial elements!' (Fig. 3.17) by Viktor Deni and Nikolai Dolgorukov, celebrates the historic and dangerous flight from Moscow to the United States via the North Pole without identifying the men directly involved. Instead, the focus is on Stalin, whose profile image sketched on a red flag sits above the city of Moscow in the mid-left of the poster. The centre of the poster is dominated by a flat view of the

---

171 *Pravda*, 8 Aug. 1936 and Georgii Baidukov, *O Chkalove*, cited in Bergman, 'Valerii Chkalov', p. 147.
172 V.P. Chkalov, 'Nash otets', *Izvestiia*, 18 Aug.1938, quoted in Bergman, 'Valerii Chkalov', p. 148.
173 Bergman postulates that an important function of the focus on aviation from 1936 onwards relates to its coincidence with the beginning of the show trials and purges. Far from distracting attention away from the trials, Bergman argues that the exploits of Soviet pilots were intended to focus attention on the trials, providing a political and ideological contrast (or binary opposition) between the selfless Soviet heroes, and the degenerate, treacherous Trotskyite–Zinovievite defendants: 'Precisely because of the moral antithesis the two events suggested, Stalin even delayed the first Moscow trial from July to August 1936 to enable Chkalov and his crew to fly across the Soviet Union before the trial began, so that when the pilots landed safely on an island off the Kamchatka peninsula, just short of their intended destination, Soviet leaders could favourably contrast their bravery and patriotism with the moral degeneracy and treason of Zinoviev and Kamenev, and of the 14 other defendants in the trial' (Bergman, 'Valerii Chkalov', p. 138).

globe from the North Pole, with the USSR positioned to the bottom, and the United States tucked away at the top. The large landmass of the USSR is coloured Soviet red, and extended by the adjoining red flag, which billows across the globe in a symbol of Soviet domination. A well-populated Moscow bustles below, the people carrying a sea of red flags and banners. The route of the historic flight is traced by a thick red line through the North Pole, the centre of the poster, which swoops upwards through Canada to the United States. While Moscow is sketched in vibrant red, features the identifiably 'Russian' towers of the Kremlin, and is densely populated, Washington is a colourless and unpopulated landscape of featureless and indistinct skyscrapers. The steep red line that marks out the route is reminiscent also of the line on a graph, the upward swoop registering success and progress, as well as the trajectory of takeoff. Almost as large as the globe itself, and larger than the whole territory of the United States, are the images of the two Soviet planes that sweep across the top of the poster, and to which Stalin's gaze directs our eye. The nearer, larger plane is marked with the number 25 (the Tupolev 25 flown on the mission), the abbreviation USSR, and its body is inscribed with the words 'Stalin's falcons'. The text reinforces the association of this historic accomplishment with Stalin, proclaiming glory to 'Stalin's falcons', rather than to the individuals involved, and also reiterates the key Soviet priority for conquering nature and the elements.

In the late 1930s the Soviet leadership watched with increasing alarm the machinations of Nazi Germany under the leadership of Adolf Hitler. It was becoming clear that war in Europe was imminent, and it was Stalin's aim to stay out of the war for as long as possible, as the forces of the Soviet Union were unprepared for battle. With the multitude of successes on the world stage in aviation, Soviet propaganda could focus on this arena of achievement and employ it as a deterrent to Germany to engage the USSR in war. Produced in 1938, 'Long live the Soviet pilots — the proud falcons of our motherland!' (Fig. 3.18) by Denisov and Vatolina, emphasises this military might by showing a sky dense with aircraft engaged in an airshow. The display is watched by Stalin (in military-style tunic but as yet no uniform of rank) and Voroshilov (in marshal's uniform). With their golden, upturned faces, and white uniforms, the two men are the centre of light in the poster. Stalin salutes the pilots in a gesture that is both a mark of respect and a form of benediction, wishing them long life and protection from the

3. STALIN IS LIKE A FAIRYTALE SYCAMORE TREE

very real dangers of their calling. Despite the defence of the nation being Voroshilov's portfolio, it is Stalin's image that predominates. It was perhaps particularly important for propaganda to play up the might of Soviet aviation with war imminent as, in reality, the Soviet Airforce was ill equipped for military battle. Substantial effort had been focused on the 'higher, faster, longer' principle in aviation, which had led to the attainment of so many world records; however, these were not the sorts of aircraft needed to engage successfully in battle, as the war would come to demonstrate.[174]

Despite the early lack of preparation, the Soviets were ultimately successful in winning the war, and aviation continued to be a field in which socialism could demonstrate considerable progress and success, culminating in Iurii Gagarin's orbit of the earth in 1961. Chkalov, and other Soviet falcons, served as an inspiration to younger generations to embark on careers in aviation, which were held in high esteem and well rewarded.[175] The 1950 poster, 'To the new achievements of Soviet aviation!' (Fig. 3.19) by Pravdin, shows a paternal Stalin in his marshal's uniform, rewarding a Pioneer youth with a view of an airshow from his balcony. They are joined by two young men in military uniform, and a pilot, and the sky is full of aeroplanes and parachutes, providing a blaze of festive colour. The youth, holding a model aeroplane, thus indicating his desire to be an aviator, is supported in this aim by the protective, encouraging arm of Stalin, who indicates by gesture that the sky is the limit for this boy's future. The youth is clean-cut, reverential, composed and determined — the sorts of qualities needed in the new Soviet man. Just as Stalin had been a father to Chkalov, his special paternal attention to this deserving youth will ensure that he follows the correct line for success in the future. Women are absent from the foreground of the poster, although may be assumed to be present among the indistinct spectators to the show. After the war, women were encouraged to focus on motherhood and the domestic sphere, rather than dangerous exploits that might take them away from their families.

---

174 Bergman, 'Valerii Chkalov', pp. 135–52.
175 As Bergman notes, after Chkalov's tragic death, the nation was in mourning: 'well over one million mourners filed past his bier in the Hall of Columns in Moscow before his body was cremated and his ashes placed in a Kremlin wall. Indeed, the government apotheosized Chkalov so successfully after his death that in 1939 fully 30 per cent of the babies born in Gorkii, not far from the town of Vasilevo where Chkalov was born, were named "Valerii"' ('Valerii Chkalov', p. 137).

Adult children: the national anthem and the morning of the motherland

The 1944 version of the Soviet national anthem includes the lines 'And Stalin raised us to be loyal to the people / Inspired us to work and to deeds', formalising Stalin's patriarchy as a matter of state. Two posters, one of 1948 and the other of 1949, quote these lines directly. The lyrics of the anthem were, of course, well known and instantly recognisable to the Soviet people, and the two lines preceding these glorify Lenin, 'Through storms the sun of freedom shone on us / And great Lenin lit up our path', although Lenin is nowhere to be seen in these posters, either in text or image. Petr Golub's 1948 poster 'Stalin raised us to be loyal to the people!' (Fig. 3.20) combines the Father and Warrior archetypes in one pastel image. Under the protective canopy of the Soviet Navy flag, Stalin inspects the troops and addresses a young sailor who has been pulled out of line. The two stand eye-to-eye, the sailor holding the leader's gaze, and they look remarkably alike in terms of facial features, as if they could be related. Unusually, Stalin is shown as the same height as the young man, although the peak of his cap makes his overall height slightly greater. The caption makes clear the dual nature of Stalin's role for the sailors — as the Generalissimus of the Armed Forces, he is their military leader and as the man who raised them, he is their symbolic father.

Leonid Golovanov's 1949 poster, 'And Stalin raised us to be loyal to the people, inspired us to work and to deeds!' (Fig. 3.21), consists of a triptych of images with Stalin's profile portrait occupying the centre panel. He is serene, wise, bathed in a sea of light that emanates from his face to fill the sky in the other two panels of the poster. The left panel shows Soviet civilians under the national flag, holding a huge sheaf of wheat, the symbol of success in agriculture and of fertility in general. People wave and cheer in the background. The right panel shows Soviet military personnel from each of the armed forces with their appropriate banners and a rifle in hand. The central image of Stalin unites the military and the civilian as Stalin again displays both the Father and the Warrior archetype in this poster, which appeared in the year of his 70th birthday celebrations.

3. STALIN IS LIKE A FAIRYTALE SYCAMORE TREE

When Stalin appears in posters as the father of the people, he stands without a female partner. Stalin had been married twice, his first wife dying young of an illness, and his second wife committing suicide in 1932. The nation saw Stalin bury Nadia and, from this point on, he did not publicly have a female partner — in fact, so little is known of this aspect of his personal life that there is only speculation as to further sexual relationships after Nadia's death. Stalin's life centred around his role as leader and it was easy to depict him as 'wedded to the nation'. Fyodor Shurpin's famous painting of 1948, *The morning of our motherland*, depicts a calm, reflective Stalin in plain white tunic, isolated and alone in a muted pastel landscape, his greatcoat draped over his sleeve. Behind him in the distance, tractors plough the fields and powerlines melt into the hazy sky. Stalin is bathed in the early morning light and looks out to the right, to the dawn of the communist utopia. This well-known painting is undoubtedly the inspiration for two posters that were both published in 1949, one in an edition of 300,000 by Golub, the other in a smaller edition of 10,000 by F. Litvinov (Fig. 3.22). Both posters share the same quotation from Stalin as a caption, 'Long life and prosperity to our motherland'. It is interesting to compare the posters to the painting that inspired them, and to each other, as the differences between them are telling. One key difference is that Stalin is slightly more face-on to the viewer in the painting than in the posters and looks considerably more tired. In the posters he is less heavily jowled, his skin brighter, and his moustache more trim. In Golub's poster, in particular, Stalin has a more military bearing, almost standing at attention while, in the Shurpin painting, he is relaxed and leans back slightly, his shoulders soft. In both posters Stalin is wearing military uniform while, in the painting, he appears as a civilian, a private individual, alone at dawn. The posters are both in portrait format, while the painting is in landscape, hence the posters emphasise the figure of Stalin, while Shurpin's painting makes much more of the landscape. Indeed, in Golub's poster, Stalin is not alone, but accompanied by a young Pioneer boy who gazes silently into the future with him, the symbolic son of the wedded union between Stalin and the motherland. The landscapes have been altered in each of the posters. The Litvinov poster was published in the Crimea and it is possible that the landscape of the poster reflects the local landscape. The Golub poster features a birch tree in the foreground, standing straight as Stalin, and a patchwork of lush green fields behind the two figures. The notion of plenitude and abundance is reinforced by the small sprig of flowers in the child's hand. A river flows through the landscape, continuing the dual association of Stalin with water, and with the golden light that illuminates him from above. By drawing so obviously on Shurpin's painting, the posters suggest the dawn of a new age of abundance for the Soviet Union, the arrival of the long-awaited communist utopia after the dark nights of the Civil War, the purges, and the Great Patriotic War. Stalin is the father of the nation who cared for, protected, and raised the nation and, in Golub's poster, the hope of the future lies in the nation's youth.

Stalin as teacher

Stalin's role as teacher and mentor overlapped substantially with his role as father, but introduced additional dimensions in which his wisdom and ability to inspire and guide were emphasised over his paternal care. As noted when discussing the politics of obligation, patronage was an accepted part of Russian life, with many aspects of culture contributing to this traditional social structure. Many of the great writers acknowledged their mentors: Isaac Babel named Maksim Gork'ii, and Gor'kii named Leo Tolstoi.[176] Mentorship, in particular, had long been a feature of Russian intellectual life, with *kruzhok*[177] to discuss poetry, critique art and argue politics an established social structure.[178] These circles provided members with access to material resources and a sense of belonging while, in return, members tended to venerate their leader with paintings, sculptures, poems and songs and, after death, with obituaries and memoirs. As Plamper notes: 'The circle members, in short, built a cult around their leader',[179] and these early experiences in their formative years may have helped the Bolsheviks internalise the mechanisms of the personality cult.

Both Lenin and Stalin had been involved in circles, Stalin claiming to have joined his first circle while still at the seminary in Georgia[180] and, over time, worked their way from membership to leadership positions. One of Stalin's keenest strengths seems to have been the ability to

---

176 Brooks, 'Stalin's politics of obligation', p. 58.
177 Circles.
178 See Plamper, *The Stalin cult*, pp. 19–21.
179 Plamper, *The Stalin cult*, p. 20.
180 Montefiore, *Young Stalin*, p. 63.

surround himself with loyal followers who were rewarded with his patronage. The need for loyalty within these circles was intensified in the cloak-and-dagger atmosphere of the revolutionary underground, where the major preoccupations were delivering Lenin's latest missives for publication abroad, obtaining Party funds by illegal means, and arguing in nitpicking detail over the finer nuances of Marxist interpretation. Arrests and exiles were commonplace and emphasis was placed on trust.

Stalin was quick to point out that he was merely Lenin's best pupil, but his propaganda made much of his role as a teacher of the people. Over time he came to take bold decisions on his own initiative and to reinterpret Marxism–Leninism in the light of his own lived experience in a socialist society. Marx and Engels did not give specific guidelines on the day-to-day business of how to make a socialist/communist society function, and Soviet society was the first such experiment of its kind. Stalin and the Bolshevik leadership found themselves very much in reactive mode and having to 'make it up as they went along', as the regime seemed to lurch from one crisis to the next. Stalin was older than the other leaders, except for the old *muzhik*,[181] Mikhail Kalinin, and as such could expect some measure of respect. As Montefiore reveals in his biographies of Stalin, Stalin was in fact widely read with a huge personal library, numbering thousands of volumes, much of which was heavily annotated in his handwriting.[182] He felt qualified to contribute to academic debates in a wide number of disciplines, with the caveat that his contribution was from the perspective of a thorough understanding of the laws of Marxism–Leninism which, it was believed among the Bolsheviks, if correctly applied, could assist in bringing 'the truth' to light in every field of human endeavour. Stalin had also endured the hardships of the 'school of life' through his underground work, arrests, exiles to Siberia, and agitation among the workers of the Caucasus. If one adds to this the high rate of illiteracy when the Bolsheviks took government and the almost total lack of any awareness or understanding of Marxist ideology among the populace, it is hardly surprising that Stalin was presented to the people as a wise and experienced teacher, the 'tried and tested' driver of the locomotive of state.

---

181 Peasant.
182 Montefiore, *Young Stalin*; and, Montefiore, *Stalin*.

As indicated earlier, this view of Stalin as intelligent, wise, canny and experienced was shared by his closest comrades in the Bolshevik leadership. Stalin was also presented as a wise teacher amongst the intelligentsia. Brooks argues that by 1934, the year of the Writers Congress, Stalin came to adopt the role of 'writer– teacher', which had a strong tradition in both Russian history in general, and amongst the Bolsheviks, with figures like Lenin and Trotskii involving themselves in literary criticism.[183] Stalin demonstrated some early promise as a poet in Georgia, with work published in leading newspapers, but abandoned this pursuit as incompatible with a career as a revolutionary.[184] In his exhaustive exploration of the content of *Pravda*, Brooks notes that Stalin was cited as a major authority on numerous topics: 'Pravda's editors cited Lenin as an authority in fewer than a fifth of the lead editorials from 1921 through 1927 and Stalin in equal measure from 1928 through 1932, but from 1933 through 1939 they mentioned Stalin in more than half.'[185] Detractors like Trotskii had, perhaps, ample motivation (including personal dislike) for claiming that Stalin was otherwise.[186]

The portrayal of Stalin as a wise teacher formed a major theme in Soviet propaganda. In posters, this was often achieved by showing Stalin in his study, or speaking to a crowd of eager listeners, but also by depicting him as a mentor to high achievers like the Stakhanovites and the Soviet falcons. In some posters, Stalin takes on a blatantly didactic role. An early example of such a poster from 1933 is Mikhail Kuprianov's 'We have overthrown capitalism ...' (Fig. 3.23). There are two similar versions of this simple poster, published in Moscow in small editions of 4,000, both featuring Stalin looking directly ahead as if meeting the eye of the viewer and making a direct request. The text is a quotation from Stalin and recounts socialist victories to date, while instructing the viewer that further education in the techniques of science is still needed.[187] A poster of the same year by

---

183 Brooks, *Thank you, Comrade Stalin!*, p. 64.
184 Montefiore, *Young Stalin*, p. 63.
185 Brooks, *Thank you, Comrade Stalin!*, p. 65.
186 Montefiore is also of the opinion that it is time to move on from Trotskii's portrayal of Stalin: 'It is clear from hostile and friendly witnesses alike that Stalin was always exceptional, even from childhood. We have relied on Trotsky's unrecognizably prejudiced portrait for too long. The truth was different. Trotsky's view tells us more about his own vanity, snobbery and lack of political skills than about the early Stalin' (*Young Stalin*, p. xxx).
187 'We have overthrown capitalism.
We took power.

Pikalov, published in Leningrad in an edition of 30,000, quotes both Lenin and Stalin as authorities, and then instructs the viewer to study the history of class struggle (Fig. 3.24). The left side of the poster is filled with the figure of Stalin, who again stares directly at the viewer. Beneath him is an authoritative caption of his own words about the importance of theory from the speech at the Conference of Marxist Agrarians on 27 December 1929.[188] The right side of the poster is filled with exemplary scenes of the history of class struggle, including scenes from the French Revolution, the *Communist manifesto*, the 1905 Revolution, the storming of the Winter Palace, the Aurora, and scenes of collectivisation and industrialisation which comprise Stalin's revolution. None of the scenes is captioned and it is assumed the viewer is familiar enough with the material to be able to identify the action in the poster.

A number of posters across the early 1930s outline Stalin's six historical conditions;[189] six guidelines for agriculture;[190] six conditions for victory;[191] Stalin's six guidelines for the transport industry;[192] the path to victory — implementation of the six conditions of Comrade Stalin, 1932;[193] and six conditions of Stalin.[194] All of these posters, which basically reproduce the same six conditions,[195] use a facial portrait

---

We built a huge socialist industry.
We are the middle peasants on the road to socialism ...
We have a bit more [to do]: to learn the techniques to master science.' (Stalin)
188 'You know that theory, if it is genuine theory, gives practical workers the power of orientation, clarity of perspective, confidence in their work, faith in the victory of our cause.'
189 Unidentified artist, 1931.
190 Unidentified artist, 1931.
191 Viktor Deni, 'Six conditions for victory', 1931.
192 Unidentified artist, (in Ukrainian) 'Six guidelines of Comrade Stalin for the transport industry!', undated.
193 Unidentified artist, 'The path to victory — implementation of the six conditions of Comrade Stalin', 1932
194 Unidentified artist, 'Six conditions of Stalin', 1938.
195 The six conditions are taken from Stalin's speech on 23 June 1931 to agricultural workers in which he lays out the main tasks and organisation of agriculture. The conditions are: 1. Recruit manpower in an organised way, by means of contracts with the collective farms, and mechanise labour; 2. Put an end to labour mobility, do away with wage equalisation, organise the payment of wages properly, and improve the living conditions of workers; 3. Put an end to the lack of personal responsibility at work, improve the organisation of work, arrange the proper distribution of forces in our enterprises; 4. See to it that the working class of the USSR has its own industrial and technical intelligentsia; 5. Change our attitudes towards the engineers and technicians of the old school, show them greater attention and solicitude, and enlist their cooperation in work more bravely; and, 6. Introduce and reinforce financial accountability and increase the accumulation of resources within industry.

of Stalin, usually looking straight at the viewer. Lenin does not appear anywhere in the visual imagery of these posters, suggesting that it was already considered appropriate to allow Stalin to offer guidance as a 'teacher' in his own right. Some early posters even feature graphs and charts related to progress on the five-year plans and other statistics indicating targets to be met.[196] Stalin usually appears in these as a cameo portrait, as if he were presenting the graphs and charts for consideration by the people. This gave the impression that Stalin was in control — he had a plan and knew exactly how progress toward it stood; that he was clever — he understood the charts and the scientific laws of Marxism–Leninism; and that he was ultimately responsible for all of this amazing progress. These didactic posters full of ideology and 'scientific data' required a considerable amount of time for reading, a high level of literacy and some mathematical sophistication. By and large, this content was inherently unsuitable to the medium and to a large proportion of the audience and, by 1934, a simpler approach was adopted that used more eye-catching images and symbolic figures, and used the poster text to make one concise point in a catchy slogan, rather than outline an entire complex plan.

By 1935 the emphasis went from mastermind to mentor, with Stalin's patronage particularly highlighted in association with the Stakhanovite movement.[197] The Stakhanovites were held up as models to be emulated by the rest of society, and were rewarded with shiny new consumer goods, like gramophone players, which the rest of the Soviet public could only dream of owning. The Stakhanovites too were emulating someone. Without fail, in all of their public speeches, they were sure to give credit to Stalin, citing his speeches as inspiring their heroic feats. Stakhanov was quoted in *Pravda* in 1935: 'To him, to the

---

196 Polenov, 'For the victory of communism in our country', 1927; Mikhail Dlugach, '10 years of the USSR Civilian air fleet', 1933; Nikolai Kochergin, 'What is the percentage increase in output', 1933.
197 The movement was named after Aleksei Grigorievich Stakhanov, a coalminer who, in 1935, exceeded his quota of seven tons of coal per shift with an output of 102 tons, and reorganised his work brigade to increase its production through the use of improved work methods. Stalin personally praised this extraordinary achievement and founded a movement in Stakhanov's name with the aim of increasing Soviet industrial output across the board. At the First All-Union Conference of Stakhanovites in November 1935, Stalin stated 'The Stakhanov movement is a movement of working men and women which will go down in the history of our socialist construction as one of its most glorious pages. / Wherein lies the significance of the Stakhanov movement? / Primarily, in the fact that it is the expression of a new wave of socialist emulation, a new and higher stage of socialist emulation' (J.V. Stalin, speech at the First All-union Conference of Stakhanovites, 17 November 1935 in Stalin, *Problems of Leninism*, p. 775).

3. STALIN IS LIKE A FAIRYTALE SYCAMORE TREE

great Stalin, we are all obligated for the happy life of our country, for the joyfulness and glory of our beautiful homeland.'[198] In fact, as Stalin pointed out in his speech to the Stakhanovite conference, the state did not owe the Stakhanovites a debt of gratitude for their hard work. Rather, the Stakhanovites owed Stalin, the Party and the state for providing them with the opportunity to work so hard.[199] The new constitution of 1936 formalised this reciprocal obligation between the worker and the state in Articles 118 and 130.[200]

The Stakhanovites were not the first record-breaking workers to be celebrated by the Soviet regime. Prior to Stakhanov's feat, *udarniki*[201] received publicity and became the theme of posters like A.M. Rumiantsev's 'Shock work at the machine is combined with the study of Marxist–Leninist theory' of 1931 (Fig. 2.4); Gustav Klutsis's 'Shock workers of the fields engage in fighting for the socialist reconstruction of agriculture …' of 1932 (Fig. 3.25); Aleksandr Polyakov's 'Worthy sons and daughters of the great party of Lenin–Stalin' of 1935; and Konev's 'Our noble people …' published in Kharkov in 1935 (Fig. 3.26). As was the case with the use of Stalin as a symbol, an individual could provide a better rallying symbol to fire the popular imagination than the collective of anonymous faces, so one man was chosen to symbolise a whole new work ethic. Sadly, there was considerable distance between the characteristics of the idealised hero and the personal qualities of the man himself, as Stakhanov apparently struggled with his new status.[202]

---

198 Aleksei Stakhanov, *Pravda*, 15 Nov. 1935 cited in Brooks, 'Stalin's politics of obligation', p. 57.
199 'The basis for the Stakhanov movement was first and foremost the radical improvement in the material welfare of the workers. Life has improved, comrades. Life has become more joyous. And when life is joyous, work goes well. Hence the high rates of output. Hence the heroes and heroines of labour. That, primarily, is the root of the Stakhanov movement. If there had been a crisis in our country, if there had been unemployment — that scourge of the working class — if people in our country lived badly, drably, joylessly, we should have had nothing like the Stakhanov movement. Our proletarian revolution is the only revolution in the world which had the opportunity of showing the people not only political results but also material results' (Stalin, 'Speech at the First All-union Conference of Stakhanovites', in Stalin, *Problems of Leninism*, pp. 783–84).
200 The first right granted to the citizen by the state was the right to work — Article 118 guarantees that 'Citizens of the U.S.S.R. have the right to work, that is, are guaranteed the right to employment and payment for their work in accordance with its quantity and quality', while Article 130 binds the citizen to the reciprocal duty of maintaining labour discipline and honestly performing public duties (1936 Constitution of the USSR, Chapter XII, Article 118, www.departments.bucknell.edu/russian/const/36cons04.html#chap12 (accessed 10 Nov. 2012)).
201 Shock workers.
202 Stakhanov and his fellow Stakhanovites were obliged to go on tour and attended conferences to promote the movement. Turovskaya records: '[Tat'iana] Fedorova told us what a "headache"

The 1935 Conference of Stakhanovites generated substantial publicity and was followed by a related publicity campaign.[203] Two posters that feature the Stakhanovites and the image of Stalin appeared in 1936, cementing in the popular imagination Stalin's mentorship of these extraordinary workers. Genrikh Mendelevich Futerfas's 'Stalinists! Extend the front of the Stakhanovite movement!' (Fig. 3.27) promotes the Stakhanovite movement and exhorts working people to join the ranks. The poster design resembles many others of the early to mid-1930s, and is a somewhat less skilful rendition of the style of poster so successfully executed by Klutsis.[204] The technique used is photomontage, and the colour scheme is monochromatic, save for the diagonal slash of red surrounding the outstanding figure of Stalin, who heartily greets the army of enthusiastic workers beneath him. The diagonal suggests movement, as if swarms of people are indeed pouring in to swell the ranks of the Stakhanovite workers, all joyously active and working together in the upward direction indicated by Stalin's guiding hand. Despite the multitude of workers featured in the poster, they are concentrated in the bottom third of the space, and it is the figure of Stalin that dominates and is the only figure to penetrate the upper part of the image. The subtitle of the poster quotes from Stalin's speech at the Stakhanovite conference: 'Life is getting better, comrades. Life has become more joyous. And when life is joyous, work goes well.'[205] The first part of this refrain became one of Stalin's major slogans, and was the inspiration for a popular song of 1936.[206]

Stakhanov was for the "other" Stakhanovites at all the forums and conferences: raising hell in the new Moscow Hotel, disappearing, having too much to drink, so that they had to dash out somewhere and bail him out, and the like. He did not fit in among the new businesslike working-class elite, but no one quite dared to send the bearer of "the name" back home' ('Easy on the heart', in Balina & Dobrenko, *Petrified Utopia*, p. 256).
203 For an in-depth discussion of how the Stakhanovite campaign was conducted at the industrial city Magnitogorsk, see Kotkin, *Magnetic Mountain*, pp. 201–15.
204 Stalin's upraised hand, his palm flat and facing outwards, is a well-known recurring motif in the work of Gustav Klutsis.
205 Stalin, 'Speech at the First All-union Conference of Stakhanovites', in Stalin, *Problems of Leninism*, p. 783.
206 *Life's getting better*, lyrics by Vasilii Lebedev-Kumach and music by General Aleksandr Aleksandrov of the Red Army Ensemble.
Beautiful as birds, all in a row
Songs fly above the Soviet land.
The happy refrain of the cities and fields:
'Life's getting better and happier too!'
The country is growing and singing as one,
It forges everyone's joys with its songs.
Look at the sun — the sun's brighter too!

3. STALIN IS LIKE A FAIRYTALE SYCAMORE TREE

Nikolai Dolgorukov's 'Swell the ranks of the Stakhanovites' also promotes the message of the Stakhanovite conference, encouraging the population to get behind the Stakhanovite movement and help spread it across the USSR. The largest of the banners publicises the organisation of a national 24-hour Stakhanovite shift on 11 January 1936, followed by a Stakhanovite Five-Day, Ten-Day, and then a Stakhanovite Month in which workers engaged in socialist competition to increase their production output.[207] The lower half of the photomontage poster shows the happy population flooding in to swell the ranks, surrounded by some of the fruits of their labour — the newly opened Metro, and power plants and factories billowing smoke in the background. The ever-present symbol of the Spassky tower is like a socialist people's church, the physical and spiritual home of the faithful, the crowning star a beacon in the sky.

The top third of the poster is occupied by a photograph of the Soviet leadership taken at the 1935 Stakhanovite conference, lined up on either side of Stalin like the saints in the Deesis. Figures from left to right are Nikita Krushchev, Anastas Mikoian, Ordzhonikidze, Stalin in the centre, Kalinin, Voroshilov, Molotov, and Kaganovich. Stalin hails the crowd with an open palm — part wave, part salute — while Krushchev and Molotov applaud. The placement of the leadership at the top of the poster provides a visual link to the widely publicised 1935 conference (the photo on which the poster is based was published in the press), and this is reinforced by the quote from Stalin appearing in red text under the photograph. It also emphasises

---

'Life's getting better and happier too!'
There's room everywhere for our minds and our hands,
Wherever you go you'll find you have friends.
Old age feels warmer, and youth braver still —
'Life's getting better and happier too!'
Know, Voroshilov, we're all standing guard —
We won't give the enemy even a yard.
There is a saying for folks old and young:
'Life's getting better and happier too!'
Let's the whole gigantic country
Shout to Stalin: 'Thank you, our man,
Live long, prosper, never fall ill!'
'Life's getting better and happier too!'
From von Geldern & Stites, *Mass culture in Soviet Russia*, pp. 237–38.
207 See Kotkin, *Magnetic Mountain*, p. 207.

the role of these leaders as overseers, organisers and inspirers of the Stakhanovite movement, viewing the activity of the ant-like workers from the heavens.

The Stakhanovite theme was popular in posters in 1935 and 1936, with the last poster I have located on this theme dated 1938. This poster, 'Long live the united communist party / Bolshevik / — vanguard of the workers of the USSR!',[208] by an unidentified artist is interesting because it is the only Stakhanovite poster I have encountered which includes an image of Lenin — Stakhanovites were a Stalinist invention. Lenin stands over the right shoulder of Stalin and both have their right arms extended: Lenin is pointing to the left, while Stalin is in almost identical pose, except that his right palm is upturned, as if he were bestowing a gift. Beneath them are two rows of distinguished Stakhanovite workers, who are introduced by a banner that reads: 'Meet the choice of the Supreme Soviet of the RSFSR, new rising Stakhanovite movement!'

While at times extraordinary results by Stakhanovite workers may have been manipulated or manufactured by ambitious bosses and officials, the movement did inspire in some people a desire to participate as fully as possible in the building of socialism and a pride in their work achievements. It also produced real results; for example, in his private diary, Fyodor Efimovich Shirnov, manager at a building materials factory in 1936, recorded the following observation:

> We brung in teachers to teach the workers and sent dozens out to take special courses. When our mechanics come back from the courses, they was already completely trained. They changed their way of working methods like it was nothing. Stakhanovites installed themselves firmly at the helm and our factory started buzzing, it went from a yearly volume of two million to thirteen million and in 1936 it rose even higher, keep pushing it higher and higher so all of us can live happier (sic).[209]

Such internalisation of Stakhanovite values was not universal. The words of one worker sound a justifiable note of cynicism: 'The Stakhanovite movement has been thought up by our rulers in

---

208 For an image, see redavantgarde.com/en/collection/show-collection/937-long-live-the-united-communist-party.html?authorId=293.
209 'Diary of Fyodor Efimovich Shirnov', in Garros et al., *Intimacy and Terror*, pp. 91–92.

order to squeeze the last juice from the toilers'[210] and, in the next decades, the term 'Stakhanovite' came to be used with a degree of contempt.

From 1937, Stalin's falcons stole the limelight and became the new Soviet heroes, with Stalin being presented in a paternal relationship with the daring young men. It is part of a father's duties to be mentor to his son, but Stalin's sudden change from teacher to father in relation to the adult population may have been due at least in part to the show trials and purges that began at this time. As Plamper has noted, an increase in terror in Soviet society was always accompanied by an increase in tenderness in the portrayals of Stalin,[211] and it makes sense that the ruthlessness of Stalin in rooting out enemies and traitors be tempered by images that showed his love for the faithful members of the Soviet family.

During the war years, propaganda was primarily focused on mobilisation for the war effort, although Stalin's guidance and leadership were invoked in a number of posters in which he was to be seen leading the troops into battle. After the war, Stalin's leadership and guidance were invoked in the name of new victories awaiting the socialist state that could now continue on the path to full communism. Stalin was often depicted in a marshal's uniform and, at times, the treatment of his image resembled an icon. In some of these posters, it is only the caption that makes reference to Stalin as a teacher. Nikolai Avvakumov's 1946 poster 'Long live our teacher, our father, our leader, Comrade Stalin!' (Fig. 3.28) is a bust portrait of a genial, avuncular Stalin that uses the caption to evoke three of the major Stalin archetypes, and glimpses of military uniform in the image evoke the fourth, that of the Warrior. In Pravdin and Denisov's 'Long live our leader and teacher the great Stalin!' of 1948 (Fig. 3.29) a dignified Stalin in military uniform gazes out to the future with the Kremlin as a backdrop. In 1949, the year of Stalin's 70th birthday, there was a renewed emphasis on the human side of Stalin in some posters, although he was still often alone, remote, or isolated from other figures in some manner. Two posters by Viktor Ivanov show Stalin alone in his study, caught in a moment of quiet reflection. 'Great Stalin is the beacon of communism!' (Fig. 3.7) shows Stalin with a book

---

210 Cited in Sheila Fitzpatrick, *Stalinism: new directions*, London, Routledge, 1999, p. 163.
211 Plamper, *The Stalin cult*, p. 48.

by Lenin in his hand, reflecting on the words he has read. Behind him are the collected works of Marx and Engels, of Lenin, and his own collected works. In 'Reach for prosperity!' (Fig. 3.30) Stalin holds a telegram and is surrounded by a pile of correspondence. Clearly many people turn to Stalin for guidance and counsel. Posters depicting Stalin in his study stress his scholarly side, the large volume of his canonical writings, his ability to act as a wise judge, and the careful consideration he gives to all matters.

After the war, emphasis was increasingly placed on technical expertise over breakneck physical labour, with the science budget of the Soviet Union tripling in 1946.[212] Toidze uses a richly symbolic visual image to illustrate this new emphasis, captioned by the familiar text, 'Under the banner of Lenin, under the leadership of Stalin, forward to the victory of communism!' (Fig. 3.31). This 1949 poster employs the preferred Toidze palette of black, white and red, with small embellishments of gold. The top half of the poster is dominated by the figures of Lenin and Stalin. Lenin appears as a life-size sculpture in characteristic pose, right arm extended and whole hand beckoning the crowd forward and appears to be shepherding Stalin forward. Stalin, only slightly less monolithic due to the higher contrast on his figure, mirrors Lenin's gesture almost exactly, except that his right index finger points and his left hand drapes over the podium. The pole of the ubiquitous scarlet banner divides the background in half vertically, at exactly the place where the heads of Lenin and Stalin meet, identifying Stalin with the banner, but not Lenin, a link that is visually reinforced by the touches of red on Stalin's uniform. The podium on which Stalin and the statue of Lenin are elevated divides the top and bottom halves of the poster. Beneath the podium, with their backs to Lenin and Stalin, are civilian members of the populace. On the left, a young female agricultural labourer, a huge sheaf of wheat over her right shoulder, stands next to a young male worker, both looking forward in the direction indicated by Lenin and Stalin. On the right, a young man holds aloft a sparkling white book with the words 'Marx, Engels, Lenin, Stalin' emblazoned on the front cover in gold. His pose mimics that of Lenin and Stalin, although his right hand does not point, but clutches the sacred text. Behind him is a young woman with windswept hair who

---

212 Ronald Grigor Suny, *The Soviet experiment: Russia, the USSR and the successor states*, 2nd edn, New York, Oxford University Press, 2011, p. 397.

adopts the same pose and looks up to Lenin and Stalin for guidance. In her right hand is a large spray of flowers, symbolising abundance and *kultur'nost*, the postwar emphasis on living a cultured lifestyle. The left or 'Lenin side' of the poster is associated with the past — the two young workers are manual labourers, in the factory and field. Stalin's side of the poster represents the present pushing on to the future. The two young people are not dressed for manual labour and rely on education and a sound knowledge of the science of Marxism, as adapted by Lenin and Stalin, for the imminent victory of communism. The early 1950s saw a continuation of the emphasis on education and the mastery of science, with a number of posters published in 1952 on these themes.[213]

A minor subgenre of posters in which Stalin appeared as teacher/mentor concerns the rights of the Soviet woman. A number of Soviet posters were produced on women's themes, with many of them designed by women, particularly in the 1920s — the 1930s saw a return to the marginalisation of women artists.[214] Of the posters that addressed women's themes, only comparatively few of them featured Stalin's image. When they did, despite overtly stressing gender equality and the independence of women, their message served to remind women that they owed their new equality in society to Stalin and the Party.

'Stalin among the delegates' is a 1937 poster by Nikolai Mikhailov, published in Moscow by Glavlit, the censorship bureau, as part of a series that included posters of 'Kalinin among the Uzbeks' and 'Peasants visiting Lenin'.[215] The poster highlights the new rights of women as enshrined in the 1936 Constitution of the USSR and features a verse at its base recalling the 'slave-like' conditions under which

---

213 Boris Belopol'skii, 'In order to build, we must have knowledge, mastery of science. And knowledge entails study. We must study perseveringly and patiently', 1952; Konstantin Ivanov, '"I wish you good health and success in teaching and social work. I hope that you successfully complete your studies and become the energetic, knowledgeable, employees, that are necessary for our country." IV Stalin', 1952; Konstantin Ivanov & M. Elt'sufen, 'Pioneer — an example to all children!', 1952; M. Solomyanii, (in Ukrainian) 'Excellent study will please the leader!', 1952.
214 According to Susan Reid, in her article about gender and power in the Soviet Union in the 1930s, 'Even in the rare cases where women held office in the art administration, they were consigned to traditionally feminine spheres of responsibility having to do with the organisation and beautification of *byt*' ('All Stalin's women: gender and power in Soviet art of the 1930s', *Slavic Review*, 57:1, 1998, pp. 133–73, p. 161).
215 Victoria E. Bonnell, *Iconography of power: Soviet political posters under Lenin and Stalin*, Berkeley, University of California Press, 1998, p. 161.

women laboured in the past.[216] The visual imagery of the poster is striking and unusual. All of the delegates are young women from the eastern republics in colourful traditional dress. A young-looking Stalin (Stalin was already 58 years old in 1937) is pictured sitting among them, as 'real' and 'fleshy' as they are, and drawn on the same scale. He is differentiated from the women only by his throne-like chair; most of the women stand. Stalin leans forward to talk intimately with a woman in blue, while a woman in a red veil listens attentively. Stalin is relaxed and friendly, superior, but not threatening, however, it is clear that he speaks, and they listen. He adopts the roles of teacher and mentor to these women from traditional societies going forth in daring new roles. Behind Stalin, the woman draped over his chair is clearly enamoured of him, as are the beaming women in the background. Two women whisper conspiratorially and giggle. The informality of the scene is reinforced by the papers scattered across the table, which imply that they have all been working together. While the purpose of the poster is to highlight Stalin's mentorship and support of women, this is the most overtly sexual image of Stalin I have encountered. Other poster images of Stalin may suggest fertility and marital union in an abstract allegorical manner, but here he appears almost as if he is presiding over his harem, while the women seem positively titillated to be in his presence. Despite the thematic emphasis on female rights and equality, the women's deference to Stalin is unambiguous in the composition and in the text. The poster was published in a large edition of 200,000 during the year of the Great Purge.

The 1938 poster, 'Long live the equal-rights woman in the USSR, an active participant in the administration of the nation's state, economic, and cultural affairs!' (Fig. 3.32) was created by two established female

---

216   As a legacy of the past,
Women laboured in the darkness of slave-like conditions
With back-breaking work and
Without any rights.
The congress of workers and peasants
Needs to address
How to get rid of
These inequities.
In his discussion with the female delegates
Stalin says:
'We are nearing a victorious conclusion'.
And the female delegates from the East,
Meditate on the clear and articulate words
Of the leader.

poster artists, Marina Volkova and Natalia Pinus. Although the subject of the poster is the new equality of women, as evidenced by high-flying women achievers in state, economic and cultural affairs, it is the figure of Stalin that dominates the poster, occupying two-thirds of the space, engulfed in a sea of holy and revolutionary red. The 'woman delegate' became something of an archetype in painting during the mid-1930s. Susan Reid notes that, at this time, 'the genre of delegates was peopled almost entirely by women',[217] and this was part of a trend in which the image of the female came increasingly to represent the stereotypic 'Soviet citizen' in visual culture. As debtors and subordinates in the politics of obligation, the role of women was to submit, to learn, and to show gratitude.

Mikhail Solov'ev's '"Such women didn't and couldn't exist in the old days." I.V. Stalin' (Fig. 3.33) of 1950 features a woman delegate making a speech, flanked on either side by attentive female delegates. Despite the depiction of women as holding positions of power, the poster again makes explicit the obligation that women have to Stalin. Stalin is positioned on a wall in a frame, removed from the action of the real world. He stands behind a lectern, an easily identifiable prop of the teacher, and his hand lies across the page of an open book. While the strong young woman on the podium in the centre dominates the image, it is clear, both visually and through the text on the poster, that it is only through Stalin's support that she can do so — it is only by virtue of his authority that she can exist at all.

Conclusion

The Stalin persona became a symbolic vessel into which a number of idealised traits, symbols and types were deposited in an attempt to give the leader the widest possible appeal. A leader who was to mobilise and unify a nation that encompassed one-sixth of the world's land mass and included numerous national groups, needed benevolence and the ability to convey the sense that he cared about each and every citizen and that he was not only concerned with weighty matters of state, but also with the small details of the personal battles of his subjects. Propagandists called upon the two mythic archetypes of Father and

---

217 Susan E. Reid, 'All Stalin's women', p. 148.

Teacher to stress the benevolent aspects of the leader persona, while at the same time reinforcing a sense of natural authority that comes with these roles. Both roles also include a notion of reciprocal rights and duties between the leader and the citizens, so that the people felt obligated to repay, with loyalty and overt displays of gratitude, the gifts bestowed upon them by Stalin, the Party and the state. While enveloping many of the same characteristics, the Father and Teacher archetypes differed primarily in the weight that each trope gave to certain characteristics. The Teacher archetype emphasised wisdom and experience, while the Father archetype focused more on notions of care and the ability to harmonise a large and divergent family as if all were brothers and sisters. The other major archetypes associated with Stalin — those of the Warrior and the Saviour — will be discussed in Chapter Four.

3. STALIN IS LIKE A FAIRYTALE SYCAMORE TREE

Fig. 3.1 'Thank you Comrade Stalin for our happy life!', Nikolai Zhukov, 1940, Iskusstvo (Moscow, Leningrad), 62 x 92 cm, edn 100,000
Source: Russian State Library

THE PERSONALITY CULT OF STALIN IN SOVIET POSTERS, 1929–1953

Fig. 3.2 'Stalin's kindness illuminates the future of our children!', Iraklii Toidze, 1947, Iskusstvo (Moscow, Leningrad), 61 x 43 cm
Source: Russian State Library

3. STALIN IS LIKE A FAIRYTALE SYCAMORE TREE

Fig. 3.3 'Stalin is the wisest of all people ...', Vartan Arakelov, 1939, Iskusstvo (Moscow, Leningrad), edn 75,000

Source: Russian State Library

Fig. 3.4 'So — greetings, Stalin, and live for a hundred years ...', Konstantin Cheprakov, 1939, UzFimGiz (Tashkent), 62 x 94 cm

Source: redavantgarde.com/en/collection/show-collection/664-greet-stalin-and-live-a-hundred-years-.html?authorId=160

3. STALIN IS LIKE A FAIRYTALE SYCAMORE TREE

Fig. 3.5 'For communism! …', Mikhail Reikh, 1948, Uzdarnashr (Tashkent), edn 10,000

Source: Russian State Library

Fig. 3.6 'We are warmed by Stalin's affection …', unidentified artist, 1949, 47 x 61 cm

Source: Russian State Library

Fig. 3.7 'Great Stalin is the beacon of communism!', Viktor Ivanov, 1949, Iskusstvo (Moscow, Leningrad), 74 x 52.5 cm, edn 300,000
Source: Russian State Library

Fig. 3.8 'Stalin takes care of each of us from the Kremlin', Viktor Govorkov, 1940, Iskusstvo (Moscow, Leningrad), 62 x 92 cm, edn 100,000

Source: Russian State Library

3. STALIN IS LIKE A FAIRYTALE SYCAMORE TREE

Fig. 3.9 'The captain of the Soviet Union leads us from victory to victory!', Boris Efimov, 1933, Izogiz (Moscow, Leningrad), 62 x 94 cm, edn 200,000
Source: Russian State Library

Fig. 3.10 'Glory to Stalin, the great architect of communism!', Boris Belopol'skii, 1951, Iskusstvo (Moscow), edn 500,000
Source: Russian State Library

THE PERSONALITY CULT OF STALIN IN SOVIET POSTERS, 1929–1953

Fig. 3.11 'Glory to great Stalin, the architect of communism!', N. Petrov & Konstantin Ivanov, 1952, Iskusstvo (Moscow), edn 200,000
Source: Russian State Library

Fig. 3.12 'Thank you beloved Stalin for our happy childhood', Viktor Govorkov, 1936, Izogiz, 71 x 103.2 cm
Source: Russian State Library

3. STALIN IS LIKE A FAIRYTALE SYCAMORE TREE

Fig. 3.13 'On the joyous day of liberation …', Viktor Koretskii, 1943, Iskusstvo (Moscow, Leningrad), edn 50,000

Source: Russian State Library

THE PERSONALITY CULT OF STALIN IN SOVIET POSTERS, 1929–1953

Fig. 3.14 'XXV years of the Komsomol', Vladimir Fedotov, 1943
Source: Russian State Library

3. STALIN IS LIKE A FAIRYTALE SYCAMORE TREE

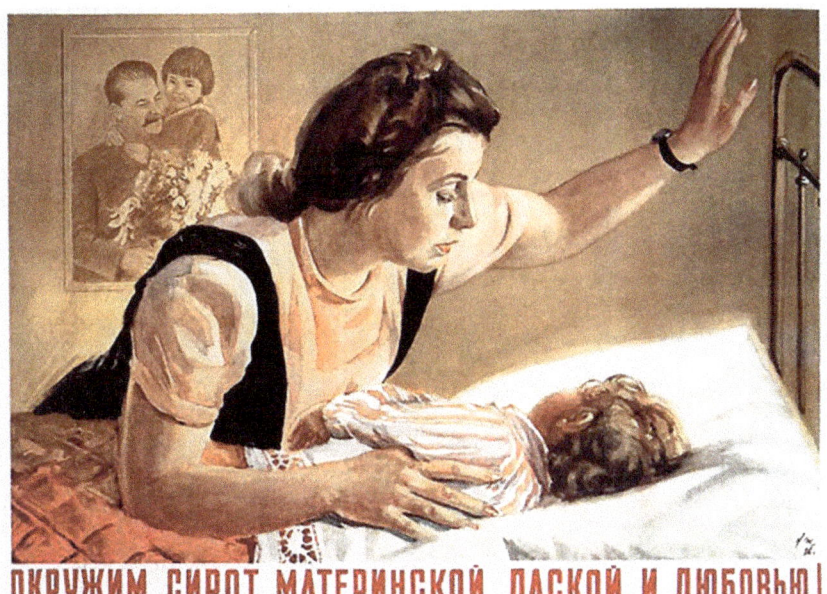

Fig. 3.15 'We'll surround orphans with maternal kindness and love', Nikolai Zhukov, 1947, 79 x 57 cm

Source: www.historyworlds.ru/index.php?do=gallery&act=2&cid=261&fid=10656

Fig. 3.16 'Best friend of children. Glory to great Stalin!', Elena Mel'nikova, 1951, Iskusstvo (Moscow), edn 50,000

Source: Russian State Library

Fig. 3.17 'Glory to Stalin's falcons — the conquerors of aerial elements!', Viktor Deni & Nikolai Dolgorukov, 1937

Source: Russian State Library

Fig. 3.18 'Long live the Soviet pilots — the proud falcons of our motherland!', Nina Vatolina & Nikolai Denisov, 1938

Source: Russian State Library

Fig. 3.19 'To the new achievements of Soviet aviation!', Vladislav Pravdin, 1950

Source: Russian State Library

Fig. 3.20 'Stalin raised us to be loyal to the people!', Petr Golub, 1948, Iskusstvo (Moscow, Leningrad), 86 x 61 cm

Source: State Historical Museum

3. STALIN IS LIKE A FAIRYTALE SYCAMORE TREE

Fig. 3.21 'And Stalin raised us to be loyal to the people, inspired us to work and to deeds!', Leonid Golovanov, 1949, Iskusstvo (Moscow, Leningrad), 76.5 x 56 cm, edn 300,000

Source: Russian State Library

Fig. 3.22 '"Long life and prosperity to our motherland!" I. Stalin', F. Litvinov, 1949, Krymizdat, edn 10,000

Source: Russian State Library

3. STALIN IS LIKE A FAIRYTALE SYCAMORE TREE

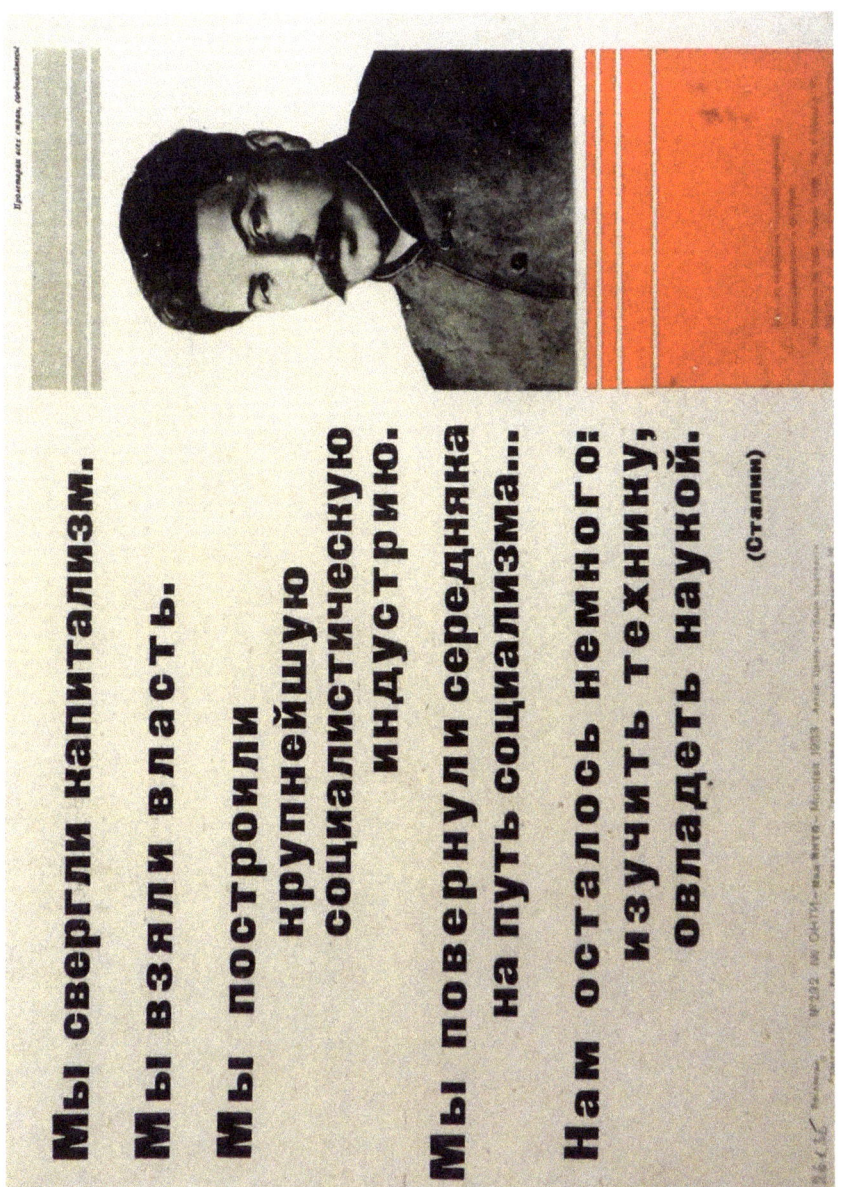

Fig. 3.23 'We have overthrown capitalism …', Mikhail Kuprianov, 1933, (Moscow), edn 4,000
Source: Russian State Library

THE PERSONALITY CULT OF STALIN IN SOVIET POSTERS, 1929–1953

Fig. 3.24 'Without a revolutionary theory there can be no revolutionary movement …', Pikalov, 1933, Izogiz (Leningrad), 77 x 109 cm, edn 30,000
Source: Russian State Library

Fig. 3.25 'Shock workers of the fields engage in fighting for the socialist reconstruction of agriculture ...', Gustav Klutsis, 1932

Source: rusarchives.ru/projects/statehood/obrazovanie-sssr.shtml

Fig. 3.26 'Our noble people', Konev, 1935, Obshchestvo sodeistviia oborone i aviatsionno-khimicheskomu stroitel'stvu SSSR (Kharkov), 85 x 60 cm, edn 20,000

Source: Hoover Institution Archives

Fig. 3.27 'Stalinists! Extend the front of the Stakhanovite movement!', Genrikh Futerfas, 1936

Source: Russian State Library

Fig. 3.28 'Long live our teacher, our father, our leader, Comrade Stalin!', Nikolai Avvakumov, 1946, Iskusstvo (Moscow, Leningrad), edn 200,000

Source: Russian State Library

Fig. 3.29 'Long live our leader and teacher the great Stalin!', Vladislav Pravdin & Nikolai Denisov, 1948, Iskusstvo (Moscow, Leningrad)

Source: Russian State Library

Fig. 3.30 'Reach for prosperity!', Viktor Ivanov, 1949
Source: Russian State Library

Fig. 3.31 'Under the banner of Lenin, under the leadership of Stalin, forward to the victory of communism!', Iraklii Toidze, 1949, Iskusstvo (Moscow, Leningrad), 85 x 61 cm

Source: Russian State Library

THE PERSONALITY CULT OF STALIN IN SOVIET POSTERS, 1929–1953

Fig. 3.32 'Long live the equal-rights woman in the USSR, an active participant in the administration of the nation's state, economic, and cultural affairs!', Marina Volkova & Natalia Pinus, 1938
Source: Russian State Library

Fig. 3.33 '"Such women didn't and couldn't exist in the old days" I.V. Stalin', Mikhail Solov'ev, 1950, Iskusstvo (Moscow), 101 x 68 cm, edn 200,000

Source: Russian State Library

4

Stalin saves the world — Stalin and the evolution of the Warrior and Saviour archetypes

Now arise, you renowned painters of the champion's brave deeds, who by your exalted art make images of the general. My praise of the crowned champion is dull compared with the wisdom that inspires your brush with its radiant colours. I will refrain from writing further of the martyr's valour, for you have crowned him and I rejoice today at the victory won by your power.

St Basil the Great[1]

The icon is a hymn of triumph, a manifestation, a memorial inscribed for those who have fought and conquered, humbling the demons and putting them to flight.

St John of Damascus[2]

The people need a hero, a saint — General Skobelev, Feodor Kuzmich, Ivan the Terrible — they are all alike to them. And the more remote, the more vague, the less accessible the hero, the more freedom for the

---

1 St Basil, 'Sermon on the blessed martyr Barlaam', quoted in Robin Edward Hutt, 'Symbolism in religion, with special reference to Orthodox worship and its relevance for the free church tradition', 1985, Masters thesis, Durham University; available at Durham E-Theses Online: etheses.dur.ac.uk/7637/.
2 'St. John of Damascus: apologia against those who decry holy images' quoted in Barasch, Moshe. *Icon: studies in the history of an idea*, New York and London, NYU Press, 1995, p. 247.

imagination ... There must be a 'Once upon a time there lived' about it — something of the fairy tale. Not a God in heaven, but here, on our dismal earth. Someone of great wisdom and monstrous power.

Vasilii Breev, monarchist[3]

While the benevolent aspect of Stalin's leadership was represented to the people by displaying Stalin as a father of the people and a wise teacher, a major component of the later years of his personality cult was his portrayal as a successful military strategist and leader of the Red Army. The identification of the Warrior archetype with the image of the leader draws from a long tradition across human societies of associating strong and successful leadership with military prowess. This association, which grew from tribal and feudal eras of human history in which the leader was usually the best warrior and one who could guarantee the safety of the tribe, has demonstrated remarkable longevity to the current era, especially in societies that are at war, in crisis or under some kind of threat, or are focused on conquest. It is also particularly prevalent in the public portrayals of charismatic leaders who have no traditional or legal legitimacy, and must ultimately rely on their ability to deliver on promises if they are to maintain their positions of power. As Napoleon commented to Metternich: 'Your sovereigns, born to the throne, can be beaten twenty times over and return to their capital; I cannot do this because I am an upstart soldier. My domination will not survive the day I cease to be strong and consequently feared.'[4]

The centrality of the Warrior archetype to propaganda for charismatic leaders is evidenced by the fact that, throughout history, even leaders who were unsuccessful in battle were portrayed in propaganda as militarily and strategically brilliant. As Simon Price notes, the Roman emperor Domitian lay claim to great military victories which were later condemned as shams and Trajan compensated for his lack of actual military achievements by being depicted as a general in his official statuary.[5] In fact, the archetype of the Warrior appears to be indispensable to a successful personality cult. Great historical figures,

---

3   Vasilii Breev, as quoted by Gor'kii in Michael Cherniavsky, *Tsar and people: studies in Russian myths*, New Haven, Yale University Press, 1961, p. 221.
4   Napoleon, quoted in Mattei Dogan, 'Comparing two charismatic leaders: Ataturk and de Gaulle', *Comparative Sociology*, 6, 2007, pp. 75–84, p. 80.
5   S.R.F. Price, *Rituals and power: the Roman imperial cult in Asia Minor*, Cambridge, Cambridge University Press, 1984, p. 183.

such as Alexander the Great, the Roman emperors, Holy Roman Emperor Maximilian I, Napoleon Bonaparte and, in the Russian context, Aleksandr Nevskii, Ivan Grozny and Peter the Great, were all portrayed as consummate warriors. St George, the 'great martyr' and warrior–saint, is one of the most celebrated saints of the Russian Orthodox Church. Indeed, even in the period immediately preceding Bolshevik rule, cults of personality based around the military archetype were flourishing.

Military cults in revolutionary Russia

In 1917, General Lavr Kornilov, an intelligence officer and Imperial Army general during the First World War, was viewed by many Russian citizens as a potential national leader and saviour. Kornilov is said to have cut a dashing figure, and to have been well-loved by his troops, whilst making a significant creative contribution himself to the dissemination of the legends behind his cult of bravery.[6] In spite of his use of illegal and unauthorised measures of terror and capital punishment against peasants and deserters in 1917, Trotskii claims: 'many of Kerensky's commissars, too, would say to themselves: there is no hope left but in Kornilov.'[7] Kornilov seems to have been not quite the military genius touted in the legends around him. Generals Aleksei Brusilov and Evgenii Martinov spoke of him as lacking a broad outlook, being strategically incompetent, and as having made catastrophic decisions in battle that cost the lives of almost an entire division of his troops.[8] 'The heart of a lion, the brains of a sheep' was how Kornilov was described by General Mikhail Alekseev.[9]

Kornilov had a regiment named for him, and enthusiasm for him among his officers was such that they went one step further than just wearing the Kornilov symbol on their uniforms — each adorned his arm with

---

6   Orlando Figes & Boris Kolonitskii, *Interpreting the Russian Revolution: the language and symbols of 1917*, New Haven, Yale University Press, 1999, pp. 97–99.
7   Leon Trotsky, 'Kerensky and Kornilov (elements of Bonapartism in the Russian Revolution)', *The history of the Russian Revolution*, vol. 2, *The attempted counter-revolution*, www.marxists.org/archive/trotsky/1930/hrr/ch29.htm (accessed 14 Jul. 2012).
8   General Evgenii Ivanovich Martinov and General Aleksei Alekseevich Brusilov, quoted in Trotsky, 'Kerensky and Kornilov'.
9   General Mikhail Alekseev, quoted in Trotsky, 'Kerensky and Kornilov'.

a tattoo of Kornilov.[10] Kornilov's cult was intense, but relatively short-lived. Orlando Figes and Boris Kolonitskii mark the symbolic height of the Kornilov cult as being his triumphal entry into Moscow for the State Conference on 13 August 1917, a huge event attended by some 2,500 people, at which Kornilov spoke. Trotskii described the scene around Kornilov's arrival:

> Kornilov's biography, together with his portrait, was generously scattered from automobiles. The walls were covered with posters summoning the people to the aid of the hero. Like a sovereign, Kornilov received in his private car statesmen, industrialists, financiers. Representatives of the banks made reports to him about the financial condition of the country.[11]

Kornilov was pelted with flowers by 'well-dressed ladies' at Aleksandrovski railway station and, after this reception, made a pilgrimage to the Iverski shrine, just outside the gates of the Kremlin, where the tsars had traditionally prayed when they visited Moscow.[12] Even this comparatively short-lived and limited cult displayed many of the phenomena that were later to become features of the cult of Stalin — leader portraits, posters, biographies, flowers, and the incorporation of religious ritual to unify secular and religious legitimacy in the person of the cult leader.[13]

Contemporaneous with the cult of Kornilov, but exceeding it in scope and imagination, was the cult of the prime minister and chairman of the Provisional Government, Aleksandr Fiodorovich Kerenskii. Kerenskii was a theatrical figure and a fiery orator, having trained as an opera singer in his youth, and with early ambitions to become an actor. Writing in 1924, Russian revolutionary Viktor Serge recalled:

> When argument fails him on the rostrum, when a rousing phrase can't make up for it, he staggers, turns pale, and sinks back as though on the verge of a fainting fit. This tribune seems ready to die for the people ... He is a demagogue, with a voice that knows how to

---

10 Figes & Kolonitskii, *Interpreting the Russian Revolution*, p. 100.
11 Trotsky, 'Kerensky and Kornilov'.
12 Figes & Kolonitskii, *Interpreting the Russian Revolution*, p. 99.
13 Kornilov was ultimately killed in action by the Red Army in April 1918, and his body buried in a secret location, which was discovered, and the body exhumed and paraded through the streets before being quartered and burned in the town square at Ekaterinodor. The location of his death became a sacred place for his followers (Figes & Kolonitskii, *Interpreting the Russian Revolution*, p. 100).

inflame, to rise, to shout, and to fade away, with its harmonies still fascinating his audience. He is an incomparable speaker. I have known worthy men, years after having heard him once or twice, who could recall his gestures, his voice and his eyes ('Oh, his eyes! What a great revolutionary he was!', a sentimental old spinster told me in Petrograd in 1919).[14]

His cult developed spontaneously 'from below' in a political atmosphere that was, for this brief period of time, quite democratic. As Trotskii sat locked away in one of Kerenskii's prisons in 1917, he penned an assessment of Kerenskii's appeal to the Russian people, noting Kerenskii's charismatic presence, his appeal to the 'common man', and his ability to demonstrate a variety of personal qualities that appealed to different sections of the population.[15] Like Kornilov, Kerenskii was showered with floral tributes and was sometimes venerated as if he were a saint,[16] appearing to believe in the sanctity of his own special mission.[17] Figes and Kolonitskii describe the adulation surrounding Kerenskii's visits to the Front during the First World War:

> During Kerensky's tour of the Front he was hailed as a hero everywhere. Soldiers carried him shoulder-high, pelted him with flowers and threw themselves at his feet … Many of them were on their knees praying; others were weeping. This kind of religious adulation had not been seen in Russia since the days when peasants believed in the 'Father-Tsar'.[18]

---

14   Victor Serge, 'Lenin in 1917', (March/April 1924). Originally published in French in *Faits et Documents*, no. 2, 1925, Al Richardson (trans.), www.marxists.org/archive/serge/1924/xx/lenin.html#f22 (accessed 16 Jul. 2012).
15   'An attorney for the defense in political cases, a Social Revolutionary who became leader of the Trudoviks, a radical without any socialist schooling whatever, Kerensky has expressed more completely than anyone else the first epoch of the revolution, its "national" formlessness, the idealism of its hopes and expectations … Kerensky made speeches about land and freedom, about law and order, about peace among nations, about the defence of the fatherland, the heroism of Liebknecht, about how the Russian revolution ought to astonish the world with its magnanimity — waving the while a little red silk handkerchief. The everyday man who was just beginning to wake up politically listened to these speeches with rapture: it seemed to him that he himself was speaking from the tribune. The army greeted Kerensky as their savior from Guchkov. The peasants heard about him as a Trudovik, as a *muzhik*'s deputy. The Liberals were won over by the extreme moderateness of idea under his formless radicalism of phrase' (Trotsky, 'Kerensky and Kornilov').
16   On 20 May the Mogilev Peasant Soviet sent him greetings, addressing him as the 'apostle of the revolution and the liberator of the peasantry' (Figes & Kolonitskii, *Interpreting the Russian Revolution*, p. 74).
17   Serge, 'Lenin in 1917'.
18   Figes & Kolonitskii, *Interpreting the Russian Revolution*, p. 88.

Badges, medals and postcards of Kerenskii were produced by the same manufacturers as had been used by the tsar, and were soon to be used in the service of the Lenin cult, and these were distributed to the general population. His portrait was painted by Ilya Repin, member of the *Peredvizhniki*[19] and one of Russia's most famous artists. Kerenskii was referred to in the press by epithets such as 'the knight of the revolution', 'the lion heart', 'the first love of the revolution', 'the people's tribune', 'the genius of Russian freedom', 'the sun of Russia's freedom', 'the people's leader', 'the leader of freedom', 'the saviour of the fatherland', 'the hero–minister', 'the prophet and hero of the revolution', 'the Prometheus of the Russian revolution', 'the good genius of free Russia', 'the leader of the Russian revolution', and 'the pride and joy of the revolution'.[20] Many of these epithets or variants thereof would later be applied to Lenin and then to Stalin.

Despite having no military background, Kerenskii was appointed war minister and, supremely conscious of his personal appearance and the impression he made on others,[21] took to wearing semi-military costumes of field shirts and puttees for appearances at the Front. Figes and Kolonitskii credit Kerenskii with initiating the fashion amongst 20th-century socialist leaders of dressing in military-style tunics.[22] Kerenskii frequently appeared in photographs adopting the 'hand-in' pose. As with all charismatic leaders throughout history, and as predicted under the model of charismatic leadership outlined by Max Weber, Kerenskii proved to be subject to the fickle nature of the crowd, especially when he failed to deliver on his promises. Soon, his fondness for the hand-in pose was lampooned, and he came under increasingly hostile attack from soldiers and sailors as he visited them

---

19   The Wanderers — a group of realist artists who in 1870 formed a movement based on freedom of movement and thought and aimed to make art that was useful for society. Many of these artists later joined the Association of Artists in Revolutionary Russia (AKhR/R).
20   Figes & Kolonitskii, *Interpreting the Russian Revolution*, p. 86.
21   Like Trotskii, Serge saw Kerenskii's revolutionary zeal as formless and lacking in real content: 'I have somewhere a photo that shows him in this role of a tragic statesman which he knew so well how to assume, crouching in oriental fashion on a divan, with this face, white, with deep, sombre eyes. He had a cult of the attitude and the phrase. In the fragments of memoirs that he published in Gatchina the words you find most often are "I" and "me". When describing the most serious events, he has phrases like this: "In the car I struck up a nonchalant pose". During the entire revolution he only struck up poses and recited phrases' ('Lenin in 1917').
22   'In the 1920s such jackets became known as *vozhdevki* ("leader suits"), and then as *Stalinki* ("Stalin suits"). In Communist China where Mao was to adopt a military tunic, they were known as the "Lenin suit"' (Figes & Kolonitskii, *Interpreting the Russian Revolution*, p. 83).

at their work.²³ Viktor Chernov, one of the founders of the Russian Socialist–Revolutionary Party, observed: 'The Russian public acted like a crowd of idol-worshippers: when their idols failed to meet their expectations they ceased to worship them, threw them to the ground and kicked them in the dirt.'²⁴

When the Bolsheviks seized power in October 1917, Trotskii, as leader of the Red Army, stood shoulder-to-shoulder with Lenin, leader of the Party, as potential leader of the nation. According to Trotskii, when the immediate post-revolutionary government was being formed, Lenin suggested that, as leader of the successful insurrection, Trotskii should lead it, but Trotskii refused the post in deference to Lenin's seniority.²⁵ Despite choosing not to take Kerenskii's political office, Lenin came to be viewed as the national leader, although it was by no means clear at the time that Lenin would retain his leadership role much beyond the October Revolution. Anatolii Lunacharskii and Serge both recorded that Trotskii was considered a candidate for leadership of the fledgling regime by virtue of his genius and his leadership abilities. Lunacharskii recalled:

> Thus for instance the late M.S. Uritsky ... once said to me ... 'Now that the great revolution has come one feels that however intelligent Lenin may be he begins to fade beside the genius of Trotsky.' This estimation seemed to me incorrect, not because it exaggerated Trotsky's gifts and his force of character but because the extent of Lenin's political genius was then still not obvious. Yet it is true that during that period, after the thunderous success of his arrival in Russia and before the July days, Lenin did keep rather in the background, not speaking often, not writing much, but largely engaged in directing organizational work in the Bolshevik camp, whilst Trotsky thundered forth at meetings in Petrograd.²⁶

---

23 French journalist, Claude Anet, elaborated some of the reasons for the swift end of the public's romance with Kerenskii: 'He frequents the imperial *loges*, he lives in the Winter Palace or at Tsarskoe Selo, he sleeps in the bed of Russian emperors. A little too much vanity and vanity a little too noticeable' (Claude Anet quoted in Trotsky, 'Kerensky and Kornilov').
24 Viktor Chernov, 'Stanitsy iz politicheskogo dnevnika', *Mysl'*, 1918, quoted in Figes & Kolonitskii, *Interpreting the Russian Revolution*, p. 95.
25 Isaac Deutscher, *The prophet armed: Trotsky, 1879-1921*, vol. 1, New York, Oxford University Press, 1954, p. 269.
26 Anatoly Lunacharsky, *Revolutionary silhouettes, Lev Davidovich Trotsky*, www.marxists.org/archive/lunachar/works/silhouet/trotsky.htm (accessed 14 Jul. 2012).

In his *Memoirs of a revolutionary*, Serge saw Trotskii as outshining Lenin on many scores:

> No one ever wore a great destiny with more style. He was forty-one and at the apex of power, popularity and fame — leader of the Petrograd masses in two revolutions; creator of the Red Army, which (as Lenin had said to Gorky) he had literally 'conjured out of nothing'; personally the victor of several decisive battles, at Sviazhsk, Kazan, and Pulkovo; the acknowledged organizer of victory in the Civil War.[27]

Clad in military uniform, Trotskii maintained a high public profile as he created, and assumed responsibility for, the Red Army throughout the Civil War. His popularity was highest amongst the members of the military, and his temperament and mode of expression suited best to rallying the troops with rousing speeches. Lunacharskii felt that Trotskii's most obvious gifts were his talents as an orator and as a writer, claiming that he was the greatest orator he had ever seen.[28] According to Isaac Deutscher, this theatricality was unassumed, and Trotskii spoke at home with his family and friends in the same manner[29] but, after the Civil War, this style connected less with the troubled masses and his popularity amongst the common people waned.

While ultimately less prominent than Lenin, Trotskii became the subject of portrait paintings, appeared on porcelain,[30] and his image was carried in processions. Viktor Deni's depiction of Trotskii as St George slaying the serpent of counterrevolution appeared in a calendar in the early 1920s.[31] In icons of St George and the dragon,

---

27 Victor Serge, *Memoirs of a revolutionary 1901–1941* Peter Sedgwick (trans.), London, Oxford University Press, 1963, pp. 140–41.
28 'His impressive appearance, his handsome, sweeping gestures, the powerful rhythm of his speech, his loud but never fatiguing voice, the remarkable coherence and literary skill of his phrasing, the richness of imagery, scalding irony, his soaring pathos, his rigid logic, clear as polished steel — those are Trotsky's virtues as a speaker ... I have seen Trotsky speaking for two and a half to three hours in front of a totally silent, standing audience listening as though spellbound to his monumental political treatise' (Lunacharsky, *Revolutionary silhouettes*).
29 Isaac Deutscher, *The prophet unarmed: Trotsky, 1921–1929*, vol. 2, New York, Oxford University Press, 1959, p. 23.
30 In 1923 an edition of porcelain mugs was released featuring a portrait of Trotskii as leader of the Red Army by Mikhail Adamovich (David King, *Red star over Russia: a visual history of the Soviet Union*, New York, Abrams, 2010, p. 15).
31 Victoria E. Bonnell, *Iconography of power: Soviet political posters under Lenin and Stalin*, Berkeley, University of California Press, 1998, p. 152.

4. STALIN SAVES THE WORLD

St George is depicted as slaying cosmic evil in the form of the serpent–dragon, the violence justifiable due to its sacred character and salvationist intent.[32]

Despite the increasing enmity between Stalin and Trotskii, resulting ultimately in Trotskii's exile in 1929 and murder in 1940, and Trotskii's considerable body of writing denouncing the fetishisation of Stalin and the Bonapartism of Stalin's regime, Trotskii himself appears to have had all the characteristic traits of a charismatic leader, and was imbued with a strong sense of his divine mission and identity as a historical personage.[33] Hungarian Marxist philosopher György Lukács reflected in 1963: 'The personal impression which I received from my meetings with Trotsky in 1931 aroused in me the conviction that he as an individual was even more inclined to "the cult" of the personality than Stalin.'[34] Trotskii appears to have been respected and perhaps even admired by those who worked with him, but was not well-liked, due to his brashness, arrogance and dictatorial attitude.[35]

While Kerenskii had consciously incorporated the Warrior archetype into his leader persona, after the October Revolution the roles of leader of the nation and leader of the military resided in separate identities — those of Lenin and Trotskii respectively. This separation

---

32   Indeed, Tsar Ivan IV was also depicted as St George slaying the dragon. See Priscilla Hunt, 'Ivan IV's personal mythology of kingship', *Slavic Review*, 52:4, 1993, pp. 769–809, pp. 783–84.
33   Lunacharskii claimed: 'Trotsky treasures his historical role and would probably be ready to make any personal sacrifice, not excluding the greatest sacrifice of all — that of his life — in order to go down in human history surrounded by the aureole of a genuine revolutionary leader' (Lunacharsky, *Revolutionary silhouettes*).
34   Georg Lukács, 'Reflections on the cult of Stalin', *Survey*, 47, 1963, p. 107.
35   Author of *Trotsky and the Jews*, Joseph Nedava wrote in 1986: 'His arrogance and inordinate self confidence, his overbearing self-appreciation and almost total disregard of the qualities of all others; in short, his sense of historical mission, all these traits removed him from the "conventional", as if he were not to be counted among "mortals"' ('Trotsky and the role of the individual in history: the acting personality in the political arena', *Modern Age*, Sep. 1986, pp. 218–25). Serge wrote: 'we had much admiration for him, but no real love. His sternness, his insistence on punctuality in work and battle, the inflexible correctness of his demeanour in a period of general slackness, all imparted a certain demagogic malice to the insidious attacks that were made against him. I was hardly influenced by these considerations, but the political solutions prescribed by him for current difficulties struck me as proceeding from a character that was basically dictatorial' (Serge, *Memoirs of a revolutionary 1901-1941*, p. 141). Lenin also commented on Trotskii's exaggerated self-confidence in his 'Testament' letter of 25 December 1922: 'Comrade Trotsky ... is distinguished not only by outstanding ability. He is personally perhaps the most capable man in the present C.C., but he has displayed excessive self-assurance and shown excessive preoccupation with the purely administrative side of the work' (I.V. Lenin, 'Letter to the Congress', 1922 www.marxists.org/archive/lenin/works/1922/dec/testamnt/congress.htm (accessed 13 Jan. 2013)).

was more than apparent, as Lenin did not present himself as a military man, always appearing in shirt, tie and jacket, and left the strategic military decisions of the Civil War to Trotskii. The separation of roles was to continue under Stalin until (somewhat ironically) a series of devastating military defeats during the Great Patriotic War saw Stalin's image become the central rallying symbol in the call to arms of the Soviet people.

Early manifestations of Stalin's Warrior archetype

Stalin's propaganda apparatus began creating a military biography for him in the early 1930s, with an increase in intensity in the late 1930s as the prospects of war loomed in Europe, but stopped short of portraying him as entirely responsible for the creation and successes of the Red Army. Stalin's pre-revolutionary Party work, which was mostly underground and largely illegal, commenced in Georgia before moving to other areas of the Caucasus.[36] While certainly full of daring exploits, and involving personal risk, time in prison and escapes from exile, Stalin could not truthfully lay claim to the same sorts of revolutionary military feats attributed to Trotskii and, in his early years of power, he usually stated that he had played only a minor role in the Revolution.

In 1930, just one year after Stalin consolidated his personal power as leader in the battle for succession after Lenin's death (and a year after Trotskii's exile), a poster with the title 'I.V. Stalin' was published (Fig. 4.1). This poster makes an interesting first tentative attempt to begin the construction of a Warrior identity for Stalin. The text of the poster provides an extensive biography purporting to summarise each year of Stalin's adult life, making mention of his revolutionary underground activities, several arrests, exiles and escapes. At this early stage in Stalin's career, his military exploits are not elaborated in detail. The Civil War years merely contain references to Stalin's roles as people's commissar for nationalities and people's commissar for the Worker–Peasant Inspectorate, as well as his appointment as general secretary of the Party in 1922. Stalin appears hatless and in

---

36 Montefiore explores Stalin's early revolutionary work in Georgia in his Stalin biography *Young Stalin* (2007).

4. STALIN SAVES THE WORLD

a vaguely military-style shirt without embellishment, although he prominently displays two military decorations, both Orders of the Red Banner, which were awarded for extraordinary heroism and courage in battle. Stalin gazes directly ahead, steadfastly meeting the viewer's eyes. His skin shows lines, and is yet to reach the flawless perfection that would characterise his image in later propaganda.[37] Behind him, sketched in a faint pale green suggestive of growth, is evidence of booming industrialisation, as a result of the implementation of the First Five-Year Plan, which was midway through in 1930. The poster serves as an introduction to Stalin as leader, as a resumé of his revolutionary and Civil War credentials and of his personal qualities of courage and Bolshevik conviction, and as a means of associating him with the goals of the Five-Year Plan.

The lead-up to the Great Patriotic War

In later years, Stalin adapted sections of Trotskii's military biography for his own, possibly as much to cover up his criminal past as to expand his warrior image. A number of propaganda posters were dedicated to the creation of a mythical biography for Stalin in order to give him revolutionary credibility. A series of posters in a hagiographical style, dating from 1938,[38] play up Stalin's role in the October Revolution, the Civil War, the growth of national cultures in the USSR and the development of the Red Army. Golomshtok claims that 'In many pictures from the first exhibitions of the AKhR/R, for example,

---

37   Plamper quotes one candid artist, I. Rerberg, who wrote to the editorial team of the photo album 'Comrade Stalin in photography' expressing his concerns about excessive retouching: 'such excessive retouching completely destroys the vitality of the photographs and everything most important in photographs, namely the rendering of the body, mannerisms, etc … . One gets the impression that the entire face is made of a single material — rubber or wax' (RGALI, f. 652, op.8, d.97, l.10, 1940, cited in *The Stalin cult: a study in the alchemy of power*, New Haven, Yale University Press, 2012, p. 183).
38   The Stalinka Digital Library gives an approximate date of 1937 for four of these posters, which appear to be undated. One can approximate the date of publishing from clues within the posters. The poster titled 'Defence of the USSR' (Fig. 4.3) makes reference to Stalin's constitution (placing it after 1936) and features a cartoon by Boris Efimov dated 1937. The poster titled 'Under the banner of the Socialist constitution' focuses on various articles of the 1936 constitution and features a photograph of the May Day celebrations of 1937. However, poster no. 11 in this series is held in the collection at the Museum of Contemporary History in Moscow, and is dated 1938, with the artist identified as Vasil'ev. I am therefore comfortable in assigning an approximate date of 1938 for the whole series.

Trotsky was depicted as the founder of the Red Army ... from the mid-twenties this role was transferred to Lenin, and from the thirties to the mid-fifties it was shared between him and Stalin'.[39]

As extensive biographical research by Simon Sebag Montefiore and Deutscher has revealed, Stalin was indeed active in both the October Revolution and the Civil War. Speaking of the early days of power after the October Revolution, Fiodor Alliluyev (Nadia's brother) noted in his unpublished memoirs: 'Comrade Stalin was genuinely known only to a small circle of people who had come across him ... in the political underground or had succeeded ... in distinguishing real work and real devotion from chatter, noise (and) meaningless babble.'[40] Lenin drafted a memo in which only he, and his personal assistants, Trotskii and Stalin, were to be permitted entry to Sovnarkom,[41] and Polish Bolshevik Stanislaw Pestkovsky noted: 'Lenin could not get along without Stalin for a single day ... Our Smolny office was under Lenin's wing. In the course of the day, he'd call Stalin an endless number of times and would appear in our office and lead him away.'[42]

Deutscher notes that Stalin was crucial to Lenin from the inception of the Soviet government due to the 'soft-heartedness' and vacillations of other Party members once the Bolsheviks seized power:

> It cannot be said that the outlook of that first team of commissars corresponded to those standards of 'ruthless determination' or 'fanatical zeal' which later came to be associated with the very term Bolshevism. On the contrary, the 'soft-heartedness' of most commissars very soon placed the Government in quite a number of tragic-comic situations ... . Their vacillations filled [Lenin] with apprehension and alarm. He saw his Government confronted with almost insuperable adversities: internal chaos, economic paralysis, inevitable counter-revolution, and a legacy of war. He looked around to see which of his colleagues in the Government and in the Central Committee could be relied upon to form a close nucleus capable of the determined and swift action which would be needed in the emergencies to come.[43]

---

39   Igor Golomshtok, *Totalitarian art in the Soviet Union, the Third Reich, fascist Italy and the People's Republic of China*, New York, Icon Editions, 1990, p. 187.
40   Fyodor Alliluyev, quoted in Simon Sebag Montefiore, *Young Stalin*, New York, Alfred A. Knopf, 2007, p. 367.
41   Council of People's Commissars, responsible to the Council of Soviets for general administration of the affairs of state.
42   Montefiore, *Young Stalin*, pp. 367–68.
43   Isaac Deutscher, *Stalin; a political biography*, 2nd edn, New York, Oxford University Press, 1966, pp. 184–85.

4. STALIN SAVES THE WORLD

During the Civil War, Lenin despatched Stalin to Tsaritsyn (later renamed Stalingrad) in mid-1918, initially to take charge of food supplies. This key strategic city looked likely to fall to White forces. Stalin took military control in July and, with his status raised to commissar, killed off a group of Trotskii's ex-tsarist specialists, and played a significant part in the victory of the Red Army in that city.[44]

Beginning in 1938, several posters highlight Stalin's achievements in the Civil War. The poster titled 'The Civil War 1918–1920' (poster no. 6 in the series — Fig. 4.2) features a black-and-white photographic portrait of the young Stalin gazing out at the viewer in military-style jacket, and includes copies of a telegram from Stalin dated 19 July 1918 and the transcript of a recorded phonecall discussing the food situation on 24 July 1918.[45] Stalin is depicted as central to the Civil War leadership, as a close and trusted comrade of Lenin, and as associated with the military effort, while Lenin is carrying out construction tasks. In one of the poster's vignettes, Stalin is shown rallying the first cavalry. In others, Lenin carries a large log during a *subbotnik*[46] and Mikhail Kalinin agitates amongst the crowd. Trotskii is nowhere to be seen.

In poster no. 13 from the same series, titled 'Defence of the USSR' (Fig. 4.3), Stalin and Kliment Voroshilov are depicted together as equals in an informal, comradely scene. Voroshilov was the centre of his own personality cult and was honoured with 'Voroshilov rations for the army', and the 'Voroshilov Marksman's Prize', as well as featuring on trading cards with other Soviet leaders.[47] His birthday was celebrated in elaborate fashion, with Stalin giving a famous speech, and he was the subject of a historical book published by English author Dennis Wheately in October 1937 — *Red eagle: the story of the Russian Revolution and of Klementy Efremovitch Voroshilov, marshal and commissar for defence of the Union of Socialist Soviet Republics*.

---

44 Simon Sebag Montefiore, *Stalin: the court of the Red Tsar*, London, Weidenfeld and Nicolson, 2003, pp. 27–28.
45 The telegram and dates are significant as propaganda in the late 1930s made much of Stalin's successful intervention in the Civil War at Tsaritsyn and the telegram provides factual proof of the trust placed in Stalin by Lenin.
46 Day of voluntary public labour.
47 Montefiore, *Stalin*, p. 170.

In poster no. 13, Stalin wears his unadorned, military-style tunic as head of the Party and the nation, while Voroshilov in full uniform is clearly a military leader. They are depicted as standing for peace, and as defenders of the world against fascism. The poster text consists of Stalin's words on the need for preparedness and defence, which follow two quotes from Lenin on the same theme. Famous cartoonist Boris Efimov's sketch at the bottom left of the poster depicts the huge fist of the NKVD[48] crushing a monstrous but small enemy while Trotskii and Hitler cower together in the corner. Trostkii has now been transformed from the creator and champion of the Red Army into its enemy, in league with Germany. Scenes of military parades on Red Square, and a sky full of aircraft illustrate Soviet might and preparedness as Europe moves closer to the brink of war.

S. Podobedov's 1939 poster 'Comrade I.V. Stalin at the Front in the Civil War' (Fig. 4.4) consists of a vast map of Soviet territories with the locations at which Stalin served in the Civil War marked with a red star. Beneath each star are the dates of service and dashed lines mark out the route between locations. Filled red stars indicate the main places on the Front at which Stalin stayed, while the unfilled stars show his field trips. The use of a map with lines, labels, dates and a key gives this content a documentary verisimilitude, providing evidence that Stalin was heavily involved in the Bolshevik military victory. The bottom of the poster contains a quotation from Voroshilov that confirms the centrality of Stalin to the Bolshevik cause, whilst also offering a plausible explanation for Stalin's apparent low profile during the Civil War years — Stalin was entrusted with the most terrible, dangerous missions and would suddenly appear in the direst circumstances to ensure victory for the Red Army:

> 'In the period of 1918–1920 Stalin was probably the only person the Central Committee sent from one battlefront to another, choosing the most dangerous, the most terrible places of a revolution. Where it had been relatively peaceful and prosperous, where we had success — there Stalin was not visible. But where, for a number of reasons the Red Army was broken, where the counter-revolutionary forces were becoming successful and threatened the very existence of the Soviet regime, where confusion and panic could at any moment turn into helplessness and catastrophe — there Stalin appeared. He did

---

48 The People's Commissariat for Internal Affairs/Secret Police.

not sleep nights, he organised, the leadership was lying in his steady hands, he broke them and was ruthless — creating a turning point, a healing environment.' K.E. Voroshilov

The golden cameo portrait of Stalin suggests a medallion or coin, with Stalin's head reminiscent of the heads of monarchs or caesars on coins and of sacred figures in icons. The map is framed in sacred colours associated with the icon — red and gold — and illustrates the mythic and sacred history of the Bolshevik Party. Voroshilov's statement allows Stalin to preserve his modesty and also contains many of the elements of the developing Stalin myth — a sense of almost magical omnipresence and the ability to appear out of nowhere whenever needed; the leader who doesn't sleep at night; and the strong but caring leader who is ruthless with his enemies. The map is stamped on the top right corner with a picture of the Order of the Red Banner, signifying Stalin's courage.

Stalin and the Party leadership may well have envisaged themselves as warriors in the battle for socialism, not only using battle metaphors from the time of the Revolution throughout the life of the regime, but also referring to themselves and each other in quasi-military terms. In conversation with Beria, Stalin referred to the Bolsheviks as 'a sort of military-religious order',[49] and, in a 1921 draft article, 'On the political strategy and tactic of the Russian communists', he wrote of: 'The communist party as a kind of order of swordbearers[50] within the Soviet state, directing the organs of the latter and inspiring its activity.'[51] When Feliks Dzerzhinskii, head of the Cheka,[52] died in July 1926, Stalin referred to him as 'a devout knight of the proletariat'.[53] In fact, Stalin himself came to be endowed with the qualities of the *bogatyr*, the mythical Russian knight–hero, along with the other Old Bolskeviks in the top Party leadership,[54] and this

---

49 Montefiore, *Stalin*, p. 88.
50 *Orden mechenostsev*. According to Erik van Ree, the 'order of swordbearers' (the *Schwertbrtider*) was an order of crusading monks founded in 1202 by Albert, bishop of Livonia, in which the brothers took the three-fold monk's vow of poverty, chastity, and 'to deny themselves to have a will of their own' ('Stalin's organic theory of the Party', *Russian Review*, 52:1, 1993, pp. 43–57, p. 45).
51 Stalin, *Sochineniia*, 5, p. 71, cited in van Ree, 'Stalin's organic theory of the Party', p. 45.
52 Extraordinary Commission for Combating Counter-Revolution and Sabotage (Secret Police), etablished by Lenin in 1917.
53 Montefiore, *Stalin*, p. 88.
54 An article in *Pravda* on 01 Jan. 1937 stated: 'Stalin, Molotov, Kaganovich, Voroshilov, Ordzhonikidze, Kalinin, and others — friends, comrades-in-arms, pupils of the great Lenin,

term was also applied to 'everyday heroes' like the Stakhanovites.[55] Lenin and Stalin were both referred to by the term *vozhd'*. This term, meaning 'leader', originally denoted a military leader and, prior to the October Revolution, was applied only metaphorically to a political leader.[56] Battle metaphors saturated Bolshevik vocabulary, beginning with the central Marxist concept of 'class war'.[57] In propaganda, each campaign involved a 'struggle' and a 'front' (e.g. the 'construction front'), and art and cultural production in general were viewed as 'a weapon'. 'Enemies' were potentially everywhere. In his analysis of the language used in *Pravda*, Jeffrey Brooks notes that '[t]he Party became an army, and a good Party member "an honest soldier of the revolution" ... To join was to enter "our ranks" ... Industry became "the production front" and slackers were traitors ...'[58]

---

a powerful *druzhina* [army] of *bogatyri* of communism — they constantly stand at the commanding bridge of the great Soviet ship, travelling on a precise course', cited in Sarah Davies, *Popular opinion in Stalin's Russia: terror, propaganda and dissent, 1934–1941*, Cambridge University Press, 1997, p. 151.

55   See Bernice Glatzer Rosenthal, *New myth, new world: from Nietzsche to Stalinism*, Pennsylvania State University Press, 2002, p. 393.

56   Bonnell cites the poem *Vozhdiu*, by Demian Bednyi, for May Day 1918, as being one of the first instances in which the term was applied to Lenin (*Iconography of power*, p. 140). Plamper notes the charismatic and sacral meaning attached to the term *vozhd'*, tracing its linguistic roots back to Old Church Slavonic (*The Stalin cult*, p. 35).

57   Kevin McDermott points out that, for Stalin and his cohort, their entire world view was filtered through the prism of actual and potential war: Revolution (which in Marxist theory is closely tied to war); Civil War; class war against internal enemies; and international war ('Archives, power and the 'cultural turn': reflections on Stalin and Stalinism', *Totalitarian Movements and Political Religions*, 2004, 5:1, pp. 5–24, p. 11). Alfred J. Rieber notes that the Georgian society in which Stalin grew up had the attributes of a warrior society, acquired by living on a long-contested frontier between empires, and with a long history of revolution and rebellion, and a cult of violence, with this culture permeating Stalin's youth and contributing to the formation of his identity ('Stalin as Georgian: the formative years', in Sarah Davies & James Harris (eds), *Stalin: a new history*, Cambridge University Press, 2004, pp. 19–20). Georgians had a reputation as excellent horsemen and brave soldiers, and had an enduring tradition of 'blood revenge', which survived into the 20th century (Alfred J. Rieber, 'Stalin, man of the borderlands', *The American Historical Review*, 106:5, 2001, pp. 1651–691, p. 1660). Stephen Kotkin argues that the Bolsheviks approached the five-year plans as military campaigns both because there had existed in Russia a centuries-long tradition of militarised society, and also because their notions of planning were basically derived from Germany's wartime experience in which the German Government had expanded state ownership of industry and increased control of private production in order to mobilise for the war effort. This brief period of German state control constituted the only concrete instance in which such a centralised system had been trialled (*Magnetic Mountain: Stalinism as a civilization*, Berkeley, University of California Press, 1995, p. 31).

58   Jeffrey Brooks, *Thank you, Comrade Stalin! Soviet public culture from revolution to Cold War*, Princeton University Press, 2000, p. 23.

In the late 1930s, as Europe teetered on the brink of war, posters of Stalin were produced on a number of domestic themes, including the constitution, elections, and industrialisation; as well as posters that focused on the Red Army and on Soviet aviation, associating Stalin with achievements related to each of these fields. In some of these, Stalin continued to appear alongside Voroshilov.[59] Deni and Nikolai Dolgorukov's 'The enemy's fate is predetermined: we have crushed them before and we will crush them again'[60] of 1938 depicts the relaxed and friendly pair of Stalin and Voroshilov, civil and military leader respectively, chatting under a portrait of Lenin, who is in characteristic collar and tie. The three figures form a 'holy trinity' that watches over and protects the Soviet Union, and the text of the poster, invoking fate and predestiny, lends a sacral aura to the notion of righteous victory. Beneath the trinity is a map of Europe in which Russia's enemies flee as a series of red flags springs up around Europe.

Another poster featuring both Stalin and Voroshilov (Fig. 4.5) takes a documentary approach to the personality cult of Stalin. The centre of Podobedov's 1939 poster is dominated by copies of the Military Oath (as it was in 1939)[61] signed and dated by Stalin and Voroshilov on 29 February 1939. The oath documents are framed in gold and surrounded by banners, the coat of arms of the USSR, a red star and hammer-and-sickle emblems. On either side of the sacred documents are black-and-white photographic portraits of Stalin (left) and Voroshilov (right) each framed in gold. Under Stalin's smiling portrait, in which he looks at the viewer, is Article 132[62] of the 1936 constitution which reminds citizens that military service is

---

59   See also, for example, 'Long live Soviet pilots — proud falcons of the Motherland!', by Vatolina and Denisov (discussed in Chapter Three).
60   For image, see redavantgarde.com/en/collection/show-collection/1342-the-enemy-s-fate-is-predetermined-we-have-crushed-them-before-and-we-will-keep-on-crushing.html?authorId=77.
61   Decree of the Presidium of the USSR Supreme Soviet, 03 Jan. 1939: Military oath. 'I, a citizen of the Union of Soviet Socialist Republics, joining the ranks of the Workers' and Peasants' Red Army, do hereby take the oath of allegiance and do solemnly vow to be an honest, brave, disciplined and vigilant fighter, to guard strictly all military and State secrets, to obey implicitly all Army regulations and orders of my commanders, commissars and superiors.
I vow to study the duties of a soldier conscientiously, to safeguard Army and National property in every way possible and to be true to my People, my Soviet Motherland, and the Workers' and Peasants' Government to my last breath' (J.V. Stalin, *Works*, vol. 14, London, Red Star Press Ltd., 1978, www.marxists.org/reference/archive/stalin/works/1939/02/23.htm (accessed 28 Jan. 2013)).
62   Universal military service is law. Military service in the Workers' and Peasants' Red Army is an honourable duty of citizens of the USSR.

their honourable duty. Under Voroshilov's stern portrait, which does not engage the viewer but looks out of the image, is Article 139,[63] a reminder of the penalties for treason. The poster serves several related functions: it emphasises the imminence of war; it educates the public about their rights and obligations under the constitution and publicises the text of the Military Oath; it highlights leadership by example, as two of the country's leaders have already signed the oath; by emphasising the sacrosanct nature of the text it enshrines it as higher than mere secular law, giving it a sense of permanence and immutability usually associated with divine or religious law; and it reinforces the identification of Stalin and Voroshilov with the tasks of leading and saving the Fatherland (as it is in this case). The grinning portrait of Stalin highlights the Father and Teacher archetypes, while the steely Warrior archetype resides in the popular military figure of Voroshilov.

This distinction between the two roles carried over into 1940, as in another poster by Podobedov featuring Stalin and Voroshilov engaged in a jolly, informal chat (Fig. 4.6). Neither of them look like they are particularly worried, or in the process of preparing for war. The black-and-white photograph of the pair is bordered with the usual formal accoutrements, banners, ribbons, stars and wreaths. In fact, the photo looks as though it may have been taken on Stalin's 60th birthday in December 1939.[64] The text is of interest in this poster, paying tribute to both Stalin and Voroshilov, and clearly differentiating their roles: 'Long live our leader and teacher, best friend of the Red Army, our dear and beloved Stalin! Long live the leader of the Red Army, first marshal of the Soviet Union, Kliment Efremovich Voroshilov!'

As discussed in Chapter Two, throughout the 25 years of his leadership, Stalin frequently appeared in posters alongside the image of Lenin. In 'Long live our dear invincible Red Army!' (Fig. 4.7) of 1938 by Dmitrii Moor and Sergei Sen'kin, Stalin and Lenin are both featured in large individual black-and-white photographic portraits, each under a red (sacred Bolshevik) aircraft, and above scenes showing battle-ready armed forces of all branches. They are both depicted as 'real' people

---

63 Defence of the homeland is a sacred duty of every citizen of the USSR. For high treason: violation of the oath, desertion to the enemy, impairing the military power of the state, espionage — is punished with the full rigor of the law as the most heinous of crimes.
64 I base this conjecture on its similarity to other photographs taken on that occasion.

and as equals. In 1938 Stalin is no longer portrayed as the disciple and student of Lenin, but as a leader and thinker in his own right. Under each of the leaders is a quotation from them which essentially makes the same point by stressing the popular nature of the Soviet armed forces as an army for the people — that is, the workers and peasants. Lenin: 'For the first time in the world an army has been created, an armed force that knows what it is fighting for.' Stalin: 'Our army is the only one in the world that has the sympathy and support of the workers and peasants. Therein lies its strength, that is its stronghold.' Facing inwards, Lenin and Stalin appear as sentries over the flags of the armed services and the text of Article 132. Everything else in the poster faces out — soldiers, aircraft, guns, turrets, tanks, horses and ships. Stalin and Lenin protect the homeland from within, while the armed forces are ever-vigilant and demonstrate their preparedness to go out to war if necessary.

In 1939, as much of the rest of Europe went to war, and Russia and Germany signed the Molotov–Ribbentrop pact that would delay their arguably inevitable engagement in battle for almost two years,[65] the Soviet Union tried to use this bought time to prepare for war. Propaganda posters featuring the image of Stalin continued to deal with a number of themes, and a number of posters were released that praised the Red Army and the airforce, and which also attempted to rally the population to mobilise around their leader. While most of the propaganda posters of 1939 exhibit a general atmosphere of bravado and battle-readiness, although not a desire for war, one Ukrainian poster by M. Kaminskii (Fig. 4.8) focuses on the desire for peace to prevail. The poster features a slab of text in large font that quotes from Stalin's 'Report on the work of the Central Committee to the Eighteenth Congress of the V.K.P.(b)' speech delivered on 10 March 1939. This speech, which is quoted more extensively in a 1940 Russian poster, is a strongly worded pronouncement on the USSR's desire to avoid war and to live harmoniously with its neighbours. This text consists of the first two of the four tasks outlined for the Party in Stalin's speech about foreign policy. The two conditions that do not appear on the poster, possibly so as not to leave any possibility of provocation or misunderstanding, are the conditions that involve strengthening the might of the Red Army and Red Navy to the utmost and strengthening

---

65   The pact was in force from 23 August 1939 to 22 June 1941.

the international bonds of friendship with the working people of all countries. Stalin himself appears in a small and relatively unobtrusive oval-shaped cameo at the top centre of the poster, perhaps as a means of authenticating the text and visually identifying the speaker. This was also the year of Stalin's 60th birthday and, although he continued to appear in posters with Lenin and occasionally Voroshilov, he was also frequently depicted alone as a central inspirational figure.

Another 1939 poster by Podobedov (Fig. 4.9) is an example of a genre of poster that was becoming predominant in the years immediately prior to the Great Patriotic War and which served to strengthen the association of Stalin with the Red Army, remind the public of the threat of war, and glorify the persona of Stalin. The text celebrates Stalin as the organiser and inspirer of the victories of the Red Army — 'Long live the organiser and leader of the victorious Red Army great Stalin!' While attempts are being made to bind the persona of Stalin to the entire history of the Red Army from its inception, and to credit him with responsibility for many of its victories, the poster caption again stops short of overtly claiming that Stalin himself created the army. The word *vdokhnovitel'* carries a connotation of leader and creator, as well as the inspiration behind. It is less explicit in expressing the notion of 'creator' as 'founder' or 'originator' than the words *sozdatel'* and *tvorets*, which are used in other posters, particularly the contemporaneous posters that celebrate Stalin as the creator of the constitution. Stalin appears as a statue on a plinth looking down protectively over the viewer and dwarfing the pale spire of the Kremlin. In his left hand is a scroll — Stalin's weapons are still his words and these words take on the nature of the sacred or divine. The statue of Stalin is monolithic and immovable, but it is also associated with history and the past. One erects monuments to founding fathers and it is the visual symbolism, more than the text, that embeds the idea that Stalin is responsible for the existence and success of the Red Army. Stalin is far less coy in claiming that he created the Red Cavalry. 'Long live the creator of the first cavalry, best friend of the Red Cavalry — Comrade Stalin!' (Fig. 4.10) by an unidentified artist makes the claim explicit and features an oval Stalin portrait with diagonally oriented banners that suggest the forward jarring motion of riding on horseback.

4. STALIN SAVES THE WORLD

A 1939 poster by Deni and Dolgorukov, 'Stalin's spirit makes our army and country strong and solid' (Fig. 4.11), depicts a Stalin of superhuman magnitude and grants him supernatural powers. Men, tanks and aircraft all take on the proportions of ants below, scurrying about in forward motion, but Stalin is still and calm, paying them no heed. His focus is upward and outward, on a vision that comes to him from the heavens. He does not act, nor seem to move — in fact he does not have legs, but emerges from the ground in a monolithic block at mid-calf. Stalin becomes fused with the banner, an extension of its protective function. The dark tones on the lower portion of his figure and the shapelessness of his greatcoat depict him as strong, solid and monolithic as the text claims. Growing out of the earth, he is the symbolic embodiment of the Russian land.

In general, in the propaganda posters of 1940, war preparation and battle-readiness is played down and, instead, the posters promote the USSR as working toward peace. An Izostat[66] poster by an unidentified artist (Fig. 4.12) has for its caption a substantial text quoted from Stalin's speech of 10 March 1939. The text stresses that the Soviet Union offers 'moral' support to the workers of all countries, and the final words state specifically that the foreign policy of the Soviet Union aligns it with countries who are not interested in breaching the peace. This landscape format poster is a colourful offering in this otherwise black, white and red era,[67] with Stalin at a podium in the foreground, papers in hand, seemingly at the beginning or end of his speech, and a crowd of multinational citizens, many in national dress, walking up behind him. They appear to be of all ages, including children, and come from all walks of life. A child holds aloft a red balloon, while on the left this action is paralleled by the raising of a red flag from the open turret of a tank. The gesture is one of salute, but is akin to the gesture of truce or surrender, which is usually made with a white flag. The tank is motionless and the personnel exposed — they are prepared, but are not heading off to war. The background is a colourful and busy tribute to Soviet achievement — tractors, lorries and harvesters are

---

66   The All-union institute of pictorial statistics of Soviet construction and economy. Izostat was set up in 1931 to train Soviet designers and technicians in the effective use of pictorial statistics, particularly as an instrument for propaganda and agitation. The institute was closed in 1940.
67   It must be borne in mind, as noted in the Introduction, that the restricted colour scheme of wartime posters may have been due to time constraints and the availability of materials.

busy in the lush green fields, smoke plumes out of the factories in the distance, aircraft fly in formation in the blue sky, and buildings at the side highlight the end results of successful construction.

The disastrous early war years

In 1941, the campaign to stay out of a war that had been raging through the rest of Europe for two years failed. During those two years, political propaganda had first indicated the Soviet Union's preparedness for war if attacked, and highlighted her military capabilities, especially with regard to aviation. Subsequently, in 1940, propaganda shifted focus to express a desire for peace and reluctance to enter the war. Throughout this time, and coinciding with Stalin's 60th birthday in December 1939, a persona was being created for Stalin that symbolised strength, unity and wisdom. Stalin was depicted as a father figure, as a wise leader and a teacher. Although Voroshilov was the marshal of the army, and Stalin held no military rank, Stalin was presented as a friend of, and inspiration to, the armed forces. Propaganda allowed Stalin to enter the war years with a mythic visual biography that depicted him as heavily involved in the Soviet Union's military affairs since the inception of the Red Army, as the creator of the Red Cavalry, and as the figure responsible for record-breaking feats in aviation.

Stalin's past as a Red warrior was not the only task that the Soviet propaganda machine approached creatively. Despite copious intelligence advising that Germany was going to invade Russia in 1941,[68] Stalin refused to believe it, trusting that Hitler would be bound by the Molotov–Ribbentrop pact. He was taken by surprise when German troops entered Russian soil on 22 June 1941. Vyacheslav Molotov[69] made the announcement of the German invasion to the

---

68 According to Christopher Andrew and Julie Elkner, the KGB later counted 'over a hundred' intelligence warnings of the German intention to invade, forwarded by Pavel Fitin, head of foreign intelligence from 1939, to Stalin in the first six months of 1941, all of which were ignored. There was also military intelligence to support Fitin's claims ('Stalin and foreign intelligence', *Totalitarian Movements and Political Religions*, 2003, 4:1, pp. 69–94, p. 78).
69 According to Montefiore, the other members of the Politburo proposed that Stalin announce the onset of war, but Stalin refused to do so, although he dominated the drafting of the speech (*Stalin*, p. 325).

Soviet people the same day,[70] and Stalin made his first public speech on the radio (or elsewhere) in two years[71] on 3 July,[72] broadcast from a room in the Kremlin at 6 am.[73]

Stalin and other members of the Politburo worked furiously for the first seven days after the German invasion. On 28 June, as he left the People's Commissariat of Defence, Stalin appeared distraught, blurting out to his comrades 'Lenin left us a great inheritance, and we, his heirs, have fucked it all up!'[74] before informing them that he was resigning from office. On 29 and 30 June, Stalin appears not to have shown up for work and may have had some sort of collapse.[75] Montefiore poses the question of whether this 'collapse' was real, or 'for effect', as Molotov and Anastas Mikoian speculated.[76] In any case, when Stalin returned to work he had the full support of his Politburo colleagues.

---

70   See www.fordham.edu/halsall/mod/1941molotov.html for text of this speech.
71   As Deutscher points out, the rarity with which Stalin spoke in public imbued those occasions on which he did with a special significance: 'To the public he spoke rarely; and every statement of his was made to appear as a milestone in history. As a rule these statements, which were in the nature of an autocrat's orders, did, indeed, have a practical significance for people in every walk of life' (Deutscher, *Stalin*, pp. 360–61).
72   See www.ibiblio.org/pha/policy/1941/410703a.html for text of this speech.
73   The speech went for 21 minutes and was not rebroadcast, although the text of the speech was re-read by others in a variety of settings, and was also published in the newspapers and a separate brochure. Thus, even on this highly significant occasion, Berkhoff claims that few people actually heard Stalin deliver the original speech condemning the Germans for breaking the non-aggression pact, and call on the population to mobilise for this life-or-death situation (*Motherland in danger: Soviet propaganda during World War II*, Cambridge, Harvard University Press, 2012, p. 25).
74   Ronald Grigor Suny, *The Soviet experiment: Russia, the USSR and the successor states*, 2nd edn, New York, Oxford University Press, 2011, p. 337.
75   'Stalin "had shut himself away from everybody, was receiving nobody and was not answering the phone". Molotov told Mikoyan and the others that "Stalin had been in such a state of prostration for the last two days that he was not interested in anything, didn't show any initiative and was in a bad way". Stalin could not sleep. He did not even bother to undress but simply wandered around the dacha'. Montefiore relies on accounts by Molotov, Mikoian, Beria via Krushchev and Chadaev, which agree on the general outline of events, although there are some variations in exact reporting of speech (Montefiore, *Stalin*, pp. 330–31).
76   'So had Stalin really suffered a nervous breakdown or was this simply a performance? Nothing was ever straightforward with this adept political actor. The breakdown was real enough: he was depressed and exhausted. It was not out of character: he had suffered similar moments on Nadya's death and during the Finnish war. His collapse was an understandable reaction to his failure to read Hitler, a mistake which could not be hidden from his courtiers who had repeatedly heard him insist there would be no invasion in 1941 … . Yet Molotov and Mikoyan were right: it was also "for effect". The withdrawal from power was a well-tried pose, successfully employed from Achilles and Alexander the Great to Ivan. Stalin's retreat allowed him to be effectively re-elected by the Politburo, with the added benefit of drawing a line under the bungles up to that point. These had been forgiven: "Stalin enjoyed our support again", Mikoyan wrote pointedly' (Montefiore, *Stalin*, pp. 333–34).

Preparations for war, although in progress, were far from satisfactory[77] and by the end of 1941 there had been numerous defeats in battle, Leningrad was under siege and the Germans were advancing towards Moscow — at one point they were only eight kilometres away.[78] As Berkhoff points out, these early disasters on the war front were covered up in the newspapers, as were the details of the implementation of the scorched earth policy[79] that Stalin had proclaimed in the 3 July speech. To reveal them would also have exposed the falsity of the propaganda leading up to the war, which had focused on the preparedness of the Red Army and on the superiority of Soviet aviation. Stalin's purges of 1937 and 1938 had also decimated the top leadership of the Red Army.[80] As Ronald Suny points out: 'Stalin killed more Soviet generals than would be killed in World War II. Fifteen out of the sixteen army commanders, 60 of the 67 corps commanders, and 136 of the 199 divisional commanders were executed.'[81]

Propaganda posters on domestic themes receded into the background and all efforts were harnessed for mobilisation of the people and the military for the Great Patriotic War. Large numbers of posters were produced on war themes, including appeals to men to protect the motherland, as well as their vulnerable women and children; depictions of the enemy as subhuman and unusually cruel (this latter appears to have some basis in fact);[82] and exhortations to kill and expel the fascist

---

77 Deutscher argues that Stalin used the time gained by the Molotov–Ribbentrop pact effectively: 'Despite all his miscalculations, Stalin was not unprepared to meet the emergency. He had solidly armed his country and reorganized its military forces. His practical mind had not been weeded to any one-sided strategic dogma. He had not lulled the Red Army into a false sense of security behind any Russian variety of the Maginot Line ... he could rely on Russia's vast spaces and severe climate' (Deutscher, *Stalin*, p. 462).
78 Deutscher, *Stalin*, p. 457. Berkhoff claims that the Germans came within 25 kilometres of Moscow (*Motherland in danger*, p. 42).
79 Part of the dam of the Dnieper Hydroelectric Station was blown up by Soviet engineers, as were mines in Kryvy Rih, and wharves in Mykolaiv. Berkhoff claims that Stalin planned to demolish Moscow with mines if it was taken by the Germans (*Motherland in danger*, p. 38).
80 Rieber argues that the rationale behind Stalin's purge of the Red Army leadership was to eliminate potential opposition that might seek to overthrow the government in the event of war. 'The precise proportions of political calculation and psychological derangement that drove Stalin to these extreme measures will always be a matter of speculation. But their effect cut two ways. When the Germans invaded there was no alternative to his leadership even though he had led the country to the brink of disaster. But in order to secure this position he destroyed what was arguably the most talented group of general staff officers in the world ...' ('Stalin as foreign policy-maker: avoiding war, 1927–1953', in Davies & Harris, *Stalin*, pp. 143–44).
81 Suny, *The Soviet experiment*, p. 285.
82 About 3 million, or approximately 57 per cent of Soviet prisoners of war in German captivity died before the end of the war, compared with only 3.5 per cent of British and

4. STALIN SAVES THE WORLD

invaders. Stephen White points out that, during the course of the war, Iskusstvo[83] alone produced about 800 posters in a total of 34 million copies, while about 700 were produced in Leningrad.[84] Despite this overwhelming propaganda effort, the incidence of images of Stalin in posters appears to have dropped during the war years, relative to the three years immediately prior to the war, which saw a boom in images of the *vozhd'* in posters. This may reflect a tendency, noted earlier in relation to unsuccessful or difficult campaigns, to dissociate the leader from failures and catastrophes, and associate his image only with success, but may also simply reflect a preoccupation with other themes. Indeed, as research by Brooks indicates, Stalin's presence in the newspapers also diminished, with some of his authority and the 'culture of obligation'[85] shifting to others and, although his portrait continued to appear, it was frequently in the form of a frame from a documentary film, rather than a photograph of a current event.[86]

Where Stalin does appear in the war posters of 1941, he is depicted as calling to the nation; inspiring the nation (along with the spirit of Lenin); and leading soldiers into battle. Stalin made few public speeches. Berkhoff cites fewer than 10 occasions on which Stalin spoke in public during the entire war, and only about 12 occasions on which his voice was heard on the radio.[87] Stalin never went near the Front; however, his image as a strong-willed leader gained in credibility when he refused to evacuate Moscow with the rest of the government. 'If the leader calls …' (Fig. 4.13), a 1941 poster by Viktor Koretskii, features a verse from Maiakovskii's poem *Barabannaia Pesnia*[88] accompanied by a black-and-white portrait bust photo

---

American prisoners (Suny, *The Soviet experiment*, p. 343). In June 1941 Adolf Hitler said to his general staff: 'A Communist is not and can never be considered a fellow soldier. This war will be a battle of annihilation … It will be very different from the war in the West. In the East harshness will guarantee us a mild future. Military leaders must overcome their humanitarian reservations' (Suny, *The Soviet experiment*, p. 342). See also Deutscher, *Stalin*, p. 474.
83   Moscow publishing house.
84   Stephen White, *The Bolshevik poster*, New Haven, Yale University Press, 1998, p. 121.
85   As Brooks points out, the 'soldiers' obligation was no longer to Stalin, but instead to their families, towns and villages, and to the nation. The press in turn stressed the population's debt to the Red Army, and published stories of citizens' gifts to ordinary soldiers' ('Stalin's politics of obligation', *Totalitarian Movements and Political Religions*, 4:1, 2003, pp. 47–67, pp. 61–62).
86   Brooks, *Thank you, Comrade Stalin!*, p. 160.
87   This includes four speeches to the Moscow City Council on the anniversaries of the October Revolution, an address to the Red Army on 7 November 1941, and the Victory Day speech on 9 May 1945 — even the annual May Day address was delivered in writing (*Motherland in danger*, p. 24).
88   *Drum Song*.

of Stalin and a quotation from his 3 July speech. At the bottom right, troops march across Red Square, the holy centre of Bolshevik ceremonial space, with Lenin's tomb occupying the central position of the background and some battle-ready soldiers photomontaged into the foreground. The diagonal thrust of their rifles and the diagonals of the platoon formations suggest motion and activity, the mobilisation of large numbers of troops for the forthcoming battle. Maiakovskii, the deceased poet of the Revolution, utters a mobilisation battle-cry that hearkens back to revolutionary days and draws an association between the two situations.[89] The suggestion is that the Soviet people should rally behind Stalin now in the same way as they rallied behind Lenin then. The excerpt from Stalin's speech announces the formation of the State Defence Committee[90] and asks the people to rally behind the committee, the government, and the army and navy. It concludes with the cry 'Forward to our victory!'[91] The poster is sombre, stark and relatively unadorned. Stalin's portrait is serious, his eyes directed at the viewer, calling him to mobilise. It was becoming less common in propaganda images for Stalin's eyes to engage the viewer, his view usually directed either down over the people assembled beneath him or up and out of the poster to a future that only he can see.

The attempt to associate the crisis situation of the Great Patriotic War with the days of Revolution is made even more explicit in a 1941 poster by an unidentified artist, '"The spirit of the great Lenin and his victorious banner inspires us now in the Patriotic War as it did 23 years ago." Stalin' (Fig. 4.14). The poster shows a tank flying a banner with a Stalin portrait, racing off to battle, accompanied by the ghostly red shadow of a Civil War tank flying the banner of Lenin. The text of the poster, taken from Stalin's speech on the

---

89 'Yesli vozhd' zovet, Ruka, na vintovku lyag! Vpered, za vzvodom vzvod! Gromche pechat' — shag!' This verse is difficult to translate sensibly into English. Its meaning is: If the leader calls, Take up your rifle, Forward! Platoon after platoon! Louder ... stamp ... march.

90 This committee consisted of Stalin as president, Molotov as deputy, and Voroshilov, Malenkov and Beria.

91 'In order to ensure the rapid mobilisation of all the forces of the peoples of the U.S.S.R. and to repulse the enemy who has treacherously attacked our country, a State Committee of Defence has been formed and the entire state authority has now been vested in it. The State Committee of Defence has entered on the performance of its functions and calls upon all our people to rally around the Party of Lenin and Stalin and around the Soviet Government, so as to render self-sacrificing support to the Red Army and Red Navy, to exterminate the enemy and secure victory. All our forces — to support our heroic Red Army and our glorious Red Navy! All the power of the people — to defeat the enemy! Forward to victory!'

23rd anniversary of the October Revolution, makes the link explicit: 'The spirit of the great Lenin and his victorious banner inspires us now in the Patriotic War as it did 23 years ago.' It is not just the situations of crisis that are paralleled in this poster but also, by extension, the role of the leader. The connection is also made explicit in a 1941 poster by A.V. Vasil'ev and S.F. Yanevich (Fig. 4.15) that pairs Lenin and Stalin as profile friezes on a red banner. The portraits of Lenin and Stalin are not photographic, nor are they sketches from life. Both the dead Lenin and the living Stalin are apotheosised onto the banner as mythic historic beings with supernatural powers. Unlike earlier uses of Lenin to bolster legitimacy for Stalin's leadership, the two are now shown as equal, with Lenin often depicted behind (or in the shadow of) Stalin. In many instances, Lenin now also serves as a means by which to apotheosise Stalin, taking him into the heavens. While in earlier propaganda Stalin used Lenin's image to legitimise his earthly powers, now he also hitches himself to Lenin's spiritual and inspirational powers.

Not all of the war posters of Stalin also featured Lenin. Iraklii Toidze's 1941 poster '"All our forces — to support our heroic Red Army and our glorious Red Navy! All the power of the people — to defeat the enemy!" Stalin' (Fig. 4.16) quotes from the same famous speech as the Koretskii poster of that year and shows a determined Stalin striding to the right accompanied by Soviet tanks and aircraft. The figure of Stalin forms a curious mixture of motion and stability. His gaze is steady and unflinching. The extended arm, showing the way forward with pointed index finger, is rigid and firm. Stalin is fixated on victory and the strength of his will carries the army and airforce with him. The force of his forward momentum is revealed by the way in which his coat lapels fly about him, and by the swirling motion of the clouds in the sky. These stormy clouds part above Stalin's head, suggesting that even the forces of nature bend to Stalin's will, making way for his unstoppable progress towards victory.

Many posters of this era are captioned with quotes from Stalin. Quoting Stalin had become akin to quoting scripture, and the posters are captioned as if these words contain deep wisdom, spiritual guidance, and unimpeachable truth. Writing in 1942 about Stalin's speeches during the war thus far, Kalinin said: 'We call these historic speeches not only in the sense that they are documents but because of their influence on our people and on our army. They are speeches that make history.'[92]

Konstantin Cheprakov's poster of 1941 (Fig. 4.17) shows Stalin (who looks slightly ethnically Uzbek in this poster) in a similar pose to the Toidze poster. He appears in profile, right arm rigidly indicating the way forward to victory. His tunic and coat-tail swirl, but here he appears to have been depicted just as he has come to a halt. Soldiers, tanks and aircraft surge forward past him, set on reaching the indicated destination. Diagonal banners and a raised bayonet in the foreground reinforce the violence of the forward motion, as do the aircraft diving in on a diagonal. The poster's caption, in Uzbek and Russian, reinforces the notion of the allegiance owed to Stalin as the wise father of the people: 'We swore an oath to our leader to fight the enemy. We will keep the covenant of our fathers. Lead us into battle victory, wise Stalin — Clear the enemy, father of fighters!' Images that appear to be photographic purport to tell the truth and, if Stalin is depicted as physically leading the troops into battle, it is easier to associate him with qualities of vision, bravery, heroism and steadfastness, even if this is at a subconscious level.

Despite the fact that Stalin was portrayed as leading the troops into battle, he was not yet depicted in military uniform. Insignia of rank were abolished in 1917, immediately after the Revolution, however, in 1935, Stalin reintroduced personal ranks and, in 1940, general officer ranks. Insignia of rank were fully restored in 1943. Stalin is usually shown hatless or, on the rare occasions when he does wear a cap, it is unadorned.[93] To represent Stalin as a military genius at this point in time may have been risky and may even have opened him up to ridicule. Lack of preparedness for war, poor decision-making, and a blatant misreading of the enemy could all be placed at Stalin's feet, as could the consequent losses of Soviet life. Despite the advantages in wartime of portraying a strong and successful warrior and military strategist, the propaganda machine was as yet unable to unambiguously drape

---

92   Mikhail Kalinin, 'Stalin and the Patriotic War', *The communist*, 1942, pp. 1000–04, www.unz.org/Pub/Communist-1942dec-01000?View=PDF (accessed 1 Nov. 2016).
93   For example, Toidze's '"All our forces — to support our heroic Red Army and our glorious Red Navy! All the power of the people — to defeat the enemy!" Stalin', 1941 (Fig. 4.16). Plamper dates the appearance of the 'general's cap' to February 1942, and Stalin can be seen in posters with the red star affixed to the band of his cap from this point forward (*The Stalin cult*, p. 53).

4. STALIN SAVES THE WORLD

Stalin in the mantle of the warrior. Instead, the established archetypes of Father and Teacher were called upon in an effort to maintain some legitimacy for the leader and to mobilise the population behind him in this crisis.

Stalin and the enemy

As discussed in Chapter Two, it was relatively uncommon for Stalin to be depicted with the enemy,[94] and even more uncommon for him to be pictured alongside any kind of brutality. The war was cruel and the Soviet people suffered harshly under German occupation. The propaganda of the preceding decades, which emphasised the unity of the working classes around the world and their shared goals and interests, had been largely successful, and some of the Russian soldiers saw this confrontation as an opportunity to reach out to the working classes of other less fortunate nations.[95] Atrocities committed on Russian soil, a series of punishing defeats, and a concerted propaganda campaign with highly emotive images that highlighted the risk to women and children under German occupation, turned this pacifist attitude on its head, and troops were encouraged to fight savagely in order to win the war. Many of the posters of the time (in which Stalin's image does not appear) focus on fear, brutality and German atrocities, as well as depicting the enemy as subhuman or vermin.

---

94   In one of Stalin's rare appearances with the enemy, a 1930 poster by Viktor Deni, 'With the banner of Lenin we won in the battles for the October Revolution ...', the small caricatures of a priest, a capitalist, an *'oblomov'*, and a Menshevik line up down the left side of the poster gesturing angrily at Stalin, who faces them off from the right with a large profile head, unperturbed gaze, and the machinery of Soviet industrialisation and construction bolstering him.

95   Ilia Ehrenburg recalled that the Russian people did not initially have any hatred for the German soldiers: 'The men defending Smolensk or Briansk repeated what they had heard first at school and later at political meetings, or read in the newspapers: in Germany the working class was strong, it was a leading industrial country; true, the fascists, supported by the Ruhr magnates and the social-traitors, had seized power, but the German people were in opposition and were carrying on the struggle. "Naturally," the Red Army men said, "the officers are fascists, and of course there must be misguided men among the rank and file, but millions of soldiers advance only because otherwise they'd be shot".' (*Men, years — life*, vol. 5, *The war: 1941–45*, Tatiana Shebunina & Yvonne Kapp (trans.), London, MacGibbon and Kee, 1964, p. 26). Ehrenburg recalls feeling enraged when gunners on the front line refused to shell a highway when commanded to do so. One of the gunners explained: '"We can't just shell the road and then retreat. We must let the Germans approach and try to explain to them it's time for them to come to their senses and rise against Hitler, and that we'll help them to do it". The others feelingly supported him. A young and intelligent-looking artillery man said: "Who are we shooting? Workers and peasants. They think we're against them, we don't leave them any choice".' (*Men, years — life*, vol. 5, pp. 27–28).

In these most desperate years of the war, a few posters contained both an image of Stalin and an image of the hated enemy. A simple war poster of 1941 by an unidentified artist (Fig. 4.18), published in Leningrad, is dominated by a large diagonal banner on which Stalin's profile appears only in white outline silhouette. Beneath Stalin's head, the words 'Under the name of Stalin we won. Under the name of Stalin we will win!' separate his faint image from the battle scene below. The crude graphic shows two aircraft above a Soviet tank that is crushing the enemy beneath it. The enemy is depicted in cartoon fashion as a skull in a helmet with long sharp-clawed paws protruding from the sleeves of its Nazi uniform — in both the Civil War and the Great Patriotic War, the enemy was often depicted with animal characteristics so as to highlight either the danger posed by the enemy, or its vermin-like, subhuman qualities. Alternately, the enemy could also be depicted in cartoon-fashion as cowardly and ridiculous.[96]

In 1942, war propaganda was at the forefront across most media, and Agitprop informed editors of the district newspapers that their main task was to:

> educate the workers in a fiery hatred of the German–fascist scoundrels, who are encroaching upon the life and freedom of our motherland; to inspire our people to a great patriotic war of liberation; and to mobilize the workers for the fulfillment of the concrete tasks in the matter of active support of the front standing before the raion ... all the work of the newspaper editors must be subordinated to the interests of the front and the tasks to organize the crushing defeat of the German–fascist invaders. The papers are obliged to daily explain to the workers the danger that is threatening our country, to overcome carelessness

---

[96] The cartoon enemy makes a brief appearance in the 1938 poster by Deni and Dolgorukov (already discussed), and in a curious undated war poster by Georgi Zarnitskii. Three-quarters of the landscape poster consists of a characteristic depiction of a young fighter (not in standard military uniform) holding a rifle and a long banner with a frieze of Lenin and Stalin and the words 'For the motherland! For Stalin!' emblazoned across it. The backdrop is full of conventional imagery — the silhouettes of fighters, rifles ready, bayonets thrust forward, and signs of successful Soviet industrialisation and agriculture in the background. The right edge of the poster, a section demarcated by the pole of the banner, is stark black with a depiction of small frightened enemies, two cowering whilst looking up at the frieze of Lenin and Stalin on the huge red banner, and the hind leg of one visible fleeing, in white outline. Above the frightened enemy is a dogfight between aircraft, with smoke and falling debris. The caption to the poster is in large, bold type and reads: 'Workers stand to defend our beloved Socialist Motherland!' While the style of the major portion of the poster is conventional and heroic, the part of the poster devoted to the enemy is cartoon-like and slightly comical. The enemy looks anything but menacing.

4. STALIN SAVES THE WORLD

and indifference, to develop Soviet patriotism, to cultivate hatred of the German occupiers and readiness to give up all one's strength for the crushing defeat of the enemy.[97]

Scenes of German callousness and brutality became a major theme in posters, as well as scenes in which the enemy was being defeated by Russian troops. A 1942 poster by Boris Mukhin, 'The spirit of the great Lenin and his victorious banner inspires us now in the Patriotic War as it did 23 years ago' (Fig. 4.19), is dominated by a large, 'fleshed-out' Lenin, while the image of Stalin on a banner on a tank is so small and finely sketched that one could almost miss it. Most of the left side of the poster is filled with the figure of Lenin with outstretched arm and pointing finger. Lenin's hand resembles the hand of God in Michelangelo's *The creation of Adam*. God reaches out to impart the spark of life to Adam. Similarly, Lenin reaches out to breathe inspiration into the Soviet troops. Behind Lenin is a large red banner showing scenes of fighting during the Civil War. The text on the banner is taken from Stalin's speech at the parade on Red Square on 7 November 1941. The foreground of the poster shows a Soviet tank rumbling forward with gun blazing, crushing German artillery and barbed wire fortifications, and about to roll over the corpses of German soldiers. Behind the tank one German soldier is falling under its tracks, and two more flee for their lives. Behind this, a similar scene is repeated in the middle distance in lesser detail. The text in the bottom left corner also looks as if it is being crushed by the tank, and refers directly to the scene of carnage above it — 'Who can deny that our Red Army makes the much vaunted German army flee in panic?'

Less graphically brutal in terms of visual imagery, but explicit in text, is V. Mirzoe's 'We can and must clear our Soviet soil of the Hitlerite filth!' (Fig. 4.20). Dating from approximately late 1942 to early 1943,[98] the poster quotes Stalin's Order no. 345, the Order of the People's Commissar of Defence, 7 November 1942. The text occupies almost half of the picture plane and instructs the Red Army to defend the front line, not retreat, wear down the enemy and destroy his machinery. It urges strict discipline and order and the expansion of a popular guerilla movement to the rear of the enemy. Above the text, a military

---

97 TsDAHOU, 1/23/67/19/21V: Upravlenie propagandy i agitatsii TsK VKP(b), rabote raionnykh gazet, March 3, 1942, cited in Berkhoff, *Motherland in danger*, pp. 11–12.
98 The poster is undated and does not include publishing details.

portrait bust of Stalin appears grave and concerned. Both Stalin and the text are coloured red and sit separated from the scene below, a black-and-white battle scene, with daubs of red provided by small red stars. Soviet tanks and troops advance on a much smaller Nazi enemy, which already appears defeated. Only one German soldier appears, sprawled over his tiny tank.

The turning tide

In his 1941 address on the anniversary of the October Revolution, Stalin cautiously told the military parade that victory was possible in 1942: 'Some more months, another half year, perhaps a year, and Hitlerite Germany will have to break under the weight of its crimes.'[99] In this speech he called on the memory of the heroic *Russian* warrior ancestors to inspire the populace to victory — Nevskii, Dimtrii Donskoi, Kuzma Minin, Dimtrii Pozharskii, Aleksandr Suvorov and Mikhail Kutuzov. This appeal to a pre-Soviet feudal or autocratic past seemed at odds with previous Soviet attempts to dissociate from the rule of the tsars, and marked an increased focus on continuity with the heroic Russian past as a society of victors against aggression and oppression.[100] It also allowed the population to interpret the current chaotic retreats from battle as a repetition of the brilliant tactical retreats of Kutuzov and Nevskii, which ultimately resulted in victory.[101] In 1942, Kalinin also suggested that the Red Army might defeat the Germans that year,[102] and evidence that at least some of the people believed this to be possible is provided by an open letter to Stalin signed by 1,017,237 people, published in the newspaper *Trud*, which stated:

---

99 I. Stalin, *O Velikoi Otechestvennoi voine Sovetskogo Soiuza*, 4th edn, Moscow, Gospolitizdat, 1944, p. 36.
100 Like D.L. Brandenberger and A.M. Dubrovsky, I interpret this apparent move toward Russian nationalism, which began around 1937, as pragmatic, rather than genuine Russian nationalism. This argument is outlined in greater detail in their essay, '"The people need a tsar": the emergence of national Bolshevism as Stalinist ideology, 1931–1941', *Europe–Asia Studies*, 50:5, 1998, pp. 873–92.
101 James von Geldern, 'Epic revisionism and the crafting of a Soviet public', in Kevin M.F. Platt & David Brandenberger, *Epic revisionism: Russian history and literature as Stalinist propaganda*, Madison, University of Wisconsin Press, 2006, p. 330.
102 Kalinin, 'Stalin and the Patriotic War'.

4. STALIN SAVES THE WORLD

For Hitler the year 1942 is a fateful date, the year of shameful ruin, of dishonorable death. In this new year that is starting, Hitler's predatory empire shall fall apart under the weight of the crimes of fascism, crushed by the grave soil of the thousands of cemeteries in Europe and Africa.[103]

It was too early yet, though, to feel confident that the Germans would be defeated.

In 1942, rather than moving forward as in 1941, Stalin's image in posters became increasingly motionless, moving into the sky or onto friezes, and banners. Sometimes he even appeared as a spirit, like Lenin. Veteran poster artist Nikolai Kogout's 'Under the invincible banner of the great Lenin — forward to victory!'[104] (Fig. 4.21) shows Soviet people of all nationalities, civilian and military, male and female, clustered under a huge red banner featuring golden portraits of Stalin and Lenin in profile, uniting for the war effort. The people carry weapons and, for the first time since the early years of the Soviet regime, women are dressed in working clothes and also carry tools. Behind the people to the left are a mass of Soviet tanks with guns blazing, and red aircraft dive in to battle in the sky. In the background to the right is a representation of Soviet industry, the source of supplies for the war effort, and the showcase of Soviet achievement.

A striking Uzbek poster featuring Lenin and Stalin, Pen Varlen's 1942 'The path to our glory is immutable — Fascism will die! ...' (Fig. 4.22), shows an infinite wedge[105] of Soviet peoples surging forward to take on the enemy. The huge mass moves as one body and consists not only of military personnel, but also of nurses and civilians of a variety of ethnicities. The sky is dominated by the huge diagonal field of a sweeping red banner, with hammer and sickle thrusting forward, and behind it the sketched figure of Stalin is shadowed by the ghostly white silhouette of Lenin. The sketch of Stalin has distinguishing features, tone and depth; however, he does not occupy the same space as the Soviet citizens. Stalin inhabits the world of the banner and simply disappears below the waist. His right arm is flung out, the hand extended to indicate the way forward to victory, palm

---

103 Cited in Berkhoff, *Motherland in danger*, pp. 44–45.
104 The text is printed in Uzbek and Russian and is a quote from Stalin's May Day order.
105 This wedge may reference the famous abstract poster by El Lissitsky 'Beat the whites with the red wedge' of 1920.

open almost as if it is he who provides the momentum for the people below. Stalin appears on a giant scale and dwarfs the silhouette of the Kremlin. The spirit of Lenin appears as Stalin's shadow, almost morphing them into the same person, and is even larger than Stalin. While Lenin's pose is almost exactly that of Stalin, the same upthrust jaw and outstretched arm, Stalin's left arm hangs at his side whereas Lenin's is bent and held high against his body. While Lenin's coat-tail flaps, Stalin's clothing is orderly and undisturbed. These minor variances highlight the difference in rhetorical style between the two men — Lenin speaking urgently, leaning forward, moving his body; Stalin calm and still — and also the fact that, while Lenin was on his way to socialism, Stalin has already arrived. The full text of the poster reads: 'The way to our glory is immutable — fascism will die! The enemy will fall! We were inspired by the great Lenin — the great Stalin leads us in battle!' The caption names Lenin as the inspiration for both Stalin and the Soviet people, although it is Stalin who now leads the battle, bridging the spiritual and corporeal worlds. Voroshilov, who had committed serious errors as marshal of the Soviet Union during the Russo–Finnish War of 1940, has disappeared.[106]

A 1942 poster by head of the Leningrad section of the Artists' Union, Vladimir Serov (Fig. 4.23), utilises the same concept of the spirit of Lenin from beyond the grave, and the spirit of Stalin in the present, but is considerably more graphic in its depiction of the war.[107] Almost the entire top half of the poster is filled by a huge red banner infused with the head of Lenin looking calmly into the distance. Lenin's sacred head emits white light which illuminates the right arm and face of Stalin below him. Stalin's right arm is raised and outstretched, but his fingers are spread and his palm turned down, and he appears to be blessing or sanctifying the action below him. The outstretched arm is a symbolic element continued from posters of Lenin.[108] Just as Stalin guides his troops and their actions, Lenin sits on Stalin's right shoulder to bless and guide him. The torso of Stalin emerges from a swirling mist of smoke above the battlefield, and in this poster Stalin is nearer to the enemy than in any other, although the implication is that he is there in spirit, not flesh. The bottom half of the poster depicts the battlefield

---

106 See Plamper, *The Stalin cult*, p. 224.
107 Serov was based in Leningrad during the siege.
108 For example, Sokolov, 'Let the ruling classes shudder before the Communist Revolution', 1922.

in closeup. In the immediate foreground is a trench with barbed wire, and a Russian soldier bayoneting a German soldier. The German has lost his gun and sprawls helpless on the ground, a dead comrade arched over barbed wire next to him. The bayonet-wielding Russian steps over the body of another dead German soldier, and next to him a comrade prepares to throw a grenade, while a poised bayonet gleams in the hands of a soldier behind him. A tank rumbles through in the background. The red text is simple and direct — 'Under the banner of Lenin, forward, to victory!'

Also in 1942, Viktor Ivanov and Ol'ga Burova (Fig. 4.24) move the portrait bust of Stalin back into the heavens and add dramatic colour with a blood-red sky and male fighters in their various coloured uniforms. The extensive text quotes Stalin's speech from Red Square in 1941: 'Comrades of the Red Army, the Red Fleet, commanders and commissars, men and women of the guerilla forces! The whole world regards you as a force capable of destroying the marauding hordes of the German invaders!'[109] A sea of bayonets symbolises the personal and heroic courage needed from each person — bayonets are an 'up close' and personal means of killing, in contrast to guns and tanks which can kill at a distance. Although the text of the poster, and the speech from which it is taken, include women among the forces defending the Soviet Union, the poster itself shows only men.[110] Depicting women (and indeed children) as combatants engaged in fighting was taboo.[111]

TASS posters

TASS window posters were a return to the earlier idea of ROSTA windows, which originated in 1919 as satirical posters that were heavily influenced by the traditional *lubok* and featured political

---

109 I.V. Stalin, 'Rech' na Krasnoy ploshchadi 7 noyabrya 1941 goda', www.marxists.org/russkij/stalin/t15/t15_14.htm (accessed 19 Aug. 2013).
110 Berkhoff claims that the Soviet leadership neither encouraged nor prevented women from becoming soldiers in the Soviet Army. In 1941, tens of thousands of women volunteered for the army, but only 300 were mobilised. In 1942 women were mobilised for both noncombat functions, such as radio operation and secretarial work, and also as anti-aircraft fighters. Berkhoff states that during the entire war about 520,000 women were members of the field army and 120,000 of these engaged the enemy as soldiers (*Motherland in danger*, p. 53).
111 Berkhoff notes that, although 25,000 children served in the Red Army, this topic was totally taboo and the press was not allowed to report the feats of any of these children (*Motherland in danger*, p. 53).

themes. In 1919 ROSTA began publishing newspapers, but chronic shortages of paper led to the idea of pasting short news articles and agitational materials up onto walls and in empty shop windows. The windows drew crowds and the idea expanded from Moscow to the provinces. By the end of the Civil War there were 47 ROSTA agencies across the Soviet Union.[112] Many notable artists and writers of the avant-garde worked on the posters in the early years — artists such as Vladimir Maiakovskii (who wrote the text for 90 per cent of the posters),[113] Aleksandr Rodchenko, Mikhail Cheremnikh and Moor.

On 23 June 1941 Aleksandr Gerasimov, head of the Organising Committee of the Union of Soviet Artists, approved a proposal by Cheremnikh, Nikolai Denisovskii and Pavel Sokolov-Skalia, to create a new propaganda studio in Moscow based on the ROSTA model. Several of the original ROSTA artists were still active, including Cheremnikh, Deni and Moor; and the revolutionary poet Dem'ian Bednyi, who was in poor health, returned from Kazan to assist the war effort. The first TASS poster appeared on 27 June 1941.[114] Some of the first windows were produced in only one copy and, until the end of December 1941, none was produced in more than 120 copies.[115] While initially the subject matter of posters was derived from Party directives, orders, news items and then Stalin's speeches, artists and writers were soon able to submit their own ideas for designs for approval. Some posters even illustrated episodes from Russian and Soviet history. TASS posters were seen as an important part of the war effort, with Sokolov-Skalia claiming in 1943: 'My weapon is the three hundred posters I created during the war.'[116]

During the war, the TASS poster workforce increased from about 12 to nearly 300 employees, and one poster was produced for nearly every day of the war. TASS was controlled by the propaganda department and, during the short-lived spirit of cooperation among Allied forces,

---

112 Peter Kenez, *The birth of the propaganda state: Soviet methods of mass mobilization, 1917–1929*, Cambridge University Press, 1985, p. 115.
113 Kenez, *The birth of the propaganda state*, p. 115.
114 N.F. Denisovsky, *Okna Tass 1941–45, (The TASS windows 1941–1945)*, Moscow, 1975, pp. 13–14, cited in D.W. Spring, 'The TASS poster series from the Hallward Library', University of Nottingham, www.ampltd.co.uk/digital_guides/soviet_posters_1940-1945/historical-introduction-dw-spring.aspx (accessed 15 Jan. 2014).
115 Spring, 'The TASS poster series from the Hallward Library'.
116 'Windows on the war: Soviet TASS posters at home and abroad, 1941–1945, art as a weapon', www.artic.edu/aic/collections/exhibitions/TASS/Art-Weapon (accessed 30 Sep. 2013).

many posters were sent abroad to Allied countries. The posters were large in scale and, unlike most other posters of the Soviet period, were usually created from complex stencils rather than lithographs, some demanding 60 to 70 different stencils and colour divisions. The use of stencils meant that each poster was printed by hand, hence the painterly look of the posters. This was a labour-intensive process and mobilised a number of artists and craftspeople in the service of the war, while limiting reliance on machinery. It also meant that editions were limited, usually to an issue of a few hundred each. Aleksei Morozov notes that edition numbers were also limited by decree — editions of 200 in posters produced in Kuibyshev and Tashkent, and 300 in Moscow, rising to 500 from the summer of 1942. Failure to comply with these restrictions could result in criminal liability for the chief editors.[117]

Like the ROSTA Windows before them, TASS posters were intended to be quickly responsive to the evolving war situation; however, in practice they often lagged behind current affairs by weeks or even months.[118] The 1942 TASS poster by Vasilii Bayuskin and A. Shpier, titled 'Great Patriotic War',[119] serves as a graphic illustration of Order of the Day, No. 55,[120] issued by Stalin on 23 February 1942, the 24th anniversary of the founding of the Red Army. The poster itself appeared in July 1942. In the order, Stalin discusses the history of the Red Army as the defender of the Soviet people, and emphasises its role in expelling foreign invaders since 1918.[121] The order concludes with

---

117 Aleksei Morozov, *Agit-Okna, Okna TASS, 1941-1945*, Kontakt-Kultura, Moscow, 2013, p. 7. Denisovsky states, however, that TASS posters were subsequently reproduced in a variety of media in large quantities: 'nearly 75,000 copies of TASS Windows were reproduced in the film cassette series *Poslednie izvestiia* (The Latest News) and from March 1943 on slide films with reproductions of 40–50 TASS Windows on each reel. Nearly 26,000 silk screen (*shelkografiki*) posters were made and over a million lithographic reduced size copies were made by the TASS collective from the beginning of 1942' (*Okna Tass 1941–45*, cited in Spring, 'The TASS poster series from the Hallward Library').
118 Morozov, *Agit-Okna*, pp. 5–7.
119 For an image, see Aleksei Morozov, *Agit-Okna, Okna TASS, 1941–1945*, Moscow, Kontakt-Kultura, 2013, p. 408.
120 Full text available in English at www.marxists.org/reference/archive/stalin/works/1942/02/23.htm; and in Russian at grachev62.narod.ru/stalin/t15/t15_19.htm.
121 Stalin states that the Red Army has already been successful in expelling the Germans once before. While acknowledging Soviet losses at the beginning of the war, he attributes these to the surprise nature of the German attack, and states that the fortunes of war are already turning in favour of the Red Army. Stalin stresses that Soviet hatred is not directed at the German people themselves, as the USSR is intolerant of racial hatred, but at Hitler's clique, and that Soviet aims extend no further than the expulsion of the Germans from Soviet territory.

several patriotic declarations, the last of which makes up the subtitle of the poster: 'Under the banner of Lenin onward to the defeat of the German-fascist invaders!' From the right, a gigantic, determined Stalin in plain greatcoat and characteristic workers' boots, strides towards the battlefield, right arm outstretched, finger pointing ahead. He is accompanied by a sky full of aircraft.

The poster uses the landscape format to display a number of battle scenes — multiple scenes and a 'storyboard effect' are reminiscent of the *lubok* and a device to which the ROSTA and TASS windows were particularly suited. Six battle scenes are featured, each captioned with a quotation from Stalin's order. The first shows the birth of the Red Army on 23 February 1918, in the battle against the Germans at Narva and Pskov. Soldiers, sailors and civilians all fight from the trenches to defend the motherland. The caption to the image reads: 'Young detachments of the Red Army, which entered war for the first time, routed the German invaders at Pskov and Narva on February 23, 1918.' Immediately beneath this image is another image relating to 1918 in which the Red Army is shown liberating Ukraine and Belarus. The caption to this image states: 'The Red Army successfully defended our country in the battles with the German invaders in 1918 and drove them beyond the confines of the Ukraine and Byelorussia.' The top middle picture juxtaposes Great Patriotic War troops in the foreground, with the cavalry of earlier days in the background, all riding forward to engage the enemy. Aircraft appear in the distant sky, accompanying the ground troops. This image is captioned: 'It is essential that in our country the training of reserves in aid of the front should not be relaxed for a moment. It is essential that ever-new military units should go to the front to forge victory over the bestial enemy.' Beneath this is an image of Soviet might in the current battle — an array of tanks rolls towards the viewer, while behind them, Soviet industry belches out smoke as it produces the weapons needed for the Front. The image shares a caption with another image that shows all means of transport — road, rail, and river — being ultilised in service of the war effort. The caption reads: 'It is essential that our industry, particularly our war industry, should work with redoubled energy. It is essential that with every day the front should receive ever more tanks, planes, guns, mortars, machine-guns, rifles, automatic rifles, and ammunition.' The bottom of the poster is dominated by a large, darker image of contemporary battle, complete with explosions, aerial bombings and troops in action. The scene is dramatic and frenetic, the sky and the earth swirling and breaking apart in the heat of the battle. It is in this scene that Stalin's feet are firmly planted. The caption for this image highlights the horrors of war and outlines the task of the Red Army: 'The Red Army's task is to liberate our Soviet territory from the German invaders; to liberate from the yoke of the German invaders the citizens of our villages and towns who were free and lived like human beings before the war, but are now oppressed and suffer pillage, ruin and famine; and finally, to liberate our women from that disgrace and outrage to which they are subjected by the German-fascist monsters.' The whole of the poster, including the figure of Stalin, is bathed in golden light, reinforcing the sanctity of the mission, the iconic nature of the image of Stalin, and the dogmatic nature of his words.

1942 saw some victories for Soviet troops, and propaganda made much of good news at last. Monumentalist and graphic artist Nadezhda Kashina's TASS poster of April 1942 (Fig. 4.25), produced for May Day festivities, celebrates Soviet success in forcing the Germans to pull back from Moscow in January. Although Moscow remained under threat for some considerable time, this constituted a significant victory after a string of heavy battle losses and was used to encourage the population in the belief that the USSR would ultimately prevail in the war. This horizontal format poster takes the form of a tryptich. The largest central image, in pastel tones with splashes of festive red, blue and yellow, shows the Spassky tower in the background, defended by aircraft flying in formation in a golden sky and a barricade of tanks. In the foreground, a partisan raises his right hand in a gesture of victory, while his left hand holds that of his wife, who carries their toddler in her arms — Moscow is now safe for women and children. The left side of the middle panel is devoted to the military sphere, which includes another partisan, a line of soldiers, and one woman in military uniform. Significantly, the military personnel are departing. The right side of the panel is devoted to the domestic sphere and is populated by women, some dressed in overalls and carrying tools, one an aviatrix, and another, perhaps, a nurse. On either side of the main image are portrait-oriented images of Soviet soldiers. On the left, the soldier wields a banner with the slogan 'Long live the 1st of May' and sharply outlined profile images of Lenin and Stalin, both with plain collars. The banner crosses over into the panel of the central image and protectively covers the departing soldiers of the Red Army, as well as the aircraft in the sky. On the right, a soldier looks to the sky with binoculars, still vigilant against the return of the enemy. Both soldiers look away from the central image, in the manner of sentries watching for external threats. The poster is captioned at the bottom with the words 'Invincible Moscow' in Uzbek and Russian. The poster was published in Uzbekistan by UzTAG[122] — many artists were evacuated during the battle of Moscow and continued to produce posters in Tashkent and Kuibyshev. This led to some confusion in numbering. All posters produced in Tashkent had to be published with text in both Uzbek and Russian.[123]

Sokolov-Skalia's November 1942 TASS poster (Fig. 4.26) shows four soldiers of various ethnicities ready for battle, rifles raised and cocked. Stalin comes down off the banners and out of the skies, and into the thick of the action alongside Soviet troops. This Stalin is 'flesh-and-blood', as real as the men beside him, and of a comparative size. Behind the figures a flash of orange and red illuminates the dark night, and one can see the silhouettes of bayonets and rifles, although no enemy is visible. The flash of colour is suggestive of both the ubiquitous protective banner, albeit with torn and jagged edges, and of the explosions occurring in battle. The caption to the poster reads: 'The sons of all the peoples of the Soviet Union go into battle for the Soviet fatherland. Long live the Red Army — army of brotherhood and friendship of the peoples of the USSR!' Not only have people of all of the republics of the USSR sent their sons off to war to fight for the nation, Stalin too sent his son, Yakov, into battle.

Stalingrad

Stalin was determined that he could not let the city named for him fall to the Germans, for both strategic and symbolic reasons,[124] and in 1942 Stalingrad became the scene of a fierce and bloody battle. On 6 November the defenders of Stalingrad took an oath to Stalin:

---

122 Uzbek Telegraph Agency.
123 See Morozov, *Agit-Okna*, p. 7.
124 Nicholas O'Shaugnessy contends that the propaganda value placed on Stalingrad was so high that the propaganda dictated political and military strategy (*Politics and propaganda*, Manchester University Press, 2004, p. 33).

'Before our battle standards and the whole Soviet country, we swear that we will not besmirch the glory of Russian arms and will fight to the last. Under your leadership, our fathers won the Battle of Tsaritsyn, and under your leadership we will now win the great Battle of Stalingrad.'[125] Toidze's 'Stalin will lead us to victory!' was released on 6 January 1943, a few weeks before the Soviet victory in Stalingrad, but already shows an increasing confidence that the tide of the war was turning in favour of the Soviets. A giant Stalin strides across the battlefield at the head of his troops, equipped with the most modern weaponry, and supported by heavy armoury and the technological excellence of Soviet aviation. Stalin's face is determined, befitting his appellation as the 'man of steel'. The steel-grey tones of the poster are broken up by the vivid red of the banner, which is picked up by the small red star on Stalin's general's cap. The use of red diagonals gives the poster a sense of inexorable movement forward. Stalin looks unstoppable, his aura of power increased by the vaguely phallic-shaped cloud of smoke on his right shoulder — even the forces of nature are harnessed by the magnetic power of Stalin.

On 2 February 1943, the Germans troops at Stalingrad surrendered. Although the war had not been won, there was finally some good news to spread to the populace and, in 1943, Stalin's image began slowly to be associated with victory. 'OKNO TASS No. 669/669A'[126] by Petr Shukhmin was published in Moscow on 20 February 1943, just weeks after this Soviet victory. A grim-faced Stalin appears amid a sea of soldiers, one of whom wields the protective palladium over all of them. The mood of the poster is serious and reflective. Despite victory in the battle, no one smiles, there is still much hardship ahead. The caption of the poster calls for the continuation of momentum: 'Under the banner of Lenin, under the leadership of Stalin, forward to the complete defeat of the German occupiers and their expulsion from our motherland!'

Many of the posters of 1943 continued on the same themes as those of 1942. The disembodied Stalin in the sky is employed in some posters, as in the 1943 poster by Vlasob' (Fig. 4.27) in which Stalin praises the Red Army for its battle victories, for defending peace and friendship, and for protecting construction. The text, in Russian and Azerbaijani,

---

125 *Pravda*, No. 310, 6 Nov. 1942.
126 For an image, see www.artic.edu/aic/collections/exhibitions/TASS/artwork/209848.

is from Stalin's Order of the Day, No. 95, 23 February 1943, the day of the Soviet victory in Stalingrad, and reflects increasing confidence in ultimate victory: 'During the war the Red Army personnel became a professional army. They learned how to defeat the enemy with a certain view of its strengths and weaknesses, as required by modern military science.' In this order Stalin describes the reversal of fortunes in the war, but warns against complacency, quoting Lenin: 'The first thing is not to be carried away by victory and not to get conceited; the second thing is to consolidate one's victory; the third thing is to finish off the enemy.' The Red Army's praises are sung again in a poster by Nikolai Zhukov and Viktor Klimashin[127] (Fig. 4.28) in which Soviet forces move forward into battle. With some victories finally in hand, the divisions advance under their identifying banners: the 331st Red Banner Smolensk Infantry Division ('Red Banner' was a special title given to Soviet armies after the award of the Order of the Red Banner); the 5th Guards Tank Corps Stalingrad (a 'Guards' army was an army that distinguished itself in the Great Patriotic War); and the Poltava Tank Regiment (instrumental in liberating the town of Poltava in September 1943). Ground forces are accompanied by ever-present aircraft in the skies, and all fly beneath a huge banner that is emblazoned with the profile portraits of Stalin and Lenin enclosed in a medallion.

In other posters, Stalin has been brought back to earth, while Lenin remains in the heavens, as in '"The spirit of the great Lenin and his invincible banner inspire us now in the patriotic war." (I. Stalin)' by People's Artist of the Soviet Union, Veniamin Pinchuk (Fig. 4.29). This poster visually references the 1942 Serov poster already discussed (Fig. 4.23), with minor but significant differences. Stalin appears before a chalky red banner, right arm outstretched and palm down in a gesture suggestive of blessing. Over his right shoulder is the ghostly head of Lenin. In these details the 1943 Pinchuk poster closely resembles the top half of the 1942 Serov poster. In the 1943 poster, the entire

---

127 Both Zhukov and Klimashin worked as military artists in the studio named after M. Grekov and also worked as artists on the battlefront. 'Klimashin Viktor Semenovich (1912–1960)' artgallery.krasno.ru/IMAGES/Grafics/Klimashin.htm (accessed 15 Aug. 2015). Zhukov was awarded People's Artist of the RSFSR (1955) and People's Artist of the USSR (1963) and was the winner of two Stalin Prizes, second degree (1943, 1951) ('Zhukov, Nikolai Nikolaevich', ru.wikipedia.org/wiki/%D0%96%D1%83%D0%BA%D0%BE%D0%B2,_%D0%9D%D0%B8%D0%BA%D0%BE%D0%BB%D0%B0%D0%B9_%D0%9D%D0%B8%D0%BA%D0%BE%D0%BB%D0%B0%D0%B5%D0%B2%D0%B8%D1%87 (accessed 15 Aug. 2015)).

bottom section of the poster — that unconventional section which shows the brutal slaying of the German enemy — has been removed. Both posters show a bust of Stalin; however, where in the 1942 poster his lower body had been dissolved in a bank of mist and battle smoke, the 1943 poster shows Stalin's body as solid to the edge of the image while his eyes directly engage the viewer.

A 1943 poster resembling a newspaper broadsheet was released by Smolgiz[128] in which the 'headline' confidently proclaims 'The Red Army crushes the enemy'. Beneath the headline is a small black-and-white portrait of Stalin and a textbox containing part of the text of the military order given by Stalin on 23 February 1943. A small banner at the top proclaims 'Death to the German occupiers!' The rest of the poster consists of documentary black-and-white photos of recent Soviet successes with explanatory captions. These captions read: 'Stalin falcons fly to perform a mission'; 'Soviet infantry storm the fascist hordes'; 'Glorious tank crews bravely advance on formidable enemy machines'; 'The heads of the fascists will come to grief on Cossack swords'; 'Our artillery is a devastating fire for the invaders'; 'Fritz Cemeteries in Vyazma. The same cemetery in Sychevka, Gzhatsk'; 'Hundreds of thousands of Nazi fighters captured by the advancing Red Army'; and 'Thousands of tanks, guns and vehicles seized from the Germans at Stalingrad'. Nothing in the poster overtly glorifies Stalin. The Red Army is given credit for its victories, and Stalin does not appear in the photographs below. His portrait is of modest proportions and merely accompanies his instructional words, identifying them with him and bolstering their legitimacy as an order to the troops and civilians.

In contrast, Koretskii's 1943 poster, 'On the joyous day of liberation …' (Fig. 3.13) lays responsibility for victory wholly at Stalin's feet. Stalin's portrait is hung in a 'Lenin corner' or 'Stalin room' as they were now sometimes called, with great reverence by a young, blond child who appears to be instructing his peasant family in the virtues of Stalin's beneficence. The little Russian boy represents the future of the motherland. Stalin is the glorious father who is to be venerated above all others. As art historian Erika Wolf observes: 'The family resembles the Holy Family, with a mother and child accompanied by

---

128 Smolensk publishing company.

an older and impotent man, akin to Saint Joseph. Stalin thus stands in as the absent father of the family, as well as the "father comrade" of the Soviet people.'[129] Stalin's portrait is soft and paternal and the icon's talismanic powers are juxtaposed with Soviet military success. The frame of the portrait balances the window frame through which a large red flag and some departing soldiers can be seen. The Red Army soldiers have restored peace and the village is intact and safe. Koretskii's poster celebrates the liberation of an occupied village and inspires the population with hope for victory in the war. The extensive text makes it clear who is responsible for the victory, and to whom a boundless and unpayable debt of gratitude is owed: 'On the joyous day of liberation from under the yoke of the German invaders the first words of boundless gratitude and love of the Soviet people are addressed to our friend and father Comrade Stalin — the organiser of our struggle for the liberation and independence of our homeland.' Stalin is addressed as 'friend and father' and does not yet appear in full military uniform. Despite being appointed marshal of the Soviet Union in 1943 and accepting the award of the Order of Suvorov, First Class, in November 1943,[130] he may still have been cautious about claiming military and strategic brilliance until ultimate victory was assured.

Stalin as marshal of the Soviet Union

One of the most significant developments in the image of Stalin as of the year 1944 is that, from this point on, he appears in the military uniform of the marshal of the Soviet Union.[131] As confidence in

---

129 Erika Wolf, *Koretsky: the Soviet photo poster: 1930–1984*, New York, The New Press, 2012.
130 The Order of Suvorov, created in July 1942, was awarded for exceptional leadership in combat operations.
131 In fact, the only poster from 1944 examined during my research that does not depict Stalin in marshal's uniform is a poster by Vasilii Nikolaev, published by Iskusstvo in Leningrad — 'Forward for the defeat of the German occupiers and their expulsion from the borders of our motherland!' This poster, for a Leningrad audience, must predate the lifting of the siege, as Vasilii Aleksandrovich Nikolaev died in Leningrad in 1943. The message of the poster encourages the population to defeat the German invaders and expel them from the motherland. Like its predecessors of the past two years, this poster places Stalin in the sky before a huge red banner, his right arm outstretched. His hand, palm down, both points the way forward and blesses the troops beneath him. The Soviet coat-of-arms, in gold on the red banner, almost forms a halo, and the sky is a golden colour reminiscent of the background in icons. Beneath the large banner is a line of soldiers stretching off into the distance, with the turrets of tanks visible above their heads. The soldiers are illumined by a golden glow over their heads, and above them, also stretching off into the infinite distance, is a row of red banners with golden medallions

ultimate victory increased, Stalin officially took his place as the head of the armed forces. Leningrad had been under a devastating siege by the Germans since 8 September 1941. This siege, which lasted 872 days and was one of the most destructive and costly in terms of loss of human life, was finally ended on 27 January 1944. A 1944 Tajik TASS poster followed closely on the heels of the lifting of the Leningrad blockade. The poster by Mikhail Karpenko[132] is dominated by a giant red head of Lenin, eyebrows furrowed, chin jutted forward, inspiring Stalin and the troops to victory. His broad red shoulders, which sit above the soldiers, have become the palladium that protects those rushing into battle. Stalin stands on the right side of the poster, his body oversized and powerful in his marshal's uniform, and his outstretched right arm points the way to victory. Beneath Lenin and Stalin, troops rush in to victory in an image that, with its sweeping lines to suggest rapid motion forward, is reminiscent of the 1942 poster by Pen Varlen (Fig. 4.22). The text, in Tajik and Russian, reads: 'Under the banner of Lenin, under the leadership of Stalin — forward to the complete defeat of the German invaders!' In Nina Vatolina's 1944 poster 'For our great motherland!' (Fig. 4.30), the familiar pairing of the profile portraits of Lenin and Stalin on a banner is employed once more. Here, although hatless, Stalin is now depicted wearing the collar of the marshal's uniform, rather than the large turned-down collar of his greatcoat.

While employing many familiar motifs, A.A. Babitskii's poster of 1944 (Fig. 4.31), shows an increase in confidence in ultimate victory. The ghostly head of Lenin on a large red banner dominates the sky; the sacred Spassky tower glows red-gold in the background; and a tank rushes forward to battle under the protective red banner. The giant figure of Stalin in his marshal's uniform dominates the poster, however here Stalin is not static and motionless, nor does he merely inspire from the sky. Stalin is rushing forward into battle, carrying a large map, the red territories showing the ground held by Soviet forces. Stalin is shown as a man of action and as an active participant in the battle — Stalin the military strategist! In the background is a little

---

with the hammer and sickle emblazoned on them. Fighter planes fly overhead and in the hazy background are the shimmering towers of the Kremlin, their red stars flashing and illuminating the sky. The mission — to defeat the Germans and expel them — is a sacred one. It is guided and blessed by Stalin, who hovers in the sky, dissolving above the row of banners.

132 For an image, see Aleksei Morozov, *Agit-Okna, Okna TASS, 1941–1945*, Moscow, Kontakt-Kultura, 2013, p. 435.

fireworks display — subtle and colourless as yet, but a precursor to what is to come. The caption of the poster makes it clear that Stalin is responsible for this latest positive turn of events — 'Under the leadership of Comrade Stalin, forward to complete victory over our enemy!'

The victorious Generalissimus

By 1945, after the surrender of Germany, Stalin could unequivocally claim victory for his troops and, with justification, lionise the Soviet role in the victory of the Allied forces. On 24 June 1945, Stalin and Marshal Zhukov stood atop Lenin's mausoleum and reviewed a parade of the Red Army. In a manner reminiscent of Kutuzov after the Patriotic (Napoleonic) War, captured German banners were thrown at Stalin's feet by the passing soldiers.[133] Victory in the Great Patriotic War was one of the greatest of Soviet achievements to be celebrated in posters and other forms of propaganda, and the image of Stalin as military genius and master tactician remained a prominent genre in his personality cult until his death in 1953. The writer Leonid Leonov wrote on 11 May 1945: 'This man defended not only our life and dignity, but the very title of the person, which fascism wished to take from us. And because of that, the first spring flowers, the first dawn light, the first sigh of joy go to him, to our Stalin!'[134] As in most other aspects of Soviet life, Stalin had been minutely involved in the conduct of the war, taking the final decisions on many military, political and diplomatic matters.[135] In June 1945, just weeks after the victory over Germany on 9 May, Stalin was awarded the Hero of the Soviet Union and, against his protestations,[136] the military rank of generalissimus. Despite Stalin's apparent modesty, Molotov claims that he changed

---

133 Deutscher, *Stalin*, p. 534.
134 Leonov, quoted in Brooks, *Thank you, Comrade Stalin!*, p. 192.
135 Deutscher, *Stalin*, p. 456.
136 Montefiore notes that Stalin's reply to the proposal by Koniev that he be made generalissimus was: 'Comrade Stalin doesn't need it ... Comrade Stalin has the authority without it. Some title you've thought up! Chiang Kai-Shek's a Generalissimo. Franco's a Generalissimo — fine company I find myself in!' (*Stalin*, pp. 504–05).

4. STALIN SAVES THE WORLD

after victory in the war: 'He became conceited, not a good feature in a statesman.'[137] Victory was celebrated exuberantly in posters, and Stalin was acclaimed for his role in this triumph.

In some posters this was done with some subtlety. Koretskii's 1945 poster 'Our banner is the banner of victory!'[138] celebrates the victory of the united Soviet people — the soldier, the munitions factory worker and the agricultural worker — although all appear to be ethnically Russian in this case. Although both military and civilian personnel contributed to this victory, it is the soldier's head that is wreathed by a victory laurel, and it is he who wields the protective banner, wearing decorations of the Order of the Great Patriotic War and the Order of Glory. Stalin and Lenin appear as small profile portraits in bas-relief on the banner that has protected the Soviet people. They too are framed by the victory laurel.

Similarly, Vladimir Kaidalov's 'Glory to the great heroic Red Army, defending the independence of our country and winning victory over the enemy!' (Fig. 4.32) pays tribute to the army, and features a line of heavily decorated personnel from the various military services, this time including women. The text of the poster is taken from Stalin's radio broadcast on 9 May, the day of the victory of the Soviet troops. In contrast to the generally subdued palettes and the stark black, white and reds of the war years, this poster is a riot of colour, with the Kremlin drenched in holy red surrounded by a brilliant sky full of fireworks. Once again, Lenin and Stalin appear in profile portrait on the banner that hovers protectively over all. The length of the portrait bust of both men extends to the high chest area, allowing Kaidalov to depict Lenin wearing a collar and tie, while Stalin is resplendent in his marshal's uniform with a chest full of war medals. Lenin's head sits at a peculiar and unnatural angle on his body, and the only reason for portraying Lenin in this way is to highlight the fact that he is dressed as a white collar worker, in direct contrast to the warrior Stalin.

---

137 F. Chuev, *Molotov remembers: inside Kremlin politics — conversations with Felix Chuev*, Albert Resis (ed.), Chicago, Terra Publishing Center as Sto sorok besed s Molotovym, Ivan R. Dee, Inc., 1993, p. 73.
138 For an image, see Erika Wolf, *Koretsky: the Soviet photo poster: 1930–1984*, The New Press, New York, 2012, p. 155.

THE PERSONALITY CULT OF STALIN IN SOVIET POSTERS, 1929-1953

It is interesting to note that, where soldiers and citizens appear in these immediate postwar posters, they all appear to be ethnically Russian. A TASS poster of 1945 No. 1291/1292[139] by Andrei Plotnov and Aleksandr Danilichev makes the association of victory with the Russian people explicit — 'Glory to the great Russian people!' The poster features the ubiquitous red banner with silhouette profiles of Lenin and Stalin[140] (both of whom are faceless in this poster) under which a soldier, a male worker, a female agricultural worker, and an old man stand, framing a plaque etched with the names of a number of great and famous Russians — Plekhanov, Lenin, Belinskii, Chernishevskii, Pushkin, Tolstoi, Glinka, Chaikovskii, Gor'kii, Chekhov, Sechenov, Pavlov, Repin, Surikov, Suvorov, and Kutuzov. Victory in the war had now become a Russian affair, and Russia was singled out as a 'big brother' and 'leader' in the family of nations that made up the Union of Soviet Socialist Republics. The text at the base of the poster continues its glorification of the heroic people who, in this case, are merely accompanied by Lenin and Stalin: 'Glory to the people, / Bulwark of the truth, / Glory to the people — a hero! / Your path is wide, / Your lot is high, / Lenin and Stalin are with you!'

Released in May 1945, TASS No. 1242, 'Long live the great organiser and inspirer of historic victory against German imperialism — our beloved leader and teacher Stalin!',[141] dates from the time of Allied victory and, like several other posters of that year, places the credit for that victory, as organiser and inspiration, with Stalin alone. TASS No. 1242 is one of 40 posters designed by Petr Shukhmin for TASS between 1941 and 1945, the period of Soviet involvement in the Great Patriotic War. Stalin's profile is emblazoned on a billowing banner with a gold aureole surrounding his head. The red flag, with its iconic emblem, flies over the nation once more. The red star, which crowns the Spassky tower, glows faintly gold, a beacon of hope in the dark sky, criss-crossed with coloured lights and fireworks. Stalin is still referred to in the text by the familiar epithets 'leader', 'teacher', 'organiser', 'inspirer', but now his profile displays the collar of his marshal's uniform and, primarily by visual association at this stage, the Warrior archetype is moving to prominence alongside the other existing archetypes of the personality cult.

---

139 For an image, see www.artic.edu/aic/collections/exhibitions/TASS/artwork/206075.
140 Stalin was, of course, Georgian, and Lenin had mixed ancestry.
141 For an image, see www.artic.edu/aic/collections/exhibitions/TASS/artwork/192613.

4. STALIN SAVES THE WORLD

This none-too-subtle promotion of the Warrior archetype is evident in posters of the time that apparently deal with other themes. The second election of candidates to the Supreme Soviet was held on 10 February 1946 and, as was the case in the historic first elections of 1937, even Stalin had to run for his own seat in the Moscow electoral district. In 1945 a poster campaign was launched that promoted Stalin's candidacy. Stepan Razvozzhaev's poster (Fig. 4.33), in the sacred colours of red and gold, contains many of the formulaic motifs of victory posters, although the text links the images firmly to Stalin's candidacy in the upcoming elections: 'Great Stalin — first deputy of the Supreme Soviet of the USSR'. A similar tactic is used in a poster released by Izdatelstvo Krasnyi Krym[142] (Fig. 4.34) around 1945,[143] captioned 'Long live the creator of the constitution of socialist society, the leader of the Soviet people, great Stalin!' In the poster, possibly produced as part of the electoral campaign, Stalin is lauded as the leader of the people and is depicted in marshal's uniform wearing a number of war medals.

In 1945, Stalin's role as hero and saviour of the nation was made even more explicit. Koretskii revisited his highly successful poster of 1943 (Fig. 3.13), made some notable alterations, and re-released it with a new caption just three days after the German surrender: 'The Soviet people are full of gratitude and love for dear STALIN — the great organiser of our victory' (Fig. 4.35). While the basic composition remains the same as that of 1943 — a young boy hangs an icon of Stalin on the wall of the family home — the scene outside the window, previously a scene of soldiers departing after making the village safe, has been replaced with a lush and blossoming orchard. The icon of Stalin has also changed. The humble, unassuming Stalin in his habitual tunic, the Stalin uncertain of ultimate victory, has been replaced with a portrait by Boris Karpov of Stalin in his marshal's regalia. Stalin looks stiff and proud, and does not look at the viewer. The use of the word *'rodnomu'* in the text continues the association of Stalin as the father of the Soviet peoples, while the marshal's uniform and the association of Stalin with victory facilitate the development of the Warrior archetype.

---

142 Izdatelstvo Red Crimea.
143 The poster itself has no date or year; however, the portrait of Stalin used in the poster is by Karpov and dated 1945.

The association of Stalin with the Warrior archetype is made most concrete with a sketched contribution by Deni (Fig. 4.36). Deni portrays Stalin with his usual sparse style in military uniform, this time without a multitude of medals or ornate braiding on the collar. According to Robert Service, Stalin felt that the title of generalissimus was too ostentatious and he refused to wear any of the new uniforms designed for this new rank, remaining in the uniform of the marshal of the Soviet Union. Stalin also asked Winston Churchill to call him marshal instead of generalissimus and frequently stated that the Red Army did not have a rank of generalissimus.[144] Stalin looks over his shoulder at the Kremlin, which flies a huge banner carrying the word 'Victory!'[145] It is the text that is most laudatory, occupying almost half of the poster area: 'Long live generalissimus STALIN — great leader and general of the Soviet people!'

In 1946 Stalin's modesty apparently prevailed and, although he is almost always depicted in marshal's uniform, regardless of the purpose of the poster,[146] the trimmings have been pared back. With one exception, the ornate gold braid on his collar either disappears or is replaced by a simple red strip, and the multitude of medals on his chest have disappeared. From this point on, the only medal Stalin wears is the Hero of Socialist Labour, a simple gold star containing the hammer and sickle emblem, dangling from a short red ribbon. The Hero of Socialist Labour was awarded for cultural and economic achievements, not military feats.

The sole exception I have discovered to this total paring back is a 1946 poster by Toidze (Fig. 4.37) which references the posters of the war years. Stalin appears in full ornamental braid amid a windswept sky, however he is wearing only two medals — the Hero of Socialist Labour and the Order of Lenin. He adopts the familiar static pose with outstretched right arm and extended index finger, but this time there is no gesture of benediction. Stalin clearly points the way forward, his head uplifted, his determined gaze directed at the future. Behind and beneath Stalin are the Soviet masses, a mix of military, urban workers, agricultural workers, men and women. In the deep

---

144 Robert Service, *Stalin: a biography*, Cambridge, Harvard University Press, 2005, p. 548.
145 *Pobeda!*
146 A large number of posters from this year which contain an image of Stalin are promoting his candidacy in the upcoming election or celebrating the 29th Anniversary of the October Revolution.

background an industrial complex puffs out smoke on the horizon. The people, who stretch as far back as the eye can see, are all travelling in the direction of Stalin's extended finger. The caption names the destination: 'Forward, to new victories of socialist construction!' and is reminiscent of the poster messages of the prewar years. In its black, white and red colour scheme (with touches of gold) this poster clearly references the tradition of the posters of the war years and is visually similar to Toidze's 1941 'All our forces ...' (Fig. 4.16) and his 1943 'Stalin will lead us to victory'.

After the war, the 'battle' was to continue on 'new fronts' and Stalin appeared in posters exhorting the public to keep making sacrifices in order to achieve full communism. The task of reconstruction after the Great Patriotic War was incredibly difficult. Official statistics list 70,000 villages, and 1,700 towns and cities in the Soviet Union as destroyed between 1941 and 1945.[147] Despite the generally festive air and visual implications of abundance of post-victory posters, hunger and hunger-related diseases took the lives of two million Soviet people in the famine of 1946–48.[148] Stalin's appearance in military uniform served as a reminder that he had already led the people to victory in the Great Patriotic War, while poster texts referred to 'new victories', 'victories of socialism', and 'new victories of socialist construction' as a reminder that Stalin had guided the nation to many victories over the years. The implications are that, with the successful achievement of socialism and victory over external foes in the war, the achievement of communism is now possible, and that it is imminent under the leadership of Stalin. Propaganda to mobilise the population for this task was particularly important because, as Robert Tucker points out, after the war the Soviet population were suffering from profound passivity and apathy:

> The root of the matter was not the incapacity of people to endure another season of privation, but rather the meaninglessness of the sacrifices they were called upon to make, the pointlessness of Russia's being in eternal conflict with the rest of the world, the total lack of prospect for tranquility in their time.[149]

---

147 James Aulich & Marta Sylvestrová, *Political posters in Central and Eastern Europe, 1945–95: signs of the times*, Manchester University Press, 1999, p. 129.
148 Brooks, *Thank you, Comrade Stalin!*, p. 196.
149 Robert C. Tucker, 'Stalin and the uses of psychology', *World Politics*, 8:4, 1956, pp. 455–83, p. 463.

THE PERSONALITY CULT OF STALIN IN SOVIET POSTERS, 1929–1953

Viktor Koretskii's '1917–1946 Glory to the Red Army, defending the gains of the great October socialist revolution!' (Fig. 4.38) of 1946 celebrates the history of the Red Army and juxtaposes the soldier of the Civil War (in *budenovka*, the pointed cap that was reminiscent of the dress of the *bogatyri*) with the soldier of the Great Patriotic War (in helmet). The arrangement of the soldiers in the foreground reflects the now habitual pairing above it, of Stalin and Lenin in bas-relief frieze. Just as Lenin led the cause in 1917 and the Civil War that followed, so Stalin led the population to victory in the Great Patriotic War and continues to lead the population to both the victory of communism and victory over the regime's enemies. Stalin, Lenin and the Red Army share credit for the war victory and for the victories of socialism.

One of Toidze's 1946 contributions (Fig. 4.39) credits the Party with victory in a poster laden with sacred overtones. The poster is dominated by the figure of the Rodina,[150] wielding a huge banner with the cameo images of Lenin and Stalin in profile enclosed in a gold medallion, and a bunch of flowers — symbol of fertility, abundance and celebration. The Rodina is serene and maternal with an ample bosom and wide hips. She is also like the Virgin in the icon, her banner serving the same protective function as the Virgin's veil. Behind the Rodina the background consists purely of rays of light and the colour scheme, rich reds and golds, is reminiscent of the icon. The text at the base of the poster reads 'Long live the V.K.P.(b) — the party of Lenin–Stalin, inspirer and organiser of our great victories!' Despite Stalin's apparent modesty in both his choice to retain the marshal's uniform and in allowing the Party and the army to be credited with victory in the war, the production of personality cult posters celebrating his leadership flourished in 1946. For example, Ukraine publisher Mistetstvo published a poster by Onufriichuk with the caption 'Long live the leader of the Soviet people — great Stalin!' (Fig. 4.40) in which a gold-tinged Stalin in marshal's uniform gazes out at the viewer, framed by oak and laurel leaves against a red background.

After several years of aborted attempts to get an appropriate biography of Stalin into the public domain, *Joseph Stalin: a short biography* was finally published in 1947.[151] In terms of Stalin's Warrior archetype,

---

150 Personification of the motherland.
151 See Chapter Two.

4. STALIN SAVES THE WORLD

the biography states that Tsaritsyn was saved due to 'Stalin's iron will and masterly foresight';[152] that Lenin conferred with Stalin on all major matters of military policy, strategy and tactics;[153] that Stalin confounded the 'military "science", "art" and "training" of the enemy';[154] that the Bolshevik Party, headed by Lenin and Stalin, created the Red Army;[155] and that Stalin alone was responsible for inspiring and organising the subsequent victories of the Red Army, having assumed leadership responsibilities once Lenin had become ill.[156] Despite the laudatory tone of the biography, the state archives reveal that the published version was substantially pared back by Stalin. His criticism of the version proposed for publication in 1946 was directed at biographers making exorbitant claims for the singularity of Stalin's role: 'It's as if [Stalin] arrived and did everything on his own. There were many people and they ought to have been listed'.[157] Stalin asked for a greater cast of characters to be added to the sections on the war, specifically those who 'gathered around the Supreme Command'.[158] Stalin's biography was able to stand as a legitimator of his rule, with Lenin's cult and his role in Bolshevik victories sliding ever further into the background. Lenin still appeared in posters as the saintly creator of the new order, but it was Stalin who was now to be seen as the leader responsible for the victories of the Party and state across a wide variety of fields of achievement.

The iconic treatment of the military portrait of Stalin became an important genre in 1947, with a number of posters produced wishing long life or glory to Stalin as the leader of the Soviet people. Mukhin (Figs 4.41 and 4.42), and the Pravdin and Denisov team (Fig. 4.43) both produced posters that focused on a framed military portrait of Stalin with the caption 'Long live the leader of the Soviet people, great Stalin!', while Georgii Bakhmutov, who was awarded the Order of the Great Patriotic War Medal, produced a similar poster in the Ukrainian

---

152 G.F. Alexandrov, M.R. Galaktionov, V.S. Kruzhkov, M.B. Mitin, V.D. Mochalov & P.N. Pospelov, *Joseph Stalin: a short biography*, Moscow, Foreign Languages Publishing House, 1947, p. 61.
153 Alexandrov et al., *Joseph Stalin*, p. 68.
154 Alexandrov et al., *Joseph Stalin*, p. 69.
155 Alexandrov et al., *Joseph Stalin*, p. 70.
156 Alexandrov et al., *Joseph Stalin*, pp. 70, 75.
157 RGASPI f. 629, op. 1, d. 54, 1.25, cited in David Brandenberger, 'Stalin as symbol: a case study of the personality cult and its construction', in Davies & Harris, *Stalin*, p. 266.
158 RGASPI f. 629, op. 1, d. 54, 1.26, cited in Brandenberger, 'Stalin as symbol' in Davies & Harris, *Stalin*, pp. 266–67.

language with the caption 'Glory to the leader of the Soviet people — great Stalin!' (Fig. 4.44). Stalin also makes a military appearance in posters encouraging the people to go forward to the victory of communism[159] and to increase their knowledge and study patiently.[160]

In 1947, Nikolai Bulganin succeeded Stalin in the role of minister of the armed forces and Victory Day was made an ordinary working day, remaining so until 1965. Posters appeared on a variety of themes, although victory in the war continued to be celebrated. Aleksandr Druzhkov and I. Shagin's 'Stalin is our fighting banner!' (Fig. 4.45) of 1948 cements the identification of Stalin with the protective banner over the motherland and the three flags of the army, navy and airforce. Mukhin's 'Glory to great Stalin!' (Fig. 4.46) features an icon-like portrait of Stalin enclosed in an oval medallion surrounded by hagiographic scenes of Stalin's life as a warrior and the three banners of the armed forces. The mid-section of the poster features painted scenes from life. On the left Stalin is instructing the soldiers in the trenches during the Civil War,[161] and on the right, Stalin is pictured, pipe in mouth and hand-in-jacket, in his office with Aleksandr Mihailovich Vasilevskii[162] during the Great Patriotic War. The lower portion of the poster depicts a military parade in Red Square in front of Lenin's mausoleum. The socialist realist style of painting in these scenes gives them a historical-factual air, suggesting that these events really happened. As in the posters of the preceding years, Stalin is portrayed as having a military biography that extends back to the days of the Civil War, and which has always brought success.

A 1948 poster by N. Petrov (Fig. 4.47) shows Stalin in uniform seated at his desk, wholly absorbed in writing in a large book. Behind him, the Spassky tower juts into a hazy sky, the red star atop the steeple blazing like a beacon, even in daylight. On the top right is a simple framed portrait of Lenin, Stalin's teacher and inspiration. The text of the poster quotes Molotov's speech of 7 November 1945, which credits

---

159 For example, Petr Grechkin, 'Under the banner of Lenin, under the leadership of Stalin — forward to the new successes of the Soviet motherland, to the full victory of communism in our country!', 1947.
160 For example, Ruben Shkhiyan', '"In order to build, we need to know, we need to master science and to know, to learn, to study hard, patiently". I. Stalin', 1947.
161 The caption reads 'Civil War. I.V. Stalin at Tsaritsyn'.
162 Vasilevskii was the chief of the General Staff of the Soviet Armed Forces and deputy minister of defence during the Great Patriotic War, and was made marshal of the Soviet Union in 1943.

Stalin with victory in the war. By putting the attribution of credit for victory to Stalin into the mouth of Molotov, Stalin can retain his personal modesty. It is interesting to note that, while the poster is in full colour, featuring soft pastel hues, Stalin is in black-and-white, except for his military insignia. His hair and flesh are in grayscale, as is Lenin's portrait in the background. Druzhkov and Shagin's poster, mentioned above, also shows Stalin in grayscale amid the bright colours of the banners that form the backdrop. Many, although certainly not all, posters depict Stalin as a photograph, a cameo, or a sketch, often amid an otherwise colourful and 'realistic' background. This tactic seems to support the idea that, although Stalin acts in the real world, he is not a real man, made of flesh and blood, but an image and symbol, whose presence in the poster stands for a number of other referenced qualities and values.

Three posters of 1948 lay credit for victory at the feet of the Party: B.I. Lebedev's 'Long live the V.K.P.(b) inspirer and organiser of the victory of the Soviet people!' (Fig. 4.48), F. Litvinov's 'Long live the party of Lenin-Stalin, inspirer and organiser of our victories!' (Fig. 4.49) and Druzhkov's 'Long live the VKP(b). The party of Lenin–Stalin, battle-seasoned vanguard of the Soviet people, inspirer and organiser of our victories!' (Fig. 4.50). In these posters the victory theme has expanded to encompass military victory in the Great Patriotic War and the multitude of other victories of the Soviet people — victories in industry, agriculture, construction and aviation.

In 1950 the focus continued to move away from the war and military battles, and onto other 'fronts'. These new fronts may be specifically named, as in Vladislav Pravdin's 'To the new achievements of soviet aviation!' (Fig. 3.19) and Kaidalov's Uzbek 'We will struggle to reap a big cotton harvest! (Fig. 4.51), or come under the more general umbrella of the 'Victory of communism' — Iosif Ganf's pared-back format and shortened slogan, 'Forward to communism!' is almost an abbreviated shorthand for this somewhat overworked theme. Boris Belopol'skii gives the slogan a slight twist and reinforces the increasingly dogmatic nature of Stalin's words by showing Stalin speaking at a podium and featuring a quotation from Stalin's Report to the Eighteenth Party Congress on 10 March 1939 — '"We move further, forward towards Communism." I.V. Stalin' — in which Stalin examines the successes of the socialist phases of Soviet society and maps out the route to be taken to full communism. Stalin's Warrior archetype is hence extended to all of the other battlefronts on which he leads the Soviet people.

Stalin: man of peace

Once victory celebrations had quietened, the task of rebuilding and getting back on track to the ultimate goal of communism moved to the forefront of propaganda. Alongside this, from 1947, was an attempt to merge Stalin's Warrior archetype into that of the Saviour by presenting him as the bringer of peace. A 1947 poster by Boris Berezovskii (Fig. 4.52) shows Stalin conspicuously out of military uniform as he proclaims the Soviet desire for peace — '"We stand for peace and we defend the cause of peace." I. Stalin', a quotation taken from Stalin's report to the Seventeenth Party Congress on the work of the Central Committee, 26 January 1934. Stalin appears softer, rounder and more genial than in most of the contemporaneous posters and, by wearing his pre-Victory plain tunic, plays down the Warrior archetype that is so prevalent in the other posters.

Toidze created two posters in 1947 which are laden with symbolism for the initiated.[163] In one (Fig. 4.53), Stalin stands in three-quarter view before a large red banner bearing the portrait frieze of Lenin. His left hand rests on the familiar red marble of Lenin's mausoleum, his right hand is raised in the air, as if taking an oath. This image immediately invokes Stalin's oration at Lenin's funeral in which he took a series of oaths, on behalf of the people, to carry on Lenin's work. The caption '"Long life and prosperity to our motherland!" I. Stalin', is from the final words of a speech that would have been immediately recognisable to the Russian people — Stalin's address to the nation on 2 September 1945 in which the unconditional surrender of Japan was announced, finally ending all Soviet war engagements.[164] The text of the speech was printed in *Pravda* on the following day.[165] The symbolism of the

---

163 'Stalin's kindness illuminates the future of our children!' (Fig. 3.2) is discussed in Chapter Three and also later in this chapter.
164 I.V. Stalin, 'Obrashcheniye k narodu 2 sentyabrya 1945 goda,' www.marxists.org/russkij/stalin/t15/t15_73.htm (accessed 29 Jul. 2013).
165 In the rest of the speech Stalin outlines the long history of Japanese aggression towards Russia and the Soviet Union and proclaims the war over and the nation at peace at last.

4. STALIN SAVES THE WORLD

poster suggests that Stalin has fulfilled his sacred vow to Lenin, by bringing peace to the nation, and also that the rest of the promised work to bring communism to the nation can continue.

By 1950, the only victory referenced in most posters of Stalin was the victory of communism and Stalin's propagandists were taking increasing pains to promote his image as a man of peace. The election propaganda of 1950 focused on Stalin as the creator of the constitution and as a friend of all peoples, rather than as victorious warrior. Stalin had proposed a 'peace-pact' between the USSR and the United States in January 1949 and a World Congress of Peace Advocates met in Paris in April of that year. The World Peace Council was set up by the VKP(b) in 1950 to promote peace and disarmament on an international scale. The Soviet Union sponsored many of the world's peace movements during the years of the Cold War and a concerted propaganda effort was made to portray the Soviet Union as the peace-loving victim of capitalist aggressive tactics.[166]

Viktor Ivanov's 1950 poster captures Stalin the peacemaker in his pristine marshal's uniform before a billowing red banner (Fig. 4.54). Stalin, looking out of the poster as if lost in contemplation, holds an edition of *Pravda*. The headline states 'The Soviet people vote for peace!' This makes a tidy symbolic reference to the 1950 election and suggests that a vote for Stalin is indeed a vote for peace. Just in case the message isn't clear enough, it is emblazoned across the banner in large gold letters — 'For peace!' — and once again in the caption: 'Stalin is our great standard-bearer of peace!' The banner, which fills more than half of the poster, billows as if in a fresh wind — the winds of change — to reveal a pale blue sky and huge white sun radiating beams of light.

Koretskii's 1950 'Great Stalin is the banner of friendship of the peoples of the USSR!' (Fig. 4.55) promotes Stalin as a unifier and saviour of the people. A smiling Stalin in marshal's uniform stands above the multinational crowd, looking down on them with paternal affection. In the background there are 16 flags, representing the 16 republics of

---

[166] As Jan Behrends observes: 'In the Stalinist peace narrative, it was the Soviet leader who prevented the outbreak of yet another world war, which was pursued by the "Anglo-American warmongers" and their "German henchman"' ('Exporting the leader: the Stalin cult in Poland and East Germany' in Balázs Apor, Jan C. Behrends, Polly Jones & E.A. Rees, *The leader cult in communist dictatorships: Stalin and the Eastern Bloc*, Hampshire, Palgrave, 2004, p. 171).

the federation.[167] The people pay floral tribute to Stalin, and the poster merges the archetypes of Warrior, Father, and Saviour. Petr Golub's poster of 1950 (Fig. 4.56) takes an audacious step further. In his white marshal's uniform, Stalin's figure fills the picture plane. His right arm points the way to a future of victorious communism and a young man and woman gaze, as in a trance, in the direction he indicates. The young man wears a suit and tie and the young woman wears the blouse of a national costume. She holds a bunch of carnations that are not offered to Stalin, and probably signify postwar abundance. The caption, which must have been particularly galling to the Latvian people,[168] states 'Great Stalin is the best friend of the Latvian people!'

Two posters of 1952 by Belopol'skii address the peace theme, one which features Stalin in military uniform, the other without. '"We stand for peace and we defend the cause of peace." I. Stalin' (Fig. 4.57) features a large red banner as a backdrop with Stalin, in marshal's uniform, standing in front of, but isolated from, a thronging crowd. The diagonal crowd filling the space suggests the movement of a never-ending river of people, and is reminiscent of the posters of the mid-1930s, although now it is no longer just the Soviet people who are giving their thanks and support to the great man, but the people of the whole world. Stalin gazes into the utopian future. He holds a pencil and a piece of paper; however, the pencil is not held in the manner in which one holds it for writing, but flat between the thumb and index finger with the tip pointing out at the viewer. It looks as if the pencil is being used as a conductor's baton, or even as a wand. This unusual gesture incorporates the suggestions that Stalin is the author of the document he is holding, which is probably some sort of declaration, that he is the orchestrator of this great mass movement, and also that he is the bearer of magic powers — a magician. This is one of the few instances I have found in posters containing Stalin's image in which the archetype of the Magician is employed, although one could argue that Stalin is associated with magical properties, such as control over

---

167 In September 1939 the number of republics in the Soviet Union increased from 11 to 16 — Russia, Ukraine, Belarus, Georgia, Armenia, Azerbaijan, Turkmenistan, Uzbekistan, Tajikistan, Kazakhstan, Kyrgyzstan, Moldavia, Finland, Latvia, Lithuania, and Estonia. The Baltic states (Latvia, Lithuania and Estonia) had been incorporated into the USSR under the Molotov–Ribbentrop pact in 1939, then occupied by the Germans in June 1941, before being 'liberated' by the Soviets in 1944.
168 The poster was published in Moscow and Leningrad in the Russian language and was most likely intended for a Russian audience.

4. STALIN SAVES THE WORLD

the elements and spiritual powers, in the visual symbolism of some of the posters produced by Toidze, and is depicted with talismanic and spiritual–inspirational properties in a number of posters. Although many of the epithets of the cult ascribe superhuman or supernatural qualities to the Stalin persona, it is only on comparatively rare occasions that the visual symbolism makes this so explicit. Stalin's figure in this poster is strangely elongated, making him appear taller and slimmer than is usually the case.

Belopol'skii's second poster on this theme, one in which Stalin appears shorter and more squat in his plain tunic, is captioned '"The world will be saved and enhanced if people take responsibility for maintaining peace into their own hands and defend it to the end." I. Stalin' (Fig. 4.58), with the words 'Peace to all nations!' inscribed in the background at the top of the poster. The caption comes from 'A conversation with the correspondent of *Pravda*' on 17 February 1951.[169] In contrast to the other Belopol'skii poster, there is no background – no banner, no crowd, just light. Stalin leans on a textbox bearing his own words and is greyer in skin and hair, and softer and more rounded, than in the other poster. His left hand rests on a copy of *Pravda,* while his right hand points loosely in the direction of the future, on which his transcendent gaze is also focused. This is a quieter, softer Stalin, the teacher or wise man who neither commands nor exhorts.

Stalin's military victory in the Great Patriotic War proved to be the ultimate tool in shoring up legitimacy for his leadership. As a result of this victory, the Soviet sphere of influence extended beyond the nation's prewar borders to include much of the territory of Eastern Europe. Molotov recalls that Stalin was in fact planning on retiring after the war, saying at an informal dinner: 'Let Vyacheslav take over now. He is younger.' Stalin apparently changed his mind after Churchill's 'Iron Curtain' speech of March 1946.[170]

While legitimacy was at its zenith in the home territories, there was an urgent need to gain legitimacy in the newly occupied territories. Highlighting the image of the victorious warrior in countries that

---

169 I.V. Stalin, 'A conversation with the *Pravda* correspondent', *Pravda*, 17 Feb. 1951, www.marxists.org/russkij/stalin/t16/t16_29.htm (accessed 04 Aug. 2013). This speech was printed but was not actually delivered publicly as a speech.
170 Derek Watson, *Molotov: a biography*, Hampshire, Macmillan, 2005, p. 235.

had been defeated by the Soviet Union would have been insensitive and counterproductive. It was essential that Stalin, and the system of government and regime for which he was a symbol, be presented as liberators who saved the world from fascism.[171] Presenting Stalin as a saviour imbued his persona with sacral and quasi-religious overtones, although these had been present in his cult from the late 1930s and were likely inevitable consequences of the nature of Bolshevism as a political religion, the cult of personality, the use of mythic archetypes to create a persona for Stalin, and the use of the Stalin symbol to represent both abstracts such as Bolshevik ideals and Marxist vision, and concrete entities like the Party, the state and the nation.

Stalin as icon

It has already been noted that while Stalin was not portrayed in posters as 'performing miracles' in the way of Christ, pictorial elements of some poster images conveyed a sense that he was able to harness superhuman or supernatural elements. This was particularly the case in some images on the battlefield, where clouds broke apart above Stalin's head, formed a fist, or swirled turbulently alongside the thundering troops led by Stalin, and where a gigantic Stalin in the sky appeared as if sanctifying Soviet troops, but was also a feature of more 'mundane' matters, such as the 'transformation of nature', the transformation into the new Soviet man and even the 'engineering of souls' by writers who were, in turn, taught and led by Stalin. Stalin was depicted as being atemporal and ubiquitous, as magically appearing where he was most needed, and as concerning himself (like Christ) with the personal matters of the 'little people'. Natalia Skradol has analysed reminiscences of encounters with Stalin for mythopoetic and folklorish elements, and quotes a number of such reminiscences in which people attribute healing knowledge and abilities to Stalin, and the ability to make the impossible come true.[172]

---

171 It is beyond the scope of this book to examine the nuances of either the Stalin cult or local leader cults in the Warsaw Pact countries. This subject is tackled extensively in Apor et al., *The leader cult in communist dictatorships*.

172 Natalia Skradol, 'Remembering Stalin: mythopoetic elements in memories of the Soviet dictator,' *Totalitarian Movements and Political Religions*, 2009, 10:1, pp. 19–41.

This phenomenon is not unique to the Stalin cult and draws on a long Russian tradition of attributing special knowledge to the tsars. The tsar was regarded as divinely instituted and fused both secular and spiritual power in his sacred personage. For example, Mikhail Bakunin said of the tsar that he is 'the ideal of the Russian people, he is a kind of Russian Christ'.[173] On hearing of the death of Nicholas I the poet Fiodor Tiutchev remarked 'it is as if one had been told that God is dead',[174] a sentiment that was echoed en masse at the time of the death of Stalin. Old Believers described the death of Tsar Aleksandr II as a second crucifixion, and similar statements to this were made when Lenin died.[175] In fact, the writers Andrei Belii, Aleksandr Blok, Sergei Esenin and Nikolai Kliuev all linked the October Revolution to the second coming of Christ.[176] Tsardom was not seen as an unequivocal blessing, but also as a burden. In the 16th century the tsar was perceived as being obligated to intercede with Christ for the souls of his subjects, while 19th-century, writer Ivan Aksakov referred to tsardom as a penance.[177] Jan Plamper cites an incident that provides a somewhat surprising parallel, in which, after Stalin's death, a woman cut his portrait from the paper and placed it in the Bible, explaining to her son[178] that 'Stalin took on his soul everybody else's sins, that everyone is going to criticize him now and that someone has to pray for him'.[179] There is also a long history, particularly amongst Western monarchs, of associating magical healing abilities with the king, and this political symbolism influenced the Russian tsars, and was carried over into the personas of charismatic leaders. Napoleon was shown as a healer and saviour in history paintings.[180] Lenin was depicted as having magical abilities, particularly after his death, including the

---

173 Mikhail Bakunin, quoted in Michael Cherniavsky, *Tsar and people: studies in Russian myths*, New Haven, Yale University Press, 1961, p. 179.
174 Fiodor Tiutchev, quoted in Cherniavsky, *Tsar and people*, p. 178.
175 Cherniavsky, *Tsar and people*, p. 188.
176 Mark D. Steinberg, 'Workers on the Cross: religious imagination in the writings of Russian workers, 1910–1924', *Russian Review*, 53:2, 1994, pp. 213–39, p. 216.
177 'The Russian Tsar with his innate, hereditary power is not ambitious or power-mad: power, for him, is a penance and a burden; to be tsar is a true sacrifice [*podvig*]' (quoted in Cherniavsky, *Tsar and people*, pp. 183–84). Nina Tumarkin argues that even after the secularisation of the monarchy under Peter the Great, the people (*narod*) still clung to their pre-Petrine beliefs in relation to the tsar (*Lenin lives! The Lenin cult in Soviet Russia*, Cambridge University Press, 1997, p. 7).
178 The future dissident Aleksandr Zinoviev.
179 Quoted in Plamper, *The Stalin cult*, p. 226.
180 See Christopher Prendergast, *Napoleon and history painting: Antoine-Jean Gros's La Bataille d'Eylau*, Oxford, Clarendon Press, 1997, esp. Chapter Four.

ability to come back to life and walk the earth.[181] In the years after Stalin, in Communist China it was taught that the correct application of Maoist thought could lead to miracles in 'every human activity and condition, such as curing cancer, healing deaf-mutes, and improving labor productivity and human understanding'.[182] In Cuba, Fidel Castro was viewed as a saviour sent from heaven, with one Presbyterian minister proclaiming: 'It is my conviction which I state now with full responsibility for what I am saying, that Fidel Castro is an instrument in the hands of God for the establishment of His reign among men.'[183]

In addition to such historical precedents for endowing the leader with superhuman or supernatural abilities, the Soviet people had a culturally specific tradition on which to draw for representations of unearthly power — the Russian Orthodox icon.[184] Ancient Rus' converted to Orthodox Christianity in the 10th century and inherited an icon tradition from Byzantium, which gradually developed local features and a tradition of its own. By the end of the 17th century, under the westernising influence of the Romanovs, the icon tradition began to lose its distinctly Russian character and to show the influences of Western art. In the late 19th century there was a revival of interest in the specifically Russian tradition of icon painting, and many icons, blackened by age, varnish and soot in the Church, were restored to their original state. Many of the avant-garde artists of the turn of the century were interested in returning to indigenous artistic forms and the tradition of icon painting had always been central to Russian art.[185] After the October Revolution, Kazimir Malevich, who held the essence of the icon to be central to his work at all stages of his

---

181 See Tumarkin, *Lenin lives!*, pp. 198–99.
182 A. James Melnick, 'Soviet perceptions of the Maoist cult of personality', *Studies in Comparative Communism*, 9:1–2, 1976, pp. 129–44, p. 133.
183 Richard R. Fagen, 'Charismatic authority and the leadership of Fidel Castro', *The Western Political Quarterly*, 18:2, part 1, 1965, pp. 275–84, p. 278.
184 Excellent sources on the Russian icon include Léonide Ouspensky & Vladimir Lossky, *The meaning of icons*, 2nd edn, Crestwood, St. Vladimir's Seminary Press, 1982; Andrew Spira, *The avant-garde icon: Russian avant-garde art and the icon painting tradition*, Aldershot, Lund Humphries/Ashgate, 2008; and, N.G. Bekeneva, *The icon collection in the Tretyakov Gallery*, Moscow, SkanRus, 2011.
185 Artists like Kazimir Malevich, Aleksandr Rodchenko, Natalia Goncharova, Mikhail Larionov, Wassilii Kandinskii, Vladimir Tatlin, Kliment Redko and the Hungarian Bela Uitz, among others, all showed the influence of the icon in their works. As Andrew Spira has noted: 'Throughout the period leading up to the Russian Revolution, icons provided a meaningful and legitimising precedent for almost every aspect of the new avant-garde art; its stylised visual languages, its sense of national identity, its universal social application, its physical materiality, its functionality and the irrelevance of self-expression' (*The avant-garde icon*, p. 120).

artistic career, employed his artwork in the service of the Revolution and the new regime. Poster artists like Moor and Deni also noted the influence of icons on their graphic work. These influences were passed on through the teaching careers of these men: for example, Malevich taught Gustav Klutsis, who subsequently taught colour theory at VKhUTEMAS (Higher Art and Technical Studios); and Moor taught the Kukryniksy, Dolgorukov and Aleksandr Deineka, all leading artists of their times.

Despite Bolshevik hostility to religion, which included the outlawing of religious practice, the burning of icons, the tearing down of churches, and the exile and murder of priests, many of the formal elements of the icon were used by artists of the regime in their propaganda work. As Andrew Spira notes: 'icons continued to be invoked — partly ridiculed, partly exploited — in the early Soviet period. Initially it was the narrative and didactic conventions of icon painting, subliminally associated with the transmission of truth by the Russian people, which were harnessed to the new ideology.'[186] Léonide Ouspensky notes that the art of the icon was 'intended not to reflect the problems of life but to answer them, and thus, from its very inception, is a vehicle of the Gospel teaching'.[187] In a similar manner, the Stalinist propaganda poster did not reflect the problems that beset the troubled regime, but portrayed them as already solved and, through the use of slogans and pictorial demonstration, portrayed the correct attitudes and demeanours by which obstacles were overcome and positive outcomes attained.

By Stalin's time, some of the forms and conventions of icon painting were employed not only for didactic purposes, but also in portrayals of the leader — without overt satirical intent. The nuances of these quasi-sacred portrayals of Stalin were not lost on people who had been raised in the tradition of engaging with icons. Images that may look similar to the uninitiated often contained subtle references to or, indeed, divergences from the canon, which would be immediately apprehended and understood by a viewer habituated by a lifetime of viewing such images. In fact, as Spira suggests, the acute interest of Stalin's regime in classical conditioning, as demonstrated by Ivan

---

186 Spira, *The avant-garde icon*, p. 10.
187 Ouspensky & Lossky, *The meaning of icons*, p. 27.

Pavlov's[188] work with dogs, meant that 'the associative power of certain physiological aspects of icon-veneration was known to be familiar and effective and it was put to new use'.[189]

The icon was a visual form that was not restricted to serving an elite, and was as available to the peasant as to the boyar. Before the Revolution, almost all Russian homes had an icon corner. The Bolsheviks established Red corners as early as 1921, which, after Lenin's death, became Lenin corners and then, in some cases, Stalin rooms. There is much evidence that Stalin's portrait was often treated like an icon. Ilia Ehrenburg noted in his memoirs that the soldiers on the front 'fervently' believed in Stalin, cutting his photograph out of newspapers or *Ogonyok*[190] and pasting it to the walls of the ruins of Berlin.[191] Plamper notes that, just as icons in the home were often covered during spousal arguments to 'block the saint's gaze', a group of war veterans turned a portrait of Stalin to face the wall when they wished to discuss their true feelings about the war.[192] Sarah Davies' research into popular opinion in Stalin's Russia found considerable evidence that people treated the portraits of Stalin and the other leaders as icons, cutting them out, pasting them up on walls, and praying to them. Davies notes that this was viewed by Party agitators as a negative practice and a distortion of official policy.[193]

---

188 Rosa Ferré notes that Lenin was influenced by Ivan Sechenov's work on conditioned reflexes and both he and Stalin gave protection to Sechenov's disciple, Pavlov, despite Pavlov's anti-Soviet stance ('Time is accelerating', in Rosa Ferré, *Red cavalry: creation and power in Soviet Russia from 1917 to 1945: 07.10.2011 – 15.01.2012*, Madrid, La Casa Encendida, 2011, pp. 46–94, p. 68).
189 Spira, *The avant-garde icon*, p. 192.
190 *Little Flame*, a weekly illustrated magazine.
191 Ehrenburg, *Men, years — life*, vol. 5.
192 Plamper, *The Stalin cult*, pp. xvi, xiv. Czeslaw Milosz quotes the example of one man who consulted a portrait of Stalin to request guidance: 'I approached Stalin's portrait, took it off the wall, placed it on the table and, resting my head on my hands, I gazed and meditated. What should I do? The Leader's face, as always so serene, his eyes so clear-sighted, they penetrate into the distance. It seems that his penetrating look pierces my little room and goes out to embrace the entire globe. I do not know how I would appear to anyone looking at me at this moment. But with my every fiber, every nerve, every drop of my blood I felt that, at this moment, nothing exists in this entire world but this dear and beloved face. What should I do?' (*The captive mind*, Jane Zielonk (trans.), New York, Knopf, 1953, p. 149). Jiehong Jiang reports an interesting ritualised parallel to this in the cult of Mao Zedong. In public interiors Mao portraits were placed high at the centre of a main wall. In the mornings workers came and asked the portrait for political instructions and at night they reported back to the portrait on their progress (*Red: China's cultural revolution*, London, Jonathan Cape, 2010, p. 60).
193 Davies, *Popular opinion in Stalin's Russia*, pp. 163–64.

Aside from the fact that both the icon and the propaganda poster were egalitarian artforms accessible to the masses, icon painting also had in common with posters of Stalin that they were part of what Ouspensky refers to, in relation to church architecture, painting, music, and poetry, as a 'liturgic whole': 'From forms of art with separate aims, they all become transformed into varied means for expressing, each in its own domain, one and the same thing — the essence of the Church. In other words, they become various instruments of the knowledge of God.'[194] This is close to the Bolshevik conception of the uses and functions of art in which all forms of art are harnessed towards the one overriding goal of mobilising the population for the achievement of communism. In addition, in both icons and posters of Stalin there existed a strict canon that did not tolerate subjectivity or divergence. Iconography was regulated by *podlinniki*,[195] while official guidelines, publications like *Iskusstvo*, and the existence of a set of approved images of Stalin, regulated and formalised the way in which Stalin could be portrayed. Both icons and posters of Stalin functioned as didactic artforms, rather than being prized for aesthetic value alone, and both featured idealised subjects rather than aiming at mimetic verisimilitude.

In the Orthodox tradition, Christ's authentic image was the *mandylion*, or image 'not made by human hands', and all subsequent images were based on this miraculous image of Christ on the cloth. Stalin's image was carefully constructed by human hands, and a small canon of officially approved images became the source material upon which all subsequent images were based. While it is true that portrait painters and graphic artists did have access to photographic images of Stalin from which to create his image, these were centrally controlled and usually heavily retouched. Plamper notes that, until 1937, when the first Stalin movie was released, press photos, most of which appeared first in *Pravda*,[196] were the 'master medium' for the canonisation of Stalin's image.[197] Stalin is not known to have sat for any portraits during the 1930s,[198] and there were few occasions on which portrait artists

---

194 Ouspensky & Lossky, *The meaning of icons*, pp. 30–31.
195 Manuals of iconography.
196 By early 1930 the circulation of *Pravda* was already one million (Matthew Lenoe, *Closer to the masses: Stalinist culture, social revolution, and Soviet newspapers*, Cambridge, Harvard University Press, 2004, p. 17).
197 Plamper, *The Stalin cult*, p. 31.
198 Plamper, *The Stalin cult*, pp. 141–42.

could get close enough to Stalin to make good sketches.[199] The painter Evgeni Katsman complained about this to Voroshilov as Stalin's 60th birthday approached:

> <u>Let us begin with the main thing</u>. There is no Stalin portrait from life. We need one! This has to be done all the more since Joseph Vissarionovich in life is so expressive and beautiful. We must depict J.V. the way he is. We owe this to history. We owe this to the peoples. We owe this to Soviet art and science ... If we accomplish this I will also paint J.V. from life — that will be the high point of my life and the good fortune of an artist.[200]

The process of photographic retouching removed pockmarks, wrinkles and uneven colourations from Stalin's skin, transfiguring his flesh into an unearthly perfection. In posters where Stalin is either portrayed as the source of light, or is lit from above, a further transformation occurs. Stalin's image comprised a set of key features that symbolised the idea of the man, making him almost unrecognisable in the flesh, as Ehrenburg noted.[201] This transformation was so pronounced that a member of the Soviet embalming team stated in a television interview that his primary task, while Stalin lay next to Lenin in the mausoleum between 1953 and 1961, was to achieve the greatest possible likeness between Stalin's corpse and the photographs and portraits of him so that people would not be shocked.[202]

With the Soviet propaganda poster becoming, in Sidorov's words, a 'contemporary icon',[203] there are three major ways in which the Stalin posters visually referenced the Orthodox icon: images in which Stalin's portrait is hung or carried like an icon;[204] images in which Stalin

---

199 Artists appear to have sometimes employed doubles, equipped with Stalin props, to sit as Stalin (Plamper, *The Stalin cult*, p. 103). As already mentioned, Klutsis complained that he needed a telephoto lens to be able to take photographs of the leaders (see Margarita Tupitsyn, *Gustav Klutsis and Valentina Kulagina: photography and montage after constructivism*, New York, International Center of Photography, 2004, p. 66).
200 Quoted in RGALI, f. 2368, op. 2, d.48, l-1ob, cited in Plamper, *The Stalin cult*, p. 144.
201 Ehrenburg, *Men, years — life*, vol.5, p. 302.
202 Plamper, *The Stalin cult*, pp. 201–02.
203 A.A. Sidorov, 'Iskusstvo plakata', *Gorn*, 1922, no. 2, pp. 122–27, cited in White, *The Bolshevik poster*, 1998, p. 5.
204 Viktor Deni & Nikolai Dolgorukov, 'Long live the Leninist VKP(b), organiser of victorious socialist construction', 1934 (Fig. 4.60); Efim Pernikov, 'The Soviet constitution is the only truly democratic constitution in the world', 1937; Galina Shubina, 'Long live the first of May!', 1937; Viktor Koretskii, 'On the joyous day of liberation ...', 1943 (Fig. 3.13); Viktor Koretskii, 'The Soviet people are full of gratitude and love for dear Stalin ...', 1945; Viktor Govorov, 'Glory to the first candidate for deputies of the Supreme Soviet of the USSR, great Stalin!', 1946; V. Paradovskii, 'Glory

4. STALIN SAVES THE WORLD

adopts a pose reminiscent of Christ;[205] and images that employ devices associated with icon painting.[206] A large number of posters of Stalin depict the *vozhd'* as a bust portrait enclosed in a sketched frame. This is often the case in election posters where Stalin is being promoted as a candidate and is in keeping with long-standing traditions around the globe for portraying electoral candidates. In some posters, whether or not they are election-themed, the frame within the poster is more elaborate, sometimes in gold colours, at other times made of flowers and plants or folkish motifs, and may even incorporate a sprig of cotton, or a branch of laurel or oak leaves. Some posters depict scenes in which these framed portraits are being carried in a procession or

---

to great Stalin!', 1947 (Fig. 4.61); Nikolai Zhukov, 'We'll surround orphans with maternal kindness and love', 1947 (Fig. 3.15); Elena Mel'nikova, 'Best friend of children ...', 1951; Unidentified artist, undated, 1952; Konstantin Ivanov, 'Happy New Year, beloved Stalin!', 1952 (Fig. 4.59).

205 Nikolai Dolgorukov, 'Swell the ranks of the Stakhanovites', 1936; Genrikh Futerfas, 'Stalinists! Extend the front of the Stakhanovite movement!', 1936 (Fig. 3.27); Viktor Koretskii, '"Our government and the party does not have other interests and other concerns than those which the people have." Stalin', 1938 (Fig. 4.64); A.I. Madorskii, 'Be as the great Lenin was', 1938 (Fig. 2.11); Marina Volkova & Natalia Pinus, 'Long live the equal-rights woman in the USSR ...', 1938 (Fig. 3.32); Nikolai Denisov & Nina Vatolina, 'Greetings great Stalin, creator of the constitution of victorious socialism', 1940; Iraklii Toidze, (in Armenian) '"... the party is unbeatable if it knows where to go and is not afraid of the difficulties." (I Stalin)', 1940; Vladimir Serov, 'Under the banner of Lenin, forward to victory!', 1942 (Fig. 4.23); Veniamin Pinchuk, '"The spirit of the great Lenin and his invincible banner inspire us now in the patriotic war." (I. Stalin)', 1943 (Fig. 4.29); Vlasob', 'During the war, the Red Army personnel became a professional army ...', 1943 (Fig. 4.27); Vasilii Nikolaev, 'Forward for the defeat of the German occupiers ...', 1944; Vladimir Serov, 'Stalin will lead us to victory', 1944; Nikolai Avvakumov, 'Long live our teacher, or father, our leader, comrade Stalin!', 1946 (Fig. 3.28); Boris Berezovskii, '"We stand for peace and defend the cause of peace." I. Stalin', 1947; I. Shagin, 'The reality of our program — it's real people ...', 1947 (Fig. 4.65); Iraklii Toidze, '"Long life and prosperity to our Motherland!" I. Stalin', 1947 (Fig. 4.53); Boris Berezovskii, Mikhail Solov'ev & I. Shagin, 'Under the leadership of the great Stalin — forward to communism!', 1951 (Fig. 4.66).

206 Unidentified artist, (in Armenian) 'June 12. With enormous gratitude and best regards, we send greetings to great Stalin', 1938; Mikhail Zhukov, 'Leader of the peoples of the USSR and workers of the whole world ...', 1938; Viktor Koretskii, 'Workers of collective and cooperative farms and machine and tractor stations ...', 1939; Vladimir Kaidalov, 'Departing from us, Comrade Lenin urged us to strengthen and extend the union of republics ...', 1940 (Fig. 2.13); Vasilii Bayuskin & A. Shpier, 'The Great Patriotic War', 1942; Viktor Ivanov & Ol'ga Burova, 'Comrades of the Red Army ...', 1942 (Fig. 4.24); Iraklii Toidze, 'Long live the VKP(b) ...', 1946; Iraklii Toidze, 'Stalin's kindness illuminates the future of our children!', 1947 (Fig. 3.2); Aleksandr Druzhkov & I. Shagin, 'Stalin is our fighting banner', 1948 (Fig. 4.45); Naum Karpovskii, 'Labour with martial persistence ...', 1948; Mikhail Reikh, 'For communism!', 1948; Vladislav Pravdin, 'Long live the Bolshevik party ...', 1950; Mikhail Solov'ev, '"Such women didn't and couldn't exist in the old days." I.V. Stalin', 1950 (Fig. 3.33); N. Talipov, 'Long live Comrade Stalin ...', 1950; B.V. Vorontsov, 'Iosif Vissarionovich Stalin', 1951; Boris Belopol'skii, '"We stand for peace and we defend the cause of peace." I. Stalin', 1952 (Fig. 4.57); Boris Belopol'skii, '"The world will be saved and enhanced if people take responsibility for maintaining peace into their own hands and defend it to the end." I. Stalin', 1952 (Fig. 4.58); Konstantin Ivanov, 'I wish you good health and success in teaching and social work ...', 1952.

hung on a wall. This treatment of the leader's portrait parallels the carrying of icons in religious processions, or the hanging of icons in the icon corner in the Russian home. Several posters in which Stalin's portrait is hung as an icon on the wall have already been discussed. Viktor Koretskii's 'On the joyous day of liberation …' of 1943 (Fig. 3.13) and 'The Soviet people are full of gratitude and love for dear STALIN — the great organiser of our victory' of 1945 (Fig. 4.35), Nikolai Zhukov's 'We'll surround orphans with maternal kindness and love' of 1947 (Fig. 3.15), and Konstantin Ivanov's 'Happy New Year, beloved Stalin!' of 1952 (Fig. 4.59) all highlight the talismanic and protective properties of the leader portrait while hung on the wall like an icon.

'Long live the Leninist VKP(b), organiser of victorious socialist construction' of 1934 by Deni and Dolgorukov (Fig. 4.60) is an early example of the Stalin portrait being carried in a parade. Five hands hold a sketched portrait of Stalin under the protective banner of the Leninist Party amid a sea of Klutsis-style open-palmed hands, all raised in the air and pointing upward in the direction of the victory of socialist construction. No other part of the body can be seen in the crowd, the hand itself symbolises the socialist worker. Efim Pernikov's 'The Soviet constitution is the only truly democratic constitution in the world' of 1937 is in tryptich format and shows a crowd of people demonstrating in support of the 1936 constitution. Two posters are carried on poles by the marching crowd: one very large poster featuring the entire upper body of Stalin with right arm raised; and a much smaller poster of the head of Lenin. Stalin's image is given precedence as the 1936 constitution supersedes the 1924 constitution drafted under Lenin's leadership. The other two panels of the poster feature Article 125 of the constitution, which guarantees freedom of speech, freedom of the press and freedom of association, and a dynamic montage image showing *Trud* and *Pravda* hot off the presses, with two men reading copies of *Pravda* and *Bolshevik*. Article 125 states:

> In conformity with the interests of the working people, and in order to strengthen the socialist system, the citizens of the USSR are guaranteed by law, a. freedom of speech; b. freedom of the press; c. freedom of assembly, including the holding of mass meetings; d. freedom of street processions and demonstrations. These civil rights are ensured by placing at the disposal of the working people and their organisations printing presses, stocks of paper, public buildings, the streets, communications facilities and other material requisites for the exercise of these rights.

4. STALIN SAVES THE WORLD

By the time of V.C. Paradovskii's 'Glory to great Stalin!' of 1947 (Fig. 4.61), the Stalin portrait on a pole has become more exalted and thus more overtly icon-like. A procession of Kyrgiz citizens holds aloft a huge portrait of Stalin in marshal's uniform with a chest full of medals, surrounded by an elaborate border of flowers, with a red banner billowing behind. No other portrait appears in the parade and the caption makes clear that, 30 years after the October Revolution, it is Stalin alone who is glorified and celebrated. In contrast to the Russian Orthodox icon, Stalin does not look directly at the viewer, but out to the left at something that we cannot see. Stalin's portrait receives similar treatment in an uncaptioned poster by an unidentified artist of 1952. This time, a huge portrait of Stalin in uniform is enclosed in a living border of lush flowers and fruits. It emerges from a sea of red banners billowing in such a way that they all converge on the Stalin portrait. Beneath the portrait and almost merging with the floral border are a crowd of children of various nationalities, wearing either national costume or Pioneer uniforms. They are smiling and many look directly at the viewer as if they had posed for a jolly family snapshot. While the children are colourful, the Stalin portrait is black-and-white and Stalin does not look at the children, nor do they look at him. His image has mere symbolic presence.

Posters of Stalin tend to show him in a relatively small number of characteristic poses. With only a few exceptions[207] he is usually static. He makes speeches, receives homage, looks to the future or, when motion is implied, is usually caught at rest the moment after arrival. Sometimes Stalin holds a newspaper[208] or book[209] or document[210]

---

207 A.A. Babitskii, 'Under the leadership of Comrade Stalin, forward to complete victory over our enemy!', 1944 shows Stalin rushing forward into battle carrying a map, while in Toidze's '"All our forces — to support our heroic Red Army and our glorious Red Navy! All the power of the people — to defeat the enemy!" Stalin' (Fig. 4.16), of 1941 shows a rigid Stalin but suggests motion through swirling coat-flaps.
208 Iu. Tsishevskii, 'Expand the ranks of the Stakhanovites of the socialist fields', 1935; Viktor Ivanov, 'Reach for prosperity!', 1949 (Fig. 3.30); Boris Karpov & Viktor Viktorov, 'VKP(b)', 1949; Viktor Ivanov, 'Stalin is our great standard-bearer of peace!', 1950 (Fig. 4.54).
209 Viktor Ivanov, 'Great Stalin is the beacon of communism!', 1949 (Fig. 3.7).
210 Vasilii Elkin, 'Be as the great Lenin was', 1938 (Fig. 2.10); E.M. Mirzoev, (in Azerbaijani), 1938; Unidentified artist, 'The electors, the people, must demand that their deputies should remain equal to their tasks', 1939; Unidentified artist, 'The foreign policy of the Soviet Union is clear and explicit ...', 1940 (Fig. 4.12); Viktor Govorkov, 'Stalin takes care of each of us from the Kremlin', 1940 (Fig. 3.8); Viktor Klimashin, 'The All-Union Agricultural Exhibition 1940', 1940; Konstantin Cheprakov, 'We swore an oath to our leader to fight the enemy', 1940; Babitskii, 'Under the leadership of Comrade Stalin, forward to complete victory over our enemy!', 1944; and, Boris Belopol'skii, 'Glory to Stalin, the great architect of communism!', 1951 (Fig. 3.10).

— often the document is rolled up in the form of a scroll. Christ Pantokrator, Christ the Teacher, is often shown in icons with his right arm raised in blessing and left hand holding a book or a scroll. There are a few Soviet variants of the 'raised right arm' gesture, although in none of these is Stalin's hand in the identical pose to Christ in the icon. Understandably, the similarities are suggestive rather than a direct appropriation. In some posters in which Stalin raises his right arm, he is saluting or acknowledging — this is particularly the case in posters in which he is watching a parade or an airshow. The meaning of the gesture is less clear in posters like Klutsis's '"Cadres decide everything." I. Stalin' of 1935 (Fig. 4.62). Stalin's right arm is raised to shoulder height, bent up at the elbow, with the palm facing out toward the viewer. This could be a form of greeting, or a means of acknowledging the homage paid by the crowd, although Stalin does not engage with the crowd. In Klutsis's 1936 'Long live the Stalinist Order of Heroes and Stakhanovites!' (Fig. 4.63) and Madorskii's 'Be as the great Lenin was' of 1939 (Fig. 2.12) Stalin speaks to a large crowd of Stakhanovites from a podium at the Bolshoi Theatre. This time his palm is turned sideways, as if to emphasise what he is saying; however, the coupling of the podium with the gesture emphasises the Teacher archetype and as such may call to mind the figure of Christ as teacher. Elkin's 1938 'Be as the great Lenin was' (Fig. 2.10) pairs a similar gesture, this time with upturned palm, with a sheaf of documents in Stalin's left hand to similar effect. A 1940 poster by Toidze[211] comes closer to the icon. In '"the party is unbeatable if it knows where to go and is not afraid of the difficulties." I.V. Stalin', Stalin is illuminated by a shaft of white light from above and is shown looking directly at the viewer in front of a billowing red Party banner. His right arm reaches forward at chest height, his fingers loosely curled in the direction of the viewer, while his left arm rests on a podium.

There are several posters that reproduce Stalin's pose in a press photograph taken at the 1935 conference of Stakhanovites. In the earliest of these posters from 1936, Stalin raises his right hand high in the air, his palm open and facing outwards towards the viewer.

---

211 The version of the poster cited in this study is in the Armenian language. redavantgarde.com/en/collection/show-collection/927--the-party-is-unbeatable-if-it-knows-where-to-go-and-is-not-afraid-of-the-difficulties-i-v-stalin-.html?authorId=197. A Tajik version of the poster published in 1940 can be viewed online at www.vnikitskom.com/ru/antique/auction/9/3604/ (accessed 03 Apr. 2014).

4. STALIN SAVES THE WORLD

This is a gesture of greeting and of acknowledgement of the crowd. In 'Stalinists! Extend the front of the Stakhanovite movement!' of 1936 (Fig. 3.27), Stalin's outstretched arm is the focal point of the image. Immediately beneath him are Nikita Krushchev and Lazar Kaganovich and beneath them are a wave of Stakhanovite workers fanned out across the poster to form a 'front' in the battle for socialist construction. The figures in the poster are arranged in a hierarchical form reminiscent of Byzantine and Russian Orthodox icons. At the top Stalin, like Christ Pantokrator, oversees all beneath him. Below, Krushchev and Kaganovich take the place of angelic messengers. Below them are the legion of saintly worker–heroes marching forward to bring to fruition the Promised Land. Dolgorukov's 'Swell the ranks of the Stakhanovites', also of 1936, shows Stalin at the Stakhanovite conference, flanked on either side by his Politburo colleagues, arranged around him in a manner reminiscent of the intercessory row on the Deesis — figures are arranged in importance from the centre outwards. Beneath the *vozhdi* are scenes of Soviet success, including the new Metro (opened in 1935) and thriving industrial complexes. Soviet sacred sites — the Kremlin and Lenin's mausoleum — are also sketched in. A crowd floods in for as far as the eye can see, a holy army on the socialist battlefront led by the famous Stakhanovite workers.

By 1938 the upraised arm gesture was slightly modified so that, instead of the open palm gesture, Stalin's right hand points straight up at the heavens, invoking a higher order of law. Koretskii's '"Our government and the Party does not have other interests and other concerns than those which the people have." Stalin' (Fig. 4.64), Madorskii's 'Be as the great Lenin was' (Fig. 2.11), and Marina Volkova and Natalia Pinus' 'Long live the equal-rights woman in the USSR …' (Fig. 3.32) all feature Stalin in this pose in posters which emphasise the democratic rights of the people as guaranteed under the constitution of 1936. In 'Long live the equal-rights woman in the USSR …' it is the figure of Stalin, engulfed in a sea of holy red, that dominates the poster, filling two-thirds of the space. The palette, the use of tone and the flat, stylised image of Stalin, all echo the Russian Orthodox icon. Stalin is the source of light. Dressed in white, with gold tones, he casts a golden hue over the entire poster, including the faces of the young women. The familiar shape of the Spassky tower is silhouetted in Stalin's golden light, rising into empty space to his right, the spire topped with a red star echoes his upraised arm and gesturing golden hand. Ouspensky's explanation of the light in religious icons can be applied equally well here:

> all that is depicted in the icon reflects not the disorder of our sinful world, but Divine order, peace, a realm governed not by earthly logic, not by human morality, but by Divine Grace. It is the new order in the new creation … All is bathed in light, and in their technical language iconographers call 'light' the background of the icon.[212]

This poster is manifestly about the new order and the new creation. The new order is symbolised by the sea of red flags on either side of the women, and also by the Kremlin. It is particularly manifest in the army of modern, professional young women, their ranks receding into the background. Though slim and attractive, there is nothing coy or frivolous about these women. They are allowed, at best, an ambiguous half-smile, and the focus is on their eyes, which do not engage the viewer, but look out of the picture and around the viewer, to the imminent future. The woman in blue is a parachutist, literally accessing the heavens under the new order. Stalin points upward and out of the picture frame, to the heaven-on-earth of the communist utopia.

By the time of the war, Stalin's right arm had moved once again, this time outstretched at shoulder level in front of him, sometimes with open palm, at other times pointing ahead. Serov's 'Under the banner of Lenin, forward to victory!' of 1942 (Fig. 4.23), Pinchuk's '"The spirit of the great Lenin and his invincible banner inspire us now in the patriotic war." (I. Stalin)' of 1943 (Fig. 4.29), and Serov and Boris Leo's Okno TASS No. 6 of 1943, all feature Stalin with his right arm outstretched and palm down in a gesture that resembles blessing and may be interpreted as Stalin protecting and sanctifying the actions of the troops beneath him.

In 1944 Stalin both sanctifies[213] and points in a posture that mimics a characteristic gesture of Lenin.[214] In the posters of the war years, Lenin is almost always shown pointing with his right arm outstretched, a

---

212 Ouspensky & Lossky, *The meaning of icons*, p. 40.
213 Vasilii Nikolaev, 'Forward for the defeat of the German occupiers …', 1944; and, Vladimir Serov, 'Stalin will lead us to victory', 1944.
214 M. Karpenko, 'Under the banner of Lenin, under the leadership of Stalin — forward to the complete defeat of the German invaders!', 1944; and, Andrei Mikhalev, '"For the complete expulsion of the German fiends from our land! Long live our Red Army! Long live our Navy!" Stalin', 1944.

4. STALIN SAVES THE WORLD

gesture already associated with Lenin for many years. The gesture is stern and commanding, suggestive of an unyielding will and absolute authority.[215] The adoption of a characteristic Lenin pose by Stalin may have helped strengthen the visual association between the two leaders in a time of crisis in Stalin's leadership.

After the war, with Stalin being presented as a man of peace, his right arm went back above his head, usually with his finger pointing to the heavens. In Berezovskii's '"We stand for peace and defend the cause of peace." I. Stalin' of 1947 (Fig. 4.52), Shagin's 'The reality of our program — it's real people ...', 1947 (Fig. 4.65) and Berezovskii, Solov'ev and Shagin's 'Under the leadership of the great Stalin — forward to communism!', 1951 (Fig. 4.66), Stalin points the way to the communist utopia above. Each of these posters uses an identical photograph of Stalin, in his old-style unadorned military tunic. With his left hand resting on a podium or, as in the Shagin poster, on a piece of paper, Stalin is associated with the Teacher archetype and with Christ as teacher.

Perhaps the most fruitful area of comparison between icons and Stalin posters lies in how the posters make use of devices and forms characteristic of the icon. It has already been noted that Stalin's pose, the arrangement of figures, and the use of light as a background in the poster might trigger an association with the icon in an acclimatised public. One of the most common features of Stalin posters is the oval or circular medallion[216] which encloses either the image of Lenin,

---

215 Maria Gough offers a religious interpretation of Lenin's gesture. In her analysis of John Heartfield's untitled photomontage for the title page of *USSR in construction*, no. 9, September 1931, Gough likens this gesture to the depiction of God on the ceiling of the Sistine Chapel by Michelangelo: 'In both scenes of creation that which the omnipotent authority (God; Lenin) is creating (Adam; Usachevka) is pictured as having already been created. Like God, however, Lenin has still more to create ... . Lenin's hand points beyond what has already been accomplished toward that which must be accomplished in the future, namely, the Central Committee's new plans for the city's development and expansion' ('Back in the USSR: John Heartfield, Gustav Klucis, and the medium of Soviet propaganda', *New German Critique*, 107, 36:2, 2009, pp. 133–84, pp. 155–56).

216 Unidentified artist, 'Six historical conditions of Comrade Stalin', undated; Unidentified artist, (in Ukrainian) 'The party of Lenin–Stalin, inspirational organiser of our great victories', undated; Semen Gel'berg, 'Long live the All-Union Party of Bolsheviks, the party of Lenin–Stalin', undated; M. Karpenko, 'On the path of Lenin to joy and glory, with Stalin in our hearts we are going to victory!', undated; Vladimir Kochegura, 'Long live the party of Lenin-Stalin ...', undated; B. Lebedev, 'Long live the party of Lenin–Stalin', undated; A.A. Mytnikov, 'Long live the candidate for deputy of the Supreme Soviet ...', undated; Georgi Zarnitskii, 'Workers stand to defend our beloved socialist motherland!', undated; Polenov, 'For the victory of communism in

the image of Stalin, or both of them together. In the icon, the medallion is usually situated at the top and encloses Christ, the Virgin or the saints, denoting their spiritual presence and sanctifying everything beneath them. In Stalin posters, the medallion also usually appears at the top, often on a banner which flies protectively over the Soviet people in the earthly realm. It symbolises the presence of the deified or apotheosised Lenin and Stalin providing guidance and protection from above. An unusual variant of the medallion can be found in Shukhmin's poster of 1945, Okno TASS No. 1242.[217] A profile portrait of a military Stalin on a banner is surrounded with an uneven glow of golden light which, irregular in form, appears to be flickering as it emanates from him.

The Stalinist medallion is sometimes surrounded by a wreath of laurel or oak leaves, which provides another set of symbolic resonances. Wreaths are associated with the dead and, in the ancient world, formed a ritual part of the cult of the dead. Wreaths have traditionally been used in a number of rituals: they were offered to someone who was being petitioned and were hung around altars and temples; when used as crowns, they formed an apotropæic circle which purified what it enclosed, protecting newlyweds and promoting fertility, cleansing

our country', 1927; P. Gorilli, 'The MTS is the organiser of our agricultural production', 1932; I. Bersian, (in Moldavian) 'We will make every Bolshevik collective farm and every collective farmer prosperous', 1933; P. Yastrzhembskii, 'Glory to the creator of the USSR constitution, the great Stalin!', 1937; Unidentified artist, 'Long live the creator of the first cavalry …', 1939 (Fig. 4.10); M. Kaminskii, 'To continue the policy of peace and of strengthening business relations with all countries …', 1939 (Fig. 4.8); Viktor Koretskii, 'Long live the Leninist–Stalinist Komsomol …', 1939; S. Podobedov, 'Comrade I.V. Stalin at the front of the civil war', 1939 (Fig. 4.4); Unidentified artist, 'State Library Museum Exhibition of Stalin in literature', 1940; Nikolai Zukhov & Viktor Klimashin, 'For the Soviet fatherland …', 1943; Unidentified artist, (in Azerbaijani) 'First deputy I.V. Stalin', 1945; Viktor Koretskii, 'Our banner is the banner of victory', 1945; Petr Shukhmin, 'Long live the great organiser and inspirer of historic victory …', 1945; Ismail Achundov, (in Azerbaijani), 1946; Iosif Ganf, 'Long live the 29th anniversary of the great October socialist revolution', 1946; Viktor Ivanov, 'Long live the Party of Lenin–Stalin!', 1946; Viktor Koretskii, '1917–1946. Glory to the Red Army …', 1946; Onufriichuk, (in Ukrainian) 'Long live the leader of the Soviet people …', 1946 (Fig. 4.40); Iraklii Toidze, 'Long live the VKP(b) …', 1946; Boris Mukhin, 'Long live the leader of the Soviet people', 1947; Ruben Shkhiyan, 'In order to build, we need to know …', 1947; Georgii Bakhmutov, (in Ukrainian) 'Glory to the leader of the Soviet people — great Stalin', 1947 (Fig. 4.44); B.I. Lebedev, 'Long live the VKP(b) …', 1948 (Fig. 4.48); F. Litvinov, 'Long live the party of Lenin–Stalin …' (Fig. 4.49), 1948; Evgeni Merega, 'Under the banner of Lenin-Stalin, forward to the victory of communism!', 1948; Boris Mukhin, 'Glory to great Stalin!', 1948 (Fig. 4.46); Unidentified artist, 'Iosif Vissarionovich Stalin', 1950; A.A. Mytnikov, 'Long live the creator of the most democratic constitution in the world, great Stalin!', 1950; P. Lukhtein, 'Glory to great Stalin!', 1951; Boris Belopol'skii, 'In order to build, we must have knowledge …', 1952.
217 For an image, see www.artic.edu/aic/collections/exhibitions/TASS/artwork/192613.

warriors returning from war, and crowning victorious athletes at games; the branches carried the vitality and power of the plants from which they were woven and in the case of athletic games, were sacred to the apotheosised hero to whom the games were dedicated.[218] Oak and laurel leaves have long been associated with victory and Stalin's portrait is often enclosed in a garland of these after victory in the war. Koretskii's 'Our banner is the banner of victory!' of 1945 encloses the bas-relief profiles of Lenin and Stalin in a small medallion on a red victory banner. The banner is wielded by a grinning soldier whose head, along with those of Lenin and Stalin, is enclosed inside a victory wreath.

The icon and the political poster share further common ground in their symbolic use of colour. It would be difficult to exaggerate the importance of the use of colour for the Soviet artist. Here, science, art and religion all merged in an attempt to engineer the 'new Soviet man'. The Soviet leadership of the Stalinist era believed that people could be totally redesigned. The psychologist Aron Zalkind advocated the conditioning of human behaviour down to the smallest detail and the planning of human reproduction on a large scale in order that the sex drive be diverted and channeled into energy for the construction of socialism.[219] In 1923 Nikolai Bukharin delivered a speech to the Komsomol in which he anticipated the production of 'living machines': 'We must now direct our efforts at creating in the shortest time possible the greatest number of specialized living machines that will be ready and willing to enter into circulation.'[220] An interest in eugenics was coupled with Lamarckian beliefs,[221] an evolutionary theory which favours environmental factors over heredity, and posits that environmentally induced mutations can be inherited. Science focused on perception and cognition, and ways in which the requisite changes could be induced. Bukharin was convinced that the science was valid, stating in 1928: 'if we took the view that racial or national

---

218 Thomas F. Mathews, *The clash of gods: a reinterpretation of early Christian art*, Princeton University Press, 1999, pp. 161–63.
219 Ferré, 'Time is accelerating', in Ferré, *Red cavalry*, p. 86.
220 Ferré, 'Time is accelerating', in Ferré, *Red cavalry*, p. 70.
221 Lamarckism sits quite well with Marxist thought.

peculiarities are so persistent that it would take thousands of years to change them, then of course our whole work would be absurd because it would be built on sand.'[222]

Colour was held to have psychological effects, often at the pre-rational level, and amongst artists and propagandists, colour theory became a key area of research and investigation. Wassilii Kandinskii wrote at length on colour in *Concerning the spiritual in art*, noting its psychic and spiritual effects:

> colour ... makes only a momentary and superficial impression on a soul but slightly developed in sensitiveness. But even this superficial impression varies in quality ... . But to a more sensitive soul the effect of colours is deeper and intensely moving. And so we come to the second main result of looking at colours: THEIR PSYCHIC EFFECT. They produce a corresponding spiritual vibration, and it is only as a step towards this spiritual vibration that the elementary physical impression is of importance. [capitals in original][223]

Malevich, El Lissitskii and Rodchenko all explored colour theory in their work, using colour with the deliberate intention of creating a direct psychological effect, and Klutsis was hired to teach 'Colour Theory for Applications other than Painting' at VKhUTEMAS in 1924. VKhUTEMAS was the site of unprecedented experimentation in the perception of colour and form, with the invention of purpose-built apparatus designed to monitor the senses.[224] As part of their research into the effectiveness of propaganda posters on their target audience, Party agitators conducted studies of how viewers reacted to the use of certain colours in posters. Victoria Bonnell summarises some of the findings in relation to peasants viewing collectivisation posters in 1934 in her article on the peasant woman in Stalinist art:

---

222 Quoted in Sheila Fitzpatrick, *Education and social mobility in the Soviet Union, 1921–1934*, Cambridge University Press, 1979, p. 141.
223 Wassily Kandinsky, *Concerning the spiritual in art, and painting in particular, (1912)*, Michael Sadleir & Francis Golffing (trans.), New York, Wittenborn, Schultz, 1947, p. 26, www.semantikon.com/art/kandinskyspiritualinart.pdf (accessed 12 Dec. 2013).
224 See Ferré, 'Time is accelerating', in Ferré, *Red cavalry*, p. 68.

viewers displayed a strong preference for soft muted colors and were especially partial to one poster with a 'delicate blue background'. They reacted negatively to bright garish colors. According to this report, the collective farmers paid attention to color and imagery and generally ignored the text.[225]

Pastel colours began to dominate Stalin posters from around 1934, and were compatible with the images of abundance that were now characteristic of Stalinist propaganda. The stark blacks and whites of the period of struggle were less apparent and only came to the fore once more during the war when time was of the essence in poster production and the theme of battle held its most dire meaning.

In his highly influential work, Kandinskii argues that, while colour may operate in an associative manner (e.g. orange is hot because it is the colour of a flame), colour also has the power to directly influence the soul:

> Colour is the keyboard, the eyes are the hammers, the soul is the piano with many strings. The artist is the hand which plays, touching one key or another, to cause vibrations in the soul.
>
> IT IS EVIDENT THEREFORE THAT COLOUR HARMONY MUST REST ONLY ON A CORRESPONDING VIBRATION IN THE HUMAN SOUL; AND THIS IS ONE OF THE GUIDING PRINCIPLES OF THE INNER NEED. [capitals in original][226]

The icon was of particular interest for many artists because of the long tradition of using standardised symbolic colours for spiritual purposes. According to Kandinskii's way of thinking, if the colour schemata of the icon (interacting with form) is suggested or reproduced in a poster, the viewer will both make an association between the icon and the poster, and also be moved at a spiritual level. Both of these phenomena can, and probably usually do, occur at a subconscious or pre-conscious level. Taking this line of thought further, if one wishes to imbue the persona of Stalin with sacrality, this can be achieved by presenting him in poses that may be associated with Christ, and by placing him against a red or gold background in a frame or in a medallion.

---

225 Victoria E. Bonnell, 'The peasant woman in Stalinist political art of the 1930s', *The American Historical Review*, 98:1, 1993, pp. 55–82, p. 73.
226 Kandinsky, *Concerning the spiritual in art*, p. 27.

THE PERSONALITY CULT OF STALIN IN SOVIET POSTERS, 1929–1953

The colour red was the dominant colour in Soviet posters throughout most of the Stalinist era, featuring in huge banners, as an undifferentiated background, and often as the colour of the poster text.[227] It also appeared on tractors, buildings, the Kremlin, scarves and blouses. As Wolfgang Holz has argued, everything that is semantically connected with socialist ideology is often coloured red, with the colour signifying ideological transformation.[228] Red was specifically associated with icons, where it often formed a background colour and represented youth, beauty and eternal life and, in posters, it imbues the figures it surrounds with an aura of sacrality. Govorov's 1946 poster 'Glory to the first candidate for deputy of the Supreme Soviet of the USSR, great Stalin!' (Fig. 4.67) in which Stalin's portrait is carried as an icon, shows Stalin sketched in gold tones against a background of pure rich red, while Onufriichuk's 1946 poster 'Long live the leader of the Soviet people — great Stalin' (Fig. 4.40) encloses a gold-toned Stalin in a medallion that is placed against a red background. Icons do not employ colour in a naturalistic fashion and the colours used for faces and clothes have symbolic resonances. In a small number of posters Stalin's face is coloured red and indistinguishable from the background. In Ivanov and Burova's 'Comrades of the Red Army, the Red Fleet, commanders and commissars, men and women of the guerilla forces!' of 1942 (Fig. 4.24), a giant blood-red Stalin head looms in a blood-red sky. In Mikhail Reikh's 'For communism! …' 1948 (Fig. 3.5), Stalin appears like the sun in the sky in two shades of red, while beneath him an ecstatic Uzbek crowd pay tribute. Denisov's 'We gathered under the red banner of Lenin …' of 1949 (Fig. 4.68) shows both Lenin and Stalin in sacred red, although Stalin's figure dominates due to its positioning in front of Lenin and to the touches of gold on his epaulettes. See also Be-Sha (Boris Shapoval) and Rozenberg, 'I would like comrades to systematically influence their deputies, to tell them to keep before them the image of the great Lenin and imitate Lenin in everything', 1940 (Fig. 4.69); and Vladimir Kaidalov, 'We will struggle to reap a big cotton harvest!' (Uzbek language),

---

[227] Much of the symbolism associated with red has already been discussed in Chapter Two.
[228] Wolfgang Holz, 'Allegory and iconography in Socialist Realist painting', in Matthew Cullerne Bown & Brandon Taylor (eds), *Art of the Soviets: painting, sculpture, and architecture in a one-party State, 1917–1992*, Manchester University Press, 1993, p. 74.

1950 (Fig. 4.51). Lenin is depicted in this way far more frequently than Stalin.[229] Where other figures appear in these posters, they usually appear in flesh tones or without colour.[230]

Gold is another colour that is found in the icon and is frequently employed as a background, representing divine light and Christ. Stalin is often depicted in gold tones against a rich red background.[231] Sometimes he is illuminated by a golden light.[232] With the early

---

229 For example, Veniamin Pinchuk, '"The spirit of the great Lenin and his invincible banner inspire us now in the patriotic war." (I. Stalin)', 1943 (Fig. 4.29); V. Reshetnikov, 'Glory to Lenin, glory to Stalin, glory to the great October', 1952 (Fig. 2.20); Vladimir Kaidalov, 'Departing from us, Comrade Lenin urged us to strengthen and extend the union republics. We swear to you, Comrade Lenin, that we will fulfill with honor your behest', 1940 (Fig. 2.13); A.A. Babitskii, 'Under the leadership of Comrade Stalin, forward to complete victory over our enemy!', 1944; Vladimir Serov, 'Under the banner of Lenin, forward, to victory!', 1942 (Fig. 4.23); Vladimir Kaidalov, 'Glory to great Stalin!', 1949 (Fig. 2.28); Nikolai Denisov & Vladislav Pravdin, 'Under the banner of Lenin, under the leadership of Stalin — forward to communism!', 1946; Unidentified artist, 'Under the banner of Lenin, under the leadership of Stalin, forward to the victory of communism!', 1948; B. Lebedev, 'Under the banner of Lenin, under the leadership of Stalin, forward to the victory of communism!', 1950; Aleksandr Druzhkov & I. Shagin, 'Under the banner of Lenin, under the leadership of Stalin — forward towards new development for the Soviet motherland and a full victory of Communism in our country!', 1947; Boris Belopol'skii, '"We move further, forward towards Communism." I.V. Stalin', 1950; Unidentified artist, (in Armenian) '12 June. With enormous gratitude and best regards, we send greetings to Great Stalin!', 1938; Anatoli Kazantsev, '1917–1944. Forward, to definitive defeat of the enemy!', 1944; Nikolai Denisov & Vladislav Pravdin, 'Under the banner of Lenin, under the leadership of Stalin — forward to the victory of communism!', 1948.
230 Some propaganda posters show Stalin in black-and-white while the environment around him appears in full naturalistic colour. For example, Druzhkov & Shagin, 'Stalin is our fighting banner', 1948 (Fig. 4.45) and N. Petrov, '… it is our blessing that in the difficult years of the war …', 1948 (Fig. 4.47). This treatment marks him out as removed from the ordinary world and as inhabiting a symbolic or allegorical plane.
231 Marina Volkova & Natalia Pinus, 'Long live the equal-rights woman in the USSR', 1938 (Fig. 3.32); Nadezhda Kashina, 'Invincible Moscow', 1942; Nikolai Kogout, 'Under the invincible banner of the great Lenin …', 1942 (Fig. 4.21); Vladimir Serov, 'Under the banner of Lenin, forward to victory!', 1942 (Fig. 4.23); Viktor Govorov, 'Glory to the first candidate for deputies of the Supreme Soviet of the SSSR, great Stalin!', 1946; Emmanuil Grabovetskii, 'Long live the 29th anniversary of the great October Socialist revolution!', 1946; M.L. Ioffe, 'Glory to great Stalin, creator of the constitution of the USSR', 1946; Onufriichuk, 'Long live the leader of the Soviet people — great Stalin', 1946 (Fig. 4.40); Mikhail Solov'ev, '29 years. long live the 29th anniversary of the great October socialist revolution', 1946; Mikhail Solov'ev, 'We have been preparing for the elections', 1946; Iraklii Toidze, 'Long live the V.K.P.(b) …', 1946; Viktor Govorkov, 'VKP(b). There is nothing greater than the title of member of the party of Lenin–Stalin!', 1947; V. Medvedev, 'Long live the 30th anniversary of the great October Socialist revolution!', 1947; Ruben Shkhiyan, 'In order to build, we need to know …', 1947; F. Litvinov, 'Long live the party of Lenin–Stalin, inspirer and organiser of our victories!', 1948 (Fig. 4.49); Mikhail Solov'ev, 'All the Soviet people are closely rallied around their government …', 1948; L. Stenberg, 'The banner of Lenin …', 1949 (Fig. 2.16); Boris Belopol'skii, '"We move further, forward towards communism." I. V. Stalin', 1950; U. Ivanov, 'Under the great and invincible banner of Lenin-Stalin for the triumph of communism', 1950 ; Aleksei Kokorekin, 'Be prepared to struggle for the cause of Lenin-Stalin!', 1951.
232 Vasilii Bayuskin & A. Shpier, 'Great Patriotic War', 1942; Petr Golub & M. Chernov, 'Under the leadership of Stalin — Forward to a new blossoming of our motherland!', 1946; Naum

exception of the 1938 women's rights-themed poster by Volkova and Pinus, golden tones became a feature of Stalin posters in 1942, as the Soviet Union experienced its first tentative victories in the war, then disappeared again until 1946, when victory was official and celebrated openly. Golden tones remain a feature of Stalin posters thereafter. By 1946 Stalin was frequently celebrated as the saviour of the USSR and of the West and propagandists became less coy in granting him a sacral aura and the talismanic properties of a miracle-working icon.

Other colours also came to take on symbolic meaning. White in the icon symbolises God the Father and eternal light. Kandinskii saw white as symbolising joy and 'spotless purity'.[233] After 1934 white began to feature not only in propaganda posters, but also in propaganda in the press. Stalin and the other leaders were often seen dressed all in white, as were the Stakhanovites and people in parades, with life becoming more 'joyous' for all Soviet citizens after the Stakhanovite conference of 1935.[234] From the earliest days of the Revolution, black, which in the language of icons is associated with evil and death, was associated with capitalists and the bourgeoisie. In posters of the war years it was often used in association with the enemy. In early propaganda posters green had traditionally been the colour of enemies, particularly associated with the Poles[235] but, in the 1930s, as enemy classes were purged and disappeared, green came to be associated with fertility, abundance and festivity. In the icon, green is associated with fecundity or the Holy Spirit.

Although the use of colours in propaganda posters did not always correspond directly with their meaning in icons, they held in common with the icon a fixity of symbolic meaning which encoded figures and objects in the posters in ways which were meaningful to the initiated. Symbolism and fixity of meaning extended beyond colour

---

Karpovskii, 'Labour with martial persistence …', 1948; Vladislav Pravdin & Nikolai Denisov, 'Long live our leader and teacher the great Stalin!', 1948 (Fig. 3.29); Vasilii Suriyaninov, 'Stalin is our banner', 1948; Leonid Golovanov, 'And Stalin raised us to be loyal to the people …', 1949 (Fig. 3.21); Petr Golub, 'Long life and prosperity to our motherland!', 1949; Viktor Ivanov, 'Great Stalin is the beacon of communism!', 1949 (Fig. 3.7); F. Litvinov, 'Long life and prosperity to our motherland', 1949 (Fig. 3.22); Vladislav Pravdin, 'Work well so that Comrade Stalin thanks you', 1949; Nikolai Denisov, 'Long live great Stalin, creator of the constitution of the victorious socialism!', 1950; Viktor Ivanov, 'Stalin is our great standard-bearer of peace!', 1950 (Fig. 4.54).
233 Kandinsky, *Concerning the spiritual in art*, p. 40.
234 J.V. Stalin, 'Speech at the First All-union Conference of Stakhanovites', 17 November 1935 in J.V. Stalin, *Problems of Leninism*, Foreign Languages Press, Peking, 1976, pp. 775–94, pp. 783–84.
235 See White, *The Bolshevik poster*, p. 5.

to include signifying and symbolic clothing, poses, gestures, props and compositional elements. Painters and art critics spoke of Stalin portraits using the same language that had long been used to discuss icon painting, for example, the terms *'zhivoi'*, which means 'alive' and 'vivid'[236] and denotes 'the discharge of sacral energy', and *obraz*, meaning 'image', which 'signifies a Russian Orthodox, nonmimetic, performative image.'[237] Plamper argues that the *obraz* functioned as the equivalent of the *podlinnik* in icon painting, and 'confined and configured' the thematic possibilities for portraying Stalin.[238] In practice, the *obraz* corresponds roughly with our archetype, so that key *obrazi* in the portrayal of Stalin were the Father of the people, the Warrior, the Teacher, the Architect, the Magician and the Saviour. The ability to merge several *obrazi* in the one image was particularly valued and *Iskusstvo* praised portrait artist Aleksandr Gerasimov with the observation that '[t]he great value of Gerasimov the portraitist lies in his ability to convey in the images of the leaders the unity of the features of the state leader, the tribune of the people, and the man'.[239]

In 1947 Toidze created a poster that combines the themes of childhood, victory in the war, and the bright communist future in one powerful image. Stalin is depicted in marshal's uniform holding a toddler aloft. At first glance, 'Stalin's kindness illuminates the future of our children!' (Fig. 3.2) appears to step back to the Stalin iconography of the mid-1930s, depicting Stalin holding a young child. The contact in 1947, however, is not fatherly, intimate or affectionate. Stalin holds the child at arm's length away from his body, his hands placed in the same manner as those of Christ in icons of the Dormition of the Virgin, and the child in the position of the soul of the Virgin which is held by Christ. The feast of the Dormition commemorates the 'falling asleep' (natural death) of the Virgin, her salvation by Christ, and her acceptance into paradise. The child in the poster (a little blond Russian boy) does not look at Stalin, but out to the right and holds a bunch of flowers and a little red flag, sacred symbol of the Revolution and blood sacrifice, protection and intercession. He wears white, as does the soul of the Virgin in Dormition icons. Stalin stands in the position of Christ in the icon. In the icon, the Virgin's soul is held by Christ who conveys

---

236 Plamper translates 'zhivoi' as 'life-giving'. Plamper, *The Stalin cult*, p. xvii.
237 Plamper, *The Stalin cult*, p. xvii.
238 Plamper, *The Stalin cult*, p. 193.
239 'Prazdnik sotsialisticheskoi kul'tury', *Iskusstvo*, 2, 1941, p. 6, cited in Plamper, *The Stalin cult*, p. 194.

it to an angel who carries it to Heaven. By depicting Stalin wearing the marshal's uniform, reference is made to his role as Russia's saviour in The Great Patriotic War. Russia has endured much pain, bloodshed and sacrifice. From this sacrifice the pure Russian soul has emerged, to be placed into the hands of Stalin and thus conveyed through the passage of worldly suffering to the waiting gates of paradise. In a socialist reading, this paradise exists here on earth, the long-promised land of the communist utopia. The text of the poster associates Stalin with light and makes it clear it is Stalin's care and kindness that has enabled the Russian people to survive the war and emerge into the communist paradise.

Stalin and the Virgin

Stalin is not only associated with the figure of Christ but, somewhat surprisingly, is endowed with many of the qualities of the Mother of God. He is often pictured with children, sometimes holding them in his arms; is surrounded by flowers, often roses; and is almost always engulfed in a sea of red which extends above him and often covers the small figures of the crowd below in a manner reminiscent of the veil of the Virgin[240] spread protectively over the congregation at the Feast of the Intercession. In Pravdin's 1950 poster, 'Long live the Bolshevik Party, the Lenin–Stalin Party, the vanguard of the Soviet people forged in battle, the inspiration and organiser of Our Victories!' (Fig. 2.22), Stalin appears with the Soviet leadership, literally situated under Lenin's banner, which protects them in a manner reminiscent of the veil of the Theotokos in Orthodox iconography.

The Virgin is often referred to as the 'joy of every living thing', a mantle that Stalin seems to have appropriated for his persona and which is made manifest in the slogans on several posters,[241] including those in which Stalin is thanked for providing a happy childhood. In their 1992 study of personality and charismatic leadership, House et al. were surprised to discover that charismatic leadership is positively correlated with the personality traits of femininity and nurturance and negatively correlated with masculinity, dominance, aggression

---

240 Often coloured blue or purple, except in Novgorodian icons where it is red.
241 For example, Viktor Koretskii, 'Beloved Stalin is the people's happiness', 1950 and Viktor Ivanov, 'For national happiness', 1950.

and criticalness.[242] Several eyewitness accounts of encounters with Stalin emphasise his softness, gentleness, solicitude, supportiveness, and even his feminine characteristics.[243]

It must be noted that the androgynous characteristic of the Stalin cult is not a unique phenomenon. Mikhail Weiskopf notes that androginal evocations in eulogistic writings on the Russian tsars had a long tradition[244] and, as has been noted earlier, Skradol has commented on the situation in which Lenin was portrayed as both father and wife to Stalin.[245] Maksim Gor'kii wrote of Lenin as 'the mother of mankind', and a man who was 'a flame of almost feminine tenderness towards humanity'.[246] Donald McIntosh argues that, in contrast to traditional leadership, prophetic charismatic leadership appears to be heavily libidinised and sometimes manifests a leader with bisexual characteristics.[247]

Conclusion

The Stalin persona contained something for everyone. It was not only ubiquitous in its presence, but all-encompassing. Stalin could be both human and divine; father, mother, husband, son; leader, teacher, warrior, saviour and magician. He had exceptional wisdom and unearthly knowledge, could appear magically when needed and heal or set a situation right, but was personally modest and unassuming,

---

242   Robert J. House & Jane M. Howell. 'Personality and charismatic leadership', *Leadership Quarterly*, 3:2, 1992, pp. 81–108, p. 88.
243   The other side of Stalin's nature, known to his intimates and close professional associates, showed a propensity to temper, impetuosity, and vindictiveness. Stalin's letters to Molotov reveal a man indifferent to the effect of his policies and decisions on the lives of the people, and quick to use arbitrary violence as a political weapon: '… definitely shoot two or three dozen wreckers from these *apparaty* [the Finance and Gosbank bureaucracies], including several dozen common cashiers' ('Letter from Stalin to Molotov', Aug. 1930, regarding plans for dealing with the coin shortage, in Lars T. Lih, Oleg V. Naumov & Oleg. V. Khlevniuk (eds), *Stalin's letters to Molotov: 1925–1936*, Catherine A. Fitzpatrick (trans.), New Haven, 1995, p. 200).
244   Mikhail Weiskopf, *Pisatel' Stalin*, Moscow, Novoe Literaturnoe Obozrenie, 2001, p. 112.
245   Skradol, 'Remembering Stalin', pp. 33–34.
246   Maksim Gor'kii, cited in Michael Smith, 'Stalin's martyrs: the tragic romance of the Russian Revolution', *Totalitarian Movements and Political Religions*, 4:1, 2003, pp. 95–126.
247   McIntosh cites Gandhi, Jesus and Joan of Arc as examples of this type of leadership ('Weber and Freud: on the nature and sources of authority', *American Sociological Review*, 35:5, 1970, pp. 901–11, pp. 905–06). Mao Zedong has also frequently been attributed feminine characteristics. For example, Agnes Smedley, *Battle hymn of China*, New York, A.A. Knopf, 1943, p. 169.

and as intimately concerned with the everyday mundane aspects of the life of the 'little man' as with affairs of state and world peace. He represented concrete entities like the Bolshevik Party, the state, and the USSR, as well as more abstract notions such as Bolshevik vision, communist ideals, the international brotherhood of workers, the victory of socialism, victory over enemies such as kulaks and fascists, world peace, and paradise on earth in the form of an imminent communist utopia. The Bolsheviks were intent on creating an entirely new type of society peopled by a new and improved type of Soviet person, but in order to do this within the space of one or two generations, a largely agricultural and illiterate people had to be inoculated with the Marxist–Leninist vision and a whole new set of principles and beliefs had to be inculcated, driving out the outdated beliefs of the past. Ideology and abstracts were of little interest, and often too complex, for the newly semi-literate and rapidly urbanising workforce whose struggle for survival in a harsh climate of deprivation consumed most of their time and energy. Bolshevik principles and teachings had to be made accessible to the public at least at a level, in the initial stages in any case, where it could serve to mobilise the population to achieve the regime's goals (and indeed to survive as a nation) and to view itself as a harmonious and united entity with a meaningful shared identity. Research by agitators and propagandists among the population indicated that these values, principles and teachings were best absorbed, at a preliminary level, if they came to be personified in the identity of the leader. As a vessel for all of these desirable qualities, the image of Stalin came to be treated by some as an icon through which one could seek comfort and spiritual guidance. This tendency, although apparently officially meeting with disapproval, was in fact facilitated by the application of many of the devices used in Russian Orthodox icons to political propaganda posters. In some ways, this may have been largely unavoidable. In order to communicate with people, it is necessary to speak a language they understand and to use concepts with which they are familiar. Early post-revolutionary attempts to overhaul the language and introduce new, specifically Bolshevik, terms met with wide incomprehension from everyone other than committed Party members. As time passed, and the leadership applied a Marxist and scientific approach to education and propaganda, with particular interest in conditioned reflexes, eugenics and Lamarckian evolution, the decision to employ a language, both verbal and visual, drawing on the pre-existing vocabulary of the Orthodox Church, national mythologies and universal archetypes, became conscious and deliberate. Icons were mass cult objects with two main functions: as liturgical cult images and with a didactic role. It can be argued that posters constituted a parallel mass visual cult with similar functions.

Fig. 4.1 'I.V. Stalin', unidentified artist, 1930, Litografia СККРО (Krasnodar), edn 25,000

Source: Russian State Library

THE PERSONALITY CULT OF STALIN IN SOVIET POSTERS, 1929–1953

Fig. 4.2 'The Civil War 1918–1920', unidentified artist, 1938, 92 x 62.5 cm
Source: Hoover Institution Archives

4. STALIN SAVES THE WORLD

Fig. 4.3 'Defence of the USSR', unidentified artist, 1938, 92 x 62.5 cm
Source: Hoover Institution Archives

Fig. 4.4 'Comrade I.V. Stalin at the Front of the Civil War', S. Podobedov, 1939, RKKA

Source: Russian State Library

4. STALIN SAVES THE WORLD

Fig. 4.5 'Military Oath', S. Podobedov, 1939
Source: Russian State Library

Fig. 4.6 'Long live our leader and teacher, best friend of the Red Army, our dear and beloved Stalin!', S. Podobedov, 1940, RKKA
Source: Russian State Library

Fig. 4.7 'Long live our dear invincible Red Army!', Dmitrii Moor & Sergei Sen'kin, 1938

Source: Russian State Library

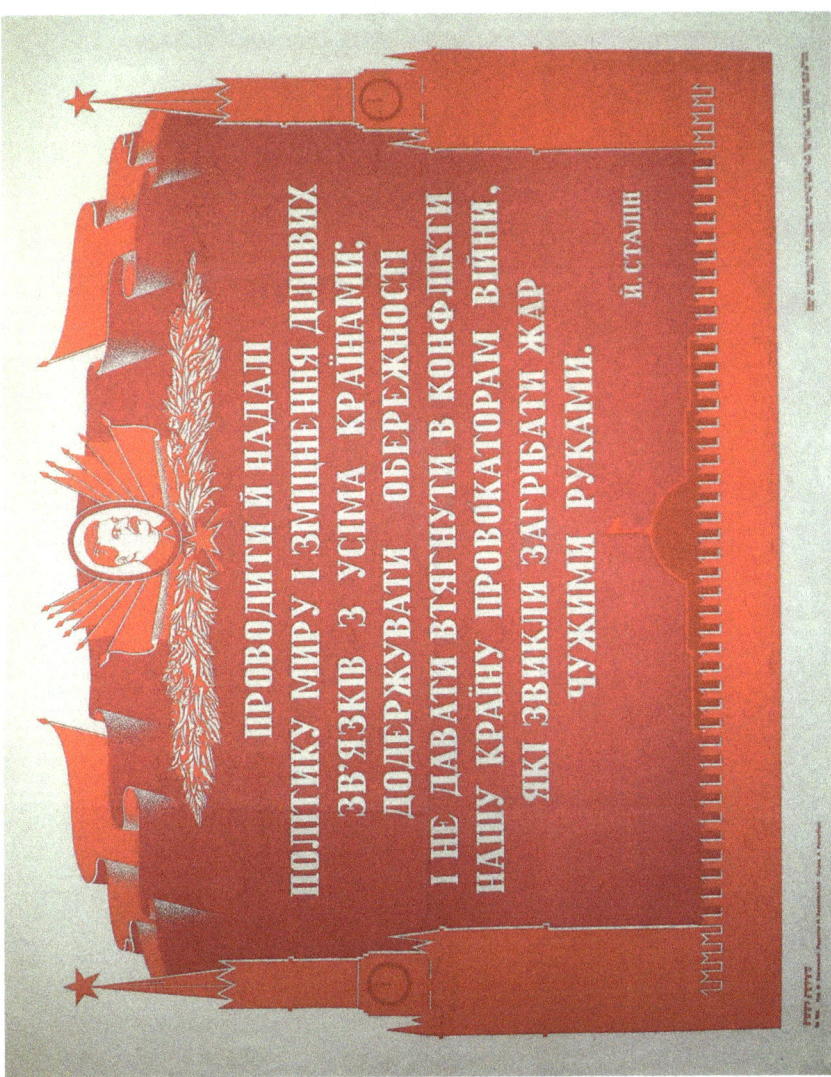

Fig. 4.8 'To continue the policy of peace and of strengthening business relations with all countries ...', M. Kaminskii, 1939, Mistetstvo (Kiev), 60 x 92 cm, edn 20,000

Source: Russian State Library

Fig. 4.9 'Long live the organiser and leader of the victorious Red Army great Stalin!', S. Podobedov, 1938, RKKA
Source: Russian State Library

Fig. 4.10 'Long live the creator of the first cavalry, best friend of the Red Cavalry — Comrade Stalin!', unidentified artist, 1939, RKKA

Source: Russian State Library

Fig. 4.11 'Stalin's spirit makes our army and country strong and solid', Viktor Deni & Nikolai Dolgorukov, 1939

Source: my-ussr.ru/soviet-posters/red-army/147-posters-of-the-ussr-red-army.html?start=1

Fig. 4.12 'The foreign policy of the Soviet Union is clear and explicit', unidentified artist, 1940, Izostat
Source: Russian State Library

Fig. 4.13 'If the leader calls ...', Viktor Koretskii, 1941, Izvestiia, 35 x 25 cm
Source: www.russianartandbooks.com/cgi-bin/russianart/Pr00233.html

Fig. 4.14 '"The spirit of the great Lenin and his victorious banner inspires us now in the Patriotic War as it did 23 years ago." Stalin', unidentified artist, 1941, Iskusstvo (Moscow, Leningrad), 82.5 x 59.5 cm, edn 10,000

Source: Hoover Institution Archives

THE PERSONALITY CULT OF STALIN IN SOVIET POSTERS, 1929–1953

Fig. 4.15 'Under the banner of Lenin–Stalin we were victorious in the great October Socialist Revolution …', A.V. Vasil'ev and S.F. Yanevich, 1941, Izdanie (Leningrad), edn 20,000

Source: Russian State Library

4. STALIN SAVES THE WORLD

Fig. 4.16 '"All our forces — to support our heroic Red Army and our glorious Red Navy! All the power of the people — to defeat the enemy!" Stalin', Iraklii Toidze, 1941, edn 6,000

Source: Russian State Library

Fig. 4.17 'We swore an oath to our leader to fight the enemy ...', Konstantin Cheprakov, 1941, Gosizdat (Tashkent), 60 x 94 cm, edn 10,000
Source: Russian State Library

4. STALIN SAVES THE WORLD

Fig. 4.18 'Under the name of Stalin we won. Under the name of Stalin we will win!', unidentified artist, 1941, Iskusstvo (Leningrad), edn 25,000

Source: Russian State Library

THE PERSONALITY CULT OF STALIN IN SOVIET POSTERS, 1929–1953

Fig. 4.19 'The spirit of the great Lenin and his victorious banner inspires us now in the Patriotic War as it did 23 years ago', Boris Mukhin, 1942, Iskusstvo (Moscow, Leningrad), 90 x 60 cm, edn 20,000

Source: Russian State Library

Fig. 4.20 'We can and must clear our Soviet soil of the Hitlerite filth!', V. Mirzoe, c. 1942, Sakhelgami, edn 1,500

Source: Russian State Library

Fig. 4.21 'Under the invincible banner of the great Lenin — forward to victory!', Nikolai Kogout, 1942, Gosizdat, edn 15,000

Source: Russian State Library

Fig. 4.22 'The path to our glory is immutable — Fascism will die! ...', Pen Varlen, 1942, Gosizdat (Tashkent), edn 10,000

Source: Russian State Library

Fig. 4.23 'Under the banner of Lenin, forward, to victory!', Vladimir Serov, 1942, Iskusstvo (Leningrad), 89 x 63 cm, edn 10,000

Source: Russian State Library

THE PERSONALITY CULT OF STALIN IN SOVIET POSTERS, 1929–1953

Fig. 4.24 'Comrades of the Red Army …', Viktor Ivanov & Ol'ga Burova, 1942, Iskusstvo (Moscow, Leningrad), 88 x 59 cm, edn 30,000
Source: Russian State Library

Fig. 4.25 'Okno UzTAG No. 123', Nadezhda Kashina, 1942, Okno UzTAG (Uzbekistan), 84 x 183 cm
Source: Russian State Library

Fig. 4.26 'Okno TASS No. 590', Pavel Sokolov-Skalia, 1942, TASS (Moscow), 218 x 102 cm, edn 400
Source: Russian State Library

Fig. 4.27 'During the war …', Vlasob', 1943, (Baku), edn 5,000
Source: Russian State Library

Fig. 4.28 'For the Soviet fatherland ...', Nikolai Zhukov & Viktor Klimashin, 1943, Iskusstvo (Moscow, Leningrad), edn 25,000

Source: Russian State Library

Fig. 4.29 '"The spirit of the great Lenin and his invincible banner inspire us now in the patriotic war" (I. Stalin)', Veniamin Pinchuk, 1943, Iskusstvo (Leningrad), edn 4,000

Source: Russian State Library

Fig. 4.30 'For our great motherland!', Nina Vatolina, 1944, Iskusstvo (Moscow, Leningrad), edn 50,000

Source: Russian State Library

Fig. 4.31 'Under the leadership of Comrade Stalin, forward to complete victory over our enemy!', A.A. Babitskii, 1944, Iskusstvo (Moscow, Leningrad), 90 x 59 cm, edn 5,000
Source: Russian State Library

Fig. 4.32 '"Glory to the great heroic Red Army, defending the independence of our country and winning victory over the enemy!" I. Stalin', Vladimir Kaidalov, 1945, Dal'giz, edn 5,000

Source: Russian State Library

Fig. 4.33 'Great Stalin — first deputy of the Supreme Soviet of the USSR', Stepan Razvozzhaev, 1945, Izdanie (Irkutsk), edn 25,000

Source: Russian State Library

Fig. 4.34 'Long live the creator of the constitution of socialist society, the leader of the Soviet people, great Stalin!', unidentified artist, portrait by Karpov, Undated, c. 1945, Izdatelstvo Krasnyi Krym, edn 10,000
Source: Russian State Library

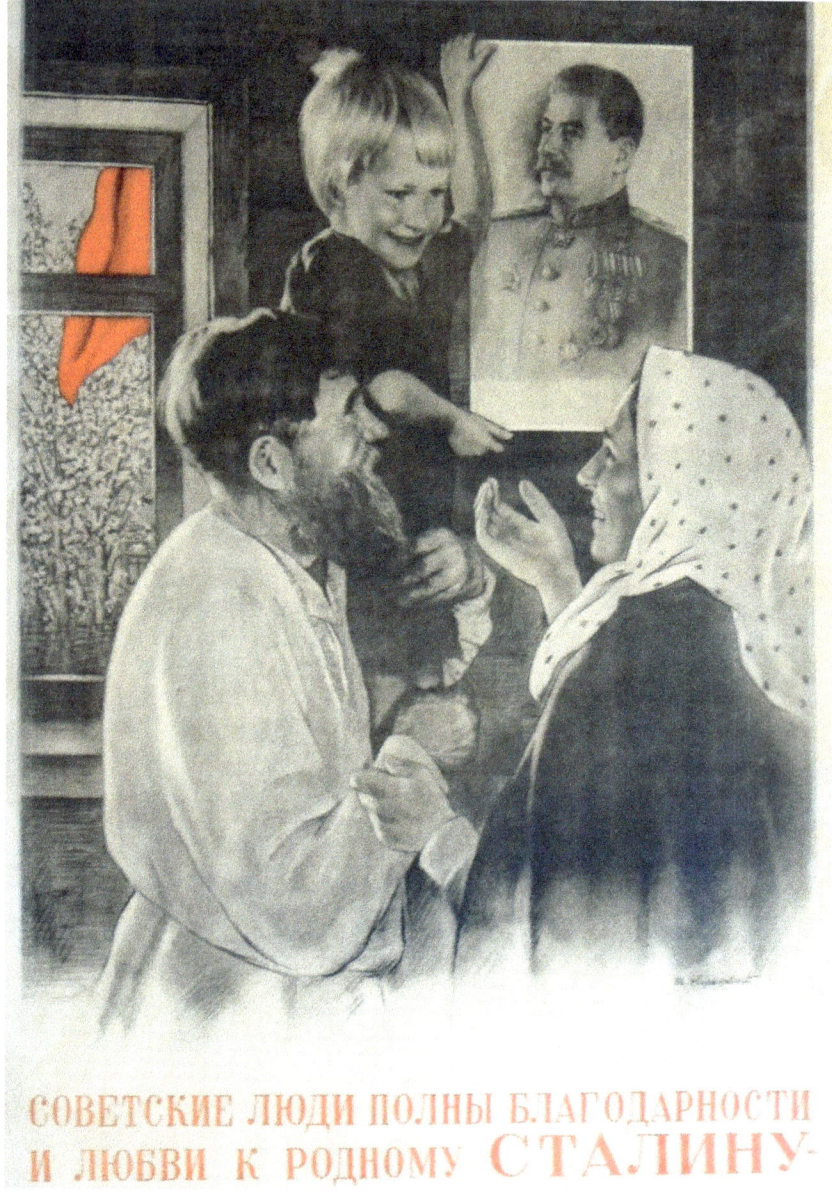

Fig. 4.35 'The Soviet people are full of gratitude and love for dear STALIN — the great organiser of our victory', Viktor Koretskii, 1945, Iskusstvo (Moscow, Leningrad), edn 75,000

Source: Russian State Library

Fig. 4.36 'Long live generalissimus STALIN — great leader and general of the Soviet people!', Viktor Deni, 1945, Iskusstvo (Moscow, Leningrad), edn 50,000

Source: Russian State Library

Fig. 4.37 'Forward, to new victories of socialist construction!', Iraklii Toidze, 1946, Iskusstvo (Moscow, Leningrad), 103 x 68 cm, edn 50,000
Source: Russian State Library

Fig. 4.38 '1917–1946 Glory to the Red Army, defending the gains of the great October socialist revolution!', Viktor Koretskii, 1946, Iskusstvo (Moscow, Leningrad), 96 x 63 cm, edn 70,000

Source: www.gelos.ru/2008/bigimages/np438-6.jpg

THE PERSONALITY CULT OF STALIN IN SOVIET POSTERS, 1929–1953

Fig. 4.39 'Long live the V.K.P.(b) — the party of Lenin–Stalin, inspirer and organiser of our great victories!', Iraklii Toidze, 1946, Iskusstvo (Moscow, Leningrad), edn 250,000

Source: Russian State Library

Fig. 4.40 'Long live the leader of the Soviet people — great Stalin', Onufriichuk, 1946, Mistetstvo, edn 50,000
Source: Russian State Library

Fig. 4.41 'Long live the leader of the Soviet people — great Stalin!', Boris Mukhin, 1947, Iskusstvo (Moscow, Leningrad), edn 300,000
Source: Russian State Library

Fig. 4.42 'Long live the leader of the Soviet people, great Stalin!', Boris Mukhin, 1947, Iskusstvo (Moscow, Leningrad)
Source: Russian State Library

THE PERSONALITY CULT OF STALIN IN SOVIET POSTERS, 1929–1953

Fig. 4.43 'Long live the leader of the Soviet people — great Stalin', Vladislav Pravdin & Nikolai Denisov, 1947, Iskusstvo (Moscow, Leningrad), edn 200,000

Source: Russian State Library

Fig. 4.44 'Glory to the leader of the Soviet people — great Stalin!', Georgii Bakhmutov, 1947, Mistetstvo, edn 70,000

Source: Russian State Library

Fig. 4.45 'Stalin is our fighting banner', Aleksandr Druzhkov & I. Shagin, 1948, Iskusstvo (Moscow, Leningrad)
Source: Russian State Library

Fig. 4.46 'Glory to great Stalin!', Boris Mukhin, 1948, Iskusstvo (Moscow, Leningrad)
Source: Russian State Library

THE PERSONALITY CULT OF STALIN IN SOVIET POSTERS, 1929–1953

Fig. 4.47 'It is our good fortune …', N. Petrov, 1948, Iskusstvo (Moscow, Leningrad)
Source: Russian State Library

Fig. 4.48 'Long live the V.K.P.(b) inspirer and organiser of the victory of the Soviet people!', B.I. Lebedev, 1948, Izdatelstvo (Moldavia), edn 5,000

Source: Russian State Library

Fig. 4.49 'Long live the party of Lenin–Stalin, inspirer and organiser of our victories!', F. Litvinov, 1948, Krymizdat
Source: Russian State Library

Fig. 4.50 'Long live the VKP(b) …', Aleksandr Druzhkov, 1948, Iskusstvo (Moscow, Leningrad)

Source: Russian State Library

Fig. 4.51 'We will struggle to reap a big cotton harvest!', Vladimir Kaidalov, 1950, 86 x 58.5 cm

Source: Tom and Jeri Ferris Collection of Russian and Soviet Culture

4. STALIN SAVES THE WORLD

Fig. 4.52 '"We stand for peace and we defend the cause of peace." I. Stalin', Boris Berezovskii, 1947, Iskusstvo (Moscow, Leningrad), 118 x 68 cm
Source: Russian State Library

THE PERSONALITY CULT OF STALIN IN SOVIET POSTERS, 1929–1953

Fig. 4.53 '"Long life and prosperity to our motherland!" I. Stalin', Iraklii Toidze, 1947, Iskusstvo (Moscow, Leningrad)
Source: Russian State Library

Fig. 4.54 'Stalin is our great standard-bearer of peace!', Viktor Ivanov, 1950, Iskusstvo (Moscow, Leningrad), 83.4 x 56.4, edn 100,000
Source: Russian State Library

Fig. 4.55 'Great Stalin is the banner of friendship of the peoples of the USSR!', Viktor Koretskii, 1950, Iskusstvo (Moscow, Leningrad), edn 200,000

Source: State Historical Museum

Fig. 4.56 'Great Stalin is the best friend of the Latvian people!', Petr Golub, 1950, Iskusstvo (Moscow, Leningrad), edn 20,000

Source: Russian State Library

THE PERSONALITY CULT OF STALIN IN SOVIET POSTERS, 1929–1953

Fig. 4.57 '"We stand for peace and we defend the cause of peace." I. Stalin', Boris Belopol'skii, 1952, Iskusstvo (Moscow), 82 x 64 cm, edn 300,000

Source: Russian State Library

Fig. 4.58 '"The world will be saved and enhanced if people take responsibility for maintaining peace into their own hands and defend it to the end." I. Stalin', Boris Belopol'skii, 1952, Iskusstvo (Moscow), 69 x 56 cm, edn 100,000

Source: Russian State Library

THE PERSONALITY CULT OF STALIN IN SOVIET POSTERS, 1929–1953

Fig. 4.59 'Happy New Year, beloved Stalin!', Konstantin Ivanov, 1952, Iskusstvo (Moscow), 55.5 x 37 cm, edn 50,000
Source: Russian State Library

4. STALIN SAVES THE WORLD

Fig. 4.60 'Long live the Leninist VKP(b), organiser of victorious socialist construction', Viktor Deni & Nikolai Dolgorukov, 1934, Izogiz (Moscow, Leningrad), 62 x 94 cm, edn 6,500

Source: State Historical Museum

Fig. 4.61 'Glory to great Stalin!', V. Paradovskii, 1947, Kirgosizdat, edn 2,190

Source: Russian State Library

Fig. 4.62 'Cadres decide everything', Gustav Klutsis, 1935, Izogiz (Moscow, Leningrad), 77 x 109 cm, edn 20,000
Source: Russian State Library

Fig. 4.63 'Long live the Stalinist Order of Heroes and Stakhanovites!', Gustav Klutsis, 1936, 71.3 x 101.2 cm
Source: David King Collection

Fig. 4.64 'Our government and the Party does not have other interests …', Viktor Koretskii, 1938, Izogiz (Moscow, Leningrad), 86 x 61.3 cm, edn 300,000

Source: Russian State Library

THE PERSONALITY CULT OF STALIN IN SOVIET POSTERS, 1929–1953

Fig. 4.65 'The reality of our program …', I. Shagin, 1947, Iskusstvo (Moscow, Leningrad), edn 300,000
Source: Russian State Library

Fig. 4.66 'Under the leadership of the great Stalin — forward to communism!', Boris Berezovskii, Mikhail Solov'ev & I. Shagin, 1951, Iskusstvo (Moscow), edn 500,000

Source: Russian State Library

Fig. 4.67 'Glory to the first candidate for deputy of the Supreme Soviet of the USSR, great Stalin!', Viktor Govorov, 1946, Ogiz
Source: Russian State Library

4. STALIN SAVES THE WORLD

Fig. 4.68 'We gathered under the red banner of Lenin …', Nikolai Denisov, 1949, Iskusstvo (Moscow, Leningrad), 89 x 60 cm, edn 100,000

Source: redavantgarde.com/en/collection/show-collection/1090-lenin-united-us-all-under-the-red-flag-and-our-destiny-is-great-glory-to-stalin-who-nurtured-the-youth-in-struggle-.html?authorId=104

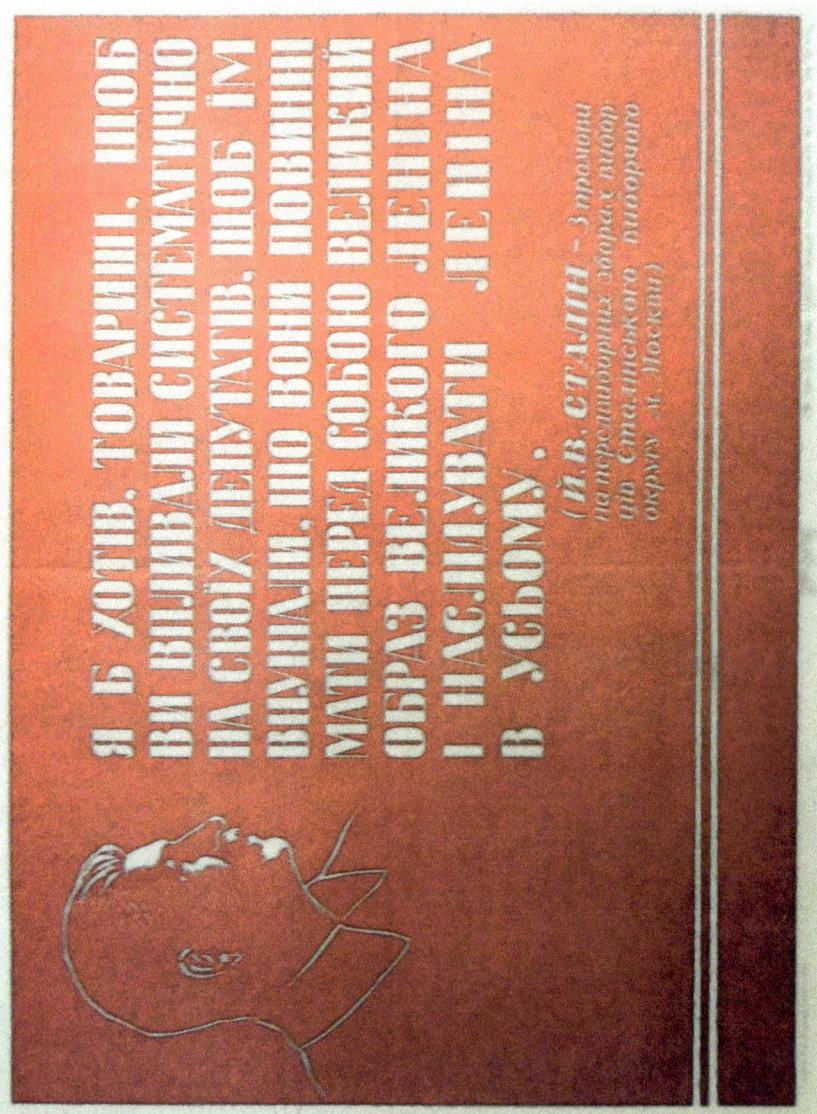

Fig. 4.69 'I would like comrades to systematically influence their deputies …', Be-Sha (Boris Shapoval) & Rozenberg, 1940, Mistetstvo (Kiev), edn 40,000

Source: Russian State Library

Conclusion

Despite Nikita Krushchev's Secret Speech condemning the personality cult of Stalin in 1956,[1] the removal of Stalin's body from Lenin's mausoleum in 1961, and the eradication of Stalin from Soviet history in the ensuing decades, some manifestations of the Stalin personality cult still exist today. In the last few years, Stalin's portrait has been (controversially)[2] carried in Victory Day parades in Russia, and his image appears on 'Soviet' tourist memorabilia such as T-shirts, mugs, calendars, bronze busts and poster reproductions. Surveys of popular attitudes in Russia suggest that Stalin has not only been 'rehabilitated' in the eyes of some sectors of the public, but that there is widespread nostalgia for the Stalinist years. A January 2005 survey carried out by the All-Russia Centre for the Study of Public Opinion in Russia reported in the *Moscow News* that 42 per cent of respondents wanted the return of a 'leader like Stalin'. When it came to respondents over 60 years of age, this figure went up to 60 per cent.[3] In 2008, Stalin ranked third in a nationwide poll to find Russia's greatest ever person.[4] Polly Jones notes that one of the major arguments against de-Stalinisation came from the military sector, which asserted that victory in the Great Patriotic War ensured Stalin a place in Soviet

---

1 Nikita Krushchev, 'Speech to the 20th Congress of the C.P.S.U', 24–25 Feb. 1956, www.marxists.org/archive/khrushchev/1956/02/24.htm.
2 A few examples of news items discussing the celebration of Stalin in Victory Day Parades can be found at *RT* (rt.com/news/stalin-history-legacy-ww2/); *Daily Motion* (www.dailymotion.com/video/xqi4sm_stalin-posters-victory-day_news); and *The Observers* (observers.france24.com/en/20120423-russia-estonia-latvia-stalinobus-kills-mood-ahead-world-war-two-victory-day-festivities). The *Moscow Times* of 12 May 2014 (p. 9) features a photograph of a Stalin portrait surrounded by floral tributes on Victory Day, 2014.
3 Figures from a 2005 survey carried out by the All-Russia Centre for the Study of Public Opinion in Russia, reported in the *Moscow News* on 4 Mar. 2005, cited in Orlando Figes, *The whisperers: private life in Stalin's Russia*, New York, Metropolitan Books, 2007, p. 641.
4 Ernest Raiklin, 'Stalinism vs Hitlerism: the basic intentions and results', *International Journal of Social Economics*, 38:4, 2011, pp. 358–81, p. 359.

history and in the national psyche.[5] The post-Stalin leadership also received numerous letters from non-military personnel claiming that the image of Stalin standing steadfastly at his post and the inspirational speeches he made to the nation were essential to the war victory. Many of these letters expressed their admiration for Stalin using the epithets of the print media and poster campaigns. A study of Soviet propaganda posters remains relevant and timely and the recent availability of extensive material in the Soviet archives has led to a burgeoning of exciting new scholarship in Stalin studies across many disciplines.

Despite the extensive literature available on the Stalin cult, there has been comparatively little focus on the visual arts under Stalin, with even fewer studies devoted to political posters of the era, and no dedicated study on the image of Stalin in posters. This book is an attempt to fill this lacuna. The political poster is shown to have been a key propaganda medium for the Stalinist regime and was central to the generation and maintenance of the cult of Stalin. Soviet public space was saturated with posters and Stalin's image was a dominant presence in many of them. Over the decades of Stalin's rule, as Stalin made fewer personal appearances in public life, his image in posters and paintings became the primary contact between the population and their leader. The leader became his portrait[6] and, in posters of the postwar years, Stalin's image sometimes took on apotropæic qualities.

In this study, Stalinist posters are analysed employing an art historical iconographic and iconologic methodology. The posters are examined as art objects and cultural artefacts, and placed in wider social, political and historical contexts. A major advantage of adopting this approach is that many interesting phenomena, trends and patterns are evident in the visual imagery employed in the posters that may not be specifically articulated elsewhere. By commencing with the images themselves, and conducting a comparative analysis across the large

---

5   Polly Jones, 'I've held, and I still hold, Stalin in the highest esteem': discourses and strategies of resistance to de-Stalinisation in the USSR, 1953–62', in Balázs Apor, Jan C. Behrends, Polly Jones & E.A. Rees, *The leader cult in communist dictatorships: Stalin and the Eastern Bloc*, Hampshire, Palgrave, 2004, p. 233.

6   Jan Plamper opens his book on the Stalin cult with an anecdote about a woman who fainted when she saw Stalin at her front door. When she recovered, Beria asked her what had happened and she answered; 'I thought that a portrait of Stalin was moving towards me' (*The Stalin cult: a study in the alchemy of power*, New Haven, Yale University Press, 2012, p. xiii).

sample of posters, subtle variations in the projections of the Stalin image over time can be detected, contributing to the discourse on the Stalin cult across a number of disciplines.

Despite the fact that Marxist systems declare themselves to be ideologically opposed to the notion of the personality cult, whether by design or default, and usually something of both, personality cults flourish in times of turbulence and strife, and particularly in circumstances when a leader needs to mobilise a population to attain urgent goals. Personality cults tap into universal myths and archetypes that provide guidance, comfort, reassurance and a spiritual dimension to a life of struggle and sacrifice. It is argued that Stalin's image in propaganda drew on mythic archetypes that tapped into unconscious forces in the popular psyche. Posters of Stalin are analysed with reference to a number of archetypes that were employed to create an all-encompassing charismatic persona for the leader. The Father, the Warrior, the Teacher, the Saviour, the Architect, the Helmsman and the Magician became various facets of the Stalin persona — sometimes confusing, contradictory and irreconcilable — but drawing on deep, unconscious associations from mythology and the Church. Stalin was simultaneously imbued with notions of blood ties and kinship with the population, teacher and mentor, brilliant warrior and military strategist, and spiritual guide with superhuman and supernatural abilities.

It is argued that this charismatic persona was intentionally crafted for Stalin in order to mobilise an initially uneducated and illiterate population behind the Party vanguard, to adopt a single ideology and to participate in a number of tangible projects and goals that transformed the immediate physical environment. The leader figure became a symbol for a surprisingly wide number of qualities and entities, both concrete and abstract. Modern personality cults make use of mass media and communication networks with vast reach to disseminate images of the leader and hence create a ubiquitous leader presence. In states like the USSR, where the leader is able to control these networks, almost total control of the dissemination of the leader's image is possible and the propaganda apparatus can craft an image which is marketed to the population, stressing desirable and charismatic characteristics and deleting anything which does not enhance the desired image. The argument that the use of archetypal qualities in portrayals of Stalin was intentional is supported by evidence from other areas of Soviet propaganda, including the creation of a hagiography constructed around a series of sacred events in which archetypal roles are highlighted, and the existence of themed rooms at exhibitions that show Stalin in his various roles.

A case has been made for the inclusion of Bolshevism in the category of 'political religion'. This concept enhances understanding of propaganda posters produced under Stalin because they borrow from, and adapt, Russian Orthodox traditions and symbolism in an attempt to induce 'religious' feeling toward the leader, the Party and the state. Belief in the new goals for the attainment of a communist state became a matter of faith, working to achieve these goals became a sacred duty, and veneration of the leader followed thereafter. Detailed analysis of the imagery in posters of Stalin has demonstrated how many of the devices used in the Russian Orthodox icon have been transplanted or adapted to the political poster, and that this occurred both because the icon provided a shared visual language for artists and the population and because several of the most successful early poster artists had studied the art of the icon as a Russian indigenous artform. These artists in turn held teaching posts at some of the most important Soviet art schools, influencing the next generations of Soviet artists.

The use of visual language associated with the icon imbued the image of Stalin with sacred qualities and, coupled with his increasing absence from public life, led to a persona that incorporated qualities of deity. His persona took on an increasingly sacral aura to the extent that when he died in March 1953, there was widespread disbelief. Many Soviet citizens viewed Stalin's death as a personal crisis and something that they found difficult to comprehend. Literary scholar Raisa Orlova wrote: 'We saw newspaper photographs of Stalin in the coffin, with arms folded and lips pressed firmly together. And it is still hard to believe that Stalin has died. Somewhere deep inside, we still keep hoping for a miracle.'[7] Writer Ilia Ehrenburg reflected: 'And we had long forgotten that Stalin was a human being. He had become an all-powerful and mysterious God. And then God died from a cerebral haemorrhage. That was unbelievable ... . I did not feel sorry for the God who died of a stroke at the age of seventy-three ... but I felt

---

7   Raisa Orlova, quoted in Irina Paperno, 'Intimacy with power', in Klaus Heller & Jan Plamper, *Personality cults in Stalinism*, Goìttingen, V&R Unipress, 2004, pp. 331–61, p. 343.

fear about what was to come.'[8] The association of Stalin with deity was complex, as Stalin's image in posters recalled both the figure of Christ and that of the Virgin and he was endowed with both masculine and feminine qualities. Research in the field of leader studies has demonstrated that it is not unusual for a charismatic leader persona to incorporate both masculine and feminine traits.

The employment of mythic archetypes and visual reference to the Orthodox icon were not the only devices used in posters to create a charismatic leader persona for Stalin. Analysis of Stalin posters reveals that Lenin appears with Stalin in approximately one-third of the posters. It appears that the image of Lenin performed important functions in the Stalin personality cult and Stalin was frequently portrayed in close proximity to Lenin as his best student and disciple. One of the devices employed by Stalin in the struggle for leadership after Lenin's death was to portray himself as the natural successor of the martyred founder of the regime. Throughout Stalin's leadership, Lenin continued to be invoked as a legitimating presence for Stalin and the Party, particularly during the years of the Great Patriotic War. Over time, Stalin came out from Lenin's shadow as a humble student and increasingly stood alongside Lenin as a revolutionary thinker in his own right. Lenin's importance as a legitimating influence was particularly evident in that it survived Stalin and was employed after Stalin's death to bestow legitimacy on the Party. It is also argued that Lenin's continual presence had an effect at an unconscious, pre-rational level. The image of Lenin invoked mortality salience in the audience, which served to increase viewer identification with Stalin as leader, and hostility toward enemies of the regime. The employment of binary coding that contrasted Stalin's image with that of despised enemies further enhanced this effect.

This study has brought to light many previously unpublished posters that illustrate in detail the evolution of the image of Stalin over the period of his leadership. The conclusions that are drawn support and supplement those arrived at in studies of other propaganda media under Stalin, making a particular contribution to the literature on the visual arts. Posters are an informative medium through which to analyse the propaganda trends under the Stalinist regime because

---

8   Ilia Ehrenburg, quoted in Paperno, 'Intimacy with power', in Heller & Plamper, *Personality cults in Stalinism*, p. 347.

poster production was particularly tightly regulated and controlled and because the medium itself invites the combination and juxtaposition of images in a stylised and symbolic manner. The addition of text to the visual image directs the viewer to the intended meaning and serves to remove potential ambiguities in the visual image. Posters thus provide an excellent record of the propagandistic priorities of the Stalinist regime, and are one of the most reliable sources of evidence for how the regime wished to present itself and its leader to the wider citizenry.

Appendix 1: Breakdown of posters in the research sample by year

Undated posters	24		1940	16
1927	1		1941	10
1928	0		1942	12
1929	1		1943	11
1930	6		1944	8
1931	8		1945	16
1932	8		1946	20
1933	23		1947	23
1934	10		1948	20
1935	12		1949	24
1936	7		1950	22
1937	14		1951	14
1938	35		1952	14
1939	29		1953	1

Source: Table prepared by the author

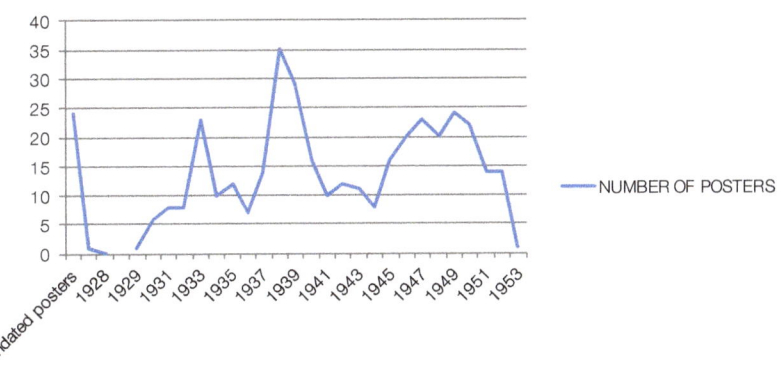

NUMBER OF POSTERS WITH AN IMAGE OF STALIN

Source: Graph prepared by the author

Appendix 2: Frequency trends in posters with images of Stalin in the research sample, and Stalin's appearances in *Pravda*

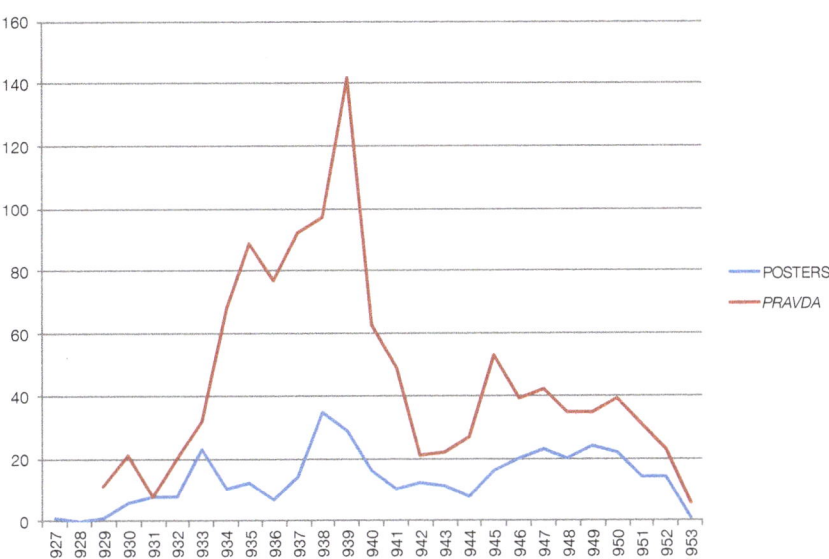

Source: Figures for Stalin's appearances in *Pravda* are from Jan Plamper, *The Stalin cult: a study in the alchemy of power*, New Haven, Yale University Press, 2012, p. 228. Graph created by author

Appendix 3: Posters of Stalin and Lenin by year

YEAR	POSTERS WITH STALIN AND LENIN	TOTAL POSTERS WITH STALIN	PERCENTAGE
1927	0	1	0
1929	0	1	0
1930	2	6	33.3
1931	2	8	25
1932	2	8	25
1933	6	23	26
1934	5	10	50
1935	0	12	0
1936	2	7	28.6
1937	5	14	35.7
1938	12	35	34.3
1939	7	29	24.1
1940	4	16	25
1941	5	10	50
1942	6	12	50
1943	6	11	54.5
1944	4	8	50
1945	6	16	37.5
1946	11	20	55
1947	7	23	30.4
1948	10	20	50
1949	7	24	29.2
1950	9	22	40.9
1951	8	14	57.1
1952	2	14	14.3
1953	1	1	100
Undated*	9	24	37.5

*Although undated, an examination of the content of these posters places them in the 1940s, either during the war years, or after victory in the war.

Source: Table prepared by the author

Bibliography

Adebanwi, Wale. 'The cult of Awo: the political life of a dead leader', *Journal of Modern African Studies*, 46:3, 2008, pp. 335–60.

Ades, Dawn. *Art and power: Europe under the dictators 1930–45*. London, Thames and Hudson in association with Hayward Gallery, 1995.

Ades, Dawn & Alison McClean. *Revolution on paper: Mexican prints 1910–1960*. Austin, University of Texas Press, 2009.

Aktűrk, Şener. 'Regimes of ethnicity: comparative analysis of Germany, the Soviet Union/post-Soviet Russia, and Turkey', *World Politics*, 63:1, 2011, pp. 115–64.

Alexandrov, G.F., M.R. Galaktionov, V.S. Kruzhkov, M.B. Mitin, V.D. Mochalov & P.N. Pospelov. *Joseph Stalin: a short biography*. Moscow, Foreign Languages Publishing House, 1947.

Alliluyeva, Svetlana. *Only one year*. Paul Chavchavadze (trans.). New York, Harper and Row, 1969.

———. *Twenty letters to a friend*. Priscilla Johnson McMillan (trans.). New York, Harper & Row, 1967.

Andersen, T. (ed.). *Malevich: the world as non-objectivity – unpublished writings, 1922–5*, vol. 3. Copenhagen, Borgens Forlag, 1976.

Andrew, Christopher & Julie Elkner. 'Stalin and foreign intelligence', *Totalitarian Movements and Political Religions*, 2003, 4:1, pp. 69–94.

Andrews, Julia F. *Painters and politics in the People's Republic of China: 1949–1979*. London, University of California Press, 1994.

Andrews, Robert. *The new Penguin dictionary of modern quotations*, Penguin, London, 2003, books.google.com.au/books?id=VK0vR4 fsaigC&pg=PT1111&lpg=PT1111&dq=marshall+mcluhan+The+ new+penguin+dictionary+of+modern+quotations&source=bl&o ts=F-iC0c8wiM&sig=BAMUDrIXRMbypg0Znsg_NMOkFgE&hl=e n&sa=X&ved=0ahUKEwiR2qiQ3IbQAhXFtpQKHa81AvoQ6AEIGz AA#v=onepage&q=marshall%20mcluhan%20The%20new%20 penguin%20dictionary%20of%20modern%20quotations&f=false (accessed 1 Nov. 2016).

Andreyanova, V.V. *Khudozhnikii Narodov SSSR: Biobibliograficheskii Slovar'*, 1. Moscow, Izdatel'stvo 'Iskusstvo', 1970.

——. *Khudozhnikii Narodov SSSR: Biobibliograficheskii Slovar'*, 2. Moscow, Izdatel'stvo 'Iskusstvo', 1972.

Andreyanova, V.V. & I.I. Nikonova. *Khudozhnikii Narodov SSSR: Biobibliograficheskii Slovar'*, 3. Moscow, Izdatel'stvo 'Iskusstvo', 1976.

Angi, Daniela. 'Three instances of church and anti-communist opposition: Hungary, Poland and Romania', *Journal for the Study of Religions and Ideologies*, 10:28, 2011, pp. 21–64.

Ansell, Joseph & James Thorpe. 'The poster', *Art Journal*, 44:1, 1984, pp. 7–8.

Apor, Balázs, Jan C. Behrends, Polly Jones & E.A. Rees. *The leader cult in communist dictatorships: Stalin and the Eastern Bloc*. Hampshire, Palgrave, 2004.

Aris, Ben. 'Stalin exhibition feeds on revived personality cult', *Daily Telegraph*, London, 21 Feb. 2003, p. 19.

Arvidsson, Claes & Lars Erik Blomquist (eds). *Symbols of power: The esthetics of political legitimation in the Soviet Union and Eastern Europe*. Stockholm, Almqvist och Wiksell, 1987.

Aulich, James. *War posters: weapons of mass communication*. New York, Thames & Hudson, 2011.

Aulich, James & Marta Sylvestrová. *Political posters in Central and Eastern Europe, 1945–95: signs of the times*. Manchester University Press, 1999.

Austin, Gilbert. *Chironomia: or, a treatise on rhetorical delivery*. London, Printed for T. Cadell and W. Davies, 1806.

Baburina, N.I. *The Soviet political poster 1917–1980: from the USSR Lenin Library Collection*. Harmondsworth, Penguin Books, 1985.

Badian, E. 'Alexander the Great between two thrones and Heaven', *Journal of Roman Archaeology*, supp. ss 17, 1996, pp. 11–26.

Baehr, Peter. *Caesarism, charisma and fate: historical sources and modern resonances in the work of Max Weber*. New Brunswick, Transaction Publishers, 2008.

Bal, Mieke & Norman Bryson. 'Semiotics and art history', *Art Bulletin*, June 1991, pp. 174–20.

Baldaev, Danzig. *Russian criminal tattoo encyclopaedia*. London, Fuel Publishing, 2009.

Balfe, Judith Huggins. 'Art style as political actor: social realism and its alternatives', *Sociologia Internationalis*, 23:1, 1 supp., 1985, pp. 3–26.

Balina, Marina & E.A. Dobrenko. *Petrified Utopia: happiness Soviet style*. London, Anthem Press, 2009.

Banks, Miranda (ed.). *The aesthetic arsenal: socialist realism under Stalin*. New York, Institute for Contemporary Art, 1993.

Barber, John. 'Stalin's letters to the editors of Proletarskaya Revolyutsiya', *Soviet Studies*, 28:1, 1976, pp. 21–41.

———. 'The image of Stalin in Soviet propaganda and public opinion during World War 2', in John Garrard & Carol Garrard (eds). *World War 2 and the Soviet people*. New York, St. Martins Press, 1993, pp. 38–49.

Barnicoat, John. *A concise history of posters: 1870–1970*. New York, Harry N. Abrams Inc., 1972.

Bartelik, Marek. 'Concerning socialist realism: recent publications on Russian art', *Art Journal*, 58:4, 1999, pp. 90–95.

Bekeneva, N.G. *The icon collection in the Tretyakov Gallery*. Moscow, SkanRus, 2011.

Belodubrovskaya, Maria. 'The jockey and the horse: Joseph Stalin and the biopic genre in Soviet cinema', *Studies in Russian and Soviet Cinema*, 5:1, pp. 29–53.

Berdichevsky, Norman. 'The politics and aesthetics of art', *Contemporary Review*, 274:1598, 1999, pp. 153–54.

Berdyaev, Nicholas. *The Russian Revolution: two essays on its implications in religion and psychology*. D.B. (trans.). London, Sheed and Ward, 1931.

Bergman, Jay. 'The image of Jesus in the Russian revolutionary movement', *International Review of Social History*, 35, 1990, pp. 220–48.

——. 'The perils of historical analogy: Leon Trotsky on the French Revolution', *Journal of the History of Ideas*, 48:1, 1987, pp. 73–98.

——. 'Valerii Chkalov: Soviet pilot as new soviet man', *Journal of Contemporary History*, 33:1, 1998, pp. 135–52.

Berkhoff, Karel C. *Motherland in danger: Soviet propaganda during World War II*. Cambridge, Harvard University Press, 2012.

Bird, Robert, Christopher P. Heuer, Matthew Jesse Jackson, Tumelo Mosaka & Stephanie Smith (eds). *Vision and communism: Viktor Koretsky and dissident public visual culture*. New York, New Press, 2011.

Bligh, Michelle C. & Jill L. Robinson. 'Was Gandhi "charismatic"? Exploring the rhetorical leadership of Mahatma Gandhi', *The Leadership Quarterly*, 21, 2010, pp. 844–55.

Blood, Carolyn. 'The motherland calls!: nationalist propaganda in the Soviet Union during the Great Patriotic War', 2010. *Senior Theses*. Paper 1. digitalcommons.linfield.edu/histstud_theses/1.

Boczar, Danuta A. 'The Polish poster', *Art Journal*, 44:1, 1984, pp. 16–27.

Bogatyrev, Sergei. 'Bronze tsars: Ivan the Terrible and Fedor Ivanovich in the décor of early modern guns', *SEER*, 88:1/2, 2010, pp. 48–72.

———. 'Reinventing the Russian monarchy in the 1550s: Ivan the Terrible, the dynasty, and the church', *SEER*, 85:2, 2007, pp. 271–93.

Bonnell, Victoria E. *Iconography of power: Soviet political posters under Lenin and Stalin*. Berkeley, University of California Press, 1998.

———. 'The peasant woman in Stalinist political art of the 1930s', *The American Historical Review*, 98:1, 1993, pp. 55–82.

Boobbyer, Philip. *The Stalin era*. London, Routledge, 2000.

Borenstein, Eliot. 'National Bolshevism', *Slavic and East European Journal*, 48:3, 2004, pp. 497–99.

Borev, Urii. *Sotsialisticheskii Realizm: Vzgliad Covremennika i covremennyi vzgliad*. Moscow, Oformlenie O.F. Nelubova, 2008.

Borg, Astrid. *The cultural history of Russia*. London, Aurum Press, 1984.

Bourdieu, Pierre. *Language and symbolic power*. Cambridge, Harvard University Press, 1991.

———. 'Selections from the logic of practice', in A.D. Schrift, *The logic of the gift: toward an ethic of generosity*. New York, Routledge, 1997, pp. 190–230.

Bowlt, John E. 'Stalin as Isis and Ra: socialist realism and the art of design', *The Journal of Decorative and Propaganda Arts*, no. 24, *Design, culture, identity: the Wolfsonian Collection*, 2002, pp. 34–63.

———. 'Russian art in the nineteen twenties', *Soviet Studies*, 22:4, 1971, pp. 575–94.

Bown, Matthew Cullerne. *A dictionary of 20th century Russian and Soviet painters, 1900s–1980s*. London, Izomar, 1998.

———. *Art under Stalin*. New York, Holmes and Meier Pub., 1991.

———. *Socialist realist painting*. New Haven, Yale University Press, 1998.

Bown, Matthew Cullerne & Brandon Taylor (eds). *Art of the Soviets: painting, sculpture, and architecture in a one-party state, 1917–1992*. Manchester University Press, 1993.

Brady, Thomas A. 'Imperial destinies: a new biography of the Emperor Maximilian I', *Journal of Modern History*, 62:2, 1990, pp. 298–314.

Brandenberger, David. *National Bolshevism: Stalinist mass culture and the formation of modern Russian national identity, 1931–1956*. Cambridge, Harvard University Press, 2002.

———. *Propaganda state in crisis: Soviet ideology, indoctrination, and terror under Stalin, 1927–1941*. New Haven, Yale University Press, 2011.

———. 'The cult of Ivan the Terrible in Stalinist Russia', *The Russian Review*, 62:1, 2003, pp. 172–73.

Brandenberger, D.L. & A.M. Dubrovsky. '"The people need a tsar": the emergence of National Bolshevism as Stalinist ideology, 1931–1941', *Europe–Asia Studies*, 50:5, 1998, pp. 873–92.

Brandenberger, David & Kevin F.M. Platt. 'Terribly romantic, terribly progressive, or terribly tragic: rehabilitating Ivan IV under I.V. Stalin', *The Russian Review*, 58:4, 1999, pp. 635–54.

Brent, Allen. *The Imperial cult and the development of church order: concepts and images of authority in paganism and early Christianity before the age of Cyprian*. Boston, BRILL, 1999.

Breuilly, John. 'Max Weber, charisma and nationalist leadership', *Nations and Nationalism*, 17:3, 2011, pp. 477–99.

Brooks, Jeffrey. 'Socialist realism in *Pravda*: read all about it!', *Slavic Review*, 53:4, 1994, pp. 973–991.

———. 'Stalin's politics of obligation', *Totalitarian Movements and Political Religions*, 4:1, 2003, pp. 47–67.

———. *Thank you, Comrade Stalin! Soviet public culture from revolution to Cold War*. Princeton University Press, 2000.

——. 'The Russian nation imagined: the peoples of Russia as seen in popular imagery, 1860s–1890s', *Journal of Social History*, 43:3, 2010, pp. 535–57.

Bryson, Norman. *Vision and painting: the logic of the gaze*. New Haven, Yale University Press, 1983.

Buchanan, George. *My mission to Russia and other diplomatic memoirs*. London, Cassell and Company Limited, 1923.

Buchanan, Sherry & David Heather. *Vietnam posters: The David Heather collection*, 1st edn. Fort Worth, Prestel Publishing, 2009.

Bullock, Alan. *Hitler and Stalin: parallel lives*. New York, Knopf, 1992.

Bulwer, J. *Chirologia: or the naturall language of the hand. Composed of the speaking motions, and discoursing gestures thereof. Whereunto is added Chironomia: or, the art of manuall rhetoricke. Consisting of the naturall expressions, digested by art in the hand, as the chiefest instrument of eloquence*. London, Thomas Harper, 1644.

Butnik-Siverskii, B.S. *Sovetskii plakat epokhi grazhdanskoi voiny, 1918–1921*. Moscow, Izd. Vses. Knizhnoi palaty, 1960.

Byman, Daniel L. & Kenneth M. Pollack. 'Let us now praise great men: bringing the statesman back in', *International Security*, 25:4, 2001, pp. 107–46.

Carleton, Greg. 'Genre in socialist realism', *Slavic Review*, 53:4, 1994, pp. 992–1009.

Cassiday, Julie A. & Emily D. Johnson. 'Putin, Putiniana and the question of a post-Soviet cult of personality', *SEER*, 88:4, 2010, pp. 681–707.

Cassidy, Brendan (ed.). *Iconography at the crossroads*. Princeton University Press, 1993.

Cattaruzza, Marina. 'Introduction', *Totalitarian Movements and Political Religions*, spec. iss., *Political religions as a characteristic of the 20th century*, 6:1, 2005, pp. 1–18.

Causey, Susan (ed.). *Tradition and revolution in Russian art*. Manchester, Cornerhouse Publications, 1990.

Cavalli, Luciano. *Charisma, dictatorship and plebiscitary democracy.* Università di Firenze, 1984.

Chamberlin, Maria. 'Charismatic leaders: Napoleon, Stalin, Mao Zedong and Kim Il Sung'. Masters thesis, California State University, 2010. gradworks.umi.com/14/87/1487113.html.

Channon, John (ed.). *Politics, society and Stalinism in the USSR.* London, Macmillan Press, 1998.

Cheetham, Mark, Michael Ann Holly & Keith Moxey (eds). *The subjects of art history.* Cambridge University Press, 1998.

Cherniavsky, Michael. *Tsar and people: studies in Russian myths.* New Haven, Yale University Press, 1961.

Chiu, Melissa. *Art and China's revolution.* New Haven, Yale University Press, 2008.

Chuev, F. *Molotov remembers: inside Kremlin politics — conversations with Felix Chuev.* Albert Resis (ed.). Chicago, Terra Publishing Center as *Sto sorok besed s Molotovym*, Ivan R. Dee, Inc., 1993.

Chuev F. *Sto sorok besed s Molotovym.* Moscow, 1991.

Chung, Hilary & Michael Falchikov. *In the Party spirit: socialist realism and literary practice in the Soviet Union, East Germany and China.* Amsterdam, Rodopi, 1996.

Cioran, E.M. & Richard Howard. 'Learning from the tyrants', *Mississippi Review* 15:1/2, 1986, pp. 7–20.

Clark, Katerina. 'Eisenstein's two projects for a film about Moscow', *The Modern Language Review*, 101:1, 2006, pp. 184–200.

———. *The Soviet novel: history as ritual.* University of Chicago Press, 1981.

Clark, Katerina & Evgeny Dobrenko. *Soviet culture and power. A history in documents, 1917–1953.* New Haven, Yale University Press, 2007.

Cliff, Tony. 'The campaign against Trotsky', *Trotsky: fighting the rising Stalinist bureaucracy 1923–1927.* www.marxists.org/archive/cliff/works/1991/trotsky3/02-campaign.html.

Cohen, Florette & Sheldon Solomon, 'The politics of mortal terror', *Current Directions in Psychological Science*, 2011, 20:316, pp. 316–20.

Collection, The USSR Lenin Library. *Soviet political posters: 1917/1980*. Boston, Penguin, 1986.

Collins, Daniel E. 'The Tower of Babel undone in a Soviet pentecost: a linguistic myth of the first Five-Year Plan', *The Slavic and East European Journal*, 42:3, 1998, pp. 423–43.

Connor, Timothy Edward. *The politics of Soviet culture: Anatolii Lunacharskii*. Epping, Bowker, 1983.

Conquest, Robert. *Lenin*. London, Fontana, 1972.

Conquest, Robert & Paul Hollander (eds). *Political violence: belief, behaviour and legitimation*. New York, Palgrave Macmillan, 2008.

Constantine, Mildred. 'The poster collection', *The Bulletin of the Museum of Modern Art*, 18:4, 1951, pp. 2–16.

Constas, Helen. 'The U.S.S.R. — from charismatic sect to bureaucratic society', *Administrative Science Quarterly*, 6:3, 1961, pp. 282–98.

Craven, David. *Art and revolution in Latin America, 1910–1990*, 2nd edn. New Haven, Yale University Press, 2006.

Craven, David, Teresa Eckmann, Tere Romo & Ilan Stavans. *Latin American posters: public aesthetics and mass politics*. Sante Fe, Museum Of New Mexico Press, 2006.

Crossman, Richard (ed.). *The god that failed*, New York, Harper, 1949.

Crowley, David. *Posters of the Cold War*. London, Victoria & Albert Museum, 2008.

Curran, John. 'Constantine and the ancient cults of Rome: the legal evidence', *Greece and Rome*, 43:1, 1996, pp. 68–80.

Czepczynski, Mariusz. 'Interpreting post-socialist icons: from pride and hate towards disappearance and/or assimilation', *Journal of Studies and Research in Human Geography*, 4:1, 2010, pp. 67–78.

D'Alleva, Anne. *Methods and theories of art history*. London, Laurence King Publishing, 2005.

Dan, Lydia. 'Bukharin o Staline', *Novyi Zhurnal*, 75, 1964.

Daniels, Robert V. 'Russian political culture and the post-revolutionary impasse', *Russian Review*, 46:2, 1987, pp. 165–75.

Davies, Sarah. *Popular opinion in Stalin's Russia: terror, propaganda and dissent, 1934–1941*. Cambridge, Cambridge University Press, 1997.

——. 'The "cult" of the Vozhd': representations in letters from 1934–41', *Russian History*, 24:1–2, 1997, pp. 131–47.

Davies, Sarah & James Harris (eds). *Stalin: a new history*. Cambridge, Cambridge University Press, 2005.

Den Hartog, Deanne N., Robert J. House, Paul J. Hanges & S. Antonio Ruiz-Quintanilla. 'Culture specific and cross-culturally generalizable implicit leadership theories: are attributes of charismatic / transformational leadership universally endorsed?' *Leadership Quarterly*, 10:2, 1999, pp. 219–56.

Deutscher, Isaac. *Stalin: a political biography*, 2nd edn. New York, Oxford University Press, 1966.

——. *The prophet armed: Trotsky, 1879–1921*, vol. 1. New York, Oxford University Press, 1954.

——. *The prophet unarmed: Trotsky, 1921–1929*, vol. 2. New York, Oxford University Press, 1959.

Dickerman, Leah. 'Camera obscura: socialist realism in the shadow of photography', *October*, 93, 2000, pp. 138–53.

Dickerman, Leah (ed). *Building the collective: Soviet graphic design 1917–1937*, 2nd edn. New York, Princeton Architectural Press, 1996.

Diggelmann, Lindsay. 'Marketing Maximilian', *Parergon*, 25:2, 2008, pp. 183–85.

Dittmer, Lowell. 'Power and personality in China: Mao Tse-tung, Liu Shaoch'i, and the politics of charismatic succession', *Studies in Comparative Communism*, 7:1–2, 1974, pp. 21–49.

Djilas, Milovan. *Conversations with Stalin*. London, Rupert Hart-Davis, 1962.

Dobrenko, Evgeny. 'Creation myth and myth creation in Stalinist cinema', *Studies in Russian and Soviet Cinema*, 1:3, 2007, pp. 239–64.

——. 'Pushkin in Soviet and post-Soviet culture', in Andrew Kahn (ed.), *The Cambridge companion to Pushkin*. Cambridge, Cambridge University Press, 2006.

Dobrenko, E.A. & Eric Naiman. *The landscape of Stalinism: The art and ideology of Soviet space*. Seattle, University of Washington Press, 2003.

Dogan, Mattei. 'Comparing two charismatic leaders: Ataturk and de Gaulle', *Comparative Sociology*, 6, 2007, pp. 75–84.

Drescher, S., Sabean, D. & Sharlin, A. (eds). *Political symbolism in modern Europe: essays in honour of George L. Mosse*. New York, Transaction, 1982.

Dulffer, Jost. 'Bonapartism, fascism and National Socialism', *Journal of Contemporary History*, 11:4, 1976, pp. 1109–28.

Dung, Nguyen Ngoc & David Kunzle. *Decade of protest: political posters from the United States, Vietnam, Cuba 1965–1975*. Santa Monica, Smart Art Press, 1996.

Dunn, Dennis J. 'Stalin's holy war', *Catholic Historical Review*, 90:1, 2004, pp. 154–55.

Dwyer, Phillip G. 'Napoleon Bonaparte as hero and saviour: image, rhetoric and behaviour in the construction of a legend', *French History*, 18:4, 2004, pp. 379–40.

Eaton, Katherine Bliss. *Daily life in the Soviet Union*. Westport, Greenwood Press, 2004.

Eatwell, Roger. 'Introduction: new styles of dictatorship and leadership in interwar Europe', *Totalitarian Movements and Political Religions*, 7:2, 2006, pp. 127–37.

——. 'The concept and theory of charismatic leadership', *Politics, Religion and Ideology*, 7:2, 2006, pp. 141–56.

Ehrenburg, Ilya. *Men, years — life*, vol. 5, *The war: 1941–45*. Tatiana Shebunina & Yvonne Kapp (trans.). London, MacGibbon and Kee, 1964.

——. *Men, years — life*, vol. 6, *Post-war years: 1945–1954*. Tatiana Shebunina & Yvonne Kapp (trans.). London, MacGibbon and Kee, 1966.

Ehrenburg, Ilia. *A vse-taki ona vertitsia*. Berlin, Gelikon, 1922.

Elliott, David. 'Guerillas and partisans: art, power and freedom in Europe and beyond, 1940–2012', *Framework, Helsinki*, 10, Supp., 2009, pp. 22–25.

——. *New worlds: Russian art and society, 1900–1937*. New York, Rizzoli, 1986.

Engel, Johann Jacob & Henry Siddons. *Practical illustrations of rhetorical gesture and action*, 2nd edn. New York, B. Blom, 1968.

Ennker, Benno. *Die Anfänge des Leninkults in der Sowjetunion*. Cologne, Böhlau, 1997.

——. 'The origins and intentions of the Lenin cult', in Ian Thatcher (ed.). *Regime and society in 20th century Russia: selected papers from the Fifth World Congress of Central and Eastern European Studies, Warsaw, 1995*. Basingstoke, 1999, pp. 118–28.

Fagen, Richard R. 'Charismatic authority and the leadership of Fidel Castro', *The Western Political Quarterly*, 18:2, 1, 1965, pp. 275–84.

Farnsworth, Beatrice. 'Conversing with Stalin, surviving the terror: the diaries of Aleksandra Kollontai and the internal life of politics', *Slavic Review*, 69:4, 2010, pp. 944–70.

'Fedor Ivanovich Panferov', *Hornos*, hrono.ru/biograf/bio_p/panferov_fi.php.

Fenander, Sara. 'Author and autocrat: Tertz's Stalin and the ruse of charisma', *Russian Review*, 58: 2, 1999, pp. 286–97.

Ferré, Rosa. *Red cavalry: creation and power in Soviet Russia from 1917 to 1945: 07.10.2011 – 15.01.2012*. Madrid, La Casa Encendida, 2011.

Feshbach, Murray. 'A different crisis', *The Wilson Quarterly*, 5:1, 1981, pp. 116–25.

Figes, Orlando. *The whisperers: private life in Stalin's Russia*. New York, Metropolitan Books, 2007.

Figes, Orlando & Boris Kolonitskii. *Interpreting the Russian Revolution: the language and symbols of 1917*. New Haven, Yale University Press, 1999.

Fitzpatrick, Sheila. 'Cultural revolution revisited', *Russian Review*, 58:2, 1999, pp. 202–09.

——. *Education and social mobility in the Soviet Union, 1921–1934*, Cambridge, Cambridge University Press, 1979.

——. *Everyday Stalinism: ordinary life in extraordinary times – Soviet Russia in the 1930s*. New York, Oxford University Press, 1999.

——. *Stalinism: new directions*. London, Routledge, 1999.

——. *The Commissariat of Enlightenment: Soviet organization of education and the arts under Lunacharsky October 1917–1921*. Cambridge, The University Press, 1970.

——. *The cultural front: power and culture in revolutionary Russia*. Ithaca, New York, Cornell University Press, 1992.

Fletcher, William C. 'Soviet sociology of religion: an appraisal', *Russian Review*, 35:2, 1976, pp. 173–91.

Foucault, Michel, Frédéric Gros, François Ewald & Alessandro Fontana. *The hermeneutics of the subject: lectures at the Collège de France, 1981–1982*. New York, Palgrave-Macmillan, 2005.

Frankel, Richard E. *Bismarck's shadow: the cult of leadership and the transformation of the German right: 1898-1945*. Oxford, New York, Berg, 2005.

From Max Weber: essays in sociology. H.H. Gerth & C. Wright Mills (eds and trans.). Oxford University Press, 1946.

Fromm, Erich. *Fear of freedom*. London, Routledge & Kegan Paul Ltd., 1966.

Fuelop-Miller, Rene. *The mind and face of Bolshevism: an examination of cultural life in the Soviet Union*, 2nd edn. New York, Harper and Row, 1962.

Fursenko, A. & V. Afiani. 'The death of Iosif Stalin', *International Affairs*, 49:3, 2003, pp. 188–99.

Galloway, George. *Fidel Castro handbook*. Kfar Saba, MQ Publications, 2006.

Gardner, Jane F. (ed.). *Leadership and the cult of personality*. London, J.M. Dent, 1974.

Garros, Véronique, Natalia Korenevskaya & Thomas Lahusen (eds). *Intimacy and terror: Soviet diaries of the 1930s*. New York, New Press, 1995.

Gellately, Robert. *Lenin, Stalin, and Hitler: the age of social catastrophe*. New York, Alfred A. Knopf, 2007.

Geller, Mikhail & Aleksandr M. Nekrich. *Utopiia u vlasti: Istoriia Sovetskogo Soiuza s 1917 goda do nashikh dnei*. London, Overseas Publication Interchange, 1982.

Gentile, Emilio & Robert Mallett. 'The sacralisation of politics: definitions, interpretations and reflections on the question of secular religion and totalitarianism', *Totalitarian Movements and Political Religions*, 2000, 1:1, pp. 18–55.

Gerschenkron, Alexander. 'The changeability of a dictatorship', *World Politics*, 14:4, 1962, pp. 576–604.

Getty, J. Arch. 'Samokritika rituals in the Stalinist Central Committee, 1933–1938', *Russian Review*, 58:1, 1999, pp. 49–70.

——. 'State and society under Stalin: constitutions and elections in the 1930s', *Slavic Review*, 50:1, 1991, pp. 18–35.

Getty, J. Arch & Oleg V. Naumov. *The road to terror: Stalin and the self-destruction of the Bolsheviks, 1932–1939*. New Haven, Yale University Press, 1999.

Gill, Graeme J. 'Personality cult, political culture and party structure', *Studies in Comparative Communism*, 17:2, 1984, pp. 111–21.

———. *Stalinism*, 2nd edn. London, Macmillan Press, 1998.

———. *Symbols and legitimacy in Soviet politics*. New York, Cambridge University Press, 2011.

———. *The origins of the Stalinist political system*, Cambridge University Press, 1990.

———. 'The Soviet leader cult: reflections on the structure of leadership in the Soviet Union', *British Journal of Political Science*, 10:2, 1980, pp. 167–86.

Ginzburg, Evgenia. *Into the whirlwind*. Paul Stevenson & Manya Harari (trans.). Penguin, Harmondsworth, 1967.

Ginzburg, Eugenia. *Within the whirlwind*. Ian Boland (trans.). London, Collins Harvill, 1989.

Glad, Betty. 'Why tyrants go too far: malignant narcissism and absolute power', *Political Psychology*, 23:1, 2002, pp. 1–37.

Glaser, Milton & Mirko Ilic. *The design of dissent: socially and politically driven graphics*. Gloucester, Rockport Publishers, 2006.

Glassman, Ronald. 'Legitimacy and manufactured charisma', *Social Research*, 42:4, 1975, pp. 615–37.

Gleason, Abbott. *A companion to Russian history*. Chichester, Wiley-Blackwell, 2009.

———. 'Views and re-views: Soviet political posters then and now: essay', library.brown.edu/cds/Views_and_Reviews/essay.html (accessed 28 Nov. 2013).

Gleason, Abbott, Peter Kenez & Richard Stites. *Bolshevik culture: experiment and order in the Russian Revolution*. Bloomington, Indiana University Press, 1985.

Glover Lindsay, Suzanne. 'Mummies and tombs: Turenne, Napoleon, and death ritual', *The Art Bulletin*, 82:3, 2000, pp. 476–502.

Godwin, Joscelyn. *Mystery religions in the ancient world*. San Francisco, Harper & Row, 1981.

Golomshtok, Igor. *Totalitarian art in the Soviet Union, the Third Reich, fascist Italy and the People's Republic of China*. New York, Icon Editions, 1990.

Gooley, Dana. 'Warhorses: Liszt, Weber's "Konzertstück", and the cult of Napoléon', *19th-century Music*, 24:1, 2000, pp. 62–88.

Gorky, Maxim. 'Soviet literature', speech delivered to the Soviet Writers Congress, 1934, www.marxists.org/archive/gorky-maxim/1934/soviet-literature.htm.

———. *Untimely thoughts: essays on revolution, culture and the Bolsheviks, 1917–18*. Herman Ermolaev (trans.). New York, Paul S. Eriksson, Inc., 1968.

Gough, Maria. 'Back in the USSR: John Heartfield, Gustavs Klucis, and the medium of Soviet propaganda', *New German Critique*, 36:2, 2009, pp. 133–84.

Grabar, Andreí. *Christian iconography: a study of its origins*. Princeton, NJ, Princeton University Press, 1968.

Gradel, Ittai. *Emperor worship and Roman religion*. Oxford, Clarendon Press, 2002.

Gregory, Paul R., Philipp J.H. Schröder & Konstantin Sonin. 'Rational dictators and the killing of innocents: data from Stalin's archives', *Journal of Comparative Economics*, 39, 2011, pp. 34–42.

Grill, Johnpeter Horst. 'The dictators', *The Historian*, 68:1, 2006, pp. 194–95.

Gromov, Evgenii. *Stalin: Vlast' I iskusstvo*. Moscow, Respublika, 1998.

Groys, Boris. 'The immortal bodies', *Res: Anthropology and Aesthetics*, 53/54, 2008, pp. 345–49.

———. *The total art of Stalinism: avant-garde, aesthetic dictatorship, and beyond*. Princeton, NJ, Princeton University Press, 1992.

Groys, Boris & Max Hollein (eds). *Dream factory communism. The visual culture of the Stalin era*. Ostfildern-Ruit, Hatje Cantz Verlag, 2003.

Gunther, Hans (ed.). *The culture of the Stalin period*. London, Macmillan, 1990.

Gutkin, Irina. *The cultural origins of the Socialist realist aesthetic: 1890–1934*. Evanston, Northwestern University Press, 1999.

Gutterman, Steve. 'Death of a dictator: In Russia, Josef Stalin still carries clout 50 years after death', *Yakima Herald*, 03 Mar. 2003.

Habachi, Labib. 'Two graffiti at Sehēl from the reign of Queen Hatshepsut', *Journal of Near Eastern Studies*, 16:2, 1957, pp. 88–104.

Halfin, Igal. 'Between instinct and mind: the Bolshevik view of the proletarian self', *Slavic Review*, 62:1, 2003, pp. 34–40.

Halperin, Charles J. 'Untitled', *The International History Review*, 28:3, 2006, pp. 587–88.

Hann, Chris. 'Problems with the (de)privatization of religion', *Anthropology Today*, 16:6, 2000, pp. 14–20.

Hariman, Robert & John Louis Lucaites. *No caption needed: iconic photographs, public culture, and liberal democracy*. Chicago, University Of Chicago Press, 2007.

Haskins, Ekaterina V. & James P. Zappen. 'Totalitarian visual "monologue": reading Soviet ers with Bakhtin', *Rhetoric Society Quarterly*, 40:4, 2010, pp. 326–59.

Hazareesingh, Sudhir. 'Napoleonic memory in nineteenth-century France: the making of a liberal legend', *MLN*, 120:4, 2005, pp. 747–73.

———. *The legend of Napoleon*. London, Granta, 2005.

Hein, Heidi. 'The leader cult in communist dictatorships', *Zeitschrift fur Ostmitteleuropa-Forschung*, 54:4, supp., 2005, pp. 582–83.

Heinzen, James. 'The art of the bribe: corruption and everyday practice in the late Stalinist USSR', *Slavic Review*, 66:3, 2007, pp. 389–412.

Heizer, James L. 'The cult of Stalin, 1929–1939', PhD thesis, University of Kentucky, 1977.

Hellbeck, Jochen. 'Fashioning the Stalinist soul: the diary of Stepan Podlubnyi (1931–1939)', *Jahrbücher für Geschichte Osteuropas, Neue Folge*, 44:3, 1996, pp. 344–73.

Heller, Klaus & Jan Plamper (eds). *Personality cults in Stalinism*. Goîttingen, V&R Unipress, 2004.

Heller, Mikhail & Aleksandr M. Nekrich, *Utopia in power, the history of the Soviet Union from 1917 to the present*. New York, Summit Books, 1986.

Hellie, Richard. 'The structure of Russian imperial history', *History and Theory*, 44, Dec. 2005, pp. 88–112.

Henderson, Elizabeth. 'Majakovskij and Eisenstein celebrate the tenth anniversary', *The Slavic and East European Journal*, 22:2, 1978, pp. 153–62.

Hernandez, Rafael, Francisco Brown, Ariel Dacal, Julio A. Diaz & Fernando Rojas. 'Cuban discussion of why Eastern European socialism fell', *Nature, Society and Thought*, 18:2, 2005.

Hernandez, Richard L. 'The confessions of Semen Kanatchikov: a Bolshevik memoir as spiritual autobiography', *The Russian Review*, 60, 2001, pp. 13–35.

Hertzler, J.O. 'Crises and dictatorships', *American Sociological Review*, 5:2, 1940, pp. 157–69.

Himmer, Robert. 'On the origin and significance of the name "Stalin"', *Russian Review*, 45:3, 1986, pp. 269–86.

Hobsbawm, E.J. *The age of revolution: Europe, 1789–1848*. London, Weidenfeld and Nicolson, 1962.

Hobsbawm, E.J. & T. O. Ranger. *The invention of tradition*. Cambridge, Cambridge University Press, 1983.

Hoffman, Bert. 'Charismatic authority and leadership change: lessons from Cuba's post-Fidel succession', *International Political Science Review*, 30, 2009, pp. 229–48.

Hoffmann, David L. (ed.). *Stalinism: the essential readings*. Malden, Blackwell Publishing, 2003.

———. *Stalinist values: the cultural norms of Soviet modernity, 1917–1941*. Ithaca, New York, Cornell University Press, 2003.

Hoisington, Sona Stephan. '"Ever higher": the evolution of the project for the palace of Soviets', *Slavic Review*, 62:1, 2003, pp. 41–68.

Hollander, Paul. 'The subordination of literature to politics: socialist realism in a historical and comparative perspective', *Studies in Comparative Communism*, 9:3, 1976, pp. 215–25.

Hollis, Richard & Elena Barkhatova. *Russian constructivist posters*. France, Pyramyd, 2010.

Holly, M.A. *Panofsky and the foundations of art history*. Ithaca, New York, Cornell University Press, 1984.

Holme, C.G. *Art in the USSR: architecture, sculpture, painting, graphic arts, theatre, film, crafts*. London, The Studio, 1935.

Holmes, Leslie. *The end of communist power. Anti-corruption campaigns and legitimation crisis*. Melbourne University Press, 1993.

Honour, Hugh & John Fleming. *A world history of art*. London, Macmillan Reference Books, 1982.

Horvath, Robert. 'The poet of terror: Dem'ian Bednyi and Stalinist culture', *The Russian Review*, 65, 2006, pp. 53–71.

Hosking, Geoffrey A. *Russia and the Russians: a history*. Cambridge, M.A., Belknap Press of Harvard University Press, 2001.

Hosking, Geoffrey. 'Thomas Lahusen, how life writes the book: real socialism and socialist realism in Stalin's Russia', *The Journal of Modern History*, 71:3, 1999, pp. 787–88.

House, Robert J. & Jane M. Howell. 'Personality and charismatic leadership', *Leadership Quarterly*, 3:2, 1992, pp. 81–108.

Huggins Balfe, Judith. 'Art style as political actor', *Sociologica Internationalis*, 23:1, 1985, pp. 3–26.

Hummel, Ralph, P. 'Charisma in politics: psychosocial causes of revolution as pre-conditions of charismatic outbreaks within the framework of Weber's epistemology'. PhD dissertation, New York University, 1972.

Hunt, Priscilla. 'Ivan IV's personal mythology of kingship', *Slavic Review*, 52:4, 1993, pp. 769–809.

Hutchings, Raymond. 'Soviet design: the neglected partner of Soviet science and technology', *Slavic Review*, 37:4, 1978, pp. 567–83.

Hutt, Robin Edward. 'Symbolism in religion, with special reference to Orthodox worship and its relevance for the free church tradition', 1985, Masters thesis, Durham University, etheses.dur.ac.uk/7637/.

Ihanus, Juhani. 'Putin and Medvedev: double leadership in Russia', *The Journal of Psychohistory*, 38:3, 2011, p. 251.

Istoriia Vsesoiuznoi Kommunisticheskoi partii (bolshevikov) Kratkii kurs. Moscow, Gospolitizdat, 1938.

Jenks, Andrew. 'A Metro on the mount: the underground as a church of Soviet civilization', *Technology and Culture*, 41:4, 2000, pp. 697–724.

Jiang, Jiehong. *Red: China's cultural revolution*. London, Jonathan Cape, 2010.

Johnson, Oliver. 'The Stalin Prize and the Soviet artist: status symbol or stigma?', *Slavic Review*, 70:4, 2011, pp. 819–43.

Jones, Polly. 'A symptom of the times: assigning responsibility for the Stalin cult in the Soviet literary community, 1953–64', *Forum for Modern Language Studies*, 42:2, 2006, pp. 152–67.

Jowett, G. S. & V. O'Donnell. *Propaganda and persuasion*, 2nd edn. London, Sage, 1992.

Jowitt, Ken. 'Soviet neotraditionalism: the political corruption of a Leninist regime', *Soviet Studies*, 35:3, 1983, pp. 275–97.

Kaganovsky, Lilya. *How the Soviet man was unmade: cultural fantasy and male subjectivity under Stalin*. Pittsburgh, University of Pittsburgh Press, 2008.

Kalinin, Mikhail. 'Stalin and the Patriotic War', *The communist*, 1942, pp. 1000–04, www.unz.org/Pub/Communist-1942dec-01000?View=PDF.

Kallis, Aristotle A. 'Fascism, "charisma" and "charismatisation": Weber's model of "charismatic domination" and interwar European fascism', *Politics, Religion and Ideology*, 7:1, 2006, pp. 25–43.

Kamenskii, Aleksandr A. *Kukryniksy: Politicheskaya satira 1929–1946*. Moscow, Izdatelstvo 'Sovietskii Khudozhnik', 1973.

Kandinsky, Wassily. *Concerning the spiritual in art, and painting in particular. (1912)*. Michael Sadleir & Francis Golffing (trans.). New York, Wittenborn, Schultz, 1947.

Kantorowicz, Ernst. *The king's two bodies: a study in medieval political theology*. New Jersey, Princeton University Press, 1957.

Keenan, Edward L. 'Muscovite political folkways', *Russian Review*, 45:2, 1986, pp. 115–181.

Keep, John. 'Recent western views of Stalin's Russia: social and cultural aspects', *Totalitarian Movements and Political Religions*, 2003, 4:1, pp. 149–66.

Keller, Adolf. *Church and state on the European continent*. London, The Epworth Press, 1936.

Keller, Bill. 'In U.S.S.R., a painful prying at roots of Stalin's tyranny', *New York Times*, 11 Jun. 1988, p. 1.

Kelly, Catriona. *Children's world: growing up in Russia, 1890–1991*. New Haven, Yale University Press, 2007.

———. *Comrade Pavlik: the rise and fall of a Soviet boy hero*. London, Granta, 2005.

———. 'Riding the magic carpet: children and leader cult in the Stalin era', *The Slavic and East European Journal*, 49:2, 2005, pp. 199–224.

Kenez, Peter. *The birth of the propaganda state: Soviet methods of mass mobilization, 1917–1929*. Cambridge, Cambridge University Press, 1985.

Kepley Jr., Vance. 'Federal cinema: the Soviet film industry, 1924–32', *Film History*, 8:3, 1996, pp. 344–56.

Keynes, John Maynard. *Essays in persuasion*. London, Rupert Hart-Davis, 1931.

Kiaer, Christina. *Imagine no possessions: the socialist objects of Russian constructivism*. London, The Mit Press, 2005.

———. 'Was socialist realism forced labour? The case of Aleksandr Deineka in the 1930s', *Oxford Art Journal*, 28 Mar. 2005, pp. 321–45.

Kiaer, Christina & Eric Naiman. *Everyday life in early Soviet Russia: taking the Revolution inside*. Bloomington, Indiana University Press, 2006.

King, David. *Red star over Russia: a visual history of the Soviet Union from 1917 to the death of Stalin: posters, photographs and graphics from the David King collection*. London, Tate, 2009.

———. *The commissar vanishes: the falsification of photographs and art in Stalin's Russia*. New York, Metropolitan Books, 1997.

Kirichenko, Evgenia. *Russian design*. New York, Harry N. Abrams, 1991.

Kirschenbaum, Lisa A. '"Our city, our hearths, our families": local loyalties and private life in Soviet World War II propaganda', *Slavic Review*, 59:4, 2000, pp. 825–47.

Khlevniuk, Oleg, Alexander Vatlin & Paul Gregory (eds). *Stenogrammy zasedanii Politburo TsKRKP(b) 1923–1938*, vol. 3, Moscow, Rosspen, 2007.

'Klimashin Viktor Semenovich (1912–1960)'. artgallery.krasno.ru/IMAGES/Grafics/Klimashin.htm.

Klugman, Jeffry. 'The psychology of Soviet corruption, indiscipline, and resistance to reform', *Political Psychology*, 7:1, 1986, pp. 67–82.

Koenker, Diane. *Republic of labor: Russian printers and Soviet socialism, 1918–1930*. Ithaca, New York, Cornell University Press, 2005.

Kohn, Hans. 'Napoleon and the age of nationalism', *Journal of Modern History*, 22:1, 1950, pp. 21–37.

Kojevnikov, Alexei. 'Rituals of Stalinist culture at work: science and the games of intraparty democracy circa 1948', *Russian Review*, 57:1, 1998, pp. 25–52.

Koloskova, T. G. *Mir o liubimom vozhde: iz istorii khudozhestvennykh kollektsii Muzeia V.I. Lenina*. Moscow, Gosudarstvennyi istoricheskii muzei, 2014.

Komar, Vitaly, Aleksandr Melamid & JoAnn Wypijewski. *Painting by numbers: Komar and Melamid's scientific guide to art*. New York, Farrar Straus Giroux, 1997.

Kotkin, Stephen. *Magnetic Mountain: Stalinism as a civilization*. Berkeley, University of California Press, 1995.

Kowalsky, Daniel. 'The Soviet cinematic offensive in the Spanish Civil War', *Film History*, 19:1, 2007, pp. 7–19.

Kravchenko, Victor. *I chose freedom: the personal and political life of a Soviet official*. New York, Garden City Publications, 1947.

Krupskaia, Nadezhda Konstantinovna. *Pedagogischeskie sochineniia v desiati tomakh*, 7. Moscow, Akademia Pedagogicheskih Nauk RSFSR, 1959.

Krushchev, Nikita. 'Speech to the 20th Congress of the C.P.S.U', 24–25 Feb. 1956, www.marxists.org/archive/khrushchev/1956/02/24.htm.

Kunzle, David. *Che Guevara: icon, myth, and message*. Washington D.C., Study of Political Graphics, 1997.

Kupper, Herbert. 'Some psychological hypotheses on Mao Tse-tung's Personality', *Studies in Comparative Communism*, 7:1–2, pp. 50–52.

Lafont, Maria. *Soviet posters: the Sergo Grigorian collection*. Fort Worth, Prestel Publishing, 2007.

Lahusen, Thomas. *How life writes the book: real socialism and socialist realism in Stalin's Russia*. Ithaca, New York, Cornell University Press, 1997.

Lahusen, Thomas & E.A. Dobrenko. *Socialist realism without shores*. Durham, Duke University Press, 1997.

Lahusen, Thomas & Gene Kuperman. *Late Soviet culture: from perestroika to novostroika*. Durham, Duke University Press, 1993.

Lambert, Peter & Robert Mallett. 'Introduction: the heroisation–demonisation phenomenon in mass dictatorships', *Totalitarian Movements and Political Religions*, 8:3–4, 2007, pp. 453–63.

Lampert, Nick & Gábor T. Rittersporn (eds). *Stalinism: its nature and aftermath*. Hampshire, Macmillan, 1992.

Lane, Christel. 'Legitimacy and power in the Soviet Union through socialist ritual', *British Journal of Political Science*, 14:2, 1984, pp. 207–17.

———. *The rites of rulers: ritual in industrial society: the Soviet case.* Cambridge and New York, Cambridge University Press, 1981.

Landsberger Stefan R., Anchee Min & Duo Duo. *Chinese propaganda posters.* Köln, Taschen, 2011.

Law, Alma H. 'A conversation with Vladimir Stenberg', *Art Journal*, 41:3, 1981, pp. 222–33.

Lawlor, Eric. 'His name meant, "Father Turk", and that he was', *Smithsonian*, 26:12, 1996, pp. 116–27.

Layton, Susan. 'The mind of the tyrant: Tolstoj's Nicholas and Solženicyn's Stalin', *The Slavic and East European Journal*, 23:4, 1979, pp. 479—49.

Ledeneva, Alena E. *Russia's economy of favours: blat, networking and informal exchange.* Cambridge, Cambridge University Press, 1998.

Lee, Chonghoon. 'Visual Stalinism from the perspective of heroisation: posters, paintings and illustrations in the 1930s', *Totalitarian Movements and Political Religions*, 8:3–4, 2007, pp. 503–21.

Lee, Simon. *Art and ideas: David.* London, Phaidon Press, 1998.

Leites, Nathan. 'Stalin as an intellectual', *World Politics*, 6:1, 1953, pp. 45–66.

Lenin, V.I. *Collected works*, vol. 29. George Hanna (trans.). Moscow, Progress Publications, 1965.

———. *Collected works*, 4th edn, vol. 31. Julius Katzer (trans.). Moscow, Progress Publishers, 1965.

———. 'Constitutional illusions', *Rabochy i soldat*, 4 & 5 (22 & 23) Aug. 1917, *Collected works*, vol. 25. Stepan Apresyan & Jim Riordan (trans.). Moscow, Progress Publishers, 1964.

Lenin, Vladimir Il'ich. *Lenin collected works,* vol. 28. Jim Riordan (trans.). Moscow, Progress Publishers, 1974.

———. 'Letter to the Congress', 1922, www.marxists.org/archive/lenin/works/1922/dec/testamnt/congress.htm.

Lenin, Vladimir Il'ich. '"What is to be done?": political exposures and "training in revolutionary activity"', 1901, www.marxists.org/archive/lenin/works/1901/witbd/iii.htm.

Lenoe, Matthew. *Closer to the masses: Stalinist culture, social revolution, and Soviet newspapers*, Cambridge, Harvard University Press, 2004, p. 17.

———. 'Sarah Davies, *Popular opinion in Stalin's Russia: terror, propaganda, and dissent, 1934–1941*', *The Journal of Modern History*, 71:3, 1999, pp. 789–91.

Levitt, Marcus C. & Tatyana Novikov. *Times of trouble: violence in Russian literature and culture*. Madison, University of Wisconsin Press, 2007.

Lewis, Ben. *Hammer and tickle: the story of communism, a political system almost laughed out of existence*. New York, Pegasus Books, 2009.

Lidov, Petr. 'Five German photographs', *Pravda*, 24 Oct. 1943.

Lih, Lars T. 'The cult of Ivan the Terrible in Stalin's Russia', *The Journal of Modern History*, 75:4, 2003, pp. 1004–05.

Lih, Lars T., Oleg V. Naumov and Oleg. V. Khlevniuk (eds). *Stalin's letters to Molotov: 1925–1936*. Catherine A. Fitzpatrick (trans.). New Haven, Yale University Press, 1995.

Lincoln, W. Bruce. *Between heaven and hell: the story of a thousand years of artistic life in Russia*. New York, Viking, 1998.

Llobera, Josep R. *The making of totalitarian thought*. Oxford, Berg, 2003.

Lobanov-Rostovsky, Nina. 'Soviet propaganda porcelain', *The Journal of Decorative and Propaganda Arts*, 11, 1989, pp. 126–41.

Loewenstein, Karl E. 'Ideology and ritual: how Stalinist rituals shaped the thaw in the USSR, 1953–4', *Totalitarian Movements and Political Religions*, 8:1, 2007, pp. 93–114.

Lotman, Iu. M., Lidiia Ginzburg, Boris Andreevich Uspenskii, Alexander D. Nakhimovsky & Alice S. Nakhimovsky. *The semiotics of Russian cultural history: essays*. Ithaca, New York, Cornell University Press, 1985.

Lowenthal, Richard. 'The post-revolutionary phase in China and Russia', *Studies in Comparative Communism*, 16:3, 1983, pp. 191–201.

Luber, Katherine Crawford. 'Albrecht Dürer's Maximilian portraits: an investigation of versions', *Master Drawings*, 29:1, 1991, pp. 30–47.

Luck, David. 'Psycholinguistic approach to leader personality: Hitler, Stalin, Mao and Liu Shao Ch'i', *Soviet Studies*, 30:4, 1978, pp. 491–515.

Lukács, Georg. 'Reflections on the cult of Stalin', *Survey*, 47, April 1963.

Lukacs, John. *June 1941: Hitler and Stalin*. New Haven, Yale University Press, 2006.

Luke, Timothy W. 'Civil religion and secularization: ideological revitalization in post-revolutionary communist systems', *Sociological Forum*, 2:1, 1987, pp. 108–34.

Lunacharsky, Anatoly. *Revolutionary silhouettes, Lev Davidovich Trotsky* www.marxists.org/archive/lunachar/works/silhouet/trotsky.htm.

Lunacharsky, Anatoly Vasilievich. *On literature and art*. Moscow, Progress Publishers, 1965.

Lyon, Christopher. 'The poster at the Modern: a brief history', *MoMA*, 48, 1988, pp. 1–2.

Lyons, Eugene. *Moscow carousel*. New York, Alfred A. Knopf, 1935.

Maasri, Zeina. *Off the wall: political posters of the Lebanese Civil War*. New York, I.B. Tauris, 2009.

MacCormack, Sabine. *Art and ceremony in late antiquity*. Berkeley, University of California Press, 1981.

MacNeal, R. (ed.). I.V. Stalin, *Sochineniya*. 13, Stanford, Hoover Institute of War, Revolution and Peace, 1967.

McLuhan, Marshall. *The medium is the message*. New York, Random House, 1967.

Maier, Hans. 'Political religions and their images: Soviet communism, Italian fascism and German National Socialism', *Politics, Religion and Ideology*, 7:3, 2006, pp. 267–81.

Malia, Martin. 'What is the intelligentsia?', *Daedalus*, 89:3, 1960, pp. 441–58.

Mandelstam, Nadezhda. *Hope against hope: a memoir*, Max Hayward (trans.). New York, Atheneum Publishers, 1970.

Marcus, Sarah & Ellen Barry. 'Georgia knocks Stalin off his pedestal', *Waterloo Region Record*, Kitchener, 26 June 2010.

Margolin, Victor. 'A look back: lessons learned', *Print*, 65:2, 2011, pp. 46–50.

——. 'Constructivism and the modern poster', *Art Journal*, 44:1, 1984, pp. 28–32.

——. *The struggle for utopia: Rodchenko, Lissitzky, Moholy-Nagy, 1917–1946*. University Of Chicago Press, 1998.

Marin, L. *Portrait of the king*. Minneapolis, University of Minnesota Press, 1988.

Marsh, Rosalind. *Images of dictatorship: portraits of Stalin in literature*. London, Routledge, 1989.

Marko, Kurt. 'The legitimacy of Totalitarianism: a pseudo-problem?', *Studies in Soviet Thought*, 31:3, 1986, pp. 239–42.

Marx, Karl. '18th Brumaire of Louis Bonaparte. Karl Marx 1852', www.marxists.org/archive/marx/works/1852/18th-brumaire/ch01.htm.

——. 'The third address May 1871 [The Paris Commune], *The Civil War in France, 1871*', www.marxists.org/archive/marx/works/1871/civil-war-france/ch05.htm.

——. 'Letters: Marx–Engels correspondence 1877'. www.marxists.org/archive/marx/works/1877/letters/77_11_10.htm.

Maryamov, G. 'J.V. Stalin: The discussion with Sergei Eisenstein on the film Ivan the Terrible', *Kremlevskii Tsenzor, Stalin smotrit kino*, Sumana Jha (trans.). Moscow, 1992, pp. 84–91. www.revolutionarydemocracy.org/rdv3n2/ivant.htm.

Mateescu, Dragoş C. 'Kemalism in the era of totalitarianism: a conceptual analysis', *Turkish Studies*, 7:2, 2006, pp. 225–41.

Mathews, Thomas F. *The clash of gods: a reinterpretation of early Christian art*. Princeton University Press, 1999.

Mauss, Marcel. *The gift: forms and functions of exchange in archaic societies*. Ian Gunnison (trans.). New York, W.W. Norton and Company, 1967 (1923).

Mawdsley, Evan. 'Untitled', *Slavic Review*, 65:4, 2006, pp. 799–800.

Mazlish, Bruce. 'Group psychology and problems of contemporary history', *Journal of Contemporary History*, 3:2, 1968, pp. 163–77.

Mazlish, Bruce. 'The French Revolution in comparative perspective', *Political Science Quarterly*, 85:2, 1970, pp. 240–58.

McCloskey, Barbara. *Artists of World War II*. Westport, Greenwood Press, 2005.

McDermott, Kevin. 'Archives, power and the "cultural turn": reflections on Stalin and Stalinism', *Totalitarian Movements and Political Religions*, 5:1, 2004, pp. 5–24.

——. 'Stalinism 'from below'?: social preconditions of and popular responses to the Great Terror', *Totalitarian Movements and Political Religions*, 8:3–4, 2007, pp. 609–22.

McIntosh, Donald. 'Weber and Freud: on the nature and sources of authority', *American Sociological Review*, 35:5, 1970, pp. 901–11.

McNeal, Robert. *Stalin: man and ruler*. New York, New York University Press, 1988.

Medvedev, Roy A. *Let history judge: the origins and consequences of Stalinism*, New York, Knopf, 1971.

——. *On Stalin and Stalinism*. Ellen de Kadt (trans.). Oxford, Oxford University Press, 1979.

Melnick, A. James. 'Soviet perceptions of the Maoist cult of personality', *Studies in Comparative Communism*, 9:1–2, 1976, pp. 129–44.

Meyer, Arline. 'Re-dressing classical statuary: the eighteenth-century "hand-in-waistcoat" portrait', *The Art Bulletin*, 77, 1995, pp. 45–64.

Miller, Frank J. *Folklore for Stalin: Russian folklore and pseudofolklore of the Stalin era*. New York, Armonk, 1990.

Milner, John. *El Lissitzky: design*. Easthampton, Antique Collectors' Club, Ltd, 2010.

Milner, John & Kirill Sokolov, 'Constructivist graphic design in the U.S.S.R. between 1917 and the present', *Leonardo*, 14:4, 1979, pp. 275–82.

Milosz, Czeslaw. *The captive mind*. Jane Zielonk (trans.). New York, Knopf, 1953.

Mocanescu, Alice. 'Practising immortality: schemes for conquering "time" during the Ceauşescu era', *Studies in Ethnicity and Nationalism*, 10:3, 2010, pp. 413–34.

'Modern history sourcebook: Khrushchev: Secret Speech, 1956'. www.fordham.edu/halsall/mod/krushchev-secret.html.

Montefiore, Simon Sebag. *Stalin: the court of the Red Tsar*. London, Weidenfeld and Nicolson, 2003.

——. *Young Stalin*. New York, Alfred A. Knopf, 2007.

Morozov, Aleksei. *Agit-Okna, Okna TASS, 1941–1945*. Moscow, Kontakt-Kultura, 2013.

Mukhametshin, Boris. *Anti-posters: Soviet icons in reverse*. Riverside, Xenos Books, 1987.

Mumford, Michael D., Jazmine Espejo, Samuel T. Hunter, Katrina E. Bedell-Avers, Dawn L. Eubanks & Shane Connelly. 'The sources of leader violence: a comparison of ideological and non-ideological leaders', *The Leadership Quarterly*, 18, 2007, pp. 217–35.

Naiman, Eric. *Sex in public: the incarnation of early Soviet ideology*. Princeton, NJ, Princeton University Press, 1997.

Nedava, Joseph. 'Trotsky and the role of the individual in history: the acting personality in the political arena', *Modern Age*, Sep 1986, pp. 218–25.

Neizvestny, Ernst. 'Art and freedom', Alfred Leong (trans.), *Studies in Comparative Communism*, 17:3—4, 1984, pp. 235—39.

Nikonova, I.I. *Khudozhnikii Narodov SSSR: Biobibliograficheskii Slovar'*, 4:1, Moscow, Izdatel'stvo 'Iskusstvo', 1983.

Nivelon, François. *The rudiments of genteel behaviour*. 1737. archive.org/details/rudimentsofgente00nive.

Nohlen, D. & Stöver, P. *Elections in Europe: a data handbook*. Baden-Baden, Nomos Publishers, 2010.

Norris, Stephen M. *A war of images: Russian popular prints, wartime culture, and national identity, 1812–1945*. DeKalb, Northern Illinois University Press, 2006.

Nove, Alec. *Stalinism and after*. London, Allen & Unwin, 1975.

Oinas, Felix J. 'The political uses and themes of folklore in the Soviet Union', *Journal of the Folklore Institute*, 12:2/3, 1975, pp. 157–75.

O'Shaughnessy, Nicholas J. *Politics and propaganda*. Manchester, Manchester University Press, 2004.

———. 'The death and life of propaganda', *Journal of Public Affairs*, 12:1, 2012, pp. 29–38.

Ouspensky, Léonide & Vladimir Lossky. *The meaning of icons*, 2nd edn. Crestwood, St Vladimir's Seminary Press, 1982.

Pakulski, Jan. 'Legitimacy and mass compliance: reflections on Max Weber and Soviet-type societies', *British Journal of Political Science*, 16:1, 1986, pp. 35–56.

Paltiel, Jeremy T. 'The cult of personality: some comparative reflections on political culture in Leninist regimes', *Studies in Comparative Communism*, 16:1–2, 1983, pp. 49–64.

Panferov, F.I. 'XVII s'yezd VKP(b) Rech' tovarishcha Panferova, Zasedaniye 8 fevralya 1934 g., utrenneye', hrono.ru/vkpb_17/25_3.html.

Panofsky, Erwin. *Meaning in the visual arts: papers in and on art history*. New York, Doubleday, 1955.

Pantsov, A.V. 'How Stalin helped Mao Zedong become the leader: new archival documents on Moscow's role in the rise of Mao', *Issues and Studies — Institute of International Relations*, 41:3, 2005, pp. 181–207.

Paperno, Irina. 'Dreams of terror: dreams from Stalinist Russia as a historical source', *Kritika*, 7:4, 2006, pp. 793–824.

Paret, Peter, Beth Irwin Lewis & Paul Paret. *Persuasive images: posters of war and revolution from the Hoover Institution archives*. Princeton, NJ, Princeton University Press, 1992.

Parker, Harold Talbot. *The cult of antiquity and the French revolutionaries; a study in the development of the revolutionary spirit*. New York, Octagon Books, 1965.

Patrikeeff, Felix. 'Stalinism, totalitarian society and the politics of "perfect control"', *Totalitarian Movements and Political Religions*, 4:1, 2003, p. 31.

Paxton, John. *Companion to Russian history*. New York, Facts on File Publications, 1983.

Perrie, Maureen. 'Folklore as evidence of peasant mentalite: social attitudes and values in Russian popular culture', *Russian Review*, 48:2, 1989, pp. 119–143.

———. *The cult of Ivan the Terrible in Stalin's Russia*. Houndmills, Palgrave, 2001.

———. *The image of Ivan the Terrible in Russian folklore*. Cambridge, Cambridge University Press, 1987.

Petrone, Karen. 'Iconography of power: Soviet political posters under Lenin and Stalin by Victoria E. Bonnell Review', *The Russian Review*, 58:2, 1999, p. 333.

———. *Life has become more joyous, Comrades. Celebrations in the time of Stalin*. Bloomington, Indiana University Press, 2000.

Petrov, Petre. 'The industry of truing: socialist realism, reality, realization', *Slavic Review*, 70:4, 2011, pp. 873–92.

Philippe, Robert. *Political graphics: art as a weapon*. New York, Abbeville Press, 1982.

Pinto, Antonio Costa & Stein Ugelvik Larsen, 'Conclusion: fascism, dictators and charisma', *Politics, Religion & Ideology*, 7:2, 2006, pp. 251–57.

Pipes, Richard (ed.). *The unknown Lenin: from the secret archive*. New Haven, Hodder and Staunton, 1996.

Pipolo, Tony. 'Eisenstein: the sound years', *Cineaste*, 28:1, 2002, pp. 42–44.

Plamper, Jan. 'Abolishing ambiguity: Soviet censorship practices in the 1930s', *Russian Review*, 60:4, 2001, pp. 526–44.

——. *The Stalin cult: a study in the alchemy of power*. New Haven, Yale University Press, 2012.

——. 'The Stalin cult in the visual arts, 1929–1953', PhD dissertation, Berkeley, University of California, 2001.

Platt, Kevin M.F. & David Brandenberger. *Epic revisionism: Russian history and literature as Stalinist propaganda*. Madison, University of Wisconsin Press, 2006.

Polonskii, Vyacheslav. *Russkii revolyutsionnyi plakat*. Moscow, Gosizdat, 1925.

Pomper, Philip. 'Nečaev, Lenin, and Stalin: the psychology of leadership', *Jahrbücher für Geschichte Osteuropas, Neue Folge*, 26:1, 1978, pp. 11–30.

Popper, Micha. 'The development of charismatic leaders', *Political Psychology*, 21:4, 2000, pp. 729–44.

Portal, Jane. *Art under control in North Korea*. New York, Reaktion Books, 2005.

Post, Jerrold M., 'Current concepts of the narcissistic personality: implications for political psychology', *Political Psychology*, 14:1, 1993, pp. 99–121.

——. 'Narcissism and the charismatic leader–follower relationship', *Political Psychology*, 7:4, 1986, pp. 675–88.

Pouncey, Carolyn J. 'Missed opportunities and the search for Ivan the Terrible', *Kritika*, 7:2, 2006, pp. 309–28.

Prendergast, Christopher. *Napoleon and history painting: Antoine-Jean Gros's La Bataille d'Eylau*. Oxford, Clarendon Press, 1997.

Price, S.R.F. *Rituals and power: the Roman imperial cult in Asia Minor*. Cambridge and New York, Cambridge University Press, 1984.

Prokhorov, A.M. & M. Waxman (eds). *Great Soviet encyclopædia*, 3rd edn. New York, Macmillan, 1973.

Prokhorov, Gleb. *Art under socialist realism: Soviet painting, 1930–1950*. East Roseville, Craftsman House, 1995.

Pujals, Sandra. 'The accidental revolutionary in the Russian Revolution: impersonation, criminality and revolutionary mythology in the early Soviet period, 1905–35', *Revolutionary Russia*, 22:2, 2009, pp. 181–201.

Radek, Karl. *The architect of socialist society*. Moscow, Co-operative Publishing Society of Foreign Workers in the USSR, 1934.

Raiklin, Ernest. 'Stalinism vs Hitlerism: the basic intentions and results', *International Journal of Social Economics*, 38:4, 2011, pp. 358–81.

Railing, Patricia. 'The idea of construction as the creative principle in avant-garde art', *Leonardo*, 28:3, 1995, pp. 193—202.

Reid, Graeme J. 'Stalin's cult of personality: the myth of legitimacy', Masters thesis, Indiana State University, 1993.

Reid, Susan E. 'All Stalin's women: gender and power in Soviet art of the 1930s', *Slavic Review*, 57:1, 1998, pp. 133–73.

——. 'Socialist realism in the Stalinist terror: the *Industry of Socialism* art exhibition, 1935–41', *The Russian Review*, 60:2, 2001, pp. 153–84.

Richter, Gisela Marie Augusta. *A handbook of Greek art*, 6th edn. London, Phaidon, 1969.

Rieber, Alfred J. 'Stalin, man of the borderlands', *The American Historical Review*, 106:5, 2001, pp. 1651–91.

Riegel, Klaus-Georg. 'Marxism–Leninism as a political religion', *Totalitarian Movements and Political Religions*, 2005, 6:1, pp. 97–126.

Rigby, T.H., Archie Brown & Peter Reddaway (eds). *Authority, power and policy in the USSR: essays dedicated to Leonard Schapiro*. London, Macmillan, 1980.

Rigby, T.H. & F. Fehér (eds). *Political legitimation in communist states*. London, Macmillan, 1982.

Roberts, Graham. *Forward Soviet!: history and non-fiction film in the USSR*. London, I.B. Tauris, 1999.

Robin, Régine. *Socialist realism: an impossible aesthetic*. Stanford University Press, 1992.

Rolf, Malte. 'A hall of mirrors: Sovietizing culture under Stalinism', *Slavic Review*, 68:3, 2009, pp. 601–30.

Rosenfeld, Alla (ed.). *Defining Russian graphic arts: from Diaghilev to Stalin, 1898–1934*. New Jersey, Rutgers University Press, 1999.

Rosenthal, Bernice Glatzer. *New myth, new world: from Nietzsche to Stalinism*. Pennsylvania State University Press, 2002.

Roth, Guenther & Claus Wittich (eds). *Max Weber: economy and society: an outline of interpretive sociology*. Berkeley, University of California Press, 1978.

Rousseau, Jean Jacques. *The social contract: or principles of political right*. G.D.H. Cole (trans.), vol. 4, chpt. 8, 1762, www.constitution.org/jjr/socon_04.htm#008 (accessed 24 May 2012).

Russell, Bertrand. *The practice and theory of Bolshevism*. London, George Allen and Unwin, 1920.

Russian and Soviet paintings 1900–1930: selections from the State Tretyakov Gallery, Moscow, and the State Russian Museum, Leningrad, rev. edn. Washington, Hirshhorn Museum and Sculpture Garden, Smithsonian Institution, 1988.

Russian art of the revolution. Ithaca, New York, Office of University Publications, Cornell University, 1971.

Rustow, Dankart A. 'Atatürk as founder of a state', *Daedalus*, 97:3, Philosophers and Kings: Studies in Leadership, 1968, pp. 793–28.

Sakwa, Richard. *The rise and fall of the Soviet Union, 1917–1991*. London, Routledge, 1999.

Salisbury, Harrison E. *Russia in revolution, 1900–1930*. New York, Holt, Rinehart and Winston, 1978.

Sandler, Åke. *Stalin and Hitler: a lesson in comparison*. Stanford, 1953.

Satjukov, S. & R. Gries. *Unsere Feinde. Konstruktionen des Anderem im Sozializmus*. Leipzig, Leiziper Universitätsverlag, 2004.

Saxl, Fritz. *A heritage of images: a selection of lectures by Fritz Saxl*. Harmondsworth, Penguin, 1970.

——. *Lectures*, vols 1 & 2. London, Warburg Institute, 1957.

Schapiro, Leonard. *The Communist Party of the Soviet Union*. New York, Random House, 1960.

Schmidt, Victor Michael. *A legend and its image: the aerial flight of Alexander the Great in medieval art*. Groningen, E. Forsten, 1995.

Schnapp, Jeffrey T. *Revolutionary tides: the art of the political poster 1914–1989*. Geneva, Skira, 2005.

Schrift, Alan D. *The logic of the gift: toward an ethic of generosity*. New York, Routledge, 1997.

Scott, Kenneth. *The imperial cult under the Flavians*. Stuttgart, Kohlhammer, 1936.

Senkevitch, Anatole, Jr. 'Art, architecture and design: a commentary', *Slavic Review*, 37:4, 1978, pp. 587–94.

Serge, Victor. 'Lenin in 1917' (March/April 1924). Originally published in French in *Faits et Documents*, no. 2, 1925. Al Richardson (trans.). www.marxists.org/archive/serge/1924/xx/lenin.html#f22.

———. *Memoirs of a revolutionary 1901–1941*. Peter Sedgwick (trans.). London, Oxford University Press, 1963.

Service, Robert. *A history of 20th century Russia*. Cambridge, Harvard University Press, 1999.

———. *Comrades!: a history of world communism*. Cambridge, Harvard University Press, 2010.

———. *Stalin: a biography*. Cambridge, Bellknap Press, 2006.

———. 'Stalinism and the Soviet State order', *Totalitarian Movements and Political Religions*, 2003, 4:1, pp. 7–22.

Shitts, I.I. *Dnevnik 'Velikogo Pereloma'* (mart 1928 – avgust 1931). Paris, YMCA Press, 1991.

Shklyariuk, A.F., A. E. Snopkov & P.A. Snopkov. *The Russian poster: 100 masterpieces during 100 years*. Moscow, Kontakt-Kul'tura, 2001.

Shub, David. 'Kamo—the legendary Old Bolshevik of the Caucasus', *Russian Review*, 19:3, July 1960, pp. 227–47.

Shukman, Harold. *Redefining Stalinism*. London, Frank Cass, 2003.

Siegelbaum, Lewis H. '"Dear comrade, you ask what we need": socialist paternalism and Soviet rural "Notables" in the mid-1930s', *Slavic Review*, 57:1, 1998, pp. 107–32.

Siegelbaum, Lewis H., A.K. Sokolov, L. Kosheleva & S.V. Zhuravlev. *Stalinism as a way of life: a narrative in documents*. New Haven, Yale University Press, 2000.

Silver, Larry. *Marketing Maximilian: the visual ideology of a Holy Roman Emperor*. Princeton, Princeton University Press, 2008.

———. 'Shining armor: Maximilian I as Holy Roman Emperor', *Art Institute of Chicago Museum Studies*, 12:1, 1985, pp. 8–29.

Simkin, John. Spartacus Educational. spartacus-educational.com/RUScivilwar.htm.

Simpson, C.J. 'Caligula's cult: immolation, immortality and intent', *Journal of Roman archaeology*, supplementary series, 17, 1996, pp. 63–71.

Skowronek, Stefan. *On the problems of the Alexandrian mint: allusion to the divinity of the sovereign appearing on the coins of Egyptian Alexandria in the period of the early Roman Empire: 1st and 2nd centuries A.D.* Varsovie, Ed. scientifiques de Pologne, 1967.

Skradol, Natalia. 'Remembering Stalin: mythopoetic elements in memories of the Soviet dictator', *Totalitarian Movements and Political Religions*, 2009, 10:1, pp. 19–41.

——. 'Laughing with Comrade Stalin: an analysis of laughter in a Soviet newspaper report', *The Russian Review*, 68, 2009, pp. 26–48.

Smart, Christopher. 'Gorbachev's Lenin: the myth in service to Perestroika', *Studies in Comparative Communism*, 23:1, 1990, pp. 5–22.

Smedley, Agnes. *Battle hymn of China*. New York, A.A. Knopf, 1943.

Smith, Michael. 'Stalin's martyrs: the tragic romance of the Russian Revolution', *Totalitarian Movements and Political Religions*, 2003, 4:1, pp. 95–126.

Smith, Philip. 'Culture and charisma: outline of a theory', *Acta Sociologica*, 43, 2000, pp. 101–10.

Smith, Trevor J. 'Lenin for sale: the rise and fall of the personality cult of V.I. Lenin in Soviet Russia', Masters thesis, Carleton University, 1995.

——. 'The collapse of the Lenin personality cult in Soviet Russia, 1985–1995', *The Historian*, 60, 1998, pp. 325–43.

Sokolov, Kirill. 'Aleksandr Drevin, Nadezhda Udal'tsova: an exhibition that never was', *Leonardo*, 35:3, 2002, pp. 263–69.

Solzhenitsyn, Aleksandr. *Lenin in Zurich*. London, Bodley Head, 1976.

——. *The first circle*. Michael Guybon (trans.). New York, Harper and Row, 1968.

Solzhenitsyn, Alexander. *The Gulag Archipelago, 1918–1956: an experiment in literary investigation*. New York, Perennial, 2002.

Speier, Hans. 'The truth in hell: Maurice Joly on modern despotism', *Polity*, 10:1, 1977, pp. 18–32.

Spira, Andrew. *The avant-garde icon: Russian avant-garde art and the icon painting tradition*. Aldershot, Lund Humphries/Ashgate, 2008.

Spiridonova, Lidiia. 'Gorky and Stalin (according to new materials from A.M. Gorky's archive)', *Russian Review*, 54:3, 1995, pp. 413–23.

Spring, D.W. 'The TASS poster series from the Hallward Library', University of Nottingham, www.ampltd.co.uk/digital_guides/soviet_posters_1940-1945/historical-introduction-dw-spring.aspx.

Srivastava, Vinay Kumar. 'Mao cult, charisma and social science', *China Report*, 1985, pp. 359–70.

Ssorin-Chaikov, Nikolai. 'On heterochrony: birthday gifts to Stalin, 1949', *Journal of the Royal Anthropological Institute*, 12, 2006, pp. 355–75.

St John of Damascus. 'St. John of Damascus: apologia against those who decry holy images', quoted in Barasch, Moshe. *Icon: studies in the history of an idea*, New York and London, NYU Press, 1995, p. 247.

Stalin, I.V. 'A conversation with the *Pravda* correspondent', *Pravda*, 17 Feb. 1951. www.marxists.org/russkij/stalin/t16/t16_29.htm.

——. *Economic problems of socialism in the USSR*. Peking, Foreign Languages Press, 1972.

——. 'Obrashcheniye k narodu 2 sentyabrya 1945 goda'. www.marxists.org/russkij/stalin/t15/t15_73.htm.

——. *O Velikoi Otechestvennoi voine Sovetskogo Soiuza*, 4th edn, Moscow, Gospolitizdat, 1944.

——. 'Rech' na Krasnoy ploshchadi 7 noyabrya 1941 goda', www.marxists.org/russkij/stalin/t15/t15_14.htm.

——. *Sochineniia*, 8. Moscow, Gospolitizdat, 1948.

——. *Sochineniia*, 13, Moscow, Gospolitizdat, 1948.

Stalin, J.V. *K shestidesyatiletiyu so dnya rozhdeniya*. Moskva, Pravda, 1940.

———. 'Speech delivered by Comrade J. Stalin at a meeting of voters of the Stalin Electoral Area, Moscow', 11 December 1937, www.marxists.org/reference/archive/stalin/works/1937/12/11.htm and www.youtube.com/watch?v=iaU_ak19YwY.

———. *Problems of Leninism*. Peking, Foreign Languages Press, 1976, pp. 483–91.

———. 'Talk with the German author Emil Ludwig', 13 December 1931. Hari Kumar (trans.), in J.V. Stalin, *Works*, vol. 13. Moscow, Foreign Languages Publishing House, 1955, pp. 106–25. www.marxists.org/reference/archive/stalin/works/1931/dec/13.htm.

———. *Works*, vol. 14. London, Red Star Press Ltd, 1978. www.marxists.org/reference/archive/stalin/works/1939/02/23.htm.

Stanley, Eliot H. 'The lively poster arts of Rockwell Kent', *The Journal of Decorative and Propaganda Arts*, 12, 1989, pp. 6–31.

Starks, Tricia. *Body Soviet: propaganda, hygiene, and the revolutionary state*, 1st edn. Madison, University of Wisconsin Press, 2008.

Stendhal. *Memoires sur Napoleon*. Paris, Le Divan, 1930.

Steinberg, Mark D. 'Workers on the Cross: religious imagination in the writings of Russian workers, 1910–1924', *Russian Review*, 53:2, 1994, pp. 213–39.

Steiner, Peter. '"Formalism" and "structuralism": an exercise in metahistory', *Russian Literature XII*, 1982, pp. 299–330.

Stites, Richard. *Soviet popular culture: entertainment and society since 1900*. Cambridge, Cambridge University Press, 1992.

Strange, Jill M. & Michael D. Mumford. 'The origins of vision: charismatic versus ideological leadership', *The Leadership Quarterly*, 13, 2002, pp. 343–77.

Strong, Carol & Matt Killingsworth. 'Stalin the charismatic leader? Explaining the "cult of personality" as a legitimation technique', *Politics, Religion and Ideology*, 12:4, 2011, pp. 391–11.

Sudakova, Elena (ed.). *See USSR: Intourist posters and the marketing of the Soviet Union*. Moscow, The Pushkin State Museum of Fine Arts, 2013.

Suetonius Tranquillus. *Lives of the twelve Caesars*. Alexander Thomson (trans.). London, G. Bell and Sons Ltd., 1914.

Sukhanov, N.N. *The Russian Revolution, 1917: a personal record*. London, Oxford University Press, 1955.

Suny, Ronald Grigor. *The Soviet experiment: Russia, the USSR and the successor states*, 2nd edn. New York, Oxford University Press, 2011.

Tarifa, Fatos. 'The quest for legitimacy and the withering away of utopia', *Social Forces*, 76:2, 1997, pp. 437–73.

Taylor, Jeremy E. 'Recycling personality cults: observations of the reactions to Madame Chiang Kai-Shek's death in Taiwan', *Politics, Religion and Ideology*, 7:3, 2006, pp. 347–62.

——. 'The production of the Chiang Kai-shek personality cult, 1929–1975', *The China Quarterly*, 185, 2006, pp. 96–110.

Taylor, Lily Ross. *The divinity of the Roman emperor*. Middletown, American Philological Association, 1931.

Taylor, Richard & D.W. Spring. *Stalinism and Soviet cinema*. London, Routledge, 1993.

Terlouw, Kees. 'Charisma and space', *Studies in Ethnicity and Nationalism*, 10:3, 2010, pp. 335–48.

'The case of the anti-Soviet bloc of rights and Trotskyites', *People's Commissariat of Justice of the U.S.S.R.*, 1938. Mathias Bismo (transcriber). www.marxists.org/archive/bukharin/works/1938/trial/.

Thompson, R. 'Reassessing personality cults: the case of Stalin and Mao', *Studies in Comparative Communism*, 21:1, 1988, pp. 99–128.

Thyret, Isolde. '"Blessed is the Tsaritsa's womb": the myth of miraculous birth and royal motherhood in Muscovite Russia', *Russian Review*, 53:4, 1994, pp. 479–96.

Tolstoi, Vladimir Pavlovich, I.M. Bibikova & Catherine Cooke. *Street art of the Revolution: festivals and celebrations in Russia, 1918–33*. New York, Vendome Press, 1990.

Tolstoy, Leo. *War and peace*, vol. 2. Rosemary Edmonds (trans.). London Folio Society, 1971.

Tompkins, Ann & Lincoln Cushing. *Chinese posters: art from the Great Proletarian Cultural Revolution*. San Francisco, Chronicle Books, 2007.

Trotskii, Leon. 'Lenin dead, Tiflis Station, January 22, 1924'. John G. Wright (trans.). www.marxists.org/archive/trotsky/1924/01/lenin.htm.

Trotskii, Leon. *My life*. www.marxists.org/archive/trotsky/1930/mylife/.

——. *Thirteenth Congress of the All-Union Communist Party (Bolsheviks): stenographic report*. Moscow, State Press for Political Literature, 1936.

Trotsky, Leon. 'Kerensky and Kornilov (elements of Bonapartism in the Russian Revolution)', *The history of the Russian Revolution*, vol. 2, *The attempted counter-revolution*, www.marxists.org/archive/trotsky/1930/hrr/ch29.htm.

——. *The challenge of the left opposition (1928–29)*. New York, Pathfinder, 1981.

——. *The history of the Russian Revolution*. Ann Arbor, University of Michigan Press, 1957.

——. 'The workers' state, Thermidor and Bonapartism', Doug Fullarton (transcriber (1998); David Walters (revised 2005). *New International*, 2:4, 1935, pp. 116–22. www.marxists.org/archive/trotsky/1935/02/ws-therm-bon.htm.

——. 'Tradition and revolutionary policy', *The new course*, December 1923, www.marxists.org/archive/trotsky/1923/newcourse/ch05.htm.

Tschabrun, Susan. 'Off the wall and into a drawer: managing a research collection of political posters', *The American Archivist*, 66:2, 2003, pp. 303–24.

Tucker, Robert C. 'Stalin and the uses of psychology', *World Politics*, 8:4, 1956, pp. 455–83.

———. *Stalin as revolutionary, 1879–1929*. New York, W.W. Norton and Company, 1973.

———. *Stalin in power: the revolution from above, 1928–1941*. New York, W.W. Norton and Company, 1990.

———. *Stalinism: essays in historical interpretation*. New York, W.W. Norton and Company, 1977.

———. 'The rise of Stalin's personality cult', *American Historical Review*, 84, 1979, pp. 347–66.

———. 'The theory of charismatic leadership', *Dædalus*, 97:3, 1968, pp. 731–56.

Tulard, Jean. *Napoleon: the myth of the saviour*. Teresa Waugh (trans.). London, Methuen, 1985.

Tumarkin, Nina. *Lenin lives! The Lenin cult in Soviet Russia*. Cambridge University Press, 1997.

———. 'Religion, Bolshevism and the origins of the Lenin cult', *Russian Review*, 40:1, 1981, pp. 35–46.

———. *The living and the dead: the rise and fall of the cult of World War II in Russia*. New York, Basic Books, 1994.

Tupitsyn, Margarita. *Glaube, Hoffnung – Anpassung: Sowjetische Bilder 1928–1945*. Oberhausen, Plitt Verlag, 1996.

———. *Gustav Klutsis and Valentina Kulagina: photography and montage after constructivism*. New York, International Center of Photography, 2004.

Turner, Stephen (ed.). *The Cambridge companion to Weber*. Cambridge, Cambridge University Press, 2000.

Valkenier, Elizabeth. *Russian realist art*. New York, Columbia University Press, 1989.

van Ree, Erik. 'Stalin's organic theory of the party', *Russian Review*, 52:1, 1993, pp. 43–57.

Velikanova, Olga. *Making of an idol: on uses of Lenin*. Göttingen, Muster-Schmidt-Verlag, 1996.

——. 'The function of Lenin's image in the Soviet mass consciousness' in Mette Bryld & Erik Kulavig (eds). *Soviet civilization between past and present*. Odense University Press, 1998.

Verdery, Katherine. *What was socialism, and what comes next?* Princeton University Press, 1996.

Vito, Maurizio. *Terra e mare: metafore e politica in conflitto*. Rome, Aracne Editrice, 2012.

Volkogonov, Dmitrii A. *Triumf i tragediia. Politicheskii portret I.V. Stalina*. 1:2, Moscow, Izdatel'stvo Agenstva pechati Novosti, 1989.

von Geldern, James. *Bolshevik festivals, 1917–1920*. Berkeley, University of California Press, 1993.

von Geldern, James & Richard Stites (eds). *Mass culture in Soviet Russia: tales, songs, poems, movies, plays and folklore, 1917–1953*. Bloomington, Indiana University Press, 1995.

Vozhatyi, 14, 1939.

Walbank, Frank William. *The Hellenistic world*. London, Fontana, 1981.

Walker, Richard L. 'The evil of personality cults', *The Wall Street Journal Asia*, 13 Feb. 2003, A7.

Ward, Alex. *Power to the people: early Soviet propaganda posters in the Israel Museum, Jerus*. London, Lund Humphries Publishers, 2007.

Ward, Chris. *The Stalinist dictatorship*. London, Arnold, 1998.

Waschik, Klaus & Nina Baburina. *Werben fur die Utopie: Russische Plakatkunst des 20. Jahrhunderts*. Bietigheim-Bissingen, Edition Tertium, 2003.

Watson, Derek. *Molotov: a biography*. Hampshire, Macmillan, 2005.

Weber, Max. *On charisma and institution building*. The University of Chicago Press, 1968.

———. *The Russian Revolution*. Gordon C. Wells & Peter Baehr (trans, eds), Cambridge, Polity Press, 1995.

Weber, Max, Hans Heinrich Gerth & Charles Wright Mills. *Max Weber: essays in sociology*. Oxford University Press, 1946.

Weinstock, Stefan. *Divus Julius*. Oxford, Clarendon Press, 1971.

Weiskopf, Mikhail. *Pisatel' Stalin*. Moscow, Novoe Literaturnoe Obozrenie, 2001.

Welch, David. 'Painting, propaganda and patriotism', *History Today*, 55:7, 2005, pp. 42–50.

White, Stephen. *Political culture and Soviet politics*. London, Macmillan, 1979.

———. *The Bolshevik poster*. New Haven, Yale University Press, 1998.

Williams, Albert Rhys. *Through the Russian Revolution*. New York, Boni and Liveright, 1921.

'Windows on the war: Soviet TASS posters at home and abroad, 1941–1945', The Art Institute of Chicago. www.artic.edu/aic/collections/exhibitions/TASS/Art-Weapon.

Wingrove, Paul. 'The mystery of Stalin', *History Today*, 53:3, 2003, pp. 18–20.

Wolf, Erika. *Koretsky: the Soviet photo poster: 1930–1984*. New York, The New Press, 2012.

Wood, Elizabeth A. 'The trial of Lenin: legitimating the Revolution through political theater, 1920–23', *Russian Review*, 61:2, 2002, pp. 235–48.

Wortman, Richard. *Scenarios of power: myth and ceremony in Russian monarchy*, vol. 1. Princeton, NJ, Princeton University Press, 1995.

Yang, Fenggang. 'Religion in China under communism: a shortage economy explanation', *Journal of Church and State*, 52:1, 2010, pp. 3–33.

Yankovskaya, Galina & Rebecca Mitchell. 'The economic dimensions of art in the Stalinist era: artists' cooperatives in the grip of ideology and the plan', *Slavic Review*, 65:4, 2006, pp. 769–91.

Yellen, Elizabeth. 'Monumental propaganda', *Slavic and Eastern European Journal*, 51:2, 2007, pp. 411–13.

Young, Glennys. 'Stalin's holy war', *The Russian Review*, 63:2, 2004, pp. 353–54.

Zarzeczny, Matthew Donald. *Meteors that enlighten the Earth: Napoleon and the cult of great men*. Newcastle-upon-Tyne, Cambridge Scholars Publishing, 2013.

'Zhukov, Nikolai Nikolaevich'. ru.wikipedia.org/wiki/%D0%96%D1%83%D0%BA%D0%BE%D0%B2,_%D0%9D%D0%B8%D0%BA%D0%BE%D0%BB%D0%B0%D0%B9_%D0%9D%D0%B8%D0%BA%D0%BE%D0%BB%D0%B0%D0%B5%D0%B2%D0%B8%D1%87.

Ziff, Trisha. *Che Guevara: revolutionary & icon*. New York, Abrams Image, 2006.

Zilberman, David B. 'Orthodox ethics and the matter of communism', *Studies in Soviet Thought*, 17:4, 1977, pp. 341–419.

Zweerde, Evert van der. 'The place of Russian philosophy in world philosophical history — a perspective', *Diogenes*, 56:2/3, 2009, pp. 170–86.

Index

abundance, 143, 205–6, 213, 232, 235, 245–46, 257, 341–42, 348, 367, 370
Achundov, Ismail (poster artist), 207, 364
Adamovich, Mikhail, 298
Agitprop, 130, 320
agit-trains, 30
agriculture, 144, 244, 249, 251, 320, 345
AKhR/R (Association of Artists of Revolutionary Russia), 93, 296, 301
Aksakov, Ivan, 351
Aksel'rod, Pavel, 131
Aleksandrov, General Aleksandr, 252
aliases, 43, 114, 120, 202
    Koba (Stalin), 112, 120, 202
    Soso (Stalin), 112, 202
Alliluyev, Fiodor, 302
All-Union Communist Party, 222
Al'menov, Bainazar (poster artist), 162
Ancient Rome, 63, 66, 68, 70, 72
Andreev, Andrei, 155
anniversary, 46, 61, 76, 148, 156, 208, 215, 218, 226, 315, 317, 322, 327, 340, 364, 369
anthem, national, 192, 244
Antony, Marc, 68
apotheosis, 22–23, 126, 139–40, 142, 145, 147, 150, 155, 317, 364

Apsit, Aleksandr (poster artist), 102
Arakelov, Vartan (poster artist), 146, 204
archetype
    the Architect, 22, 76, 212–14, 359, 371, 443
    the Father, 22, 24, 34, 45, 75, 78, 107, 204–7, 215, 218, 224, 225–46, 255, 259–60, 292, 295, 318–19, 331, 333–34, 371, 373
    the Helmsman, 22, 209–13, 443
    the Magician, 22–23, 47, 57, 69, 82, 85, 113, 142, 164, 195, 201, 305, 311, 317, 348–50, 352, 371, 373, 443
    the Saviour, 23–24, 34, 45, 47, 58, 72, 85, 88, 108, 192, 199–200, 215, 219, 260, 291, 293, 296, 339, 346–72, 373, 443
    the Teacher, 22, 24, 34, 45–47, 75, 77, 139, 146, 151, 207, 215, 224, 246–60, 308, 312, 319, 338, 344, 349, 357, 360, 363, 370–71, 373, 443
    the Warrior, 23–24, 45, 66, 70–72, 75, 107, 115–16, 237, 244, 255, 260, 291–346, 348–49, 364–65, 371, 373, 443
archetypes, 3, 16, 21–23, 45–47, 67, 71–72, 83–84, 192, 215, 220, 224–25, 255, 259–60, 292, 338, 348, 371, 375, 443

499

architecture, 23, 30, 51, 68, 157, 207, 355
archives, Soviet state, 2, 5, 13, 14, 77, 91, 112, 115, 133, 194–95, 343, 442
Arctic explorers, 107, 128, 204, 224, 238–39
armed forces, 157, 222, 229, 244, 309, 312, 323, 329, 335, 344
  Airforce, 203, 243, 309, 317, 344
  military ranks, 39, 233, 242, 318, 340
  Red Army, 99, 138, 141, 144, 146, 148, 207–8, 222, 226, 292, 294–95, 297–98, 300–304, 306–12, 314–19, 321–22, 325, 327–34, 336–37, 340, 342–44, 357, 359, 362, 364
  Red Cavalry, 223, 310, 312
  Red Navy, 226, 244, 296, 309, 316–18, 325, 328, 344, 359, 368
Armenian, 223, 357, 360, 369
art history, 4
Arzhilovsky, Andrei Stepanovich, 191
aviation, 38, 73, 120, 128, 141, 143–44, 146, 158, 199, 203, 223–24, 230, 238–43, 304, 307–9, 311–12, 314, 317, 320, 328, 330–31, 345
  aircraft in posters, 223, 229–30, 235, 240–43, 307, 312, 318, 329, 332, 335, 360
  parachutes, 230, 243
  Stalin's falcons (pilots), 128, 144, 146, 203, 223, 234, 239–43, 248, 255, 307
Avvakumov, Nikolai (poster artist), 207, 255, 357
awards
  Hero of Socialist Labour, 148, 223, 340

  Honoured Artist of the RSFSR, 209
  Order of Lenin, 147, 210, 234, 340
  Order of Suvorov, 334
  Order of the Great Patriotic War Medal, 343
  Order of the Red Banner, 234, 305
  Order of the Red Star, 234
  People's Artist of the RSFSR, 210
  People's Artist of the USSR, 210, 332
  Stalin Prize, 108, 111, 115, 208, 332
Azerbaijani, 207, 331, 359, 364

Babel, Isaac, 246
Babitskii, A.A. (poster artist), 148, 208, 359, 369
Baidukov, Georgii, 241
Bakhmutov, Georgii (poster artist), 343, 364
Bakst, Leon, 98
Bakunin, Mikhail, 351
banner, 132, 139–41, 143–46, 148–50, 152–55, 158–62, 196, 198, 207–8, 222–23, 242, 244, 254, 307–8, 316–17, 319–21, 323–24, 328–31, 335, 337, 344–45, 347, 359–60, 364–65, 368–70
  captured German, 153, 336
  of Lenin, 137, 139–41, 148–50, 155, 157, 198, 207–8, 222–23, 234, 256, 316, 319, 325, 331, 335, 344, 357, 362, 369, 372
  of Lenin–Stalin, 148, 364, 369
  of Marx–Engels–Lenin–Stalin, 156, 158–60, 162
Barbusse, Henri, 113, 201
battle metaphors, 305–6
battle-readiness, 309, 311–12
battle scenes, 157, 320, 322, 328

battle standards, 146, 153, 331
baucans, 153
Bayuskin, Vasilii (poster artist), 207, 327, 357, 369
Bednota, 130
Bednyi, Dem'ian, 306, 326
Belii, Andrei, 76, 351
Belinskii, Vissarion, 338
Belomor Canal, 89
Belopol'skii, Boris (poster artist), 149, 162, 208, 213, 222, 257, 345, 348–49, 357, 359, 364, 369
Berezovskii, Boris (poster artist), 207, 222, 346, 357, 363
Beria, Lavrenti, 75, 112, 305, 313, 316, 442
Bersian, I. (poster artist), 364
Be-Sha. *See* Shapoval, Boris (poster artist)
binary coding, 22, 26, 121, 123, 241, 370, 445
biography, 2, 5, 12–13, 39, 43, 73–74, 78, 85, 88, 117–20, 160, 194, 237, 247, 294, 300–301, 312, 342–44
birthdays, Stalin, 43, 115, 117, 138, 142, 146, 161, 194, 204, 216, 244, 255, 303, 308, 310, 312, 356
blat, 219–20
Blok, Aleksandr, 351
bogatyr, 305, 306, 342
Bogdanov, Aleksandr, 28, 59
Bolsheviks, 21, 24–29, 31–33, 36, 43, 45, 48, 70, 74–75, 80, 84, 111, 114, 117, 131–32, 135, 247–48, 254, 297, 302, 305–6, 354, 358, 363–64, 374
Bonch-Bruevich, Vladimir, 28, 132
Bondar, N. (poster artist), 222
Breev, Vasilii, 292
Brodskii, Isaak, 134
Bronshtein, Lev Davidovich. *See* Trotskii, Lev Davidovich

Brusilov, General Aleksei Alekseevich, 293
Brutus, 68
Bukharin, Nikolai, 122–24, 193, 365
Bulganin, Nikolai, 344
Burgkmair, Hans, 14, 70
Burova, Ol'ga (poster artist), 325, 357, 368

cadres, 38, 118, 122, 161, 198, 360
censorship, 104, 196, 199, 257
centralisation of artistic production, 90, 103, 199
Chaikovskii, 338
Chapaev
    film, 117
    Vasilii, 117–18
charisma
    manufactured, 81–83, 113
    routinisation of, 34–35, 81, 112
charismatic leadership. *See* leadership, charismatic
Charlemagne, 72
Cheka (Extraordinary Commission for Combating Counter-Revolution and Sabotage), 42, 58, 64, 195–96, 305
Chekhov, Anton, 338
Cheprakov, Konstantin Pavlovich (poster artist), 38, 75, 205, 233, 318, 359
Cheremnikh, Mikhail (poster artist), 326
Chernishevskii, Nikolai, 76, 338
Chernov, M. (poster artist), 369
Chernov, Viktor, 297
children, 34, 38, 77, 85, 119, 132, 143, 147, 199, 204–7, 217, 222, 225–37, 243, 245–46, 311, 314, 319, 325, 329, 333, 339, 357, 359, 371–72
    toys, 229–30

children of Stalin
  Alliluyeva, Svetlana, 12
  Artiom (adopted), 112
  Vasilii, 42, 45
  Yakov, 42, 330
China, 197, 296, 352
Chkalov, Valerii Pavlovich, 128, 240–41, 243
Christ, 17, 47, 127, 130, 152–54, 200, 214, 350–51, 355, 357, 360–61, 363–64, 367, 369, 371–72, 445
Christian symbolism, 59, 127, 154, 352
Churchill, Winston, 340, 349
  Iron Curtain speech, 349
Civil War, 25–27, 32, 34, 57, 65, 81, 99, 102, 107–9, 118–19, 122, 143–44, 151, 200, 225, 246, 298, 300–304, 306, 316, 320–21, 326, 342, 344, 364
class, 25–26, 28, 37, 46, 58, 64–65, 73, 75, 80, 85, 113, 121, 123, 138, 221, 225, 251–52, 306, 319, 324, 370
  history of, 249
  intelligentsia, 26, 28–29, 31, 46, 48, 58, 74, 115, 248
  kulaks (wealthy peasants), 65, 121, 374
  working, 29, 85, 114, 123, 138, 220, 226, 249, 251, 319
coins (numismatics), 68–70, 134, 192, 305
collective principles, 37, 41, 48, 55, 60, 63–64, 83, 87, 90, 117, 130, 197, 228, 251
collectivisation, 23, 28, 62, 89, 96, 104, 122, 139, 146, 157, 207, 221, 223, 249, 357, 364, 366–67
congress
  Eighteenth Party, 149, 229, 309, 345
  Extraordinary Eighth Party, 143

Fifteenth Party, 136
First All-Union of Soviet Writers, 90–91, 93
Seventeenth Party, 62, 91, 346
Sixteenth Party, 140
Sixth Party, 141
Thirteenth Party, 123
Twelfth Party, 131
Twentieth Party, 52
Constantine, Emperor, 70, 134
Constitution of 1936, 37–38, 107, 120, 142–43, 145, 198, 223, 251, 257, 301, 307–8, 310, 339, 347, 356–58, 361, 364, 369–70
criminal past, Stalin, 24, 120, 301
cult, 13, 50–55, 57, 60, 71, 74–76, 78, 82, 86–87, 134, 192, 202, 246, 306
  Alexander the Great, 13, 52, 66, 71, 134, 293, 313
  ancient world, 21, 60, 86, 364
  Attaturk, Kemal, 73
  Bonaparte, Napoleon, 13–14, 52, 66, 71–73, 83, 116, 134, 153, 199–200, 204, 215, 292–93, 299, 336, 351
  Caesar, Julius, 13, 68, 71, 83, 134
  Caesar Augustus, 13, 52, 66, 71, 83, 134
  Castro, Fidel, 352
  Ceauşescu, Nicolae, 129
  Chiang Kai-Shek, 197, 336
  Darius the Great, 68, 134
  Kerenskii, Aleksandr Fiodorovich, 33, 74, 231, 294–97, 299
  Kornilov, General Lavr, 74, 231, 293–95
  Kosmodemianskaia, Zoia, 77
  leader, 21–22, 50, 53, 61, 71, 73, 115, 192–93
  Lenin, Vladimir, 47, 60, 81, 87, 129–30, 133–34, 142, 216, 227, 296, 343

Liszt, Franz, 72
Lysander, 66
Mao Zedong, 15, 52, 197, 209, 296, 354
Marat, Jean-Paul, 71
Maximilian I, Holy Roman Emperor, 13, 52, 70–71, 134, 293
military, 293, 300
Mussolini, Benito, 15, 54, 114
Napoleon, Louis (Napoleon III), 73
personality cult, 2, 13–17, 20–21, 34–36, 39, 47, 49–54, 61–62, 66, 69–71, 74–75, 82–83, 86–87, 129, 133, 158, 292–93, 303, 307, 336, 338, 342, 441, 443, 445
  modern, 50, 54, 443
Putin, Vladimir, 85, 201
Robespierre, Maximilien de, 71, 83
Roman imperial, 61
Stalin, Iosif, 15, 17, 20–21, 33, 44, 50, 60, 66, 70, 72, 85, 87, 114, 119, 134, 137, 142, 200–201, 215–16, 294, 442–43
Washington, George, 73

Danilichev, Aleksandr (poster artist), 338
David, Jacques-Louis, 14, 71
death
  Lenin, 36, 61, 89, 123, 130, 133, 135, 193, 225, 300, 354, 445
  Stalin, 52, 227, 351, 445
death penalty, 58
Deineka, Aleksandr (poster artist), 93–94, 107, 353
deity, 13, 17, 28, 36–37, 40, 45–46, 53–54, 60–61, 68–71, 130, 133, 143, 159–60, 192, 195, 201, 203, 205–6, 208, 232–33, 321, 351–52, 355, 363, 444–45

demonisation, 121–22
Deni, Viktor Nikolaevich (poster artist), 38, 103, 105, 107, 139–41, 144, 198, 207, 221–23, 241, 249, 298, 307, 311, 319–20, 326, 340, 353, 356, 358
Denisov, Nikolai (poster artist), 144, 160, 207, 223, 230, 235, 242, 255, 307, 343, 357, 368–70
Denisovskii, Nikolai (poster artist), 94, 326
Denon, Vivant, 71
de-Stalinisation, 441–42
Detizdat, 39
Dizzy with success, 221
Dlugach, Mikhail (poster artist), 250
Dnieper Dam, 37, 157, 208, 314
Dolgorukov, Nikolai Andreevich (poster artist), 38, 141–42, 144, 158, 207, 223, 241, 253, 307, 311, 320, 353, 356–58, 361
Domition, Roman emperor, 292
Donskoi, Dmitrii, 322
Druzhkov, Aleksandr (poster artist), 146, 223, 344–45, 357, 369
Dürer, Albrecht, 13–14, 70, 134
Dzerzhinskii, Feliks, 58, 127, 305
Dzhambul, 191, 204–5
Dzhugashvili, Iosif (Stalin), 24, 42, 120, 202

education, 22, 46, 57, 64, 76, 90, 94, 100, 118, 121, 137, 198, 237, 248, 257, 374
Efimov, Boris (poster artist), 105, 210, 301
Ehrenburg, Ilia, 12, 24, 38, 112, 319, 354, 356
elections to the Supreme Soviet, 33, 96, 144, 207, 254, 307, 339–40, 347, 356, 363, 368–69
electrification, 38, 151, 208–9, 214
Elkin, Vasilii (poster artist), 105, 107, 127, 145–46, 223, 359–60

Elt'sufen, M. (poster artist), 257
embalming team, Stalin, 356
enemy, German, 77, 85, 148, 154, 207, 226, 239, 313–14, 319–23, 325, 327–31, 333–35, 348, 357, 362
enemy in posters, 28, 32, 84–85, 121–22, 124, 145, 148, 207–8, 210, 221–22, 233–34, 253, 255, 304–6, 308, 314, 316–21, 323–25, 328, 330, 332, 336–37, 359, 369–70, 445
Engels, Friedrich, 52, 72, 84, 97, 118, 129, 131, 137, 154, 156–63, 208, 212, 247, 256
Enukidze, Avel, 112
Esenin, Sergei, 351
eugenics, 365, 374
exiles and escapes of Stalin, 119, 144, 247, 300
Ezhov, Nikolai, 39, 75

faith
  political, 17, 51
  spiritual, 38, 237
family, 26, 44–45, 77–78, 85, 95, 107, 130, 220, 225, 229, 233, 237, 243, 255, 260, 315, 333–34, 338, 359
Fatherland, 148, 225, 232, 295, 308, 330, 364
Fedotov, E. (poster artist), 223
Fedotov, Vladimir (poster artist), 234
festivals, 30, 57, 61, 68
Feuchtwanger, Lion, 113
film, 2, 29–30, 76, 117–18, 229
Five-Year Plan, First, 104, 121, 301
folklore, 26, 59, 95, 100, 240
formalism, 93, 105–6, 108
Freud, Sigmund, 34, 83
Frunze, Mikhail, 127
Futerfas, Genrikh Mendelevich (poster artist), 142, 223, 252, 357

Gagarin, Iurii, 243
Gandhi, Mahatma, 39, 83
Ganf, Iosif (poster artist), 345, 364
Gapon, Georgii, 79
Gel'berg, Semen (poster artist), 222, 363
Generalissimo, 39, 217, 222, 244, 336, 340
Georgian accent (Stalin), 39
Gerasimov, Aleksandr, 87, 326, 371
Gerasimov, Sergei, 209
gesture, 116, 146, 153, 224, 242–43, 256, 332, 340, 348, 360–63, 371
gifts, 45, 62, 150, 215–20, 229–30, 232, 235, 254, 260, 315
Gints, Stefan (poster artist), 153, 207–8
Glavlit, 104, 194, 257
Glinka, Mikhail, 338
god-builders, 28, 58–60, 95
Goethe, Johann von, 53
Golovanov, Leonid (poster artist), 207, 223, 244, 370
Golub, Petr (poster artist), 148, 208, 222, 244–45, 348, 369–70
Goncharov, Ivan, 101
Goncharova, Natalia, 352
Gordon, Mikhail (poster artist), 207
Gorilli, P. (poster artist), 364
Gor'kii, Maksim, 28, 76, 89–90, 93, 95, 127, 132, 237, 246, 298, 338, 373
Gorky, Maxim. *See* Gor'kii, Maksim
Gosizdat, 161
Govorkov, Viktor (poster artist), 150, 209, 221, 228, 359, 369
Govorov, Viktor (poster artist), 207, 356, 368–69
Grabovetskii, Emmanuil (poster artist), 369
Grandfather Frost (Stalin as), 231
Grandpa Lenin, 132, 225

gratitude, 46, 62, 191, 205–6, 217–18, 221–24, 226–27, 229–30, 235–36, 251, 259–60, 334, 339, 356–58, 369
Great Fergana Canal, 205
Great Patriotic War (*see also* World War Two), 23–24, 39, 42, 45, 47, 75, 77, 147–48, 153–54, 206–8, 213, 215, 217, 224, 226, 232–33, 300–301, 314, 316, 320, 327–28, 336–38, 341–45, 369, 372
Grechkin, Petr (poster artist), 207, 344
Grekov Studio of War Artists, 159, 234, 332
Grinets, Dmitrii (poster artist), 221, 229
Gros, Antoine-Jean, 14, 71

hagiography, 22, 119, 444
hand-in gesture, 116, 140, 195, 296, 344
happiness and joy, 21, 107, 147, 207, 222, 228, 232, 251–52, 370
happy childhood, 207, 216, 221–22, 224, 227–30, 232, 235–37, 372
Heartfield, John, 7, 92, 363
heavens in posters, 158, 232–33, 254, 311, 317, 325, 332, 352, 361–63, 372
Helvétius, Claude Adrien, 49
heroes, 33, 37, 57, 59, 78, 99, 101, 106–7, 120, 123, 128, 132, 156, 160, 194–95, 223, 240–41, 251, 291, 294–96, 316, 318, 320, 336, 338–40
historical materialism, 161
history painting, 351
Hitler, Adolf, 15, 40, 52, 114, 242, 304, 312–13, 315, 319, 321, 323, 327

iconography, 6, 32, 138, 150, 154, 355, 371–72
icons, 9–10, 47, 60, 67, 78–79, 100, 102–3, 108, 145, 150, 152–55, 195, 199, 231, 233, 235–36, 305, 329, 334, 342, 350, 352–65, 367–72, 374–75, 444
  avant-garde, 9
  Dormition, 371
  Novgorodian, 145, 372
  Theotokos, 153–54, 372
  veil of the Virgin, 153, 234, 372
Ikramov, Akmal, 44
illiteracy, 4, 24, 31, 86, 98, 117, 247, 250, 374
image, sexual Stalin, 245, 258
Immortalisation of Lenin's Memory, 36, 134
immortality, 58–59, 67, 126, 129, 134, 205
imperial cult, 61, 69
industrialisation, 23, 28, 37, 50, 101, 106, 137, 198, 203, 208, 221, 239–40, 249–50, 301, 306–7, 319–20, 323, 328, 341, 345, 361
Ingres, Jean-Auguste-Dominique, 14, 71, 134
intercession, 153, 371–72
Invincible Moscow, 330, 369
Ioffe, M.L. (poster artist), 223, 369
Iron Lazar, 75, 203. *See also* Kaganovich, Lazar
Iskusstvo (journal), 195, 355
Iskusstvo (publishing house), 315, 334, 371
Ivanov, Konstantin (poster artist), 214, 235, 257, 357–58
Ivanov, U. (poster artist), 369
Ivanov, Viktor (poster artist), 208, 222, 255, 325, 347, 357, 359, 364, 370, 372
Izdatelstvo Krasnyi Krym, 339
Izogiz, 103–5, 110, 139

Izostat, 311
Izvestiia, 31, 78, 228, 230, 241

Kaganovich, Lazar, 39, 42, 75, 82, 127, 140–41, 203, 239, 253, 305, 361
Kaidalov, Vladimir (poster artist), 127, 147, 161, 207–8, 222–23, 337, 345, 357, 368–69
Kalinin, Mikhail, 74–75, 112, 140, 247, 253, 257, 303, 305, 317, 322
Kamenev, Lev, 120, 122–23, 128, 131, 135, 202, 241
Kaminskii, M. (poster artist), 309, 364
Kandinskii, Wassilii, 352, 366–67, 370
Kaplan, Dora. *See* Kaplan, Fania
Kaplan, Fania, 129, 154
Karpenko, Mikhail (poster artist), 148, 207, 212, 335, 362–63
Karpov, Boris (poster artist), 339, 359
Karpovskii, Naum Pavlovich (poster artist), 38, 151, 207–8, 223, 357, 370
Kashina, Nadezhda (poster artist), 329, 369
Katsman, Evgeni, 112, 134, 356
Kazantsev, Anatoli (poster artist), 207, 369
Kazbegi, Alexander, 120
Khitryi Lenin, 59, 227
Khudfond (Khudozhestvennyi Fond), 89
kings, 1, 67, 69, 226, 351
Kirov, Sergei, 127, 140, 198, 237
Klimashin, Viktor Semenovich (poster artist), 148, 207, 332, 359, 364
Kliuev, Nikolai, 351
Klucis, Gustavs. *See* Klutsis, Gustav

Klutsis, Gustav (poster artist), 6–7, 38, 94, 104–6, 111, 125, 137–42, 156–58, 197–98, 223, 251–52, 353, 356, 360, 366
Kochegura, Vladimir (poster artist), 222, 363
Kochergin, Nikolai (poster artist), 250
Kogout, Nikolai (poster artist), 323, 369
Kokorekin, Aleksei (poster artist), 224, 369
Kollontai, Aleksandra, 12
Komsomol (All-Union Leninist Young Communist League), 38, 114, 119, 132, 137, 141, 148, 206, 223, 234, 236, 364
Konev (poster artist), 223, 251
kontraktatsiia, 89–90, 164
Koretskii, Viktor (poster artist), 6, 107–8, 110, 144, 146, 207, 222, 224, 233, 315, 333, 337, 339, 342, 347, 356–58, 361, 364–65, 372
Korovin, O. (poster artist), 77
Kossior, Stanislav, 140
Kossov, A. (poster artist), 162
Krasin, Leonid, 59
Kratkii kurs (History of the All-Union Communist Party (Bolshevik) Short Course), 114
Kremlin, 86, 147, 158, 161, 203–4, 209, 229, 232–33, 242, 255, 294, 310, 313, 324, 335, 337, 340, 359, 361–62, 368
Krupskaia, Nadezhda, 135
Krushchev, Nikita, 42, 52, 75, 253, 313, 361
Krylov, Porfiri (poster artist), 105
Kuibyshev, Valerian, 82, 127, 140
Kukryniksy (poster artists), 105, 353
Kulagina, Valentina (poster artist), 6, 94, 104–5, 110, 124, 138
Kul't lichnosti, 52

kultur'nost, 257
Kun, Gleb (poster artist), 223
Kuprianov, Mikhail (poster artist), 105, 248
Kutuzov, Mikhail, Field Marshal, 73, 322, 336, 338

Lamarckism, 365, 374
Lansere, Evgenii, 98
Larionov, Mikhail, 352
Latgosizdat, 151
Latsis, Martin, 64
Latvian, 138, 151, 222, 348
leader, 4, 6, 21–22, 24, 33–34, 36, 40–42, 47, 50–51, 67, 84, 86–87, 96, 114, 128, 192–93, 196, 200, 221, 246, 292, 306, 374, 442–46
  beloved, 106, 142, 144, 146, 193, 198, 223, 234, 308, 338
  great, 138, 144, 151, 208, 222, 340
leader persona, 21, 33, 42, 54, 66–67, 70, 75, 82, 121, 192, 315
  Stalin, 3, 22, 24, 42–44, 87, 111, 116, 120–21, 136, 141, 148–49, 163–64, 192–93, 200–201, 207–8, 256, 260, 331, 335, 341, 343–44, 350, 369, 372, 444
leaders, Bolshevik Party, 29–31, 33, 43–44, 46, 74, 80, 111, 113, 122, 126, 136, 138, 140, 155, 163–64, 197–98, 231, 237, 240–42, 247–48, 253, 303, 305, 365, 372
leadership, 2–3, 21, 23, 41, 67, 70–72, 80, 82, 111, 117–18, 125, 148, 155, 192–93, 203, 207–9, 213, 239, 253, 255, 357, 359, 363, 369, 374
  charismatic, 16, 21–22, 24, 33–37, 39–42, 50, 54, 71, 81–83, 86, 112–13, 121, 125–26, 129, 134, 164, 193, 200, 292, 296, 299, 306, 372–73, 443, 445

followers, 27, 34, 36, 40–41, 51, 56, 121, 247
  ideological, 41
  hereditary/traditional, 82, 373
  Lenin, 29, 43, 133, 135, 138
leadership emblems, 22
leader violence, 41
Lebedev, B.I. (poster artist), 146, 208, 222, 345, 363, 364, 369
Lebedev, M. (poster artist), 146
Lebedev, Vladimir (poster artist), 107
Lebedev-Kumach, Vasilii, 252
legitimation, 14, 21, 27, 33, 37, 45, 67, 70, 72, 81–82, 87, 129, 131, 133, 138, 147, 154, 162, 216, 221, 226, 317, 319, 343, 349
  charismatic, 33, 35, 82
  traditional, 70–71
Lenin, Vladimir, 23–24, 27–29, 34–35, 56–57, 60, 80–83, 126–27, 129–33, 135–41, 145, 148–51, 161–64, 193, 200–202, 207–9, 212–14, 222–23, 225–27, 296–300, 302–6, 317, 321, 362–63, 368–69, 445
  cult. *See* cult, Lenin, Vladimir
  decree on dismantling of monuments, 83
  funeral, 127, 133, 147, 346
  gesture, 321, 363
  head of, 140, 143–44, 146, 150, 156, 324, 332, 335, 337, 358
  image of, 126, 136, 138, 141, 254, 308, 317, 363, 445
  infallibility, 81, 133
  inspiration, 139–40, 146, 162, 315–16, 324, 332, 335, 344, 357, 362, 369
  legacy, 106, 146, 199
  testament, 135, 299

Lenin and Stalin (*see also* Stalin and Lenin), 23, 35, 46, 67, 68, 83, 96, 129, 136, 137, 139, 141–45, 148–51, 156, 162, 209, 246, 249, 256–57, 306, 308–9, 317, 320, 323, 329, 332, 335, 337–38, 343, 365, 368, 451
Lenin corners, 67, 89, 333, 354
Lenin Mausoleum, 46, 231, 316, 336, 344, 346, 361, 441
Lenin–Stalin, party of, 129, 143, 148, 150, 162, 208, 222–23, 251, 316, 342, 345, 363–64, 369
Leningrad, 92–93, 119, 249, 314–15, 320, 324, 334–35
Leninism, 39, 56, 58, 130–31, 136, 140, 162–63
Leo, Boris (poster artist), 362
Leonov, Leonid, 336
Lidov, Petr, 77
lineage, 13–14, 35, 70, 72, 133–34, 151
 ideological, 72, 134, 156
Lisovskii, Kazimir, 234
Lissitskii, El (poster artist), 97, 366
literature, 2, 7, 30, 43, 51, 62, 86, 89–93, 117–18, 149, 209, 228, 364
Litizdat, 100
Litvinov, F. (poster artist), 207–8, 222, 245, 345, 364, 369–70
Logvin, G. (poster artist), 141
lubok, 32, 85, 100–101, 103, 325, 328
Ludwig, Emil, 41–42, 131, 238
Lukács, György, 299
Lukhtein, P. (poster artist), 364
Lunacharskii, Anatolii Vasilievich, 28, 58–59, 297–99
Lysenko, Trofim, 76

Madorskii, A.I. (poster artist), 127, 146, 357, 360–61
Maiakovskii, Vladimir, 29, 37, 48, 101, 221, 227, 252, 315–16, 326
Makarenko, Anton, 76, 237
Malenkov, Georgi, 52, 316
Malevich, Kazimir, 100, 130, 352–53, 366
Malkin, Boris, 139
Mandelshtam, Nadezhda, 76, 78, 228–29
Mandelshtam, Osip, 76
Markizova, Dominika Fedorovna, 231
Markizova, Gelia, 231, 234
Marr, Nikolai, 76, 163, 237
marshal of the Soviet Union, 23, 46, 75, 112, 148, 161, 213, 242–43, 255, 303, 308, 312, 324, 334–40, 342, 344, 347–48, 359, 371–72
Martinov, General Evgenii Ivanovich, 293
Martov, Julius, 131
martyrdom, 57, 78, 127, 152–54, 293
Marx and Engels, 84, 131, 156–57, 160, 163, 208, 212, 247, 256
Marx, Engels and Lenin, 88, 156, 159, 161, 164
Marx, Karl, 24–25, 47, 139, 152, 213, 238
Marxism, 26, 52, 84, 119, 163, 238, 257
 Marxist–Leninist theory, 28, 31, 57, 118, 139, 154, 161–64, 247, 250
masses, 20, 22, 28, 31–32, 36, 41, 50, 54, 57–58, 69, 84, 88, 92, 99, 101, 114, 118, 121–22, 124, 132, 138, 155, 192, 198, 298
Matvievskii, V., 231
medallion, 143, 148, 305, 332, 344, 363–65, 367–68

Medvedev, V. (poster artist), 208, 369
Mel'nikova, Elena (poster artist), 207, 236, 357
mentors, 45, 215, 220, 246, 248, 250, 252, 255, 258, 443
Merega, Evgeni (poster artist), 364
Merovingian kings, 72
Mikhailov, Nikolai (poster artist), 222, 257
Mikhalev, Andrei (poster artist), 362
Mikoian, Anastas, 42, 82, 112, 140, 155, 220, 253, 313
Mikoyan, Anastas. *See* Mikoian, Anastas
Military Oath, 307–8
military-style tunics, 296, 304
Minin, Kuzma, 322
Mirzoe (poster artist), 321
Mirzoev, E.M. (poster artist), 159, 359
Mizin (poster artist), 141
modesty, Stalin, 113–16, 206, 305, 336, 342, 345
Moldavian, 364
Molotov, Vyacheslav, 12, 39, 42, 75, 106, 112, 127, 134, 140, 144–45, 194, 202, 205–6, 253, 305, 312–13, 316, 345, 349, 373
Molotov–Ribbentrop pact, 128, 309, 312, 314, 348
monuments, 71, 76, 83, 310
Moor, Dmitrii (poster artist), 99–103, 105, 107, 144–45, 209, 308, 326, 353
mortality salience, 17, 125–28, 445
Moscow, 39, 46, 68, 75, 90, 93, 99–102, 105, 138–39, 144, 146, 154, 194, 203, 214–15, 220, 228, 235, 240–43, 294, 314–15, 326–27, 329–30, 339
  Metro, 37–38, 75, 141, 203, 209, 223, 253, 361

Moscow-Volga Canal, 37, 146, 223
MOSSKh (Moscow Section of the Union of Soviet Artists), 93
Motherland, 132, 142–44, 148, 198–99, 207–8, 223, 225–26, 228, 230, 232, 234, 242, 244–45, 307, 314, 320, 328, 331, 333–34, 342, 344, 346, 357, 363, 369–70
Mukhin, Boris (poster artist), 208, 222, 321, 343–44, 364
Musinov, V. (poster artist), 208, 222
myths, 15, 21, 44, 55, 59, 77, 79, 82–85, 94–95, 97, 119–20, 137, 164, 192, 200, 209, 215, 231, 233, 237, 301, 305, 312, 443, 445
Mytnikov (poster artist), 149–50, 212, 223, 363–64

Nadia, Stalin's wife, 127, 245, 313
name of Stalin, 194, 320
Napoleonic pose, 116. *See also* hand-in gesture
national costume, 258, 311, 348, 359
Nehru, Jawaharlal, 83
NEP (New Economic Policy), 109, 157
Nevskii, Aleksandr, 14, 293, 322
new Soviet man, 240, 243, 350, 365
New Year, 230, 235, 357–58
Nietzsche, Friedrich, 63, 84
Nikolaev, Vasilii Aleksandrovich (poster artist), 334, 357, 362
North Pole, 240–42
Novaya Zhizn, 26–27, 132

obligation, 22, 45, 60–61, 65, 215, 218–21, 223, 227, 236, 246, 251, 259, 308, 315
oblomov, 101, 319
obraz, 371
Octavian, 68

October Revolution 1917, 24, 29, 34, 118, 122, 124, 138–41, 144, 148, 151, 208, 212, 218, 222–23, 226, 231, 295–97, 299, 301–2, 306, 317, 319, 351–52, 364, 369
Ogonyok, 208, 354
Oktiabriata, 132
Old Bolsheviks, 23, 39, 48, 114, 123–24, 132
Onufriichuk (poster artist), 342, 364, 368–69
Ordzhonikidze, Sergo, 112, 135, 140, 237, 253, 305
orphans, 231, 234–35, 357
ORPP (Russian Revolutionary Poster Artists), 103

Panferov, Fedor Ivanovich, 62
Panofsky, Erwin, 3
parades and processions, 30, 57, 61, 68, 74, 78, 104, 106, 153, 157–59, 226, 232, 235, 298, 304, 321–22, 336, 344, 357–60, 370, 441
Paradovskii, V.C. (poster artist), 356, 359
Paris Commune, 152
partiinost', 123, 220
Party, Bolshevik/Communist, 27–28, 31, 58, 78, 81, 84, 118, 120, 129, 132–33, 135, 138, 142, 144, 149–50, 191, 193, 220, 223, 225, 305–6, 343, 345, 372, 374
patronage, 45–46, 219–20, 241, 246–47
Paulus, General Friedrich von, 42
Pavlov, Ivan (engraver), 102
Pavlov, Ivan (psychologist), 76, 338, 354
peace, 23, 45, 85, 107–8, 151, 162, 191, 199, 207–8, 222, 226, 295, 304, 309, 311–12, 331, 334, 346–49, 357, 359, 362–64, 370, 374

peasants, 25–26, 31, 38, 48, 62, 75, 77–78, 97–98, 100, 102, 104, 122, 128, 130, 139, 141, 225, 233, 247, 249, 258, 293, 295, 309, 366
peasant woodcuts, 102
Pen Varlen (poster artist), 212, 323, 335
Pernikov, Efim (poster artist), 142, 356, 358
personality cult. *See* cult, personality
Peters, Yakov, 44
Petrov, N. (poster artist), 214, 222, 344, 369
photographs, 19, 43–44, 75, 108, 110, 116, 136, 144, 146, 152, 156, 196, 231, 240, 253, 296, 301, 307–8, 315, 317–18, 345, 354, 356, 360, 363
Piatikov, Iurii, 123
Pikalov (poster artist), 249
Pinchuk, Veniamin (poster artist), 332, 357, 362, 369
Pinus, Natalia (poster artist), 107, 207, 222, 259, 357, 361, 369–70
Pioneers, 114–15, 119, 132, 205, 229–30, 235–36, 243, 245, 257, 359
pipe, Stalin's, 195, 213, 217, 344
Plekhanov, Georgi, 28, 131, 338
Plotnov, Andrei (poster artist), 338
podium, 140, 143, 146–47, 149, 235, 256, 259, 311, 345, 360, 363
podlinniki, 355
Podobedov, S. (poster artist), 146, 304, 307–8, 310, 364
Polenov (poster artist), 250, 363
Politburo, 43, 63, 74, 91, 131, 136, 142, 195, 312–13, 361
Polonskii, Vyacheslav, 99–100, 109
Polotskii, Simeon, 203
Poltava Tank Regiment, 332

Polyakov, Aleksandr (poster artist), 223, 251
porcelain, propagandistic, 30, 109, 219, 298
portrait busts, 66–67, 71, 76, 160, 322, 325, 337
portraits, 23–24, 42, 66–69, 71–74, 76, 78–79, 109–11, 113, 128, 130, 139, 141, 144, 146, 159–60, 195–98, 200, 233, 235–36, 294, 298, 307–8, 323, 354–59, 364–65
poster campaigns, 32, 37, 96, 339, 442
poster exhibitions, 96, 98, 100
poster mania, 99
poster production, 5, 98–99, 103, 108–9, 139, 367, 446
posters, photomontage, 7, 38, 92, 106, 111, 139, 252–53, 363
Postyshev, Pavel, 230
Pozharskii, Dmitrii, 322
Pravda, 31–32, 43, 46, 77, 94, 101, 107, 127–28, 130, 139, 145, 156, 160, 163, 204, 221, 241, 248, 250, 305–6, 346–47, 349, 355, 358, 449
Pravdin, Vladislav (poster artist), 154, 158, 207, 221–24, 230, 235, 243, 255, 343, 345, 357, 369–70, 372
Pravdina, Zoia (Rykhlova-Pravdina) (poster artist), 158–59, 230, 235
priests, 60, 65, 101, 121, 152, 154, 214, 225, 319, 353
prison camps, 76, 89, 125, 154
prisoners of war, 314
propaganda, 2–5, 20–24, 27–29, 31–33, 35–37, 40–41, 45–46, 50, 64–65, 68–71, 81, 84–85, 103–4, 121, 126–27, 198–200, 203, 212–13, 221, 238–39, 241–43, 311–12, 314–15, 329–30, 443–45
protection of the population, 153–54, 219, 233–34, 242, 364, 371

pseudo-folktales, 86
purges, 64, 94, 124–25, 127–28, 213, 241, 246, 255, 258, 314
Pushkin, Aleksandr, 76, 338
Putin, Vladimir, 85, 201

RABIS (Worker's Art), 111
Radek, Karl, 212
railways, 47, 74, 203, 211
Razvozzhaev, Stepan (poster artist), 339
reciprocity, 22, 45, 143, 215, 218, 220, 225
Red corners, 89, 354
Red Square, 44, 110, 124, 144, 158, 226, 304, 316, 321, 325, 344
Redko, Kliment, 352
Reikh, Mikhail (poster artist), 206, 357, 368
religion, 23, 28, 48, 54–58, 60, 63, 98, 100, 204, 237, 353, 365
  civil, 55
  mythological, 55
  political, 21, 50, 54–55, 60, 63, 79, 154, 350, 444
Repin, Ilya, 296, 338
republics of the USSR, 127, 144, 147, 158, 161, 205, 207, 223, 258, 330, 338, 347–48, 357, 369
  Belarus, 328, 348
  RSFSR (Russian Soviet Federative Socialist Republic), 144, 151, 210, 254, 332
  Ukraine, 25, 328, 348
  Uzbekistan, 31, 147, 205, 330, 348
Reshetnikov, V. (poster artist), 151, 369
resurrection, 59, 152
retouched image of Stalin, 23, 106, 196
Reznichenko, A. (poster artist), 142, 223

ritual, 21, 50, 54–55, 57, 60–66, 83–84, 91, 97, 133, 137, 154, 193, 218, 220, 232, 294, 354, 364
Oktiabrina, 62, 154
samokritika, 65, 128, 220
Rodchenko, Aleksandr, 29, 44, 326, 352, 366
rodina, 232
Rodina (personification of the Motherland), 143, 342
Romain, Rolland, 113
Roman emperors, 13, 66, 68–71, 134, 293
Rosenfeld, Lev. *See* Kamenev, Lev
ROSTA (Russian Telegraph Agency), 101–2, 195, 210, 325–28
Rousseau, Jean-Jacques, 55, 59
Rumiantsev, A.M. (poster artist), 139, 251
Russell, Bertrand, 56
Russian art, 9, 15, 100, 352
Russian folklore, 26, 59, 95, 100, 240
Russian Orthodox Church, 6, 10, 21, 32, 47, 59–61, 78, 102, 119, 127, 150, 152, 154, 293, 352–53, 355, 374, 443
Russian scientists, 240
Russian State Library, 6, 19, 110
Rykov, Aleksei, 120
Ryvkin, K. (poster artist), 146

sacrality, 33, 145, 367–68
sacrifice, 14, 37, 58, 107, 113, 130, 143, 150, 153–54, 341, 351, 372, 443
saints, 22, 78, 102, 119, 145, 150, 154, 208, 253, 291, 293, 295, 364
George, 293, 298–99
John Chrysostom, 145, 209
Nicholas, 150
Paul, 49, 83, 145, 152
Peter, 83, 145, 152

saluting, 106, 231, 236, 253, 311, 360
salvation, 58, 63, 69, 121, 127, 299, 371
sanctifying, 324, 350, 362, 364
satire, 101–3, 107, 325, 353
Saxl, Fritz, 3
Schiller, Friedrich, 53
School of Inter-Planetary Communications, 212
schools, 74, 137, 218, 229–31, 319
science, 1, 28–29, 51, 59, 88, 161–63, 202, 248, 256, 332, 356, 365
Scriabin, Vyacheslav, 202. *See also* Molotov, Vyacheslav
searchlights, 206, 208
Sechenov, Ivan, 338, 354
Secret Speech 1956 (Krushchev), 52, 441
Selivanov, V. (poster artist), 207, 208, 222
Sen'kin, Sergei (poster artist), 144–45, 308
Serge, Victor, 12, 75
Serov, Vladimir (poster artist), 148, 207, 324, 332, 357, 362, 369
Shagin, I. (poster artist), 146, 207, 344, 357, 363, 369
Shakhty Trial, 157
Shapoval, Boris (Be-Sha) (poster artist), 368
Shatunovskii, M., 114
Shirnov, Fyodor Efimovich, 254
Shkhiyan, Ruben (poster artist), 207, 344, 364, 369
shock work, 139, 204, 223, 251
Sholokhov, Mikhail, 42
show trials, 65, 124, 128, 241, 255
Shpier, A. (poster artist), 207, 327, 357, 369
Shtange, Galina Vladimirovna, 40
Shubina, Galina (poster artist), 143, 356

Shukhmin, Petr (poster artist), 207–8, 222, 331, 338, 364
Shurpin, Fyodor, 245
Sidorov, Aleksei, 102, 356
Simonov, Konstantin, 194
Skobelev, General Mikhail, 291
slogans, 30, 38, 97, 107, 109–10, 138, 149, 151, 155, 158–60, 162, 197, 208, 214, 228–29, 231–32, 250, 252, 329, 345, 353, 372
Smolgiz, 333
Sobolevskii, Konstantin (poster artist), 223
socialism, 25, 27, 37, 93–94, 107, 118, 120, 132–33, 140, 143, 148–49, 157, 159–60, 164, 210, 212–13, 216–17, 222–24, 226, 230, 249, 254, 341–42, 370, 374
socialist construction, 38, 89, 107, 128, 137, 141, 146, 157, 162, 199, 203, 207, 223, 250, 303, 306, 311, 319, 331, 341, 356, 358, 361, 363, 365
socialist realism, 2, 44, 92–95, 106, 126, 237
Sokolov (poster artist), 324
Sokolov, Nikolai (poster artist), 105
Sokolov-Skalia, Pavel (poster artist), 159, 207, 211, 326, 330
Solomyanii, M. (poster artist), 224, 257
Solov'ev, Mikhail (poster artist), 207–8, 222, 259, 357, 363, 369
Solzhenitsyn, Aleksandr, 59–60
songs, 23, 75, 78, 86, 106, 204, 207, 216, 229, 241, 246, 252
sons, 148, 223, 226, 237–38, 240–41, 246, 251, 255, 330, 373
Sosnovskii, Lev, 130
Soviet life, 45, 62, 95, 220, 336
Soviet parenting, 34
Soviet rule, 31, 38, 44, 88, 212, 223
Stakhanov, Aleksei Grigorievich, 142, 250–52

Stakhanovite conference 1935, 37, 146, 250–53, 360–61, 370
Stakhanovite movement, 37, 107, 120, 128, 142, 223, 248, 250–55, 306, 357, 359–61, 370
Stal, Ludmilla, 202
Stalin and Lenin (*see also* Lenin and Stalin), 23, 35, 46, 67, 68, 83, 96, 129, 136, 137, 139, 141–45, 148–51, 156, 162, 209, 246, 249, 256–57, 306, 308–9, 317, 320, 323, 329, 332, 335, 337–38, 343, 365, 368, 451
Stalin biography, 88, 117, 119, 121, 300, 343
Stalin speeches, 40, 249, 252, 309, 311, 316–17, 321, 325–26
Stal'noi, Soslan, 202
Stalskii, Suleiman, 204
Stanislavskii, Konstantin, 76
statuary, 23, 53, 57, 68, 70, 73, 78, 214, 292
Stebaev, I.V. (poster artist), 141
Stenberg, L. (poster artist), 149, 369
Stenberg (poster artist), 143, 223
succession crisis, 35, 81, 123, 133–35, 300
Sudoplatov, Pavel, 42
Sukhanov, Nikolai, 112
Surikov, Vasilii, 338
Suryaninov, Vasilii, 207, 370
Suvorov, General Aleksandr, 322, 338
symbolism, 23–24, 28, 30, 32, 45, 53–54, 61, 69–72, 83–86, 89, 91, 97–98, 120–21, 143, 153, 191–94, 197, 199, 201, 203, 214–15, 217, 224–25, 242, 259–60
    abstracts, 111, 164, 191, 193, 350, 374, 443
    aureole, 153, 155, 299, 338
    bayonets, 318, 320, 325, 330
    clothing, 195, 201, 205, 324, 371

colour, 101–2, 108–9, 152–53, 161, 195, 197, 229, 243, 325, 337, 345, 365–70
   black-and-white, 137, 152, 214, 303, 307–8, 315, 322, 333, 345, 359, 369
   gold, 149, 159, 161, 217, 256, 305, 307, 334, 338–39, 341–42, 361, 368–70
   pastel, 213, 367
   red, 152, 342, 368
   sacred, 152, 305, 339
cotton, 161, 205–6, 208, 345, 357, 368
embalmed corpse, 59
flags, 146, 152–53, 192, 210, 241–42, 244, 309, 311, 334, 338, 344, 347, 362, 371
flowers, 205–6, 229–33, 235–36, 246, 257, 294–95, 336, 342, 357, 359, 372
hammer and sickle, 153, 307, 323, 335, 340
journey, 123, 160, 210–11
light, 144, 158, 197, 203–5, 207–9, 214, 229, 232–33, 236, 242, 244–46, 324, 329, 336, 338, 342, 347, 349, 356, 360–64, 369, 372
   lamps, 131, 208–9
   sun, 22, 38, 197, 203–7, 241, 244, 252, 296, 347, 368
red star, 204, 210, 230, 233, 235, 241, 253, 304, 307, 318, 322, 331, 335, 338, 344, 362
right arm, 151, 254, 256, 318, 323–24, 328, 332, 334, 340, 348, 358, 360, 362–63
scroll, 213, 310, 360
ship, 209–11, 213, 229–30, 306
Spassky tower, 86, 147, 150, 161, 206, 233, 242, 253, 310, 324, 329, 335, 338, 340, 344, 361, 368

steel, 22, 75, 120, 201–3, 213, 240, 298, 331
train, 159–60, 209, 211–12, 229
train driver, 159, 211–12
wedge, 140, 323
wheat, 206, 244, 256
wind, 144, 256, 340, 347
wreath, 69, 149, 161, 206, 308, 337, 342, 357, 364–65

Talipov, N. (poster artist), 207, 223, 357
tanks, 141, 309, 311, 317–18, 320–23, 325, 328–29, 333–34
TASS (Telegraph Agency of the Soviet Union) posters, 7, 159, 210, 325–28, 330–31, 338, 364
Tatgosizdat, 161
Tatlin, Vladimir, 29, 352
Tchaikovskii. *See* Chaikovskii
terror, 62, 81, 91, 124, 255, 293
threat, 72, 85, 121, 127, 192, 202–3, 210, 233, 239, 292, 304, 310, 320, 329–30
Tito, Josip Broz, 76
Tiutchev, Fiodor, 351
Toidze, Iraklii (poster artist), 140–41, 143, 200, 207, 222–23, 256, 317–18, 331, 340–42, 346, 349, 357, 359–60, 364, 369, 371
Tolstoi, Leo, 73, 228, 246, 338
Trajan, 292
transformation
   nature, 4, 30, 95, 111, 147, 350, 443
   political, 39, 57, 63, 85, 99, 214, 223, 350, 368
transition socialism to communism, 37
Tretiakov, Pavel, 29
Trotskii, Lev Davidovich, 13, 39, 44, 54, 74, 87, 99, 112–13, 120, 122–24, 131, 133, 135–36, 202, 225, 248, 294–300, 302–4

Trud, 322, 358
Tsaritsyn, 303, 331, 343–44
tsars, 14–15, 26, 33, 39, 45, 66, 72, 78–80, 83, 109, 114, 155, 218–19, 225–26, 294, 296, 299, 322, 351, 373
    Aleksandr II, 26, 153, 351
    Ivan IV, the Terrible (Grozny), 72, 79, 291, 293, 299, 313
    Nicholas I, 351
    Nicholas II, 26, 30, 79
    Peter I, the Great, 14, 72, 225, 293, 351
Tsishevskii, Iu. (poster artist), 223, 359
Tupolev, 25, 242

Ugarov, Aleksandr, 198
Uitz, Bela, 352
Ukrainian, 141, 224, 230, 249, 257, 343, 363–64
USSR, 31, 36, 144, 148, 151, 197–98, 207, 210, 222–23, 234, 239, 242, 251, 253–54, 307–9, 311, 327, 329–30, 332, 347–48, 356–58, 361, 363, 368–70, 374
utopia, 28, 34, 37, 57, 75, 85, 96, 106–7, 113, 127, 157, 206, 232, 237, 245, 348, 362–63, 371–72, 374
Uzbek, 75, 205–6, 233, 257, 318, 323, 330, 345, 368
UzTAG, 330

Vasil'ev, A.V. (poster artist), 148, 317
Vasilevskii, Aleksandr Mihailovich, 148, 301, 344
Vasnetsov, Apollinari, 98
Vasnetsov, Viktor, 98
Vatolina, Nina (poster artist), 144, 160, 207, 221–23, 230, 232, 235–36, 242, 307, 335, 357

Venediktov, Aleksandr (poster artist), 38, 212, 223
Vialov, Konstantin (poster artist), 223
victory, 45–46, 141, 147–49, 152–55, 161–62, 194, 205, 207–8, 210, 212, 222, 224, 249–50, 256–57, 303–4, 316–18, 322–23, 329, 331–39, 341–45, 347, 357–58, 362–65, 369–72, 374
    Stalingrad, 46, 330–33
Victory Day, 46, 315, 344, 441
Viktorov, Viktor (poster artist), 359
violence, 41, 128, 306, 373
Virgin Mary, 153–54, 234, 342, 364, 371–72, 445. *See also* icons, Theotokos
visual literacy of Soviet population, 31–32, 47, 352, 444
VKhUTEMAS (Higher Art and Technical Studios), 353, 366
Vlasob (poster artist), 331, 357
Volga-Don Canal, 60
Volkova, Marina (poster artist), 146, 207, 222, 259, 357, 361, 369–70
Vorontsov, B.V. (poster artist), 207, 223, 357
Voroshilov, Klementy Efremovitch, 23, 75, 82, 104, 106, 112, 116, 127, 134, 140–41, 144–45, 158, 237, 242–43, 253, 303–5, 307–8, 310, 312, 316, 324, 356
vozhd', 6, 114, 118–19, 133, 198, 237, 306, 315, 357, 361
Vrubel, Mikhail, 98
Vsedusha, 58
VseKoKhudozhnik, 89–90, 104

war, 153, 192, 292, 306, 315, 354
War and Peace, 73
Weber, Max, 21, 33–35, 37, 81, 83, 296

wisdom of Stalin, 24, 39, 88, 146, 204, 210–11, 233, 244, 246, 256, 260, 312, 317, 349, 373
women, 6, 77, 148, 208, 222, 224, 232, 234, 243, 250, 257–59, 319, 323, 325, 329, 337, 340, 357, 361–62, 366, 368–70
  female delegates, 222, 257–59
workers, 26, 38, 92, 94, 97, 104, 106, 119, 122, 146, 197–98, 201, 207, 214, 217, 247, 249, 251–54, 257–58, 309, 311, 319–20, 357–58, 361, 363
World War One, 24, 56, 74, 101, 293, 295
World War Two (*see also* Great Patriotic War), 14–15, 23–24, 45, 47, 75, 77, 119, 121, 147–48, 153–54, 199–200, 206–8, 213, 215, 217, 224, 226, 232–33, 300–301, 310, 312–14, 319–20, 327–28, 336–38, 341–45
worship, 28, 54, 114, 132, 200, 204–5, 297
writers, 26, 42, 48, 62, 76, 86, 88, 93, 113, 118, 131, 163, 194, 213, 246, 248, 298, 326, 336, 350, 444

Yanevich, S.F. (poster artist), 148, 317
Yang, I. (poster artist), 144
Yastrzhembskii, P. (poster artist), 38, 146, 223, 364
youth, 78, 119, 132, 137, 149, 206, 230, 234, 243, 246, 253, 368

Zarnitskii, Georgi (poster artist), 320, 363
Zasulic, Vera, 24–25
Zdrogova, Nina, 231
Zhdanov, Andrei, 75, 91, 127
Zhdanov, Yuri, 42
Zhitomirskii, Aleksandr (poster artist), 222

zhivoi, 371
Zhukov, B. (poster artist), 147
Zhukov, M. (poster artist), 207
Zhukov, Marshal Georgii, 46, 112, 336
Zhukov, Nikolai (poster artist), 147–48, 194, 207, 222, 231, 234, 332, 357–58, 364
Zinoviev, Grigorii, 67, 75, 123, 128–29, 135, 241
Zotov, K.V. (poster artist), 141
Zubov, U. (poster artist), 207

www.ingramcontent.com/pod-product-compliance
Lightning Source LLC
Chambersburg PA
CBHW062024290426
44108CB00025B/2773